Democratizing the Metaverse:

Accessibility, Inclusivity, and Human-Centric Innovation

Jyotir Moy Chatterjee
https://orcid.org/0000-0003-2527-916X
Graphic Era University, India

Pawan J. Lingras
Saint Mary's University, Canada

Ravi Samikannu
https://orcid.org/0000-0002-6945-6562
Botswana International University of Science and Technology, Botswana

Sujatha Radhakrishnan
https://orcid.org/0000-0002-1993-7544
Vellore Institute of Technology, India

IGI Global
Scientific Publishing
Publishing Tomorrow's Research Today

Vice President of Editorial	Melissa Wagner
Director of Acquisitions	Mikaela Felty
Director of Book Development	Jocelynn Hessler
Production Manager	Mike Brehm
Cover Design	Jose Rosado

Published in the United States of America by
IGI Global Scientific Publishing
701 East Chocolate Avenue
Hershey, PA, 17033, USA
Tel: 717-533-8845 | Fax: 717-533-7115
Website: https://www.igi-global.com E-mail: cust@igi-global.com

Library of Congress Cataloging-in-Publication Data

LCCN: 2025041403 (CIP Data Pending)
ISBN13: 9798337367217
Isbn13Softcover: 9798337367224
EISBN13: 9798337367231

British Cataloguing in Publication Data
A Cataloguing in Publication record for this book is available from the British Library.

Table of Contents

Detailed Table of Contents

Often described as the next phase of the internet, the Metaverse brings together immersive technologies such as virtual reality, augmented reality, artificial intelligence, and blockchain to create shared and persistent digital environments. This chapter focuses on the broader social implications of these environments, particularly their influence on human interaction, communication, identity formation, learning, and cultural practices, rather than limiting the discussion to technical aspects. As digital experiences become more immersive and integrated into everyday life, traditional social norms and values are being reshaped. Drawing on perspectives from technology studies, sociology, psychology, and ethics, the chapter examines both the transformative potential and associated risks, including psychological effects, changes in social behavior, inclusivity, accessibility, surveillance, and regulation. The aim is to offer educators, researchers, technologists, and policymakers a clearer understanding of how these virtual environments influence society.

Urban public spaces plays a vital role in enhancing social cohesion through the support of interaction, cultural exchange and identity collectively. In smart city era, the public spaces are oriented towards digital technologies that reshape how people meet each other, communicate and participate. Traditional design principles of accessibility, safety, proximity in modern public life is now through digital layer like participatory apps, real time data applications, smart mobility systems and advance technology like metaverse. Combing digital and physical world resulted in creation of hybrid public spaces which enables communities to cocreate and experience in multiple dimensions. Case Studies including Amsterdam, Barcelona, Singapore, Bhopal and Seoul show on how various tools for designing apps to integrated command centres and metaverse platforms can enhance inclusion and civic management. In spite of the opportunities for extended participation are growing, challenges must be addressed to ensure resilient and equitable smart cities.

The fast-paced development of the design education field demands a radical re-assessment of the traditional pedagogical methods in order to equip future design professionals for complex, interdisciplinary challenges that are brought on by technological innovations. This chapter responds to these demands through an investigation of the need for an innovative pedagogical toolkit. Utilizing a comprehensive approach to synthesizing the research and pedagogical strategies, the study compiles current research and pedagogical strategies, explores innovative digital tools and analyses their potential to support critical thinking, problem-solving and adaptability in design students. Key findings reveal that advanced digital and immersive technologies, especially in the context of developing the Metaverse ecosystem, hold unprecedented benefits in terms of advancing customization, creativity and immersive learning experiences that ultimately lead to greater understanding of spatial relationships and better design communication

The management of agricultural waste and the sustainability of resources continue to be major obstacles, and waste-to-wealth practices are not widely used because of a lack of knowledge, expertise, resources, and technology. Farmers can safely learn and test circular solutions thanks to the agricultural metaverse, which makes use of AR/VR, digital twins, and simulations. Results indicate that immersive platforms accelerate the transition to a circular economy by improving knowledge, cooperation, recycling behavior, and resource recovery.

India is undergoing rapid urbanisation. This has increased the demand for affordable rental housing for the urban poor and migrants, which is also inclusive in nature. Since time immemorial, the focus of the government has been on promoting ownership models, leaving policies for rental housing inefficient and ineffective. The reverse migration witnessed during COVID-19 pandemic exposed the precarious conditions in which the urban poor lived in the city. This phenomenon propelled the launch of Affordable Rental Housing Complexes (ARHC) policy under Pradhan Mantri Awas Yojna Urban (PMAY-U). Despite of noble intentions, the policy faces challenges in scaling up, monitoring, integration of existing policies and is yet not inclusive in nature. This chapter proposes a transformative strategy through the Policy Metaverse Model (PMM), a socio- technological innovation integrating ideas of digital twins, immersive community engagement, blockchain enabled contracts and AI data analytics to improve transparency, accountability and inclusivity in the digital governance space.

Metaverse is making education more interesting and interactive by making learning spaces that are more like real life. Metaverse education is different from traditional e-learning since it uses AI, IoT, and augmented and virtual reality (AR/VR) to make classrooms which are more welcoming, interesting, and available to all students. This chapter looks at how these technologies can work together and change how teachers teach and students learn. The chapter is about human-centered design that means making learning systems flexible enough to meet the needs of each student, make it easier for students with disabilities to learn, and give everyone the same chances to learn, no matter where they live. IoT devices, AI-driven personalization, and immersive simulations can enhance the learning experience and student outcomes, as demonstrated by real-world use cases like smart classrooms and AR-based campus navigation. This chapter offers a road map for developing an inclusive and democratized metaverse for education by combining case studies, current trends, and future directions.

The rapid convergence of immersive technologies and artificial intelligence has accelerated the rise of the metaverse—dynamic, contactless digital ecosystems encompassing social, cognitive and economic dimensions. However, these evolving environments also present complex challenges in trust, privacy and digital forensics. This chapter demonstrates a unified, explainable and ethically grounded metaverse security framework by integrating Sanskrit epistemology, specifically Nyāya logic, with Explainable Artificial Intelligence (xAI) and incremental learning paradigms. The framework adopts the Nyāya epistemic structure, rooted in Pramā a and a fivefold reasoning process. Symbolic reasoning modules are combined with incremental learning algorithms to enable continuous adaptation and evidence-based inference without catastrophic forgetting. Experimental results compare the Nyāya-driven xAI framework through its interpretability and adaptability on forensic explainability. The logical traceability of its decision process strengthens trust and accountability in metaverse investigations.

Preface

INTRODUCTION

This book explores deep ways in which the metaverse is revolutionizing industries in human life and making humanity stronger. It provides an in-depth understanding of real-time metaverse technologies that are revolutionizing industries like education, healthcare, business, and entertainment while solving ethical, social, and economic issues. With such information by way of case studies and future outlook, the reader can now employ actionable insights to navigate and tap the metaverse's potential both for innovation as well as social good. The intention behind writing this book is to bridge the gap between technological innovation and human-oriented applications. While the metaverse tends to be considered from a technological or entertainment perspective, this book changes the focus to its potential to address actual problems and make humanity stronger. It presents a comprehensive view as a handbook for professionals, scholars, and policymakers in the effective and responsible utilization of the metaverse's potential.

The accelerated rhythm of the metaverse has resulted in an acute need for a resource that seeks to reconcile technical depth with useful application and moral consideration. What is currently in the literature is either excessively technical or conceptually speculative, and therefore it is creating a lack of knowledge around its actual practical applications. It is this space that the current book bridges, offering a mature, interdisciplinary discourse, making the book a key guide to stakeholders of varied inclinations.

Unique Selling Points:

- Brings together technical, social, and economic views to present a balanced picture of the metaverse.

- Contains case studies that highlight how sectors such as health care, education, and urban planning are evolving via the metaverse.
- Provides practical frameworks to solve society's problems, responsibly and fairly utilizing the technologies of the metaverse.

OVERVIEW OF CHAPTERS

Chapter 1: Metaverse and Societal Effects

Often described as the next phase of the internet, the Metaverse brings together immersive technologies such as virtual reality, augmented reality, artificial intelligence, and blockchain to create shared and persistent digital environments. This chapter focuses on the broader social implications of these environments, particularly their influence on human interaction, communication, identity formation, learning, and cultural practices, rather than limiting the discussion to technical aspects. As digital experiences become more immersive and integrated into everyday life, traditional social norms and values are being reshaped. Drawing on perspectives from technology studies, sociology, psychology, and ethics, the chapter examines both the transformative potential and associated risks, including psychological effects, changes in social behavior, inclusivity, accessibility, surveillance, and regulation. The aim is to offer educators, researchers, technologists, and policymakers a clearer understanding of how these virtual environments influence society.

Chapter 2: Public Spaces, Smart Cities, and the Metaverse Future

Urban public spaces plays a vital role in enhancing social cohesion through the support of interaction, cultural exchange and identity collectively. In smart city era, the public spaces are oriented towards digital technologies that reshape how people meet each other, communicate and participate. Traditional design principles of accessibility, safety, proximity in modern public life is now through digital layer like participatory apps, real time data applications, smart mobility systems and advance technology like metaverse. Combing digital and physical world resulted in creation of hybrid public spaces which enables communities to cocreate and experience in multiple dimensions. Case Studies including Amsterdam, Barcelona, Singapore, Bhopal and Seoul show on how various tools for designing apps to integrated command centres and metaverse platforms can enhance inclusion and civic management. In spite of the opportunities for extended participation are growing, challenges must be addressed to ensure resilient and equitable smart cities.

Chapter 3: Metaverse Technologies for Architectural Pedagogy: A Scoping Review and Taxonomic Framework

The fast-paced development of the design education field demands a radical re-assessment of the traditional pedagogical methods in order to equip future design professionals for complex, interdisciplinary challenges that are brought on by technological innovations. This chapter responds to these demands through an investigation of the need for an innovative pedagogical toolkit. Utilizing a comprehensive approach to synthesizing the research and pedagogical strategies, the study compiles current research and pedagogical strategies, explores innovative digital tools and analyses their potential to support critical thinking, problem-solving and adaptability in design students. Key findings reveal that advanced digital and immersive technologies, especially in the context of developing the Metaverse ecosystem, hold unprecedented benefits in terms of advancing customization, creativity and immersive learning experiences that ultimately lead to greater understanding of spatial relationships and better design communication

Chapter 4: Harnessing Agricultural Metaverse Platforms to Convert Farm Waste Into Circular Economic Value

The management of agricultural waste and the sustainability of resources continue to be major obstacles, and waste-to-wealth practices are not widely used because of a lack of knowledge, expertise, resources, and technology. Farmers can safely learn and test circular solutions thanks to the agricultural metaverse, which makes use of AR/VR, digital twins, and simulations. Results indicate that immersive platforms accelerate the transition to a circular economy by improving knowledge, cooperation, recycling behavior, and resource recovery.

Chapter 5: Policy Metaverse Model (PMM) Towards Affordable and Inclusivity in Rental Housing Policy in India

India is undergoing rapid urbanisation. This has increased the demand for affordable rental housing for the urban poor and migrants, which is also inclusive in nature. Since time immemorial, the focus of the government has been on promoting ownership models, leaving policies for rental housing inefficient and ineffective. The reverse migration witnessed during COVID-19 pandemic exposed the precarious conditions in which the urban poor lived in the city. This phenomenon propelled the launch of Affordable Rental Housing Complexes (ARHC) policy under Pradhan Mantri Awas Yojna Urban (PMAY-U). Despite of noble intentions, the policy faces challenges in scaling up, monitoring, integration of existing policies and is yet not inclusive in nature. This chapter proposes a transformative strategy through the Policy Metaverse Model (PMM), a socio- technological innovation integrating ideas of digital twins, immersive community engagement, blockchain enabled contracts and AI data analytics to improve transparency, accountability and inclusivity in the digital governance space.

Chapter 6: Immersive Service Value Co-Creation in the Metaverse: A Strategic Framework for Telecom Transformation

The merging of immersive technologies such as augmented reality, virtual reality, blockchain, and artificial intelligence are accelerating the development of the Metaverse - an organized virtual environment where people will be able to interact, exchange value and co-create experiences. Within this context of the possible, the telecommunications sector goes beyond its traditional role as a provider of connectivity services and takes on a leading role in facilitating immersive digital services. The present chapter introduces the Immersive Service Value Co-Creation Framework (ISVCCF) by elucidating how the telecom operators can design and deliver value-rich experience in Metaverse EcosystemThe chapter culminates by stating research propositions, managerial implications, and avenues for further research for establishing trust, ethics, and accessibility as a crucial part of the sustainable adoption of Metaverse.

Chapter 7: A Sequential DL-Based Approach for MRI-Based Brain Tumor Classification With Metaverse

The classification of brain tumors (BTs) from magnetic resonance imaging (MRI) images is of paramount importance in facilitating precise analysis and medication planning for healthcare professionals. This study presents an innovative approach to BT classification, employing sequential deep learning techniques. Customized CNN architectures are made with brain tumor classification in mind, accounting for the special characteristics and patterns found in medical pictures. Our methodology harnesses the capabilities of convolutional neural networks (CNNs) to obtain spatial features from both MRI pictures and MRI masks. The research commences with the preprocessing of the MRI dataset and the curation of a diverse collection of labeled BT scans. To ensure consistent and stable training conditions, we normalized the MRI images. The CNN layers are instrumental in extracting spatial features from individual MRI slices, significantly contributing to optimal classification accuracy.

Chapter 8: Human-Centric Educational Revolution in the Metaverse: Integrating AI, IoT, and AR for Inclusive Learning

metaverse is making education more interesting and interactive by making learning spaces that are more like real life. Metaverse education is different from traditional e-learning since it uses AI, IoT, and augmented and virtual reality (AR/VR) to make classrooms which are more welcoming, interesting, and available to all students. This chapter looks at how these technologies can work together and change how teachers teach and students learn. The chapter is about human-centered design that means making learning systems flexible enough to meet the needs of each student, make it easier for students with disabilities to learn, and give everyone the same chances to learn, no matter where they live. IoT devices, AI-driven personalization, and immersive simulations can enhance the learning experience and student outcomes, as demonstrated by real-world use cases like smart classrooms and AR-based campus navigation. This chapter offers a road map for developing an inclusive and democratized metaverse for education by combining case studies, current trends, and future directions.

Chapter 9: Integrating Sanskrit Epistemology With xAI for Trustworthy Metaverse Systems

The rapid convergence of immersive technologies and artificial intelligence has accelerated the rise of the metaverse—dynamic, contactless digital ecosystems encompassing social, cognitive and economic dimensions. However, these evolving environments also present complex challenges in trust, privacy and digital forensics. This chapter demonstrates a unified, explainable and ethically grounded metaverse security framework by integrating Sanskrit epistemology, specifically Nyaya logic, with Explainable Artificial Intelligence (xAI) and incremental learning paradigms. The framework adopts the Nyaya epistemic structure, rooted in Prama?a and a five-fold reasoning process. Symbolic reasoning modules are combined with incremental learning algorithms to enable continuous adaptation and evidence-based inference without catastrophic forgetting. Experimental results compare the Nyaya-driven xAI framework through its interpretability and adaptability on forensic explainability. The logical traceability of its decision process strengthens trust and accountability in metaverse investigations.

Chapter 10: Learning in the Metaverse Through a Mixed-Methods Investigation of Immersion, Engagement, Performance, and Governance in Higher Education

This paper reviewed metaverse based learning in a 6 week course with 142 learners. The great learning achievement was captured and the presence and the engagement were found to be the strong predictors of performance. Behavioural information showed an indication of the gradual engagement, frequent interaction, and frequent movement within the virtual learning zones. The qualitative examination demonstrated three primary themes, namely, enhanced immersion, enhanced social relationship as a result of communication via avatars, and initial difficulties in the domains of usability and safety. The results indicate that the metaverse learning settings may be beneficial provided that the instructional design makes use of the immersive affordances and the learners are provided with proper developmental support in the process of adapting. Governance, safety-related guidelines, and technical scaffold should be able to provide meaningful and safe learning experiences.

Chapter 11: Moral Foundations for Infinite Digital Realities: Navigating Ethics in AI-Powered Metaverses

This chapter examines moral foundations for navigating ethics in AI-powered metaverses, where traditional ethical frameworks prove inadequate for addressing unprecedented digital realities. The authors analyze key challenges including algorithmic responsibility in virtual economies, informed consent in AI-mediated interactions, data sovereignty in immersive environments, and the moral status of AI entities. This chapter demonstrates that conventional ethical theories require significant adaptation to address the unique characteristics of persistent, immersive virtual worlds where physical and digital boundaries increasingly blur. The authors propose universal ethical principles for implementing cross-reality moral standards while protecting human dignity and fostering responsible AI development. This chapter contributes to digital ethics discourse by defining governance frameworks for AI-enabled metaverses grounded in fundamental human values.

Chapter 12: Human-Oriented Sustainability Pathways for an Eco-Friendly and Digitally Inclusive Metaverse

The Green Metaverse is not yet eco-friendly due to limited research. This paper assesses the Green Metaverse's potential for human well-being and planetary health. Using a mixed-method approach, sustainable infrastructure accessibility and human-centred value creation are explored. Findings show that combining energy-efficient design with applications like digital learning and global collaboration offers transformative potential for a sustainable virtual future.

CONCLUSION

We sincerely thank the authors for their valuable contributions and dedication, which have been instrumental in shaping the quality of this book. We also extend our heartfelt appreciation to all the reviewers for their timely and insightful feedback, enabling us to maintain high scholarly standards and complete the project within the scheduled timeline.

Jyotir Moy Chatterjee
Graphic Era University, India

Pawan Lingras
Saint Mary's University, Canada

Ravi Samikannu
Botswana International University of Science and Technology, Botswana

Sujatha Radhakrishnan
Vellore Institute of Technology, India

Acknowledgement

I extend my heartfelt gratitude to my Late Grandfather, Mr. Gopal Chatterjee; my Late Grandmother, Ms. Subhonkori Chatterjee; my Late Ms. Mother, Nomita Chatterjee; Father Mr. Aloke Moy Chatterjee; and Uncle Mr. Moni Moy Chatterjee, the most significant persons in my life, whose grace has transformed my long-cherished dream of this book into reality. I also express appreciation to my friends for their steadfast support, encouragement, and blessings, which have infused this work with unconditional love and patience.

Jyotir Moy Chatterjee
Graphic Era University, India

Chapter 1
Metaverse and Societal Effects

Pradip Karmakar
http://orcid.org/0009-0004-7325-907X
Global Institute of Management and Technology, India

Parag Chatterjee
http://orcid.org/0000-0003-1243-9582
Global Institute of Management and Technology, India

Sanju Ghosh
http://orcid.org/0009-0006-0688-323X
Global Institute of Management and Technology, India

Tarunjit Biswas
http://orcid.org/0009-0004-1329-6274
Global Institute of Management and Technology, India

Deboprasad Modok
http://orcid.org/0009-0002-4883-5528
Global Institute of Management and Technology, India

ABSTRACT

Often described as the next phase of the internet, the Metaverse brings together immersive technologies such as virtual reality, augmented reality, artificial intelligence, and blockchain to create shared and persistent digital environments. This chapter focuses on the broader social implications of these environments, particularly their influence on human interaction, communication, identity formation, learning, and cultural practices, rather than limiting the discussion to technical aspects. As digital experiences become more immersive and integrated into everyday life, tra-

DOI: 10.4018/979-8-3373-6721-7.ch001

ditional social norms and values are being reshaped. Drawing on perspectives from technology studies, sociology, psychology, and ethics, the chapter examines both the transformative potential and associated risks, including psychological effects, changes in social behavior, inclusivity, accessibility, surveillance, and regulation. The aim is to offer educators, researchers, technologists, and policymakers a clearer understanding of how these virtual environments influence society.

1. INTRODUCTION

In consideration of the future internet and digital world, one thing that always pops into people's minds is the metaverse. This is not a location or even a technology; it is a series of interconnected areas on a digital world, on which users can interact with one another. In these areas, individuals can communicate with one another, trade goods and services, as well as express themselves through various means. This is distinct from other environments as it combines a number of related technologies such as Virtual Reality, Artificial Intelligence, Networking Technology, and Digital Currencies into one continuous process. This allows for sustained environments for platforms to exist on for a period of time, as well as sustained identity on these environments by users. Social media platforms such as Facebook allow for continuous presence, identity, so well as continuous interactions through their various functions, which enable users to remain connected for a considerable amount of time (Dwivedi et al., 2022).

Although the concept has become popular these days, yet its origin is not very old. People have been interacting with each other through digital platforms for many years now. People have been enjoying virtual games, virtual worlds, as well as social networks. The difference between previous digital platforms and the present concept of the metaverse is its realism and persistency. Users can feel immersed as well as stay for longer periods. These digital platforms are no more used temporarily; instead, they are an everyday affair. People can feel its absence even when they are not using them. This proves that metaverse technology is not an invention but is an evolving process related to digital platforms (Mystakidis, 2022).

In recent years, the interest shown by the business community, institution, and academia has widened the need to study its overall impact on society per se. History shows that all innovative technologies that came along in the past have sometimes allowed unexpected issues along with the benefits that come with the use of the innovative platforms. Platforms that were supposed to facilitate creativity and openness have sometimes led to a heightened level of inequality, surveillance, and the overall concentration of power held in the hands of a few organizations. Since such environments have great dependency on the use of data and interaction with the platform, such issues could be intensified. Thus, studying the overall impact on society is essential to understand how digital environments could affect social relationships, economic participation, or governance systems (Kim, 2021).

1.1. Definition of the Metaverse

In scholarly research, the metaverse has been described in general as a virtual world where multiple users can interact in a virtual world through virtual figures, called avatars. In general, persistence is described as a virtual world that always persists and grows, regardless of users being offline. In general, synchronicity is described as a world where multiple users have multiple opportunities to instantly connect, regardless of geographical location, and respond instantly, no matter where they are in geographically different locations (Dwivedi et al., 2022).

However, it is not possible to understand the metaverse solely based on its definition from an engineering perspective since it is much more than that. The metaverse is also a place where social processes intersect with economic processes, alongside other activities, including creative pursuits. These individuals are not those who consume much but are also active participants in these virtual spaces in terms of space creation, including all other economic activities. This level of participation is essential because it shows how it is related to other sectors of user-generated content, but also creates other frontiers in terms of user engagement with the said technology. After all, it seeks "interoperability," allowing individuals to keep their identities regardless of the platforms they use (Park & Kim, 2022).

First and foremost, the metaverse is a type of sociotechnical system. The development and implications of the metaverse are based on its technological platform interaction with strategies and incentives at both socioeconomic and societal levels. The nature of platform governance, data ownership, and accessibility mechanisms shapes user agency and participation and inclusivity that emerge within virtual spaces of such platforms. To better grasp the metaverse, there is a need to explore various sociotechnical settings that surround its enactments, as mentioned by Mystakidis (2022).

1.2. Evolution and Technological Roots

The metaverse did not appear overnight or in a vacuum, separate from other developments in the digital world. The metaverse is an experimental work with network computing, dating back several decades to virtual environments and virtual societies. Early virtual worlds proved that virtual environments can support persistent identities, common social interaction, and even a rudimentary economy. Over time, the power of computing, graphics, and network capabilities has enabled these more immersive and interactive environments.

As digital interaction was widely adopted, the boundaries among these worlds began to blur. This is the reason why the metaverse has again received importance in recent years. It does not symbolize a historic breakthrough; it symbolizes a cumulative effect resulting from long-standing technological trajectories and social practices. Looking at the metaverse from this historical perspective offers a more realistic foundation for judging its potential importance and avoids hyperbole, novelty, or inevitability claims (Dwivedi et al., 2022).

1.3. Importance of Studying Societal Effects

The social implications of the metaverse go beyond matters of technological viability and commercial viability. First, consider the issue of social interaction. Immersives allow people to experiment with identity presentation in a manner that could encourage creativity, self-expression, and inclusivity. At the same time, such environments can introduce psychological pressures, boundaries between what is public and what is private, or new forms of social exclusion, especially where there may not be equal access or cultural practices that may differ.

Another area of consideration would be the issue of privacy and data governance. Metaverse platforms are reliant on significant behavioral and biometric data in order to be effective. This data can be seen in the form of movement and presence tracking. There are also potential challenges related to data exploitation and misuse or loss of user autonomy. The design of regulatory systems was not intended for levels of immersion found in this kind of environment (Kim, 2021).

Economic implications also reinforce the importance of critical analysis. Indeed, the metaverse presents novel concepts of digital labour, ownership, and value, in which platforms or operators exert control over access. For instance, these platforms require producers to sign a contract when selling items in the metaverse. Nevertheless, in creating new opportunities, they are also poised to perpetuate established trends. In this regard, knowledge about the phenomenon is central in being able to understand how the metaverse could transform economic and stratification systems (Dwivedi et al., 2022).

2. HISTORICAL AND TECHNOLOGICAL BACKGROUND OF THE METAVERSE

The metaverse did not appear as a result of innovation in technology but as a result of research and development in virtual reality, online communities, and digital economies that have been conducted over several decades. The development of the metaverse can be seen as a continuation of a socio-technical trajectory where technological innovation in networking, virtual reality, and interactive technology has made possible a new way of interacting with each other and with technology to create a shared virtual space. The early virtual reality environments and online communities formed the conceptual basis for the metaverse.

2.1. Early Virtual Worlds and Online Communities

The history of the metaverse can be traced back to the early virtual worlds and massive online worlds that allowed users to interact with each other in virtual worlds. Before the development of immersive technologies, online worlds allowed users to interact with each other, work together with each other, and build communities through text-based communication and avatars. The online worlds proved that social presence and collective identity could be achieved in virtual worlds by creating patterns of governance, economy, and culture similar to those of physical societies.

It was suggested that virtual worlds are socio-economic systems and not merely entertainment platforms. Castronova (2005) suggested that virtual worlds have the potential to create complex economies, societies, and politics, which are examples of the potential of virtual worlds to rebuild and recreate social interactions. Massively multiplayer online games have significantly improved these interactions by allowing individuals to collaborate in real time, although they were geographically dispersed all over the world. Research has suggested that individuals have been able to form long-term relationships, coordinate group activities, and even create new economic systems on these platforms (Taylor, 2006). These early developments created a proof-of-concept paradigm for understanding identity, property, and social interactions in virtual worlds, which created the foundation for the development of virtual worlds. The development of virtual worlds was also affected by the development of massively multiplayer online games, which created a platform for individuals to interact and socialize with each other.

It is important to point out that online communities were not limited to online gaming platforms. Online forums, social networking platforms, and collaborative software platforms proved that people with similar interests could use technology to build lasting communities regardless of the interface quality. From a socio-technical perspective, online communities prove that technology and social behavior can interact in such a way as to support the notion that the metaverse is more than just a technological achievement.

2.2. Role of VR, AR, AI, and Blockchain

The modern metaverse is defined by the integration of various cutting-edge technologies that make it possible to create immersive, interactive, and decentralized spaces. Virtual reality (VR) and Augmented Reality (AR) technologies improve the presence experience by enabling users to interact with virtual spaces using embodied interaction. Immersive interfaces exceed screen-based interaction, encouraging spatial interaction that improves social and emotional ties in virtual spaces

Artificial intelligence is a deal when it comes to managing virtual ecosystems. Things like agents and automated tools use artificial intelligence to make things more personal for people. Artificial intelligence is also used in environments and generative content tools to do the same thing.

There is a problem with using artificial intelligence. It can be unfair. People do not always know what is going on, which is are big issue. These issues can be fixed by responsibly designing intelligence, as some people suggested in 2022.

When we think about how artificial intelligence works with people and technology, we should remember that artificial intelligence is not a technical thing. Artificial intelligence also affects how people control things in environments, so it is a big part of the system. Artificial intelligence plays a role in this.

The metaverse is a place where people talk about who owns things, who people are, and how things are run. Blockchain technology is a part of this conversation. It helps keep track of things in a way that is not controlled by one person. This means people can manage their stuff, like money and items, without needing someone in charge to say it is okay.

Blockchain technology also gives us ways to think about trust and trading things with each other. Even though some people are not sure if blockchain is an idea because it can be slow, and we are not sure about the rules, it is still an important idea. It helps people make decisions together without needing someone in charge. It gives users control over their digital money and things. The metaverse is made up of layers like a big stack. Blockchain technology, immersion, intelligence and decentralization all work together to create ways for people to take part in the digital world.

2.3. Transition from Web 2.0 to Web 3.0

The metaverse is really connected to the change from Web 2.0 to Web 3.0. Web 2.0 made the internet a place where people can interact with each other create their content use social media and be in digital spaces that are controlled by companies. This allowed for a lot of ideas and economic growth, but it also made people concerned about who owns the data, big companies having too much power, and being watched all the time.

Web 3.0 is a mindset that is all about making things more decentralized so that multiple systems can be used together, and users have more control. In this regard, the metaverse is considered a way to further make digital systems more decentralized so that users have power over their own identity, assets, and activities online. (Park and Kim in 2022) this is a significant transition where the power is being removed from the companies and given to the users, which is a major shift in how online platforms are governed. Even though we do not know yet how much of this will actually happen, the metaverse and Web 3.0 show that technology and society are changing how they work together in spaces, and the metaverse is a big part of this change.

2.4. Convergence of Technologies Shaping the Metaverse

The metaverse is something that we should consider to be a system that is comprised of many different pieces, such as virtual reality, artificial intelligence, and new methods of accessing the internet. It is not one website or one application, but many different systems that are all connected and allow us to communicate with each other in a virtual reality. This is occurring as a result of changes in the way that we use technology, and it is becoming increasingly difficult to distinguish what is real and what is virtual.

If we consider the metaverse in an abstract manner, we can observe that it is a large ecosystem that encompasses many different technologies, users, and organizations that work together. Some researchers, such as Ning and his team, have argued that the metaverse is a system that encompasses both technology and social aspects, and that these are all interrelated and impact each other. The metaverse could be a place where people can collaborate, be creative, and make money, but it also poses some big questions about who is in charge, how everything will work together, and what the right thing to do is. In order to understand the metaverse, we must consider it in a detailed manner and not only consider what it is, but also consider what it means to society and how it will impact our lives.

3. SOCIETAL DOMAINS AFFECTED

The metaverse embodies the shift in paradigm between digital technologies and the real-life social world. What has evolved from being a platform for communication or entertainment is now most likely to revolutionize interaction, learning, labor, and governance. As these spaces evolve, so too does their impact across a multidimensional landscape of social relations, education, economic activity, healthcare, identity-building, and regimes of governance. Because many of these effects are intersectional, there is a need to consider how immersive digital ecologies are reconfiguring human practices, the distribution of life chances, and struggles over power in society.

3.1. Social Interaction and Communication

3.1.1. Virtual Communities and Real-Time Collaboration

One of the most apparent consequences of the metaverse is related to social interactions. Since it enables users to socialize with each other through embodied avatars, the metaverse gives these users an immense sense of presence. Unlike social networking sites like Facebook, Instagram, or Twitter, since the metaverse presents an immersive environment where users communicate with each other through gestures of motion as if they were socializing in reality, it enables the user to socialize with others not just at an intellectual or cognitive level but at an emotional level as well (Schroeder, 2016).

Virtual communities in the metaverse tend to extend past physical, as well as cultural, spaces. People from different places would be able to work on different activities in a real-life manner without necessarily being in the same location. Virtual conferences, design studio work, and even social meetings would be examples of such activities, emphasizing how collective participation can now be exhibited in new forms in such realms. After a certain period of time, certain norms and practices can be established in such realms and, in turn, give way to the development of new virtual cultures in such spaces. In terms of work and creativity, the capabilities of working collectively provided in the metaverse would be of great advantage. Such capabilities would give collective virtual space to different activities such as encounter, communication, and working, which could, in turn, help to improve innovation and working even in globally dispersed companies.

3.1.2. Impact on Offline Relationships

On the other hand, immersive environments provide increased opportunities for socializing, although these environments have offline impacts as well. When players spent a significant amount of time within a virtual environment, it could change the way players allocated their attention between their offline and online interactions. For some individuals, virtual environments supplement offline relationships in terms of interacting with their online friends and communities in a way that would otherwise be impossible offline. For others, too much immersion in virtual environments could reduce offline interactions and give rise to social withdrawals due to overimmersion (Turkel, 2017).

Offline relations are affected and influenced by personal circumstances, usage patterns, and the context of society. The immersive technology can add value to the societal experience, given that its usage is in good balance. Unrestricted or dominating usage can have the potential to create strain within the context of family relations and could make people uninterested in their surrounding communities. It is crucial to understand this aspect, given that one may have to assess the immersive impacts of the communication technology.

3.2. Education and Learning

3.2.1. Virtual Classrooms and Immersive Simulations

Education is one of the sectors that has been readily identified as having the potential to be affected by the metaverse. The days when schools would have to rely on traditional means of education, which entail listening as compared to physically interacting with the information, are now a thing of the past. Virtual classrooms would give learners a chance to work in virtual labs, virtual historic events, or even complex systems, thereby giving them the ability to experiment with the information (Radianti et al., 2020).

Such settings foster learning methods that focus on engagement, cooperation, and problem-solving. The talents that the students gain include those associated with team-building in cyber settings, which could be too expensive, risky, and complex to undertake in real life. The students get an opportunity to get immediate responses concerning the effects of their engagement. This results in high levels of motivation and understanding in those topics associated with science and technology, such as architecture and medicine.

In addition to the conventional processes of learning, the metaverse will also ensure learning outside the classroom setting. Learning or development of certain skills can be done online via virtual training, workshops, and so on. This will help learning to be made accessible to various sections of society because of the accessibility of the metaverse.

3.2.2. Opportunities and The Digital Divide

However, with advantages, embracing metaverse-based education brings considerable concerns about fairness and accessibility. Generally, immersive learning would involve the latest technology, internet connectivity, and basic digital competencies. Therefore, some students from poorer families or areas where such technology infrastructure is not available may be excluded, hence the existing gaps will be widened further.

Additionally, immersion technology will also be effective in the educational field, with the effectiveness of its implementation of such technology into the educational process. If untrained and without a specific framework in mind, immersion technology might be used only as a simple enhancement and nothing else than a tool of learning. It calls for developing digital infrastructure to overcome these challenges.

3.3. Work and Economy

3.3.1. Digital Workplaces and Decentralised Markets

The Metaverse is also impacting the work and business sectors. Virtual workplaces have been created, which help employees communicate and work through their avatars, and these workplaces have been made similar to office workplaces and work sessions. And they can have an ability to improve the collaboration of the employees when working from distant locations, and they lack in the standard video conferencing software (Dionisio et al., 2013).

Organizations that also have physically dispersed workers can benefit significantly from virtual workspaces, which also offer new possibilities for collaboration, training, or even informal networking. In virtual workspaces, workers can collaborate over shared resources, conduct training simulation exercises, or have informal meetings that can aid productivity as well as enable bonding, which can lead to new relationships.

In terms of the economy, the metaverse ensures the development of a decentralized virtual market where a range of products and services can be generated and exchanged. This is especially affirmative news to entrepreneurs in creative industries like digital art, virtual fashion, and so on. In view of the increasing amount of economic activity taking place in these virtual social platforms, the lines between work, leisure, and creativity are becoming less defined.

3.3.2. Implications for Labour And Employment

Apart from this requirement, new challenges arising from labor conditions and practices, the Metaverse introduces unique immersive work environments that foster an expectation of continuous availability, which in effect makes it challenging for an employee to demarcate time between personal and professional life. Should this issue remain unchecked, this blurring of boundaries may be a causative agent for growing stress and burnout. Sennett, 2018

The international virtual labour market increases competitiveness, and the normalized power disparities tend to be reaffirmed. Issues of fair compensation, job security, and rights of labour become more complicated as virtual work spans international borders. The challenge of ensuring fair and sustainable working practices will demand changes in labour policies to respond to a new reality that is still emerging from within virtual economies.

3.4. Health and Well-Being

3.4.1. Applications of Virtual Reality In Healthcare

The role of immersive technologies in the current state of the healthcare sector has just begun, and the applications of virtual reality as part of various therapeutic processes, such as the treatment of pain, psychology, and exposure-based therapies, are already numerous. Moreover, during rehabilitation treatments, the presence of virtual environments can increase the effectiveness of the exercise for the patient (Rizzo and Koenig, 2017).

Beyond therapy and rehabilitation, immersive systems are increasingly being explored within telemedicine. Virtual consultations can improve patient-provider communication through an interactive platform offering a far more appealing option than the conventional remote consultation. It is a highly applicable development for people in remote areas where medical care is relatively limited. Simulation training can improve the skills of healthcare providers in a realistic setting without putting the patient or the provider at risk.

3.4.2. Health Risks and Responsible Use

However, the presence of such benefits does not mean that protracted immersion in virtual reality does not carry any risks. The risk involves physical fatigue or mental exhaustion that may occur when one spends considerable time engaging in virtual interaction at the expense of emotional and social engagements (Kuss & Griffiths, 2017).

To ensure that these novel technologies are rather helpful than harmful to our health, their use must be responsible. We need ethical design for these devices to prevent misuse. It is also important to note that these should be supervised or monitored by professionals in the field of health to result in a healthy digital life.

3.5. Identity And Representation

3.5.1. Avatars as Self-Expression

One of the key characteristics of the metaverse is the capability to build and customize these virtual identities via the use of avatars. These users can choose how they opt to represent themselves in a manner not physically or socially possible in the real world. This kind of experimentation is very empowering to people, especially those who are socially marginal in nature (Yee & Bailenson, 2007).

Interactions via the avatar can also help foster more inclusive public spaces by diminishing the importance attributed to the visually observable physical self, which so often informs offline processes of discriminatory exclusion. Inclusion can, then, be promoted through the design of cyberspace to positively foster acceptance of the differences associated with various identities.

3.5.2. Authenticity, Bias, and Accountability

Nevertheless, the ability to choose new forms of identification also generates concerns regarding authenticity and responsibilities. Anonymity or multiple forms of identification could serve to ensure the lack of accountability for negative action on the part of players. Moreover, there could exist implicit bias within avatar systems, including culture, races, and gender, especially when few alternatives are available by default (Nakamura, 2015).

To tackle these issues, there needs to be deliberate design choices made while keeping in mind cultural sensibilities and inclusivity. On the other hand, there must be measures to strike a balance between freedom of expression and accountability in online communities so that these spaces are safe and trustworthy.

3.6. Governance And Law

3.6.1. Privacy, Responsibility, and Digital Rights

The development of immersive virtual reality spaces raises substantial issues of governance for the metaverse, especially concerning matters of privacy and digital rights. Currently, a significant aspect of data can be held within the metaverse, including data obtained from the behavior and biometric characteristics of users. The aspect of ensuring data security and still enabling realistic levels of user interaction can pose a challenge. The aspect of accountability can also be an important aspect. Harmful behaviors or activities, financial problems, or rights violations within virtual spaces can be difficult to control through the use of existing legal frameworks.

3.6.2. Legal Frameworks for Virtual Worlds

As the metaverse develops further, there comes an increasing need for the development of regulatory frameworks that treat virtual spaces as socially and economically relevant environments. Data protection regulations and those about labor and intellectual property must adapt to the new digital realities brought by the immersive virtual worlds presented by the metaverse. Governments and associated stakeholders must collaborate on creating regulatory frameworks that are adaptable and robust for virtual worlds (Lessig, 2006).

3.7. Environmental Impacts: Energy Consumption and Carbon Footprint of Blockchain and VR Infrastructure

The emergence of immersive digital spaces has brought with it the term "metaverse" as a virtual world sustained by blockchain technology and virtual reality. Although these technological developments bring with them revolutionary changes in communication, business, education, and entertainment, they also pose serious environmental issues. The energy-hungry aspect of decentralized computing and immersive graphical environments is a concern for sustainability and carbon emissions. It is important to study the environmental implications of these developments to ensure that technological advancements are in line with global sustainability targets (Sedlmeir et al., 2020).

3.7.1. Energy Consumption in Blockchain Systems

The blockchain technology employs the use of distributed computing systems in order to ensure that the systems are transparent, decentralized, and secure. Most of the blockchain platforms that have been developed in the past are based on proof of work consensus algorithms, which require a lot of computational power in order to ensure that the blockchain network is secure. The process involves solving mathematical problems using specialized computer hardware, which consumes a lot of energy in the process. The more the blockchain network grows, the more the computational power required. The impact of energy consumption is quite significant, especially if the energy source is fossil fuel (Krause & Tolaymat, 2018). While blockchain technology has its strengths in terms of transparency and trustless systems, its sustainability has been a topic of debate. In reaction to these issues, new blockchain frameworks have shifted towards different consensus algorithms like proof-of-stake, which significantly cuts down energy consumption by moving away from the computational competition model and towards validation models based on the stake (Truby, 2018).

3.7.2. Carbon Footprint and Environmental Sustainability

The carbon footprint of blockchain technology is not just about the electricity usage. It involves all the steps in the production, usage, and disposal of the hardware. Graphics cards, processors, and mining computers are all part of the depletion of resources and the production of electronic waste. The use of rare earth materials and energy-intensive processes is necessary for the production processes and adds to the carbon footprint (Krause & Tolaymat, 2018).

Geographic location and energy sources also influence the carbon footprint. While regions with coal or non-renewable energy resources will enhance the carbon footprint, regions with renewable energy resources will reduce the carbon footprint. Therefore, the impact of blockchain technology on the environment is not experienced by all geographical regions. Research projects related to carbon-neutral blockchain applications, mining networks based on renewable energy resources, and sustainable design strategies focusing on resource conservation and energy efficiency have been promoted by the increasing awareness of climate change (Sedlmeir et al., 2020).

3.7.3. Energy Demands of Virtual Reality Infrastructure

One of the most important technologies in the metaverse is virtual reality. However, virtual reality technology needs powerful computers capable of processing high-resolution environments in real time. This is particularly true for graphics processing units, cloud computing, and high-speed networks. As the metaverse grows in size and more people use it, the energy consumption required by virtual reality applications is also expected to increase (Kim et al., 2021).

The environmental issue associated with VR infrastructure is the operational energy consumption and cost required in the manufacturing process. The manufacturing process of VR components such as headsets and sensors, as well as other hardware components, consumes raw materials and industrial energy, hence the production of carbon. In addition, the requirement to upgrade hardware components from time to time as a result of technological advancements may accelerate the production of electronic waste. The remedy for these issues is to make hardware components energy-efficient and seek ways to recycle (Kim et al., 2021).

3.7.4. Role of Data Centers in Metaverse Sustainability

Data centers are a significant component of metaverse technology because they are the ones that store virtual worlds and user data. In the field of cooling and computing infrastructure that supports this stability, data centers are huge energy consumers.

Data centers are expected to consume more energy as virtual environments become more complex and the number of users increases (Jones, 2018).

There are efforts being made to make data centers more environmentally sustainable. This includes the adoption of advanced cooling systems, effective server space usage, and the adoption of renewable energy. Edge computing can also ensure that data centers are environmentally sustainable by reducing the amount of energy required for data transmission, hence making data centers environmentally sustainable (Jones, 2018).

3.7.5. Lifecycle Environmental Costs and Resource Management

Environmental impact studies must consider the entire lifecycle of the technology, from resource extraction to disposal. The production of semiconductors, GPUs, and VR products is a huge energy hog and uses rare materials, which is a problem in terms of resource depletion and the environment. A lifecycle analysis can identify areas where sustainability improvements can be achieved, such as material savings, energy conservation, and recyclability (Krause & Tolaymat, 2018).

Moreover, effective resource management also demands collective efforts on the part of manufacturers, developers, and policymakers. This is because sustainability policies and regulations can promote eco-friendly design principles, which in turn will ensure that technological development does not disrupt the ecological equilibrium.

3.7.6. Strategies for Sustainable Development

Sustainable development in the blockchain and VR environment requires innovation in technology, government intervention, and awareness among the community. The shift to energy-efficient consensus algorithms, the use of renewable energy resources, and the promotion of green data centers are some of the most important steps towards achieving sustainability. In addition, research on low-power rendering and software architecture can help reduce energy consumption without affecting performance (Sedlmeir et al., 2020).

Public awareness and corporate accountability are also critical in ensuring sustainability. Companies that adopt environmental responsibility policies can set the pace for the adoption of environmentally friendly practices. The inclusion of sustainability metrics in technology development ensures that the environment remains at the forefront of innovation.

3.8. Ethical ai and algorithmic governance in the metaverse

The metaverse is a digital ecosystem that enables users to interact with each other through virtual reality environments that are supported by artificial intelligence systems. The ethical implications and algorithms are core in defining how these environments should work. The growing impact of AI systems on decision-making in virtual worlds has made it important to have responsible governance to avoid any misuse of these systems (Floridi et al., 2018).

3.8.1. Role of Artificial Intelligence in the Metaverse

Artificial intelligence is the main force behind the operation of many metaverse features, such as content management, personalized experiences, virtual economies, and user interactions. The algorithms used in artificial intelligence handle a large amount of data to create a personalized environment for users based on their preferences. Although the personalized environment is an incentive for users to interact more with the system, it also generates some concerns regarding privacy and data ownership. If biased data is used to train AI, it may end up contributing to the inequality of society. It is important that ethical design principles are followed when designing algorithms. Algorithm transparency can ensure that users are aware of how decisions are made (Floridi et al., 2018).

3.8.2. Algorithmic Governance and Decision-Making

Algorithmic governance may be described as the application of algorithms to govern behavior and interactions within a virtual world. In the metaverse, algorithms can be applied to govern access permissions, visibility, and economic transactions. Although algorithms are more efficient, they also pose challenges in terms of accountability. In order to ensure ethical governance, there is a need for guidelines on how the algorithms operate and how the users can dispute the decisions made by the algorithms. Human intervention is still necessary to prevent unintended consequences and ensure that ethical principles are followed.

3.8.3. Privacy and Data Protection

The immersive nature of the metaverse also allows for the collection of a lot of data, such as behavior patterns, biometric data, and social interactions. Therefore, ethical AI governance also has to prioritize the protection of privacy to ensure that sensitive data is not abused. Data protection also encompasses reducing risks of surveillance. Excessive surveillance can undermine the autonomy and freedom of expression of users. Moral values must therefore ensure that data is collected with the purpose of achieving legitimate objectives and not for exploiting users for profit (Floridi et al., 2018).

3.8.4. Digital Identity and Ownership

Digital identity is a very important aspect of metaverse interaction. Users can create avatars and digital identities that represent personal identity. Ethical governance must address issues of identity authenticity, ownership rights, and protection from impersonation or any form of fraud. Blockchain technology may provide a solution through the use of decentralized identity platforms that enable users to control their own information. However, there are ethical considerations that emerge in relation to accessibility. Governance systems should ensure that identity platforms do not discriminate against marginalized groups.

3.8.5. Moderation, Safety, and Inclusivity

The issue of creating a safe and inclusive environment is a concern in immersive virtual reality. AI-powered moderation systems are useful in identifying and preventing negative behaviors, harassment, and undesirable content. But these systems can be prone to biases or misunderstandings of cultural nuances. In ethical governance, moderation systems are constantly evaluated, taking into consideration various viewpoints to ensure that there is no bias. Open appeal processes allow users to contest decisions, ensuring that justice is done. Inclusive design principles ensure that people with different abilities and cultures can access the platform.

3.8.6. Economic Governance and Virtual Economies

The virtual economy in the metaverse includes digital goods, virtual currencies, and peer-to-peer markets. Algorithmic regulation is used to control transactions, avoid fraud, and ensure economic stability. There are ethical issues related to market manipulation, resource inequality, and user exploitation. The creation of the ethical economic systems requires regulation, transparency in transactions, and user education. The issue of how to ensure that the process of decentralization is well balanced with consumer protection is still a challenge that needs the cooperation of technology developers and regulators.

3.8.7. Ethical Challenges and Future Directions

The dynamic nature of the metaverse also gives rise to new ethical issues that have to be addressed by new approaches to governance. The development of new technologies such as generative AI and immersive simulation technologies also gives rise to new ethical issues. Future governance frameworks of the metaverse may also include decentralized decision-making systems that enable community members to take part in decision-making processes related to rules and regulations.

4. BENEFITS AND OPPORTUNITIES

One key aspect of this transition is that while the metaverse introduces many innovative ideas and abilities, the metaverse may also result in other social, economic, educational, and cultural benefits. In addition, as it evolves into a shared, collaborative, and interactive environment, the metaverse could provide many people, including those who have historically been constrained by physical, financial, and geographic limitations, with access to new ways of connecting. By definition, these new opportunities will not come about unless they are designed correctly, governed effectively, and provided with sufficient access; however, the opportunities created by the metaverse will lead to dramatic changes in how humans will interact, be creative, and connect throughout the world in the coming decades (Dwivedi et al., 2022).

4.1. Inclusivity and Equitable Participation

The metaverse offers a unique opportunity for inclusiveness, and this stands out as one of its key benefits. The use of virtual reality means people have more options on how to connect without necessarily being in the same space for a physical visit. Such people who suffer from social anxiety, disabilities, or discrimination have a better opportunity to connect with others via virtual reality. With the expansion of the metaverse into various fields, it has the potential to mitigate social stratification on the same considerations (Park & Kim, 2022).

The accessible technology is also expected to allow individuals with difficulty with their senses, understanding a language, or physical restrictions to be better engaged with or experience their surroundings. Such technologies include the use of speech-to-text software, spatial sound, the ability to alter the avatar, or the ability to create the environment. The use of these technologies gives better engagement options compared to traditional use. The ability of virtual services to evolve, the capacity of the metaverse to improve this ability, especially in areas with poor infrastructure, is set to improve (Mystakidis, 2022).

However, universal inclusive designs may not always be realized. The lack of access to devices, internet connectivity, and technology skills and competencies may worsen and create greater inequities in the metaverse. It should all be considered when there is a need to develop metaverse platforms that should focus on inclusivity and create opportunities for those who lack modern technology (Dwivedi et al., 2022).

4.2. Innovation and Creative Industries

The Metaverse also holds numerous opportunities in various areas, including arts, business, and innovations. Artists will be able to create three-dimensional artworks that do not necessarily have to be made out of physical matter. There will be the power to create immersive products, environments, and performances that are limitless in terms of resources (Lee et al., 2021).

In the metaverse, the creative economies will rely heavily on the concept of User-Generated Content, which will facilitate the transfer from consumer centric behaviour to production-centric behaviour. It will be an opportunity for creatives to monetize their efforts through the metaverse via virtual money or the use of blockchain, depending on whether this platform is developed or not in the marketplace environment. It will hence result in an environment that promotes self-directed, self-organized production of cultural products, since the structural constraint to the creative industries will be eliminated (Park & Kim, 2022).

Entertainment industries such as virtual concerts, social gaming, and immersive storytelling are only a few examples of the potential for spatial digital media to be groundbreaking. Businesses can be supported through new ways of visualizing products and customer interaction. Organizations can create simulations for tests or training purposes for applications in the real world, thus promoting innovation at lower costs of development (Dwivedi et al., 2022).

With more experimentation and innovation, the metaverse can possibly become a breeding ground for new ways of culture and economic models that go beyond the present digital worlds.

4.3. Accessibility in Education, Healthcare, and Work

Great Opportunity to Improve Accessibility and Service Delivery in the Institutional Sector Using Metaverse Technologies in the Core Institutional Sector, including but not limited to: Education &c. The Immersive Virtual Environment allows for Simulation Laboratory Experiments, a Historical Reconstruction, and a Representation of Abstract Concepts, giving Students an Engaging and Experiential Way of Learning. Students from an Ocean Away can participate in The Same classroom and in Real Time, giving Them Access to The Best Class Quality.

The Virtual Environment offers a chance for Medical Students and Professionals to learn in A Realistic Environment by Practicing Procedures with No Risk to the Patient. Patients Can Benefit from a Virtual Consultation, Therapy, and Rehabilitation with Improved Access through Body-Based Interaction, Reducing Travel to Hospitals or Specialist Facilities. Currently, Immersive Impact Therapeutics for Phobias, Cognitive Disabilities, and Mental Health Support has demonstrated efficacy in a controlled environment.

The Metaverse will transform the Method of Work by A Mode of Remote Work, Offering Colleagues a Far Higher Level of Presence in the Workspace than That Provided by Typical Video-Conferencing. This Could Enable a Far More Inclusive Mode of Employment for People with Care-Giving Responsibilities, Mobility Issues, or a Rural Lifestyle.

Companies Currently Testing Out This Hybrid Approach to Virtual Workspaces Have Shown Promise to Enhance Productivity, Innovations, and Social Interaction Through an Integration of Online and Real Environments.

4.4. Global Collaboration and Cultural Exchange

Perhaps the most revolutionary potential with the metaverse is in the affordance to provide international collaboration irrespective of time differences and geographical location. Individuals from varied countries, cultures, and languages can collaborate in the same digital setting, promoting cross-cultural collaboration. Virtual worlds provide the means for instant cross-cultural collaboration, allowing collaboration to be experienced rather than a mere idea (Levy et al., 2022).

International academic conferences, exhibitions, and performances could take place in immersive environments. That could reduce the carbon cost associated with international travel for conferences and the cost associated with attending exhibitions and performances. That could potentially democratize access to the global knowledge network and the global culture network for people who may have had limited access due to geographical and financial constraints.

Culture can also develop within the metaverse, as local cultures, languages, and arts are reflected in virtual worlds. Such virtual worlds could serve as a platform for the preservation of heritage cultures or even the development of a new form of digital culture. However, these same platforms also need to be mindful of cultural representation and balance for globalization to relate to, but not be a form of cultural supremacy.

5. RISKS AND CHALLENGES

Alongside a whole range of potential benefits, the metaverse introduces a whole range of risks that will demand serious critical consideration and engagement. As it is a very rapidly developing sociotechnical space, it encompasses a whole range of challenges that relate to social equity, privacy and surveillance, psychological well-being, and trust in information. While a whole range of risks will apply in different contexts and to different individuals and groups within different regions of the world, they do have in common that they relate very intimately to existing societal and digital inequalities in their respective contexts and environments (Dwivedi et al., 2022).

5.1. Digital Inequality and Accessibility Gaps

While the metaverse is presented as a domain of expanded participation, the availability of the technologies required to participate in it is still a decidedly unequal process. Superior hardware and quality broadband connectivity, and enhanced digital literacy skills, still tend to favour richer individuals and geographic areas. Such a state of affairs threatens to vouchsafe a division in society with full participation in the metaverse reserved for the current privileged of the digital global economy (Ning et al., 2021).

If a country or a community has limited and/or expensive internet access, a lot of people may be excluded from gaining access to the metaverse. Additionally, even in technologically advanced nations, factors such as income levels, age, disability, and educational attainment will affect users of metaverse technology. Some users may be unable to wear head-mounted devices due to physical discomfort and/or medical concerns. Additionally, users may find certain interfaces complicated to handle. If major sectors such as education and employment depend on metaverse technology infrastructure, users who do not access the technology may be barred from social mobility (Park & Kim, 2022).

There is a culture-based digital divide as well. The choices made to ensure a certain level of functionality and usability, while shaped by leading technology companies around the world, can end up ignoring or failing to address a variety of cultures and modes of communication, creating spaces where others feel alien or excluded. The metaverse, if not managed carefully, could become a space where Western technology values dominate, thereby undermining rather than enhancing global diversification (Levy et al., 2022).

5.2. Privacy Risks, Surveillance, and Data Misuse

The metaverse is founded on a large amount of data collection, such as movement, looking, facial expressions, interaction, and even biometric data. The amount and delicacy of the data collected create a level of data that is unprecedented in former platforms (Mystakidis, 2022). Even as it makes immersion possible, it tends to create great privacy concerns.

The high-risk factor includes corporate or governmental surveillance. The behavior and biometric data can identify one's cognitive patterns and emotional and personal desires and preferences. Misuse of such information may lead to highly invasive data usage for corporate advertising. As current legislation addresses conventional web data, it has failed to synchronize its tenets with those of the embodied Internet environment.

Other categories are more related to property and control of digital identity because the bottom line is that when users put so much emotional and financial investment into their digital assets and digital identity, control remains in the hands of the people who run the platforms. This situation raises specific concerns with respect to data loss, theft of assets, or one-sided decisions when it comes to moderation (Ning et al., 2021).

It also reveals risks associated with security. Lack of security, identity theft, and virtual harassment are certain to not only disturb the virtual experience but also that of psychological security associated with it. As a function of presence, it is likely that these problems might have more serious implications associated with them, ensuring that appropriate security measures are put in place from inception.

5.3. Addiction and Mental Health Concerns

Immersive online worlds are typically designed to promote engagement. Some of these include factors like continuous interaction, content customization, and the presence of continuous worlds. While interaction and fun are great experiences, engagement could be detrimental to work, sleeping, and health offline for some people (Damar et al., 2023).

The virtual environment can also affect the separation of one's online and offline identity, leading to possible stress and feelings of disconnection from reality. Since youths are still developing emotional control and even identity, they are more susceptible to these factors. The development of supportive settings and guidelines from caregivers then becomes critical in ensuring that youths safely navigate through the virtual world (Kim, 2021).

Harassment, lack of inclusion, or negative comparison with others through social media is not unique, but problems could be exacerbated in visually realized environments. Negative experiences can happen through the internalization of poorly experienced interactions through avatars, even if there is a reliance on these environments for confidence building. It is a challenge that needs the combined effort of technologists, psychologists, teachers, and policymakers working together to retain well-being as a key design goal.

5.4. Spread of Misinformation and Trust Issues

The credibility and security of the information in the metaverse are challenges as well. Digital environments are capable of creating misleading but credible information through immersive images and interactive social environments that display misleading information not related to the credibility of the information. Digital environments that create persuasive images of reality through electronic media, and immersive social environments that interact with it, are likely to offer challenges different from the usual in addressing misleading information (Lee et al., 2021). This is specifically true for misleading information in areas such as politics, healthcare, and emergency.

Avatars are also poised to become the norm within digital communication, and the challenge of whether one is actually who he or she claims to be will soon become impossible. Avatars of those who are hiding information related to politics or a corporation will also heighten the possibility of fraud and trickery. Nor will it be possible to date or state as factual avatars that have the same characteristics as real-life beings, posing a heightened possibility of fraud or legal culpability (Park & Kim, 2022). As this is ongoing, the degree of trust users will have towards a metaverse will depend on the creation of a system designed to verify not only the identity but also the information of the avatars, as well as a balance between creating a secure environment for users and the users' freedom.

The management of speech and behavior will be more complex due to the fact that there are many people from other cultures and legal jurisdictions. Thus, the design and improvement over time of an approach to the fair and transparent moderation of the system will be difficult. The platform operators will have the strongest influence on the information to which the users will have access and on the prioritization of the information presented to the users, and will also play an important role in the design and implementation of the approach that will be responsible for the users and to themselves (Levy et al., 2022).

6. ETHICAL AND REGULATORY CONSIDERATIONS

This raises a new set of ethical issues different from the old ones, simply because the metaverse itself represents permanence and immersion. The presence of the metaverse and the virtual engagement that happens over actual physical engagement is itself transforming the manner of the representation of identities, the manner of the depiction of ownership, the manner of sharing responsibilities, as well as the manner of application of governance. The new issues that emerge are to be tackled, keeping in mind the issues associated with equity, accountability, user consent, and the sufficiency of policy mechanisms, or else this metaverse may become a reality where technological superiority precedes social accountability.

6.1. Fairness, Accountability, and Safety

Fairness in the Metaverse refers to the treatment of participants in the Metaverse in a range of ways: socially, economically, or culturally. In many Metaverse environments, there are systems of automated decision-making to manage the extent to which views are restricted through the use of the economy or the interactions between participants. Although the Metaverse's use of automation ensures higher levels of efficiency in these systems, there still exists the problem of the negative impact of these systems upon marginalized groups in favor of the primary group or a desirable behavior (Mittelstadt et al., 2016).

Issues surrounding responsibility or accountability are another area that can be complex. However, this becomes even more so in the context of immersive environments because this would hold implications for the platform provider, the software/app provider, the content provider, and the users. With matters relating to intimidation, discrimination, or economic exploitation where there are issues with the individual or group who are affected, and any injury caused to them becomes difficult to hold any person or institution accountable from the point of the legal system, since there are juridical boundaries for the legal entities in play (Helberger et al., 2020).

Safety remains the underlying ethical issue here, since the immersive nature of the technology enhances social presence. Perceptions of harassment or aggressive intent might have greater psychological trauma than in the text-based community. While safety may demand safeguarding primarily through the use of human moderators or enforcers, the need to design the environment carefully to reduce unhealthy socializing while allowing users to care for one another would remain essential. The safety paradigm supporting the underlying ethics will then tread the thin line between safeguarding and autonomy to avoid control and build trust as well as well-being (Floridi et al., 2018).

6.2. Digital Ownership and User Consent

"Digital ownership encompasses more than just virtual goods and may be exercised over one's identity, self-expression, and social presence." Users tend to invest considerable amounts of time, labor, and emotional capital into creating avatars and virtual worlds. Nonetheless, the terms of service tend to undercut the notion of digital ownership as a means to advocate the agenda of the corporation that runs the digital platform (Zuboff, 2019).

Also, the aspects of consent in immersive scenarios are more complex due to the ongoing and sometimes imperceptible data processing. In addition to simple data regarding user interactions, the metaverse system may be processing data regarding movement patterns, location behaviors, and biometric data. The common consent approach in the form of a simple agreement or consent form cannot be applicable in such pervasive data processing. The ethical approach to consent in the metaverse requires all these aspects to be ongoing, transparent, and dynamic to facilitate well-informed decisions regarding changes in contexts (Nissenbaum, 2010).

Moreover, the persistence offered by digital identity establishes long-term implications for autonomy and the right to privacy. Deeds undertaken by the avatar could be tracked, analyzed, and repurposed. If not guarded properly, the user can lose control over the representation and construction of their identity. As stipulated above, governing the formation and construction of digital identity must take precedence in user agency.

6.3. Responsible Design Principles

Regulatory systems were not cognizant of the immersive transnational digital world of the metaverse. Because regulations, such as those concerning data protection, consumer rights, and intellectual property, typically draw distinctions between the digital and physical worlds, and the metaverse represents the darkening of such distinctions.

Apart from that, the question of jurisdiction is one of the main challenges that exist. Online interactions can take place among people from different countries governed by different jurisdictions. The challenge that exists here is the rules that are to be used in addressing the disputes, the transactions, as well as the damaging activities.

"Governance of the metaverse will certainly involve both formal regulation and ethical frameworks. They could offer flexibility in their application as well as ensure the protection of fundamental human rights. Ethical and regulatory success depends finally on aligning innovations with valued public purposes."

6.4. Policy Gaps and Governance Challenges

The previous system of laws was not designed for the immersive global space that can be created with a metaverse. The system of laws that regulates data protection, consumer rights, and intellectual property rights is delineated in a manner that makes a clear demarcation between the physical world and the online world. In a metaverse, these distinctions will fade away, thus challenging laws and jurisdictions where these laws must be amended (Brownsword, 2020).

Jurisdiction is another field that offers an immense level of challenge to the individual involved in the virtual communication process. In virtual communication, the concerned parties may belong to diverse countries. These countries fall under the jurisdiction of different authorities. It was difficult to conclude under which jurisdiction the concerned parties would fall in case of conflicts or even negative acts.

The future of managing the metaverse may very well call for the application of hybrid models, which enable the combination of formal rule-making with ethical values. This approach could result in the allowance for flexibility while preserving human rights. Ultimately, the success of ethics and regulations would depend on innovation and the greater good.

7. FUTURE OUTLOOK

The future of the metaverse is not an already determined path, but rather an outcome of the interplay of innovation, institutional decisions, and social negotiation. The metaverse is more than a mere destination of the future. Its development depends on the various ways immersive technologies can be incorporated into daily lives. It includes many possibilities for the future, such as the sectors of education, healthcare, work, and governance, among others (Castells, 2010).

7.1. Integration in Education, Healthcare, Work, and Governance

Turning to education, the potential use of immersive technologies lies in experiential learning, as they can be used to engage with complex systems or models. Virtual classrooms can be created for learning. However, issues may emerge in terms of accessibility and learning overload as immersive technologies are used to engage educational programs. These issues are identified by a study cited by Selwyn (2016).

Applications in the health sector can vary from training simulators to treatment environments and remote health clinics. It is, on the other hand, an important fact that such applications can do the trick of offering greater accessibility for health care and training, especially within those areas lacking such infrastructure.

Integration in the workplace is also envisioned to introduce a paradigm shift in workplace interaction. Virtual offices or collaborative spaces may also ensure that geographically distanced teams function with improved interactive tools. Questions also emerge in terms of observation and separation of working and non-working life, or "virtual fatigue". Organisational policy will significantly influence whether immersion in working environments frees or entrenches managerial control over employees as envisioned in Sennett (2018).

Applications of governance remain an area to investigate, with great significance. Forums and virtual publics might serve as arenas for governance engagement and civic education. This would demand transparency and trust in the role of the actors of the institution.

7.2. Scenarios of Immersive Adoption

Various adoptive futures for these emerging technologies are possible. One may involve the integration of immersive tech into the fabric of society, while another could involve an adoption pattern where these platforms offer a niche solution to professionals. Social acceptability will rest upon perceived usefulness, credibility, and relevance.

Cultural issues will play an even more significant part in the adoption processes. Each culture has its own perspectives on privacy issues, automation, and the use of technology as a mediating device. This results in the growth of the metaverse being uneven across the world. Here, the need for contextual study (Castells, 2010) comes into prominence.

7.3. Research and Policy Recommendations

In the next research, focus and emphasis should shift away from short-term and technological performance and focus instead on the longer-term social implications and outcomes. An important area of study, interestingly, lies at the interface of various disciplines, and the knowledge and expertise of multiple fields need to come together to help understand the implications of immersive environments on cognition, relationships, and institutions.

Frameworks for policy must incorporate flexibility, making it easier for regulatory development to keep pace with technological developments. Instead of regulatory determinism, principles-based regulation may provide an effective way to safeguard basic human rights while permitting innovation. International debate will also be needed to respond to global issues with joint approaches to ethics (OECD, 2019).

7.4. Building Inclusive and Sustainable Digital Ecosystems

The metaverse will have to be designed and managed in certain ways so that it is going to be inclusive and sustainable. Sustainability will involve more than efficiency, incorporating aspects such as social resilience, cultural diversity, and ethical integrity. Virtual worlds must facilitate creativity and collaboration, but not drain or widen the gap of attention.

Ultimately, the future of the metaverse and the role it plays within society is determined by the needs and desires of the collective as it pertains to technology and society as a whole. By turning their focus towards inclusion, responsibility, and the welfare of humanity, the digital realms of the metaverse can develop as an enhancement of the real world, not an alternative.

CONCLUSION

This chapter has examined how the metaverse presents as a dynamic socio-technical system that not only exceeds innovation but in effect Transformation affects how we interact in society as well as how institutions and cultures are framed in the current digital age. From foundational frameworks and technologies backtracked in this respect towards respective origins, in effect builds as how societies are perceived in terms of immersive technologies, smart technologies, and blockchain technologies in respect towards how these non-entities are understood in building towards dynamic socio-technical frameworks as spin-offs associated with innovation in effect. Within key areas in society as explored in respect towards key domains in effect in how innovations in these areas interact in respect towards rebuilding how these innovations shape society in key areas including learning and work as discussed in detail in this respect in effect; healthcare and wellness as explored towards understanding; identity within these areas as understood within building towards transforming towards how representation in these key areas are imperative in forging identities in respect towards innovation within these areas as understood in effect. It also represents a shifting focus from technology and innovation to themes of governance and regulation. Today, there is a challenge in dealing with data protection and digital ownership in these immersion environments. In fact, in future projections, it will not necessarily be technology that will ensure the social benefit of this society in the future. Actually, with future visions in place regarding the benefits of the metaverse society in society at large, it would make sense that instead of reducing social interaction in reality, it becomes one of the places.

REFERENCES

Brownsword, R. (2020). *Law, technology and society: Re-imagining the regulatory environment*. Routledge.

Castells, M. (2010). *The rise of the network society* (2nd ed.). Wiley-Blackwell.

Castronova, E. (2005). *Synthetic worlds: The business and culture of online games*. University of Chicago Press.

Damar, M., Kaleci, D., & Kılıç, E. (2023). Educational opportunities and challenges in the metaverse: A systematic review. *Computers & Education: Artificial Intelligence*, *4*, 100154. Advance online publication. DOI: 10.1016/j.caeai.2023.100154

Dionisio, J. D. N., Burns, W. G., & Gilbert, R. (2013). 3D virtual worlds and the metaverse: Current status and future possibilities. *ACM Computing Surveys*, *45*(3), 34. Advance online publication. DOI: 10.1145/2480741.2480751

Dwivedi, Y. K., Hughes, L., Baabdullah, A. M., Ribeiro-Navarrete, S., Giannakis, M., Al-Debei, M. M., Dennehy, D., Metri, B., Buhalis, D., Cheung, C. M. K., Conboy, K., Doyle, R., Dubey, R., Dutot, V., Felix, R., Goyal, D. P., Gustafsson, A., Hinsch, C., Jebabli, I., & Wamba, S. F. (2022). Metaverse beyond the hype: Multidisciplinary perspectives on emerging challenges, opportunities, and agenda for research. *International Journal of Information Management*, *66*, 102542. Advance online publication. DOI: 10.1016/j.ijinfomgt.2022.102542

Floridi, L., Cowls, J., Beltrametti, M., Chatila, R., Chazerand, P., Dignum, V., Luetge, C., Madelin, R., Pagallo, U., Rossi, F., Schafer, B., Valcke, P., & Vayena, E. (2018). AI4People—An ethical framework for a good AI society. *Minds and Machines*, *28*(4), 689–707. DOI: 10.1007/s11023-018-9482-5 PMID: 30930541

Floridi, L., Cowls, J., Beltrametti, M., Chatila, R., Chazerand, P., Dignum, V., & Vayena, E. (2018). AI4People—An ethical framework for a good AI society. *Minds and Machines*, *28*(4), 689–707. DOI: 10.1007/s11023-018-9482-5 PMID: 30930541

Helberger, N., Pierson, J., & Poell, T. (2020). Governing online platforms: From contested to cooperative responsibility. *The Information Society*, *36*(1), 1–14. DOI: 10.1080/01972243.2017.1391913

Jones, N. (2018). How to stop data centres from gobbling up the world's electricity. *Nature*, *561*(7722), 163–166. DOI: 10.1038/d41586-018-06610-y PMID: 30209383

Kim, J. (2021). Advertising in the metaverse: Research agenda. *Journal of Interactive Advertising*, *21*(3), 141–144. DOI: 10.1080/15252019.2021.2001273

Kim, J., Lee, H., & Lee, J. (2021). Energy consumption and sustainability of virtual reality systems. *IEEE Access : Practical Innovations, Open Solutions*, *9*, 123456–123470.

Krause, M. J., & Tolaymat, T. (2018). Quantification of energy and carbon costs for mining cryptocurrencies. *Nature Sustainability*, *1*(11), 711–718. DOI: 10.1038/s41893-018-0152-7

Kuss, D. J., & Griffiths, M. D. (2017). Social networking sites and addiction: Ten lessons learned. *International Journal of Environmental Research and Public Health*, *14*(3), 311. Advance online publication. DOI: 10.3390/ijerph14030311 PMID: 28304359

Lee, L. H., Braud, T., Zhou, P., Wang, L., Xu, D., Lin, Z., Kumar, A., Bermejo, C., & Hui, P. (2021). All one needs to know about metaverse: A complete survey on technological singularity, virtual ecosystem, and research agenda. *Journal of Information Technology Case and Application Research*, *23*(4), 1–20. DOI: 10.1080/15228053.2021.1996899

Lessig, L. (2006). *Code version 2.0*. Basic Books.

Levy, S., Bender, E. M., & Tsvetkov, Y. (2022). Cross-cultural communication and collaboration in virtual environments. *Journal of Virtual Worlds Research*, *15*(2), 45–60.

Mittelstadt, B. D., Allo, P., Taddeo, M., Wachter, S., & Floridi, L. (2016). The ethics of algorithms: Mapping the debate. *Big Data & Society*, *3*(2), 1–21. DOI: 10.1177/2053951716679679

Mystakidis, S. (2022). Metaverse. *Encyclopedia*, *2*(1), 486–497. DOI: 10.3390/encyclopedia2010031

Nakamura, L. (2015). The unwanted labour of social media: Women of color call out culture as venture capital. *New Formations*, *86*, 106–112. DOI: 10.3898/NEWF.86.06.2015

Ning, H., Wang, H., Lin, Y., Wang, W., Dhelim, S., Farha, F., Ding, J., & Daneshmand, M. (2021). A survey on metaverse: The state-of-the-art, technologies, applications, and challenges. *IEEE Internet of Things Journal*, *10*(4), 2927–2946. DOI: 10.1109/JIOT.2021.3124546

Nissenbaum, H. (2010). *Privacy in context: Technology, policy, and the integrity of social life*. Stanford University Press.

OECD. (2019). *Artificial intelligence in society*. OECD Publishing., DOI: 10.1787/eedfee77-

Park, S. M., & Kim, Y. G. (2022). A metaverse: Taxonomy, components, applications, and open challenges. *IEEE Access : Practical Innovations, Open Solutions, 10*, 4209–4251. DOI: 10.1109/ACCESS.2021.3140175

Radianti, J., Majchrzak, T. A., Fromm, J., & Wohlgenannt, I. (2020). A systematic review of immersive virtual reality applications for higher education. *Education and Information Technologies, 25*, 1–38. DOI: 10.1007/s10639-019-10003-6

Rizzo, A. A., & Koenig, S. T. (2017). Is clinical virtual reality ready for primetime? *Neuropsychology, 31*(8), 877–899. DOI: 10.1037/neu0000405 PMID: 29376669

Schroeder, R. (2016). *Social theory after the Internet: Media, technology, and globalization*. UCL Press.

Sedlmeir, J., Buhl, H. U., Fridgen, G., & Keller, R. (2020). The energy consumption of blockchain technology: Beyond myth. *Business & Information Systems Engineering, 62*(6), 599–608. DOI: 10.1007/s12599-020-00656-x

Selwyn, N. (2016). *Education and technology: Key issues and debates*. Bloomsbury Academic.

Sennett, R. (2018). *The corrosion of character: The personal consequences of work in the new capitalism*. W. W. Norton & Company.

Taylor, T. L. (2006). *Play between worlds: Exploring online game culture*. MIT Press. DOI: 10.7551/mitpress/5418.001.0001

Truby, J. (2018). Decarbonizing Bitcoin: Law and policy choices for reducing the energy consumption of blockchain technologies and digital currencies. *Energy Research & Social Science, 44*, 399–410. DOI: 10.1016/j.erss.2018.06.009

Turkle, S. (2017). *Alone together: Why we expect more from technology and less from each other*. Basic Books.

Yee, N., & Bailenson, J. N. (2007). The Proteus effect: The effect of transformed self-representation on behavior. *Human Communication Research, 33*(3), 271–290. DOI: 10.1111/j.1468-2958.2007.00299.x

Zuboff, S. (2019). *The age of surveillance capitalism*. PublicAffairs.

Chapter 2
Public Spaces, Smart Cities, and the Metaverse Future

C. V. Subramanian
http://orcid.org/0000-0001-9313-0311
Periyar Maniammai Institute of Science and Technology, India

J. Janani
http://orcid.org/0009-0005-8145-7807
Periyar Maniammai Institute of Science and Technology, India

ABSTRACT

Urban public spaces plays a vital role in enhancing social cohesion through the support of interaction, cultural exchange and identity collectively. In smart city era, the public spaces are oriented towards digital technologies that reshape how people meet each other, communicate and participate. Traditional design principles of accessibility, safety, proximity in modern public life is now through digital layer like participatory apps, real time data applications, smart mobility systems and advance technology like metaverse. Combing digital and physical world resulted in creation of hybrid public spaces which enables communities to cocreate and experience in multiple dimensions. Case Studies including Amsterdam, Barcelona, Singapore, Bhopal and Seoul show on how various tools for designing apps to integrated command centres and metaverse platforms can enhance inclusion and civic management. In spite of the opportunities for extended participation are growing, challenges must be addressed to ensure resilient and equitable smart cities.

DOI: 10.4018/979-8-3373-6721-7.ch002

INTRODUCTION

Open Space such as squares, parks, Plazas, and marketplaces are considered as Urban Public spaces, which are accessible to all citizens to enhance social interactions, recreational activities and community building. In the ancient period, these public spaces shaped the social identity of the city and provided a way for people to gather, engage and interact (Jacob,1961; Gehl 2011). Urban class theory suggests that public spaces demonstrate spatial stories which promote inclusive decision making, encourage active citizen participation and in turn promote social cohesion (Habermas, 1989; Senett, 2018). According to Lefebvre (1991), it is rather through the dynamics of the interactions between physical form and identity that a public space truly comes to function as the very heart of urban life.

In the last few years, globally urbanisation, socioeconomic development and challenges in the environment have changed the scenario of public space usage and its purpose (Madanipour, 2003). Meantime, the advancement in the development of information and communication technologies (ICT), mobile networking and networking in sensors have evolved in smart city mission which intensely fit in digital infrastructure into urban management and everyday life (Allam & Newman, 2018; Kitchin, 2015). Public spaces are not only a physical setting but also acts as a node where social entity and technical knowledge merges together through real time data collection, predictive examination and collaborative services through public participation (Batty, 2018; Komninos, 2020).

The above-mentioned conditions lead to evolution of Hybrid public spaces which was quoted by many research scholars, in which the digital and physical layers intersect in the environmental condition (Graham & Marvin, 2001; Aurigi & Willis, 2020). ICT enabled technologies like charging ports enabled smart benches, AI enabled heritage building tour and participatory mapping apps are new ICT enabled features in cities (Foth st al, 2016; Townsend, 2013). People meet and interact with one another in two ways like physically in real places and also through the digital world (Hampton, 2016). Public participation in real time scenario is mediated not only by proximity but also connectivity through availability of Wi-Fi, Apps, and other digital technology (Nam & Pardo, 2011; Cardullo & Kitchin, 2019).

Recently, the development in the technologies including metaverse, three-dimensional virtual environment is achieved through interfaces like extended reality (XR) and has led way to the new idea of research on public spaces for the researchers (Dwivedi et al. 2022; Maier et al, 2025). Cities such as Seoul are experimenting with metaverse technologies where these platforms host virtual city halls, virtual cultural fest, enabled residents to participate through various embodiments in spite of its physical location or mobility constraints (Owojori, 2023). Researchers, Scholars and Experts are beginning to ask how physical and hybrid spaces will blend each other and whether metaverse will form a new idea of urban public spaces (Bibri & Allam, 2022; Sharifi & Amirzadeh 2025).

In the middle of all these developments, the question of social cohesion lies as how strongly people that they belong to a group or community and how much they trust each and further how actively they take part in activities together (Forrest & Kearns, 2001; Chan et al, 2006). Urban public space has historically been the primary creators of space that promotes social cohesion, to foster everyday activities to create a familiar spaces and supportive network system (Ujang & Zakariya, 2015; Peters et al, 2010). According to Lai, Wang and Wen (2024) show that public spaces designed to enhance people comfort, accessibility and value significantly contribute to people sense of belongings particularly in resettlement communities. In research by Li et al (2024), explains how social cohesion can be reinforced thorough demonstration of heritage public spaces by anchoring collective memory and identity.

The emergence of ICT enabled smart city technologies and metaverse spaces complicates this relationship in uncertain ways. On one hand, to enhance inclusion digital tools acted as initiators thorough which people who are geographically apart to unite together, further physically impaired to access information and to involve themselves in public processes (Meijer & Bolivar, 2016; Calzada, 2021; Itair et al, 2023). Information about historical events, environmental conditions or community developments, extending attachment and stewardship are provided by hybrid environments (Garau et al, 2017; Batty, 2018). Metaverse platforms may qualify safe and playful engagement with development circumstances particularly for young generation people (Dwivedi et al, 2022; Maier et al, 2024).

Over the last three years, digital transformation in urban areas has developed far beyond the platform-based governance towards immersive, Ai assisted decision making environment. Post pandemic the urban recovery strategies have included data analytics, artificial intelligence, extended reality and digital twins reshaping on how cities are experienced and managed. Recent research argue that smart cities are transitioning from sensor-based model to participatory ecosystem where algorithmic system mediate planning, service and citizen engagement (Sharifi & Amirzadeh, 2025). These developments tells that public space is no longer a physical encounter but also a hybrid socio technical interface.

The evolution of AI assisted planning platforms has introduced few forms of urban simulation in which pedestrian flows, environmental comfort, behavioural response and even social interaction patterns can be modelled before physical application. Such predictive systems promise efficiency and awareness. Contemporary research in 2025 highlights concerns about algorithmic bias, data asymmetry and digital sovereignty, particularly when proprietary technologies shape civic infrastructure (Bibri & Allam, 2022).

In parallel to AI expansion, immersive technology platforms are also being tested as extensions of civic participation. Rather than simply hosting online forums, these environments enable citizens to enter spatially stimulated urban setting, visualize proposal based on developments and interact with officials (Maier et al, 2024). This change marks a movement from informational participation towards practical participation. This implication of social cohesion is significant.

Despite growing literature on smart cities, digital twins and metaverse governance, few studies systematically examine on how hybrid and immersive public spaces influence social cohesion across different governance model and socio-economic context (Maier et al, 2025). Existing trend tend to isolate either technological efficiency or social participation without integrating them into comprehensive framework. Moreover, comparison between global north and global south remain limited particularly on how digital integration intersects with public trust. This study addresses that gap by synthesising theories of public spaces, social cohesion, hybrid urbanism and metaverse governance into a unifies analytical framework.

On the other hand, public spaces which are digitally equipped will produce risk of inequalities tied to connectivity, accessibility to device and digital literacy (Hollands, 2015; Townsend, 2013;

Sharifi et al, 2021). The power from citizens will be shifted to corporates and algorithm designers by date driven governance and it will supress transparency and accountability (Kitchin, 2014; Zuboff, 2019). The use of sensor cameras and behaviour monitoring devices in public spaces can erode the sense of freedom and spontaneous vibrant character of public life by turning the space into venues of surveillance capitalism (Bibri & Allam, 2022; Calzada, 2021). In addition to this, over dependency on virtual forms of interaction may weaken embodied sociability, reducing the change that nurtures empathy and social resilience (Sennett, 2018; Hampton, 2016).

Figure 1. Methodology Flow Chart

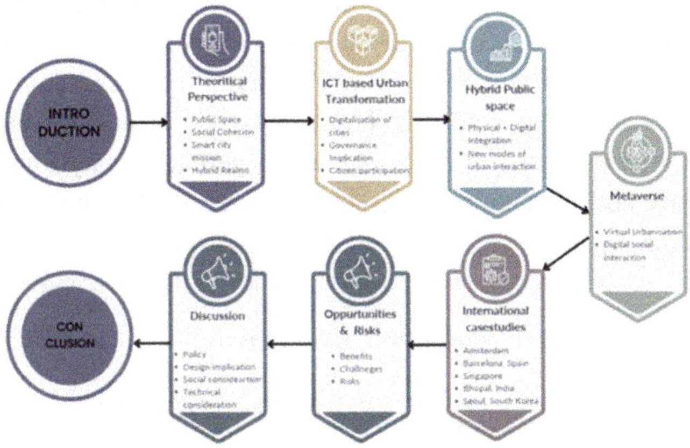

This chapter addresses the dilemma created by exploring how metaverse environment and hybrid spaces in Urban public spaces in smart cities can influence social cohesion as shown in Figure 1. It has three main objectives:

1. Developing a theoretical framework that combines urban public space, social cohesion, smart city, hybrid space and metaverse environment.
2. Analysing real time examples where digital technology is mediated in public spaces across various global contexts including Amsterdam, Barcelona, Singapore, Bhopal and Seoul.
3. To propose design and principles for human centered hybrid public open spaces that enhance inclusion, trust and democratic participation while mitigating risks.

THEORETICAL FRAMEWORK – URBAN PUBLIC SPACE, HYBRID REALMS AND SOCIAL COHESION

Public Space and the Public Sphere

The ideology of public is closely connection to the concept of the public sphere. A space where people get along to share their ideas, exchange opinions, discuss issues and make decisions for the betterment of the society (Habermas, 1989; Mitchell, 2003). In Habermas (1989) view this public sphere has originated in coffeeshops, salons and early media networks where people met to discuss social and political issues. Urbanist highlighted the importance of public spaces like parks, plazas and streets in cities, where people gather, met each other, get exposed to different opinions and cultures (Low, 2000; Madanipour, 2003). Jane Jacobs (1961) added that ordinary urban public space like sidewalks and street corners help build safety and trust because people constantly watched what happens around them: eyes on the street, which encourages care, protection and shared sense of responsibility within a community as shown in Figure 2. The importance of human scale, proximity, walkability and active corners for encouraging people to stay longer in a place, interact socially and engage in joyful activities rather than just passing through quickly (Gehl, 2011).

Figure 2. Changing Urban Place into Urban Square

Public space is not neutral. Public space is shaped by social networking and systems of power (Lefebvre, 1991). In capitalist cities, urban development often breaks apart genuine public area and replaces them with commercial spaces like shopping malls that are accessible only to paying customers. In view of the "right to the city" movement argues that all citizens should have the power to influence on how urban space can be designed, used and access to public space should be fair and equal (Harvey, 2012; Purcell, 2002). In this perspective social cohesion does not happen just because of people sharing space rather it requires efforts towards inclusion, depiction and respect for varied groups.

Social Cohesion

Social Cohesion denotes that how strongly people feel connected to their community including a sense of belonging, shared values, mutual trust and motivation to work together for the growth of the community (Forrest & Kaerns, 2001; Chan et al, 2006). Key dimensions of social cohesion include social networking, social interactions, inclusion, participation, engagement and shared identity. In urban contexts, public space plays a critical role by providing environments where people from various background can informally meet each other, perceive standards, negotiate conflicts and develop mutual tolerance (Peters et al, 2010; Francis et al, 2012).

Lai et al. (2024) expresses that citizens perception of social cohesion when they offer comfort, safety, amenities and opportunities for interaction were contributed by public spaces in resettlement communities. Placemaking elements such as seating area, shade structures, walkable pathways, cultural symbols create a sense of community and it strengthen attachments among people (Ujang and Zakariya, 2015). Temple, public square and other heritage open spaces enhances social cohesion by anchoring the history and rituals (Li et al, 2024). All these studies show that the way public spaces are designed and managed has a strong impact on how people form relationships and support each other which helps communities stay strong during challenges.

Smart Cities and Urban Governance

Smart cities are commonly known as urban systems that use latest technologies like ICT, sensors networks and data analytics to optimize service, increase efficiency and promote innovation (Caragliu at al, 2011; Giffinger at al, 2007). Researchers strongly disagree on what smart technologies in cities mean for society. One group focuses on the technocentric perspective view focusing on efficiency, economic development and smooth integration of digital infrastructure through positive smart urban development (Batty, 2013; Hollands, 2015) Another group focuses on critical perspective warns that smart cities can lead to corporate control, increased surveillance, reducing democratic decision and social inequality (Kitchin, 2014; Calzada, 2021).

Nam and Pardo (2011) suggest that smart city should balance technology, people and institutions rather focusing on technology alone. Smart urban development should promote smart governance enabling that digital tools should be used to improve transparency, collaboration and public participation instead of concentrating control in the hands of authorities (Meijer and Bolivar, 2016). Cardullo and Kitchin (2019) warn that these participation platforms give residents only the illusion of being involved and people may provide with data or feedback but it rarely influences real decision making or power relations. Together these arguments show that the arguments on smart cities are difficult to understand on how hybrid public space should be designed, managed and regulated so that the technology supports democracy rather than replacing it.

Hybrid Public Spaces

Hybrid public spaces are described as urban environments where digital technologies and physical spaces are connected together. They are neither purely material not fully virtual but a fusion of both (Graham & Marvin, 2001; Foth et al, 2016). Digital layers like data networks, apps, sensors and smart service are embedded in streets, building and everyday infrastructure. Aurigi and Willis (202) refer this as augmented city where information overlays guide how people understand and navigate the urban environment. Figure 3 shows that mobile networking enables people to be physically present in public space while simultaneously connected to other online communications which give rise to hybrid spatial experiences.

Figure 3. Hybrid Public Space where Digital Technologies and Physical spaces are combined together

Publicness in these spaces is partly constructed through digital visibility including selfies, location tags, check-ins, livestreams and online discussions linked to physical events (Evans, 2015). Hybrid spaces also support participation and cocreation as seen in digital kiosk, participatory mapping tools and sensor based artistic installations that allow citizens to contribute information and aesthetics (Foth et al, 2016; Duarte at al, 2018). However, these technologies can also fragment collective experience and introduce new exclusions, especially for those people without smartphones, data access and digital literacy (Hollands, 2015; Townsend, 2013).

The Metaverse as Public Realm

The metaverse is described as a network of persistent, immersive and interoperable virtual environments in which users interact with one another with digital objects in real time (Dwivedi et al, 2022; Smart et al, 2007). Even though these technologies initially associated with gaming and entertainment only, recently many researches highlight it broader implication for education, commerce, governance and urban life (Allam & Newman, 2022; Maier at al, 2024). Bibri and Allam (2022) describes the metaverse as virtual layer of smart urbanism where the city data network and digital twins are merged into simulated environments that can directly experienced by users for their benefits.

Emerging countries initiatives such as Seoul's metaverse platform for public services and citizen participation raise the question of whether metaverse environments may constitute a new form of public space (Owojori, 2023). Expanding accessibility to public with mobility challenges, offering risk free environments for experimental learning and fostering cultural exchange across nation will be potentially possible through these platforms (Sharifi & Aminzadeh, 2025). Yet the metaverse also introduce ethical challenges which includes the extraction and commercialisation of personal data, tracking of behavioural patterns, concentration of power among major corporates and possibility of algorithmic systems shaping public interaction without democratic freedom (Zuboff, 2019; Calzada, 2021),

Synthesis

Collectively these theoretical standards of public space, social cohesion, smart governance, hybrid environments and the metaverse form a comprehensive framework for examining how public spaces in smart cities are being transformed. They suggest that the issue extend far beyond technology and are fundamentally social and political like who is allowed to participate in these spaces? who controls the digital platforms and the data they generate? How are norms, visibility and opportunities for interaction shaped or restricted? These concerns determine whether technologically enabled public spaces will promote inclusion and engagement among citizens or reinforce inequality and control. The following sections use this framework to analyse real world case studies and evaluate how emerging public spaces operated in practice. Table 1 shows the Urban public relation and their role in social cohesion

Table 1. Public space and their role in social cohesion

Aspects	Key Idea	Implication for Design
Social Cohesion	• Encounters every day in public space • It builds trust and community engagement	Creates environments that encourage casual, unplanned social interactions
Inclusion	• Public spaces should be accessible • Public spaces should welcome wide range of people	Design with sensitivity to age, gender, ability, socioeconomic status and cultural differences
Heritage and Identity	• Historical open spaces create a sense of place and memory	Preserving heritage sites making them as active, modern community spaces.
Quality of Place	• Should enhance comfort, safety. • Should strongly shape how long people will stay and how will they use the space	Providing seating, shades under trees, green spaces, proper lighting and overall comfort for the people
Equity	• Free and accessible public space for all citizens	Over commercialisation should be prevented to ensure that space remains open, affordable and inclusive for all people.

Conceptual Model: Hybrid Public Space and Social cohesion matrix

Earlier theoretical discussion explains that public space, digital infrastructure and governance are deeply interconnected. However, to evaluate their collective impact on social cohesion, a more structured analytical model is required. A proposal of hybrid public space social cohesion matrix participates physical design, digital integration and institutional governance into a layered evaluative framework.

The first layer consists of physical design quality, encompassing accessibility, comfort, safety, spatial diversity and environmental performance. Basic urban research show that walkability, huma scale, seating, shading and mixed-use activity generate conditions for everyday encounters thar fostering trust and awareness (Gehl,2011; Jacobs, 1961). Without this spatial foundation, digital enhancements cannot compensate for poor public realm design.

The second layer involves digital integration intensity. This includes the presence of sensor, data dashboards, participatory platforms, AR overlays, interactive installation and digital twins. Such technologies can increase responsiveness and transparency; extreme technological intervention may portion shaded experience or privilege digitally literate population (Maier et al, 2025). Hybrid environments therefore need calibrated integration rather than technological saturation.

A fourth-dimension addresses digital equity and access. Infrastructure availability, device affordability, multilingual interfaces and digital literacy programmes regulate whether hybrid space are inclusive or exclusionary. Without active equity actions, digital augmentation risks amplifying existing socio-economic divides.

Lastly, institutional trust functions as the mediating variable linking these layers to social cohesion outcomes. Trust emerges when governance processes are transparent, privacy protections are respected and date stewardship remains accountable. Recent scholarship emphasises that algorithmic systems embedded in urban infrastructure must be subject to public audit, consent protocols and ethical review boards to preserve democratic legitimacy (Bibri & Allam, 2022).

The interaction between these five dimensions decides whether hybrid public spaces reinforce or weaken social cohesion. High physical quality combines with moderate digital integration, strong governance transparency, deep participation and robust equity strategies tend to enhance belonging and collective identity. Conversely high technological intensity without transparency or access protections risks surveillance normalisation and civic disengagement.

This matric will be applies to case study analysis to evaluate on how different cities balance these dimensions and what implications arise for social cohesion in both physical and immersive public environment.

Smart Cities and ICT Driven Urban Transformation

ICT Infrastructures in smart cities

Smart cities heavily depend on ICT such as monitoring networks for infrastructures, cloud platforms, urban systems to manage and analyse and these infrastructures include mobile applications, network broad banding, sensors, cloud computing platforms that helps to collect and process the real time data form the real time urban environment (Batty, 2013; Komninos, 2020). ICT enabled applications for coordinating traffic lights, public transport, parking, shared mobility are part of Intelligent Transport Systems (ITS) through which live information streams are gathered to improve flow and reduce congestion (Zhang et al, 2017). Environmental monitoring systems like tracking air pollution, noise levels and microclimate enable better planning principles and adaptive policy responses, especially in places where there is climate challenges are pertaining as shown n Figure 4 (Baklanov et al, 2018). In addition, open data initiatives allow people, researchers and planners to access data information, stimulate innovation and enabling people to oversee government and service providers (Kitchin, 2015).

Transformation of Public Space

Figure 4. ICT enabled Public Space Design.

The infrastructure changes reshape on how public spaces function and how they are perceived by the people. Dynamic sensing tools like adaptive lighting networks and live population dashboards allow urban environments to respond to changing conditions through real time adjustments of lighting, safety interventions and crowd management (Naranjo et al, 2016 Vieira et al, 2020). Digital platform such as Fix my Street and similar other applications allows residents to identify potholes, damaged lights, waste issues which allow residents can effectively take care of urban maintenance rather than to be passive user (Meijer & Bolivar, 2016). Digital twin such as high-fidelity virtual model of cities allows urban planner to simulate people flow, shading, movement pattern and behavioural responses before implementing any physical changes in urban context there by reducing the risk and cost associated with tail and error in public space design (batty, 2018; Duarte et al, 2018). These advancements collectively lead to more responsible public environments.

Governance, Accountability and Power Dynamics

ICT integration also transformed government structures. Integrated Command and Control Centres (ICCCs) centralise the date from traffic system, public safety cameras, emergency network, sanitation systems and other services into combined dashboards that allow officials to make decision with proper coordination similar to one in Bhopal, India (Ajaj,2020). These systems enhance efficiency, coordinate response and crisis management, they also centralise the power within government institutions and corporate vendors (Sharifi et al, 2021). Figure 5 shows the combination of this relationship between government authorities and private technology firms complicated accountability by merging public and commercial interest leaving citizens uncertain who controls the data and how data are being managed and how decisions are taken.

Figure 5. Urban Public Space transferred into a Community Interaction Space

This raises concerns about surveillance, data extraction and emergence of new urbanism concept where private companies hold increasing influence over public infrastructure.

Implications for Social Cohesion and Equity

In the view of social cohesion, transformation based on ICT has both positive and negative impacts. On the positive side, responsive government, improved services and safer society play a vital role to enhance the quality of life and improve the trust between citizens and government institution (Allam & Newman, 2018; Giffinger at al, 2007). Civic engagement in planning and economic management can be improved through digital participation portals and e-governance tools, particularly when the merge with each other and replace offline forms of participation (Meijer & Bolivar, 2016; Vieira et al, 2020). However, these technocentric approaches lead to the risk of prioritising efficiency over equality and imposing on model solutions that overlook local differences (Hollands, 2015). Citizens are primarily the data providers rather than decision makers which reinforces exclusion rather empowering them (Cardullo& Kitchin, 2019). Moreover, the data driven profiling and predictive policing tools have targeted marginalised groups in several ways, resulting in reduced trust and increased anxiety about sense of surveillance rather than safety (Brayne, 2017; Calzada, 2021). Table 2 explains the relation between study aspects and their implication in reality which summarize the relation between smart cities and ICT technology.

Table 2. Blending Real and Digital World in Public Space Design

Aspect of Study	Key ideology	Implication for Practice
Hybrid Spaces	Digital and Physical experiences overlap each other	Public spaces are treated as multilayers systems
AR and media facades	Interaction Media	Used to enhance place identity not distract from it.
Participatory Tools	Citizen create ideology in planning through feedback systems.	Inputs are integrated into real time decision making
Exclusion risks	Not every citizen is digitally equipped	Providing public devices and digital alternatives.
Data Ethics	Behavioural data is collected through sensors and apps	Use clear agreement, transparency and limits

HYBRID PUBLIC SPACES

Convergence of Digital and Physical Layers

Hybrid public spaces evolves when physical setting is integrated with digital infrastructures which results in urban spaces which are both materialistic and virtual. This integration takes multiple forms including information overlays, interactive installations, Smart Street furniture, participatory platforms. Augmented reality (AR) heritage trails and mobile applications can display historical narratives over modern landscape, wherein QR codes link visitors to educational content (Garau et al, 2017). Interactive installation like projection mapping, responsive facades and sensor-based installation invite citizens by reacting to movement, sound which transforms public space into interactive interface (Foth et al, 2016). Wi-Fi enabled street furniture, charging stations, sensor enabled seating provide connectivity among people and gather usage of data to inform planning and maintenance (Townsend, 2013; Aurigi & Willis, 2020). Digital tools allow residents to register their ideas on design proposals, report issues, upload stories based on places and collectively gather context knowledge. (Vieira at al, 2020).

Benefits of Hybridisation

Recent research explain that hybrid public (Figure 6) spaces can enhance the experience and social value of any public space. Hampton (2016) explain that mobile connectivity can strengthen and unite people by helping them to coordinate interactions and convert online weak ties into face-to-face interactions. Evans (2015) shows that social media can amplify place-based event, attracting larger and more varied audiences for public gatherings. Foth at al, (2016) finds that interactive urban screens as digital third places that host civic, creative and cultural activities fostering a sense of **belonging and shared expression.**

Inequalities and Frictions

Despite these frictions, hybrid space will lead to new tensions also. Access to digital platforms will remain uneven fostering to user who own gadgets and can afford data services, while excluding the citizen who cannot (Hollands, 2015; Townsend, 2013). Personalized digital layers can fragment share experience to each user may encounter a different representation of the same physical environment, potentially weaking e=collective perception and symbolic unity (Aurigi & Willis, 2020). In addition, sensors and platforms embedded in public spaces often collect behavioural data without full consent or comprehension raising ethical concern about privacy, surveillance and ownership (Greenfield, 2013; Calzada, 2021).

Figure 6. Hybrid Public Space – where Physical setting is integrated with Digital Infrastructure

Implication for Design and Governance

Hybrid spaces require planned and responsible governance as shown in Table 3. Effective design should ensure transparency in data collection, provide various modes of engagement and involve communities in design process to reflect native identities (Foth et al, 2016; Aurigi & Willis, 2020, Vieira at al, 2020). In this way, hybrid space can increase the benefit of digital reality which protecting publicness, inclusivity and trust.

Table 3. Technological Influence on Urban Design

Aspect of Study	Key ideology	Implication for Planning
Digital tools	Simulation and Optimisation are enabled	Using them as testing options rather than replacing them
Smart Infrastructure	Streets and parks can respond in real time scenario	Improves safety and efficiency
Data Drive design	Evidence based decisions are supported	Community knowledge can be combined with site information
Invisible qualities	Data base rarely consider people emotions and local culture	Participation based qualitative research should be included
Ethical Design	Algorithms affect the beneficiaries	To check for bias, fairness and accidental effects

METAVERSE AS EMERGING PUBLIC REALM

Metaverse platforms represents as development of hybrid public spaces which is fully into virtual and immersive environment. Emerging technologies including virtual reality (VR), augmented reality (AR) and mixed reality (MR) enabling user so interact with each other and with digital artefacts inside simulated or entirely fictional urban settings (Dwivedi et al, 2022; Smart et al, 2007). Recently in urban planning, the usage of AR and VR are increasingly linked to digital twin models, allowing professionals, researchers and citizens to walk through proposed development before they are been physical constructed (Batty, 2018; Duarte et al, 2018). In this way, the metaverse provides spatial imagination of the city, providing a platform for experimental and participatory engagement.

Municipal Applications and Emerging Practices

Many cities around the world are experimenting with metaverse platforms as initiation of governance systems. Seoul's metaverse is the one of the most frequently cites examples as it hosts virtual municipal offices, consultation halls and civic event spaces where people can interact with each other in a personalized manner (Owojori, 2023). Citizens can access to all infrastructure services, attend public hearing, submit documents and participate in all cultural activities without travelling physically. This model paves us the way to reduce participation barrier particularly for young people, migrants and citizens with limited access (Sharifi & Amirzade, 2025). Similar model such as VR based planning studios and immersive participatory simulations are being tested in various global cities (Maier et al, 2024; Allam & Newman, 2022). These application model gives a change in way people engage and public discussion are increased which are mediated through virtual as well as physical environments.

Opportunities for Publicness

The metaverse platform has several significant opportunities for public space reimagining as follows

Inclusivity: Designing virtual spaces need not physical barriers and it allows customisation according to people need.

Experimentation: High risk urban design proposal can be digitally modelled with minimal material cost and political cost through which we can understand the feasibility.

Cultural: People from different regions can co-experience places and events without physically visiting it in person.

Exchange: Virtual space enhances cross border interactions.

These development in urban environment indicate that metaverse can act as a new civic arena, enabling discourse, involves cultural participation and allows collective imagination beyond physical geographical limits.

Risk and Ethical Concerns

Metaverse platforms raise major ethical and governance challenges. Most of the data are owned and accumulated by privation corporations, where their networking model relies on data extraction, attention monetisation and predicting behaviour (Zuboff, 2019; Dwivedi et al, 2022). Without proper regulatory frameworks, the potential risk of metaverse public realms is governed by algorithms, proprietary terms of service and commercial incentive in spite being democratic principles (Bibri & Allam, 2022; Calzada, 2021). In addition, manipulation of identity, harassment, dilemmas on moderating contents and psychological effects associated with extended immersion are serious concerns (Oh & Bailenson, 2017; Nowak & Fox, 2018).

Implications for Social Cohesion

In the perspective of social cohesion, the metaverse offers a new channel for civic participation and ownness, but researchers warns that virtual interaction cannot replace fully the embodied forms of co-presence, chance encounters and sensory engagement that characterise traditional public spaces (Sennett, 2018; Hampton, 2016. As a result of this hybrid models linking virtual deliberation with physical public environments, one to one interaction and formal decision-making processes are needed for ensuring that metaverse development strengthens rather than replacing the democratic and social functions of public space design as shown in Table 4.

Table 4. Role in ICT to enhance Social Cohesion in Smart Cities

Aspect of Study	Key ideology	Implication for Governance
Reporting Tools	Citizens can standardise problem easily	Outcomes to be shown based on building quick response systems.
Open data	Make operation more visible in cities	Using clear and understandable dashboards
Social media	Community supported networks	Encourage local constructive communication
Digital Literacy	All citizens are not comfortable with ICT	Offering training, creating help desks and offline options
Trust	People need output from the engagement activities	Close loop to the feedback systems and communicate clearly in them.

GLOBAL CASE STUDIES

Amsterdam: Participatory Digital Urbanism

Amsterdam is widely recognised as a global frontier in smart city development, especially in its commitment towards open data, transparency and participation by citizen (Meijer & Bolivar, 2016; Cardullo & Kitchin, 2019). Participatory digital urbanism model was emphasised rather than adopting a pure technocentric model as it involves citizens not only as data subjects but as active contributor in urban design making. Smart City mission in Amsterdam act as a collaborative measure linking government officials, private companies, universities, civic organisations and neighbourhood communities to jointly design solutions across energy, mobility and public space management.

Figure 7. Amsterdam – Participatory Digital Urbanism model

Residents are supported by participatory digital platforms through which they can visualize mobility patterns, evaluate street configurations and suggest alterations. The use of temporary tactical urbanism interventions, including pedestrian zones pop-upped and pilot traffic calming schemes is outcome of this approach which allows proposal to be tested and refined before permanent implementation.

City design philosophy can be demonstrating hybrid public spaces (Figure 7). The smart light system located in city center adapts LED lighting that responds to real time pedestrian activity, adjusting brightness to balance safety, ambience and energy efficiency (Naranjo et al, 2016). Other neighbourhood application display energy consumption, air quality levels and local sustainability indicators which encourages residents to monitor environmental conditions and adopt stewardship behaviours.

In spite of Amsterdam being strong participation-oriented development, the challenges remain constant. Researchers show that digital application usage is unevenly distributed with higher involvement among well-educated and digitally equipped group of people (Cardullo & Kitchin, 2019). In this condition, the city has worked strategy to extend their inclusion through outreach programs, multilingual interface creation, community workshops and neighborhood level facilitations. Over all, Amsterdam demonstrated how smart city can combine both technology and participatory processes to enhance public space design.

Barcelona, Spain: Super Blocks and Smart Mobility

Barcelona had developed an influential globally acclaimed references in people centric smart urbanism through Superblocks programme (Figure8). This initiative programs encourage pedestrian prioritised micro neighbourhood by restructuring the traditional car dominated grid where the vehicle traffic route is directed to the perimeter streets allowing the interior streets for walking, cycling and community life (Russo, 2020). These interior spaces in streets incorporated green infrastructure, playgrounds, seating areas and multifunctional community zones, which redefine the role of streets from transport corridors to social, ecological and cultural environments.

Smart mobility applications play a major role out in the management of the superblocks Programme. To reroute vehicles, optimise public transport and monitor air quality and noise levels resulting pedestrianisation, smart technologies like GPS, environmental and traffic data can be used (Zhang et al, 2017). Digital twin models support planning processes by simulating alternative configurations before physical implementation, reducing uncertainty and enabling evidence-based decision making.

Figure 8. Barcelona: Superblock model – creating community engaging public spaces in interior street.

Citizen participation is a defining element of Barcelon's approach. Residents to redesign reclaimed public spaces, influencing decisions on street furniture, pay areas, cultural programming and the allocation of greenery through participatory workshops, neighbourhood consultations and online platforms (Garau et al, 2017). This collaborative methodology ahs been associated with increased social interaction, enhanced sense of belonging and stringer neighbourhood identity (Russo, 2020).

Despite these achievements, social equity challenges have emerged. The increased attractiveness of pedestrian friendly neighbourhood has coincided with rising tourism intensity and real estate speculations, raising concerns about displacement and affordability (Russo, 2020; Calzada, 2021). Critics warn that without supporting housing policies, Super blocks risk becoming catalyst for gentrification and uneven benefit distribution particularly affecting low-income group. Overall, Barcelona illustrated how urban design, digital mobility interface and participatory governance can be established to reshape public spaces.

Singapore: Smart Nation and Public Life

Singapore's smart nation agenda initiatives digital infrastructure as the foundation of daily life, governance and economic development. This programme emphasises on integrated ICT development, monitoring real time data and citizen facing digital services across multiple sectors (Allam & Newman, 2018; Komninos, 2020). A leading example is virtual Singapore(Figure 9), a high-resolution digital twin that models land use, climate, transport flows and pedestrian density to support data driven planning. By using the 3D interface, the public can explore proposed developments and environmental scenarios bridging the gap between expert analysis and public understanding (Batty, 2018).

Figure 9. Singapore – Initiation of digital infrastructure into public space design.

Public spaces such as parks, plazas, streets, waterfronts are equipped with sensors measuring the number of visitors, thermal comfort, humidity measurement and environmental quality which enables the adaptive management such as dynamic lighting, shading structures and crowd management systems (Baklanov et al, 2018).Singapore initiatives programs like Smart Nation Ambassadors to improve the conditions of digital literacy and inclusion by providing training to senior citizen, low income community people and particularly for migrant workers. (Allam & Newman, 2018).

Singapore model shows, how technology can increase the safety, efficiency of model and resilience towards development, even though its model highlights the ongoing tension between top-down technocratic planning and grassroots cocreation (Calzada, 2021). In spite of practicing participation mechanism, Singapore retains strong control over the digital platforms and data governance.

Bhopal, India: Smart City in an Emerging Economy

Bhopal model demonstrates on how smart city system are being adapted to resource constrained and socially diverse contexts. The Bhopal Smart City Development Corporation developed an Intergraded Command and Control Center (ICCC) to manage and coordinate infrastructure facilities like traffic, solid waste systems, water supply, public safety and emergency responses through unified dashboards (Ajaj, 2020). Public spaces like Upper Lake promenade (Figure 10) were been transformed in which smart lighting systems. Smart seating, pathways and Wi-Fi access are supported by sensors and feedback platforms.

Figure 10. Bhopal - Integrated Command and Control Center (ICCC) to manage Infrastructure Services

Recognising profound digital divides, Bhopal's model help residents to report issues, learn navigation applications and access government services through incorporation of capacity building programmes and digital kiosk (Sharifi et al, 2021). Even though there exist the challenge related to funding, coordination among institution and digital access unequally, early information suggests then even modest but well targeted technological interventions can strengthen governance and improve the usability and safety of public spaces when grounded in transparency and education (Ajaj, 2020). Bhopal model demonstrated an incremental, socially oriented pathway to smart urbanism in developing economies.

Seoul, South Korea: Metaverse – Based Governance

Seoul established one of the world's most determined researches in metaverse enabled public administration. Seoul – The Metaverse city (Figure 11) initiative extends municipal services into immersive virtual environments, enabling citizens to attend civic events, access administrative services, submit documents and consult with officials via personalized applications (Owojori, 2023; Maier et al, 2024). District wise model of redevelopment helps the citizens to visualize the urban development projects and provide with feedback mechanism before the implementation by adapting transparency and experimental participation.

Figure 11. Seoul – Metaverse enabled Public Administration

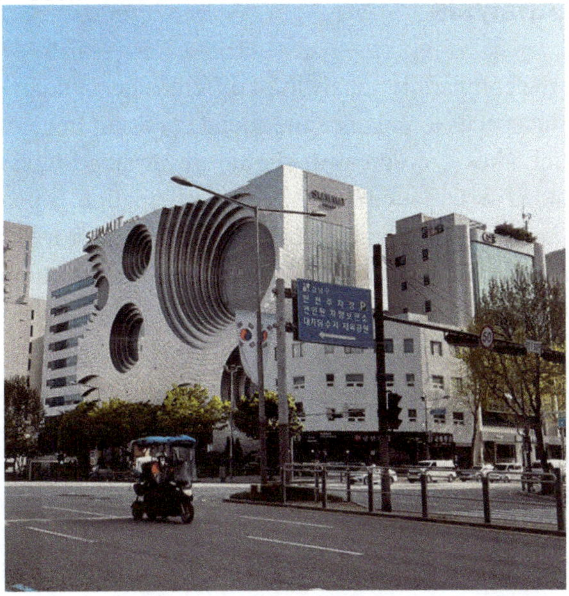

Prior investigation suggests that the high engagement among young people who use the metaverse platforms not only for public involvement but also for volunteering, educational and cultural activities (Owojori, 2023). Though Seoul model experience reveals the difficulty in governing virtual public realms. Challenges including digital access, moderation of content, harassment prevention, psychological wellbeing and data governance together with fundamental questions about the ownership and accountability when civic interaction occurs in privately claimed platforms.

Seoul highlights the possibilities and threat of treating the metaverse as an addition of public space design. Wherein the immersive platforms can extend participation and reduce physical and social barriers, sustained inclusion requires parallel attention of confidentiality, oversight regulatory and alignment with offline democratic process.

Besides the administrative purpose, Seoul's metaverse projects also serves as an experimental space for urban learning and collective imagination. By allowing citizens to visualize redevelopment projects in immersive 3D spaces, the project decreases the level of information asymmetry between policy makers and citizens because they ca nget a better understanding as non-experts. Additionally educational programs included in the metaverse enable younger generations to learn about citizen activities through gamified participation programs. These enable the creation of awareness among them regarding urban governance. The metaverse spec also serves as a venue for cultural events, history exhibitions and citizen forms which expand the symbolic space in the digital world.

Comparative Analysis

Table 5 shows the comparative analysis of different case studies – worldwide and its impact on public spaces to enhance the social cohesion in urban public spaces.

Amsterdam embodies a co-creative digital governance model in which tech systems are grounded within a culture of city participation. Open date programs, local workshops and tactical urbanism experiments suggest relatively high levels of citizen engagement. While digital layers become used as but not limited to the command and control of public space, institutional transparency adds trust attached between institutions.

Barcelona's superblocks program focuses on spatial configuration as the method of cohesion. But digital working methods focus above all the efficient mobility and green performance than reconfiguring our participating structures. More face to fae interaction in pedestrian areas helps build community, but higher property values can create issues.

Singapore follows a technocratic model focused in efficiency with strong digital integration and central governance. The virtual Singapore digital twin plans help with planning and resilience. Still, participation is mostly managed by the state which raises questions about how much real democratic input there is.

Bhopal Illustrated an incremental inclusion model within resource constrained conditions. The integrated command and control center centralises service coordination, while digital kiosks and training initiatives attempt to reduce digital divides, Cohesion improvements appear linked more to improved service delivery and safety rather than immersive participation.

Seoul introduces an immersive civic model by extending governance into metaverse environments. Avatar based interaction expands access and reduce physical barriers. Yet, questions of platform ownership, behavioural moderation and digital fatigue complicate long term cohesion prospects.

A comparative look at cities within which digital integration actually adds to rather than replaces bodily experiences indicates that these cities possess better potential for cohesion. Over reliance on the technological aspect tend to encourage surveillance, while over reliance on the bodily aspect without any form of technological governance innovation appears to be unsustainable for maximum inclusivity in the participation aspect.

Table 5. Comparative Analysis of Case studies globally

City / Case Studies	Primary Focus / Model	Major Technology and Digital Tools	Impact on Public Space	Outcomes – Social Cohesion
Amsterdam	Participatory Digital platforms	Open data analysis, of mobility dashboards Visualization and design tools	Temporary urban interferences, adaptive street networks, community base improvements.	Higher engagement among digitally equipped people, improved inclusion through outreach programs and multilingual interface.
Barcelona, Spain	Superblocks and Smart mobility	Digital twins, GPS based traffic management and environmental sensors.	Pedestrianisation of neighbourhood, adaptive sensor enabled streets, community-based improvements.	Strengthened social interaction, Redevelopment pressure creates uneven benefits
Singapore	Smart nation & smart public life	Virtual Singapore, Digital Twins, Environmental sensors. Apps for citizens,	Sensor managed public spaces like water fronts, parks and environmental adaptation.	Improved safety and service access. Tension between planning and re development
Bhopal, India	Smart City Model	ICCC, Mobile applications, Digital kiosks and public space enabled with Wi-Fi	Upgraded waterfront developments, smart lighting	Digital gaps and challenges on coordination exists, capacity building enhances inclusion and transparency.
Seoul, South Korea	Metaverse based governance	Metaverse city platform, VR consultation spaces, 3D redevelopment models.	Enhance virtual civic participation, application-based services, physical engagement.	Active youth participation, access-based risk, content moderation, private and platform governance.

OPPORTUNITIES AND RISKS OF HYBRID AND METAVERSE ENABLED PUBLIC SPACES

Opportunities

Expanded participation: Digital Platforms decrease traditional barriers to public involvement making more residents to express their preference, report their issues and co-design public spaces (Meijer & Bolivar, 2016; Cardullo & Kitchin, 2019).

Enhance Transparency and Accountability: Open resources dashboards and visualizations of data make organisational performance and environmental conditions visible in real time which supports liability and informed decision making (Kitchin, 2015, Vieira et al, 2020).

Adaptive and Evidence Based Spatial Management: To enable continuous usage of lighting, shading and activity programming based on real behavioural and environmental data interfaces like sensors, simulations and digital twins are used (Batty, 2018; Naranjo et al, 2016).

Increased Inclusivity for Specific User Groups: Hybrid and metaverse based participation can benefit individual citizen who may be under represented in physical public spaces such as people with mobility limitations, caregiving responsibilities or social anxieties (Sharifi & Amirzadeh, 2025; Itair et al, 2024).

Risks

Digital Divides: Inadequate access to network connectivity, devices and digital knowledge restricts from people who can benefit from digital layers of public spaces, possibly widening rather than reducing the inequalities (Hollands, 2015; Townsend, 2013).

Surveillance and Data Misuse: Universal identification and behavioural tracking may compromise on privacy, changes personal data and depress free public expression (Greenfield, 2013; Zuboff, 2019; Bibri & Allam, 2022).

Technology Based Governance: Over dependency on algorithmic decision systems risks the chance of marginalising experimental knowledge, local history and democratic freedom in urban planning (Kitchin, 2014; Calzada, 2021).

Erosion of Embodied Sociability: Replacing one to one interaction with virtual interaction can decrease everyday meeting thereby reducing empathy and weaken neighbourhood ties (Sennett, 2018; Hampton, 2016).

Implication for Social Cohesion

The interchange between opportunities and risks will majorly decide on whether hybrid public spaces can strengthen or weaken social cohesion. When digital layers are governed ethically and used to complement each other rather than replacing personal interaction, hybrid public spaces can improve the sense of belonging, enhance collective civic life and democratic people participation. Equally implementation risk exists when poorly regulated implication happens and can deepen exclusion, normalise surveillance and weaken the social fabric the public space which have been historically supported.

DISCUSSION

Technology by itself do not automatically empower or control people and the outcome depends on how its planned, designed and governed. The social effects depends on the way and how it is being designed, governed and embedded into native context both socially and culturally (Nam & Pardo, 2011; Allam & Newman, 2018). Hybrid public space and metaverse can extend the types of civic interaction, but only when guided by human centered principles and democratic misunderstanding.

Irreplaceability of Physical Public Space

The evidence through research show that physical space remains as basic element to social cohesion. Even high-end virtual environments cannot replace the depth of multisensory, embodied encounters or the substantiate social learning generated through closeness to strangers (Jacobs, 1961; Gehl, 2011; Sennett, 2018). So digital and metaverse platforms should be placed as replacements rather than substitute for investments in accessible, inclusive and well-maintained urban public spaces.

Hybridisation Succeeds When Grounded in Local Civic Cultures

The above discusses case studies shows that hybridisation us most effective way when built upon social networks and civic cultures rather imposing as a technological blueprint. Initiatives like Amsterdam's participatory platforms, Barcelona's Superblock design and Bhopal skill enhancement programs shows that digital tools succeed when combined with community engagement, capacity building and sensitivity towards culture (Meijer & Bolivar, 2016; Garau et al, 2017; Ajaj, 2020).

Digital Equity, Data Rights and Algorithmic Impartiality are Pre-conditions Not Additions

Hybrid and virtual public space must be ensured with advance equity rather than creating inequalities, clear attention must be given to the digital gaps, surveillance practices and algorithmic bias (Hollands, 2015; Brayne, 2017; Calzada, 2021). Regulatory frameworks should support data minimisation, informed consent, transparency and the right to challenge automated decisions (Zuboff, 2019; Sharifi et al, 2021). Data collected should remain under civic stewardship and to be treated as a common good rather than a proprietary resource (greenfield, 2014; Kitchin, 2015).

Multi-Sensory and Inclusive Design of Hybrid Public Space

In the aspect of design, hybrid public spaces should encourage multiple modes of participation such as visual, auditory, tactile and social so that people with varied abilities and preferences ca meaningfully engage to deliver potential output (Aurigi & Willis, 2020; Itair et al, 2023). Integrating "calm technology" principles can stop digital overload principle and ensure that technological layers can be updated without dominating, leaving he space for quiet and unmediated experiences (Weiser & Brown, 1997; Foth et al, 2016).

Expanding the Definition and Governance of the Public Realm

Metaverse has raised the challenges for planners and policy makers to extend their understanding towards what will constitute public domain. Virtual spaces that conduct civic activities must be planning according to public values such as openness, fairness, safety and accountability even it is run by a private operator (Bibri & Allam, 2022; Maier et al, 2024). Involving citizens panels, ethics boards and cross section partnership may be requires to assure that metaverse infrastructure corelate with broader urban goals and human rights in urban governance model (Sharifi & Amirzadeh, 2025; Calzada, 2021).

Synthesis

Altogether, the research findings underline that the value of hybrid and metaverse enable d public space design lies not only in their novelty but in their ability to reinforce existing societal function such as copresence, interaction, sense of belonging and democratic freedom. When technological systems are planned thoughtfully and governed ethically resulting in strengthening the social cohesion, similarly when they are poorly implemented, they create rick of exclusion, surveillance and fragmentation. The Challenge for future planning lies in balancing innovation with public values to ensure that hybrid environments are human-centred.

Governance Framework for Hybrid Public Space

Transformation of public space into hybrid and immersive domains requires new governance paradigms. While traditional urban planning frameworks were very much focused on land use and spatial regulation, hybrid environments call for regulatory attention of data stewardship, algorithmic accountability and digital rights.

A civic stewardship model places urban data as a public good not a proprietary commodity. In this model, municipalities retain custodianship, while procurement is transparent, standard are open and algorithmic systems are auditable by the public (Maier et al, 2025). Proposals for digital infrastructure are subject to review by citizen oversight committees and interdisciplinary ethics boards before implementation.

Public private partnership should, in turn be built into explicit clauses on data minimisation, user content and interoperability that can prevent technological lock in. In as much as metaverse platforms host civic functions governance principles must be aligns to democratic norms of accessibility, non-discrimination and procedural fairness.

Embedding these principles within urban policy will ensure that hybrid public space enhances rather than undermines trust, equity and participation.

Evaluation Framework for Measuring Social Cohesion in Hybrid Cities

In order to determine if hybrid and immersive public spaces effectively promote social cohesion, specific indicators must be developed. These includes

Belonging and Identity Indices: Resident survey, number of repeat visits to a place and percentage of residents participating in civic events. Trust metrics which measure safety perception, transparency of institution and date protection.

Interaction Diversity Indicators: These are indicators used to measure the diversity of cross group engagement within physical and virtual environments. Digital quality metrics regarding access to connectivity, device ownership and support for device literacy.

Depth of participation measures that differentiate consultation form co-decision processes. Accomplishing this through the use of qualitative perception survey as well as quantitative behavioural date enables planners to not just evaluate the performance of the technology, but alsoi its impact on society. Analysis of data iver time is critical to assess whether novelty becomes factor.

CONCLUSION AND WAY FOWARD

Urban public space is undergoing a thoughtful evolution as it reshapes how people interact with each other, participate and construct shared meaning through digital infrastructures, hybrid environments and emerging metaverse platforms. This chapter has exposed that these technologies create new possibilities of inclusion, transparency and adaptive spatial planning, yet they have critical risk associated with it like inequality, surveillance and the weakening of embodied sociability. The key insight is that future of public space will be envisioned as hybrids commons which includes adaptive socio and technical environment that integrate physical and digital layers which keeping human values, social equity and democratic governance as the main concern.

Public space should retain the core function of social cohesion to achieve socially sustainable hybrid urban environments with integration of digital layer to complement rather than replacing it. To achieve this, closing digital divides through affordable connectivity, device access and digital empowerment are required. Hybrid public spaces are most effective when communities are actively involved in the design and governance when technological development incorporates local cultural, values and everyday practices instead of imposing standard city models. The outcome should not be measured only in the values of efficiency and performance metrics rather their contributions to wellbeing, social support systems, inclusivity and sustainable environment.

Further research should extend on long term impacts of hybrid public space and metaverse public spaces on varied demographic locations and across different people in different context, understanding that governance models and social norms are the outcome. In short public spaces guided by human centric and democratic principles, can become more powerful drivers of social cohesion and more approachable in urban futures.

REFERENCES

Ajaj, S. (2020). Smart city governance and integrated command and control centres in India: The case of Bhopal. *Journal of Urban Management, 9*(3), 285–297.

Allam, Z., & Newman, P. (2018). Redefining the smart city: Culture, metabolism and governance. *Smart Cities, 1*(1), 4–25. DOI: 10.3390/smartcities1010002

Allam, Z., & Newman, P. (2022). The metaverse as a virtual form of smart cities: Opportunities and challenges for governance. *Smart Cities, 5*(1), 1–16. DOI: 10.3390/smartcities5010001

Aurigi, A., & Willis, K. (2020). *The programmable city: Digital urbanism and its discontents*. Routledge.

Baklanov, A., Molina, L., & Gauss, M. (2018). Megacities, air quality and climate. *Atmospheric Environment, 199*, 210–227. DOI: 10.1016/j.atmosenv.2018.11.028

Batty, M. (2013). *The new science of cities*. MIT Press. DOI: 10.7551/mitpress/9399.001.0001

Batty, M. (2018). Digital twins. *Environment and Planning. B, Urban Analytics and City Science, 45*(5), 817–820. DOI: 10.1177/2399808318796416

Bibri, S. E., & Allam, Z. (2022). The metaverse as a virtual form of data-driven smart urbanism: On post-pandemic governance through the prism of surveillance capitalism. *Smart Cities, 5*(2), 715–727. DOI: 10.3390/smartcities5020037

Brayne, S. (2017). Big data surveillance: The case of policing. *American Sociological Review, 82*(5), 977–1008. DOI: 10.1177/0003122417725865 PMID: 38322733

Calzada, I. (2021). Smart city citizenship: A critical perspective. *Journal of Urban Technology, 28*(1–2), 21–46. DOI: 10.1080/10630732.2020.1798179

Caragliu, A., Del Bo, C., & Nijkamp, P. (2011). Smart cities in Europe. *Journal of Urban Technology, 18*(2), 65–82. DOI: 10.1080/10630732.2011.601117

Cardullo, P., & Kitchin, R. (2019). Being a 'citizen' in the smart city: Up and down the scaffold of smart citizen participation. In Kitchin, R., Cardullo, P., & Di Feliciantonio, C. (Eds.), *The right to the smart city* (pp. 219–231). Emerald. DOI: 10.1108/9781787691391

Chan, J., To, H., & Chan, E. (2006). Reconsidering social cohesion: Developing a definition and analytical framework for empirical research. *Social Indicators Research, 75*(2), 273–302. DOI: 10.1007/s11205-005-2118-1

Duarte, J., Martí, P., & González, C. (2018). City information modelling: Parametric urban models including design guidelines and rules. *Sustainable Cities and Society*, *36*, 322–332. DOI: 10.1016/j.scs.2017.10.031

Dwivedi, Y. K., Hughes, L., Baabdullah, A., Ribeiro-Navarrete, S., Giannakis, M., Al-Debei, M., & Wamba, S. F. (2022). Metaverse beyond hype: Multidisciplinary perspectives on emerging challenges, opportunities and agenda for research, practice and policy. *International Journal of Information Management*, *66*, 102542. Advance online publication. DOI: 10.1016/j.ijinfomgt.2022.102542

Evans, L. (2015). Locative social media: Place in the digital age. *First Monday*, *20*(3). Advance online publication. DOI: 10.5210/fm.v20i3.5457

Forrest, R., & Kearns, A. (2001). Social cohesion, social capital and the neighbourhood. *Urban Studies (Edinburgh, Scotland)*, *38*(12), 2125–2143. DOI: 10.1080/00420980120087081

Foth, M., Brynskov, M., & Ojala, T. (2016). *Citizen's right to the digital city: Urban interfaces, activism, and placemaking*. Springer.

Francis, J., Giles-Corti, B., Wood, L., & Knuiman, M. (2012). Creating sense of community: The role of public space. *Journal of Environmental Psychology*, *32*(4), 401–409. DOI: 10.1016/j.jenvp.2012.07.002

Garau, C., Annunziata, A., & Yamu, C. (2017). A walkability assessment tool coupling multi-criteria analysis and space syntax: The case study of Iglesias, Italy. *European Planning Studies*, *25*(12), 2215–2236. DOI: 10.1080/09654313.2017.1345868

Gehl, J. (2011). *Life between buildings: Using public space* (6th ed.). Island Press.

Giffinger, R., Fertner, C., Kramar, H., Kalasek, R., & Meijers, E. (2007). *Smart cities: Ranking of European medium-sized cities*. Centre of Regional Science, Vienna University of Technology.

Graham, S., & Marvin, S. (2001). *Splintering urbanism: Networked infrastructures, technological mobilities and the urban condition*. Routledge.

Greenfield, A. (2013). *Against the smart city*. Do Projects.

Habermas, J. (1989). The structural transformation of the public sphere: An inquiry into a category of bourgeois society (T. Burger, Trans., with the assistance of F. Lawrence). MIT Press.

Hampton, K. N. (2016). Persistent and pervasive community: New communication technologies and the future of community. *The American Behavioral Scientist*, *60*(1), 101–124. DOI: 10.1177/0002764215601714

Hollands, R. G. (2015). Critical interventions into the corporate smart city. *Cambridge Journal of Regions, Economy and Society*, *8*(1), 61–77. DOI: 10.1093/cjres/rsu011

Jacobs, J. (1961). *The death and life of great American cities*. Random House.

Kitchin, R. (2015). Making sense of smart cities: Addressing present shortcomings. *Cambridge Journal of Regions, Economy and Society*, *8*(1), 131–136. DOI: 10.1093/cjres/rsu027

Komninos, N. (2020). *Smart cities and connected intelligence: Platforms, ecosystems and network effects*. Routledge.

Lai, Y., Wang, P., & Wen, K. (2024). Exploring the impact of public spaces on social cohesion in resettlement communities from the perspective of experiential value. *Buildings (Basel, Switzerland)*, *14*(10), 3141. Advance online publication. DOI: 10.3390/buildings14103141

Lefebvre, H. (1991). *The production of space*. Blackwell.

Li, H., Ikebe, K., Kinoshita, T., Chen, J., Su, D., & Xie, J. (2024). How heritage promotes social cohesion: An urban survey from Nara city, Japan. *Cities (London, England)*, *149*, 104985. Advance online publication. DOI: 10.1016/j.cities.2024.104985

Low, S. (2000). *On the plaza: The politics of public space and culture*. University of Texas Press.

Madanipour, A. (2003). *Public and private spaces of the city*. Routledge. DOI: 10.4324/9780203402856

Maier, F., Reuter, C., & Schwab, M. (2025). AI-driven urban digital twins and participatory governance: Opportunities and ethical constraints. *Environment and Planning. B, Urban Analytics and City Science*. Advance online publication. DOI: 10.1177/2399808325123456

Maier, F., & Weinberger, M. (2024). Metaverse meets smart cities—Applications, benefits, and challenges. *Future Internet*, *16*(4), 126. Advance online publication. DOI: 10.3390/fi16040126

Meijer, A., & Bolívar, M. P. R. (2016). Governing the smart city: A review of the literature on smart urban governance. *International Review of Administrative Sciences*, *82*(2), 392–408. DOI: 10.1177/0020852314564308

Mitchell, D. (2003). *The right to the city: Social justice and the fight for public space*. Guilford Press.

Nam, T., & Pardo, T. (2011). Conceptualizing smart city with dimensions of technology, people, and institutions. In *Proceedings of the 12th Annual International Digital Government Research Conference* (pp. 282–291). ACM. DOI: 10.1145/2037556.2037602

Naranjo, P. G., Shojafar, M., Mostafaei, H., Pooranian, Z., & Baccarelli, E. (2016). Big data streaming applications scheduling in datacenter: A survey. *Journal of Parallel and Distributed Computing*, *89*, 1–16. DOI: 10.1016/j.jpdc.2015.11.015

Nowak, K., & Fox, J. (2018). Avatars and computer-mediated communication. In *The Oxford handbook of networked communication*. Oxford University Press.

Oh, S. Y., & Bailenson, J. (2017). Virtual reality. *The Journal of Communication*, *67*(5), 703–708. DOI: 10.1111/jcom.12393

Owojori, S. (2023). Metaverse Seoul: Exploring virtual public services and citizen participation. *Smart Cities*, *6*(4), 221–240. DOI: 10.3390/smartcities6040011

Peters, K., Elands, B., & Buijs, A. (2010). Social interactions in urban parks: Stimulating social cohesion? *Urban Forestry & Urban Greening*, *9*(2), 93–100. DOI: 10.1016/j.ufug.2009.11.003

Purcell, M. (2002). Excavating Lefebvre: The right to the city and its urban politics of the inhabitant. *GeoJournal*, *58*(2–3), 99–108. DOI: 10.1023/B:GEJO.0000010829.62237.8f

Russo, A. (2020). Superblocks: Reclaiming public space in Barcelona. *Sustainable Cities and Society*, *52*, 101864. Advance online publication. DOI: 10.1016/j.scs.2019.101864

Sennett, R. (2018). *Building and dwelling: Ethics for the city*. Farrar, Straus and Giroux.

Sharifi, A.. (2021). A critical review of smart city development in India. *Sustainable Cities and Society*, *72*, 103045. Advance online publication. DOI: 10.1016/j.scs.2021.103045

Sharifi, A., & Amirzadeh, A. (2025). The metaverse as a future form of smart cities: Co-benefits and trade-offs for sustainable development goals. *Cities (London, England)*. Advance online publication. DOI: 10.1016/j.cities.2025.105879

Smart, J., Cascio, J., & Paffendorf, J. (2007). *Metaverse roadmap: Pathways to the 3D web*. Metaverse Roadmap Report.

Townsend, A. (2013). *Smart cities: Big data, civic hackers, and the quest for a new utopia*. W. W. Norton.

Ujang, N., & Zakariya, K. (2015). The notion of place, place meaning and identity in urban regeneration. *Procedia: Social and Behavioral Sciences*, *170*, 709–717. DOI: 10.1016/j.sbspro.2015.01.073

Vieira, R.. (2020). Integrating participatory mapping and smart-city dashboards. *Journal of Urban Technology*, *27*(2), 3–26. DOI: 10.1080/10630732.2019.1699449

Weiser, M., & Brown, J. S. (1997). The coming age of calm technology. *IEEE Pervasive Computing*, *1*(1), 1–5.

Zhang, L.. (2017). Data-driven intelligent transportation systems: A survey. *IEEE Transactions on Intelligent Transportation Systems*, *18*(11), 3019–3032. DOI: 10.1109/TITS.2017.2680200

Zuboff, S. (2019). *The age of surveillance capitalism: The fight for a human future at the new frontier of power*. PublicAffairs.

Chapter 3
Metaverse Technologies for Architectural Pedagogy:
A Scoping Review and Taxonomic Framework

C. V. Subramanian
http://orcid.org/0000-0001-9313-0311
Periyar Maniammai Institute of Science and Technology, India

G. Tamil Ezhil
http://orcid.org/0009-0003-5547-3171
Periyar Maniammai Institute of Science and Technology, India

ABSTRACT

The fast-paced development of the design education field demands a radical re-assessment of the traditional pedagogical methods in order to equip future design professionals for complex, interdisciplinary challenges that are brought on by technological innovations. This chapter responds to these demands through an investigation of the need for an innovative pedagogical toolkit. Utilizing a comprehensive approach to synthesizing the research and pedagogical strategies, the study compiles current research and pedagogical strategies, explores innovative digital tools and analyses their potential to support critical thinking, problem-solving and adaptability in design students. Key findings reveal that advanced digital and immersive technologies, especially in the context of developing the Metaverse ecosystem, hold unprecedented benefits in terms of advancing customization, creativity and immersive learning experiences that ultimately lead to greater understanding of spatial relationships and better design communication

DOI: 10.4018/979-8-3373-6721-7.ch003

INTRODUCTION

The Necessity for an Innovative Pedagogical Toolkit

Architecture as a profession in this century is trying to cope with the ever-changing advancement in construction techniques, software, technology and the way buildings are being built. This situation demands an equally advanced approach in architecture and design education and a critical approach to revamp the current mode of teaching and learning architecture. Environmental, social and political factors have a strong influence on the practice of architecture, as the students have to compete with these challenges along with design innovation and creativity, which are the foundations of architecture or any creative course (Kee et al., 2023).

At the onset, many institutions are updating their curriculum to cater to the changing academic landscape by prioritizing practical and applicable teaching methods to develop the skills necessary for today's digital scenario. The challenge is to develop an approach that is relevant to design education and connected to future innovations. Shifting the teaching and learning methods beyond the dimensions of space and time and boundaries of classroom limits resulted in the emergence of a hybrid platform for education that had a significant impact of education on society. (Kee et al., 2023). However, the hybrid mode encourages exploration of problem-solving methods and nurtures creative thinking in a better way and provides an opportunity to combine intuitive thinking and technical skills in the learning environment. (Al-Rqaibat et al.,2025). The design thinking process in this hybrid mode encourages the learners to ideate, reflect and to criticise, the core of the constructivist approach in pedagogy, in an efficient way.

The Historical Development of Technology Within the Design Studio

The technological nature of the design studio is not a very new phenomenon, but a continuous development under the influence of technical innovations and the changing pedagogical paradigm. The adoption of Computer-Aided Design systems in the 1990s was a defining point in time that transformed the field of architecture education and practice by introducing new environments to operate in (Toprak and Hacıhasanoğlu, 2019). Development of the digital perspective of architecture started in the 1960s along with the industrialization that emphasized on efficiency, mechanical reproduction, and the systematization of the design process (Soulikias et al., 2021). Initially, digital innovations were mostly considered the cause of construction boom and mass production (Soulikias et al., 2021).

Nevertheless, such an approach to history also underlines the pervasive distrust on the part of the educational paradigms that were historically preoccupied with material, analogous output and face-to-face studio communications (Soulikias et al., 2021). The substitution of physical model prototypes in the pre-Renaissance period by the use of perspective illustrations in the Renaissance period which were later supplemented by the use of computer assisted strategies can be seen as an attempt to take the design representation and conceptualization to the next level. The 21st century digital technology is intensively incorporated into the educational programs and the methodology of the design studios, and it has contributed to the architectural structure of any educational institution as well as pointed to the element of computational literacy that is a secondary skill, especially in the context of material exploration (Riskiyanto, 2023). With the emergence of modern digital tools, processes, and resources, the key principles of the Bauhaus have been expanded, and material investigation is no longer conducted through traditional manual techniques but through digital craftsmanship, with a conceptual framework of a digital tectonic also contributing to forming a historical opposition between a digital world of ephemeral images and a tectonic structure of functional production (Riskiyanto, 2023).

Whereas conventional design studios mostly align with the existing pedagogical practices and focus on reflection on action, non-traditional design studios are marked by the excessive number of digital technologies to support communication and collaboration (Hettithanthri and Hansen, 2021). In the conventional studios, digital instruments play a supportive role in promoting the idea of creative design thinking and communication (Hettithanthri and Hansen, 2021). Studio development has been a highly discussed topic, and schools of architecture have faced the challenge of changing their teaching methods and incorporating the necessary knowledge and skills that are relevant to the careers in architecture (Özorhon & Sarman, 2023).

Complexity and Ambiguity in the Existing Framework

Regardless of the ever-increasing use of technology, current design education models are often not sufficient to equip design students with the inherent complexity and ambiguity of contemporary design practice. The failure to combine knowledge gained with the application of design studios, the lack of knowledge of the students about how the elements of design impact the users, and the inability to realize the design process completely is among the significant problems of architectural education (Al-Rqaibat et al., 2025; Maghool et al., 2018).

The current excessive dependency on a few digital tools tends to shift the emphasis to the end-result, hence overlooks the dynamic thinking involved in its creation and, therefore, diminishes the versatility of the designer (Al-Rqaibat et al., 2025). The method lessens human responsiveness which may result in development of designs that do not emphasize on human needs and are not responsive to psychological needs (Al-Rqaibat et al., 2025). One of the biggest problems is the lack of competencies to transfer theoretical knowledge into practice (Maghool et al., 2018).

Moreover, an overdependence on digital technologies can lead to the inability of learners and designers to study architectural design issues effectively, which will further decrease the skills of the former in solving problems, as well as the capacity of the former to think in space and structure. According to research, high reliance on specific digital platforms may also prevent the flexibility in generating different design solutions and may affect the development of the design process (Al-Rqaibat et al., 2025).

Additionally, a thorough conceptual model for the inclusion of Building Information Modelling in architectural learning is still not sufficiently advanced (Maharika et al., 2020). Nevertheless, the amalgamation of various digital systems—such as the integration of CAD with engineering, manufacturing, or immersive-reality applications—has been shown to positively affect designers' creative processes, thus presenting a viable approach to overcoming these limitations (Al-Rqaibat et al., 2025).

Objectives, Aims, and Scoping Review Methodology

The three interconnected goals of this chapter are

- to develop a consistent taxonomy of Metaverse technology as an architecture pedagogy based on pedagogical affordance as opposed to commercial branding;
- to develop a framework that operationalizes the main pedagogical properties of immersiveness, collaboration, interoperability, accessibility, and specialized qualities into action criteria that facilitate technology adoption; and
- to curate implementation strategies and practical recommendations on the basis of documented case studies to support evidence-based adoption.

In order to meet these goals, a strict scoping review process was used. Scoping reviews are especially suitable in mapping and synthesizing studies in the fields that are new and actively developing. Scoping reviews are systematic literature reviews, which ought to be transparent, exhaustive, and repeatable and ought to entail systematic processes, which include scoping, planning, searching, screening, and determining eligibility (Moon & Lee, 2022) PICO can be adjusted to define the main parameters of search questions, which leads to the structuring of the analysis (Mogaji and Newton, 2020). In addition, systematic reviews can incorporate both quantitative and qualitative synthesis approaches by combining bibliometric techniques with content analysis, and they typically follow established reporting frameworks such as PRISMA.

Phase 1: The Research Question(s) Identification

This review followed three research questions:

- RQ1: What types of Metaverse technologies are being implemented in the architecture pedagogy and what their technical and pedagogical characteristics arc?
- RQ2: Which pedagogical qualities are the most salient to measure the use of Metaverse technologies in design studio settings, and how various types of technologies perform in these criteria?
- RQ3: What are the implementation strategies, implementation barriers, and success factors based on the documented case studies and what can be used to guide institutions to adopt them?

Phase 2: Relevant Studies Identification

A series of systematic searches in various databases and conference proceedings were undertaken in order to access both peer-reviewed scholarship and practice-oriented reports. Search terms were used in the form of the combination of technology descriptors (extended reality, VR, AR, MR, XR, virtual reality, metaverse, game engine, BIM, augmented reality, mixed reality) and educational contexts (design studio, architecture pedagogy, teaching, learning, architecture education) with the help of Boolean operators. Web of science and Scopus databases were searched in addition to specific searches of conference proceedings and journals in architectural education.

Phase 3: Study Selection

Studies were selected based on the following criteria: includes architectural education (landscape architecture, urban design, interior design); uses Metaverse, XR, or game-engine technology as a pedagogical intervention; provides empirical evidence (case studies, experiments, surveys) or suggests conceptual models based on educational theory; and published within 2020-2025 to capture relevant recent developments. The exclusion criteria eliminated research in which the application of professional practice was the sole subject, only the description of a technical tool without pedagogical analysis, or research that were not within the temporal context.

First searches resulted in 1,200 papers. This was narrowed down to 480 potentially relevant studies with title and abstract screening. The evidence base of this chapter was generated as 345 papers were found after a full-text review with inclusion/exclusion criteria. This collection contains both empirical case studies, systematic reviews and theoretical frameworks and implementation reports across a variety of institutional settings, geographic areas, and levels of education (undergraduate to graduate).

Phase 4: Charting the Data

Included studies were analysed using a structured template that stored data on: technology category and tools used; pedagogical context (type of course, learning objectives, level of students); theoretical frameworks used; and implementation (hardware, software, duration); reported outcomes (qualitative and quantitative); barriers and challenges; and recommendations. The presented charting process led to identifying common themes that were used in the construction and evaluation framework of the taxonomy proposed in the further sections (Avinç & Yildiz, 2025).

Phase 5: Results Collation, Summarizing and Reporting

The synthesis was done in an interpretive manner, finding patterns within studies to develop the four-category taxonomy, defining five major pedagogical attributes to be evaluated, and condensing implementation strategies based on successful and failed deployments. All along, the goal was to focus on practical advice to be provided to the educators, though the evidence gaps and the gaps that need to be filled in the form of additional research were recognized.

Towards a Taxonomy: Organizing the Metaverse Ecosystem

The quickly changing world of digital technologies and especially the use of the Metaverse offers opportunities and challenges to the field of design education. The Metaverse is envisioned as a continuous, interrelated and immersive virtual world that combines a variety of emerging and developed technologies to form a simulated reality that allows users to interact, collaborate and create. Such a revolutionary digital boundary requires an organized intelligence regarding its building technological elements to fully utilize its pedagogical capability in design professions

(Avinç & Yildiz, 2025). The goal of this section is to formalize the Metaverse ecosystem through the suggestion of a taxonomy that outlines the main types of tools and platforms and shows their functionality and the effects on innovative design pedagogue. Figure 1 tabulates the categories of the metaverse taxonomy and give a comparative account of the characteristic features of the different models.

Figure 1. Metaverse Ecosystem Taxonomy

Metaverse Ecosystem Taxonomy

Characteristic	Immersive Conceptual Modelers	BIM & Design Visualization Plugins	Collaborative Social Platforms	Game Engines for Simulation
Function	Ideate, sculpt, create in 3D space	Real-time, high-fidelity design visualization	Foster shared virtual environments for co-creation	Create realistic, interactive, dynamic simulations
Examples	Gravity Sketch, Shapelab	Enscape, Twinmotion	Spatial.io, NVIDIA Omniverse	Unreal Engine, Unity
Pedagogical Value	Enhance creative process, immediate feedback	Rapid assimilation of spatial designs	Facilitate interactive learning, enhance creative potential	Merge gamification with design pedagogy

Category 1: Immersive Conceptual Modelers (e.g., Gravity Sketch, Shapelab)

One of the fundamental forms of the Metaverse ecosystem is immersive conceptual modelers that enable the designers to ideate and sculpt and create in the three-dimensional virtual environment. Such applications are usually available in virtual reality applications, which allow virtual 3D sketching and computer-aided design, allowing one to interact naturally with virtual objects in a collaborative space (Roberts et al., 2020). This scale of working of design 1:1 constructs more understanding of the relation and shape of space and transcends the limitation of the 2D representation of the model (Gómez-Tone et al., 2022). The pedagogical interest of immersive conceptual modelers is that they allow developing the creative process and offer an opportunity to explore and convey ideas using the immediacy and feedback unavailable in the traditional means (Gómez-Tone et al., 2022).

Figure 2. Components of Immersive Conceptual Modelers

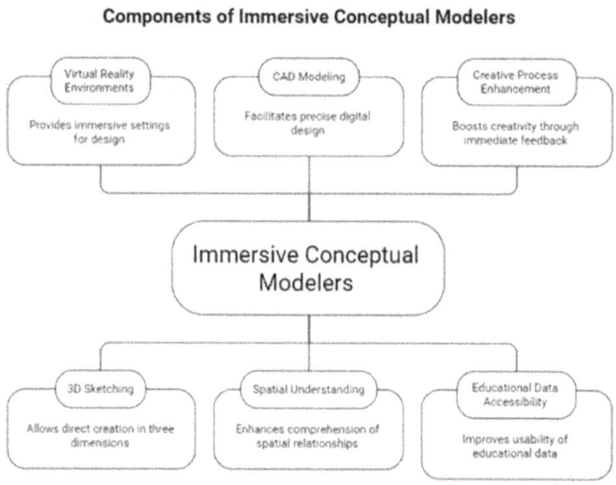

In particular, the fact that the extended reality technologies used, including VR in the design studios, allow fully consuming the experience of visualization, allows having a more fruitful conversation and make more informed decisions when looking at the design (Crolla et al., 2024). These technologies provide designers with an opportunity to interact with synthetic objects in the environment of so-called rich immersive 3D experiences, which, in its turn, has a significant impact on the design creativity (Gomez-Tone et al., 2022, Roberts et al., 2020). Moreover, the use of interactive modeling tools is becoming helpful in enabling even unskilled users to be involved in the generation and selection of ideas process. Figure 2 summarises the components of the immersive conceptual modellers. The ease and convenience of the educational data access by the means of the immersive visualization opportunities offered by such technologies is also sought in the conditions of the multidisciplinary design environment (Fonseca et al., 2020a, 2020b).

Category 2: Building information model and design visualisation Plugins (e.g., Enscape, Twinmotion)

This type is devoted to the association of Building Information Modeling processes with high-tech tools of design visualization, which is one of the important elements of the Metaverse ecosystem in the sphere of architecture and engineering. Modern professional practice can always use BIM systems, which offer detailed and data-rich models that simplify the process of design, construction, and operation (Alizadehsalehi et al., 2021; Ehab et al., 2023). The use of real-time rendering and visualization plugs, including Enscape and Twinmotion, allows BIM to be greatly extended into high-fidelity and instantaneous visualization at real time of design concepts. Such plugins enable the visualization and comprehension of spatial designs faster and in a more all-encompassing way than conventional plans or physical models (Fonseca et al., 2021). They play a significant role in improving communication and teamwork of project stakeholders using immersive and realistic visualizations (Ehab et al., 2023). As an illustration, Enscape directly supports a BIM system, such as Revit, allowing designers to make real-time updates to their design, and thus high-level visualization is available to users without a deep background in programming Ehab et al., 2023).

Figure 3. Integrating BIM with Visualization Plugins

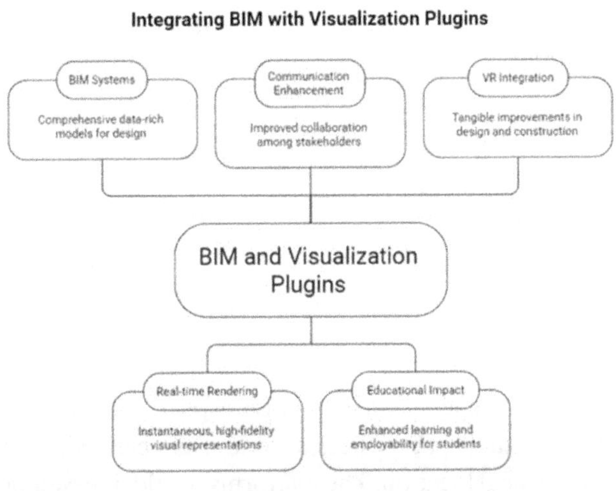

Figure 3 presents the different role of the BIM Models and the functions of visualisation plugins that can be introduced into the model. These technologies and their effects on student learning, engagement, and employability in education on the built environment are common knowledge (Ghanbaripour et al., 2024). Moreover, the adoption of the BIM and VR has shown practical advancements in design and construction project, such as quality and efficiency, and this is valuable in AEC education and training (Alizadehsalehi et al., 2021). Academic curricula are progressively adapting towards instruction focused on BIM to enhance the readiness of students for professional standards, as BIM facilitates the amalgamation of visualization, data governance, and collaborative processes within the educational paradigm (Maharika et al., 2020).The fact that these tools assist users in determining the relations between people and their surroundings, passing the ideas across, and modifying spaces according to the requirements of the users highlights their pedagogical importance (Fonseca et al., 2021).

Category 3: Collaborative Social Platforms (e.g. Spatial.io, NVIDIA, Omniverse)

Figure 4. The Social dimension of the Metaverse

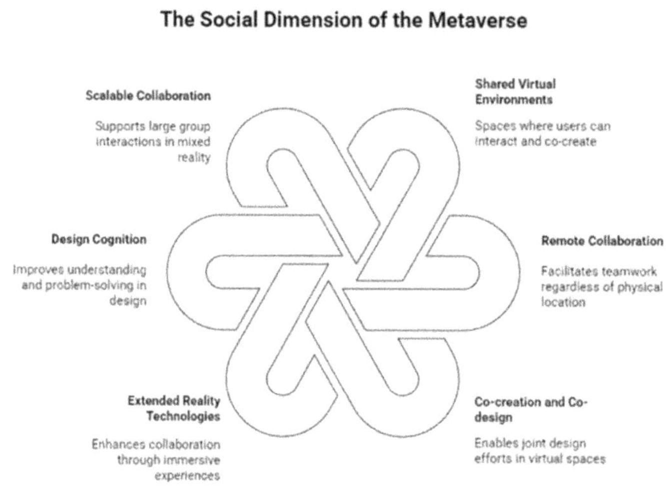

Social platforms are the social and interactive aspect of the Metaverse ecosystem that creates a shared virtual space where several users can exist, interact, and co-create despite their physical location. The platforms would be essential in solving the increasing demand of the remote and distributed collaboration in design education and professional practice.

Figure 4 demonstrates the social dimension of the metaverse graphically. Co-creation and co-design is possible through these virtual spaces through the use of extended reality technologies, which enhances the early design process and breaks down geographies (El-Jarn & Southern, 2020). Studies emphasize the advantages of computer-based collaborative workplaces and computer-based collaborative design systems in widening the design scope to dynamic digital space, allowing remote and online design processes to take place (Lee & Ostwald, 2022). These tools are supposed to amplify the cognition of design when working remotely and creating a more fluid exchange of ideas and collectively solving problems. Moreover, the construction of practice-based models of organizing large groups of people in distributed mixed reality collaboration offers an outlay of scalable collaborative experiences (Wong et al., 2024). The combination of such social VR space provides a powerful solution to promote interactive learning and stimulate creative possibilities in design studios, which can promote hybrid learning practices (Avinç & Yıldiz, 2025).

Category 4: Game Engines with Improved Simulation (e.g. Unreal Engine, Unity)

Game engines, including Unreal Engine and Unity, are a strong and growing category of the Metaverse ecosystem and can be characterized as a powerful framework that may be used to create highly realistic, interactive, and dynamic simulations. Designed with the gaming sector in mind, these engines are currently being extensively used in architectural and design processes due to their sophisticated visualization, simulation, and user experience research (Fonseca et al., 2021).

These platforms allow building realistic, interactive spaces where one can navigate and manipulate virtual space in real-time, which effectively combines gamification with pedagogy of architecture and urban design (Ehab et al., 2023; Fonseca et al., 2021). Game engines promote the quick visualization and integration of design spaces, which is essential in perceiving the complicated models (Fonseca et al., 2021). They also have broad potentials of creating realistic, immersive surroundings that are powered by a variety of simulation applications and interactive design functions (Ehab et al., 2023). An example of this is the Unreal engine where it is easy to add interactive elements such as X-ray, object manipulation, virtual annotations, and virtual camera features, which are indispensable when it comes to exploration of specific designs and feedback (Ehab et al., 2023). BIM integration with real-time game engines is changing the AEC sector by improving design solutions, simplifying the construction process, and enhancing more effective stakeholder collaboration (Rehman et al., 2025). Moreover, the engines are used to create virtual reality educational games to assist students with assessing and reviewing the BIM-based designs to prove their usefulness in terms of both practical learning and assessment. BIM systems combined with video-game engines are also relevant in education to make ephemeral projects in urban and architectural proposals (Fonseca et al., 2020).

Table 1. Comprehensive Technology Comparison Matrix

Attribute	Immersive Conceptual Modelers	BIM Visualization Plugins	Collaborative Social Platforms	Game Engines
Primary Purpose	Early ideation, spatial exploration	Technical coordination, stakeholder communication	Remote critique, distributed design	Gamified learning, advanced simulation
Presence Fidelity	High (9/10)	Medium-High (7/10)	Medium-High (7/10)	High (9/10)
Scale Perception	High (9/10)	Medium-High (7/10)	Medium (7/10)	High (9/10)
Synchronous Collaboration	Yes (real-time co-modeling)	Limited (screen-share based)	Strong (designed for multi-user)	Yes (multiplayer capable)
Concurrent Users	Small groups (2-8)	Typically single user	Varies (10-50+ documented)	Server-dependent (tested 5-20)
BIM Metadata Preservation	Limited (5/10)	High (8/10)	Medium (6/10)	Medium (6/10 with custom scripts)
File Format Support	FBX, OBJ, glTF	IFC, RVT, FBX via plugins	Common 3D formats (FBX, OBJ)	Universal (FBX, OBJ, glTF, USD)
Round-Trip Editing	Limited	Some support with caveats	Weak	Possible with custom tools
Hardware Requirements	VR headset (Quest/Vive) + controllers	VR-capable PC (high-end GPU) or desktop	Desktop/mobile or VR headset	High-end PC (powerful GPU) for VR
Estimated Cost (USD)	$300-1000 (HMD) + $0-50/mo (software)	$1000-3000 (PC) + $100-500/yr (licenses)	$0-500 (varies by platform) + HMD if VR	$2000-4000 (dev PC) + $0 (Unity/Unreal free)
Learning Curve	Moderate	Moderate-High	Gentle-Moderate	Steep
Faculty Development	Moderate (UI training needed)	High (BIM + VR workflow)	Moderate (facilitation skills)	High (programming + pedagogy)
Construction Pedagogy	Limited	Strong (LOD, sequencing)	Domain-specific (VRArch Education)	Very Strong (custom modules)
Performance Simulation	Minimal	Moderate (lighting, basic)	Limited	Very Strong (scripted)
Assessment Integration	Basic (session replay)	Moderate (BIM analytics)	Variable (platform-dependent)	Strong (custom analytics)
Technology Maturity	Emerging to Moderate	Moderate to Mature	Emerging (rapid growth)	Mature (engines); emerging (educational use)
Implementation Complexity	Medium	Medium-High	Low-Medium	High

continued on following page

Table 1. Continued

Attribute	Immersive Conceptual Modelers	BIM Visualization Plugins	Collaborative Social Platforms	Game Engines
Scalability	Good for small cohorts	Scales with BIM infrastructure	High (distributed access)	Highly scalable technically
Equity Considerations	Motion sickness 20-40%; device access varies	Requires institutional BIM licenses	Accessible for remote students; HMD optional	High development barrier; resource-intensive

Table 1 is a complete technology comparison matrix of 19 evaluative attributes. These qualities form a practical comparison matrix that helps educators match learning goals, resources, and technology, such as choosing immersive modelers for low-budget studios focused on spatial learning, or BIM visualization tools for advanced courses with existing BIM infrastructure.

A FRAMEWORK FOR EVALUATION: PRINCIPAL PEDAGOGICAL ATTRIBUTES

A solid framework in evaluation would be needed to successfully assimilate and evaluate the wide range of Metaverse technologies that exist in design education. This framework should specify and support the criteria that can have an opportunity to compare the pedagogical effectiveness of these tools based on their ability to improve learning outcomes and prepare students to meet complex professional problems Kee et al., 2023. The given framework is necessary due to the shortcomings identified in the integration of digital tools, as well as the required lack of specific knowledge on the proper usage of such tools in the context of design pedagogy (Ummihusna & Zairul, 2022., Al-Rqaibat et al., 2025). In this section, the most important pedagogical qualities to be considered as the measure of assessing the immersive and digital design tools will be formulated based on the existing research to give a complete picture of their capabilities and constraints.

Simulation and Sensation of Size

One of the most important pedagogical features of design education is immersiveness, which is supported by virtual reality and augmented reality technologies, and has a direct impact on the perception of scale and space of a student Darwish et al., 2023; Kee et al., 2023. Immersive environments promote experience learning, during which learners will be able to experience the concept of design in a real-life setting, which will develop their practical, spatial, and kinesthetic skills Kee et al.,

2023. This in-person interaction has a huge impact on the design creativity, as it is possible to explore and understand the relationships in space much deeper and better. 3. As an example, VR has been demonstrated to increase the level of spatial ability of students regarding architectural design education Darwish et al., 2023. The richer fidelity of learning scenarios in terms of visual, spatial, and audio, available in immersive learning environments, is helpful to develop holistic competency and self-directed learning (Kee et al., 2023).

Cooperation and Multiuser Functionality

Teamwork and multi-user functionality are essential learning qualities, since the modern design practice is becoming both interconnected and collaborative. Multi-User Virtual Environments provide mutual virtual spaces, where students get to interact, communicate, and collaboratively create, thus contributing to collaborative learning (Sopher & Lescop, 2023). This helps buttress the more interactive, collaborative and student centered learning in design education (Kee et al., 2023). These platforms are important in creating collaborative review spaces, to make traditional procedures become active and interactive, where students, teachers, and external professionals can have a positive conversation and share criticism with each other (Crolla et al., 2024). Pedagogical and societal contributions to the process of co-creation in the architectural field are also observed through the use of digital whiteboards as a collaborative tool in the same study by (Brandão et al., 2021). Moreover, it has discussed the creation of real-time multiplayer building systems in the form of video games to allow collaborative building of models and imparting of tacit design knowledge (Yuan et al., 2023).

Inter-operability and Cohesion in Workflow

The inter-operability and cohesion of workflows are required in ensuring seamless exchange data and integration of the tools in the digital design education ecosystem. Combination of the separate digital systems, or CAD with Computer-Aided Engineering, Computer-Aided Manufacturing, and Extended Reality systems, affects the creative behaviors of the designers positively (Al-Rqaibat et al., 2025). Though there is a possibility, workflow integration problems between different 3D digital design tools and Building Information Modeling platforms continue to arise and usually cause interruptions to the design fidelity and ineffective data transfers (El-Khouly & Abdelhalim, 2024). The idea of conceptual design continuity between platforms demands strategies to improve interoperability and ensure a smooth exchange of data (El-Khouly & Abdelhalim, 2024). The study will help in the creation of teaching strategies that would enable students to acquire the skills to cope with the obstacles of digital design and attain effective management of workflow (El-Khouly & Abdelhalim, 2024.) Tailoring studio needs to facilitate high-level tool implementation and promoting serious technological thinking are essential measures towards creating technologically knowledgeable workflows, which can facilitate innovation and optimization of the architectural profession (Crolla et al., 2024).

Availability, Economic factors, and Learning Curve

The practical use of the Metaverse technologies largely depends on the accessibility, financial viability, and learning curve considerations. There is a visible gap in skills between students and teachers in using the advanced technologies; moreover, there are complexities of curriculum integration (Crolla et al., 2024). The Head-Mounted Displays and Computer-Assisted Virtual Environment have prohibitive costs that present significant barriers to widespread use (Crolla et al., 2024). This subject holds considerable relevance within the educational landscape, in which academic institutions often present a deficiency in adequate technological support and thorough career development efforts, thereby obstructing the widespread application of (Kee et al., 2023). Nevertheless, there is also evidence that immersive technologies may provide a predictable and affordable study experience (Kee et al., 2023). Although VR may save development time and costs over real-world investments on physical prototyping, especially during the initial stages of the design process (Roberts et al., 2020), it still takes time and practice to achieve high-level skills, and it is recommended that teachers should combine immersive technologies with other learning experiences to reinforce the actual experience and abstract cognition (Kee et al., 2023). It should be focused on an adequate level of institutional and technical support and the general structure and arrangement of teaching and learning material (Kee et al., 2023).

3.5 Specialization of Pedagogical Characteristics

The metaverse technologies possess special pedagogical features that present some exclusive benefits to design education. They encompass the promotion of digital literacy and experiential learning, which result in the creation of a more holistic and interactive curriculum (Kee et al., 2023). Virtual reality and augmented reality are becoming more integrated to provide deep immersive learning experience that encourages active experimentation, reflective observation, and skills and knowledge acquisition (Kee et al., 2023). The use of immersive technology can equally contribute to bringing the students close to the realm of design (Crolla et al., 2024) by increasing the visualization possibilities and closing the divide between theory and practice of architectural design. This assists students to acquire critical skills in design process which include design-based learning and appreciation of digital technology (Kee et al., 2023). Among the issues of architectural education addressed by XR technologies, there is the necessity to have practical experience, the necessity of profound self-reflection when working with a design, and the successful combination of theoretical knowledge and technical skills (Crolla et al., 2024). AR/VR application in design education provides new possibilities of fully immersive, open, creative, collaborative, and dialogic knowledge construction (Kee et al., 2023).

COMPARATIVE ANALYSIS: EDUCATORS RESOURCE

This section presents a comparative analysis of Metaverse tools based on the proposed taxonomy, highlighting key pedagogical attributes to help educators understand the strengths, limits, and appropriate use of immersive and digital technologies in design education.

Analysis of Immersive Conceptual Modelers

The immersive conceptual modelers (like Gravity Sketch and Shapelab) allow the designer to generate and edit 3D models in virtual reality spaces. The tools have been proven to be very useful in developing a profound experience of spatial relations and scale because of their nature of immersion Gomez-Tone et al., 2022. They permit a 1:1 interaction with digital objects, which enables experiential learning, as students can subconsciously experiment with design forms and volumes Gomez-Tone et al., 2022. This also plays a major role in the growth of the practical, spatial and kinesthetic skills allowing to explore the design forms to a deeper level and expressing them Kee et al., 2023. Virtual environments are also valuable in that the process of designing also plays an important role in design creativity Roberts et al., 2020.

Regarding collaboration, although there are those which are multi-user in nature, some immersive modelers do not always focus on collaborative conceptualization. Nonetheless, the models designed can often be exported to be reviewed in collaboration in other platforms Roberts et al., 2020. Inter-operability may also pose issues because a lot of immersive content may be locked into certain hardware or software systems, which may complicate its compatibility with other design tools Fernandes et al., 2023. The development of a system of interoperability between conceptual data modeling languages and hybrid modeling tools is one of the current research topics Braun et al., 2022. Initial users also have a steep learning curve when learning how to use it at basic level, and the immediate interaction of 3D sketching can be developed into an asset within not a long time Sim & Jung, 2025. The accessibility is also closely related to the accessibility of VR hardware, which may be a cost barrier to institutional and individual students. These tools are outstanding in terms of initial design ideation, creativity, and enhanced spatial cognition due to the ability to redo and engage the theory practically in a virtual learning environment Kee et al., 2023.

Analysis of Building Information Modelling and Build Plugins Design Visualization

BIM software, with real-time visualization extensions, such as Enscape and Twinmotion, is a potent design ecosystem of detailed design development and communication in architecture education. These applications improve the sense of scale with highly realistic and navigable 3D models that enable users to more quickly view and internalize designs at a more comprehensive scale than 2D plans do Fonseca et al., 2021. This gap is also further closed with the use of BIM and VR, which provide an opportunity to review the project in an immersive manner and get a better understanding of the spatial implications, which positively affects the quality and efficiency of the design project Alizadehsalehi et al., 2021; Xiberta et al., 2022.

BIM is a collaborative tool with its fundamental principle being the support of multi-disciplinary workflows full of data. This is further complemented by visualization plugins which enable the stakeholders to view the designs in real-time with each other, making it easier to communicate and make decisions Ehab et al., 2023. BIM and emerging technologies promote collaboration and effective communication in building management training Abouelkhier et al., 2024. Interoperability is also one of the most important factors; although the BIM platforms are designed to exchange the data freely, a close attention to the integration with different extensions and other software may still be needed to balance the working process coherence Urban et al., 2022; Wong et al., 2020. The use of the Metaverse to teach BIM is still an emerging method of assessing the attitudes of students towards the workflow and integration Bartels & Hahne, 2023. BIMS software may have a steep learning curve because it is a complex and data-intensive software ÇAKIR & Uzun, 2020. Nevertheless, more complex rendering can usually be accessed with a relatively lower learning curve when using visualization plugins Fonseca et al., 2021. Availability of software BIM is common in higher educational institutions, although the high-performance hardware might be needed to use visualization plug-ins effectively. BIM should be integrated into academic programs to meet the industry demands Lite et al., 2022. These systems can be used, pedagogically, as a learning instrument to real-life building activities and communicative activity to ensure that students perform and engage better Ghanbaripour et al., 2024; Maharika et al., 2020.

Analysis of Collaborative Social Platforms

Social platforms Collaborative social platforms could be defined as Spatial.io or NVIDIA Omniverse, which are tailored to the multi-user interaction inside the common virtual environment, and collaboration is their most salient pedagogical feature. These are the platforms that enable co-creation and co-design processes, which enable students to communicate, collaborate, and solve problems together despite geographical barriers Wong et al., 2024. They encourage interactive, dynamic reviewing, and turn the above-mentioned traditional critiques into an interactive conversation between learners and their instructors and external specialists Crolla et al., 2024.

As much as these platforms are different in their levels of immersiveness, their main advantage is their ability to promote social presence and mutual comprehension, but not accurate conceptual modeling. Nevertheless, participatory immersive virtual reality has the potential to enhance spatial abilities and augment user experience Pastor et al., 2023. One of the reasons that could hinder the increased usage of the XR technologies is the lack of interoperability since immersive content can be confined to certain hardware or software Fernandes et al., 2023. Nonetheless, the progress in the interoperability of the architecture of the multi-user AR based-curricula has a potential to create a seamless integration in the future Masneri et al., 2024. The navigation and interaction in these platforms have a relatively low learning curve to follow, which facilitates easy adoption of the tool because the students tend to introduce new communication and design of projects to projects through online platforms Tavares & Steagall, 2020. The barrier to entry is comparatively low with numerous platforms being web based or having free/low-cost options, which do not need elaborate hardware. Nevertheless, the obstacles of VR implementation are the cost, skills, and cultural shift in the industry Badamasi et al., 2021. In terms of pedagogy, these platforms are more effective in terms of communication, collaboration, and critical dialogue, where remote learning settings can have gaps, and student learning and interest are fostered (Sopher & Lescop, 2023; Tavares and Steagall, 2020).

Analysis of Game Engines as an Increased Simulation

Game engines such as Unreal Engine and Unity offer powerful platforms to produce highly realistic, interactive and dynamic simulations with massive pedagogical benefits to design education. They can be used to create a more detailed and immersive setting, making their perception of scale and realistic exploration of the space essential in being able to comprehend complex architectural models Fonseca et al., 2021. To create realistic and interactive environments, they are applied to make users explore and manipulate virtual spaces in real-time to appear to merge the idea of gamification with design pedagogy Ehab et al., 2023; Meier et al., 2020.

Game engines are essentially designed to facilitate multi-user interaction, and can be set up to facilitate collaborative design and review works using the strong networking potential of game engines Shakeri & Örnek, 2023. The combination of BIM and real-time game engines is changing the AEC sector by improving the design procedures, simplifying the construction process, and improving stakeholder cooperation Rehman et al., 2025. There has been an improvement in interoperability, with game engines providing powerful pipelines to import BIM and CAD software assets, enabling professional models to be simulated with high fidelity Rehman et al., 2025. Simple programming can be the lowest learning curve of basic operation of certain game engines, where certain programming languages such as Roblox Studio do not need prior knowledge of programming Meier et al., 2020. Nevertheless, to use the full capabilities of the advanced game engines, such as Unreal Engine or Unity, particularly when one is performing complex architecture simulations, their learning commitment may still be significant Fonseca et al., 2021. Game engines are pedagogically unique because of its ability to produce detailed simulations, which can be followed with an experiential experience, study of user experience, and design hypothesis testing within the dynamic virtual environment Aydin and Aktaş, 2020; Elsemahy, 2020. They allow more interactive elements, including X-ray visualization, the ability to manipulate objects, and virtual annotation, which helps to explore the design in detail Ehab et al., 2023.

Figure 5. Pedagogical Use Cases and Technology Suitability

Learning Objective / Use Case	Immersive Modelers	BIM Plugins	Collaborative Platforms	Game Engines
Early-stage conceptual ideation	●●● Highly Suitable	◐ Limited	•• Suitable	•• Suitable
Scale and proportion understanding	●●● Highly Suitable	•• Suitable	•• Suitable	●●● Highly Suitable
Construction sequencing education	◐ Limited	●●● Highly Suitable	◐ Limited	●●● Highly Suitable
BIM coordination and clash detection	◐ Limited	●●● Highly Suitable	•• Suitable	•• Suitable
Remote design critique and review	•• Suitable	◐ Limited	●●● Highly Suitable	•• Suitable
Synchronous collaborative design	•• Suitable	◐ Limited	●●● Highly Suitable	•• Suitable
Stakeholder/client communication	•• Suitable	●●● Highly Suitable	•• Suitable	•• Suitable
Environmental performance visualization	◐ Limited	•• Suitable	◐ Limited	●●● Highly Suitable
Gamified procedural learning	◐ Limited	◐ Limited	◐ Limited	●●● Highly Suitable
Measurement and survey skills	•• Suitable	•• Suitable	●●● Highly Suitable	•• Suitable
Material and tectonic understanding	•• Suitable	•• Suitable	•• Suitable	●●● Highly Suitable
Interdisciplinary coordination	◐ Limited	●●● Highly Suitable	•• Suitable	•• Suitable

It is evident that the matrix shown in Figure 5, delineates pedagogical niches based on categorical frameworks: Immersive Modelers excel in preliminary ideation and spatial awareness, BIM Plugins are paramount in construction sequencing and coordination, Collaborative Platforms facilitate remote critiques and distributed design, while Game Engines enhance gamified learning and sophisticated simulations. No single tool fits all needs; therefore, an objective-driven selection is required. Figure 5 supports this by linking learning goals to appropriate tools, enabling a phased approach such as using immersive modelers in early studios, BIM plugins in intermediate years, collaborative platforms throughout, and game engines in electives to match student development.

Trade-offs and New Trends Overview

The comparative analysis shows that each Metaverse tool offers distinct benefits and trade-offs: immersive modelers support intuitive ideation but face cost and interoperability limits; BIM tools enable professional design and communication but require high investment; collaborative platforms enhance teamwork and access but lack advanced design features; and game engines provide the most realistic simulations but demand significant learning effort.

There are new trends of increased convergence and integration between these categories. The boundaries between conceptual modeling, BIM, and game engine visualization are becoming blurry, with more and more attempts to develop smooth processes that enable designers to transition between the various phases of design without any interruption Rehman et al., 2025. The continued growth of AI and machine learning will enable automated design, smart feedback, and personalized learning, leading to flexible hybrid pedagogical tools that support interdisciplinary and problem-based learning for future design challenges.

BETWEEN THEORY AND PRACTICE: IMPLEMENTATION AND INTEGRATION

It is important to translate theoretical frameworks into practical pedagogical practices to successfully incorporate advanced technologies in design education. The effective introduction of new tools into the design studio requires the close attention to the education goals, real issues, and new tendencies in technologies. This part presents some of the main points that should be considered when transitioning between theoretical knowledge and practice so that technology can be used to optimize, not to impede the learning process.

Strategic Choice: Adapting Technology to Education Results

The desired results of utilizing digital tools should be carefully matched with the targeted educational outcomes and allow promoting creativity and enhancing the design thinking processes (Hettithanthri and Hansen, 2021; Kee et al., 2023). The use of hybrid tools in conceptual design modules can be a valuable implication in terms of increasing creativity, yet their performance depends on a responsible design of course material considering various phases of the design process (Kee et al., 2023). Enhancing the control of those tools by designers is essential to enhance efficiency and facilitate design thinking so that technology could become a partner and not a constraint of creative problem-solving (Hettithanthri and Hansen, 2021).

As an example, the design curriculum must be modified with the integration of immersive technologies to increase the importance of hands-on exercises and reflection that are essential to the development of skills and knowledge (Kee et al., 2023). But these technologies should be complemented with other learning activities by the instructors which can help to support the real-world experiences and abstract conceptualization since immersive tools do not necessarily fully address these phenomena (Kee et al., 2023). The purposes of selection should also focus on developing abstraction and metacognition in the students, whereby teachers must employ certain methods and design learning activities and assessment to facilitate these high-order thinking abilities (Kee et al., 2023). The idea is to select tools that will help to have a more profound integration with the constructivist learning theories, including the concepts of design thinking: ideation, reflection, and critiquing (Kee et al., 2023).

Solving Practical Problems: Financial, Access, and Training Issues

The implementation of extended reality technologies in architecture education has a number of practical issues, which include high cost, lack of skills, and curriculum challenges (Crolla et al., 2024). The cost of the prohibitive hardware such as Head-Mounted Displays and Computer-Assisted Virtual Environment systems is also a significant barrier to mass adoption (Crolla et al., 2024). This economic obstacle is especially severe in the educational sphere, where inadequate funding of technology support and the absence of long-term planning may become an impediment to a wider adoption (Kee et al., 2023).

In addition, there is an evident skills gap both among the educators and the students in the areas of the successful use of these new technologies, and multiple schools of thought are offered in the context of widespread training programs to prepare educators and students with the skills to implement XR into their activities (Crolla et al., 2024). In spite of these issues, immersive technologies may provide a predictable and affordable learning process (Kee et al., 2023). Although Virtual Reality may be less time-consuming and cheaper than a physical prototype, especially at an early design phase Roberts et al., 2020, it is more time-intensive and practice-based to be fully integrated (Roberts et al., 2023). Thus, the primary success of implementation is the sufficient institutional and technical support, as well as a well-structured teaching and learning content (Kee et al., 2023). It is also important to tackle the problem of accessibility, so that more privileged groups should not be the only ones who have access to advanced technologies, but a larger student population should be included in this category (Kee et al., 2023). Other issues that tend to create barriers to VR adoption in the industry include the challenge of cost, skills shortage, and cultural change (Badamasi et al., 2021).

In the future, AI, haptics, and the enduring campus will emerge. Trends such as AI and haptic feedback will reshape design education within the digital ecosystem, subsequently redefining the function of the physical campus. The convergence of AI and immersive technologies is opening the door to the personalized learning process which can be developed through AI in the real-time where the performance and engagement of students can be recorded and reacted to through the creation of personalized learning environments in real-time as these learning environments adapt accordingly to optimize student learning (Mallek et al., 2024). AI can be used as a virtual tutor offering adaptive cues and additional resources, performance analysis, and personal feedback to achieve better skills in solving problems (Mallek et al., 2024). An important field of future research, particularly to provide designers, customers, and final users with the opportunity to effortlessly contribute to the design process, is the effect of AI on increasing the VR capabilities to provide real-time design and collaboration capabilities (Ehab et al., 2023).

Such developments are indicating that there will be a day when the physical campus, even though always important in terms of community, face-to-face learning and practical learning, will be supplemented by a very rich digitally enriched learning environment. Due to new forms of hybrid virtual learning and new educational technologies, the possibilities of breaking the teaching and learning process of the space and time are gigantically large (Kee et al., 2023). ARVR integration provides the prospects of an entirely immersive, open, creative, collaborative, and dialogic knowledge construction (Kee et al., 2023). Nevertheless, with the advancement of learning settings towards becoming more technologically oriented, the loss of physical touch between a student and a teacher should be considered, and the attempts should be aimed at making the technological achievements available and reachable by every educational facility and individual (Pérez et al., 2023).

CONCLUSION: CURATING THE DIGITAL STUDIO

The adoption of new high-tech and immersive technologies, especially among the emerging Metaverse ecosystem, is a critical concept that has fundamentally changed the design education. The chapter has examined the historical process of technology in design studios, its failures and shortcomings in current pedagogical strategies, and suggested a taxonomy of the most important Metaverse technologies. In addition, it has also defined key pedagogical characteristics of their analysis that will be evaluated, and gave a full comparative analysis of these tools. The ongoing change of the traditional analog approach to the advanced digital simulations explains the necessity of an active and creative pedagogical set of tools to prepare future designers to work in a more diverse and global professional environment.

Overview of Findings

Table 2 below summarises the key findings on the benefits of Metaverse technologies in design education, the proposed tool taxonomy, and the core pedagogical insight emerging from the review.

Table 2. Key Findings on the Advantages of Metaverse Technologies in Design education

Aspect	Key Points
Educational Benefits	Enables customization, creativity, and interactive learning; improves spatial understanding and design communication (Tlili et al., 2022; Villegas-Ch et al., 2024)
Learning Experience	Supports deeper engagement with complex design concepts; allows more iterations and may reduce student anxiety compared to traditional methods (Crolla et al., 2024; Kee et al., 2023)
Tool Taxonomy	Tools classified as Immersive Conceptual Modelers, BIM & Design Visualization Plugins, Collaborative Social Platforms, and Game Engines for Improved Simulation
Strengths of Tool Categories	Immersive tools support early ideation; BIM tools enable professional workflows; collaborative platforms enhance teamwork; game engines allow dynamic and realistic simulation (Alizadehsalehi et al., 2021; Ehab et al., 2023; Fonseca et al., 2021; Gomez-Tone et al., 2022)
Key Pedagogical Insight	Effective use depends more on intentional pedagogy and teaching methods than on technology novelty or availability (Wong et al., 2024)

The table 3 summarizes these methods and the learning outcomes they are designed to evaluate.

Table 3. Summary of Assessment Methods in Metaverse Studios

Metaverse Technology Category	Assessment Integration Level	Specific Assessment Methods & Features	Primary Learning Outcomes Evaluated
Immersive Conceptual Modelers	**Basic**	**Session replays**; Exporting models for collaborative review in other platforms.	Spatial literacy, intuitive ideation, and 3D sketching ability.
BIM Visualization Plugins	**Moderate**	**BIM analytics**; Real-time review of spatial implications and design quality.	Technical knowledge, construction sequencing, and coordination.
Collaborative Social Platforms	**Variable**	**Dynamic interactive review sessions**; Shared virtual spaces for "remote critique".	Communication, teamwork, and critical discussion skills.
Game Engines	**Strong**	**Custom analytics**; Educational games used to "assess and review" BIM designs; Design hypothesis testing.	Advanced simulation, gamified learning, and complex problem-solving.
Emerging AI-Driven Tools	**Advanced** (Potential)	**Performance and engagement recording**; AI virtual tutors providing "performance analysis" and personalized feedback.	High-order thinking, metacognition, and individualized skill acquisition.

The study arrives at defining a "Framework for Evaluation" that identifies five principal attributes used to measure the pedagogical effectiveness of these tools, that is summarised in table 4

Table 4. The Assessment Framework

Evaluation Attribute	Focus of Assessment
Simulation & Sensation of Size	Student perception and understanding of scale, proportion, and spatial experience
Cooperation & Multi-user Functionality	Ability to collaborate, interact, and co-create within shared digital environments
Interoperability & Workflow Cohesion	Effectiveness of data exchange and continuity across multiple design tools
Accessibility & Learning Curve	Cost feasibility and ease of skill acquisition for student users
Pedagogical Specialization	Support for digital literacy, experimentation, and active learning practices

Table 5 outlines the key ethical, accessibility, and inclusivity challenges associated with integrating Metaverse technologies into design studios and Table 6 summarises the main challenges related to faculty readiness and training for Metaverse-based pedagogy.

Table 5. Ethical, Accessibility and Inclusivity Concerns

Concern Area	Key Issues Identified	Implications for Design Studio Integration
Economic Barriers & Inequality	High cost of HMDs and CAVE systems limits access, (Crolla et al., 2024)	Risk of exclusion and unequal learning opportunities; need for inclusive access strategies
Physical Discomfort & Well-being	20–40% users experience motion sickness; physical and mental strain	Limits duration and intensity of use; requires alternative modes and health-aware deployment
Ethical & Privacy Concerns	Continuous data capture of student performance and engagement	Necessitates clear ethical guidelines, data protection policies, and informed consent
Loss of Human Connection	Reduced physical interaction between students and faculty, ((Kee et al., 2023)	Risk of diminished studio culture; need for hybrid or blended pedagogical models
Institutional Constraints	Insufficient infrastructure and long-term planning	Slows adoption and scalability; demands institutional commitment and policy support

Table 6. Challenges related to Faculty Readiness and Training

Aspect	Key Observations	Pedagogical / Institutional Implications
Skills Gap	Mismatch between faculty expertise and technological complexity	Requires structured capacity-building and continuous upskilling
Training Intensity by Tool Type	Immersive Conceptual Modelers – Moderate BIM Visualization Plugins – High Collaborative Social Platforms – Moderate Game Engines – High	Training programs must be tool-specific, not uniform
Institutional & Technical Support	Effective adoption depends on time, support, and resources	Faculty readiness is tied to institutional investment and technical assistance
Pedagogical Planning	Risk of tool-driven rather than learning-driven implementation	Faculty must design intentional tasks targeting higher-order thinking
Implementation Success Factors	Training, support, and planning identified as critical	Long-term success depends on aligned pedagogy, technology, and policy

Educator Recommendations

To embrace the maximum potential of these emerging technologies, teachers need to be strategic and considerate to integrate them in the design curriculum. Recommendations for the academic brains are summarised in the table 7.

Making use of multi-user functions of different platforms, the above can be used to establish dynamic interactive review sessions that promote communication, teamwork, and critical discussion between students, instructors and external experts (Crolla et al., 2024).

Table 7. Recommendations for integrating emerging technologies in the Design Curriculum

Recommendation Area	Description
Align Technology to Educational Outcomes	Methodically select and integrate digital tools to ensure alignment with desired learning goals, supporting creativity and design thinking (Kee et al., 2023).
Holistic Learning	Use immersive technologies to complement hands-on activities and reflective observation essential for skill and knowledge acquisition. These tools must be paired with exercises that offer real-life experience and abstract conceptualization, as immersive environments may not fully address these aspects (Kee et al., 2023).
Develop Critical Skills	Strengthen students' higher-order thinking, abstraction, and metacognition through targeted teaching strategies and intentionally designed learning tasks and assessments (Kee et al., 2023).
Address Practical Implementation	Provide extensive training, support, and time for faculty and students to adapt to new learning modalities, ensuring adequate access to infrastructure (e.g., well-equipped VR labs) (Crolla et al., 2024; Kee et al., 2023).
Balance Traditional and Digital Methods	Ensure digital tools complement, rather than replace, conventional design practices such as freehand sketching and model making to avoid overreliance on technology and reinforce foundational design principles.
Reorganize Curricula to Support Innovation	Merge educational frameworks to unite Building Information Modeling (BIM) and programming with essential design and environmental studies, rather than seeing them as unrelated disciplines. Implement instructional frameworks that facilitate individualized learning adapted to the varied requirements and learning preferences of students (Onu et al., 2023; Villegas-Ch et al., 2024).
Leverage Multi-User Platforms	Use multi-user features of emerging technologies to create dynamic, interactive review sessions that encourage communication, teamwork, and critical discussion among students, instructors, and external experts (Crolla et al., 2024).

Restrictions and Future Research Perspectives

Although Metaverse technologies show a lot of potential, their use in design education is still limited. The major barriers come from the high cost, lack of needed skills, difficulty of fitting these tools into current curricula, and gaps in infrastructure and device capability. Many learners experience discomfort during the use of these systems, while there are ongoing concerns about privacy and mental well-being. Future studies should investigate these issues for longer periods and from different perspectives. This involves researching further technological integrations such as the role of artificial intelligence, the development of better interoperability between tools, and clearer guidelines concerning ethics and accessibility. In addition, it is relevant to better understand how students' engagement in gaming is linked to learning behaviour and data analysis. Addressing such challenges, coupled with an expanded scope of research, can lead design education toward a more efficient, equitable, digitally enhanced studio environment, better positioned for future technological shifts.

REFERENCES

Al-Rqaibat, S., Al-Nusair, S., & Bataineh, R. (2025). Enhancing architectural education through hybrid digital tools: Investigating the impact on design creativity and cognitive processes. *Smart Learning Environments*, *12*(1), 26. Advance online publication. DOI: 10.1186/s40561-025-00370-9

Avinç, G. M., & Yıldız, A. (2025). A bibliometric and systematic review of scientific publications on metaverse research in architecture: Web of Science (WoS). *International Journal of Technology and Design Education*, *35*(2), 825–849. DOI: 10.1007/s10798-024-09918-1

Brandão, E., Adelfio, M., Hagy, S., & Thuvander, L. (2021). Collaborative pedagogy for co-creation and community outreach: An experience from architectural education in social inclusion using the Miro tool. In Ahram, T., Taiar, R., & Groff, F. (Eds.), *Human factors in architecture, sustainable urban planning and infrastructure* (pp. 118–126). Springer., DOI: 10.1007/978-3-030-80415-2_15

Braun, G., Fillottrani, P. R., & Keet, C. M. (2022). A framework for interoperability between models with hybrid tools. *Journal of Intelligent Information Systems*. Advance online publication. DOI: 10.1007/s10844-022-00731-7 PMID: 35919102

Çakir, H., & Uzun, T. (2020). *Building information modelling in architectural education: Contribution of BIM in design process*. Turkish Online Journal of Design Art and Communication., DOI: 10.7456/11004100/009

Crolla, K., Song, J., Bunica, A., & Sheikh, A. (2024). Integrating extended reality in architectural design studio teaching and reviews: Implementing a participatory action research framework. *Buildings (Basel, Switzerland)*, *14*(6), 1865. Advance online publication. DOI: 10.3390/buildings14061865

Crolla, K., Song, J., Bunica, A., & Sheikh, A. T. (2024). Integrating extended reality in architectural design studio teaching and reviews: Implementing a participatory action research framework. *Buildings (Basel, Switzerland)*, *14*(6), 1865. Advance online publication. DOI: 10.3390/buildings14061865

Darwish, M., Kamel, S., & Assem, A. (2023). Extended reality for enhancing spatial ability in architecture design education. *Ain Shams Engineering Journal*, *14*(6), 102104. Advance online publication. DOI: 10.1016/j.asej.2022.102104

Ehab, A., Burnett, G., & Heath, T. (2023). Enhancing public engagement in architectural design: A comparative analysis of advanced virtual reality approaches in building information modeling and gamification techniques. *Buildings (Basel, Switzerland)*, *13*(5), 1262. Advance online publication. DOI: 10.3390/buildings13051262

Fonseca, D., Cavalcanti, J., Peña, E., Valls, V., Sánchez-Sepúlveda, M., Moreira, F., Navarro, I., & Redondo, E. (2021). Mixed assessment of virtual serious games applied in architectural and urban design education. *Sensors (Basel), 21*(9), 3102. Advance online publication. DOI: 10.3390/s21093102 PMID: 33946868

Gómez-Tone, H., Chávez, M., Samalvides, L., & Martín-Gutiérrez, J. (2022). Introducing immersive virtual reality in the initial phases of the design process—Case study: Freshmen designing ephemeral architecture. *Buildings (Basel, Switzerland), 12*(5), 518. Advance online publication. DOI: 10.3390/buildings12050518

Gomez-Tone, H. C., Alpaca Chávez, M., Vásquez Samalvides, L., & Martin-Gutierrez, J. (2022). Introducing immersive virtual reality in the initial phases of the design process—Case study: Freshmen designing ephemeral architecture. *Buildings (Basel, Switzerland), 12*(5), 518. Advance online publication. DOI: 10.3390/buildings12050518

Hettithanthri, U., & Hansen, P. (2021). Design studio practice in the context of architectural education: A narrative literature review. *International Journal of Technology and Design Education, 32*(4), 2343–2364. DOI: 10.1007/s10798-021-09694-2

Kee, T., et al. (2023). An empirical study on immersive technology in architectural education: The impact of virtual and augmented reality on design learning.

Kee, T., Zhang, H., & King, R. (2023). An empirical study on immersive technology in synchronous hybrid learning in design education. *International Journal of Technology and Design Education*. Advance online publication. DOI: 10.1007/s10798-023-09855-5

Maghool, S., Moeini, S., & Arefazar, Y. (2018). An educational application based on virtual reality technology for learning architectural details: Challenges and benefits. *Archnet-IJAR, 12*(3), 246. Advance online publication. DOI: 10.26687/archnet-ijar.v12i3.1719

Maharika, I., Irsan, A., Susanto, A., Abma, V., & Yuriandala, Y. (2020). Building information modelling (BIM) adoption model for architectural education. Journal of Design and Built Environment. DOI: 10.22452/jdbe.vol20no3.2

Mallek, F., Mazhar, T., Shah, S., Ghadi, Y., & Hamam, H. (2024). A review on cultivating effective learning: Synthesizing educational theories and virtual reality for enhanced educational experiences. *PeerJ. Computer Science, 10*, e2000. Advance online publication. DOI: 10.7717/peerj-cs.2000 PMID: 38855256

Masneri, S., Domínguez, A., Pacho, G., Zorrilla, M., Larrañaga, M., & Lasa, A. (2024). A collaborative AR application for education: From architecture design to user evaluation. *Virtual Reality (Waltham Cross)*, *28*(1), 1–13. DOI: 10.1007/s10055-024-00952-x

Mogaji, I. M., & Newton, P. (2020). School leadership for sustainable development: A scoping review. *Journal of Sustainable Development*, *13*(5), 15–30. DOI: 10.5539/jsd.v13n5p15

Onu, P., Pradhan, A., & Mbohwa, C. (2023). Potential to use metaverse for future teaching and learning. *Education and Information Technologies*, *29*(7), 8893–8924. DOI: 10.1007/s10639-023-12167-9

Ozorhon, G., & Sarman, G. (2023). The architectural design studio: A case in the intersection of the conventional and the new. Journal of Design Studio. DOI: 10.46474/jds.1394851

Rehman, S. U., Kim, I., & Hwang, K.-E. (2025). Advancing BIM and game engine integration in the AEC industry: Innovations, challenges, and future directions. *Journal of Computational Design and Engineering*, *12*(4), 26–54. DOI: 10.1093/jcde/qwaf030

Riskiyanto, R. (2023). Material-based learning in architecture design studio: From 'Beaux-Arts' to 'Bauhaus' into current educational era. Journal of Architectural Design and Urbanism. DOI: 10.14710/jadu.v5i2.18448

Roberts, S., et al. (2020). Designing in virtual environments: The integration of virtual reality tools into industrial design research and education.

Sim, Y. W., & Jung, E.-C. (2025). Comparative analysis of hand and VR sketching: Impact of immersion on idea generation in product design education. *International Journal of Technology and Design Education*. Advance online publication. DOI: 10.1007/s10798-025-10023-0

Soulikias, A., Cucuzzella, C., Nizar, F., Hazbei, M., & Goubran, S. (2021). We gain a lot… but what are we losing? A critical exploration of the implications of digital design technologies on sustainable architecture. *Open House International*, *46*(4), 548–562. DOI: 10.1108/OHI-04-2021-0085

Tlili, A., Huang, R., Shehata, B., Liu, D., Zhao, J., Metwally, A., Wang, H., Denden, M., Bozkurt, A., Lee, L., Beyoglu, D., Altınay, F., Sharma, R., Altınay, Z., Li, Z., Liu, J., Ahmad, F., Hu, Y., Salha, S., & Burgos, D. (2022). Is metaverse in education a blessing or a curse: A combined content and bibliometric analysis. *Smart Learning Environments*, *9*(1), 24. Advance online publication. DOI: 10.1186/s40561-022-00205-x

Toprak, İ., & Hacihasanoglu, O. (2019). Terms and concepts on design studio in the research articles of 2010's. *Journal of Design Studio*, *1*(2), 13–22.

Ummihusna, A., & Zairul, M. (2022). Exploring immersive learning technology as learning tools in experiential learning for architecture design education. *Open House International*, *47*(4), 605–619. Advance online publication. DOI: 10.1108/OHI-01-2022-0020

Villegas-Ch, W., García-Ortiz, J., & Sánchez-Viteri, S. (2024). Educational advances in the metaverse: Boosting learning through virtual and augmented reality and artificial intelligence. *IEEE Access : Practical Innovations, Open Solutions*, *12*, 59093–59112. DOI: 10.1109/ACCESS.2024.3393776

Yuan, X., Li, Y., & Wang, Y. (2023). A game engine based interactive and collaborative architectural education model proposal. In *International Conference on Innovative Academic Studies (Proceedings).*

Chapter 4

Harnessing Agricultural Metaverse Platforms to Convert Farm Waste Into Circular Economic Value

Durga Gurumoorthy
http://orcid.org/0009-0002-6633-9587
Periyar Maniammai Institute of Science and Technology, Thanjavur, India

Umamaheswari Durairaj
http://orcid.org/0000-0003-3655-1800
Periyar Maniammai Institute of Science and Technology, Thanjavur, India

Sylvestre Toe
Norbert Zongo University, Burkina Faso

ABSTRACT

The management of agricultural waste and the sustainability of resources continue to be major obstacles, and waste-to-wealth practices are not widely used because of a lack of knowledge, expertise, resources, and technology. Farmers can safely learn and test circular solutions thanks to the agricultural metaverse, which makes use of AR/VR, digital twins, and simulations. Results indicate that immersive platforms accelerate the transition to a circular economy by improving knowledge, cooperation, recycling behavior, and resource recovery.

DOI: 10.4018/979-8-3373-6721-7.ch004

1. INTRODUCTION

The rapid digitalization of global food systems has ushered in a transformative era in which advanced technologies are increasingly integrated into agricultural production, management, and decision making processes. Among these innovations, the emergence of the agricultural metaverse an immersive digital ecosystem that merges virtual environments, real time data, and interactive tools has gained considerable attention for its potential to reshape farming practices around the world. As agriculture grapples with an array of urgent challenges, including climate stress, resource scarcity, labor shortages, and rising demands for efficiency, the metaverse presents a compelling opportunity to reimagine how farmers access knowledge, monitor environmental conditions, and engage with global markets. However, realizing the full promise of this technology requires far more than innovation alone; it demands a systematic, inclusive, and ethically grounded framework to ensure that its benefits are equitably distributed and its implementation is sustainable.

Central to this vision is the need for substantial infrastructural investment across rural landscapes, where technological gaps continue to hinder participation in the digital economy. While metaverse tools offer sophisticated simulations, remote monitoring capabilities, and collaborative virtual networks, their effectiveness is fundamentally dependent on robust digital infrastructure. Reliable broadband connectivity, high quality smart sensors, and well maintained digital service platforms form the backbone of any successful integration of metaverse applications into farming. Without these foundational components, rural farmers particularly those in developing economies remain excluded from the very innovations designed to improve their livelihoods. As such, governments, local authorities, and international development organizations play a critical role in expanding rural technological capacity, ensuring that geographically remote communities are not marginalized in the transition toward digital agriculture.

Moreover, technological access alone does not guarantee meaningful engagement. Digital literacy remains a major barrier for numerous farming communities, many of whom have limited experience with advanced equipment or virtual platforms. To bridge this divide, comprehensive training programs must be implemented, offering hands on workshops, tailored instruction, and ongoing technical support. These initiatives should emphasize not only how to operate metaverse tools but also how to interpret data outputs, apply insights to farm management, and integrate digital practices into existing workflows. By empowering farmers with the knowledge required to navigate the digital agricultural landscape, capacity building frameworks can prevent the emergence of new inequalities between technologically adept farmers and those who lack exposure to modern tools. Equitable participation must remain a guiding principle, ensuring that metaverse technologies enhance, rather than disrupt, socioeconomic stability in rural communities.

A critical dimension of metaverse development is the incorporation of transparent and verifiable environmental monitoring systems. As global consumer markets become increasingly sensitive to sustainability claims, the demand for trustworthy environmental data has intensified. Metaverse based agricultural platforms can respond to this demand by integrating blockchain technology, IoT sensors, and automated verification protocols to track waste, emissions, soil quality, water usage, and other key environmental indicators. Blockchain's decentralized architecture ensures that environmental records remain tamper proof, enhancing the credibility of sustainability reporting. These monitoring mechanisms not only help ensure responsible land management but also protect farmers and companies from accusations of greenwashing, which can undermine consumer trust and harm market access. By embedding environmental accountability directly into digital agricultural platforms, developers can reinforce the legitimacy and ethical grounding of the agricultural metaverse.

Economic incentives also play a fundamental role in motivating the adoption of environmentally conscious and technologically advanced farming practices. Token based reward systems where farmers earn digital assets for sustainable behaviors have emerged as a promising mechanism to encourage positive environmental outcomes. These tokens may function as credits, tradable assets, or discounts on essential agricultural supplies, thereby directly linking ecological stewardship with tangible benefits. Yet, for such incentive structures to be effective and equitable, pricing strategies must be carefully designed to accommodate diverse economic contexts. In many low-income countries, farmers operate with narrow profit margins and limited capital; thus, pricing models that burden smallholder farmers could inadvertently widen disparities. Fair, transparent, and adaptable economic systems are essential to ensure that the metaverse becomes a tool for empowerment rather than exclusion.

Equity and fairness extend beyond economic considerations to encompass data governance, ethical design, and equal access to emerging technologies. As farmers increasingly rely on digital platforms that collect vast amounts of personal, environmental, and behavioral data, the need for strong data protection policies becomes paramount. Developers must adopt rigorous protocols to ensure data privacy, informed consent, and secure storage. In addition, algorithmic transparency is crucial to prevent biases that could disadvantage specific groups of farmers. Fairness in digital agriculture means not only providing access but safeguarding rights, protecting autonomy, and preventing technological systems from perpetuating historical inequalities.

Despite the transformative potential of the agricultural metaverse, its successful implementation depends on addressing persistent gaps in technological accessibility.

A significant portion of the global farming population lacks access to advanced devices, updated software, and stable network coverage. Without intervention, the rollout of metaverse tools risks reinforcing the digital divide. To avoid this outcome, comprehensive strategies such as device subsidies, community technology centers, and mobile based metaverse interfaces must be prioritized. These approaches ensure that even farmers with limited resources or outdated hardware can participate meaningfully in virtual agricultural ecosystems. Equal access must be seen not as a secondary concern but as an essential prerequisite for systemic digital transformation.

Before full scale deployment, rigorous empirical evidence is required to determine the practical value of metaverse applications in agriculture. Field trials, pilot programs, and participatory research initiatives serve as indispensable mechanisms for evaluating usability, accuracy, and impact under real world conditions. Agricultural environments are inherently complex and influenced by numerous variables ranging from soil composition to weather fluctuations which cannot be fully replicated in controlled simulations. Therefore, farmer led experimentation is vital to identify limitations, refine system designs, and tailor tools to diverse agricultural contexts. Through iterative testing, metaverse technologies can evolve into practical and responsive instruments that align with farmers everyday needs and realities.

Importantly, the transition from conceptual innovation to field level implementation requires patience, continuous evaluation, and long term commitment. Rushing the deployment of untested metaverse tools risks producing inefficiencies, frustrating users, and undermining the credibility of digital agriculture. A thoughtful, research driven approach ensures that technological advancements are both effective and sustainable. It also fosters trust among farmers, who must feel confident that these tools genuinely address their challenges rather than impose new complexities.

In summary, the agricultural metaverse represents a profound opportunity to reshape the future of farming by integrating real time data, immersive environments, and intelligent systems into a cohesive digital framework. Yet its promise can be realized only through a holistic, inclusive, and ethical strategy that encompasses infrastructure development, digital literacy, transparent environmental governance, equitable economic models, and rigorous field validation. Collaboration among governments, local institutions, private companies, and farming communities will be essential in creating a digital ecosystem that is accessible, secure, and capable of supporting sustainable agricultural growth. By centering fairness, environmental integrity, and practical usability, the agricultural metaverse can emerge not merely as a technological innovation but as a transformative force that empowers farmers, strengthens food systems, and contributes to global sustainability.

Objectives of the Study:

1. To explore the role of agricultural metaverse platforms in enabling waste to wealth practices.
2. To evaluate their effectiveness in promoting recycling and resource efficiency,
3. To assess their socio economic and environmental impacts on farming communities.

1.1. Research Problem

Despite a growing emphasis on sustainability and circularity in agriculture worldwide, farm waste management is still a major concern, especially in developing nations where efficient waste valorization is hampered by a lack of market incentives and inadequate technology. For small scale producers, traditional circular economy methods like physical recycling, composting, and bioenergy frequently lack digital integration, traceability, and financial attraction. New technologies like blockchain and the metaverse, meantime, present fresh opportunities to encourage environmentally conscious behavior, virtualize sustainability initiatives, and establish online marketplaces for environmental goods. However, little is known about how these digital ecosystems may be used to create real benefits for the circular economy and whether they can share value among many agricultural stakeholders in a fair manner.

1.2. Research Methodology

To assess how agricultural Metaverse platforms impact circular economy transitions by facilitating waste reduction, digital adoption, and sustainable practices among farmers, the study used a quantitative, descriptive, and inferential research design. Through correlation, chi square, and ANOVA analyses, the design was selected to measure attitudes, preparedness, and obstacles pertaining to the Agricultural Metaverse and to find statistically significant relationships between important variables.

Primary data was gathered from farmers, agricultural entrepreneurs, and agritech specialists using a survey based methodology. This method was suitable for assessing respondents' preparedness, knowledge, familiarity, and perceived influence of the Metaverse on circular economy concepts like resource efficiency, reuse, and waste reduction.

Sample Size: For analysis, 197 respondents in all were chosen from the Delta Region.

Sampling Method: Because the study was exploratory in nature and the idea of the Agricultural Metaverse was still in its infancy, a convenience sampling method was employed. In order to represent regions with both traditional and technologically integrated farming systems, the Delta Region was specifically selected

1.3. Research Gap

The absence of knowledge and data regarding the true contributions of agricultural metaverse platforms to the shift to a circular economy in agriculture is the research gap mentioned in the document. The extent to which these platforms offer tangible circular advantages beyond merely symbolic digital interaction is still unknown, despite their enormous potential to virtualize agricultural waste into digital assets and advance sustainability. Knowledge regarding how these digital ecosystems may fairly share value among agricultural stakeholders is also lacking, particularly in underdeveloped nations where traditional circular economy models are hindered by a lack of market incentives and technology. The technological, financial, and socio environmental aspects that affect the uptake and scalability of agricultural metaverse platforms must also be investigated, as must the possible dangers, restrictions, and moral dilemmas related to the virtualization of sustainability and agricultural waste.

1.4. Background of the Study

Crop residues, animal manure, and processing byproducts are among the substantial amounts of waste produced by agriculture. These wastes contribute to soil pollution, greenhouse gas emissions, environmental deterioration, and decreased agricultural productivity when they are not managed. In order to turn agricultural waste into useful resources like compost, biofertilizers, bioenergy, and recycled nutrients, the circular economy framework's waste to wealth concept has received a lot of support in recent years. However, grassroots adoption of circular farming practices is still comparatively low despite extensive promotion.

Farmers frequently deal with issues like low awareness, poor technical proficiency, expensive initial investment costs, and limited access to contemporary technologies. In order to facilitate experimentation, demonstration, and skill acquisition for sustainable waste management, traditional training and extension methods have proven inadequate.

Digital and immersive technologies present promising prospects in this regard. Agricultural training and practice could be revolutionized by the emergence of the agricultural metaverse, an integrated virtual environment utilizing digital twins, augmented and virtual reality, simulation models, and interactive GIS tools. Farmers can investigate recycling methods, assess environmental effects, and test new technologies without facing risks or financial loss in the real world by building realistic virtual environments. Additionally, these platforms facilitate shared problem-solving, peer collaboration, and expert guidance. The study looks into how these platforms can increase awareness, encourage recycling, and hasten farming communities' adoption of circular economy practices.

2. LITERATURE REVIEWS

2.1. Digital Platform Engagement and User Behavior in Agriculture

Digital platform engagement in agriculture is significantly impacted by user familiarity and regular online behavior, which affects both the likelihood of consistent usage and the intention to adopt technology enabled services. User commitment is strengthened by purpose driven design features like responsive support, seamless interfaces, and added value services. Especially for early adopters, trust serves as a psychological anchor that boosts self esteem and influences positive behavioral intentions. The credibility and long term acceptability of the platform are further strengthened by easily accessible contact details and clear communication channels. (Pienwisetkaew et al., 2023)

2.2 Institutional, Regulatory, and Social Factors Influencing Adoption of Circular Economy Practices

Adoption is further facilitated by supportive policies, subsidies, and transparent regulatory frameworks however, complicated compliance processes and legislative changes frequently pose risks. Additionally important are social acceptance and open communication with the community, particularly in cases where waste processing facilities may cause odor or environmental issues.(Donner et al.,2021)

Favourable policies, targeted subsidies, and clear regulatory guidelines significantly accelerate the adoption of circular economy practices by reducing financial uncertainty and improving regulatory compliance. However, these institutional frameworks can also introduce challenges, as complex approval procedures, evolving legal requirements, and administrative delays often impede smooth implementation. Beyond policy considerations, social acceptance plays a vital role, with communities frequently expressing concerns related to odour, environmental risks, and land-use changes associated with waste-processing facilities. (Amran et al., 2021)

2.3. Integrated Resource-Recovery Approaches for Advancing Circular Economy Practices in Agrifood Systems

Circular economy Integrated strategies that recover water, energy, and nutrients from farm and food processing waste are essential for agricultural system transitions. In addition to lowering environmental pressures, practices like anaerobic digestion, wastewater reuse, nutrient recycling, and green extraction technologies improve resource efficiency and generate new value streams. Since complicated regulations and high capital requirements frequently impede progress, successful implementation necessitates supportive policies, dependable financing and well coordinated logistics. Social acceptance is also important because project viability may be impacted by worries about odor, environmental hazards, and changes in land use. More resilient and sustainable circular agri food systems are made possible by combining cutting edge resource recovery technologies with robust institutional support and proactive community involvement. (Rodias et al.,2020)

2.4. Valorizing Agricultural Waste for Sustainable Crop Production

Significance of turning agricultural waste into products with added value, like biostimulants, biofertilizers, and biopolymers, in order to transition to sustainable and circular agriculture. Soil degradation, a heavy reliance on chemical fertilizers, and rising greenhouse gas emissions are some of the major issues facing modern farming. Rich in phenolics, amino acids, organic acids, sugars, and lignocellulosic components, agricultural residues present a substantial opportunity for repurposing. According to studies, the bioactive compounds in biostimulants made from fruit waste, crop husks, seaweed residues, and lignin rich biomass can improve crop yield, nutrient uptake, photosynthesis, stress tolerance, and seed germination. Similarly, biofertilizers made from composted waste or helpful microorganisms enhance soil structure, nutrient availability, organic matter stability, and carbon sequestration while lowering the need for synthetic fertilizers. (Puglia et al., 2021)

2.5. Circular Economy as a Driver of Agricultural Transformation

The implementation of circular economy principles holds great promise for converting agricultural waste streams into useful resources, opening up new revenue streams for farmers, and bolstering the stability of the national economy. Agricultural resilience and profitability rise when circularity is incorporated into production systems, transforming waste into a marketable asset that lessens environmental stress and improves local livelihoods. (Sarpong et al., 2022).

Financial incentives and extended producer responsibility are two examples of targeted policy tools that are essential to the advancement of circular agricultural systems. These resources support sustainable practices, lessen implementation difficulties, and increase farmers involvement in circular economy initiatives. Long term sustainability and increased income stability are experienced by stakeholders through these integrated frameworks. (Chenavaz & Dimitrov, 2024).

2.6. Waste Reduction and Resource Efficiency Strategies in Agriculture

For the agricultural industry, circular economy strategies that prioritize resource efficiency, waste reduction, and creative business models open up revolutionary possibilities. These tactics lessen reliance on finite natural resources and diversify economic opportunities. Agricultural systems progress toward increased productivity, sustainability, and environmental resilience by incorporating circularity into farm operations. (Vladimirova, 2017).

2.7. Resource Recovery and Upcycling Innovations in Farming

Recycling, resource recovery, and upcycling focused agricultural techniques show great promise for turning waste into valuable goods. These strategies ease environmental stress while opening new income channels, thereby enhancing farmers financial stability. Circular farming becomes an essential means of attaining low impact economic growth as a result of such advancements. (V. Reddy et al., 2023).

2.8. Enhancing Value Through Agricultural By Product Utilization

Operational effectiveness, profitability, and cost control are all greatly enhanced by initiatives to reduce food waste and raise the value of agricultural byproducts. Sustainable production systems are supported and farmers' incomes are increased through circular practices that turn waste into useful resources. These steps help create agricultural frameworks that are robust and prepared for the future. (Bigdeloo et al.,, 2021).

2.9. Circular Growth Models for Sustainable Agriculture

Business models founded on circular growth illustrate how economic development and environmental responsibility can coexist. Approaches that prioritize regeneration over resource depletion support farmers by maximizing value creation and reducing waste. These models strengthen both profitability and sustainability, positioning agriculture within a more balanced economic ecosystem. (Lacy & Rutqvist, 2015).

2.11. Community Engagement and the "Waste is Wealth" Approach

Community based "Waste is Wealth" campaigns stress how crucial it is to communicate policies clearly and raise public awareness in order to improve recycling and waste management practices. Farmers gain indirectly from improved circular practices, less waste, and more revenue opportunities when communities actively engage in resource recovery. (Jongsuksomsakul 2024)

2.12. Pathways for Transforming Agricultural Waste into Sustainable Agricultural Inputs

Circular economy (CE) methods can reduce environmental harms while converting livestock and agricultural residues into valuable inputs. This view is backed by both micro level case studies and comprehensive reviews of agricultural waste valorization. Reviews emphasize the need for integrated, bio-based valorization technologies and enabling policies to scale these solutions and highlight methods for turning agro-residues into biostimulants, biofertilizers, and biopolymers that enhance soil health, nutrient efficiency, and crop resilience. Reversing declining processing trends requires targeted responses, institutional strengthening, consistent technical support, and market development. CE outcomes rely on reinforcing feedbacks and balancing constraints. In order for CE interventions to transition from pilot success to long term success, the literature generally suggests combining technological valorization with governance, finance, and market strategies. (Latif et al., 2023)

2.13. Challenges in Circular economy

The shift of a traditional linear economic model to Circular Economy (CE) presupposes extensive structural, behavioral, and technological changes. The available literature points out that though Information and Communication Technology (ICT) solutions do have the potential of transforming enabling CE practices including resource optimization, waste minimization, and closed loop production, there are many obstacles to their large scale implementation. The studies determine that there are severe challenges such as poor consumer and business awareness, unwillingness to change behavior, high startup implementation costs, and uncertainty too on the environmental impact assessment. Moreover, the absence of education about the principles of CE and insufficient knowledge of the recent digital tools are one more limitation to the successful implementation of ICT into the framework of the circular system. It has been noted that these barriers mostly interplay to form multifaceted obstacles at the social, economic, and technological levels. Multidisciplinary research has also been identified to be essential in the design of integrated ICT CE frameworks, which have the capacity to consider the environmental, economic, and social fronts. All in all, current studies emphasize the fact that although ICT is an essential component in the development of the Circular Economy, the current issues can only be addressed through concerted efforts by the stakeholders, institutions, and knowledge systems. (Demestichas & Daskalakis, 2020).

2.14. Digital Technology in Circular Economy

Digital Technologies (DTs) and their application to the development of the Circular Economy (CE) demonstrate the increasing literature interest, though the sources are disjointed. Most of the studies focus on the discrete technologies, including IoT, blockchain, big data analytics, or AI, and their capacity to assist certain CE functions, including waste tracking, resource recovery, or product lifecycle extension. Although these concentrated observations are useful, they do not provide an insight into the wider systemic effect that DTs may exert in facilitating a full scale CE transition. Lack of coherent perspective complicates the evaluation of how various technologies depend on each other, or work together to create a net effect of operation, environment and economic aspect of circularity. (Cagno, E et al., 2021).

The circular economy principles can reduce waste, improve sustainability, and enhance farm profitability, while challenges such as policy limitations, lack of awareness, and technological barriers still need to be addressed. (Muñoz et al., 2021).

2.15. Circular Economy Policies & Impacts

CE action plans portray how the demand of recycled content or extended producer responsibility (EPR) can provide upstream solutions to redesign and downstream solutions to invest in recycling infrastructure. Repair, remanufacture, composting, recycling, in some way or other, generate work, although the quality, safety, and availability of the work varies extensively. Informal workers, especially waste pickers, are usually essential to the circular economy but not formally part of the CE plan, which results in precariousness or displacement when waste management is formalized or privatized by the municipalities. (Vanhuyse et al., 2021)

Macroeconomic research exhibits that the policies of the CE like the extended producer responsibility, the mandate of recycled content, the eco design regulations and fiscal incentives can lead to the creation of new employment opportunities and at the same time impact other sectors. A number of modeling based studies indicate that circular practices have the potential to spur both green employment and energy security as well as diminish virgin resource reliance, resulting in long term GDP benefits. The literature, however, also cautions that these advantages are not equally shared among the sectors, and transition risks (e.g. job loss in extractive industries, the need to raise capital requirements of SMEs) should be evaluated in order to achieve equitable and inclusive results. (Hernandez, et al., 2021)

Reuse, remanufacturing, recycling, and product life extension it offers a strong potential for creating more sustainable and efficient waste management systems and it maximizing product utility and prolonging the lifespan of components. Circular Economy practices provide theoretical foundation and future sustainability of various sectors. (Yang et al., 2022) Educational programs, Incentives, agricultural extension services are need to strengthened to improve circular economy farming practices. (Vliert et al., 2024)

3. RESEARCH METHODOLOGY

To assess how agricultural Metaverse platforms impact circular economy transitions by facilitating waste reduction, digital adoption, and sustainable practices among farmers, the study used a quantitative, descriptive, and inferential research design. Through correlation, chi square, and ANOVA analyses, the design was selected to measure attitudes, preparedness, and obstacles pertaining to the Agricultural Metaverse and to find statistically significant relationships between important variables.

Primary data was gathered from farmers, agricultural entrepreneurs, and agri-tech specialists using a survey based methodology. This method was suitable for assessing respondents preparedness, knowledge, familiarity, and perceived influence of the Metaverse on circular economy concepts like resource efficiency, reuse and waste reduction.

Sample Size: For analysis, 197 respondents in all were chosen from the Delta Region.

Sampling Method: Because the study was exploratory in nature and the idea of the Agricultural Metaverse was still in its infancy, a convenience sampling method was employed. In order to represent regions with both traditional and technologically integrated farming systems, the Delta Region was specifically selected.

4. DATA ANALYSIS AND RESULTS

The correlation analysis showed the statistically significant and negative correlation between the degree of readiness to implement practices connected to the metaverse based circular economy and the conviction that the agricultural metaverse platforms can be used to help decrease agricultural waste. The correlation coefficient with a significance level of p = 0.010 was r = 0.184 using a sample of 197 respondents. It means that with the growing willingness to implement metaverse facilitating practices related to the circular economy, the faith in the beneficial effect of metaverse based practices on the farm waste reduction is inclined to diminish marginally. The correlation is not that strong, but because it is statistically significant, it can be concluded that there can be some underlying concerns or skepticism on the part of the participants towards the practical waste cutting potential of metaverse technologies. The two variables had perfect internal correlations with each other (r = 1.000) and the measurement was therefore reliable.

The chi square test has shown that the distribution of the gender of the respondents is statistically significant, 5% =.000, 18.89, df = 1, which means that the difference is highly significant. There were 197 respondents out of which 129 were male and 68 were female versus an anticipated 98.5 representatives of both genders. The remaining values indicate that the males have a positive deviation (30.50) whereas the females have a negative deviation (30.50), which has proven the imbalance in the representation. These findings indicate that more men (65.5%) than women (34.5%) would engage or respond to concerns concerning adoption of agricultural metaverse based services, which may indicate a high level of awareness, exposure, or preparation of male respondents in the field of using metaverse practices in agriculture.

The chi square test, which compared familiarity with the concept of the Agricultural Metaverse, turned out the highly significant difference between the categories of answers, 2(3) = 163.39, p =.000, which means that distribution of familiarity levels is not the same as it would be under the influence of chance only. The proportion of respondents who claimed to know about the concept, but were not aware of the details was the largest (126 respondents, 64%), with a large positive residual of +76.75, out of 197 respondents. Conversely, the responses of the categories Not familiar at all and Somewhat familiar had only 18 respondents each, and the residuals were negative -31.25 and -14.25 respectively, and 35 respondents were very familiar, and this corresponded to a -14.25 residual. These findings indicate that the general awareness of the Agricultural Metaverse is present, but not much knowledge and profound understanding. The results suggest that more educational outreach, training, and information dissemination needs to be done to enhance familiarity and meaningful engagement in agricultural projects based on the metaverse.

The chi square test to analyse the relationship between the primary barriers to the adoption of agricultural metaverse tools and the level of readiness to adopt the tools showed a significant level of association of a value of 129.82, df = 15, and p =.000, meaning that the level of readiness to adopt the tools significantly differ according to the type of perceived barrier. The greatest barriers among the respondents (N = 197) were low digital literacy (28.4) and low internet connectivity (25.9), indicating the problematic infrastructural and skills based issues. The respondents who answered the question by being Not sure about their readiness mostly referred to unclear policy frameworks thus expressing doubts in the regulatory and governance systems. In the meantime, the most frequently used responses amongst those who identified themselves as the Very ready were those who specified poor digital literacy as a significant obstacle meaning that willing adopters still encounter knowledge and training gaps. Altogether, the outcomes indicate that the willingness to implement technologies of the agricultural metaverse is determined by several barriers which are interconnected and the necessity of such capacity building, infrastructure development, and policy clarity is highlighted to increase the possibilities of adoption.

The ANOVA test that was used to compare the degree of preparedness to use the Metaverse related practices of the circular economy among various groups of agricultural experience demonstrates the significant difference between the respondents ($F = 8.70$, $p = .000$). This result shows that the years of experience contribute to the formation of the level of readiness. Those having a more profound agricultural experience are more likely to be more willing to adopt the idea of the Metaverse based circular economy solutions, which could be explained by the fact that they are more exposed to technological innovations, novel farming techniques, and interventions aimed at enhancing the sustainability of the sector.

The same situation can be observed when it comes to the ANOVA test that determines the interconnection between the familiarity with the Agricultural Metaverse and the perceptions of its effectiveness in fostering circular economy principles, as significant differences among groups can also be identified ($F = 3.26$, $p =.013$). Those respondents who hold stronger belief over the capability of the Metaverse to improve the results of the circular economy are more familiar with the technology. This finding indicates that the increased level of perceived efficacy is directly linked to the increased level of awareness, understanding, and exposure, which implies that perception of the value of the Metaverse has a significant positive influence on the familiarity and acceptance of the users.

Figure 1.

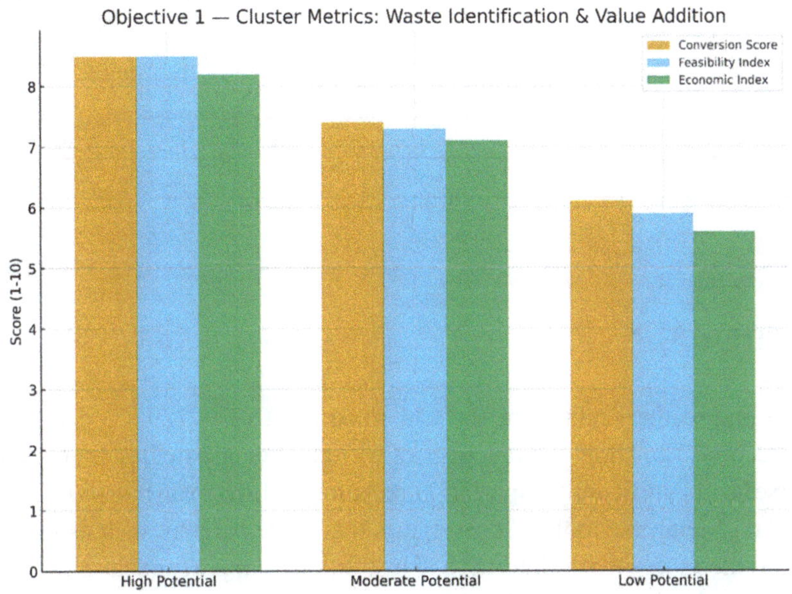

Table 1. Main Barriers to Adopting Agricultural Metaverse Tools × Level of Readiness to Adopt Metaverse Based Circular Economy Practices

Main Barriers	Not Ready	Not Sure	Somewhat Ready	Very Ready	Total
Lack of awareness	1 (20%)	3 (60%)	0 (0%)	1 (20%)	5 (100%)
High technology cost	4 (21.1%)	0 (0%)	12 (63.2%)	3 (15.8%)	19 (100%)
Poor digital literacy	12 (21.4%)	7 (12.5%)	5 (8.9%)	32 (57.1%)	56 (100%)
Limited internet access	11 (21.6%)	8 (15.7%)	6 (11.8%)	26 (51%)	51 (100%)
Lack of institutional support	10 (32.3%)	5 (16.1%)	16 (51.6%)	0 (0%)	31 (100%)
Unclear policy frameworks	3 (8.6%)	27 (77.1%)	2 (5.7%)	3 (8.6%)	35 (100%)
Total	41 (20.8%)	50 (25.4%)	41 (20.8%)	65 (33%)	197 (100%)

Table 2. Chi-Square Tests:

Test	Value	df	Sig. (2 tailed)
Pearson Chi-Square	129.82	15	.000
Likelihood Ratio	127.47	15	.000
Linear-by-Linear Association	9.79	1	.002
N of Valid Cases	197		

5. INFERENCE

According to the findings of the Chi square test (2 = 129.82, p =.000), the level of readiness to adopt the practices of a circular economy based on the use of Metaverse has a significantly important correlation with the main barriers to adopting Agricultural Metaverse tools. This suggests that some barriers such as low digital literacy, limited access to the internet and institutional support and favor act as major influences in the difference in levels of preparedness. Although, less affected by awareness and cost related issues, not ready respondents are more influenced by these factors as compared to very ready respondents who tend to be more digitally literate and internet connected.

Table 3. Gender and Familiarity with Agricultural Metaverse

Gender of Respondents	Observed	Expected	Residual
Male	129	98.5	30.5
Female	68	98.5	-30.5
Total	197		

Table 4. Test Statistics

Familiarity with Agricultural Metaverse	Observed	Expected	Residual
Not familiar at all	18	49.25	-31.25
Heard of it but not familiar with details	126	49.25	76.75
Somewhat familiar	18	49.25	-31.25
Very familiar	35	49.25	-14.25
Total	197		

Table 5. Inference

Variable	Chi-square	df	Sig.
Gender of the respondents	18.89	1	.000
Familiarity with Agricultural Metaverse	163.39	3	.000

More of the male respondents are involved in agricultural research on the Metaverse and the gender distribution is skewed (2 = 18.89, p <.001).

The difference in the degrees of acquaintance with the concept of the Agricultural Metaverse is also very significant (χ 2 = 163.39, p <.001). Awareness and training programs are required to make people know more about the practical familiarity with Metaverse technologies in agriculture because most respondents have heard about the term but do not understand it in detail.

6. RESULTS

Principal Findings

1. The agricultural metaverse systems allow transforming real farm waste into digital or tokenized form using the latest technologies of blockchain, artificial intelligence, the Internet of Things and extended reality. These platforms provide an efficient and open minded valuation of agricultural byproducts through the development of digital twins of pieces of farms and the creation of traceable processes of waste conversion.
2. Through the integration of digital technology and sustainable farming, such systems enhance better use of resources and reduce waste as well as promote the value recirculation. The waste virtualization and tokenized value chains can prompt the stakeholders to engage in the Circular economy programs by closing the gap between the virtual economic value and the physical sustainability implementation.
3. Adoption and scalability of agricultural metaverse platforms are affected by various factors: Technical: It is important to have reliable internet access, availability of IoT devices, and user friendly interfaces in order to succeed in its implementation. Economic: There are the costs of the application of new technologies, economic incentives of the market on virtual assets, and possible financial benefits that affect the participation of farmers. Socio Environmental: Fair value distribution among the small scaled producers, awareness and disciplineness to digital literacy all influence the sustainability and inclusiveness of these platforms.

4. Agricultural metaverse platforms also have many issues, although they are potentially beneficial: The usefulness of virtualized sustainability initiatives remains not fully known. Developing something symbolic as digital engagement and not substantially supporting the environment is dangerous. Ethical issues relate to privacy of data, fair access and the possibility of marginalization of stakeholders who lack technological know how.
5. Existing circular economy agricultural systems, such as composting and bioenergy generation, in most cases are not interconnected with digital ecosystems. This restricts the access of smallholders to monetary appeal and traceability, which could be offered through metaverse by allowing online markets and gamification of environmentally friendly conducts.

7. LIMITATIONS

Agricultural metaverse platforms have a number of important drawbacks despite their potential advantages. Adoption is difficult for small and marginal farmers due to high initial investment and deployment costs, and accessibility is further limited by low digital literacy and poor rural internet infrastructure. The actual environmental and economic outcomes of virtual sustainability initiatives remain uncertain, raising concerns about the effectiveness of tokenized waste to wealth models. Ethical and operational risks are also brought about by concerns about data privacy, security, and ownership. Legal ambiguity is increased by the lack of standardized regulations for virtual marketplaces and digital asset valuation, and an excessive reliance on technology providers may lead to an uneven distribution of value. Social and technological divides may further widen the gap between large and small producers, limiting inclusivity.

Furthermore, it is still difficult to integrate traditional circular economy practices with digital ecosystems, and there is a chance that virtual participation will only serve as a token gesture rather than producing real environmental benefits. Therefore, although promising, agricultural metaverse systems need to get past these ethical, social, and structural obstacles in order to be implemented in a way that is both equitable and sustainable.

8. FUTURE RESEARCH DIRECTIONS

Agricultural metaverse is a promising prospect of transforming the farming process and agricultural sector in general. This virtual ecosystem is likely to increase the control over the resources, become better decision-makers and provide new opportunities to the farmers to interact with digital tools and technologies. Nevertheless, along with such positive opportunities, the agricultural metaverse has a number of serious negative factors that could compromise the advantages. These are the high cost of high technology, lack of digital literacy and rural connectivity, the issue of sustainability, privacy of data, and the absence of legal frameworks to regulate the digital asset ecosystems. Moreover, digital divide can further widen the socioeconomic disparities between farmers, which could restrict their access to the fair markets and cause barriers to adoption. Future studies should therefore concentrate on.

Conquering these obstacles and making it possible to have the agricultural metaverse reach its maximum capabilities to meet the concerns of the real world.

The capability to combine virtual asset ecosystems with the physical waste management process is one of the main issues of the agricultural metaverse. As much as the metaverse can recreate and replicate resource management, there is a difference between virtual achievements and the actual results. As an example, the principles of the circular economy advocated on the Internet might not be easily transferred to the real world of environmental improvement. There is a necessity to seek hybrid frameworks that would help bridge the two worlds virtual and physical.

Further research would explore the potential of digital models to complement the actual agricultural activities. This may involve examining the possibilities of agricultural metaverse operation in conjunction with physical waste management and sustainability activities that may involve composting, organic farming, and management of soil health. Hybrid models would potentially enable more realistic resource flows simulation in the real world, and the virtual models would assist farmers to optimize their practices on the basis of predictive data. Through the pilot projects done on these hybrid models, researchers are likely to get a better insight into how the virtual solutions can be directly implemented to address acute agricultural problems, such as waste management, crop rotation, and nutrient cycling.

Also, it is important to come up with scalable and economical models which can fit the smallholder farmers. In developing areas or communities in the rural rural environment, many farmers lack high quality technology and infrastructure to integrate fully into the metaverse. Therefore, it is necessary to conduct research on the feasible, locally applicable metaverse models. These models may involve integrating low cost virtual tools with the traditional agricultural knowledge that can enable smallholder farmers enjoy the metaverse without being crushed by the cost of technology. Furthermore, it would be useful to research the ways in which smallholder farmers can utilize the agricultural metaverse to receive information, training, and market opportunities to reduce the technology gap and develop resilience in susceptible agro ecosystems.

Another obstacle to the widespread implementation of the agricultural metaverse is the poor degree of online literacy, especially on smallholder farmers in rural and underserved regions. Digital literacy plays a critical role in making sure that farmers have the ability to use the digital tools in order to make informed decisions, to optimize resources and to be able to engage in virtual value chains. Poor digital literacy may restrict the capacity of farmers to adopt the novel technologies and put them behind in an ever digitizing agricultural environment.

The future studies ought to center on devising interventions to enhance digital literacy of farmers. This may involve the establishment of easy to use training and workshops, educational material, etc. that are available in various languages and formats. Additionally, efforts ought to be directed towards developing the basic digital tools before introducing the more sophisticated metaverse applications. Researchers may investigate how local community centers, agricultural cooperatives, and Non Governmental Organizations may help in implementing these literacy programs. Moreover, AI based learning systems will be able to customize the learning process of farmers, making it more effective and applicable to the requirements of the farmers.

Besides digital literacy, lack of connectivity among rural areas is also a major challenge. In most parts of the world, the rural locations do not have a strong internet connection to support smooth metaverse experiences. This is not only a problem with access to virtual farming devices but it also drives away online market and collaboration network. The studies on affordable connectivity, including satellite internet connectivity, low pricing data plans, or internet sharing communities will be necessary to eliminate this gap. More to the point, technologies such as 5G, edge computing, and Internet of Things (IoT) networks may help to increase the connectivity in remote areas, which would allow more farmers to access the agricultural metaverse and use its tools.

With the farmers interacting with the agricultural metaverse, issues related to data privacy and security will emerge with greater intensity. The agricultural metaverse gathers enormous amounts of data such as crop performance, weather trends and even personal data, of farmers. In the absence of robust data protection solutions, misuse, unauthorized access, and exploitation of the data of the farmers by the third party companies can occur.

Further studies ought to aim at coming up with safe data sharing programs that would enable farmers to retain ownership of their data without necessarily losing the benefits of the tools offered by the metaverse. This may include the adoption of blockchain technology to generate transparent and non manipulative data exchange records. Also, decentralized data storage solutions can contribute to overcoming the fear of centralized control and ensure that farmers have a greater degree of control over their information.

9. SUGGESTIONS

The governments, local institutions, and individual stakeholders would have to work together in a strategic effort to support the growth and scalability of farming oriented metaverse tools in the long term. With the continuous development of digital agriculture, rural areas should not be disadvantaged; thus, the government agencies and local communities need to focus on enhancing technological infrastructure within those territories. This involves improving the reach of good and effective broadband network, deployment of smart sensors in areas of agriculture and also ensuring that the farmers can find access to digital service platforms without much resistance. This kind of infrastructural investment forms the necessary basis of the implementation of the advanced metaverse in the daily activities of farming, which will allow the collection of data more accurately, real time monitoring, and cooperation in the online world.

Besides the development of infrastructure, it is essential to develop long term capacity building programs among the farmers. Hands on training, training in digital literacy, and easy to use demonstration programs can play a major role in making the farmers confident in the use of emerging technologies. A large number of small scale farmers, especially those in the developing economies, are restrained by barriers associated with the lack of exposure to digital tools. Thus, systematic training can be used to balance the involvement of the agricultural metaverse and lessen the chance of the technological gap between the first adopters and marginalized groups. These kinds of programs must be participatory, context based and sensitive to the existing educational and technological differences.

Agricultural metaverse apps should also add transparent and reliable environmental observation aspects to gain trust in the technologies and to make them effective. These will incorporate the integration of highly developed waste monitoring devices based on blockchain technology, Internet of Things (IoT) sensors, and automated data verification systems. Blockchain (especially) has provided a decentralized, impossible to change system that can ensure the quality of environmental data, including carbon emissions, the use of fertilizers, and the practices of waste management. These tools can be integrated to ensure that the level of accountability is not only improved, but also contributes to checking whether the claims on sustainability linked to new digital products are true and not a case of green washing. As it is necessary to farmers, investors, and policy makers alike, such transparency is the key to confidence in technological interventions, as well as the assurance of the environmental benefits being both measurable and credible.

Incentive systems are very vital in promoting the universal use of the green friendly practices. The introduction of token based reward systems can offer farmers with a concrete incentive in the use of sustainable farming practices in the metaverse ecosystem. These tokens, be it in the form of credits, discounts, or digital goods can be traded in farm supplies, services, and technological upgrades. Notably, these models of incentives should be sensitive to the economic situation in a region. There should be fair and flexible pricing strategies to meet the realities of the smallholder farmers, particularly those located in lower income countries. This will be achieved by avoiding cost designs that disfavor such farmers in a disproportionate manner to trigger inclusive growth and avoid a further established digital inequality.

With the rise in the level of technological integration, issues of fairness, ethics, and data security will continue to be of growing concern. To ensure protection of personal information and promote non reinforcement of the existing inequities, the developers should embrace sound governance structures, where digital agricultural systems are designed to promote equity. This involves the establishment of stringent data privacy principles, offering clear consent forms and formulation of algorithms that are not systematically discriminatory against specific groups of people or agricultural groups. The principle of fair access should be considered as a pillar of the design of agricultural metaverse systems because it is only under such a scenario that the transformative power of digital innovation can be achieved when the benefits are distributed equitably among all the players in the agricultural value chain.

Innovation is never enough without meeting the gaps in technological access. There are numerous rural regions with the absence of the newest hardware, software, and network coverage to operate advanced metaverse tools. Thus, aggressive measures to overcome this digital divide include subsidies of devices, creating a mutual digital point in rural areas, and providing specific technical assistance to farmers who might not be conversant with sophisticated technologies. With these supports in place, technological adoption is not only open to farmers that have the means to take it up but it has a chance to be accessible to a significant portion of the population.

Field testing also cannot be excluded in testing the feasibility and functionality of metaverse applications in agriculture. Although the possible results can be modeled with the help of laboratories and simulations, a farm is a highly unpredictable environment, depending on weather patterns, soil conditions, and types of crops as well as localized farming techniques. Pilot studies, on farm research and participation based research projects will enable developers and researchers to acquire empirical evidence concerning usability, accuracy, and the general effectiveness. These types of studies also allow farmers to give immediate feedback so that the digital tools can be continuously improved before large scale adoption.

This is a testing time that requires patience. The process of the conceptual innovation and its transfer to the real world application takes time and necessitates the consideration and the modifications on the basis of empirical information. Early adoption before adequate evidence would result in frustration inefficiency on the part of the farmers or the environmental sustainability unintended results. A staged and scientifically informed implementation plan can be beneficial in making sure that metaverse tools are not only technologically sophisticated, but also actually helpful and responsive to the everyday reality of agricultural labor.

On the whole, the development of the agricultural metaverse should be comprehensive and ethically based, which incorporates the development of infrastructure, capacity building programs, open environmental monitoring systems, fair pricing methods, and strict field testing. Governments, institutions, and technology developers should work together to come up with digital ecosystems, which are accessible, secure, and sustainable. Focusing on fairness, environmental sustainability, and usability shall make the farming metaverse become a disruptive platform that would increase productivity, create sustainability, and empower farmers in various socioeconomic backgrounds.

10. CONCLUSION

The fundamental aspect of this possibility is that the metaverse is able to transform traditionally underutilized or discarded products of agriculture into valuable digital information, with this redesigning economic and informational worth to the waste streams. In traditional agricultural systems, waste valorization is usually impaired due to the infrastructural issues, lack of knowledge, and the absence of economic benefits. By allowing virtual representations of waste to be tokenized, such as nutrient content or biomass quality, carbon offsets or ecological regeneration potential, and more, metaverse platforms have the potential to break these constraints and integrate them into a digital simulation. These processes could trigger new environmental accounting practices that would enable farmers, cooperatives, and agribusiness to tap into new value in by products, which are not used to date. As a result, not only the material, but also informational recirculation of value is strengthened, the new paradigm of data directed representations of waste that inform real world decision making, investment flows, and sustainability performance monitoring is established.

In addition, agricultural metaverse ecosystems help bring together producers, consumers, regulators, researchers, and technology providers in a manner never seen before. Such interconnectedness would be able to bring about more collective and cooperative methods of implementation of the CE. On farm digital twins, workflows of livestock or the supply chain can be used to conduct real time monitoring and scenario analysis, and provide farmers with dynamic information about the nutrient cycles, energy use, soil condition, and resource flows in the farmland. Virtual markets are able to increase supply chains transparency, whereas, immersive learning environments democratize access to agronomic education, sustainable production methods, and CE. This decentralization of knowledge may minimize the barriers which particularly impact the smallholders that are often not aware of the advanced extension services or financial mechanisms. In this way, interactions through the metaverse can enhance fairness in the process of agricultural transition to the circular economy since various stakeholders can access complex information in engaging and visual rich formats.

However, such benefits can only be realized when big financial, technological, ethical and socio environmental problems are mitigated. The world has become increasingly technologically advanced at a very high pace but the difference in the digital literacy, the availability of the infrastructure and the internet connectivity continues to exist especially in the rural areas where the agricultural industry is concentrated the most. The development of metaverse platforms will potentially increase existing disparities instead of reducing them unless specific interventions are done. The introduction of these platforms should be however accompanied by investment in digital infrastructure broadband expansion, cloud computing capacity, inexpensive hardware, and technology design geared towards farmers. Besides, it is essential to increase the level of cybersecurity and data protection, since the agricultural metaverse is bound to rely on the mass scale gathering, analysis and sharing of sensitive information. Ethics models with transparency, consent, fairness in the allocation of profits, and safeguarding against exploitation should be integrated into the developmental process at the very beginning.

Socio environmental consideration is at the center stage besides infrastructural and ethical factors. Even though virtual platforms can replicate sustainability results, the simulation should be converted into physical changes in the utilization of the resources, biodiversity protection, and cut of emissions in the real world. One of the main critiques of metaverse based sustainability tools is the possibility of an absence of connection between the virtual interaction and the real life environmental care. In case virtual practices produce little or no material ecological payoffs, then the agricultural metaverse may turn into a performative or abstracted sustainability space instead of a material determinant of change. Thus, it is important to have strong systems of justifying, checking, and measuring the environmental effects of metaverse interactions. Traceability based on blockchain, remote sensing information, and non differentiated sustainability measurements may be capitalized upon to make sure that virtual certifications, digital tokens, and ecological credits are linked with the verifiable changes in reality.

The management of agricultural metaverse ecosystems should also be well organized. The framework of inclusive policy is required to promote equal access and safeguard the interests of the smallholder, as well as to avoid the monopoly of large agritech corporations. The policymakers should take into account the intersection of metaverse mediated transactions, trading virtual waste assets or engaging in a decentralized sustainability financing scheme, with the current environmental regulations, carbon credit markets, and farm subsidy schemes. The overall circularity transition of the sector can be multiplied by establishing frameworks that can make virtual incentives align with national priorities on sustainability. Moreover, intellectual property, ownership of digital assets, and liability in case of algorithmic error, and the environmental effects of digital infrastructure (or data centers and blockchain networks) should be regulated more clearly.

Interest in the multi stakeholder cooperation is also necessary to practically implement agricultural metaverse solutions. Researchers, technologists, environmental scientists and financial institutions should collaborate to codevelop systems that are technologically and agriculturally sound. Bringing agronomic experience to the digital world will be crucial to making sure that virtual models capture the dynamics of the ecosystem and can be used to make reasonable decisions. Pilot projects, living labs, and testbeds may also be used as experimental environments to assess the viability, scalability, and acceptability of these platforms by the users. These programs can help to produce empirical data to prove theoretical assumptions and enhance the modeling of metaverse based CE instruments.

Although the existing doubts and constraints persist, a paradigm shift in the world of agriculture through the use of metaverse platforms cannot be underestimated. With the advancement of technologies, some of the previously hypothetical ideas can turn into the elements of the sustainable farming. Soil health evaluations carried out with the help of VR, AI controlled circular crop planning, cryptocurrency based nutrient credit markets, and digital twins that can simulate regenerative practices all represent new concepts that will help the world to become more circular and resilient in terms of its agri food systems. Consumer engagement can also be improved as the metaverse will provide consumers with immersive farm to table experience, transparent product history, and interactive sustainability education. This can be helped by the ability to enhance cultural awareness on resource stewardship and promote behavioral change towards responsible consumption and therefore reinforce the circular economy on both the supply and demand side.

Besides, the metaverse facilitates emergent financial streams of circular agriculture. The farmers can be offered diversified sources of revenue by means of tokenized waste assets, decentralized sustainability bonds, and transparent carbon offset mechanisms. The models would be useful in mitigating the financial risks involved in implementing regenerative or circular practices, particularly among small scale farmers who have poor credit access. The virtual marketplaces may also help to make the exchange of farmers more efficient, by allowing them to share equipment, biomass, compost, or renewable energy in more systematized and data-optimal methods. In this regard the metaverse acts as a digital platform that makes the collaborative circular networks to scale a major requirement to the success of the CE initiatives.

Another critical point to be made is that there is still the baby stage of the agriculture metaverse nexus. Research on this topic is growing at the academic level, technology potential is developing fast, and there is little empirical evidence. Although preliminary theoretical frameworks indicate that the potential is great, application usefulness of metaverse tools will rely on strict field testing, involvement in designing, and tracking over a long period. The studies have to continue on not only the technical aspects of the use of the agricultural metaverse but also its socio cultural, economic, ecological, and geopolitical implications. It involves analysing the perception of farmers, rates of adoption, gender effects, labour change, and the danger of becoming digital addicts. Complexity in integrating virtual innovation with sustainable agricultural development will be unavoidable that will require holistic and interdisciplinary investigation.

Finally, the ultimate goal on how to attain maximum impact is by developing open, just and profitable ecosystems benefitting small farmers and large agribusiness enterprises. In the way of designing and implementing interventions on the metaverse based circular economy, equity has to be one of the primary principles rather than a secondary factor. Participatory decision making instruments, inclusive governance structures as well as community based digital literacy programs can serve to ensure that the metaverse is democratizing and not a source of digital stratification. The overall vision of the agricultural sector should also be straightforward: to use digital innovation in a manner that actually positively impacts environmental health, food security, rural livelihoods, and resilience to global uncertainty.

Synthetically, the advancement of a collaboration between the principles of the circular economy and the new metaverse technologies is a promising but complicated way of attaining the sustainability of agriculture in the digital era. Agricultural metaverse platforms have the capacity to trigger regenerative agricultural systems and material loops by making it possible to recycle values, minimize waste, improve resource efficiency, and amplify the collaboration of stakeholders. What will make them a successful case is their ability to defeat the infrastructural and socio economic hurdles, integrate powerful ethical protection, and make virtual activities meaningful in terms of physical environmental changes. When developed and regulated with care, these technologies have the potential to revolutionize the way in which we think about agricultural sustainability, and offer an innovative mode of how to build the 21st century food system, resilient against any form of challenge. The complementary relationship of the circular economy concepts and the virtual innovation therefore represents a considerable move in the realization of agricultural activities as not only a productive business but also a regenerative and adaptive system, which can be operated under the limits of planetary opportunities.

REFERENCES

Aguilar-Hernandez, G. A., Dias Rodrigues, J. F., & Tukker, A. (2021). Macro-economic, social and environmental impacts of a circular economy up to 2050: A meta-analysis of prospective studies. *Journal of Cleaner Production*, *278*, 123421. DOI: 10.1016/j.jclepro.2020.123421

Amran, M. A., Palaniveloo, K., Fauzi, R., Satar, N. M., Mohidin, T. B. M., Mohan, G., Razak, S. A., Arunasalam, M., Nagappan, T., & Sathiya Seelan, J. S. (2021). Value-Added Metabolites from Agricultural Waste and Application of Green Extraction Techniques. *Sustainability (Basel)*, *13*(20), 11432. DOI: 10.3390/su132011432

Bigdeloo, M., Teymourian, T., Kowsari, E., Ramakrishna, S., & Ehsani, A. (2021). Sustainability and Circular Economy of Food Wastes: Waste Reduction Strategies, Higher Recycling Methods, and Improved Valorization. *Materials Circular Economy*, *3*(1), 3. Advance online publication. DOI: 10.1007/s42824-021-00017-3

Cagno, E., Neri, A., Negri, M., Bassani, C. A., & Lampertico, T. (2021). The Role of Digital Technologies in Operationalizing the Circular Economy Transition: A Systematic Literature Review. *Applied Sciences (Basel, Switzerland)*, *11*(8), 3328. DOI: 10.3390/app11083328

Chenavaz, R. Y., & Dimitrov, S. (2024). From waste to wealth: Policies to promote the circular economy. *Journal of Cleaner Production*, *443*, 141086. DOI: 10.1016/j.jclepro.2024.141086

de Vliert, A. V., & Peij, J. V. (2024). Circular Economy Implementation in Dutch Agriculture: Assessing Sustainable Practices and Economic Impact. *Law and Economy*, *3*(1), 20–31. DOI: 10.56397/LE.2024.01.03

Demestichas, K., & Daskalakis, E. (2020). Information and Communication Technology Solutions for the Circular Economy. *Sustainability (Basel)*, *12*(18), 7272. DOI: 10.3390/su12187272

Donner, M., Verniquet, A., Broeze, J., Kayser, K., & De Vries, H. (2021). Critical success and risk factors for circular business models valorising agricultural waste and by-products. *Resources, Conservation and Recycling*, *165*, 105236. DOI: 10.1016/j.resconrec.2020.105236

Jongsuksomsakul, P. (2024). "Waste Is Wealth": Circular Economy Strategies from Media Persuasion to Utilization. *Sustainability (Basel)*, *16*(12), 5205. DOI: 10.3390/su16125205

. Lacy, P., & Rutqvist, J. (2015). Gaining the Circular Advantage. Waste to Wealth, 24–32. https://doi.org/.DOI: 10.1057/9781137530707_3

Latif, A., Cahyandito, M. F., & Utama, G. L. (2023). Dynamic System Modeling and Sustainability Strategies for Circular Economy-Based Dairy Cow Waste Management. *Sustainability (Basel)*, *15*(4), 3405. DOI: 10.3390/su15043405

Pienwisetkaew, T., Wongsaichia, S., Pinyosap, B., Prasertsil, S., Poonsakpaisarn, K., & Ketkaew, C. (2023). The behavioral intention to adopt circular economy-based digital technology for agricultural waste valorization. *Foods*, *12*(12), 2341. DOI: 10.3390/foods12122341 PMID: 37372552

Puglia, D., Pezzolla, D., Gigliotti, G., Torre, L., Bartucca, M. L., & Del Buono, D. (2021). The Opportunity of Valorizing Agricultural Waste, Through Its Conversion into Biostimulants, Biofertilizers, and Biopolymers. *Sustainability (Basel)*, *13*(5), 2710. DOI: 10.3390/su13052710

. Reddy, V. V., Kumar, P., Rao, A. L. N., Kumar, R., Singh, S., Asha, V., & Kareem, S. H. (2023). Waste to Wealth Generation: Innovative Methodologies in Resource Utilization and Minimization in Circular Economy. E3S Web of Conferences, 453, 01035. https://doi.org/.DOI: 10.1051/e3sconf/202345301035

Rodias, E., Aivazidou, E., Achillas, C., Aidonis, D., & Bochtis, D. (2020). Water-Energy-Nutrients Synergies in the Agrifood Sector: A Circular Economy Framework. *Energies*, *14*(1), 159. DOI: 10.3390/en14010159

Sarpong, S., & Alarussi, A. S. (2022). Waste to wealth: Enhancing circularities in the Malaysian economy. *Technological Sustainability*, *1*(2), 145–159. DOI: 10.1108/TECHS-01-2022-0001

Vanhuyse, F., Fejzić, E., Ddiba, D., & Henrysson, M. (2021). The lack of social impact considerations in transitioning towards urban circular economies: A scoping review. *Sustainable Cities and Society*, *75*, 103394. DOI: 10.1016/j.scs.2021.103394

Velasco-Muñoz, J. F., Mendoza, J. M. F., Aznar-Sánchez, J. A., & Gallego-Schmid, A. (2021). Circular economy implementation in the agricultural sector: Definition, strategies and indicators. *Resources, Conservation and Recycling*, *170*, 105618. DOI: 10.1016/j.resconrec.2021.105618

Vladimirova, D. (2016). Waste to wealth: The circular economy advantage. Production Planning &amp. *Production Planning and Control*, *28*(4), 349–349. DOI: 10.1080/09537287.2016.1249131

Yang, M., Chen, L., Wang, J., Msigwa, G., Osman, A. I., Fawzy, S., Rooney, D. W., & Yap, P.-S. (2022). Circular economy strategies for combating climate change and other environmental issues. *Environmental Chemistry Letters*, *21*(1), 55–80. DOI: 10.1007/s10311-022-01499-6

Chapter 5

Policy Metaverse Model (PMM) Towards Affordable and Inclusivity in Rental Housing Policy in India

C. V. Subramanian
http://orcid.org/0000-0001-9313-0311
Periyar Maniammai Institute of Science and Technology, India

Prakriti Mehta
http://orcid.org/0000-0001-8698-0131
Periyar Maniammai Institute of Science and Technology, India

ABSTRACT

India is undergoing rapid urbanisation. This has increased the demand for affordable rental housing for the urban poor and migrants, which is also inclusive in nature. Since time immemorial, the focus of the government has been on promoting ownership models, leaving policies for rental housing inefficient and ineffective. The reverse migration witnessed during COVID-19 pandemic exposed the precarious conditions in which the urban poor lived in the city. This phenomenon propelled the launch of Affordable Rental Housing Complexes (ARHC) policy under Pradhan Mantri Awas Yojna Urban (PMAY-U). Despite of noble intentions, the policy faces challenges in scaling up, monitoring, integration of existing policies and is yet not inclusive in nature. This chapter proposes a transformative strategy through the Policy Metaverse Model (PMM), a socio- technological innovation integrating ideas

DOI: 10.4018/979-8-3373-6721-7.ch005

of digital twins, immersive community engagement, blockchain enabled contracts and AI data analytics to improve transparency, accountability and inclusivity in the digital governance space.

INTRODUCTION

Need for Affordable and Inclusive Urban Rental Housing in India

India's Population is 1.4 billion, which is 31.13% of the total population of India, and by 2030, 40% of India's population will be residing in urban areas. (United Nations Department of Economic and Social Affairs, 2019) This rapid urbanisation exerts immense pressure on cities and, particularly, on housing. The economically weaker section particularly faces a consistent challenge in residing in urban areas. (Kundu, 2014; UN-Habitat, 2003)

The policy discourse has historically focused on ownership-centric approaches, which gave occupants social security and economic stability. (Tiwari & Rao, 2016). Yet in 2020, during Covid 19 Pandemic, India witnessed the phenomenon of reverse migration, and the need for a framework to safeguard the urban poor and migrants was identified. (Williams et al., 2022) Moreover, studies show the shift from ownership centric approach to a rental approach. However, rental housing witnessed an increase in informal housing arrangements with very limited protection from the Rental Control Act, thus disincentivizing private engagement and investment. Figure 1 shows, as per the Census of India 2011, 28% of the population were in rental urban housing. However, 11.9 million houses remain vacant, and 1.77 million are homeless in Urban India. (Census Tables | Government of India, 2011) Policy design inefficiencies can be seen in this paradox of vacant housing stock amidst the scarcity of housing. (Gandhi et al., n.d.; Sharma, 2023).

Figure 1. Rental Household and Vacant Stock in India

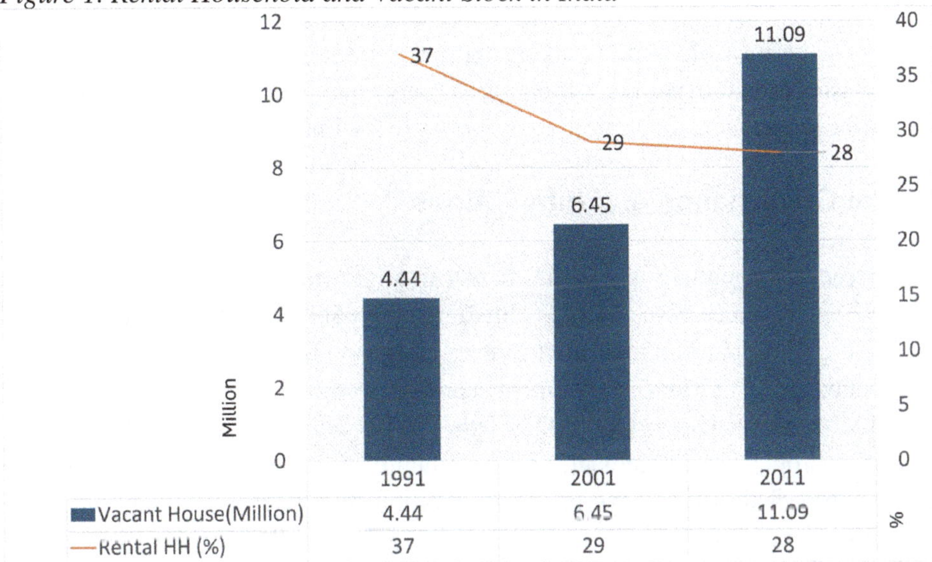

(Data Source: Census of India, Visual Source: Author)

The paradox of high rental requirements and significant vacant housing stock shows a housing market failure stemming from stern regulation and weak institutional support. A lot of the vacant stock is presumed as speculative asset. It reflects a greater preference given to capital income over rental appreciation because of low yields and complicated and tiring tenancy legal frameworks. Landlords find renting a risky option, given the time-consuming judicial process and lack of enforcement of the rental agreement. (Gandhi et al., 2022) On the other hand, the tenant lacks power and is likely excluded from the formal process due to documentary requirements and discrimination. This incongruity in demand and supply is a housing issue and at the same time a challenge in terms of governance that needs fresh thinking towards data, incentives, and legal regulatory frameworks, and how they all interact with each other. This paradox needs an ecosystem that can integrate real-time data, minimize transaction costs, and build trust in the governance system.

Covid as a Policy Catalyst

The mass exodus of migrants, workers, labours and urban poor in 2020(Ayushmaan & Chaudhry, 2020) highlighted the crucial role of rental housing in the city's economic resilience. Reverse migration witnessed in urban areas of India exposed the precarious conditions of the workers, informal renters, and urban poor. (Bhagat et al., 2020; Naik, 2015) To address the issue, the Government of India launched the

Affordable Rental Housing Complexes (ARHC) programme under Pradhan Mantri Awas Yojana (PMAY-Urban)(Ministry of Housing & Urban Affairs, 2020), aiming to formalise affordable rental housing and institutionalise it through PPP models, incentivising private developers (Mehta & Subramanian, 2025). The programme does seem to be progressing; however, a substantial gap is witnessed in its implementation.

Digital Governance and Innovations

Governance is undergoing digital transformation worldwide. (Gil-Garcia et al., 2018). E- governance have evolved from digitisation of records to open data portals to now engaging participation platforms in isolation (Janssen & Estevez, 2013a). The metaverse is a virtual environment seamlessly curating simultaneous real and digital worlds. (Dwivedi et al., 2022) This can be seen in pilot projects in urban planning, property management, and community engagement. These platforms aid in approachability to governance, integration of services, unifying data, and fostering interaction.

Rationale for Policy Metaverse Model (PMM)

PMM has the potential to create a robust, transparent, inclusive, and evidence-based ecosystem that can innovatively address India's rental housing challenge. Its objective is to fill gaps in data integration, stakeholder engagement, accountability, and implementation where previous policy and governance have not succeeded holistically. (Saha et al., 2025) This innovative model aligns with the global discourse and the Digital India Programme in accelerating governance capacity.

Theoretical Foundations of the Policy Metaverse Model

The Policy Metaverse Model (PMM) is rooted in multidimensional theoretical frameworks that converge on governance theory, socio-technical systems thinking, and participatory urban planning. In essence, the PMM responds to the notion that results of public policy are influenced not only by regulatory intentions but also by the interplay among institutions, technologies, and social actors. In India, Traditional governance of rental housing has predominantly functioned with hierarchical and isolated administrative structures. These are inadequate to handle issues of informality, spatial inequality, and exclusion of stakeholders.

PMM diverges from this conventional approach by framing governance as a dynamic and interactive ecosystem instead of a straightforward administrative procedure. PMM acknowledges that the technological infrastructures and social institutions evolve together, addressing the socio- technical systems requirement.

Technologies like digital twins, artificial intelligence, and blockchain are not merely neutral instruments. They influence decision making process, power dynamics, and access to services. Consequently, the PMM incorporates these technologies in a defined policy-driven and institutionally integrated framework, ensuring that the technological advancements are consistently aligned with the objectives of affordability, inclusivity, and accountability.

The model also incorporates governance theory, which perceives digital platforms as facilitators of interactions among stakeholders. It transcends beyond a simple service delivery mechanism. In the realm of rental housing, this suggests a change in the state's role from being merely a regulator or provider to a facilitator that promotes transparent interactions among tenants, landlords, developers, and local authorities. PMM operated as a public interest platform where regulations, data flows, and participation mechanisms are seen by public institutions. This reduces the risks of market capture or exclusion.

Participatory planning theory further supports the PMM's objective of immersive engagement. The conventional consultation process in the housing policy remains superficial, restricting meaningful participation from the marginalised groups, such as the migrants and informal renters. By integrating participatory mechanisms within immersive digital environments, the PMM puts into practice deliberative governance principles. This enables stakeholders to visualise policy effects, engage in scenario testing, and share experiential knowledge. This methodology aligns with the right-based urban theories that insist on" Right to City" as inclusive access to decision - making processes rather than merely physical shelter.

Together, these theoretical positions position PMM as a governance innovation that transcends mere incremental digitisation. It signifies a transition towards adaptive, evidence-based, and engagement-based policy ecosystems that are capable of addressing the complexities of the urban rental housing in India.

Objective and Methodology

This paper contributes to urban policy studies by synthesizing secondary data on rental housing policies its evolution in India. It offers a literature-based understanding of data driven approach towards affordability and Inclusivity while proposing a Policy Metaverse Model framework, in the Indian and global context. The study also suggests future research directions for model experimentation.

LITERATURE REVIEW

The section of the research paper provides a critical analysis of the development of rental housing in India and in other nations. It aims to uncover structural, institutional, and governance-related deficiencies that have hindered affordability and inclusivity. Instead of merely offering a chronological summary of policies, the review delves into how frameworks focused on ownership, regulatory fragmentation, and marginalisation of informal rental arrangements have influenced the current policy landscape. Additionally, this section contextualises India's experiences within the broader framework of international rental housing policy practices to derive applicable governance lessons. These findings collectively build a conceptual and empirical foundation for suggesting an innovation in the alternative governance framework. The Policy metaverse Model is a culmination of the same that would be elaborated in the following sections.

Evolution of rental housing and its policies in India

There has been an evolution of housing policies for the urban poor in India from 1949 to 2020. There has been a gradual shift from ownership to a rental approach framework. The Industrial Housing Scheme and 1st Five Year Plan focused on the institutional development of a segment of the population. 1950's and 1960's The Slum Areas (Improvement and Clearance) Act 1956 (The Slum Areas(Improvement and Clearance)Act 1956, n.d.) displaced people without any alternative arrangements. (Tiwari & Rao, 2016) HUDCO gave financial support, but not to the urban poor. Environmental Improvement of the Slums (EIUS) 1972 (Ravindra Prasad & Malla Reddy, 1994) and EWS Housing in 1970 (Chowdhury & Samanta, 2024) didn't expand the formal rental housing market but improved slum living conditions. (Mehta & Subramanian, 2023) Urban Basic Services for the Poor (UBSP) (Tahir, 2022) and National Housing Policy 1988(Kumar, 1989) integrated shelter with poverty alleviation, though favoured ownership models. Implementation of the National Slum Development Programme (NSDP) 1996 (Charumitra et al., 2014), Valmiki Ambedkar Awas Yojana VAMBAY(2001), and Jawaharlal Nehru National Urban Renewal Mission (JNNURM) in 2003 (JAWAHARLAL NEHRU NATIONAL URBAN RENEWAL MISSION, n.d.) remained fragmented. National Urban Housing & habitat Policy 2007 (NUHHP)(National Urban Housing & Habitat Policy 2007, n.d.), National Urban Rental Housing Policy Draft 2015 (NURHP) (National Urban Rental Housing Policy (Draft), n.d.) and Draft Model Tenancy Act (MTA) (2015,2019) (The Model Tenancy Act, 2019, n.d.) recognised formal rental housing but excluded informal renters. (Mukherjee et al., n.d.) Pradhan Mantri Awas Yojana -Urban (PMAY-U) 2015 focused on ownership models until 2020 with the introduction of Affordable Rental Housing Complexes (ARHC) (Ministry of Housing & Urban Affairs, 2020). The ARHC was introduced with a noble intention to provide respectable rental housing to the Economically Weaker Section and Lower Income Groups strata, yet it faces the challenge of scaling, low investment returns, implementation, site selection, monitoring, evaluation, and integration with the informal rental market as a result of inadequate institutional and government support (Mehta & Subramanian, 2024). In 2025, the operational guidelines under PMAY Urban 2.0 (Operational-Guidelines-of-PMAY-U-2. Pdf, n.d.) with a greater focus on rental housing for the urban poor and migrant was launched.

A significant yet unexplored orientation of India's rental housing is the enormous informal rental housing market that exists beyond the legal regulatory frameworks. Informal rental housing typology, from shared rooms to dormitories to ad hoc temporary dwelling units are the predominant housing typology for a lot of migrants and lower-income groups. (Srivastava & Sutradhar, 2016) These informal arrangements are identified by verbal agreements with no written or formal agreements, which give them legal protection. These are devoid of access to necessities like sanitation, hygiene, water, electricity, natural light, and ventilation. (Zhang, 2018). Although there are so many significant numbers, these remain absent from policy discourse. This results in interventions that are delusional of the lived experiences and realities of the urban poor. The absence of any kind of data on informal rental occupants further complicates the design and planning of the policies. The PMM has the potential to bridge the gap and map them in real time through participation of the residents and take decisions in the best interest of human living.

The history of India's rental housing policy indicates a continuous gap between the intentions of the policy and the lived experiences of its citizens, especially the urban poor and migrants. In spite of the acknowledgement of the significance of the rental housing, the execution and implementation have been inconsistent, lacking in data, and institutionally fragile. The lack of updated information, restricted involvement of stakeholders, and insufficient coordination among regulatory, fiscal, and planning mechanisms have limited the success of initiatives like ARHC. These inconsistencies highlight the crisis in rental housing. The crisis is not only of supply and /or financing but is rooted in governance failures. The insight serves as a foundation for analysing global rental housing trends where governance frameworks have influenced the achievement of affordability and inclusivity.

Global Insights on Rental Housing

In 2005, 53% of Germany's Household is renting. (Gilbert, 2016) It has strong rent caps, tenant security regulations, and cooperatives to ensure affordability. (Hanhörster & Ramos Lobato, 2021) India, perhaps, could understand balancing regulation from

Germany and the Netherlands (Scanlon et al., 2014). The Netherlands integrates social housing into urban planning. The housing associations manage 30% of the housing stock, and the rent cap avoids exploitation (Priemus & Dieleman, 2002).

Measures like associating inflation with mortgage rates ensure affordability in Switzerland, which has 65% of the tenant population in the year 2000. (Gilbert, 2016) While Canada has institutionalised financing through the design of mixed-income housing supported by government subsidies. In 2023, a policy was rolled out on affordability through inclusivity and supplements. (Suttor, 2025)

Singapore, for its low-income households, offers public rental housing with subsidies, improving affordability. (Groves, 2016) Similarly, Hong Kong accommodates 30% of its population in such public rental housing. (Ming Yip, 2001). Affordability has been a challenge, but the government provides tenurial security to the low-income groups. These two countries demonstrate how inclusivity can be scaled through such state-led initiatives.

In the United States of America, affordability in the private rental market is backed by subsidies such as Section 8 and vouchers. (Schwartz, 2021). Their schemes are facing challenges of upkeep and maintenance of housing. Affordability is beginning to become a challenge in a few areas due to rising rents. (Hulchanski, 1995) . Affordability remains a challenge in Australia. (Gurran & Phibbs, 2015)

It is essential to integrate these learnings from both developing and developed nations on contextual adaptations, informal market, weak implementation or enforcement of policy, and financial viability, to deepen the necessity of a new governance model like the PMM.

The international experiences discussed above emphasise that success in rental housing systems does not depend on financial tools but also robust governance structures, data integration, and institutional responsibility. Although the above models give deep insights, their straightforward application in India is limited by informality, scale, and fragmented governance. This disparity underscores the need for a flexible, technology - driven governance model. The subsequent section examines the perspectives of the metaverse-based digital governance.

THE METAVERSE OF DIGITAL GOVERNANCE

This section presents the idea of metaverse-enabled digital governance as a progression beyond traditional e-governance models. It positions the metaverse not merely as a technological innovation but as a governance framework that can unify data, stakeholders, and the decision-making process in a cohesive virtual space. Through real-time simulations, immersive engagement, and transparent oversight, the metaverse governance structure provides a novel opportunity for handling policy intricacies and execution deficiencies. In the realm of rental housing, these features are especially pertinent due to the informal nature of the sector, diversity in participants, and inequality in spatial dynamics.

Evolution from Data-collecting portals to immersive policy governance platforms

In the last few decades, governments have globally accepted, adopted, and supported digital transformation to improve effectiveness and efficiency, increase transparency, and encourage citizen participation. Initially E- Governance oriented itself to digitising existing and future records and providing access to online services. It gradually advanced to open-data dashboards and citizen participatory portals. Today, technologies in the metaverse allow governance to integrate advancements such as Augmented Reality (AR) and Virtual Reality (VR) to collaborate virtually in citizen engagement, scenario modelling, and real-time data analysis in a multiverse environment. (Lnenicka et al., 2024) Application of Digi- Governance has enabled virtual collaborations, scenario modelling, participatory engagement, and transparent monitoring. (Allam et al., 2022; Uzun, 2023) This has already been tested in a pilot in a smart city planning project, property management, and budgeting. (Gupta & Pal, 2023) . Figure 2 shows the transformation of India's E-Governance model to a Metaverse Governance model.

Figure 2. Transforming from E-Governance to Metaverse Governance

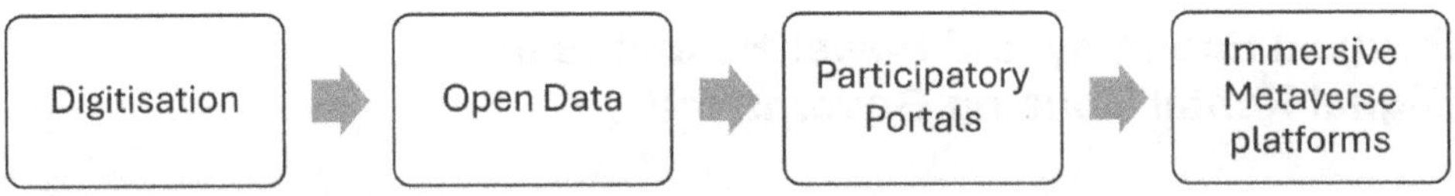

(Source: Author)

Opportunities for Metaverse in Housing Policy

The opportunities that the Metaverse in Housing Policy holds are multifold and at various levels. The metaverse could help in identifying the vacant stock of housing through mapping with digital twins. It could also identify demand hotspots. This model could simulate subsidies or incentives in real time and thus develop strategies for affordability. (Bibri, 2022) The virtual model can encourage inclusivity through participation of stakeholders (Urban poor, migrants, and informal groups) in policy design. The model also becomes a training and capacity-building platform for

Fiscal policy designers and implementers, urban designers, urban planners, policy makers, policy implementers, lawyers, and architects through an immersive and engaging ecosystem.

Risks and Challenges of the Metaverse in Housing Policy Design

While the model does highlight great opportunities, the risks and challenges are equally significant. India yet does not claim 100% digital literacy or access to technology and its devices. It does possess a cybersecurity threat (Lnenicka et al., 2024), with systems becoming vulnerable to breaches. Integration of several sources of data raises concerns of misuse. An algorithm may become biased, which may lead to inequalities, since India is yet to develop a clear legal framework (Ana Mercedes López Rodríguez, 2024) for such mapping, integration of data, and virtual contracts. (Digital Future Society, 2023).

Although these risks are considerable, they do not reduce the importance of governance in the metaverse. Instead, it highlights the need for a thoughtfully constructed policy-driven and ethically sound framework. Challenges of digital exclusion, data privacy, and algorithm bias necessitate the incorporation of protective measures in the governance structure itself. The PMM introduced in the next section addresses these issues by combining regulatory supervision, participatory design, and accountability systems. This converts technological possibilities into a responsible governance approach.

Political Economy and Power Relations in Digital Rental Housing Governance

The governance of rental housing is influenced by the power dynamics between the state, market participants, and tenants. In India, these disparities are evident due to informal tenancy agreements, the absence of security of tenure, and speculative land markets. The implementation of digital governance tools like platform based don't address these structural inequalities. It may instead perpetuate or even exacerbate existing power disparities if not designed in detail.

Landlords and private developers have higher access to financial resources, legal knowledge, and digital skills. This allows them to maneuver through formal systems more adeptly than low-income group tenants. The technology providers and platform operators can wield considerable power over data, algorithm decision-making, and system priorities. In the absence of strong public oversight, digital governance may transform tools of platform capture where private interests dictate policy execution under the pretense of efficiency.

PMM explicitly recognises the dynamics of political economy by incorporating governance controls into public institutions. Data ownership, access protocols, and decision-making rules are framed as regulatory issues rather than technical options. Through the integration of public audit trails, clear eligibility criteria, and participatory oversight mechanisms. PMM aims to shift informational power towards tenants and the community who have been overlooked within formal housing systems.

Additionally, PMM addresses spatial power imbalances by providing real-time data on vacant housing stock, demand hotspots, and service disparities. This approach reduces information monopolies that currently benefit speculative actors. The model reinterprets digital governance as a means of redistributive urban policy designed to rectify enduring inequities in the rental housing market in India.

POLICY METAVERSE MODEL (PMM) – AN INNOVATION

The idea of PMM is developed as a socio- technological innovation that integrates immersive technologies with evidence-based housing policy for ensuring affordable and inclusive rental housing in India. This model offers a modular system that can be integrated with existing housing policy and its implementing systems. (Allam et al., 2022; Anurag Wasnik & Anisha Bhasin, 2022)

Key Pillars of PMM

The conceptual architecture of the PMM can be understood in the form of its key pillars, visualised in Figure 3.

Figure 3. PMM's conceptual architecture

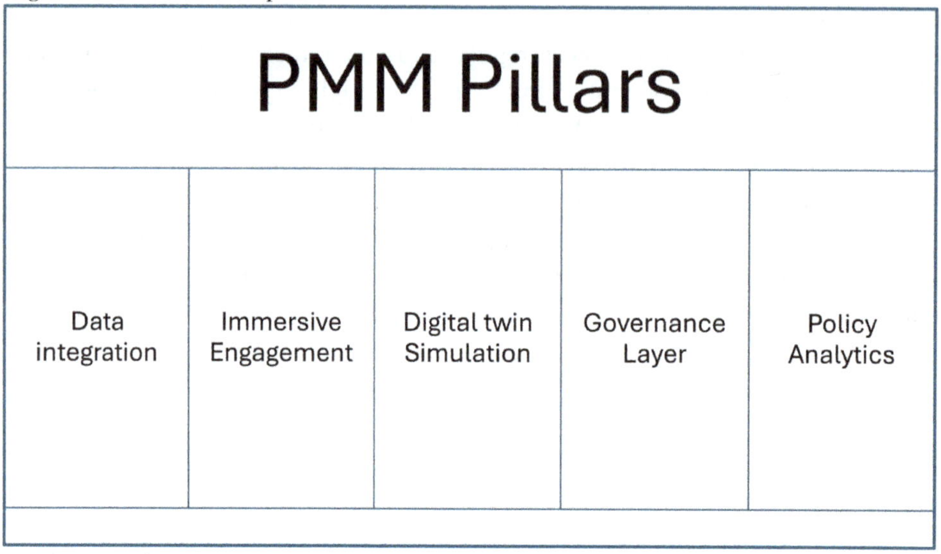

(Source: Author)

Data Integration: The model aggregates data streams (Kitchin, 2014) from various sources like census records, municipal databases, market trends, IoT sensors on land use, built use, occupancy, crowdsourcing data, and old policy data. This integration of data will aid in the identification of correct beneficiaries, mapping vacant dwelling units, and areas of demand.

Immersive engagement: Stakeholder engagement is a key distinctive feature of PMM. The stakeholders may include policymakers, tenants, and owners. They interact in a 3D environment modelled on the geography of a real city. The end user can virtually walk through the rental housing complex, participate in policy design, and engage in relevant discussions. The model being multilingual with sufficient audio and visual aids encourages inclusivity even to the marginalised groups like differently-abled users.

Digital Twin Simulation: Digital Twin is a real-time replication of a city or a region with information inputs on housing, infrastructure, occupant type, and quantitative and demographic data. (Batty, 2018) This integrated real-time data will help in the development and planning of scenarios for subsidy, incentives, rent control, and most importantly, equitable spatial distribution. Research highlights the role of computing in urban studies in predictive simulation modelling and experimentation. (Hooli, 2025)

Governance Layer: Smart Contracts based on blockchain (Ølnes et al., 2017). Unique Digital Identity Management, like UIDAI registration and audit trails into the PMM, encourages transparency, accountability, and responsibility. Research suggests e-governance mechanisms reduce disputes and automate benefits to potential end users or beneficiaries identified.

Ethics, Consent, and Data Justice Considerations: The implementation of immersive and data-intensive governance brings about ethical dilemmas when used for vulnerable groups. PMM recognises it should adhere to the principles of consent, proportionality, and data justice rather than just focusing on efficiency. Informal renters fear surveillance due to concerns over eviction. PMM stresses informed consent mechanisms that are accessible, multilingual, and sensitive to context. Participation on the platform must be voluntary with transparent communication regarding data usage, retention, and the right to withdraw. Visual and audio-based consent can help overcome literacy challenges, promoting inclusivity without coercion.

Data justice necessitates the examination of algorithmic bias. Machine learning systems that are trained on incomplete or historically biased datasets risk perpetuating exclusionary trends. PMM advocates for ongoing algorithm auditing, human-in-the-loop decision-making systems, and grievance redressal mechanisms to mitigate these risks. Privacy by design ensures the data collected is anonymous and sharing with other agencies is limited to specific purposes.

Policy Analytics: Historical and real-time data are both procured by Machine Learning Algorithms. (Sen & Kumar, 2023) This helps identify trends, foresee risks, and effectively implement policies. Machine Learning flags anomalies, monitor and proposes dynamic resource allocation and optimisation. (Janssen & Kuk, 2016).

Deployment of PMM and Use Cases

PMM can be embedded as a measure to policy management in the ARHC Programme, state housing portals, or as a national dashboard for rental housing policy. The following are the use cases of the PMM in the Indian scenario.

E- marketplace for Rental Housing: The PMM would act as a secure platform for Artificial Intelligence (AI) moderated listing and exchanging rental properties. This list could be for formal, informal, co- living, employee service apartment, or dormitory type housing for the stakeholders. (Allam & Dhunny, 2019)

Stakeholder participatory planning: The PMM supports online consultation of all stakeholders on identified subjects like site identification and selection for ARHC and rent setting, along with its terms and conditions for maintenance. This becomes a record that remains unchanged for monitoring and evaluation for identifying any deviations. (Gupta & Pal, 2023)

Identification of Beneficiaries: The PMM using AI will set eligibility criteria. This would aid in identifying potential beneficiaries amongst EMS or LIG. It would also help in allocation, procedures, cross-linking other subsidies, and in conflict resolution for both the owner and the tenant. (Kulal et al., 2024)

Monitoring: Digital Twins of cities allow monitoring of the performance of the ARHC. This monitoring by local authorities can help in understanding occupancy trends, and compliance with an issue could also be done in real time, virtually. (Batty, 2018)

Open Access: The data on rental prices, potential beneficiaries in future cycles, new subsidies, state advisory, and support could be made available to the stakeholders at the click of a button through the PMM. (Janssen & Estevez, 2013b)

Community-focused: The PMM can encourage community-focused initiatives that bond social cohesion with rental housing. Virtual Spaces for communities can be integrated into PMM. It is easier for tenants to attend neighbourhood meetings, give feedback, and be aware of information on health camps, awareness campaigns, policy workshops, etc. The virtual modules can host training for the health and safety of building, maintenance, waste management, and digital literacy. Persons with disabilities or senior citizens would be assisted while being heard on this platform, as it gives a safe avenue for engagement. (Smart Nation 2.0 " A Thriving Digital Future for All, 2024)

Climate Responsive Rental Housing: With a global discussion on the climate responsiveness of built spaces, a significant importance is given to the role of housing. Climatic data through heat maps, vulnerable zones like flood risk, earthquakes, cyclones, etc., air quality, and soil quality indices are available to be integrated in the digital twin simulation. It is easier for policymakers to simulate potential environmental risks on rental housing complexes and suggest strategies for resilience, relation, and retrofitting. The PMM could also integrate simulations done on building design, like for ventilation, natural and artificial light, shading, thermal performance, and energy efficiency parameters. (Bibri, 2022)

Enhancing Private Sector Participation: The private sector participation can be boosted through the PMM. The biggest challenge currently is that the private sector has limited access to credible data on occupancy and yields in rental housing. PMM could address the challenge by giving real-time data intelligence through AI and data dashboards. The private sector could identify and analyse demand hotspots, assess risk, and demand specific rental housing designs. The PMM also gives a highly predictable and transparent system of digital monitoring and service delivery to the occupants, with the advantage of minimised legal uncertainty. (Casey et al., 2022)

Assume a scenario of PMM deployed to an ARHC complex in India. The Municipal Corporation would identify the vacant stock and relate the rice price trends, accessibility in terms of transport, and employment opportunities. With the use of interaction and engagement tools, tenants can participate in online consultations to address any potential issues the occupant may have faced or is likely to face. E.g., Safety, privacy, maintenance, tenure security, access to livelihood, and services. The beneficiary can be AI-identified with preset eligibility criteria, priority, and transparency. Digital twin simulation can impact the expected rent based on occupation and affordability, enabling evidence-based decisions. Rents can be automated along with maintenance requests, and conflict resolution through blockchain enables smart contracts. This reduces the burden on the administration and ensures accountability. This integration shows the potential of PMM to transform rental governance from a fragmented system that performs in isolation to a cohesive system, developing an efficient ecosystem.

Road Map for Implementation

1. Phasing for Implementation of PMM in the Indian Rental Housing Policy Context

The process of implementation of PMM through transformative technology would have been done gradually, including stakeholders, and within the regulatory frameworks. Research scholars state that regulatory governance frameworks are within which institutional reforms need to be embedded. (Lodge & Wegrich, 2012). Table 1 shows the short-term, medium-, and long-term actions that could be taken stage-wise to implement the PMM.

Table 1. Timeline and key initiators of each stage (Source: Author)

Stage	Action	Duration	Term	Key initiators
1	Building Stakeholder and Policy Consensus	3 to 6 months	Short Term	Ministry of Housing & Urban Affairs, ULBs, local organisations, and NGO's, Community
2	Technical Architecture and Pilot Development	6 to 12 months	Medium Term	Technical professionals like IT, marketing, and the design team
3	Service Integration and Feedback Mechanisms	6 to 8 months	Medium Term	Industry experts, NGO's, Academic institutions, Technology team
4	Monitoring, Continuous Improvement & Scaling up	12 to 24 months	Long Term	Legislation, state and Central Government, ULBs

Stage 1 – Building Stakeholder and Policy Consensus

The initiating phase would require focusing on establishing legitimacy and stakeholder consensus. Participatory governance highlights the role of multiple stakeholders, which in turn fosters trust.

National Working Group: The policy metaverse taskforce under the MoHUA should include representation from state governments, technical experts, local civic organisation and private sector representatives.

Institution Digital Capacity: It may be essential to assess the digital readiness of the MoHUA, ULBs, State Housing boards, and agencies before implementing digital initiatives.

Data Policy: Integrated with India's Digital Personal Data Protection Act 2023 (Digital Personal Data Protection Act, 2023, n.d.), develop a data policy emphasising the requirement for cohesive data frameworks.

Stage 2 – Technical Architecture and Pilot Development

The feasibility of any project can be assessed through testing at the pilot stage as an experimental ground for scalability.

Platform Design and Development: The core platform for PMM should be based on standards, a modular architecture, and should be compatible and can be integrated with existing PMAY or ULB dashboards or platforms.

City Identification and Selection: Selection of 2 or 3 cities from Tier- I like Bangalore, Delhi, Ahmedabad, and 2 or 3 from Tier – II or Tier- III cities for pilot testing. These selected cities should represent all forms of social, cultural, and scale diversity and typical rental housing challenges.

Digital Twin: Simulating environments for each city through a co- designing process. It should be with the civic society, associations of tenants, market trends analysts, etc., to improve credibility, integrity, and legitimacy.

Experience Centers: These centers could be established at common community centers as kiosks or information booths to create awareness and citizen engagement. This will minimise digital exclusion.

Stage 3 – Service Integration and Feedback Mechanisms

End-to-end Integration: The PMM must integrate the entire rental housing workflow from listing of properties, application process, verifications, contract development, agreements, information on rental subsidies, disbursement procedures, and conflict resolution mechanisms.

Participatory Sessions: PMM could include participatory sessions, which could be AR or VR-enabled. The sessions could be on rent control amendments, their design and planning for ARHC, and service delivery audits.

Feedback Mechanisms: The updates based on pilot implementation and learningss-hould be integrated with real-time reporting tools for ULBs, community, architects, urban planners and designers, policy makers, and implementers.

Stage 4- Monitoring, Continuous Improvement & Scaling up

Evaluation Matrix: Periodic evaluation of defined performance index like rental occupancy rates, economic strata like LIG or EWS, category, gender, grievance resolution timeline, indices in user satisfaction, feedback, rate, and kind of participation in digital form(Ye et al., 2024).

Policy updates and Act amendments: Synthesis of learnings from pilots could inform the model. This would be essential for updating the Draft Model Tenancy Act, ARHC policy guidelines, and could also aid in setting up new legal benchmarks for smart contracts.

Cross-Sectoral Linkages: The PMM could scale up to the center and state level. This model could enable cross-linkages with other metaverses of transport planning, education, and economic employment. This would help in monitoring global trends in digital governance.

2. Institutional Policy Enablers

The PMM should be alignment in regulatory Framework. Amendments in Draft Model Tenancy Act or ARHC policy should recognise digital contracts, AR or VR, and grievance redressal systems. Capacity Building: Holistic and Integrated training for ULBs, platform operators, the community, and technical professionals is necessary as a capacity-building exercise. (Debarpita Roy et al., 2022) This capacity-building exercise could be formalised by Skill India Digital Hub. (Ministry of Skill Development & Entrepreneurship, n.d.) and the All India Council for Technical Education (AICTE) (AICTE FLAGSHIP SCHEMES AND INITIATIVES 2025, n.d.). The PMM would have a structured requirement for financing. A separate budget from the centre and state could be set aside, along with CSR funds, and challenge grants could be secured to operationalise this model. At the same time, institutions that engage in designing fiscal policies, i.e. Ministry of Finance and its various departments, should be integrated and engaged at appropriate stages.

3. Scaling based on Evaluation and Monitoring

An impact evaluation should be conducted on clear and pre- defined parameters. The following is a list of non- exhaustive parameters that may be included in the monitoring and evaluation matrix:

a. Percentage of marginalised tenants who have access to affordable rental housing through PMM
b. Transparency could be gauged through the number of participatory sessions conducted, open data accessibility rating, grievance redressal rates, and feedback on it
c. Frequency of policy updation, periodic implementation of policy updations through pilot projects, followed by corrective measures on feedback received.

The impact evaluation need not necessarily be at the complete end of the project or pilot project. These should be periodic and independent in nature to assess appropriateness and effectiveness in outcomes.

4. Evaluation Framework for Assessing PMM Effectiveness

PMM requires a structured evaluation framework to ensure accountability and continuous improvement. The framework would capture both governance performance and social outcomes. The evaluation model can be structured around 5 key dimensions: Inputs, Processes, Outputs, Outcomes, and Impacts.

Inputs consist of technology infrastructure, institutional capacity, and levels of stakeholder participation. Process indicators evaluate transparency, responsiveness, and adherence to ethical safeguards. Output indicators concentrate on quantifiable governance improvements such as occupancy rates in affordable rental housing, timelines for grievance resolution, and frequency of participation. Outcome indicators assess affordability, security of tenure, and access to services for marginalised groups. Long-term impact indicators measure reductions in spatial inequality, reliance on informal housing, and responsiveness of policies.

PMM views evaluation as a mechanism for learning and not a compliance task. Regular feedback loops facilitate policy adjustments, refinements of the algorithm, and updates to regulations. Independent audits and collaborations with academic institutions can increase credibility. An iterative evaluation strategy ensures PMM adapts in tandem with urban dynamics and strengthens its function as a flexible governance framework.

GLOBAL RELEVANCE

This section places the PMM within the larger global discussion on digital governance and innovations in housing policy. The aim is not to showcase these international examples as best practices, but to highlight how the conversion emphasises governance frameworks to use digital tools to improve transparency, participation, and responsiveness in policy making. These experiences offer insights that highlight the importance of the PMM, especially in the global south, which is facing challenges of informality, rapid urbanisation, and institutional limitations.

The PMM resonated with global digital governance trends in housing policy. Research shows how nations are experimenting with metaverse models and platforms designed for civic engagement, legal redressal, framework development, implementation models, and service delivery. India, through its federal system of governance and multitude of urban challenges, is a unique testing ground for metaverse-enabled housing policy for the Global South.

Similar Models implemented

The best practices (Stephens & Hick, 2024) across the world highlight the importance of policy-compliant, end-user centric, private in nature, yet participative and adapting continuously to new regulations. Table 2 shows the metaverse policy models implemented in the world in recent years.

1. Metaverse Soul, South Korea

South Korea's Metaverse Seoul represents the benchmark of advanced metaverse–enabled public governance. The initiative was launched in 2021, and the platform was developed by integrating municipal services, stakeholder consultations, and virtual administrative offices in an interactive and engaging digital environment. The focus has not only been on service delivery but also extended to experimentation with urban planning and architectural tools. It allows citizens to visualise redevelopment design proposals, land use changes, and housing layouts in a 3D format. This promoted residents' engagement, specifically the younger generation, who are more comfortable with digital interfaces. (Seoul to Provide Public Services through Its Own Metaverse Platform, 2021)

2. Shanghai Digital Twin Pilot project, China

The Shanghai Digital Twin City in China is a model that shows how empowering is the real time simulation is in housing governance. The model mirrors the city through its physical infrastructure, population dynamics, and climatic or environmental situations. The platform monitors traffic movement and flows, civic utilities, predicts disasters and responses, and plans for new development in the built environment. The platform has been particularly useful in the rental housing context. The Shanghai Digital Twin project has been able to identify unutilised buildings, assessing demands and foreseeing the implications of policy interventions on affordability, accessibility, and spatial equality. The AI integration with Big Data analysis has been able to predict models for migration trends and patterns and future needs in housing. (The First Digital Twin City at the Neighborhood Level in Shanghai: Huamu Subdistrict, 2022)

3. Dubai Metaverse Strategy, United Arab Emirates, Dubai

Dubai Metaverse Strategy was launched in 2022, and the city is pioneering as a global focal point for immersive technologies with a strong orientation towards digital governance, real estate, and innovation in public service. The strategy foresees the use of the metaverse for transactions of properties, virtual inspection, and blockchain-enabled smart contracts. The pilot project in Dubai has been conducted on virtual Municipal offices where citizens can be aware of services, submit documents, and interact with officials online. The strategy supports virtual property visits, online land registration, and AI-enabled land valuation in the Real estate sector. This creates an open and transparent citizen and an investor-cohesive environment. (Dubai Metaverse Strategy, 2024)

4. Smart Nation 2.0, Singapore

Smart Nation 2.0 in Singapore is a national transformative strategy to create a "Thriving digital future for all". This strategy is built on the decade-long progress made under Smart Nation 1.0 in 2014. The new Vision is focused on 3 major goals of Growth, Community, and Trust. The country claims that it has been able to transform the daily lives of its citizens through the initiative, with 99% of the government services available online, and digital payment and broadband connectivity are ubiquitous. Singapore's digital economy has contributed approximately 18% to the GDP in 2023. Singapore, with Smart Nation 2.0, has moved ahead from the pure requirement of efficiency to now inclusivity and citizen centric approach. It has also strategized for improving digital infrastructure, updating workforce capacities, amending and updating laws and regulations, and encouraging digital inclusion through subsidised access to broadband and devices to lower-income groups. They have also stressed the significant role of cybersecurity, protection against online scams, and responsible use of AI to gain public trust. As a part of the initiative, the use of smart technologies was adopted to improve the quality of citizens. The initiative intends to plan, develop, and manage newer Housing & Development Board towns. Sensors automatically inform town councils of faults in services such as water pumps and lifts, ensuring quicker responses. The residents play a key role in neighbourhood issue reporting through Kaki (the OneService Chatbot)6 or the OneService mobile application. They play a part in maintaining a clean, hygienic, and safe neighbourhood. Artificial Intelligence is used to efficiently direct residents' feedback to concerned agencies, and in turn, provide real-time updates on responses on the platform. (Smart Nation 2.0 " A Thriving Digital Future for All, 2024)

5. Research on Terner Housing Policy Dashboard, United States of America

The Terner Center for Housing Innovation at UC Berkley is researching the development of a Terner Housing Policy Dashboard. This dashboard is an immersive simulation tool to help policy makers, planners, designers, and researchers understand how land use and housing policies play a key role in impacting the production of new housing in Los Angeles. The tool predicts the financial implications of development along several parcels of land by assimilating data on zoning, construction cost, rental yields, land valuation, and legal and regulatory requirements.

The research concludes that any minor policy amendments result in significant influence on feasibility, especially where development margins are low. The research dashboard also highlights spatial occupancy patterns. Higher value pockets are tougher to develop due to higher land value costs, and low value pockets require incentives to attract investment. On the whole, the dashboard shows how evidence-based data modelling can encourage transparency and help the government to evaluate and estimate trade-offs prior to implementing reforms and policies. (Casey et al., 2022)

Table 2. Metaverse Models across the globe (Source: Author)

S.no.	Country	Name of the Initiative	Initiating Year
1	South Korea	Metaverse Seoul	2021
2	China	Shanghai Digital Twin Pilot Project	2021
3	United Arab Emirates – Dubai	Dubai Metaverse Strategy	2022
4	Singapore	Smart Nation 2.0	2024
5	USA	Research on Terner Housing Policy Dashboard	2022

Global experience of implementing Metaverse governance, Digital twin Simulation, and AI – driven systems shows that technology plays an important role in strengthening transparency, engagement of citizens, and evidence-based policy development. India needs to move away from paper based, fragmented, and reactive approach to rental housing governance frameworks and focus on integration and digital mediums.

Concept of Lex Metaversi

The Lex Metaversi approach is gaining global support. (Rodríguez, 2024) The approach defines the idea of developing legal frameworks for visual environments. (Radhakrishna, 2022) A metaverse platform is likely to integrate public administration, rental housing policies, and its implementation strategies and legal frameworks designed and developed for administrative and physical jurisdictions. Thus, there is a challenge to address issues of identity, consent, liability, and enforcement. Lex Metaversi has the potential to bridge this gap through the definition of digital identity, legal validity of smart contracts, and conflict resolution and redressal of grievances through legal institutional mechanisms. India has multiple regulatory frameworks, and PMM may be a good environment to test with sandboxed legal protocols in a controlled environment, assessing adherence to current laws and identifying gaps in regulatory frameworks. This would integrate the metaverse at both the national and state levels.

VISION FOR PMM

In the long term, PMM is likely to develop into a national digital infrastructure that could integrate housing with other critical urban systems like transportation, healthcare, education, and social infrastructure. Policy designers could encourage interventions that encourage economic mobility and minimise spatial inequality by integrating rental housing data with labour market information and labour laws. The model could advance climate-responsive housing strategies through integration with GIS and environmental real-time updates. This model would also give a chance to innovate in the fiscal policy domain, like rent insurance, vouchers, real-time subsidies, and performance-based grants. As India seeks to promote towards being a pioneer in digital governance, the PMM is a blueprint for metaverse governance in the Global South. This model addresses socio-economic challenges of the country through highlights on inclusivity, transparency, and evidence-based policy making. The model is a fundamental change in how governance is thought and implemented.

CONCLUSION

India's rental housing challenges of affordability, accessibility, viability, tenure security, and inclusivity are a reflection of a larger governance paradox of rapid urbanisation and socio-demographic change, with poor policy adaptation. Despite a noble intent of providing and safeguarding the urban poor or migrants through acts like rent control act and draft model tenancy act and policies like the ARHC, the effectiveness is undermined. Global studies demonstrate how stability is achieved with strong rental housing frameworks. The Policy Metaverse Model (PMM) is an innovative and transformative strategy. To address issues of transparency, accountability, coordination, responsibility, and inclusivity, the PMM exploits the potential of participative technology. This transcends the digitisation of records and their automation. It is repositioning itself as an adaptive, collaborative, dynamic, and transparent system. The model requires a strong system with equally strong leadership, ensuring data protection as an utmost priority, sustainability in terms of financing the model, and developing cultures of civic engagement. The risks of digital divide, privacy, ethics, and legality should be acknowledged, but the "privacy by design" approach could be adopted as a resolution strategy. PMM, through an inclusive and iterative process, can not only improve the policy capacities and outcomes but also establish benchmarks for global practice in the metaverse of city policy and design.

Further studies should explore outcomes from pilot projects, collaborating between disciplines like urban studies, policy studies, information technology and sciences, urban design, and management. As the adoption of the PMM grows, a detailed matrix for evaluation could be researched for benchmarking in global models of digital governance. A legal framework innovation could be developed through the Lex Metaversi for smart contracts, dispute resolution, defining rights, duties, and responsibilities of the stakeholders, to encourage inclusivity and participation. Figure 4 represents, through a visual, the potential advantages of adopting the PMM in the Indian governance system as a transformative strategy.

Figure 4. Advantages of Policy Metaverse Model (PMM) in Indian Metaverse Governance

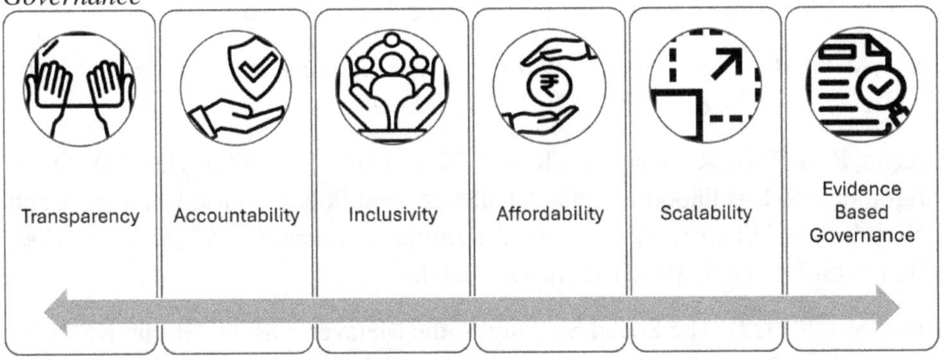

(Source: Author)

REFERENCES

AICTE FLAGSHIP SCHEMES AND INITIATIVES. 2025. (n.d.). AICTE. Retrieved https://aicte.gov.in/downloads/initiatives/AICTE-VISION-MERGED.pdf

Allam, Z., & Dhunny, Z. A. (2019). On big data, artificial intelligence, and smart cities. *Cities (London, England)*, *89*, 80–91. DOI: 10.1016/j.cities.2019.01.032

Allam, Z., Sharifi, A., Bibri, S. E., Jones, D. S., & Krogstie, J. (2022). The Metaverse as a Virtual Form of Smart Cities: Opportunities and Challenges for Environmental, Economic and Social Sustainability in Urban Futures. *Smart Cities*, *5*(3), 771–801. DOI: 10.3390/smartcities5030040

Ana Mercedes López Rodríguez. (2024, June 13). Law Applicable to Virtual Real Estate in the Metaverse. Proceedings of the International Congress Towards a Responsible Development of the Metaverse, 13-1 4 June 2024, Alicante. Academic Chair for the Responsible Development of Metaverse.

Anurag Wasnik & Anisha Bhasin. (2022, April 25). Meta-governance: Role of the metaverse in India's E-governance. NITI Aayog. https://www.niti.gov.in/meta-governance-role-metaverse-indias-e-governance

Ayushmaan, A., & Chaudhry, S. (2020). *Search of home: A study on migrant workers' access to housing and land*. Housing and Land Rights Network.

Batty, M. (2018). Digital twins. *Environment and Planning. B, Urban Analytics and City Science*, *45*(5), 817–820. DOI: 10.1177/2399808318796416

Bhagat, R. B., R.S., R., Sahoo, H., Roy, A. K., & Govil, D. (2020). The COVID-19, Migration and Livelihood in India: Challenges and Policy Issues: Challenges and Policy Issues. *Migration Letters : An International Journal of Migration Studies*, *17*(5), 705–718. DOI: 10.33182/ml.v17i5.1048

Bibri, S. E. (2022). The Social Shaping of the Metaverse as an Alternative to the Imaginaries of Data-Driven Smart Cities: A Study in Science, Technology, and Society. *Smart Cities*, *5*(3), 832–874. DOI: 10.3390/smartcities5030043

Census tables | Government of India. (2011). [Dataset]. https://censusindia.gov.in/census.website/data/census-tables#

Charumitra, B., Krishna Kumar, D., & Anupama, S. (2014). Slum Redevelopment Strategy: A Way forward to Urban Environment Management through an Inclusive Approach. *Research Journal of Engineering Sciences*, *3*(7), 28–37.

Chowdhury, P., & Samanta, G. (2024). Slum Development Initiatives in India: An Insight into Policy Shifts. NIUA. *Urban India*, *44*(1), 148–156.

Digital Future Society. (2023). Ethical and social challenges posed by the future metaverse. https://digitalfuturesociety.com/app/uploads/2023/07/Ethical-and-social-challenges-posed-by-the-future-metaverse_ENG.pdf

Digital Personal Data Protection Act. (2023). Retrieved https://www.dpdpa.in/

Dubai Metaverse Strategy. (2024, December 30). U.AE. https://u.ae/en/about-the-uae/strategies-initiatives-and-awards/strategies-plans-and-visions/government-services-and-digital-transformation/dubai-metaverse-strategy

Dwivedi, Y. K., Hughes, L., Baabdullah, A. M., Ribeiro-Navarrete, S., Giannakis, M., Al-Debei, M. M., Dennehy, D., Metri, B., Buhalis, D., Cheung, C. M. K., Conboy, K., Doyle, R., Dubey, R., Dutot, V., Felix, R., Goyal, D. P., Gustafsson, A., Hinsch, C., Jebabli, I., & Wamba, S. F. (2022). Metaverse beyond the hype: Multidisciplinary perspectives on emerging challenges, opportunities, and agenda for research, practice, and policy. *International Journal of Information Management*, *66*, 102542. DOI: 10.1016/j.ijinfomgt.2022.102542

Gandhi, S., & Green, K. R., & Patranabis, S. (n.d.). India's housing paradox: Empty houses and housing shortages. Centre for Social and Economic Progress.

Gandhi, S., Green, R. K., & Patranabis, S. (2022). Insecure property rights and the housing market: Explaining India's housing vacancy paradox. *Journal of Urban Economics*, *131*, 103490. DOI: 10.1016/j.jue.2022.103490

Gil-Garcia, J. R., Dawes, S. S., & Pardo, T. A. (2018). Digital government and public management research: Finding the crossroads. *Public Management Review*, *20*(5), 633–646. DOI: 10.1080/14719037.2017.1327181

Gilbert, A. (2016). Rental housing: The international experience. *Habitat International*, *54*, 173–181. DOI: 10.1016/j.habitatint.2015.11.025

Groves, R. (2016). Housing and the New Welfare State (A. Murie, Ed.; 0 ed.). Routledge. DOI: 10.4324/9781315587103

Gupta, R., & Pal, S. K. (2023). Metaverse for Public Sector. In R. Gupta & S. K. Pal, Introduction to Metaverse (pp. 91–114). Springer Nature Singapore. DOI: 10.1007/978-981-99-7397-2_5

Gurran, N., & Phibbs, P. (2015). Are Governments Really Interested in Fixing the Housing Problem? Policy Capture and Busy Work in Australia. *Housing Studies*, *30*(5), 711–729. DOI: 10.1080/02673037.2015.1044948

Hanhörster, H., & Ramos Lobato, I. (2021). Migrants' Access to the Rental Housing Market in Germany: Housing Providers and Allocation Policies. *Urban Planning*, *6*(2), 7–18. DOI: 10.17645/up.v6i2.3802

Hooli, M. (2025). Digital Twins and Urban Planning: Designing Smarter, More Inclusive Cities. *European Journal of Computer Science and Information Technology*, *13*(44), 104–112. DOI: 10.37745/ejcsit.2013/vol13n44104112

Hulchanski, J. D. (1995). The concept of housing affordability: Six contemporary uses of the housing expenditure-to-income ratio. *Housing Studies*, *10*(4), 471–491. DOI: 10.1080/02673039508720833

Janssen, M., & Estevez, E. (2013a). Lean government and platform-based governance—Doing more with less. *Government Information Quarterly*, *30*, S1–S8. DOI: 10.1016/j.giq.2012.11.003

Janssen, M., & Estevez, E. (2013b). Lean government and platform-based governance—Doing more with less. *Government Information Quarterly*, *30*, S1–S8. DOI: 10.1016/j.giq.2012.11.003

Janssen, M., & Kuk, G. (2016). The challenges and limits of big data algorithms in technocratic governance. *Government Information Quarterly*, *33*(3), 371–377. DOI: 10.1016/j.giq.2016.08.011

Kitchin, R. (2014). *The Data Revolution: Big Data, Open Data, Data Infrastructures & Their Consequences*. SAGE Publications Ltd., DOI: 10.4135/9781473909472

Kulal, A., Rahiman, H. U., Suvarna, H., Abhishek, N., & Dinesh, S. (2024). Enhancing public Service delivery efficiency: Exploring the impact of AI. *Journal of Open Innovation*, *10*(3), 100329. DOI: 10.1016/j.joitmc.2024.100329

Kumar, A. (1989). National Housing Policy: The Implications. [JSTOR.]. *Economic and Political Weekly*, *24*(23), 1285–1294.

Kundu, A. (2014). Exclusionary Growth, Poverty, and India's Emerging Urban Structure. *Social Change*, *44*(4), 541–566. DOI: 10.1177/0049085714548538

Lnenicka, M., Rizun, N., Alexopoulos, C., & Janssen, M. (2024). Government in the metaverse: Requirements and suitability for providing digital public services. *Technological Forecasting and Social Change*, *203*, 123346. DOI: 10.1016/j.techfore.2024.123346

Lodge, M., & Wegrich, K. (2012). *Managing regulation: Regulatory analysis, politics, and policy*. Palgrave Macmillan. DOI: 10.1007/978-1-137-26552-4

Mehta, P., & Subramanian, C. V. (2023, October 12). RIGHT TO LIFE AND HOUSING POLICIES IN INDIA: AN UNDERSTANDING OF HOUSING POLICIES SINCE INDEPENDENCE. One- Day International Conference on Changing Dimensions of Human Rights : Contemporary and Upcoming Role.

Mehta, P., & Subramanian, C. V. (2024). A Study of Rental Housing and Its Policies for the Urban Poor in India. In Nandineni, R. D., Ang, S., & Mohd Nawawi, N. B. (Eds.), *Sustainable Resilient Built Environments* (pp. 687–698). Springer Nature Singapore., DOI: 10.1007/978-981-99-8811-2_58

Mehta, P., & Subramanian, C. V. (2025). AN INTERSECTIONAL THEORETICAL ANALYSIS OF THE SOCIOLOGICAL IMPACT OF RENTAL HOUSING POLICIES ON THE URBAN POOR. *Journal of Applied Bioanalysis*, •••, 10–20. DOI: 10.53555/jab.v11i3.217

Ming Yip, N. (2001). Tenant participation and the management of public housing - The Estate Management Advisory Committee of Hong Kong. *Property Management*, *19*(1), 10–18. DOI: 10.1108/02637470110366176

Ministry of Housing & Urban Affairs. (2020). ARHC [Policy concept note]. https://arhc.mohua.gov.in/

Ministry of Skill Development & Entrepreneurship. (n.d.). Skill India Digital Hub (SIDH). Retrieved https://www.skillindiadigital.gov.in/home

Mukherjee, A., Dasgupta, S., & Das, A. (n.d.). State of Urban Poor Rental Housing in India and Emerging Policy Trends.

Naik, M. (2015). Informal Rental Housing Typologies and Experiences of Low-income Migrant Renters in Gurgaon, India. *Environment & Urbanization Asia*, *6*(2), 154–175. DOI: 10.1177/0975425315591425

Nation, S. (2024). *2.0: A thriving Digital future for all.* Ministry of Digital Development and Information., https://file.go.gov.sg/smartnation2-report.pdf

National Urban Housing & Habitat Policy. (2007). *National Urban Rental Housing Policy*. Draft.

Ølnes, S., Ubacht, J., & Janssen, M. (2017). Blockchain in government: Benefits and Implications of distributed ledger technology for information sharing. *Government Information Quarterly*, *34*(3), 355–364. DOI: 10.1016/j.giq.2017.09.007

Operational-Guidelines-of-PMAY-U-2.pdf. (n.d.). Retrieved December 17, 2024, from https://pmay-urban.gov.in/uploads/guidelines/Operational-Guidelines-of-PMAY-U-2.pdf

Priemus, H., & Dieleman, F. (2002). Social Housing Policy in the European Union: Past, Present and Perspectives. *Urban Studies (Edinburgh, Scotland), 39*(2), 191–200. DOI: 10.1080/00420980120102911

Radhakrishna, G. (2022). Legal Issues with Real Estate in the Metaverse. In Adam, Y. C., & Abdull Manaf, A. W. B. (Eds.), *Proceedings of the International Conference on Law and Digitalization (ICLD 2022)* (pp. 74–82). Atlantis Press SARL. DOI: 10.2991/978-2-494069-59-6_7

Ravindra Prasad, D., & Malla Reddy, A. (1994). Environmental improvement of urban slums: The Indian experience : an evaluation of Environmental Improvement of Urban Slums Programme in South Indian states. Regional Centre for Urban and Environmental Studies, Osmania University, Hyderabad, and Booklinks Corp.

Rodríguez, A. M. L. (2024). Towards a Lex Metaversi? The law applicable to virtual real estate in the metaverse. *Interactive Entertainment Law Review*, *7*(2), 110–121. DOI: 10.4337/ielr.2024.02.05

Roy, D. Meera ML, Haque, I., & Gupta, E. (2022). Institutional provisioning of affordable rental housing in urban India. In Policy Series by ICRIER & Ford Foundation. ICRIER. https://icrier.org/pdf/Rental-policy-series_261222.pdf

Saha, D., Banerji, H., & Kumar, U. (2025). Critical Success Barriers (CSB) to Rental Housing Policy Implementation in Urban India. *Journal of Contemporary Urban Affairs*, *9*(1). Advance online publication. DOI: 10.25034/ijcua.2025.v9n1-4

Scanlon, K., Whitehead, C., & Arrigoitia, M. F. (Eds.). (2014). *Social Housing in Europe* (1st ed.). Wiley., DOI: 10.1002/9781118412367

Schwartz, A. F. (2021). *Housing Policy in the United States* (4th ed.). Routledge., DOI: 10.4324/9781003097501

Sen, S., & Kumar, G. (2023, March 8). The Metaverse: A Tech and Policy Brief For India. National Law School of India University, Bengaluru. https://www.nls.ac.in/publications/the-metaverse-a-tech-and-policy-brief-for-india/

Seoul to provide public services through its own metaverse platform. (2021, November 5). Seoul Metropolitan Government. https://english.seoul.go.kr/seoul-to-provide-public-services-through-its-own-metaverse-platform/

Sharma, S. (2023). Analysing For Affordable Rental Housing Policies and Parameters in India. *International Journal of Advances in Engineering and Management*, *5*(4), 1473–1485. DOI: 10.35629/5252-050414731485

Srivastava, R., & Sutradhar, R. (2016). Labour Migration to the Construction Sector in India and Its Impact on Rural Poverty. *Indian Journal of Human Development, 10*(1), 27–48. DOI: 10.1177/0973703016648028

Stephens, M., & Hick, R. (2024). Comparative housing research. In Jacobs, K., Flanagan, K., De Vries, J., & MacDonald, E. (Eds.), *Research Handbook on Housing, the Home and Society* (pp. 141–157). Edward Elgar Publishing., DOI: 10.4337/9781800375970.00017

Suttor, G. (2025). Housing Policy. In Béland, D., Mahon, R., & Smith, A. (Eds.), *The Oxford Handbook of Social Policy in Canada* (1st ed.). Oxford University Press., DOI: 10.1093/oxfordhb/9780197766859.013.0026

Tahir, M. (2022). URBAN BASIC SERVICES FOR THE POOR: CRITICAL EVALUATION AND ITS AVAILABILITY AND UTILISATION BY THE URBAN POOR. *International Journal of Multidisciplinary Research Review, 8*(8), 50–61.

The First Digital Twin City at the Neighborhood Level in Shanghai. Huamu Sub-district. (2022, May 23). Urban Planning Society of China- City Initiatives. https://en.planning.org.cn/nua/view?id=646

The Model Tenancy Act. (2019). Retrieved https://mohua.gov.in/upload/whatsnew/5d25fb70671ebdraft%20Model%20Tenancy%20Act,%202019.pdf

The Slum Areas(Improvement and Clearance) Act. (1956). Retrieved https://www.indiacode.nic.in/bitstream/123456789/1709/1/195696.pdf

Tiwari, P., & Rao, J. (2016). Housing Markets and Housing Policies in India. 565. https://www.adb.org/publications/major-challenges-facing-small-and-medium-sizedenterprises-asia-and-solutions/

UN-Habitat (Ed.). (2003). Rental housing: An essential option for the urban poor in developing countries (Reprod. without formal ed. by the United Nations).

United Nations Department of Economic and Social Affairs. (2019). World Urbanization Prospects: The 2018 Revision. UN. DOI: 10.18356/b9e995fe-en

Uzun, M. M. (2023). Metaverse Governance. In Esen, F. S., Tinmaz, H., & Singh, M. (Eds.), *Metaverse* (Vol. 133, pp. 231–244). Springer Nature Singapore., DOI: 10.1007/978-981-99-4641-9_16

Williams, G., Charlton, S., Coelho, K., Mahadevia, D., & Meth, P. (2022). (Im) mobility at the margins: Low-income households' experiences of peripheral resettlement in India and South Africa. *Housing Studies, 37*(6), 910–931. DOI: 10.1080/02673037.2021.1946018

Ye, X., Zhao, G., Peng, Q., Dawkins, C., Kim, J., & Wu, L. (2024). Global Trends in Housing Research over the Past three Decades. *Computational Urban Science*, *4*(1), 17. DOI: 10.1007/s43762-024-00129-x

Zhang, Y. (2018). The credibility of slums: Informal housing and urban governance in India. *Land Use Policy*, *79*, 876–890. DOI: 10.1016/j.landusepol.2017.05.029

KEY TERMS AND DEFINITIONS

Policy Metaverse Model (PMM): A socio- technological innovation that integrates virtual ecosystems' ideas of digital twins, immersive community engagement, blockchain-enabled contracts, and AI data analytics, followed by implementation and monitoring mechanisms in the housing policy domain.

Affordable Rental Housing: A category in housing typology, where rent is about 30% or less of the total household income. This typology is usually accessible to the Economically Weaker Section or Lower Income Group, which are termed as the Urban Poor.

Metaverse Governance: It is an ecosystem of laws, rules, regulations, processes, institutional framework, and digital governance that includes all stakeholders, including local authorities, community, to engage and interact in decision making, implementation of policies and services, regulate workflows, and feedback mechanisms. It blends digital and real mediums through digital twins.

Digital Twin: It is real time replication of a physical environment received through sensors, data simulated, and analyzed for actual performance and monitoring. This system is based on dynamism.

Lex Metaversi: The evolution of a legal framework developed to govern the virtual ecosystem, addressing, but not limited to, data protection, privacy, conflict management and resolution, contracts, and agreements.

Affordable Rental Housing Complexes (ARHC): After Covid- 19, India aimed to promote the economy through the Atma Nirbhar Bharat Mission. The Ministry of Housing and Urban Affairs, with related ministries, states, the private and public sector, initiated the ARHC for the urban poor and migrants. The objective was to improve the living conditions of the segment living in slums / informal settlements and peri – urban areas of the urban areas.

Immersive Engagement: It refers to a multi-modal and multi-sensory ecosystem, like AR, VR, and simulations in 3D, for stakeholders to interact and participate in the policy design, planning, and implementation process.

Inclusivity: It is a qualitative term that intends to define the intentional design and planning of policies and systems that ensure engagement of all human beings as a human right. It is regardless of age, gender, economic class, culture, demography, geography, and has access to the benefits of the public services and systems equitably. It intends to remove any barriers that may exist, like structural, social, or technological in nature, which exclude the marginalised from decision-making or participation in policy outcomes.

Chapter 6
Immersive Service Value Co-Creation in the Metaverse:
A Strategic Framework for Telecom Transformation

Kritika Pancholi
http://orcid.org/0009-0002-6564-6374
Narayana Business School, India

Indra Meghrajani
http://orcid.org/0000-0003-2555-4483
Narayana Business School, India

ABSTRACT

The merging of immersive technologies such as augmented reality, virtual reality, blockchain, and artificial intelligence are accelerating the development of the Metaverse - an organized virtual environment where people will be able to interact, exchange value and co-create experiences. Within this context of the possible, the telecommunications sector goes beyond its traditional role as a provider of connectivity services and takes on a leading role in facilitating immersive digital services. The present chapter introduces the Immersive Service Value Co-Creation Framework (ISVCCF) by elucidating how the telecom operators can design and deliver value-rich experience in Metaverse EcosystemThe chapter culminates by stating research propositions, managerial implications, and avenues for further research for establishing trust, ethics, and accessibility as a crucial part of the sustainable adoption of Metaverse.

DOI: 10.4018/979-8-3373-6721-7.ch006

1. INTRODUCTION

Society 5.0 envisions a fully interconnected digital and physical world where technological progress will be in harmony with human desires with a focus on resilience, sustainability and openness (Hitachi- UTokyo Laboratory, 2020). The Metaverse - a shared and persistent collaborative digital environment powered by AR, VR, blockchain and AI - emerges as a key enabling factor in this paradigm (Mystakidis, 2022). By providing socially networked terrains, decentralized economies, and multimodal interactions, it goes beyond the traditional experiences of the online.

Historically considered a utility service provider, the Telecommunications industry is currently going through an immense phase of transformation. As owners of 5G infrastructure, edge computing facilities and low latency networks, telecom operator are innocently positioned to support immersive experiences (Dwivedi et al., 2022). They are moving from providers of connectivity to being orchestrators of immersive experiences - positioning avatar-based customer support, virtual retail storefronts and tokenised loyalty programmes. (Future Today Strategy Group [FTSG], 2025) The evolution of the Metaverse does not depend on technological innovation only but on the delineations and development of user-driven design, participatory interactions and co-creation frameworks; these are areas where service industries like telecom can play a leading role (Wider et al., 2023).

This change requires a re-examination of traditional service marketing strategies. Unlike traditional 2D service platforms, in the Metaverse, not only are people active participants and co-creators but also immersed into the behavioral activities that allows for redefining the perception and exchange of value (Vargo & Lusch, 2008). Immersive service models in telecom are not just a way to improve, but a strategic imperative in a world moving quickly towards Web 3 (Ball, 2022).

2. LITERATURE REVIEW

2.1 Telecom and the Metaverse

Telecom companies form key enablers of Metaverse that can provide infrastructural requirements by means of 5G connections, the fibre network, edge computing and cloud integration (Kshetri et.al., 2025). AI mediates interaction and act as a brand guardian in Metaverse which ensures consistency of tone, identity, and values using intelligent virtual agents (Khalil & Ahmed, 2024). These immersive applications represent a shift away from the delivery of services and towards experience. One salient point is the necessity for telcos and platform providers to have device application intersection security that focus on continuous authentication, biometrics validation and running protection for immersive applications (Kshetri et al., 2025). Such measures allow the telecoms to make the shift from "product push" models to "experience design."

A strong shift is noticeable in the form of service delivery. Telecom providers no longer offer only SIM cards or data plans; instead, they now co-create environments for service in virtual spaces. These include 3D service kiosks, virtual customer lounging, and interactive planners. Such touchpoints blur the demarcation between service and experience.

Security has become a new layer of services. In its final form, it is a multi-faceted approach to data security beyond the firewall, which includes real-time biometric authentication, device-level access control, and immersive levels of identity validation at the hardware-application convergence. (Kshetri et al., 2025). This is important in spatial compute environments where users are never disconnected.

The Metaverse is envisioned and consolidated as an evolutionary convergence of a multi-layered ecosystem that incorporates extended reality (XR), blockchain for validating ownership, AI for intelligent interaction, and digital twins for digital service replication (Lee et al., 2024). These partnerships make the development of decentralised and scalable environments necessary for persistent 3D interactions and virtual economies and it allows users to co-make and actualize these in real time, with telecom players playing a central role in actualizing this potential. For example, Reliance Jio, India, made a JioDive, a VR headset at low price, that provides its immersive 360-degree experience through JioImmerse app. But, its efficacy is dependent on high expecting speed, low and low latency 5G networks - demonstrating the direct influence from telecommunication logistics on immersive consumer applications (GSMA, 2024; Tesseract, 2023).

Globally, telecom providers are also getting into immersive engagement. Verizon, for instance, built a virtual 5G stadium in Fortnite during the Super Bowl to highlight its implementation of Ultra Wideband network, which enabled fans to have branded engagement in a gamified virtual world (Brodkin, 2022). SK Telecom introduces Ifland, an avatar-based virtual meeting metaverse. Although it was terminated in early 2025 because of strategic changes, it was still an interesting experiment as a telco-led Metaverse integration (Fierce Wireless,2025).

To sum it all up, telecom companies are no longer the passive pipelines of connectivity but are evolving to become active experience platforms in the Metaverse, building real-time and multisensory touchpoints that redefine the user experience with telecom services.

Recent empirical studies further substantiate the evolving role of telecommunications firms as immersive service orchestrators rather than passive connectivity providers.

Large-scale empirical investigations conducted across multiple countries demonstrate that network performance indicators—such as latency, bandwidth stability, and edge computing proximity, have a statistically significant impact on users' perceived immersion, satisfaction, and continued usage intention in Metaverse environments (Lee et al., 2024; GSMA, 2024). These findings empirically validate earlier conceptual claims that telecom infrastructure quality directly shapes experiential value in immersive services.

Moreover, cross-industry empirical evidence suggests that telecom-led immersive platforms enhance customer engagement when service interactions move beyond transactional interfaces to avatar-based and spatially interactive environments (Gursoy et al., 2023). Such results reinforce the notion that immersive service delivery represents a strategic extension of telecom service portfolios rather than an experimental add-on.

Recent telecom initiatives provide illustrative evidence of how immersive services are operationalized in practice. For example, Reliance Jio in India has introduced low-cost virtual reality devices and mobile-first immersive applications, demonstrating how telecom infrastructure can enable scalable Metaverse access in emerging markets. In contrast, Verizon in the United States has leveraged virtual environments primarily for branded engagement and network capability demonstration, while SK Telecom in South Korea experimented with avatar-based communication platforms for social and enterprise interaction. Collectively, these cases highlight how telecom-led Metaverse applications vary by market maturity while reinforcing the central role of network infrastructure in enabling immersive service experiences.

2.2 Theoretical Foundation

In order to understand how telecom services can be changed under immersive platforms, four key theories are used in this framework: Service Dominant Logic (S-D Logic), Technology Acceptance Model (TAM), Experience Economy, and the E-SERVQUAL model. These theories explain the creation and delivery of value and perceived value in the Metaverse.

Service-Dominant Logic (Vargo & Lusch, 2008) sees value as co-created through interaction as the basis for understanding value. In the case of Metaverse, service avatars, customization and interactive interfaces are some of the key enablers of this logic. These elements are what give users control and participation which are at the heart of value co-creation. For example, to make a personalised service plan for a telecom customer using a virtual assistant, the customer co-creates that service experience.

The Technology Acceptance Model (Davis, 1989), places a strong emphasis on perceived ease of use and usefulness for user adoption - an important aspect for immersive platforms, which are characterised by complex ways of navigation and interaction in the virtual environment. If the virtual environment is intuitive and offers value to the customer's experience (e.g. more efficient support or better service demonstrations), users are more likely to adopt and continue to use the service. This helps to retain customers and also adds to digital engagement.

The Experience Economy (Pine & Gilmore, 1999) contends that for businesses to drive high customer self-satisfaction, they need to create satisfying, memorable experiences, a proposition that can be met through gamified, sensory-flooded service designs for telecoms. In the Metaverse, telecoms have the opportunity to provide emotive and playful experiences through the use of AR/VR, gamification, and tokenised rewards. Such engagements make service interactions change from utilitarian tasks to holistic experiences. A virtual plan selection kiosk, for example, including an immersive walkthrough, can make service exploration fun.

E-SERVQUAL (Parasuraman et al., 2005) adaptation to virtual environments provides a framework for measuring quality in terms of responsiveness, assurance and interactivity in digital service environments. Such dimensions are particularly relevant when services are provided in immersive, real-time situations. Telecoms need to ensure that their immersive platforms are able to offer timely aids, secure processes, and human-like responsiveness with AI agents.

Empirical studies integrating Service-Dominant Logic and immersive technologies show that co-creation mechanisms, such as avatar personalization, collaborative virtual spaces, and AI-driven service agents, positively influence perceived service value and psychological ownership (Kumar & Shankar, 2024). These outcomes empirically confirm that value in immersive environments is co-created through interaction rather than delivered unilaterally.

Similarly, empirical validations of the Technology Acceptance Model in immersive contexts reveal that perceived usefulness and ease of use remain significant predictors of adoption; however, sensory immersion and emotional engagement act as complementary drivers in XR-based services (Lee et al., 2024). This suggests that traditional adoption models retain relevance but require experiential augmentation in Metaverse settings.

Comparative insights across regions indicate that Metaverse adoption in telecom services follows distinct global and local trajectories. In developed markets, immersive telecom applications are often oriented toward brand experience, enterprise collaboration, and premium services, whereas in emerging economies, the emphasis lies on affordability, mobile accessibility, and digital inclusion. These contrasts suggest that while the underlying technological enablers of immersive telecom services are globally shared, their value realization is strongly shaped by local socio-economic, regulatory, and infrastructural conditions.

2.3 Research Gap

Despite a growing body of literature on Metaverse and its technological underpinnings, a big gap lies in the aspects of service marketing implications especially in the telecom domain (Dwivedi et al., 2022). While the research about Metaverse has erupted in areas like gaming, retail, and entertainment, there is little research on the immersive service delivery in the telecom space and thus, this is a gap in the empirical findings (Miles, 2017).

Secondly, though concepts like Service-Dominant Logic, Technology Acceptance Model and the Experience Economy are widely used, they are not applied together in a framework to explain immersive telecom services. The lack of an integrated theoretical model that ties together the nature of avatar interactions, AI-disseminated support, trust, privacy and perceived value of service for the context of telecom forms a distinct conceptual gap (Miles, 2017).A third issue relates to context. Most Metaverse research is based on Western markets and focuses on industries like fashion or gaming. But in countries like India, telecom providers are experimenting with immersive experiences (e.g., Reliance Jio's JioDive or Vi's gamified recharge journeys). These practices are not well documented in academic literature. This reveals a contextual gap, where findings from other sectors or regions cannot be directly applied to telecom in emerging markets (Miles,2017).

Telecommunication firms are increasingly putting up avatar based service kiosks, virtual onboarding platforms and token based loyalty programmes. However, they still lack strong design models to guide these innovations. A framework is needed that connects service architecture with user trust, identity control and personalised value co-creation within immersive platforms, which is necessary given the practical gaps that have been identified by Miles (2017). In this lack of direction, companies are seeking limited theoretical support.

While the mainstream scholarly agenda has thoroughly examined technological enablers such as augmented and virtual reality, the underlying psychosocial dimensions - trust, privacy and identity - to Metaverse services are insufficiently conceptualised (Gursoy et al., 2023). Accordingly, theorisation over how immersive environments help in facilitating value co-creation is still in the early stages of maturity, and current literature often fails to see the moderating force of trust and privacy in customer experiences within virtual ecosystems. Kumar and Shankar (2024) identify a lack of theoretical integration on the relationship between immersive service delivery and influencer-led co-creation in high-involvement service sectors, such as telecommunications.

Finally, although immersive applications have been explored in healthcare and tourism, there is still a lack of studies dedicated to telecom-specific use cases, such as real time AR overlays, biometric supporting bots and virtual plan customisation.

As such, there is a large empirical and theoretical gap regarding the impact of these immersive features on user loyalty, perceived service value and continued engagement in telecom contexts (Alimamy & Jung, Hajernik, & Jung (2024)) Kumar & Shankar (2024)

While early Metaverse research was largely conceptual, a growing body of empirical work from 2023–2025 has begun to examine immersive services across diverse geographic contexts. Studies from North America and Europe emphasize brand engagement, virtual commerce, and experiential marketing outcomes (Gursoy et al., 2023). In contrast, research emerging from Asia-Pacific highlights the role of telecom providers in enabling scalable immersive platforms for communication, collaboration, and service access (Lee et al., 2024).

In emerging economies such as India, empirical observations indicate that affordability, mobile-first design, and cultural relevance strongly influence Metaverse adoption in telecom contexts (GSMA, 2024). Telecom-led initiatives that combine immersive experiences with low-cost access models demonstrate higher engagement and perceived value, underscoring the need for contextual sensitivity when theorizing immersive service ecosystems.

Table 1. Key Constructs Table

Theory	Key Construct	Empirical Support (2023–2025)	Telecom Metaverse Use Case
Service-Dominant Logic	Value co-creation	Co-creation + perceived value (Kumar & Shankar, 2024)	Avatar-based service kiosks
TAM	Usefulness, ease of use	Immersion + usability ↑ adoption (Lee et al., 2024)	VR plan customization
Experience Economy	Experiential value	Sensory immersion + loyalty (Gursoy et al., 2023)	Virtual retail stores
E-SERVQUAL	Responsiveness, assurance	AI responsiveness + trust (Alimamy & Jung, 2024)	AI-driven customer support

3. METHODOLOGICAL APPROACH

This study uses a conceptual and qualitative research approach to derive a new framework for immersive service provision of the telecommunications industry, specifically, Metaverse environments. Given the nascent nature of this field and lack of empirical models, the investigation uses only extant academic literature, industry reports and established theoretical constructs as the basis from which to derive a grounded and contextually relevant frame of reference.

3.1 Rationale behind Thematic Analysis

Thematic analysis provides a flexible and systematic approach to identifying, analysing and reporting patterns in qualitative data. It is especially helpful in cases where conceptual clarity is still evolving and multiple interdisciplinary perspectives still need to be brought together. In this study, analysis of the secondary data is carried out by Braun and Clarke's (2006) approach to the thematic analysis. This methodology is appropriate to the objective of identifying recurring themes across a diversity of data sources where new or multidisciplinary fields are concerned. Unlike meta-analysis, which requires large amounts of numerical data, thematic analysis allows researchers to explore concepts, categories and interrelationships. Consequently, it helps building a theoretical structure that bridges both known models (e.g., TAM and S-D Logic) and new trends (e.g., immersive avatars and tokenisation) with telecom service marketing.

3.2 Data Sources and Collection

To feed into the framework, a multi-source review of data was carried out covering the following categories:

At this point (2023), there are no specific business focus areas.

- **Academic Literature**: The theoretical foundations of this research are Service-Dominant Logic (Vargo & Lusch, 2008), the Technology Acceptance Model (Davis, 1989), the Experience Economy (Pine & Gilmore, 1999), and E-SERVQUAL, which were consulted to offer conceptual grounding.
- **Industry reports and white papers:** FTSG from 2025, and the document Chi et al from 2023 are discussed, focusing on the move of telecommunications companies towards decentralized company models and identity solutions where blockchain is the essential technology.
- **Emerging research studies:** Bibliometric and conceptual analysis of research studies for example Wider et al. (2023), Lee et al. (2024), Kumar and Shankar (2024) were reviewed for the dominant constructs and future research agendas.

Searches were conducted using Scopus, Web of Science, and Google Scholar with keywords such as *"Metaverse and telecom"*, *"immersive service marketing"*, *"AR/VR in service co-creation"*, and *"trust in virtual environments"*.

3.3 Data Analysis Procedure

Thematic analysis followed Braun and Clarke's (2006) six-phase model:

1. **Familiarization with Data**: All literature and reports were read thoroughly to identify recurring ideas, key constructs, and theoretical linkages.
2. **Generating Initial Codes**: Concepts such as *interface immersion*, *co-creation*, *perceived value*, *trust*, *privacy*, and *gamification* were coded across different data sources.
3. **Searching for Themes**: Codes were clustered under broader themes that align with immersive service experiences and value co-creation in the Metaverse.
4. **Reviewing Themes**: Themes were refined through iterative comparison with both theoretical models and real-world practices in telecom service design.
5. **Defining and Naming Themes**: Final themes were defined as: (1) Service Interface Immersion, (2) Co-Creation Capabilities, (3) Perceived Service Value, (4) Trust & Privacy Moderators, and (5) Behavioral Outcomes.
6. **Framework Development**: These themes were then logically connected into a conceptual framework showing how immersive technologies can transform telecom services through co-created value experiences.

3.4 Trustworthiness and Rigor

In order to guarantee methodological rigor and credibility, several attested qualitative validation strategies have been implemented during this study. As the research is conceptual and based on secondary data rather empirical collection, the quality and trustworthiness of the findings were ensured through themes consistency, triangulation methods of sources and transparent analytics interpretation.

Credibility: First, credibility was ensured through the analysis of a variety of and reputable data sources: academic journal articles, white papers by industry experts, and market reports by institutions such as GSMA Intelligence, Deloitte, Accenture and Statista. Each source of data was considered in terms of authenticity, publication reliability and contextual relevance to the research problem. This multi- source approach addressed researcher bias and provided strength to the confidence in the conceptual framework.

Transferability: Second, transferability was provided for by clearly defining the scope and setting of the investigation. The study focuses on the AI-enabled retail environments, especially on emerging economies like India. By unpacking the context or shaping factors - technology maturity, cultural factors, and consumer behaviour - the research provides practical information that can be adapted to other markets with similar socio-digital characteristics.

Dependability: Third, dependability was addressed by having a transparent and systematic research process. The study followed Braun and Clarke's (2006) six-step thematic analysis approach, which offered an appropriate audit trail from coding the literature to generating themes. Each stage including data familiarisation, coding, theme identification, review, definition and synthesis were documented to ensure replicability of the conceptual reasoning process.

Confirmability: Fourth, the confirmability was reinforced by upholding an explicit link between theoretical constructs and data interpretation. Concepts, such as the AI trust paradox, algorithmic fairness, and privacy concerns, were not taken for granted: instead, they were built on the foundation of verified literature and cross-compared between sources to ensure that interpretations were based on evidence rather than personal prejudice.

Furthermore, the narrative synthesis approach (Popay et al., 2006) and the best fit framework synthesis approach (Carroll et al., 2011) were used to synthesize the findings across disciplines. Narrative synthesis was used to support thematic integration of various streams of the literature, ranging from AI to understanding consumer psychology to marketing services, whereas best fit framework synthesis was used to refine existing models such as the Technology Acceptance Model and the Service-Dominant Logic to reflect AI-enabling retail contexts. This theoretical triangulation helped to insure that the emergent conceptual model would be both coherent and defensible.

Last but not least, ethical rigor was maintained throughout. As the research was exclusively made up of secondary data, there was no human subject, therefore ensuring that the research equips were in place in terms of research ethics. All secondary materials were cited correctly using APA 7th edition standards to ensure academic transparency and intellectual integrity.

In nut shell, the methodological rigour of this conceptual study is based on four pillars; credibility, dependability, transferability and confirmability which ensures that the study findings are credible, theoretically based, transferrable for academic and practical applications. The resulting framework thus forms a strong basis for future empirical validation and strategic implementation in intelligent retail environments.

Figure 1. Trustworthiness and Rigor Framework

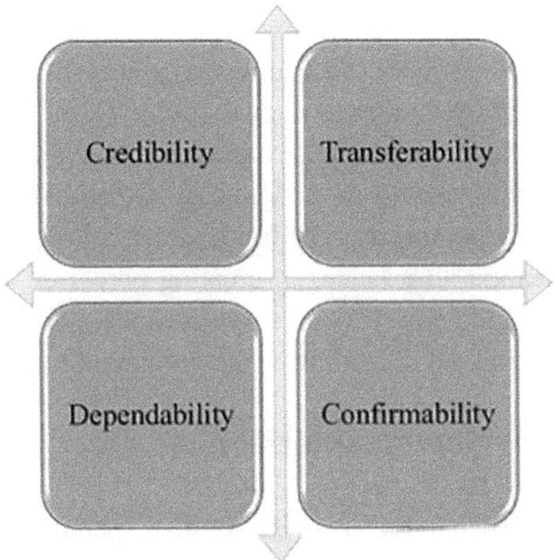

Source: Developed by Authors

The methodological approach outlined in this chapter was able to constitute a systematic and reliable foundation of the development of the proposed conceptual model. Secondary literature, industry reports and emergent Metaverse case studies were consulted in order to ensure that what we found had both meaning in theory and real-world application. Braun and Clarke's thematic analysis was used to distil reoccurring themes of immersion, co-creation, trust, privacy and value perception, while following the criteria of credibility, transferability, dependability and confirmability helped to make the results robust. As a result, the constructs and interrelations that emerged from the review were systematized with a grounding in the evidence and were not arbitrary. This rigorous foundation enables a smooth transition from thematic insights to the Immersive Service Value Co-creation Framework, illustrated in the section that follows.

The resulting conceptual model combines the major themes that emerged from the analysis and considers established theoretical frameworks to explain how the services of immersive telecom within the Metaverse engender value and influence customer behaviour.

4. CONCEPTUAL MODEL DEVELOPMENT

The conceptual model presented in this chapter is a synthesis of the main themes identified in the thematic analysis (Section 4) and places them in the context of established theories of service and technology research. Based on Service-Dominant Logic, Technology Acceptance Model, Experience Economy and E-SERVQUAL, the research proposes Immersive Service Value Co-Creation Framework (ISVCCF) of telecom services in the Metaverse. The framework explains the role of immersive interfaces and co-creation affordances in creating perceived value and customer behaviour, where trust and privacy issues serve as moderators. Subsequent sections describe each construct in detail leading to the integrated model and propositions.

4.1 Immersion into Service Interface

Service Interface Immersion refers to the sensory, spatial and interactive characteristics of the virtual environment in which the customers interact with the telecom services. Immersive interfaces are comprised of high resolution AR/VR displays, spatial audio, haptic feedback, realistic 3D environments and smooth low latency communication, facilitated by 5G and edge computing (Lee etálních., 2024). These characteristics increase the sense of presence, that is a psychological sense of "being inside" the virtual environment which is highly correlated with heightened feelings of enjoyment, engagement, and perceived usefulness (Davis, 1989).

Within immersive telecom applications, users can walk though virtual stores for service, interact with avatar-based service agents or customize plans via holographic tools. Such interfaces make mundane tasks into experiential touchpoints. The Experience Economy states experience has great influence, arguing that sensory richness and emotional involvement raises substantially the symbolic and hedonic value (Pine & Gilmore, 1999). Consequently, Service Interface Immersion acts as a key antecedent of Perceived Service Value in the context of telecom services in Metaverse.

4.2 Co-Creation Capabilities

Co-creation Capabilities refer to how much the users can actually influence their experience on the service within immersive environments. These capabilities include the ability to customize avatars, interactive plan builders, shared virtual spaces, customer communities and collaborative interfaces with AI. Rooted in Service-Dominant Logic, co-creation involves customers as active participants who make contributions, including skills, preferences and creativity during value formation (Vargo & Lusch, 2008).

In cases of Metaverse driven telecoms a co-creation process enhances user autonomy and involvement. Users can set up service plans visually and create avatars to reflect a personal identity, engage with their peers, as well as give direct feedback in a participatory virtual environment (Kumar; & Shankar, 2024). These kinds of activities are methods of social emotional connection and symbolic value because these activities feel owned by the user. As a result, co-creation capabilities have a positive contribution to perceived service value and represent a key mechanism of value co-creation in immersive ecosystems.

4.3 Perceived Service Value (Mediator)

Perceived Service Value is the user's overall assessment of the benefits from immersive telecom experiences as compared to costs, effort or emotional commitment. In the Metaverse, value goes beyond "functional utility to include emotional, experiential and symbolic areas" (Pine & Gilmore, 1999). For example, pleasure while engaging in a virtual consultation, ease in navigating 3D self service kiosks, or pride of creating a unique avatar help to add to perceived value.

Research has shown its ability to empirically assess emoticons as a function of emotional and symbolic value is a key predictor of loyalty and engagement in technology mediated service contexts (Gursoy et al., 2023). Immersive experiences increase the level of sensory stimulation and emotional resonance; so, perceived value represents the mediating construct between immersive features (Service Interface Immersion and Co-creation capabilities) and behavioural outcomes. Perceived Service Value thereby describes the translation between immersion and participation on the one hand and meaningful behavioural intent on the other.

4.4 Moderators: Trust, Privacy issues

4.4.1 Trust (Positive Moderator)

Trust is the user's perception that the telecom provider, the immersive platform and the AI-driven virtual agents will conduct themselves in a safe, reliable and ethical manner. Trust reflects confidence in data governance, identity protection, algorithmic transparency and platform integrity. In the past research, however, trust has been identified to increase the connection between perceptions of gain and behavioural goals on the Internet (Gefen et vše., 2003). In telecom settings of Metaverse, where biometric data and persistent identities are common, trust is a key for reducing perceived risk while creating greater engagement. High levels of trust increase the effect that Perceived Service Value has on behavioural outcomes.

4.4.2 Privacy Issues (Negative Moderator)

Privacy Concerns refer to the user's fears about the misuse of data, tracking of biometric data, lack of control, and surveillance in immersive spaces. Given the potential in the Metaverse for real-time behavioural tracking and identity replication, higher levels of privacy concern can potentially undermine user comfort and engagement (Alimamy & Jung, 2024). When privacy issues are important, users will not fully enjoy immersive experiences, therefore reducing the positive way that Service Interface Immersion has on Perceived Service Value. Accordingly, privacy concerns act as a negative moderator to weaken the immersion-value pathway.

Together, Trust and Privacy Concerns reflect the socio-psychological factors affecting immersion in telecom services.

The expansion of immersive telecom services also intensifies regulatory, compliance, and accessibility challenges. Immersive platforms depend on continuous data collection, including biometric and spatial data, raising concerns related to consent, surveillance, and data governance under evolving regulatory regimes. In parallel, accessibility considerations are critical, as immersive environments may unintentionally exclude differently-abled users or individuals with limited digital literacy. Addressing these issues requires telecom providers to embed regulatory compliance, inclusive interface design, and accessibility-by-design principles into immersive service architectures to ensure responsible and equitable Metaverse adoption.

4.4.3 Governance, Compliance, and Data Protection in Immersive Telecom Services

The deployment of immersive telecom services in the Metaverse raises complex governance, compliance, and data protection challenges that extend beyond traditional digital service environments. Immersive platforms rely on continuous data streams, including biometric identifiers, spatial movement data, voice interactions, and behavioral patterns, which heighten regulatory and ethical concerns related to consent, surveillance, and data ownership (Alimamy & Jung, 2024; Phattanaviroj et al., 2024).

From a regulatory perspective, telecom operators operating immersive platforms must comply with evolving data protection regimes such as GDPR, India's Digital Personal Data Protection Act, and sector-specific telecom regulations. Empirical policy studies indicate that inadequate governance mechanisms reduce user trust and limit the adoption of XR-based services, particularly when biometric data are involved (Dwivedi et al., 2022).

Consequently, governance in immersive telecom ecosystems must shift from static compliance models to dynamic, design-embedded governance, incorporating transparent consent architectures, explainable AI agents, identity protection frameworks, and auditable data flows. These governance mechanisms function not merely as compliance safeguards but as strategic enablers of trust and sustained value co-creation in Metaverse services.

4.5 Behavioural Outcomes

Behavioural Outcomes include sustained use of the platform, subscription renewal or upgrade, loyalty and electronic word of mouth (e-WOM). Perceived Service Value is a strong predictor of these behaviours in digital and immersive service situations (Parasuraman et al., 2005. When users experience high experiential, symbolic and functional value, they tend to be more engaged with the platform and advocate for the platform.

In the Metaverse the behavioural outcomes are amplified through social mechanism. Users participate in, share their experiences, and create content in the virtual communities and strengthening peer influence, collective identity (Wider et al., 2023). These outcomes not only describe satisfaction but also provide a feedback that adds more value to the service ecosystem through Co-creation Capabilities. For instance, user generated tutorials, avatar interactions, and shared experiences enhance users and in turn open up opportunities for co-creation.

4.6 Integrated Model and Propositions

Based on the constructs described above, the Immersive Service Value Co-Creation Framework argues that the following relationships exist:

P1: Service Interface Immersion has a positive influence on Perceived Service Value.

P2: Co-creation Capabilities positively affect on Perceived Service Value.

P3: Perceived Service Value positively impacts on Behavioural Outcomes

P4: Trust has a positive interaction with Perceived Service Value on Behavioural Outcomes

P5: Privacy Concerns has a negative moderating effect on the relationship Service Interface Immersion and Perceived Service Value.

P6: Behavioural Outcomes Positively reinforce Co- Creation Capabilities through community participation and e- WOM.

These propositions define a coherent value cocreation cycle where immersive design and active participation are driving force for value perceptions and behaviour which are modrable through socio-psychological moderators.

5.6 Immersive Service Value Co-Creation Framework (ISVCCF) Model

Figure 2.

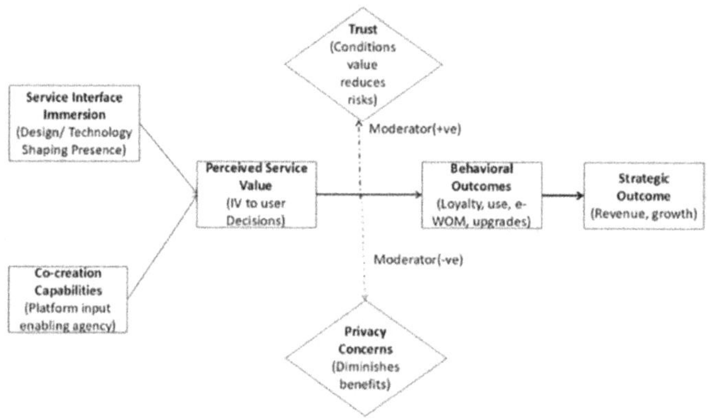

Source: Developed by Authors

The Immersive Service Value Co-Creation Framework illustrates how immersive interfaces and co-creation affordances influence perceived service value and behavioural outcomes in telecom Metaverse environments. Trust and privacy concerns function as moderators that condition these relationships, while behavioural outcomes reinforce co-creation capabilities over time.

5. RESEARCH PROPOSITION

Based on the Immersive Service Value Co-creation Framework (ISVCCF) a set of propositions is developed which are theoretically grounded. These propositions translate the conceptual relationships into something that is empirically testable and can be used to guide future research as the result of the integration of Service-Dominant Logic, the TAM Model, the Experience Economy, and the digital trust and privacy literature. Each proposition is an exact match to the structural pathways within the model.

H1: Service Interface Immersion has a positive impact on Perceived Service Value.

Immersive interfaces allow customers to feel the telecom services in the form of realistic, engaging, and interactive 3D environments. Such environments are associated with greater spatial presence and an increase of cognitive and emotional engagement and therefore with higher value perceptions (Lee et al., 2024). Studies in digital and immersive services have shown that the more senses are involved and the more responsive the systems are, the more useful or entertaining they appear to be (Davis, 1989). Consequently, stronger immersion should improve the evaluation of the service provided to the users.

P2: Co-creation Capabilities has a positive influence on Perceived Service Value.

Co- creation enables the customer to actively design their service experience. Tools such as avatar personalisation, interactive plan builders and collaborative virtual spaces contribute to a sense of ownership and agency. Service-Dominant Logic argues that the value is created by the consumption and integration of resources by users and not by passive consumption (Vargo & Lusch, 2008). Thus, higher co-specification capability should boost the perceived value of services in terms of increased functional, emotional and symbolic benefits.

P3: Perceived Service Value has a positive effect on Behavioral Outcomes.

Perceived service value is the momentary psychological precursor of customer behaviour. When customers perceive that they are getting meaningful functional benefits, emotional fulfilment and symbolic expression in immersive telecom environments, they are more likely to continue using the service, to upgrade or recommend it to others (Gursoy et al., 2023). Consistent with previous value-based research in the digital services domain, value is the principal determinant of loyalty and persistence (Parasuraman et al., 2005).

P4: Trust has a positive moderating relationship with the relationship between Perceived Service Value and Behavioral Outcomes.

Trust decreases perceived risk in virtual environments by increasing the perceived security of platforms and stimulates users to have faith in the platforms status security agents and immersive interfaces that are AI-based. In fact, previous research has shown that trust exaggerates the impact of value judgement on behavioural intention in cyberspace Gefen et al. (2003). In telecom services based on metaverse, higher trust should amplify the way of perceived value in the form of loyalty, e-WOM and upgrades of subscription.

P5: Privacy Concerns is one of the moderating variables that has a negative effect on the relationship between Service Interface Immersion and Perceived Service Value.

Immersive interfaces are based on biometric data, spatial tracking and behavioural monitoring; as a result, privacy may create a feeling of unpleasantness or cognitive resistance. Users that fear misuse of data or surveillance may avoid deep engagement with immersive features thereby reducing value perceptions (Alimamy and Jung,

2024). Therefore, privacy issues reduce the positive impact that immersion has on perceived service value.

P6: Behavior Results back from Co-Creation Capabilities on a Feedback loop.

Positive behavioural responses such as content sharing, peer recommendations and community participation contribute to the growth of platforms and the richening of co-creation environments. Assistive technologies provide a foundation for a growing pool of user-generated resources, peer learning, and community-driven service improvements as the number of users that engage and interact with them increases (Wider et al., 2023). This feedback loop enhances the constantly ongoing co-creation process and ecosystem development.

Together, these propositions (as displayed in Figure 2) form a basis for future empirical testing through experiments using survey-based techniques, experiments based on simulations or through metaverse environments. They also inform researchers and practitioners on the most important levers that shape immersive telecom service experiences.

6. MANAGERIAL IMPLICATIONS

The gathering of immersive, user-directed Metaverse environments soon requires that telecommunications companies change the way they think about their services, management of customer relationships and the building of digital ecosystems. The Immersive Service Value Co-Creation Framework (ISVCCF) outlines new strategic priorities that telecommunications providers need to undertake to provide real value to their customers and shape long-term customer engagement. The following managerial implications turn the theoretical model into practical advice that leaders in the industry can apply:

6.1 Designing Immersive Service Interfaces

Telecommunications firms should consider immersive interfaces as the main outlets of service delivery instead of ancillary experiments. Empirical evidence suggests that better sensory and spatial design significantly increases perceived value (Lee et.al.,2024). As such, bosses should secure resources for:

* One realistic 3-dimensional environments of services,
* Latency-reduction for augmented- and virtual- realities facilitated by 5G and edge computing, and
* Responsive avatar based for multilingual support, and
* Virtual onboard venues for customers to explore service options.

In keeping with the Experience Economy, memorable and affectively engaging experiences produce more robust value perceptions and forms of behavioural response (Pine & Gilmore, 1999). As such, telecommunications providers should create immersive designs that are intuitive, culturally relevant and interoperate across devices.

6.2 Facilitating Co-Creation With Participatory Platforms

Co-creation is one of the central mechanisms of customer value creation in immersive situations. The framework shows that active customer participation in the construction of their service experience amplifies the value, both emotional and symbolic (Vargo & Lusch, 2008). Managers should implement:

* Avatar based customisation platforms,
* Virtual plan configurators,
* Troubleshooting lounges with teams of collaborative
* Community review forums & user generated knowledge repositories;

Research shows that the human rights of participants in co-creation build greater psychological ownership and brand affinity (Kumar 2024). Accordingly, telecommunications firms should reconceptualise customers not just as recipients, but as creative partners who will enrich the service ecosystem.

6.3 Trust and Ethics of Data and Virtuality

Trust is a key moderator in changing perceived value to actual behaviour. Within service environments of immersion, AI-aided assistance mechanisms that can guarantee trust are indispensable (Gefen et al., 2003). Telecom managers have to set priorities:

* Transparent data policies,
* Clear explanation about what is AI and immersive agent operations,
* Identity protection mechanism of avatars and of digital twins,
* Resilient authentication systems using secure biometrics.

Considering that environments in the Metaverse rely on steams of data and identities that endure over time, trust-building measures enhance low levels of uncertainty between the user and the trust levels in Metaverse environments (Dwivedi etigado, 2022). Trust should not so much be seen as one feature but as an ongoing governance function.

6.4 Overcoming Privacy Issues Proactively

Privacy concerns lessen the impact of immersive interactions on perceived value. Many users are apprehensive about behavioural tracking, biometic scanning and spatial monitoring within extended reality systems (Alimamy and Jung, 2024). Telecom companies should thus:

* Providing granular data-share of data controls,
* Be able to offer real time privacy dashboards,
* Reduce unnecessary capture of biometric data,
* Make communication about use of data transparent from immersive interface data.

Providing users agency over their data helps to reduce cognitive discomfort and increases willingness to participate. Privacy cannot be seen as a compliance requirement but has to be built into the design of the virtual services.

6.5 Establishing Sustainable Behavioural Outcomes

Behavioural outcomes-behavioural outcomes such as continued use, electronic word-of-mouth and subscription upgrades can be a direct indicator of perceived value. Telecom companies should track these behaviours in real time in order to optimize immersive services. Empirical studies show that emotional and symbolic value are highly predictive of digital loyalty (Gursoy et kujnyy, et al, 2023). To reinforce these behaviours, the telecom managers can:

* Integrate token-based loyalty programmes,
* Allow social sharing within the Metaverse,
* Curate virtual events and/or gamified missions,
* Create exclusive immersive experiences for the premium clientele.

These strategies bring the telecom services from a transactional service towards being an engaging digital journey to reinforce long-lasting relationships.

6.6 Exploiting Feedback Loops to Support Platform Growth

The conceptual model shows that there is a feedback loop wherein positive behavioural outcomes boost co-creation capabilities. As the user engagement increases, immersive communities grow in size and supply further content (Wider et al., 2023). Telecom companies should exploit this dynamic by:

* Increasing user generated content,
* Rewarding community participation, and
* Organizing virtual town halls for customer co-designing,
* Metaverse- based customer support scaling using both AI and trained human agents.

This recursive growth model fits well with the platform economics, where the participation of users enhances network effects, capturing and concentrating competitive advantage.

Collectively these managerial implications point to the need for telecommunications firms to outgrow their role of providing connectivity and move instead towards orchestrating immersive experiences.

6.7 Inclusivity, Accessibility, and Digital Equity in Metaverse Adoption

While immersive telecom services promise enhanced engagement, concerns related to inclusivity and digital equity remain critical. Empirical studies emphasize that immersive platforms risk reinforcing existing digital divides if accessibility considerations are not embedded in service design (Mystakidis, 2022; Dwivedi et al., 2022).

Differently-abled users, older adults, and individuals with limited digital literacy may face barriers due to device requirements, sensory overload, or interface complexity. Inclusive design research highlights the importance of adaptive interfaces, multimodal interaction options, assistive avatars, and low-bandwidth immersive alternatives to ensure equitable access (Lee et al., 2024).

In emerging economies, affordability and infrastructure availability further shape Metaverse adoption. Telecom providers play a pivotal role in promoting digital equity by offering low-cost immersive access, mobile-first Metaverse experiences, and community-oriented virtual services. Embedding inclusivity within immersive telecom ecosystems aligns with the broader Society 5.0 vision of human-centric and socially responsible digital transformation.

7. FUTURE RESEARCH DIRECTIONS

The advent of Metaverse is a paradigm shift that leads to numerous new research opportunities for the telecommunications industry. While the conceptual framework outlined in this chapter provides a systematic basis, future researches can help address a number of methodological, theoretical, and contextual lacunae.

7.1 Empirical Validation of ISVCCF Model

Prospective work should test empirically the associations defined in the Immersive Service Value Co-creation Framework (ISVCCF). Quantitative methodologies like Structural Equation Modeling, survey based research, or machine learning capabilities that allow behavioural tracking, hold the potential to measure the extent of interrelating immersion, co-creation, perceived value and behavioural outcomes (Gursoy et al., 2023). Experimental configurations within virtual reality environments could be used to support the role of sensory richness on value perception under experimentally controlled conditions.

7.2 Cross Cultural and Market Specific Studies

Currently, Metaverse research is focused mostly on western systems. Nevertheless, there are significant patterns of telecommunications adoption across markets, which are due to differences in social norms, digital literacy, and privacy expectations. Comparative investigations between emerging economies like India and more developed nations may help understand the moderating role of the cultural factors on the immersive experience of services (Dwivedi et al., 2022). Future research should continue to explore the role of regional differences in the development of trust, co-creation behaviour and the willingness to interact in immersive telecommunication environments.

7.3 Role of Artificial Intelligents (AI Agents) and Autonomous Delivery of Services

Increasingly, Metaverse ecosystems depend on AI-powered agents, such as virtual assistants, conversational avatars, and self-sustaining agents for problem solving, for service transactions. Subsequent research should scrutinise the role of these agents in affecting trust, emotional response and perceived service value. Understanding customer differentiation between human and AI-led service in the immersive context will be indispensable, especially as generative AI technologies are becoming increasingly sophisticated (Kumar & Shankar, 2024).

7.4 Privacy and Data Ownership & Ethical Governance

Privacy concerns remain a key barrier to the use of immersive technologies. Of the future, exploration of the psychological, behavioural and regulatory aspects of privacy within XR as well as the Metaverse should be undertaken. This involves analysis of biometric data sensitivity, consent framework, and privacy dashboard or data transparency tool impact (Alimamy & Jung, 2024). There is an additional research imperative of building ethical governance structures which allow for telecommunications operators to foster safe and inclusive virtual ecosystems.

7.5 Behavioural Outcome Longitudinal Studies

Consequent studies should assess the over time evolution of behavioural outcomes such as loyalty, electronic word of mouth and as a result, sustained usage. Longitudinal research can track this development of the customer relationship as immersive platforms are matured and telecommunications companies are constantly improving their service line of offers (Wider et al., 2023). Such investigations will make it clear whether immersive experiences lead to more permanent value creation or to temporary novelty effects only.

7.6 Metaverse Driven Service Innovation and Business Model

The Metaverse presents a potential for telecommunications companies to move beyond traditional connectivity service offerings with new connectivity services like the Metaverse-as-a-service, digital twin services, virtual retail, and mixed-reality customer support. Future research should focus on how these modalities alter competitive advantage, partnering ecosystems, and organisational design (Lee et al., 2024). In addition, there should be an investigation on the role of tokenisation, virtual economies, and gamified rewards in enhancing and amplifying customer engagement and revenue streams.

7.7 Accessibility and Inclusion and Social Impact of Immersive Telecommunications Services

In the context of Society 5.0, which places humancentric digital transformation at the fore, the future work needs to question the issue of accessibility and inclusion in immersive telecommunications services. Studies should examine the experiences of people with disabilities, older adults or populations with low digital literacy in their experience of virtual environments. Design of inclusive immersive interfaces need to be a priority of research in order to address issues of digital inequalities and establish widespread adoption (Mystakidis, 2022).

7.8 Innovations to Methodology in Immersive Research

The use of immersive environments requires new approaches to data acquisition and data analysis. Possible research questions include:

- behavioural analytics (based on sensors),
- VR eyes tracking and movement tracking,
- Sentiment mining based on AI on the avatars interacting,
- mixed reality experimental designs.

These novel methods will allow scholars to record holistic insights on user behaviour, decision making processes and co-creation processes within 3D service ecosystems.

Across the directions discussed in the preceding section, there is the theme that runs through them in which a call for interdisciplinary synthesis of telecommunications services is made. This synthesis incorporates aspects of both service marketing and XR technology, artificial intelligence, ethical and behavioural science, and platform economics. Consequently, researchers are given a solid chance to examine how Metaverse-driven value co-creation can be implemented in the telecommunications sector.

7. CONCLUSION

The coming together of immersive tech, the ability of advanced telecommunications infrastructure and user-driven digital ecosystems is fundamentally changing the future of the delivery of services. This chapter has investigated the role of telecommunication providers as a potential experience orchestrator for the future Metaverse and for this purpose presented the Immersive Service value Co-creation Framework (ISVCCF) as an explanatory model for such a transformation. By creating a synthesis between insights from Service- Dominant Logic and the Technology Acceptance Model, and its alignment with the framework of the Experience Economy and the broader literature on digital service quality, the framework aims to provide conceptual clarity on the nature of joint relationships between immersive interfaces and co-creation mechanisms in the creation of customer value and behaviour.

In particular, the analysis shows that value in immersive telecommunication services is generated not only through high - quality interfaces but also through participatory design features that allow customers to contribute, customise and collaborate in virtual worlds. Perceived service value acts as the crucial psychological link between immersive stimulation and co-creation opportunities and manifest behavioural drivers, such as loyalty, consumption loyalty and e-word-of-mouth. The impact of trust and privacy issues exposes the need for digital trust and ethical governance, particularly in cases where we really depend on biometric sensing to support persistent identity and AI - driven interactions.

Finally, the model highlights the dynamic nature of the immersive telecommunication ecosystem. Customer behaviour is iteratively informing service design as part of communal participation, user generated content and social interactions, so service providers are required to adopt iterative, participatory and user centred service architectures.

From a practical perspective, the chapter describes practical ways for interface design, facilitation of co-creation, building trust, privacy protection, and building a community. These insights can help telecommunication companies move away from network utilities towards immersive service leadership in order to support the Society 5.0 visions of human-centric, inclusive and connected digital experiences.

Finally, this chapter argues some areas of future research. As immersive ecosystems evolve, scholars can study new behavioral, cultural, technological and ethical issues that would have been irrelevant for study in conventional telecommunication contexts. The ISVCCF forms a basis for empirical validation and further conceptual refinement to endorse both researchers and industry practitioners for the understanding of the role that immersive service value is playing in the future of telecommunication services.

REFERENCES

Alimamy, S., & Jung, T. (2024). The AR cloud: Navigating metaverse augmentation technologies for enhanced co-creation of value within services. *Journal of Service Research*. Advance online publication. DOI: 10.1177/10946705241265753

Ball, M. (2022). *The metaverse: and how it will revolutionize everything*. Liveright Publishing.

Braun, V., & Clarke, V. (2006). Using thematic analysis in psychology. *Qualitative Research in Psychology*, *3*(2), 77–101. DOI: 10.1191/1478088706qp063oa

Brodkin, J. (2022, February 12). *Verizon builds metaverse stadium in Fortnite to show off 5G*. Ars Technica. https://arstechnica.com/gaming/2022/02/verizon-builds-metaverse-stadium-in-fortnite-to-show-off-5g/

Carroll, C., Booth, A., & Cooper, K. (2011). A worked example of "best fit" framework synthesis: A systematic review of views concerning the taking of some potential chemopreventive agents. *BMC Medical Research Methodology*, *11*(1), 29. DOI: 10.1186/1471-2288-11-29 PMID: 21410933

Chi, C., Lin, D., Ramadoss, R., Yuan, Y., Yin, Z., Luo, C., . . . Ma, R. (2023). White paper-The industrial Metaverse report. *The Industrial Metaverse Report*, 1-20.

Davis, F. D. (1989). Perceived usefulness, perceived ease of use, and user acceptance of information technology. *Management Information Systems Quarterly*, *13*(3), 319–340. DOI: 10.2307/249008

Dwivedi, Y. K., Hughes, L., Baabdullah, A. M., Ribeiro-Navarrete, S., Giannakis, M., Al-Debei, M. M., Dennehy, D., Metri, B., Buhalis, D., Cheung, C. M. K., Conboy, K., Doyle, R., Dubey, R., Dutot, V., Felix, R., Goyal, D. P., Gustafsson, A., Hinsch, C., Jebabli, I., & Wamba, S. F. (2022). Metaverse beyond the hype: Multidisciplinary perspectives on emerging challenges, opportunities, and agenda for research, practice and policy. *International Journal of Information Management*, *66*, 102542. DOI: 10.1016/j.ijinfomgt.2022.102542

Dwivedi, Y. K., Hughes, L., Baabdullah, A. M., Ribeiro-Navarrete, S., Giannakis, M., & Wamba, S. F. (2022). Metaverse beyond the hype: Multidisciplinary perspectives on emerging challenges, opportunities, and agenda for research, practice and policy. *International Journal of Information Management*, *66*, 102542. DOI: 10.1016/j.ijinfomgt.2022.102542

Future Today Strategy Group. (2025). *Metaverse & new realities: Strategies for a digitized future.* https://ftsg.com/wp-content/uploads/2025/03/Metaverse-New-Realities_FINAL_LINKED.pdf

Gefen, D., Karahanna, E., & Straub, D. (2003). Trust and TAM in online environments: An integrated model. *Management Information Systems Quarterly*, *27*(1), 51–90. DOI: 10.2307/30036519

GSMA. (2024). *The Fast Mode: Unlocking Metaverse with 5G and immersive tech.* Retrieved from https://event-assets.gsma.com/Shanghai/Doc/media/publication-2024-the-fast-mode.pdf

Gursoy, D., Lu, L., Nunkoo, R., & Deng, D. (2023). Metaverse in services marketing: An overview and future research directions. *Service Industries Journal*, *43*(15-16), 1140–1172. DOI: 10.1080/02642069.2023.2252750

Hitachi-UTokyo Laboratory. (H-UTokyo Lab.) (Ed.). (2020). Society 5.0: A people-centric super-smart society. Springer Nature.

Kshetri, N., Pokhrel, B. P., Rahman, M. M., Mishra, R., & Hutson, J. (2025). SecureMetaEnd—Endpoint Security in the Metaverse: Securing devices and applications. In *Defending the Metaverse* (pp. 319–333). CRC Press. DOI: 10.1201/9781003581659-16

Kumar, A., & Shankar, A. (2024). Investigating the role of metaverse influencers' attributes for the next generation of services. *Journal of Services Marketing*, *38*(7), 816–838. DOI: 10.1108/JSM-09-2023-0320

. Lee, L. H., Braud, T., Zhou, P. Y., Wang, L., Xu, D., Lin, Z., ... & Hui, P. (2024). All one needs to know about metaverse: A complete survey on technological singularity, virtual ecosystem, and research agenda. *Foundations and trends® in human-computer interaction, 18*(2–3), 100-337.

Miles, M. P. (2017). A taxonomy of research gaps: Identifying and defining the seven research gaps. *Journal of Research in Marketing and Entrepreneurship*, *19*(1), 2–8.

Mystakidis, S. (2022). Metaverse. *Metaverse. Encyclopedia*, *2*(1), 486–497. DOI: 10.3390/encyclopedia2010031

Nowell, L. S., Norris, J. M., White, D. E., & Moules, N. J. (2017). Thematic analysis: Striving to meet the trustworthiness criteria. *International Journal of Qualitative Methods*, *16*(1), 1–13. DOI: 10.1177/1609406917733847

Parasuraman, A., Zeithaml, V. A., & Malhotra, A. (2005). ES-QUAL: A multiple-item scale for assessing electronic service quality. *Journal of Service Research*, *7*(3), 213–233. DOI: 10.1177/1094670504271156

Phattanaviroj, T., Moslehpour, M., & Walawalkar, A. M. (2024). Data ethics and privacy. In *Challenges in Large Language Model Development and AI Ethics* (pp. 321–353). IGI Global. DOI: 10.4018/979-8-3693-3860-5.ch010

Pine, B. J., & Gilmore, J. H. (1999). *The experience economy: Work is theatre & every business a stage*. Harvard Business Press.

Popay, J., Roberts, H., Sowden, A., Petticrew, M., Arai, L., Rodgers, M., & Duffy, S. (2006). *Guidance on the conduct of narrative synthesis in systematic reviews*. ESRC Methods Programme.

Rurianto, J., Sumarwan, U., Suharjo, B., & Hasanah, N. (2021). Sustainable value co-creation in mobile advertising in cellular telecommunication industry: A conceptual framework. [IJBE]. *Indonesian Journal of Business and Entrepreneurship*, *7*(2), 172–172. DOI: 10.17358/ijbe.7.2.172

Tesseract. (2023). *JioDive: Step into the immersive world*. Retrieved from https://tesseract.in/jiodive/

Vargo, S. L., & Lusch, R. F. (2008). Service-dominant logic: Continuing the evolution. *Journal of the Academy of Marketing Science*, *36*(1), 1–10. DOI: 10.1007/s11747-007-0069-6

Wider, W., Jiang, L., Lin, J., Fauzi, M. A., Li, J., & Chan, C. K. (2023). Metaverse Chronicles: A Bibliometric Analysis of Its Evolving Landscape. *International Journal of Human-Computer Interaction*, *40*(17), 4873–4886. DOI: 10.1080/10447318.2023.2227825

Wider, W., Jiang, L., Lin, J., Fauzi, M. A., Li, J., & Chan, C. K. (2023). Metaverse chronicles: A bibliometric analysis of its evolving landscape. *International Journal of Human-Computer Interaction*, *40*(17), 4873–4886.

Wider, W., Jiang, L., Lin, J., Fauzi, M. A., Li, J., & Chan, C. K. (2023). Metaverse chronicles: A bibliometric analysis of its evolving landscape. *International Journal of Human-Computer Interaction*, *40*(17), 4873–4886. DOI: 10.1080/10447318.2023.2227825

Wireless, F. (2025, March 10). *SK Telecom drops ifland metaverse service in favour of AI strategy*. https://www.fierce-network.com/operators/sk-telecom-drops-ifland-metaverse-service-favour-ai-strategy

Chapter 7

A Sequential DL-Based Approach for MRI-Based Brain Tumor Classification With Metaverse

R. Sujatha
http://orcid.org/0000-0002-1993-7544
Vellore Institute of Technology, India

Jyotir Moy Chatterjee
http://orcid.org/0000-0003-2527-916X
Graphic Era University, India

Ahmed Amine Souayeh
École de Management Léonard de Vinci, Paris, France

ABSTRACT

The classification of brain tumors (BTs) from magnetic resonance imaging (MRI) images is of paramount importance in facilitating precise analysis and medication planning for healthcare professionals. This study presents an innovative approach to BT classification, employing sequential deep learning techniques. Customized CNN architectures are made with brain tumor classification in mind, accounting for the special characteristics and patterns found in medical pictures. Our methodology harnesses the capabilities of convolutional neural networks (CNNs) to obtain spatial features from both MRI pictures and MRI masks. The research commences with the preprocessing of the MRI dataset and the curation of a diverse collection of labeled

DOI: 10.4018/979-8-3373-6721-7.ch007

BT scans. To ensure consistent and stable training conditions, we normalized the MRI images. The CNN layers are instrumental in extracting spatial features from individual MRI slices, significantly contributing to optimal classification accuracy.

1. INTRODUCTION

MRI has arisen as a crucial diagnostic means in the field of medical imaging, enabling detailed visualization of anatomical structures & pathological conditions within the human brain. Among the various applications of MRI, the identification and classification of BTs are of paramount importance in guiding clinical decisions and treatment strategies. The increasing prevalence of BTs, coupled with the complexity of their morphological and temporal characteristics, necessitates advanced computational techniques that can harness the inherent information within sequential MRI scans (Vankdothu & Hameed, 2022).

The challenge of BT classification is twofold: capturing the intricate spatial patterns present in individual MRI slices and discerning the temporal evolution of tumors across sequential scans. Traditional machine-learning (ML) approaches have made significant strides in obtaining spatial features from MRI pictures using procedures like region-based analysis and handcrafted feature extraction (FE). However, these methods often fall short of capturing the dynamic progression of tumors over time, where the subtle changes between consecutive scans contain vital diagnostic information (Kumar et al., 2023).

Recently, deep learning (DL) has transmuted medical image analysis by autonomously learning features from raw data, obviating the necessity for automatic feature engineering. CNNs, a class of DL models specialized for image analysis, have established amazing success in single-image classification responsibilities, involving BT discovery. Nevertheless, the sequential nature of MRI scans remains largely unexplored in the context of CNNs. This leads to the necessity for a framework that can fuse the power of CNNs for spatial FE with a mechanism for handling sequential data (Hu et al., 2022). The advent of RNNs, tailored for sequential data analysis, presents an opportune solution to address the temporal dimension of sequential MRI scans. RNNs, equipped with memory cells to retain information over time, have shown promise in capturing temporal dependencies in various domains. When applied to BT classification, RNNs could unveil hidden patterns within the evolution of tumors and facilitate more accurate and timely diagnoses (Kumar et al., 2022).

Motivated by the limitations of existing methods and the potential for sequential DL techniques, the central focus of the work is summarized as follows:

- Customized CNN architectures are made with brain tumor classification in mind, accounting for the special characteristics and patterns found in medical pictures.
- Integration of multiple layers, involving fully connected, pooling, and convolutional layers, that are tailored to extract pertinent characteristics.
- Incorporating approaches to advance the interpretability of CNN models, assisting medical professionals in comprehending the model's decision-making method & boosting confidence in forecasts.
- Multiclass classifiers that can discern between distinct kinds of brain malignancies, including meningioma, glioma, and lymphoma, have been developed using customized CNNs. Given the variety of appearances that brain tumors can have, this is a difficult endeavor.

The remaining sections of this article are structured as follows: Section 2 bestows a summary of similar work done in the domains of BT classification, DL in medical imaging, and sequential data analysis. Section 3 elaborates on the methodology, detailing the dataset, preprocessing steps, model architecture, and training procedures. Section 4 presents our investigational setup & discusses the findings obtained from the proposed approach. Lastly, section 5 offers concluding remarks, highlights the contributions to our work, and outlines possible future work.

2. LITERATURE REVIEW

Machine Learning Approach

Efficient BT detection is vital for prompt treatment; the variability of BTs demands tailored approaches. Physical diagnosis by radiologists is time taking & error-prone. This work introduces a practical solution for BT diagnosis with MRI imaging. The process improves image superiority and uses morphological analysis for nontumor exclusion. Segmentation & clustering identify high-quality tumor regions, further enhanced by multiple neural networks extracting features. An adaptive fusion net builds a fusion feature vector for SVM-based classification, supplemented by training data to prevent overfitting. Evaluated on a public dataset, this approach achieves a high accuracy of approximately 98.98%, improving diagnostic efficiency and automation (Aamir et al., 2023).

Accurate BT detection through MRI is vital, but manual evaluation can be inaccurate due to fatigue and expertise limitations. This study proposes a segmentation method to support experts by accurately detecting and classifying BTs. Achieving 98.81% pixel-level segmentation & 98.93% classification accuracy on the MICCAI

BraTS'20 dataset, the projected technique outperforms previous studies, offering a promising solution for improving BT diagnosis accuracy (Farajzadeh et al., 2023).

Fractal analysis is a versatile approach used across various fields to efficiently analyze irregular objects. The fractal dimension, an effective measure of natural element roughness, can serve as a feature for irregular objects such as breast masses, that can extent from malignant to benign tumors. The study focuses on applying fractal geometry as an FE technique in mammograms, using the box count method for FE and SVM for classification. By combining SVM and fractal dimension, the methodology attained a high accuracy of 98.13% in classification of benign and malignant breast cells, showcasing the potential of this combined method in medical imaging (Swain et al., 2020).

Deep Learning Approach

Emerging technologies are revolutionizing brain morphology analysis. Diagnosing BTs accurately is challenging, with early treatment hinging on precise diagnosis and segmentation. Neuroimaging modalities enhance tissue resolution, but manual segmentation is hindered by noise, tissue merging, and overlapping. Computer-aided diagnosis (CAD) systems employing DL, such as Unet, are gaining traction. Using a novel residual model, this study segments tissues with a focus on FLAIR-modality multispectral images. Their model achieved high performance with a Jaccard index of 0.8293 & a Dice coefficient of 0.9056, outperforming existing frameworks in BT segmentation using the Kaggle LGG dataset (Kumar et al., 2023).

DL has gained significant attention as a powerful tool in ML, effectively solving complex problems. (Mohsen et al., 2018) employed a DL classifier to categorize a brain MRI dataset of 66 samples into 4 classes. The classifier is enhanced with principal component analysis (PCA) & discrete wavelet transform (DWT) for FE. A DWT breaks down a given signal into many sets, each of which is a time series of coefficients that describe how the signal changes over time in the associated frequency range. By shrinking a huge pool of variables to a miniature one that still preserves the mass of the information in the larger set, PCA is a dimensionality reduction procedure which is frequently exercised for reducing the dimensionality of large datasets. The assessment demonstrates a favorable presentation across various measures, showcasing the effectiveness of this approach.

Clinical decisions and cancer treatment depend on patient-specific data and clinical reasoning. Biomedical imaging aids noninvasive disease assessment for better clinical outcomes. Early brain cancer characterization used statistical modeling of neuroimaging. DL has become standard due to computer vision advances. This study reviews statistical, DL, and probabilistic DL models for MRI-based BT segmentation, showing the potential of combining classical statistics and data-driven

DL for automated clinical oncology systems. Integrated methods unify medical, statistical, and AI knowledge (Zulfiqar et al., 2023).

This paper explores utilizing DL to predict BT phases, aiding practitioners in patient assessment and future anomaly prediction. The approach offers a remote medication solution, which is particularly relevant during the pandemic. DL's success in the supervised classification of complex patterns is leveraged for automated analysis, providing quick impressions and reducing manual computations. The study focuses on classifying brain images with different tumor types using MATLAB, achieving 89% to 95% accuracy via standard metrics. The outcomes are equated with CNN and artificial neural network (ANN) models (Atmakuri et al., 2023). An ANN is a hybrid approach modeled after the neural architecture of the human brain.

The study (Sujatha et al., 2023) focused on utilizing DL, specifically TL, for ranking breast invasive ductal carcinoma for more accurate diagnosis. Five TL approaches, including VGG16 and VGG19, were employed and evaluated for their accuracy. Experimental outcomes flourished that DenseNet121 got the utmost accuracy of 92.64%, while InceptionResNetV2 had the lowest accuracy among the models tested. The study emphasized the potential of DL in improving breast cancer analysis, especially in cases involving dense breasts, and provides insights into effective model selection for accurate grading.

The collection of features by CNN is performed arbitrarily, without considering the global & local features, which leads to overfitting issues. This study introduces a new topology called the parallel deep convolutional neural network (PDCNN) which addresses this problem. The PDCNN architecture is designed to extract both global & local features from two parallel stages. Additionally, to mitigate overfitting, the PDCNN utilizes a dropout regularizer in conjunction with batch normalization (Rahman & Islam, 2023).

The study (Mundru et al., 2023) highlighted the clinical utilization of Deep Q-learning systems for decisions for patient treatment and other appropriate parts of medication. Compared to other well-known DL approaches utilized in personalized health care, the experimental results demonstrate superior performance. The study (Asif et al., 2023) introduced an innovative deep-stacked ensemble model named 'BMRI-NET,' to achieve high recall & precision in the detection of BTs from MRIs.

Deep Transfer Learning Approach

(Kumar et al., 2022) aimed at enhancing BT detection accuracy while reducing errors and computational complexity. A deep CNN (DCNN) with a nature-inspired ResNet 152 transfer learning (TL) approach is introduced for brain image categorization. Preprocessing involves noise removal and image quality enhancement with Otsu binarization. The hybrid model, Hyb-DCNN-ResNet 152 TL, pairs DCNN with ResNet 152 for the classification of normal, benign, and malignant images. Weight parameters are fine-tuned utilizing the COVID-19 optimization algorithm (CoV-19 OA). The proposed method achieves high accuracy and lower error rates compared to existing methods on MATLAB.

BTs pose a significant global health threat, potentially leading to death due to tissue damage and increased pressure. Early diagnosis is crucial, and in this study, the GrabCut method accurately segmented lesion symptoms. A TL model, VGG-19, is fine-tuned for FE, linked through handmade features via a serial approach. Entropy optimization enhances classification with the fused vector feeding classifiers. The model is tested on MICCAI challenge databases (BRATS 2015, 2016, and 2017), yielding high dice similarity coefficients (DSCs) of 0.99, 1.00 & 0.99, respectively, showcasing accurate BT diagnosis (Saba et al., 2020).

Gliomas, prevalent malignant BTs, influence patient survival based on grade. MRI-based tumor segmentation and grading are crucial for diagnosis and planning. A DL approach, uniting U-net-based CNN for segmentation and transfer learning with VGG16 for grading, was developed in (Naser & Deen, 2020). BT grading via invasive biopsies poses risks; noninvasive methods are crucial. A noninvasive MRI-based BT grading method utilizing DL and ML techniques is introduced. Five DL and five ML-based models are trained and tested on four clinically applicable datasets. An ensemble MajVot algorithm optimizes classification performance. DL-based MajVot improves accuracy against individual DL models by 1.04% to 2.67% and outperforms ML by 10.12%. Validation on synthetic face data achieves up to 2.88% accuracy improvement. The MajVot algorithm shows promise for BT classification, harnessing the strengths of multiple models (Tandel et al., 2021).

Accurate BT classification is crucial for treatment decisions, and MRI offers superior imaging quality. Manual BT division is time-consuming, leading to the growth of AI and ML procedures. The study proposed a BT detection approach using ResNet50, FE, and CNN pre-trained datasets for transfer learning. The enhanced ResNet50 model is designed with additional layers. The novel deep-learning method improves brain cancer categorization accuracy, leveraging transfer learning. Performance metrics validate the model's effectiveness and are assessed through state-of-the-art techniques, showcasing advancements in noninvasive diagnosis (Sharma et al., 2023).

BTs are severe, necessitating accurate diagnosis for effective treatment. Experiments on the Figshare MRI BT dataset achieved high accuracy scores, with ResNet50V2 achieving 99.68%, outperforming other models. The proposed model's accuracy aids neurologists and doctors in swift and accurate investigative conclusions for BT patients (Talukder et al., 2023). BT classification poses challenges in clinical image analysis, with ML enabling noninvasive diagnosis. This study addresses the complexity of designing accurate DL architectures for BT classification. To overcome the need for expert manual design, the proposed framework combines a deep convolutional ResNet model with an enhanced form of ant colony optimization (IACO), integrating a differential evolution approach and multi-population operator. The approach achieves high accuracy (0.98694) in automatic BT classification, demonstrating the effectiveness of IACO-ResNet in optimizing DL architectures (Mehnatkesh et al., 2023).

Accurately identifying the extent of BT from MRI volumes is crucial for treatment planning. Manual segmentation is time-consuming; hence, computer-aided detection and DL have gained prominence. This study presents an improved U-Net edifice with residual networks and subpixel convolution, improving accuracy while avoiding overlaps. Evaluated on the BraTS challenge datasets, the suggested U-Net achieves segmentation accuracies of 93.40% & 92.20%. Furthermore, it outperforms existing methods in classifying tumor subregions (TC, WT, EC), demonstrating its effectiveness in BT segmentation (Pedada et al., 2023).

Hybrid Approach

Medical image processing is a rapidly growing field focused on diagnosing and treating illnesses. BTs, potentially fatal abnormal growths in brain cells, are a key concern. This study explores computer tomography (CT) based BT segmentation to enhance efficiency and reduce complexity. CT scans are common for diagnosing head traumas, malignancies, and skull fractures. Using an adaptive median filter, image clarity is improved by removing noise and artifacts. FE methods are updated regardless of the preprocessing technique. Classification with an adaptive neuro-fuzzy inference system (ANFIS) & support vector machine (SVM) followed, identifying normal & abnormal images. Aberrant images are segmented using fuzzy c-means (FCM) clustering with optimized centroids from genetic algorithm (GA), social spider optimization (SSO) & gray wolf optimization (GWO). The hybrid technique (SSO-GA) achieves 99.24% accuracy, outperforming other algorithms. Implementation is performed in MATLAB 2014 (Vankdothu & Hameed, 2022).

The study (Khairandish et al., 2022) focused on classifying brain MRI images into malignant & benign tumors utilizing a hybrid way by combining SVM & CNN for classification, along with threshold-based segmentation for detection. This approach reached an impressive accuracy of 98.4959%, topping earlier models that ranged from 94.233% to 97.5%. Brain cancer detection is challenging due to its complex characteristics, but the proposed hybrid model offers enhanced accuracy and effectiveness compared to conventional techniques, which rely on manual features and radiologist expertise. The study's innovative approach addresses the critical need for improved BT classification in medical imaging.

Ensemble Approach

BT segmentation faces challenges due to tumor diversity. Ensembling models to mitigate generalization errors is effective, but conventional methods train members separately. A novel method, mutual ensemble learning (MEL), trains multiple 3D segmentation nets through mutual learning. In order to help every unit congregate to a superior local minimum than whilst trained on its own, mutual learning can facilitate information sharing across networks and allow them to educate one another throughout the training process. This allows knowledge exchange and convergence to better local minima, reducing errors on test data. The proposed consensus dice loss facilitates information convergence between networks during training, improving segmentation performance on the BRATS 2015 and 2018 datasets (Hu et al., 2022).

The present work aims to address challenges in the classification of brain tumors from MRI scans by proposing a novel approach based on sequential deep learning techniques.

3. MATERIAL AND METHODS

3.1. Dataset Description

From 233 patients, the BT data set includes 3064 T1-weighted contrast-enhanced pictures from 3 different types of BTs: meningioma (708 slices), pituitary tumor (930 slices) & glioma (1426 slices). Spanning the years 2005 to 2010, these pictures were obtained at Nanfang Hospital, Guangzhou, China & General Hospital, Tianjin Medical University, China. Using a 512×512 matrix, the imaging technique gave spin-echo weighted pictures with a 0.49×0.49 mm^2 pixel dimension. The pictures display a slice spacing of 6 mm and a slice gap of 1 mm. Furthermore, gadolinium (Gd) was given 0.1 mmol/kg at a speed of 2 ml/s (Cheng, 2017).

3.2. Image Preprocessing

The MRI images under consideration were subdivided into three subsets: 80% for training, 10% for testing & 10% for validation. This partitioning scheme aligns with recommended pedagogical practices to enhance the learning process (Aslan et al., 2021). The dataset consists of three different classes: glioma, pituitary tumor & meningioma. These class-specific sets are employed for subsequent processing. To optimize performance, data resizing and rescaling are imperative. In our approach, resizing is performed to achieve dimensions of 256×256, while rescaling is carried out using a factor of 1/255, as detailed in (Chatterjee & Sujatha, 2023).

Figure 1 illustrates the application of the customized CNN to differentiate MRI data of brain cancers. The MRI scans are preprocessed and separated among training, validation, and test kits. Performance of the CNN model in differentiating the tumors into three groups— glioma, pituitary tumor & meningioma —are judged based on metrics such as accuracy, loss, AUC, recall & precision.

Figure 1. Customized CNN BT classification

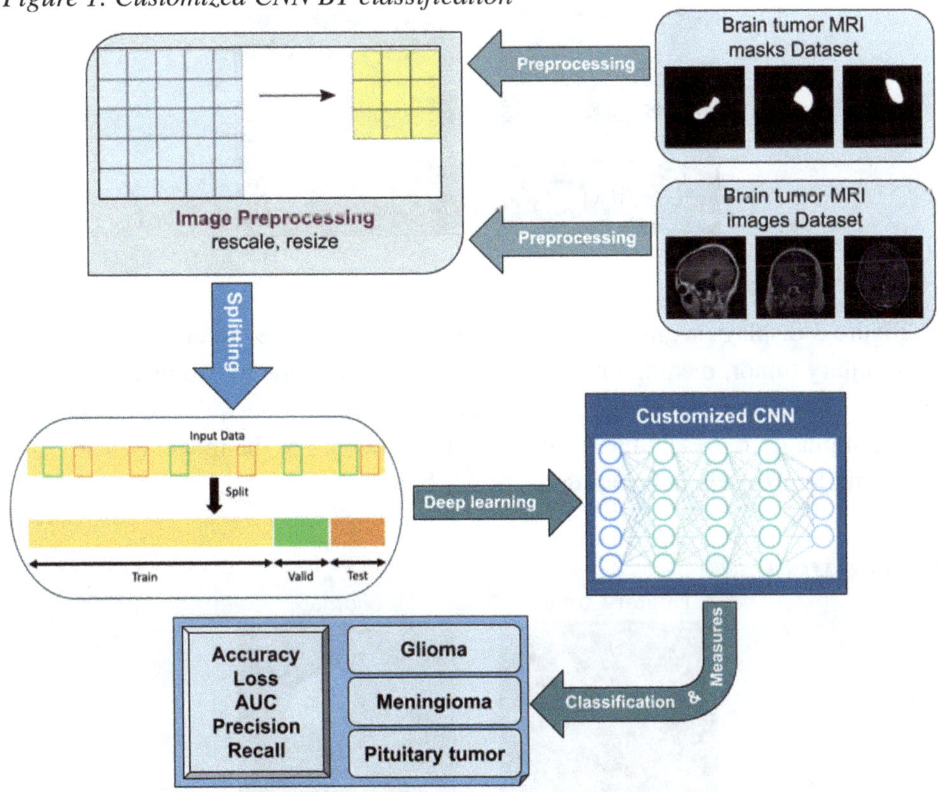

Figure 2 displays two distinct perspectives of gliomas, a meningioma, and a pituitary tumor together alongside their corresponding MRI images. The MRI pictures are utilized for categorizing tumors since they show unique features that correspond to each type of tumor. The pictures show the variations in appearance that a customized CNN would be able to recognize and classify.

Figure 2. MRI Images

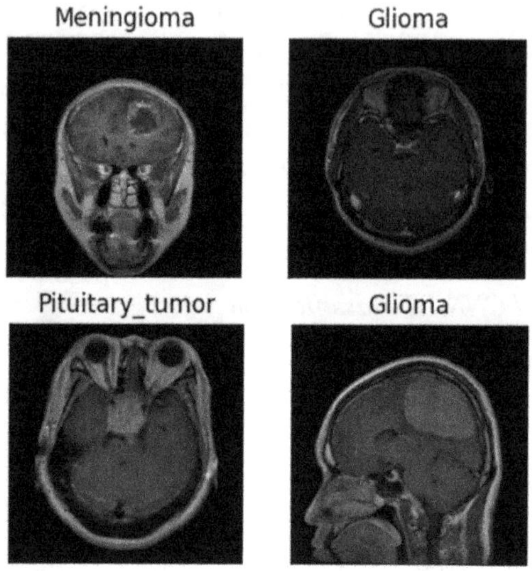

Figure 3 displays segmented MRI masks that emphasize the areas affected by the pituitary tumor, meningioma, and gliomas (which come in two distinct sizes). To train a CNN to precisely detect and categorize these tumors, the white spots in the brain images represent the locations of the lesions. For the model to learn, the masks aid in precisely delineating the tumor borders.

Figure 3. MRI Masks

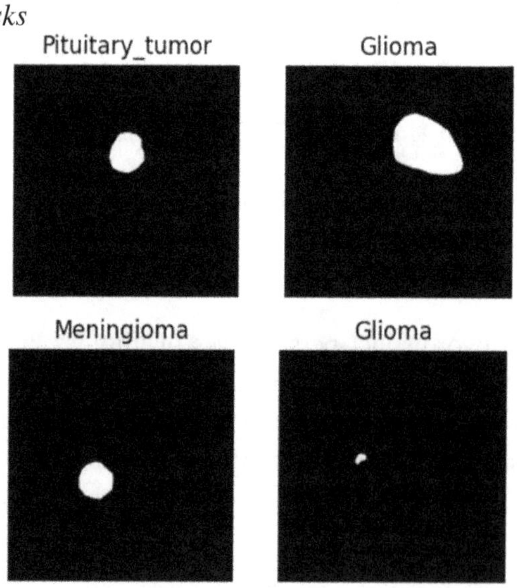

3.3. Fifteen-Layered Architecture

The sequential arrangement of these layers significantly contributes to the precision of the classification process. For a comprehensive understanding of the hyperparameters employed at each stage of the workflow, please refer to Figure 4, which is illustrated using a neural network diagram. It is worth noting that the ReLU activation function is used in the convolutional layer, and a pooling size of 2 is utilized in the max pooling layer. The batch size is 32, the filter size is 64, the kernel size is 3 & the total number of epochs is 20.

The choice between a 15-layer and a 16-layered architecture, or any specific number of layers for that matter, be contingent on various aspects such as the complexity of the dataset, computational resources & the desired trade-off amongst generalization ability & model complexity (Salamat et al., 2021). Here are a few reasons why a 15-layered architecture might be chosen over a 16-layered one:

1. Adding more layers doesn't always lead to better performance. After a certain point, the marginal benefit of adding additional layers diminishes, and the model becomes more prone to overfitting.
2. More computer power and a longer training time are needed by deeper networks. Compared to a 16-layered architecture, a 15-layered one finds a happy medium between training speed and model complexity.
3. Simpler models with fewer layers are easier to interpret and understand.
4. In scenarios where computational resources are limited, a 15-layer architecture is more practical to train & deploy competed to a deeper network.

Different architectures may perform differently varying on the nature of the data & the task being addressed.

Figure 4. 15-layered architecture

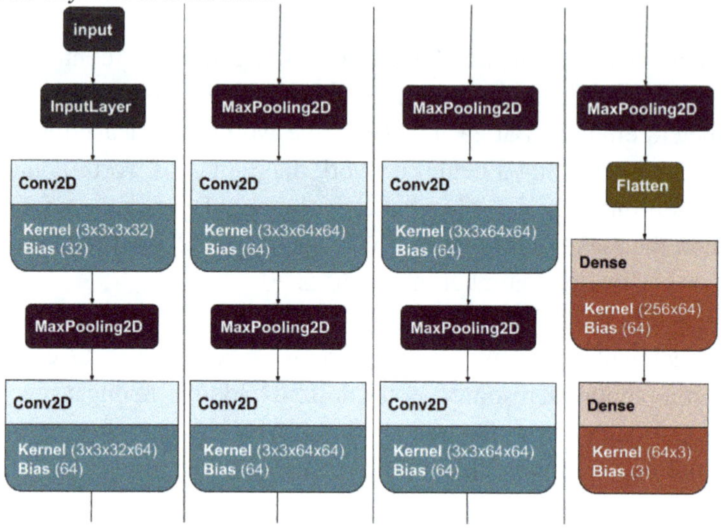

3.3.1. Convolutional Layers (Conv2D)

The initial Conv2D with kernel size 3×3 and filter sizes 32 and 64 are engaged to mine relevant features from the input MRI pictures. These layers capture local patterns within the images. The ReLU activation function is applied after each convolutional layer to establish non-linearity & enhance the model's capacity to understand intricate features.

3.3.2. MaxPooling Layer (MaxPooling2D)

Max-pooling is a well-established technique that extracts the most prominent features from a given input region (Latif et al., 2020). The subsequent max-pooling layers with pooling size 2 × 2 are incorporated to condense the dimensionality of the data & introduce some level of translation invariance. This helps to alleviate the effects of minor shifts in the location of the BT within the MRI image.

3.3.3. Flatten Layer

Flattening transforms the data into a 1D array, preparing it to be passed to the subsequent layer by converting the outcome of the convolutional layers into a single, elongated feature vector. This step connects to the final classification layer, effectively consolidating all pixel information into a linear format for association with the last layer (Reinhold, 2019).

3.3.4. Dense Layer

This fully connected layer is in charge of mapping the input to the correct class. This defines the connectivity pattern between neurons in the present layer and those in the next level, therefore guaranteeing that every neuron in the transitional layer is linked to every neuron in the next layer (Jeong, 2019). Classifying the input image into one of three groups—normal, benign tumor, or malignant tumor—is done by the last dense layers with a kernel size of 64 and 3. Data dimensionality is even lower in the 64-unit second dense layer and more advanced features are gleaned. With softmax activation and three units, the last dense layer outputs the chances of the photograph belonging to every one of the three groups. Figure 5 shows a modeling summary of the created sequential layer.

The selection of hyperparameters, including the number of layers, kernel size, filter size, pooling size, and batch size, was informed by a combination of factors.

- A kernel size of 3×3 was selected based on empirical evidence suggesting that it effectively captures local features in medical image analysis tasks (Niyas et al., 2022).
- The filter sizes 32 and 64 were chosen based on a similar rationale, considering the trade-off between model complexity and capacity to learn complex features (Vrbačič et al., 2022).
- A pooling size of 2×2 was selected to shrink the dimensionality of the data by saving relevant features (Wei, 2022).
- A batch size of 32 was opted based on computational effectiveness considerations & hardware limitations (Xue et al., 2022).

Figure 5. Layer types and parameters in Customized CCN

Model: "*sequential_1*"		
Layer (type)	**Output Shape**	**Param**
conv2d (Conv2D)	(32, 254, 254, 32)	896
max_pooling2d	(MaxPooling2D (32, 127, 127, 32)	0
conv2d_1 (Conv2D)	(32, 125, 125, 64)	18496
max_pooling2d_1	(MaxPooling (32, 62, 62, 64)	0
conv2d_2 (Conv2D)	(32, 60, 60, 64)	36928
max_pooling2d_2	(MaxPooling (32, 30, 30, 64)	0
conv2d_3 (Conv2D)	(32, 28, 28, 64)	36928
xmax_pooling2d_3	(MaxPooling (32, 14, 14, 64)	0
conv2d_4 (Conv2D)	(32, 12, 12, 64)	36928
max_pooling2d_4	(MaxPooling (32, 6, 6, 64)	0
conv2d_5 (Conv2D)	(32, 4, 4, 64)	36928
max_pooling2d_5	(MaxPooling (32, 2, 2, 64)	0
flatten (Flatten)	(32, 256)	0
dense (Dense)	(32, 64)	16448
dense_1 (Dense)	(32, 3)	195
	Total params: 183,747	
	Trainable params: 183,747	
	Non-trainable params: 0	

3.4. Performance Measures

3.4.1. Accuracy

It is a highly intuitive classification metric that is straightforward to comprehend (Humayun & Alsayat, 2022) (Khalil et al., 2021). It represents the ratio of accurate estimation to the entire number of forecasts made (Humayun et al., 2022):

$$Accuracy = \frac{TP + TN}{TP + FP + FN + TN} \tag{1}$$

3.4.2. Precision

It is the fraction of predicted pertinent results to the actual applicable results (Gouda et al., 2022) (Khalil et al., 2022):

$$Precision = \frac{TP}{TP + FP} \quad (2)$$

3.4.3. Recall

It is the fraction of applicably foreseen positive values amid all the genuine positive values. As follows:

$$Recall = \frac{TP}{TP + FN} \quad (3)$$

3.4.4. F1-score

It is a performance measure for classification tasks and is computed as the harmonic mean of exactness & recall (Talukder et al., 2023). It is commonly expressed using:

$$F1 \quad score = \frac{2*(Recall * Precision)}{(Recall + Precision)} \quad (4)$$

4. RESULTS AND DISCUSSIONS

4.1 Various Performance Measures Using Customized CNNs for MRI Images

The accuracy of the CNN model applied to MRI images increases significantly from an initial value of 0.4884 to an impressive 0.9880 over the epochs for the training data. Correspondingly, the loss decreases substantially from 1.0285 to a minimum of 0.0356, indicating improved predictive capabilities and reduced prediction errors, and is represented in Table 1. for training data and Table 2. for testing data.

Table 1. Performance measures over customized CNNs for training data for MRI images

Epochs	Loss	Accuracy	AUC	Precision	Recall	F1-score
1	1.0285	0.4884	0.7687	0.5796	0.4998	0.4767
5	0. 4517	0. 8106	0. 9718	0. 8835	0. 8429	0. 8543
10	0. 1312	0. 9493	0. 9966	0. 9590	0. 9589	0. 9586
15	0. 0792	0. 9703	0. 9990	0. 9736	0. 9751	0. 9741
20	***0. 0356***	***0. 9880***	***0. 9999***	***0. 9957***	***0. 9933***	***0. 9945***

Table 2. Performance measures over customized CNNs for testing data for MRI images

Epochs	Loss	Accuracy	AUC	Precision	Recall	F1-score
1	0. 9096	0. 5590	0. 7552	0. 5517	0. 4847	0. 4569
5	0. 3880	0. 8438	0. 9658	0. 8857	0. 8276	0. 8476
10	0. 2414	0. 9201	0. 9852	0. 9367	0. 9378	0. 9370
15	0. 2033	0. 9444	0. 9930	0. 9472	0. 9518	0. 9493
20	***0. 2096***	***0. 9583***	***0. 9947***	***0. 9580***	***0. 9555***	***0. 9567***

The AUC value that assesses the representation's capability to differentiate between positive and negative cases shows a remarkable increase from 0.7687 to 0.9999 over the course of 20 epochs. This implies that the model efficiently learns to differentiate amongst various image features & it is graphically represented in Figure 6.

Figure 6. AUC vs Epoch

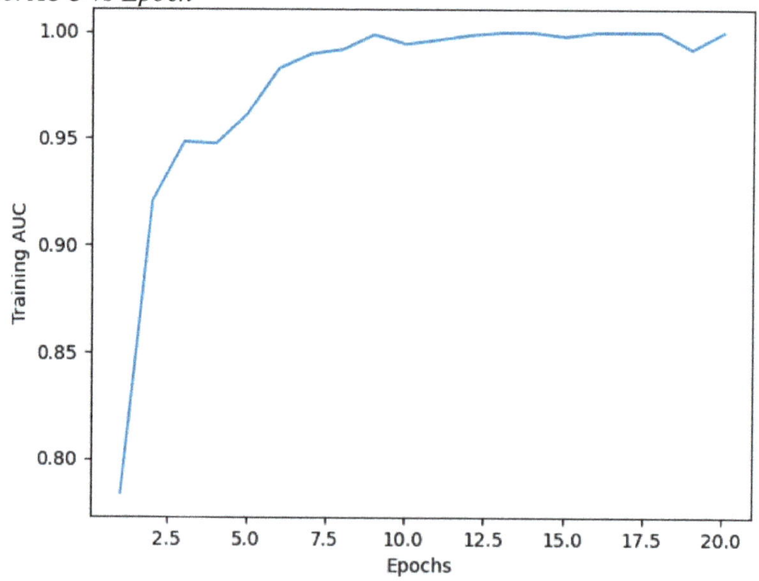

Moreover, when considering precision, recall, and the F1-score, all metrics experience steady improvements across epochs. The precision increases from 0.5796 to an impressive 0.9957, the recall rises from 0.4998 to 0.9933, and the F1-score advances from 0.4767 to 0.9945. These increments show that the prototypical becomes more accurate at recognizing positive occurrences whilst preserving a balance between false negatives & false positives, as indicated in Figure 7.

Figure 7. Precision & Recall vs Epoch

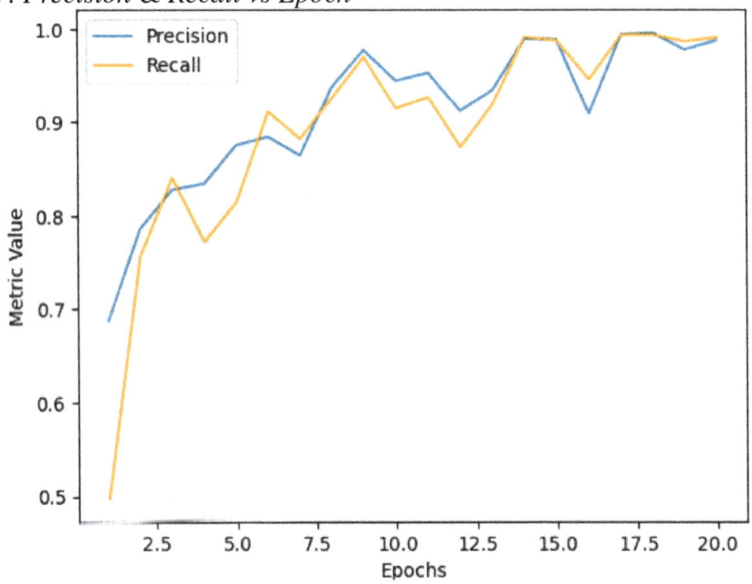

Maximum values in the diagonal of the confusion matrix (CM) indicate that correct classification according to the target is at the optimal level for training data, as presented in Figure 8.

Figure 8. CM For Training Images

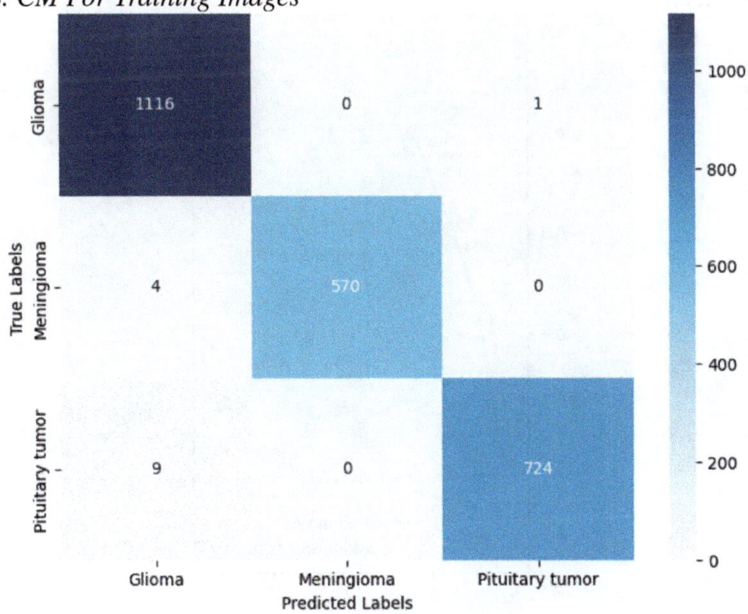

Loss declined for the constructed sequential layer for the BT MRI images, as depicted in Figure 9, and accuracy increased over the epochs, as graphically represented in Figure 10 for training vs. validation data.

Figure 9. Loss vs Epoch

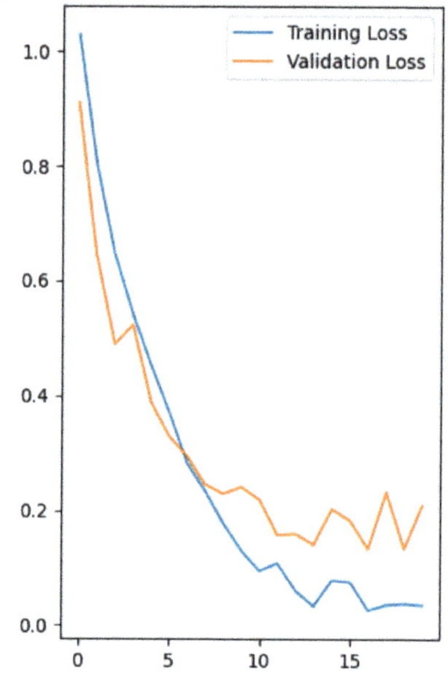

Figure 10. Accuracy vs Epoch

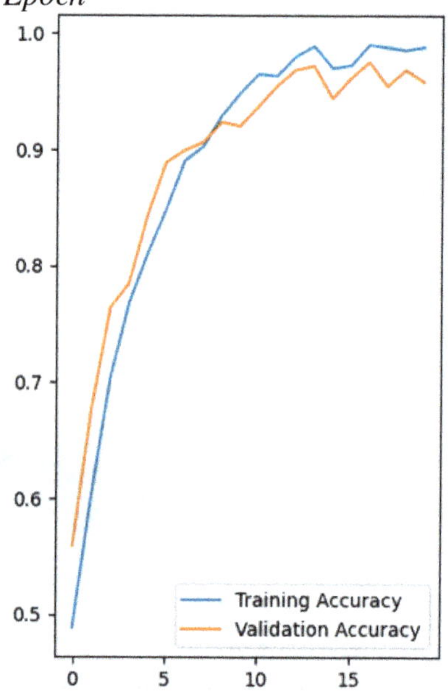

Maximum values in the diagonal of the CM indicate that correct classification according to the target is at the optimal level for testing data, as shown in Figure 11.

Figure 11. CM For Testing Images

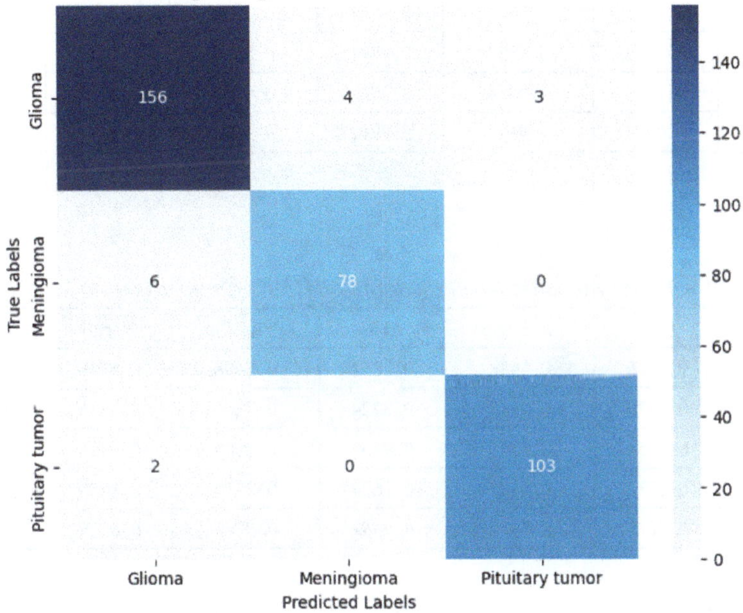

4.2 Various Performance Measures Using Customized CNNs for MRI Masks

Similarly, the customized CNN model applied to MRI masks demonstrates notable improvements. The accuracy improves notably from 0.5536 to 0.9633 over 20 epochs, indicating an enhanced ability to classify mask classes. Concurrently, the loss decreases from 0.9299 to 0.0942, implying a reduction in prediction errors, as given in Table 3. for the training data & Table 4. for the testing data.

Table 3. Performance measures over customized CNNs for training data for MRI images

Epochs	Loss	Accuracy	AUC	Precision	Recall	F1-score
1	0. 9299	0. 5536	0. 7823	0. 5720	0. 5872	0. 5735
5	0. 7108	0. 6625	0. 8851	0. 7555	0. 6814	0. 7004
10	0. 4039	0. 8333	0. 9741	0. 8809	0. 8535	0. 8631
15	0. 1763	0. 9369	0. 9945	0. 9533	0. 9508	0. 9520
20	***0. 0942***	***0. 9633***	***0. 9992***	***0. 9723***	***0. 9798***	***0. 9758***

Table 4. Performance measures over customized CNNs for testing data for MRI images

Epochs	Loss	Accuracy	AUC	Precision	Recall	F1-score
1	0. 8125	0. 5938	0. 7851	0. 5498	0. 5730	0. 5501
5	0. 6120	0. 7188	0. 8724	0. 7265	0. 6815	0. 6905
10	0. 3851	0. 8368	0. 9557	0. 8665	0. 8478	0. 8549
15	0. 2732	0. 9167	0. 9624	0. 8519	0. 8650	0. 8574
20	***0. 2115***	***0. 9410***	***0. 9682***	***0. 8747***	***0. 8929***	***0. 8820***

The AUC values also exhibit a substantial increase from 0.7823 to 0.9992 over the same 20 epochs, signifying the replica's improving capacity to differentiate among diverse mask patterns, as graphically presented in Figure 12.

Figure 12. AUC vs Epoch

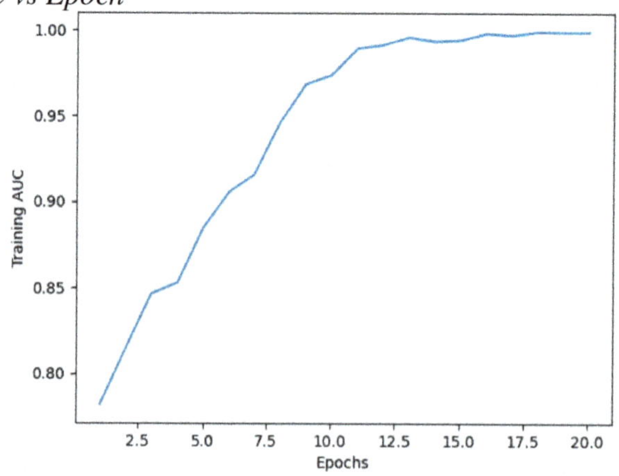

Precision, recall & the F1-score for MRI masks demonstrate consistent improvements. The precision progresses from 0.5720 to 0.9723, the recall increases from 0.5872 to 0.9798, and the F1-score increases from 0.5735 to 0.9758. These advancements highlight the replica's enhanced capacity to recognize positive cases by maintaining an equilibrium between precision and recall, as shown in Figure 13.

Figure 13. Precision & Recall vs Epcoh

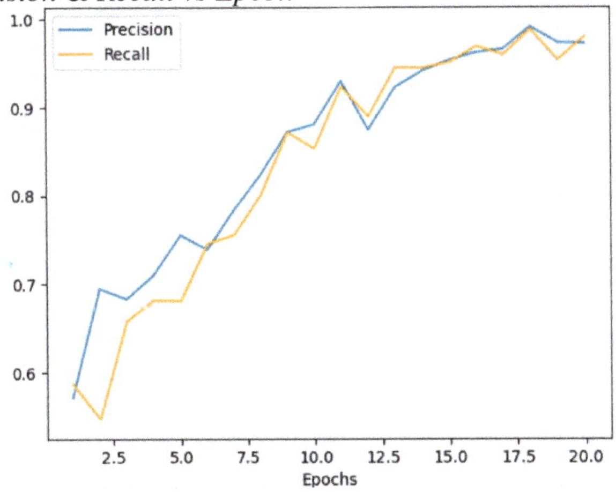

Maximum values in the diagonal of the CM indicate that correct classification according to the target is at the optimal level for testing data, as presented in Figure 14.

Figure 14. CM For Training Images.

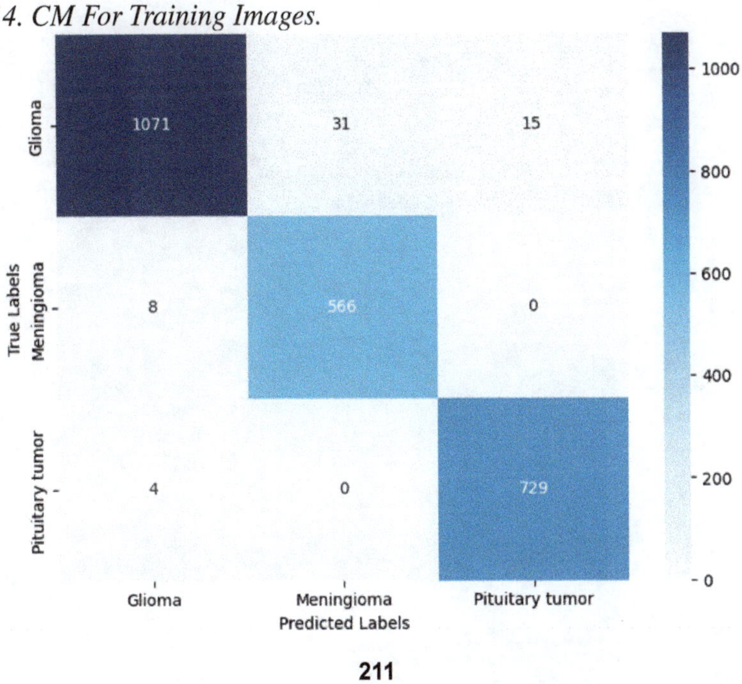

Loss declined for the constructed sequential layer for the BT MRI masks, as depicted in Figure 15, and accuracy increased over the epochs, as graphically represented in Figure 16 for training vs. validation data.

Figure 15. Loss vs Epoch

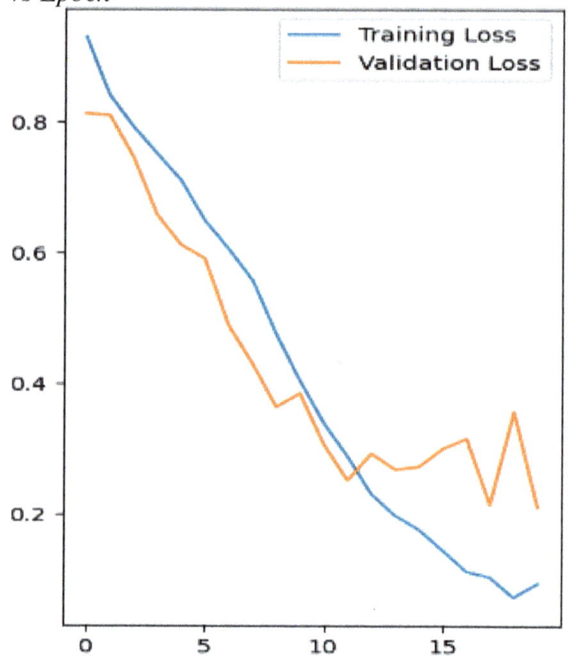

Figure 16. Accuracy vs Epoch

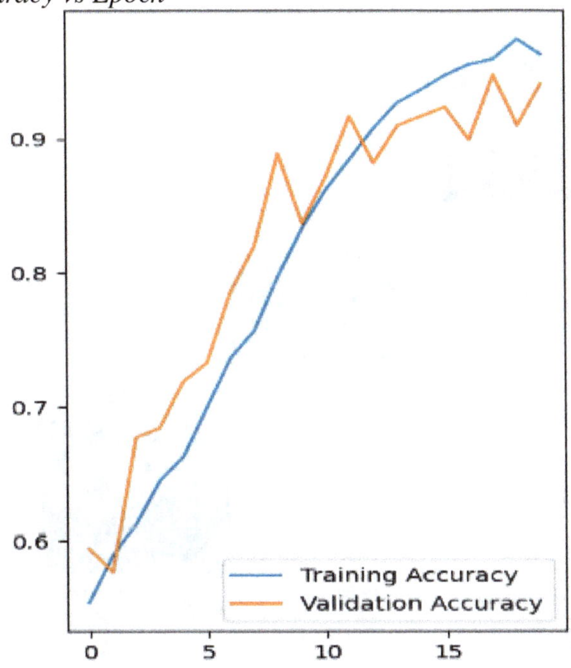

Maximum values in the diagonal of the CM indicate that correct classification according to the target is at the optimal level for testing data, as shown in Figure 17.

Figure 17. Confusion Matrix For Testing Images.

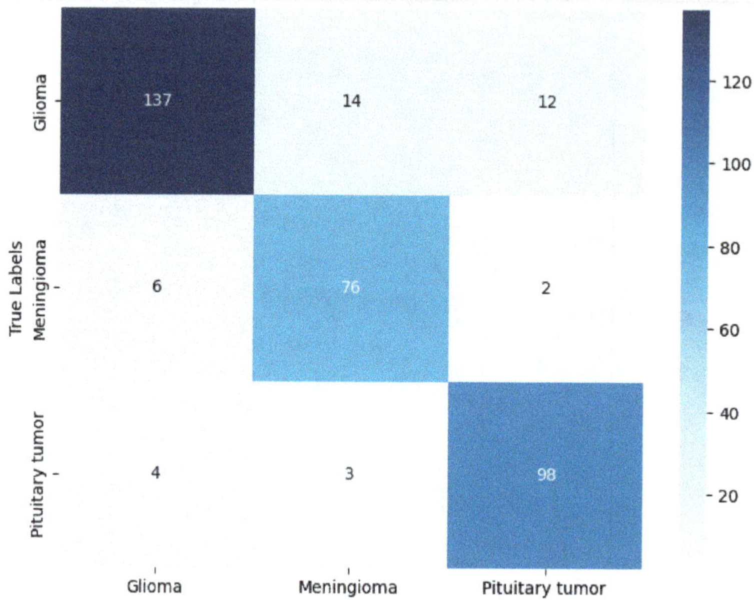

4.3 Result Analysis

Our study involved the application of customized CNNs to analyze MRI pictures and masks, focusing on various performance measures. The CNN models showed remarkable accuracy and loss reduction improvements over epochs, indicating enhanced predictive capabilities and reduced errors. Table 5. presents the comparison between the loss and accuracy.

Table 5. Loss vs Accuracy

	Metrics	Loss	Accuracy	Val_loss	Val_accuracy
Image	VGG16	0.1661	0.9484	1.43	0.5047
	VGG19	0.3875	0.85	0.983	0.5078
Mask	VGG16	0.197	0.9323	1.5	0.4967
	VGG19	0.3843	0.84	0.969	0.5002

✓ **For MRI images:** The CNN model's accuracy increased significantly from 0.4884 to an impressive 0.9880 over 20 epochs, accompanied by a substantial decrease in loss from 1.0285 to 0.0356. This improvement is further supported by the rise in AUC from 0.7687 to 0.9999, indicating the model's ability to effectively differentiate between negative & positive cases. Additionally, metrics such as recall, precision & F1-score experienced steady improvements, with precision increasing from 0.5796 to 0.9957, recall rising from 0.4998 to 0.9933, and the F1 score advancing from 0.4767 to 0.9945.

- ✓ **For MRI masks:** The CNN model demonstrated notable improvements in accuracy, increasing from 0.5536 to 0.9633 over 20 epochs, with a subsequent decline in loss from 0.9299 to 0.0942. AUC values also increased significantly from 0.7823 to 0.9992, indicating improved differentiation among mask patterns. Precision, recall, and the F1 score also showed consistent enhancements, with precision progressing from 0.5720 to 0.9723, recall increasing from 0.5872 to 0.9798, and the F1 score increasing from 0.5735 to 0.9758.
- ✓ The comparison between MRI images and masks revealed similar trends in performance improvements, emphasizing the effectiveness of customized CNN models for medical image analysis. Our proposed approach outperformed existing research efforts, attaining an accuracy of 98.80% assessed to other prior works, showcasing the superior performance and advancements introduced by our research.
- ✓ These results emphasize the capability of customized CNN models in accurate medical image analysis & classification, with implications for various medical applications requiring precise image interpretation.

Comparing MRI images and masks, both exhibit similar trends in their performance improvements. Accuracy increases, and loss decreases as epochs progress, indicating effective learning. AUC values increase substantially, demonstrating improved class differentiation. Precision, recall, and the F1-score all consistently improve, suggesting better classification performance. The numerical trends in performance measures underscore the efficacy of customized CNN models for medical image analysis. The consistent improvement in metrics reflects the model's capability to realize & distinguish meaningful features. These models show promise in medical applications that require accurate image analysis and classification. Table 6. presents a comprehensive comparison between our innovative approach and existing research efforts, and we are delighted to report that our proposed work has demonstrated superior performance. This achievement stands as a testament to the effectiveness and advancements introduced by our research.

Table 6. Performance Comparison

References	Approach	Accuracy	Recall
(Khairandish et al., 2022)	SVM (BRATS 2015 dataset)	67.98%	--
	CNN (BRATS 2015 dataset)	97.84%	--
	Hybrid (BRATS 2015 dataset)	98.67%	--
(Masood et al., 2021)	Custom Mask-RCNN (Figshare brain tumor dataset + Brain MRI Dataset)	98.34%	95.30%
(Masood et al., 2021)	Traditional Mask-RCNN (Brain Tumor Figshare Dataset + BrainTumor Kaggle Dataset)	95.10%	95%
(Rahman & Islam, 2023)	Resize + Grayscale conversion + Augmentation + PDCNN (Binary dataset-I)	97.33%	97.50%
	Resize + Grayscale conversion + Augmentation + PDCNN (Figshare dataset-II)	97.60%	97%
	Resize + Grayscale conversion + Augmentation + PDCNN (Kaggle daset-III)	98.12%	97.75%
(Balasubramanian et al., 2024)	Residual fused Shepherd convolution neural network (RF-ShCNN) (BRATS 2018 dataset + Brain Tumor Figshare Dataset)	94.00%	95%
(Kaur et al., 2023)	CNN (Brain Tumor Image Dataset + Brain Tumor Classification (MRI) Dataset)	97.50%	--
(Alam et al., 2019)	TKFCM (BT MRI Images)	97.5%	97.43%
(Priyadarshini et al., 2024)	ResNet50 (Brain MRI Image)	98.48%	98.50%
(Vasavi et al., 2025)	EfficientNet-DbneAlexnet (Figshare + BRATS 2018 dataset)	92.77 %	90.36%
Proposed Work	***Sequential Deep Learning (Figshare brain tumor dataset)***	***98.80%***	***99.33%***

The figure 18 presents the comparison of the existing works with the proposed work.

Figure 18. Comparative Analysis

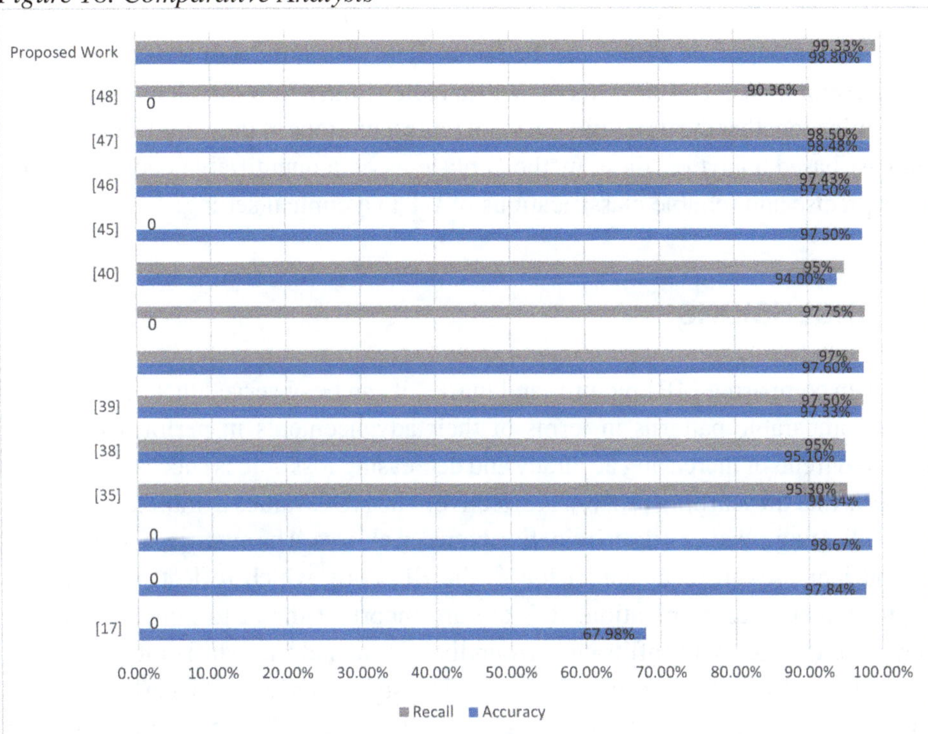

5. BT RESEARCH WITH METAVERSE APPROACH

The classification of BT can be improved by taking advantage of metaverse-based systems that combine shared three-dimensional visualizations with AI tools. Clinical datasets in the form of MRI, CT, histopathological images and genomic information are able to be represented as inter-connected three-dimensional models and not traditional flat slices to aid in making a more accurate assessment of tumour morphology, extent and time course. At the same time, AI algorithms can work in the same spatial context, superimposing predictive results such as risk stratification and salient regions in the imaging, directly onto the three-dimensional image. This integrated presentation makes the interpretation of the results simpler and gives confidence in prescribing system. Such platforms also facilitate institutional-to-institutional collaborative workflows without having to transfer raw patient data. Clinicians and investigators can proceed to virtual world (secure environment) to annotate images, study outcomes and try to iteratively optimize models. Federated learning methodologies allow the training of computational models on the data keeping it local, in consideration to the privacy. Moreover, virtual clinics can create realistic synthetic tumour cases with controlled variations, which reduces the challenges of limited sample sizes and class imbalance that often limit neuro-oncological research. By coming together the three-dimensional representations of the same tumour along with AI-based analytics, these methods place us on a quantifiable course towards more precise and reliable classifications of BT in a clinical setting.

6. CONCLUSIONS

When comparing MRI pictures and masks, it can be observed that both demonstrate comparable patterns in terms of their advancements in performance. The observed trend of increasing accuracy and decreasing loss across successive epochs suggests that the learning process is effective. The AUC values exhibit a significant rise, indicating enhanced discrimination between classes. The outcomes consistently exhibit increases in recall, precision & the F1 score, which reflect performance improvement in categorization. BTs are an important threat to human health as they have the ability to infiltrate surrounding tissue and metastasize to regions of the body far from their original location. The significance of BT early detection for prompt medical treatment has long been recognized. This research proposes a special CNN architecture designed for BT identification and classification from MRI images and masks. The custom proposed CNN model is tested on the BT dataset that involves multiclass tumor images and masks that include three different types of tumors. Surprisingly, the model shows high accuracy, precision, recall, and F1 scores for these varied BT datasets. As part of the upcoming work, the intended architecture will be further extended to include a 3D framework for tumor detection based on using 3D brain MRI images. Investigating deeper optimization techniques, like Grid Search and Bayesian Optimization, for adjusting the CNN model for improved performance will be among the highlights of upcoming work in an attempt to improve accuracy and efficiency even more.

REFERENCES

Aamir, M., Rahman, Z., Abro, W. A., Bhatti, U. A., Dayo, Z. A., & Ishfaq, M. (2023). Brain tumor classification utilizing deep features derived from high-quality regions in MRI images. *Biomedical Signal Processing and Control, 85*, 104988. DOI: 10.1016/j.bspc.2023.104988

Alam, M. S., Rahman, M. M., Hossain, M. A., Islam, M. K., Ahmed, K. M., Ahmed, K. T., Singh, B. C., & Miah, M. S. (2019). Automatic human brain tumor detection in MRI image using template-based K means and improved fuzzy C means clustering algorithm. *Big Data and Cognitive Computing, 3*(2), 27. DOI: 10.3390/bdcc3020027

Alamin Talukder, M., Islam, M., Ashraf Uddin, M., Akhter, A., Alamgir Jalil Pramanik, M., Aryal, S., ... & Moni, M. A. (2023). An efficient deep learning model to categorize brain tumor using reconstruction and fine-tuning. arXiv e-prints, arXiv-2305.

Asif, S., Zhao, M., Chen, X., & Zhu, Y. (2023). BMRI-NET: A Deep Stacked Ensemble Model for Multi-class Brain Tumor Classification from MRI Images. *Interdisciplinary Sciences, Computational Life Sciences, 15*(3), 1–16. DOI: 10.1007/s12539-023-00571-1 PMID: 37171681

Aslan, M. F., Unlersen, M. F., Sabanci, K., & Durdu, A. (2021). CNN-based transfer learning–BiLSTM network: A novel approach for COVID-19 infection detection. *Applied Soft Computing, 98*, 106912. DOI: 10.1016/j.asoc.2020.106912 PMID: 33230395

Atmakuri, M. K., Ram, A. G., & Prasad, V. V. K. D. V. (2023). Reliable image metrics-based brain tumor analysis using sensor deep learning technologies. *Measurement. Sensors, 29*, 100864. DOI: 10.1016/j.measen.2023.100864

Balasubramanian, S., Mandala, J., Rao, T. V. M., & Misra, A. (2024). RF-ShCNN: A combination of two deep models for tumor detection in brain using MRI. *Biomedical Signal Processing and Control, 88*, 105656. DOI: 10.1016/j.bspc.2023.105656

Chatterjee, J. M., & Sujatha, R. (2023). Detection of COVID-19 Cases from X-ray and CT Images Using Transfer Learning and Deep Convolution Neural Networks. In *Artificial Intelligence in Medical Virology* (pp. 81–98). Springer Nature Singapore. DOI: 10.1007/978-981-99-0369-6_6

Cheng, J. (2017). brain tumor dataset. figshare. Dataset. https://doi.org/DOI: 10.6084/m9.figshare.1512427.v5

Farajzadeh, N., Sadeghzadeh, N., & Hashemzadeh, M. (2023). Brain tumor segmentation and classification on MRI via deep hybrid representation learning. *Expert Systems with Applications*, *224*, 119963. DOI: 10.1016/j.eswa.2023.119963

Gouda, W., Almurafeh, M., Humayun, M., & Jhanjhi, N. Z. (2022, February). Detection of COVID-19 based on chest X-rays using deep learning. In Healthcare (Vol. 10, No. 2, p. 343). MDPI.

Hu, J., Gu, X., & Gu, X. (2022). Mutual ensemble learning for brain tumor segmentation. *Neurocomputing*, *504*, 68–81. DOI: 10.1016/j.neucom.2022.06.058

Humayun, M., & Alsayat, A. (2022). Prediction Model for Coronavirus Pandemic Using Deep Learning. *Computer Systems Science and Engineering*, *40*(3), 947–961. DOI: 10.32604/csse.2022.019288

Humayun, M., Sujatha, R., Almuayqil, S. N., & Jhanjhi, N. Z. (2022, June). A transfer learning approach with a convolutional neural network for the classification of lung carcinoma. In Healthcare (Vol. 10, No. 6, p. 1058). MDPI. DOI: 10.3390/healthcare10061058

Jeong, J. The most intuitive and easiest guide for CNN, The Medium (2019) [cited 2022Aug14]. Available from: https://towardsdatascience.com/the-most-intuitive-and-easiest-guide-for-convolutional-neural-network-3607be47480#:w:text%C2%BCFlattening%20is%20converting%20the%20data

Kaur, M., Mann, P., Rani, R., Jaiswal, G., Sharma, A., & Kumar, R. (2023, March). MRI Image Segmentation using Deep Learning for Brain Tumor Detection. In 2023 10th International Conference on Computing for Sustainable Global Development (INDIACom) (pp. 939-944). IEEE.

Khairandish, M. O., Sharma, M., Jain, V., Chatterjee, J. M., & Jhanjhi, N. Z. (2022). A hybrid CNN-SVM threshold segmentation approach for tumor detection and classification of MRI brain images. *Ingénierie et Recherche Biomédicale : IRBM = Biomedical Engineering and Research*, *43*(4), 290–299. DOI: 10.1016/j.irbm.2021.06.003

Khalil, M. I., Humayun, M., Jhanjhi, N. Z., Talib, M. N., & Tabbakh, T. A. (2021). Multi-class segmentation of organ at risk from abdominal CT images: A deep learning approach. In Intelligent Computing and Innovation on Data Science [Springer Singapore.]. *Proceedings of ICTIDS*, *2021*, 425–434.

Khalil, M. I., Tehsin, S., Humayun, M., Jhanjhi, N. Z., & AlZain, M. A. (2022). Multi-Scale Network for Thoracic Organs Segmentation. *Computers, Materials & Continua*, *70*(2).

Kumar, K. A., Prasad, A. Y., & Metan, J. (2022). A hybrid deep CNN-Cov-19-Res-Net Transfer learning architype for an enhanced Brain tumor Detection and Classification scheme in medical image processing. *Biomedical Signal Processing and Control, 76*, 103631. DOI: 10.1016/j.bspc.2022.103631

Kumar, P. S., Sakthivel, V. P., Raju, M., & Satya, P. D. (2023). Brain tumor segmentation of the FLAIR MRI images using novel ResUnet. *Biomedical Signal Processing and Control, 82*, 104586. DOI: 10.1016/j.bspc.2023.104586

Latif, S., Usman, M., Manzoor, S., Iqbal, W., Qadir, J., Tyson, G., Castro, I., Razi, A., Boulos, M. N. K., Weller, A., & Crowcroft, J. (2020). Leveraging data science to combat COVID-19: A comprehensive review. *IEEE Transactions on Artificial Intelligence, 1*(1), 85–103. DOI: 10.1109/TAI.2020.3020521 PMID: 37982070

Masood, M., Nazir, T., Nawaz, M., Javed, A., Iqbal, M., & Mehmood, A. (2021). Brain tumor localization and segmentation using mask RCNN. *Frontiers of Computer Science, 15*(6), 156338. DOI: 10.1007/s11704-020-0105-y

Masood, M., Nazir, T., Nawaz, M., Mehmood, A., Rashid, J., Kwon, H. Y., Mahmood, T., & Hussain, A. (2021). A novel deep learning method for recognition and classification of brain tumors from MRI images. *Diagnostics (Basel), 11*(5), 744. DOI: 10.3390/diagnostics11050744 PMID: 33919358

Mehnatkesh, H., Jalali, S. M. J., Khosravi, A., & Nahavandi, S. (2023). An intelligent driven deep residual learning framework for brain tumor classification using MRI images. *Expert Systems with Applications, 213*, 119087. DOI: 10.1016/j.eswa.2022.119087

Mohsen, H., El-Dahshan, E. S. A., El-Horbaty, E. S. M., & Salem, A. B. M. (2018). Classification using deep learning neural networks for brain tumors. *Future Computing and Informatics Journal, 3*(1), 68–71. DOI: 10.1016/j.fcij.2017.12.001

Mundru, Y., Yogi, M. K., & Chatterjee, J. M. (2023). Application of Deep-Q learning in personalized health care Internet of Things ecosystem. In *Deep Learning in Personalized Healthcare and Decision Support* (pp. 39–47). Academic Press. DOI: 10.1016/B978-0-443-19413-9.00024-2

Naser, M. A., & Deen, M. J. (2020). Brain tumor segmentation and grading of lower-grade glioma using deep learning in MRI images. *Computers in Biology and Medicine, 121*, 103758. DOI: 10.1016/j.compbiomed.2020.103758 PMID: 32568668

Niyas, S., Pawan, S. J., Kumar, M. A., & Rajan, J. (2022). Medical image segmentation with 3D convolutional neural networks: A survey. *Neurocomputing, 493*, 397–413. DOI: 10.1016/j.neucom.2022.04.065

Pedada, K. R., Rao, B., Patro, K. K., Allam, J. P., Jamjoom, M. M., & Samee, N. A. (2023). A novel approach for brain tumor detection using deep learning based technique. *Biomedical Signal Processing and Control, 82*, 104549. DOI: 10.1016/j.bspc.2022.104549

Priyadarshini, P., Kanungo, P., & Kar, T. (2024). Multigrade brain tumor classification in MRI images using Fine tuned efficientnet. e-Prime-Advances in Electrical Engineering. *Electronics and Energy*, *8*, 100498.

Rahman, T., & Islam, M. S. (2023). MRI brain tumor detection and classification using parallel deep convolutional neural networks. *Measurement. Sensors*, *26*, 100694. DOI: 10.1016/j.measen.2023.100694

Rahman, T., & Islam, M. S. (2023). MRI brain tumor detection and classification using parallel deep convolutional neural networks. *Measurement. Sensors*, *26*, 100694. DOI: 10.1016/j.measen.2023.100694

Reinhold, J. Dropout on convolutional layers is weird. Medium, Data Science (2019) [cited 2022Aug14]. Available from: https://towardsdatascience.com/dropout-on-convolutional-layers-is-weird-5c6ab14f19b2

Saba, T., Mohamed, A. S., El-Affendi, M., Amin, J., & Sharif, M. (2020). Brain tumor detection using fusion of hand crafted and deep learning features. *Cognitive Systems Research*, *59*, 221–230. DOI: 10.1016/j.cogsys.2019.09.007

Salamat, N., Missen, M. M. S., & Surya Prasath, V. B. (2021). Recent developments in computational color image denoising with PDEs to deep learning: A review. *Artificial Intelligence Review*, *54*(8), 6245–6276. DOI: 10.1007/s10462-021-09977-z

Sharma, A. K., Nandal, A., Dhaka, A., Zhou, L., Alhudhaif, A., Alenezi, F., & Polat, K. (2023). Brain tumor classification using the modified ResNet50 model based on transfer learning. *Biomedical Signal Processing and Control, 86*, 105299. DOI: 10.1016/j.bspc.2023.105299

Sujatha, R., Chatterjee, J. M., Angelopoulou, A., Kapetanios, E., Srinivasu, P. N., & Hemanth, D. J. (2023). A transfer learning-based system for grading breast invasive ductal carcinoma. *IET Image Processing*, *17*(7), 1979–1990. DOI: 10.1049/ipr2.12660

Swain, M., Kisan, S., Chatterjee, J. M., Supramaniam, M., Mohanty, S. N., Jhanjhi, N. Z., & Abdullah, A. (2020). Hybridized machine learning based fractal analysis techniques for breast cancer classification. *International Journal of Advanced Computer Science and Applications*, *11*(10), 179–184. DOI: 10.14569/IJACSA.2020.0111024

Talukder, M. A., Islam, M. M., Uddin, M. A., Akhter, A., Pramanik, M. A. J., Aryal, S., Almoyad, M. A. A., Hasan, K. F., & Moni, M. A. (2023). An efficient deep learning model to categorize brain tumor using reconstruction and fine-tuning. *Expert Systems with Applications*, *230*, 120534. DOI: 10.1016/j.eswa.2023.120534

Tandel, G. S., Tiwari, A., & Kakde, O. G. (2021). Performance optimization of deep learning models using majority voting algorithm for brain tumor classification. *Computers in Biology and Medicine*, *135*, 104564. DOI: 10.1016/j.compbiomed.2021.104564 PMID: 34217980

Vankdothu, R., & Hameed, M. A. (2022). Brain tumor segmentation of MR images using SVM and fuzzy classifier in machine learning. *Measurement. Sensors*, *24*, 100440. DOI: 10.1016/j.measen.2022.100440

Vasavi, G., Rani, V. V., Ponnada, S., & Jyothi, S. (2025). A hybrid EfficientNet-DbneAlexnet for brain tumor detection using MRI images. *Computational Biology and Chemistry*, *115*, 108279. DOI: 10.1016/j.compbiolchem.2024.108279 PMID: 39631224

Vrbačič, G., Pečnik, Š., & Podgorelec, V. (2022). Hyper-parameter optimization of convolutional neural networks for classifying COVID-19 X-ray images. *Computer Science and Information Systems*, *19*(1), 327–352. DOI: 10.2298/CSIS210209056V

Wei, D. (2022). An Online Extraction Algorithm for Image Feature Information Based on Convolutional Neural Network. *Mobile Information Systems*, *2022*, 1–11. Advance online publication. DOI: 10.1155/2022/1606438

Xue, Z., Liang, J., Song, G., Zong, Z., Chen, L., Liu, Y., & Luo, P. (2022). Large-batch optimization for dense visual predictions. *Advances in Neural Information Processing Systems*, •••, 1.

Zulfiqar, F., Bajwa, U. I., & Mehmood, Y. (2023). Multiclass classification of brain tumor types from MR images using EfficientNets. *Biomedical Signal Processing and Control*, *84*, 104777. DOI: 10.1016/j.bspc.2023.104777

Chapter 8

Human-Centric Educational Revolution in the Metaverse: Integrating AI, IoT, and AR for Inclusive Learning

Amit Sagu
http://orcid.org/0000-0002-0129-7665
MVN University, Palwal, India

Susheel Kumar
http://orcid.org/0009-0001-0783-3422
MVN University, Palwal, India

Sumit Kumar
http://orcid.org/0009-0007-3877-0907
MVN University, Palwal, India

Shashi Kant Singh
MVN University, Palwal, India

ABSTRACT

Metaverse is making education more interesting and interactive by making learning spaces that are more like real life. Metaverse education is different from traditional e-learning since it uses AI, IoT, and augmented and virtual reality (AR/VR) to make classrooms which are more welcoming, interesting, and available to all students. This chapter looks at how these technologies can work together and change how teachers teach and students learn. The chapter is about human-centered design that

DOI: 10.4018/979-8-3373-6721-7.ch008

means making learning systems flexible enough to meet the needs of each student, make it easier for students with disabilities to learn, and give everyone the same chances to learn, no matter where they live. IoT devices, AI-driven personalization, and immersive simulations can enhance the learning experience and student outcomes, as demonstrated by real-world use cases like smart classrooms and AR-based campus navigation. This chapter offers a road map for developing an inclusive and democratized metaverse for education by combining case studies, current trends, and future directions.

1. INTRODUCTION

Advances in immersive technologies, artificial intelligence (AI), and the Internet of Things (IoT) are driving a paradigm shift in the educational landscape. The idea of the metaverse a persistent, immersive, and networked digital environment where students and teachers engage through avatars, simulations, and intelligent systems is central to this change (Lee et al., 2021). Unlike conventional e learning infrastructures that rely on fixed materials and web conferencing tools, the metaverse integrates the convergence of augmented reality (AR), virtual reality (VR), AI-driven personalized learning, IoT-driven smart learning spaces, and blockchain is secured credentialing in an integrated system. Such integration allows for the development of human centric learning spaces in which inclusivity, accessibility, and flexibility become integral parts of the design of learning. Learning engagement can be modeled as a function of interactivity, immersion, and personalization:

$$E = \alpha I + \beta M + \gamma P$$

Where E is engagement, I is interactivity, M is immersion, and P is personalization, with α, β, γ as weighting factors determined empirically.

Inclusivity and accessibility are of utmost importance. Traditional learning spaces and virtual learning spaces often leave out students with disabilities, students from disadvantaged socioeconomic statuses, or learners from isolated regions (Dwivedi et al., 2022). On the contrary, the educational metaverse offers features such as real-time language translation, voice-controlled avatars, haptic responses, and virtual reality navigation, allowing for fair play for varied learners. Such technologies are instrumental in narrowing the gap in digital opportunity, subject to overcoming infrastructural and resource limitations (Ning et al., 2021).

In spite of the proliferation of Massive Open Online Courses (MOOCs) and virtual learning platforms, existing infrastructure is constrained by low engagement, lack of customization, and limited availability (Veletsianos & Houlden, 2019). The metaverse can eliminate these shortcomings through real-time adaptive and immersive learning procedures for enhancing higher learning outcomes. For example, reinforcement learning models are capable of adapting difficulty in real-time, while Internet of Things (IoT) wearables are capable of monitoring engagement and stress indicators for the AI tutor to shift learning approaches dynamically (Huang et al., 2022).

The goal of this chapter is to:

1. Explain what the metaverse means in education and discuss the technology that makes it possible.
2. Ensure that everyone can use it and that everyone is involved in the design.
3. Identify the issues with current e-learning systems and demonstrate how the metaverse can address them.
4. Provide a plan for creating educational metaverses that focus on people, ethics, and the environment.

This chapter argues that the educational metaverse goes beyond just a technological improvement. It combines recent research, mathematical modeling, and case studies. It represents a shift towards more human-centered learning, which will help students prepare for jobs and life in our digital world.

1.1. Background of the Metaverse in Education

The metaverse, first introduced in Stephenson's (1992) novel Snow Crash, is now becoming a technological reality. It can be defined as an extended reality (XR) ecosystem that combines physical and digital spaces through continuous, immersive environments. In education, the metaverse goes beyond just replicating physical classrooms. It creates dynamic learning environments where students can collaborate, explore, and experiment in ways that traditional systems do not allow.

The metaverse can be conceptualized as a graph:

$$G = (V, E)$$

Where V represents entities such as avatars, digital objects, or classrooms, and E represents interactions such as communication, collaboration, or resource exchange. Unlike conventional e-learning, where interactions are mostly linear, such as lectures leading to assignments and then assessments, the metaverse encourages non-linear, multi-dimensional interactions. Real-time data from IoT devices and adaptive AI agents improve this experience (Duan et al., 2021).

The metaverse is based on three waves of digital learning. In the 1980s, the first wave of computer-assisted instruction was all about practice exercises that were driven by software. The second wave, which included web-based e-learning and MOOCs, made things more accessible but relied a lot on video-based content that didn't change. The third wave, which is the metaverse, brings in immersive simulations, AI tutors, and classrooms that connect to the Internet of Things. This method allows for experiential and collaborative learning (Kye et al., 2021).

It has a lot of potential, as shown by case studies. Stanford University has taught whole courses in VR, which has led to clear improvements in retention and engagement (Bailenson, 2022). Teachers can use Roblox Education to make problem-solving environments that are fun and work together. The University of Tokyo has also made AR-based tools for students with disabilities to help them find their way around campus. These examples highlight the educational metaverse's ability to combine inclusivity, immersion, and innovation.

Still, there are problems that need to be fixed. If everyone doesn't have equal access to devices and high-speed networks, the digital divide could get bigger. Ethical concerns, including data privacy, cybersecurity, and algorithmic fairness, necessitate attention (Dwivedi et al., 2022). The metaverse's background in education shows how it could change things and how important it is to use design principles that focus on people.

1.2. Why Inclusivity and Accessibility Matter

Despite educational rights being fundamental, students are often discriminated against by formal systems due to geography, income, or disabilities (UNESCO, 2020). Inclusivity entails providing equitable educational chances to every learner, irrespective of background or capability. The Activating of thoughtful removal of barriers is what we mean by Developing Inclusive Systems in the Metaverse

For instance, haptic feedback devices enable tactile representation of graphical data to blind students. Students who are multilingual or deaf are served from real-time translation and captioning (Zhang et al., 2022). Accessibility is also exemplified mathematically as the optimization of several variables:

$$\mathrm{A}(x) = \sum_{i=0}^{n} \alpha_i f_i(x)$$

Where $f_i(x)$ represents accessibility features (visual aids, haptic feedback, NLP tools), and α_i represents weights based on learner requirements. Maximizing $\mathrm{A}(x)$ ensures optimal support for diverse learners.

Equity considers disparities across the globe. The Metaverse can help students in less developed areas by giving them better access to quality education (Ning et al., 2021). Achieving this goal, however, involves significant infrastructure, cost, and digital literacy challenges.

Thus, access, and inclusivity are not optional considerations. They are fundamental elements of design. The Metaverse has the potential to change the inequitable distribution of educational resources from being a privilege to a fundamental right and thereby strengthen its purpose as a means of social equity.

1.3. Gap in Current Virtual Learning Systems

Although there are several educational opportunities made available through MOOCs or e-learning portals, there remains room for improvement particularly regarding;

1. Integration in learning: Many e-learning portals are simply passive by which engagement is only through video lectures, leading to disengagement and boredom. (Veletsianos & Houlden, 2019)
2. Adaptation in education: Simple student-learning adaptations are through recommendation systems (Huang et al., 2022)
3. Underrepresented learners: Most educational platforms are not built with students with learning esc disabilities in mind.
4. Equity in education: Most learners remain disadvantaged due to lack of devices and internet support.
5. Integration with other learners: Electronic discussions, in comparison, sorely lack the integration or engagement found in a traditional classroom (Krause et al., 2019)

The shortfalls of the traditional classroom are supported by the educational metaverse. VR/AR can enhance immersion through the use of digital and virtual worlds, personal learning through Artificial Intelligence and varied modalities, collaboration through Avatars learners can work in shared environments. Wearable Internet of Things devices can track levels of stress and engagement. Through this, AI instructors can adapt in the moment in response to changes in student response.

To this point, the education systems that are in use have increased equity by providing access to wide-ranging opportunities. However, these systems have not been particularly effective in providing quality engagement. The metaverse offers the opportunity to change the extent to which the learning environments are human centric, and inclusive.

1.4. Chapter Objectives

The objectives of this chapter are:

1. To define the metaverse in education and explore its technological ecosystem.
2. To explore how AI, IoT, and AR/VR increase accessibility and engagement for diverse learners.
3. To analyze practical examples of metaverse education.
4. To address the ongoing issues of inclusivity, ethics, security, and data privacy.
5. To formulate a set of solutions that compromise democratized and sustainable educational metaverse.

By achieving these objectives, the chapter contributes to the growing literature on digital education, emphasizing that the metaverse is not merely about technological novelty but about redefining education around human needs.

2. UNDERSTANDING THE EDUCATIONAL METAVERSE

The educational metaverse is a significant development in digital learning environments. It combines cloud infrastructures, blockchain, IoT, immersive technologies, and artificial intelligence (AI) to create dynamic, interactive, and human-centered learning environments. Massive open online courses (MOOCs) and traditional e-learning are mostly limited to passive content consumption and two-dimensional interfaces. In contrast, the metaverse offers a vast ecosystem in which educators and students coexist in persistent, interactive, multisensory digital realities. In these settings, students build, cooperate, and experiment in ways that mimic or expand on interactions in the real world in addition to consuming knowledge (Mystakidis, 2022).

2.1. Definition and Scope of the Metaverse in Learning

The metaverse in education encompasses a broad application, ranging from immersive classrooms that either replicate or reimagine on-ground spaces, to personalized AI tutors that are capable of tailoring their interaction to dynamically suit a learner's strengths and weaknesses: for example, when IoT-enabled ecosystems link a student's physiological and cognitive state with the virtual learning tools available to them, digital classrooms may be able to adapt to, and respond to, real time conditions.

The global reach of the metaverse is one of its fundamental features. In addition to providing students from various cultural and geographic backgrounds with the opportunity to collaborate in real time on group projects, virtual labs, and shared experiments, cross-border collaboration enables students to collaborate from any location. For example, engineering students from Brazil, Germany, and India could collaborate on problems that call for a variety of disciplinary viewpoints in a metaverse virtual laboratory. This is not only a sensible response to the logistical and economic barriers to mobility between regions, but an equitable opportunity to enable international academic-based exchange (Duan et al., 2021).

2.2. Key Components

The metaverse rests upon several interconnected technological pillars, each of which contributes to its inclusivity, adaptability, and interactivity.

2.2.1. Virtual and Augmented Reality (VR/AR)

Virtual reality (VR) produces worlds that are immersive and disconnect learners from their actual reality, whereas augmented reality (AR) fills in or overlays information and interactivity in phenomenological space. Technology practically provides learners with embodied learning experiences in which abstract concepts including (but not limited to) molecular structures in chemistry and three-dimensional vector spaces in mathematics are experienced in June.

The success or performance of using VR/AR in education depends on the amount of latency, which mathematically can be described as:

$$L_{total} = L_{render} + L_{network} + L_{device}$$

Where L_{render} is the rendering latency, $L_{network}$ the network transmission delay, and L_{device} the hardware-specific processing time. Minimizing L_{total} is crucial for preventing motion sickness and ensuring seamless immersion. Advanced solutions, such as edge computing and 5G-enabled networks, play a pivotal role in reducing delays, thereby enabling smooth educational simulations (Moro Visconti & Piroli, 2023).

2.2.2. Artificial Intelligence (AI)

The AI capabilities classified within the educational metaverse promotes personalization. AI can provide personalized curricula considering students' cognitive levels and their paces through adaptive learning models, intelligent tutoring systems, and natural language processing (NLP).

Reinforcement learning (RL) frameworks are especially relevant in adaptive education. In RL, the learning agent selects an action a in a given state s to maximize the expected cumulative reward:

$$\pi^*(s) = \arg \max_{a} \mathrm{E}\left[\sum_{t=0}^{\infty} \gamma^t R(s_t, a_t)\right]$$

Here, $\pi^*(s)$ represents the optimal policy, $R\left(s_{t,}\ a_t\right)$ denotes the reward function measuring incremental learning progress, and γ is the discount factor controlling the weight of future outcomes. Such models enable intelligent tutors to dynamically adjust learning complexity, delivering content that is neither too easy nor too overwhelming for the learner (Chen et al., 2020).

2.2.3. Internet of Things (IoT)

The Internet of Things (IoT) is situated at the intersection of the physical and virtual realities of education. Wearable technologies, such as EEG headbands, smart watches, or augmented reality (AR) glasses, combine data in real time from the physical and behavioral realm (e.g., heart rate, attention span, emotional responses). Each one of these signals can be include in adaptive learning and instruction by analyzing and responding to them as engagement data.

The delivery of multiple heterogeneous sensor data can be modeled using a sensor fusion equation to characterize what is happening in the learning environment:

$$S_{\text{combined}} = \sum_{i=1}^{n} w_i S_i$$

Where S_i represents the reading from the ith sensor and w_i is the corresponding weight denoting its accuracy or reliability. This formulation enables a holistic assessment of a learner's state, ensuring that instructional interventions are personalized not only to cognitive needs but also to physical well-being (Sharma et al., 2022).

2.2.4. Blockchain

Blockchain supports trust and transparency in learning credentials in the metaverse. It promises academic certificates, records, and even micro-credentials can be stored and verified without reliance on a central authority, using distributed ledger technology. Smart contracts enable more than just storage; they enhance the grading and assessment verification process while reducing overhead, and maintain fairness.

And, blockchain provides portability for academic mobility through universally verifiable certificates. As an example, there would be no bureaucratic delays in validating certificates earned in a metaverse-based course in India at an institution in Europe or North America (Tapscott & Tapscott, 2018).

The comprehensive framework of the educational metaverse synthesizes AI, IoT, blockchain, AR/VR, and cloud computing into one intelligent ecosystem as shown in Figure 1.

Figure 1. Layered system architecture of the educational metaverse

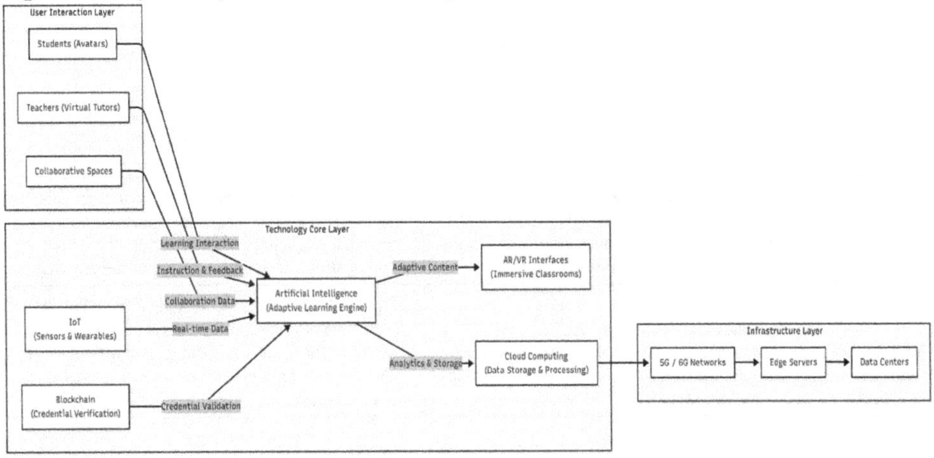

2.2.5. Cloud Computing

The cloud infrastructures support the metaverse's computational and storage needs. Cloud platforms allow real-time rendering, AI-driven analytics, and continuous storage to support immersive classrooms. Edge computing functions in concert with cloud computing as it processes everywhere by moving the processing as close as possible to the end-user by leveraging only the most local resource available. One very broad purpose of edge computing is to reduce latency to enable seamless learning experiences in augmented reality (AR) and virtual reality (VR) based learning environments. Together, cloud computing and edge computing form the technological infrastructure that enables the metaverse to function at scale (Dwivedi et al., 2022).

2.3. Comparison with Traditional E-learning and MOOCs

Table 1 illustrates the differences between the metaverse and conventional e-learning systems highlight the revolutionary potential of the former.

Table 1. Comparative Analysis of Traditional E-learning and Educational Metaverse Environments

Feature	Traditional E-learning/MOOCs	Educational Metaverse
Interface	Utilizes 2D screens with static content like video lectures, PDFs, and text. The interaction is limited to clicking, scrolling, and typing.	Provides 3D immersive worlds that users can navigate with a VR headset or a desktop. This allows for spatial learning and a more natural sense of presence.
Personalization	Offers basic recommendation engines that suggest courses or content based on a user's past viewing history. This is often a one-size-fits-all approach.	Features AI-driven adaptive tutors that can tailor the learning path in real-time based on a student's performance, cognitive load, and emotional state, creating a truly personalized experience.
Accessibility	Has limited disability support, often relying on simple features like closed captions or screen readers, which may not be fully integrated or effective for all needs.	Supports multi-modal accessibility, including AR (Augmented Reality) for overlays, haptics (touch feedback) for hands-on learning, and IoT (Internet of Things) devices to create a more inclusive environment for people with diverse needs.
Collaboration	Collaboration is generally forum-based, asynchronous, and text-heavy. Students might work on group projects, but the interaction lacks a sense of shared space or real-time co-presence.	Facilitates real-time VR laboratories and group projects where students can interact with each other and virtual objects in a shared 3D space, fostering a deeper sense of teamwork and cooperation.
Engagement	Can suffer from low engagement, often leading to "video fatigue" and high dropout rates due to the passive nature of content consumption.	Promotes high engagement through gamification, immersion, and interactive simulations. The active participation required by the user keeps them more focused and motivated.
Assessment	Typically uses quizzes and assignments that test knowledge recall. This method is often summative and doesn't provide real-time insights into the learning process.	Employs IoT and AI real-time tracking to monitor a user's actions, eye movements, and even physiological responses. This provides a more holistic and continuous assessment of a student's understanding and skill acquisition.

Traditional platforms, though valuable for scalability, often suffer from low engagement and accessibility barriers. The metaverse, in contrast, creates participatory, inclusive, and immersive learning environments that better align with diverse learner needs (Mystakidis, 2022).

2.4. Case Examples

Several real-world implementations illustrate the transformative capacity of the educational metaverse.

1. Meta's Horizon Education - A collaborative VR platform that allows students to interface with digital objects and peers in 3D immersive classrooms to support experiential learning.
2. Roblox Classrooms - Popular with K–12 educators in gamified learning environments, educators can develop interactive simulations using Roblox to improve student motivation and engagement.

3. Stanford's Virtual Human Interaction Lab - The Impacts of Immersive Learning Environments on Cold and Hot Learning: The course delivery method in immersive VR spaces demonstrates 20% higher retention rates and significantly greater evidence of empathy bulding than didactic lectures (Bailenson, 2018).
4. University of Tokyo's AR Campus Navigation - Hotspots of IoT and AR technology have provided college and university administrators with evidence of inclusive applications in the metaverse for differently abled students to access navigation tools across campuses.

These use cases demonstrate that the metaverse is not merely a futuristic concept but an evolving paradigm that is already reshaping educational experiences globally.

3. HUMAN-CENTRIC DESIGN PRINCIPLES

A metaverse as an online learning environment is not sustainable wholly through technology; it requires the infusion of values that connect to human experience. In developing learning environments that leverage the metaverse, the imperative question is not, "What can the technology do?" it is "What do learners need?" This implies that human-centered design is the essential foundation of educational systems, and that equity, access, personalization, and community engagement should be valued as fundamental rather than as an enhancement (Zhang et al., 2022). This method ensures that immersive learning environments are not simply an extension of dangerous or flawed systems and ultimately an equitable and empowering educational experience.

3.1. Accessibility: Addressing Differently-Abled Learners

Accessibility is the first step in designing for people. It means that people with physical, sensory, or cognitive limitations can fully engage in the metaverse (Huang et al., 2022). The metaverse can offer more ways to participate than traditional e-learning platforms, which mostly use closed captions or screen readers. For example, haptic gadgets let pupils who can't see "feel" three-dimensional things like chemical structures or architectural models. Gesture-controlled avatars and real-time voice-to-text transcription also make it simpler for students with hearing loss to participate.

In theory, accessibility may be thought of as a multi-variable optimization problem. The success of an educational system depends on how many adaptive characteristics it has:

$$A = \sum_{i=1}^{n} w_i f_i$$

Where A represents the accessibility score, f_i represents the presence of a feature such as haptic feedback, voice navigation, or adaptive contrast, and w_i is the weight assigned based on learner needs. By maximizing, A designers can ensure equitable access to immersive learning for diverse students (Dwivedi et al., 2022).

Case examples demonstrate that universities have begun the integration of these aspects. The University of Tokyo has built AR-based navigation tools that let visually impaired students get around campus on their own. Other schools have tried using VR sign language interpreters for classroom presentations (Duan et al., 2021). These practices not only show how far technology has come, but they also show a philosophical commitment to making sure that no student is left out of digital classrooms.

3.2. Inclusivity: Bridging the Digital Divide

Inclusivity also involves cultural, regional, and societal obstacles to education, not just disabilities (UNESCO, 2020). There are still digital access gaps across the world. For example, children in some rural locations, poorer homes, or lesser-developed countries lack the infrastructure for immersive learning. As reported by UNESCO, almost half of students in the world continue to lack access to reliable connectivity, and thus modern digital learning environments.

The metaverse can, however, help close these gaps by allowing for a tiered structure of access. Lightweight mobile apps, VR laboratories in schools that everyone can use, and smart classrooms powered by IoT devices that are run by the community are all affordable ways to get started. These approaches allow students in more rural areas to engage with the same immersive labs as their urban counterparts, thus improving accessibility to education for all (Mystakidis, 2022) Inclusivity also means recognizing and being sensitive to cultural differences, something that is especially important. For example, avatars and learning environments should allow students from around the world to modify aspects of their environment that resonate culturally, allowing them to recognize their identities in the metaverse.

Equity is also conceptually linked to inclusivity. Equity means that learners with different disadvantages have extra assistance to obtain comparable learning outcomes. Leveraging AI-driven analytics, the metaverse can identify learners who are under-accessed and provide additional support, such as more feedback, language translation, or more intuitive interfaces, to alleviate burdens on their learning experience (Chen et al., 2020). This will allow digital transformation to not exacerbate inequality, but instead, help to empower learners.

3.3. Personalization: AI-Driven Adaptive Learning

Personalization is perhaps the most important way that the metaverse is better than older digital learning methods. MOOCs and e-learning platforms provide uniform content, but the metaverse facilitates highly personalized routes (Sala, 2021). AI is a big part of how this customization works. AI tutors may change the difficulty of activities, provide more resources, and even change how they teach based on how students behave by using reinforcement learning models and real-time analytics.

An adaptive AI teacher might keep an eye on stress levels by employing IoT gadgets like smartwatches or EEG headbands. If the system sees that someone is very stressed, it may slow down the lessons or add fun activities to help them relax. On the other hand, if the student shows that they have mastered the material, the system may speed up development to find the best balance between difficulty and competence. Reinforcement learning algorithms that improve actions based on cumulative rewards help with this process:

$$Q(s,a) \leftarrow Q(s,a) + \alpha[r + \gamma maxQ(s',a') - Q(s,a)]$$

Where $Q(s,a)$ is the expected reward for taking action α in state s, r is the immediate reward, γ is the is the discount factor, and α is the learning rate (Mayer & Bailenson, 2024).

In the metaverse, personalized learning is not only about making things easier; it's also about fairness. Studies indicate that individualized digital interventions markedly enhance retention and motivation, particularly for learners who have challenges in conventional classroom settings (Krause et al., 2019). So, customization makes sure that learning environments change to fit the learner, not the other way around.

3.4. Engagement: Gamification and Immersive Experiences

One of the major drawbacks of online learning is still engagement. Because traditional e-learning systems usually incorporate passive content like films and PDFs, they tend to have high dropout rates. The metaverse supports engagement through immersive environments, gamification and learning together.

Gamification includes things like point systems, rewards, challenges, and quests that learners can work on together. These elements transform learning from a mundane chore to an intriguing adventure (Lee et al., 2021). For example, medical students might take part in a gamified VR lab for performing surgery, where learners must complete each procedure before moving on to a higher difficulty level. Engineering students might work together in quests where they solve design issues in VR spaces facilitated for all participants.

Research supports the effects of immersive engagement. Stanford University has conducted research on virtual reality classrooms and has found that students not only had improved rates of memory, but also had a heightened sense of empathy towards their peers, after lectures were simulated and offered through avatars (Kye et al., 2021). The metaverse similarly enhances engagement through making learners "feel" as if they are "there," in the digital classroom. This has resulted in more psychological absorption, leading to more stimulation, collaboration, and performance.

So, being in the metaverse isn't only for fun; it's also an important part of teaching. The metaverse changes learning from a passive, meaningless, and emotionally distant experience to an active, meaningful, and emotionally connected one by combining gamification, immersion, and collaboration.

4. TECHNOLOGICAL FRAMEWORK

To make a human-centered metaverse in education a reality, there has to be a strong technical base that brings together many digital advances into a single ecosystem (Sutton & Barto, 2018). The driving philosophy is centered on human-centered design principles while the underlying infrastructure Artificial Intelligence, the Internet of Things, Augmented and Virtual Reality, blockchain, and high-speed connection via edge computing and 5G enables these principles to come to life. Each of these technologies has a specific but related contribution to improving the immersive quality and welcome-ness of classrooms.

4.1. Artificial Intelligence and Machine Learning for Personalization

AI has increased the personalization of the educational metaverse. AI algorithms analyze students' behaviors in real-time and develop malleable pathways for learning, modifying the pathways depending on what different students need. AI tutors are able to change the pace of the instruction, the method of instruction, and the assessment of each student in a way that traditional systems can't do, in which evidence of all students engage with the same material at the same pace.

Reinforcement learning (RL) and natural language processing (NLP) are two of the strongest areas of AI education. RL will allow AI agents to continue improving their teaching based on the appropriate balance between short and long term learning outcomes. For example, if a student doesn't understand anything, the AI tutor can keep giving them exercises with different levels of difficulty until they do. The Bellman equation uses a formal architecture to show that the value of a choice is not only based on a current reward, but finally relies on future rewards.

NLP further provides conversational modalities where students can interact with virtual assistants in a more natural, spoken fashion. Such assistants may immediately answer questions, live translate languages, or provide spoken turn-by-turn navigation in virtual spaces. These features make education more flexible and accessible, especially for students who speak multiple languages or otherwise may not have easy access to resources (Zawacki-Richter et al., 2019).

Research shows that personalization induced by AI can effectively strengthen engagement and retention. Broad-based research conducted in higher education contexts reflected that adaptive AI tools improved test results by approximately 15% over static online modular content (Atzori et al., 2019). This research indicates ways in which AI may radically shift how people interact with each other and maintain learner engagement within the metaverse contexts.

4.2. Internet of Things for Connected Learning Environments

The Internet of Things (IoT) links the physical or external environment to the digitalized or virtual environment of the metaverse. Smartboards, wearables, and classroom sensors active to the Internet of Things (IoT), allow for settings that immediately react to the requirements of the learners (Stankovic, 2020). Smart classrooms, for example, may alter the light, sound, and temperature of the classroom to maximize students' attention. IoT devices can capture physiological data indicating heart rate and attention span for Artificial Intelligence (AI) teaching strategies or interventions.

From a mathematically analyzed perspective, the superposition of data from the IoT can be treated as a sensor fusion problem:

$$S = \sum_{i=1}^{n} w_i x_i$$

Here, S is the combined signal representing the learner's state, x_i denotes input from sensor i (such as EEG readings or environmental sensors), and w_i represents the weight corresponding to reliability or importance of that signal (Gao et al., 2021). This fusion allows AI systems to construct a holistic understanding of learner engagement, enabling interventions tailored to both cognitive and physiological conditions.

IoT also makes things more accessible. IoT devices can help students with disabilities find their way around by giving them adaptive navigation, real-time warnings, and AR-based wayfinding tools. In rural areas, community-based IoT networks might make it possible for people to share access to smart laboratories at a low cost. This way, the advantages of technology can reach places other than cities (Radianti et al., 2020). IoT is the basis for a responsive, human-centered learning environment because it makes it easy for devices to connect to each other.

4.3. Augmented and Virtual Reality for Immersive Teaching

Augmented Reality (AR) and Virtual Reality (VR) have been two of the clearest aspects of the educational metaverse to date. AR provides digital information in the real world, while VR places learners in a completely digital environment. As a result, they provide tactile interaction and as much hands-on experience as traditional education can allow. For example, in school for medical students, VR simulations allow students to perform surgery in safe, immersive virtual labs. AR overlays allow engineering students to see how complicated mechanical systems function by adjusting 3D models and aiding their comprehension of the abstract (Herrera et al., 2018). Research in history has demonstrated that immersive experiences may elicit emotional responses and allow the person to experience some empathy. For example, VR courses on social issues made students far more likely to take other people's points of view than studying from a textbook (Slater & Sanchez-Vives, 2016).

Latency is a major problem for anyone who want to use AR and VR. Delays longer than 20 milliseconds can break immersion, make people nauseated, and make it harder to learn (Grech & Camilleri, 2017). Edge computing and 5G networks can help with this problem by processing data closer to the user and providing connections with very low latency.

Empirical research highlights the efficacy of AR/VR in educational contexts. An investigation at Stanford University found that students remembered 20% more when they took classes in VR than when they took them in person (Turkanović et al., 2018). These results show that immersive education is not just an improvement; it is a change in how we educate that helps students remember what they learn by doing it.

4.4. Block chain for Credentials and Certification

The metaverse needs to do more than just provide immersive learning; it also needs to make sure that academic credentials are real and authentic. Blockchain technology provides a decentralized way to certify that makes academic records that are safe from tampering, clear, and can be checked anywhere in the world. Blockchain-based credentials can be checked right away across borders, unlike traditional credentialing systems that sometimes have long wait times and the possibility of fraud.

Furthermore, smart contracts provide additional utility to blockchain technology; they can even automate and create greater objectivity when it comes to verifying assessments and lessen administrative burdens. For example, the blockchain could automatically log a student's outcomes and award a certificate once a student has completed a VR-based assessment without anyone having to do anything.

Verifying credentials using blockchain is less expensive for less developed countries, when compared to centralized processes. Blockchain also makes it easier for students to navigate their academic pathways through the ability to seamlessly transfer academic credits from schools to schools around the globe. In this manner, the blockchain creates more educational accessibility for everyone, confirming students' achievements regardless of where they may be, and what school they are attending.

4.5. Edge Computing and 5G for Real-Time Experiences

Finally, the architecture of edge computing and 5G networks is what makes real-time immersive learning possible. Cloud computing can be scaled up, but AR/VR simulations, IoT analytics, and AI customization need ultra-low latency. Edge computing moves processing away from the center and closer to the consumer. 5G, on the other hand, may reach speeds of up to 10 Gbps with latency of only a few milliseconds (Porambage et al., 2018). This combination makes it possible for students in remote or less resourced places to have high-quality immersive experiences without any problems. A remote student with a light VR headset may join the same virtual physics lab as students at metropolitan colleges thanks to local edge nodes that cut down on latency (Zhang & Li, 2023). The potential of edge and 5G technology is that they can grow. As more people and gadgets connect to the metaverse, centralized cloud infrastructures alone can't keep up with demand. Edge-enabled designs spread out the workload, making sure that performance and accessibility are always the same in different areas (Zhao et al., 2022).

5. CASE STUDY: AI + AR NAVIGATION IN A SMART CAMPUS

This case study presents an augmented reality (AR) system for navigation on campus that seamlessly integrates indoor and outdoor navigation using an AR Core-based approach. Traditional 2D/3D navigation systems do not support localization in both indoor and outdoor environments, which leads to ineffective navigation and a poor experience for the user. The proposed system integrates GPS localization, a visual-inertial odometry (VIO) model, and AR Core technology to provide accurate, continuous localization. Whereas the GPS will localized the user in an outside environment, AR Core uses the mobile device camera and motion sensors for localizing the user's position and its orientation with respect of the surroundings. Users will also be able to switch modes depending if they are indoors or outdoors (Porambage et al., 2018). In contrast to Gaode's (Amap) AR navigation, the AR Core-based product offers greater level of interactivity and localization accuracy, and the near-real-time 3D AR visualizations provide a spatial context for the user by overlaying the 3D route guidance, building labels, and directional indications seamlessly on the camera feed. Four groups of university students participated in experimental testing, and results indicated significant improvements in the areas of navigation efficiency, usability, and user satisfaction. An AR system will facilitate effective smart practice campus management in the use phase by providing the user with a more intuitive, intelligent, and immersive experience in the spatial dimension for navigation. By overlaying 3D trail directions, building labels, and direction markers, the AR system enhances spatial understanding. Experimental research with four sets of college students indicated substantial increases in user satisfaction, usability, and navigation efficiency. Through a more intelligent, immersive, and intuitive navigation approach the AR system streamlines smart campus management.

5.1. Problem Definition

They distinguish between interior and outdoor navigation; Wi-Fi or Bluetooth-based localization is required indoors, while GPS-based devices are only effective outdoors. The abrupt change between the two contexts causes user confusion and a bad experience.

The systems lack the spatial awareness of actual buildings and are frequently 2D-based.

Users have trouble recognizing landmarks, orienting themselves, and comprehending the architectural plan. Therefore, the primary objective of this article is to use AR Core (Google's Augmented Reality SDK) to design a unified 2D/3D navigation framework that combines inside and outdoor positioning into a single seamless system. The suggested AR Core-based AR Navigation System combines GPS, map data, and visual-inertial odometry (VIO) to provide continuous tracking and navigation in both indoor and outdoor settings.

With the help of the phone's camera and IMU sensors, AR Core Engine tracks the environment in real time. The localization module provides hybrid location by combining visual-inertial odometry (inside) and GPS (outside).The best path between the user's present location and their goal is determined by the navigation algorithm (Tseng et al., 2021). Using augmented reality overlays, 3D scene rendering displays building labels, distance markers, and direction arrows straight on the camera feed. The User Interaction Layer offers visual feedback, search, and route query capabilities.

5.2. Integration With IoT Devices & Cloud

It's become harder to find some places on campus, including offices, labs, and classrooms, because campuses are developing so quickly. Traditional 2D/3D campus navigation systems can only handle one location at a time, whether it's indoors or outside. They typically use GPS outdoors, and since it cannot work indoors, it cannot adapt to changes in real-time or visualize the best options in a dynamic way. Now that we have cloud computing, augmented reality (AR), artificial intelligence (AI), and the Internet of Things (IoT), we have created a new solution to this problem. Cloud computing provides scalable storage and computation, IoT devices give real-time environmental data, AI will help to make smart decisions, and AR will allow people to see everything in a more direct way. Therefore, it is possible to construct a Smart Campus Navigation System that offers constant, precise and tailored directions.

We propose an AI + AR Smart Campus Navigation System that incorporates four fundamental technology pillars: Use AI for predictive navigation, object detection, and optimization of routes. The AR Core system uses augmented reality (AR) to deliver navigation cues and geographic data in real time. Humans are using IoT devices to procure contextual data and sense the environment as they navigate through it. Cloud computing synchronizes all symmetrical systems, wages data processing, and helps storage. The connection allows for continuous navigation inside versus outside, live updates, and user interactivity in various forms.

The Cloud Layer is the AI + AR Smart Campus Navigation System's brain and data management platform. It stores, calculates, and syncs all of the connected devices and apps. The Cloud Layer houses the building models, floor plans, and geospatial data necessary for route calculations and augmented reality visualization, all within the 3D Digital Twin of the campus. The Cloud Layer is also responsible for continually collecting and interpreting data from the IoT sensors scattered across the campus, such as motion sensors, Bluetooth beacons, and monitoring devices, to maintain real-time situational awareness of environmental conditions and crowd movement (Tran et al., 2024). The navigation service will synchronize this information in real-time and deliver the most relevant route and situational data to the user.

The cloud monitors user behavior, anticipates congestion, and optimizes routes through AI-supported analytics on a continuous basis. The cloud continued to refine accuracy, efficiencies, and flexibility through machine learning processes and real-time and historical data. The cloud allows for safeguarding system and user data through authentication and encryption using API processes. With these infrastructures, multiple users and devices can access synchronized real-time information, and administrators can monitor resource use, evaluate system performance, and manage all campus operations from one consolidated dashboard. This immersive augmented reality experience makes use of a user's spatial awareness by creating a physical connection with digital orientations in order to allow users greater efficiency when locating buildings, departments or facilities. The app also shows useful information like building names, floors, or event locations in the AR perspective. The AI engine also customizes the trip by modifying the routes based on data from IoT sensors, information from the environment, and how the user behaves. The interface allows real-time transitions, so if a route gets busy or isn't available, it will quickly recalculate routes and show the new interaction on the screen. This clever, good-looking, and easy-to-use interface gives students and educators a personalized and dynamic experience on a smart campus, replacing the old way of getting around.

5.3. Enhancing Student Orientation, Safety & Engagement via AI + AR Navigation

AI uses computer vision and machine learning techniques to identify terrain and contexts, anticipate user goals, and interpret routes creatively in relation to warnings, avoidance of hazards, or unexpected delays. Within a set of AR overlays, learners can view real-time notifications of events and attendee conversation, building names and directions, all compared to traditional two-dimensional map representations. Improved spatial cognition and reduced cognitive load in the students' experience follows from a more direct presentation of the spatial data when using AR maps. AR-based smartphone orientation apps will enhance engagement in onboarding experiences and help to alleviate freshman anxiety. (Toma et al., 2025) AI-driven personalization, including voice assistants and adaptive recommendations, makes navigation more accessible, inclusive, and relevant for users.

5.3.1. Enhancing Student Orientation

AR systems augmented by AI can set up interactive, gaming, and playful capabilities to promote academic span including lab settings or administrative settings. One example is that of the study, AR-LabOr (2025) which found that an AR-based orientation tool for the lab settings promoted knowledge retention and student confidence. Similarly, AI can enhance the space by assessing student performance and adjusting the difficulty of navigation, and hints, which support autonomy and spatial awareness. Orientation for new students can also involve complicated building navigation and learning facilities.

5.3.2. Improving Campus Safety

Safety is another key consideration for smart campus design. Leveraging real-time IoT data feeds, AI-enabled AR navigation could deliver proactive warnings to students in crowded areas, maintenance areas, and restricted areas. To evaluate safety risks from visual overload and distraction, simulated wearable AR settings. (Tran et al., 2023) The results help inform interface design aiming to support sustained situational awareness and agent efficient wayfinding. With AI in the system, it would allow the system to learn and adapt to safety alerts by gathering data from the environment; integrating this ability would be especially useful when in darkness or safety emergencies.

5.3.3. Fostering Student Engagement

Engagement is more than just navigation; it also relates to how students engage with their environment on emotional and cognitive levels. When AR markers, coupled with AI-powered sentiment and behavior analytics, can contextualize activities (events, artwork, sustainability indicators) based on user preferences, the user experience becomes individualized. Nguyen and usability studies confirm that AR navigation improves student engagement and immersion above traditional apps resulting in sustained engagement and positive impressions of campus. (Prandi et al., 2021) Next-generation smart campus navigation systems are being created using the AI and AR technology platform as the foundation. This integration enables seamless orienting and enhances engagement by creating immersive learning environments that support safety through context-based alerts.

5.4. Potential for hybrid/remote learners

AR front-end (wearable and mobile): AR Core/Unity client that superimposes interactive markers, building names, and arrows on the video stream. The implementation strategy adheres to the AR Core design patterns for mixed indoor/outdoor navigation developed. (Toma et al., 2025)

Semantic location classification, computer-vision landmark identification, and a route optimizer that modifies routes based on accessibility requirements (elevators/ramps), crowding (from IoT sensors), and time of day. Additionally, AI tailors "hint levels" for users who are novices versus experts. Features of hybrid/remote support include:

a) Synchronous AR tours, in which a live instructor can remotely place AR markers that distant students can observe on a 3D map or in their own camera view;
b) Asynchronous guided tours, which are voice-overed recorded augmented reality sessions with hotspots that distant learners can explore;
c) For users who are single-handed or have disabilities, there are haptic prompts, voice instructions, and larger overlays in the accessible mode.

Previous research demonstrates that AR-oriented apps improve perceived utility and onboarding engagement a helpful design argument. Orientation gain:

Compared to 2D maps in controlled studies, AR overlays increased task success and decreased navigation errors for inexperienced and hybrid users (Lu et al., 2021). Empirical AR campus studies that demonstrate enhanced orientation and engagement are consistent with this. Compared to text-based orientation packs, gamified AR orientation (such as quizzes and hotspots) greatly improved emotional engagement and retention throughout orientation week deployments. Additionally, remote learners expressed greater confidence following synchronous AR tours. Wearable AR can cause attentional shifts and potential hazards if overlays are dense or obscure the scene, according to simulations and VR-based evaluations (Romli et al., 2024). However, many risks were reduced in prototypes by using safety-focused interaction patterns, which include quick-exit gestures, audio/haptic cues, and minimal persistent overlays.

6. ETHICAL AND SECURITY CHALLENGES

Data reduction and privacy-by-design: only gather what is required (e.g. coarse attendance rather than continuous location logs). Before storing, aggregate or down sample telemetry. Keep visual odometry, instantaneous AR overlay, and raw sensor fusion on the device if possible. If necessary, upload only derived, anonymised metadata for campus analytics. The literature on AR navigation suggests hybrid edge/cloud designs.

Analytical anonymization and differential privacy: use verifiable privacy measures prior to sharing navigation telemetry or learning analytics with other campus services (research direction; see privacy literature reviews). TLS in transit, encryption at rest, and stringent RBAC for datasets (including teacher and admin access boundaries) are examples of encryption and robust access restrictions. Preserve biometric and gaze data by treating eye tracking and behavioral traces as extremely sensitive, storing them only when required, obtaining explicit informed consent, and implementing stricter safeguards (short retention, severe purview constraints). (Holstein et al., 2019)

6.1. Governance & Policy

Provide students and staff with unambiguous consent and disclosures about the use of navigation and virtual classroom data, how long it will be retained, and any sharing with third parties. Make the opt-out method for unnecessary processing as simple as possible. Data processing agreements that require restrictions (no secondary use, no selling), localization requirements, and audit rights are required for evaluating vendors and their contracts. Designate a privacy officer and a privacy and data protection impact assessment (DPIA) for new installations of XR/AR technology, and especially ensure data flows are compliant with FERPA, GDPR, and other applicable laws. When sensors (camera, microphone, gaze) are in use, provide explicit UX cues and privacy-preserving defaults (e.g., pseudonymized classroom metrics). Studies caution that privacy measures boost adoption and trust. (Mehrabi et al., 2021)

6.1.1. Existing Gaps and Future Opportunities

a) We require threat models tailored to AR/VR classroom scenarios as well as benchmark datasets for standard metrics and evaluation of privacy in AR education.
b) Make SLAM/place recognition and learning analytics accessible without cloud exposure with on-device machine learning for augmented reality that offers verifiable privacy guarantees.
c) Privacy-aware gaze analytics are techniques that deduce educational cues (such engagement) while demonstrably avoiding identify or sensitive characteristic reconstruction.

6.2. Bias in AI Recommendations

The application of artificial intelligence (AI) recommendation systems is growing quickly in e-learning platforms, smart campuses, and AR-based navigation systems that provide recommendations for routes, resources, or educational materials to customize user experiences. However, the potential fairness of the AI models used is a critical component of trusting those recommendations. In AI, bias occurs when certain people or certain groups are treated unfairly based on data/ algorithms/ users.

6.2.1. Sources of Bias

Data bias can lead to AI making erroneous predictions, as the training datasets may not be representative of the population or situation. For example, a campus navigation AI trained with users who are able-bodied may fail to offer accessible routes for persons with disabilities.

6.2.2. Algorithmic Bias

Decisions associated with various aspects of a model's architecture, such as weighting schemes; optimization objectives, and loss functions, may be biased towards certain outcomes. As Barocas notes, a course recommendation engine, for example, may privilege conventionally viewed measures of engagement over fair exposure generating potential gender or subject bias (Raji & Buolamwini, 2019). Interaction Bias: User behavior (e.g. clicks, words, or gestures) can inadvertently reinforce bias. Technology may recommend more known locations, in an AR navigation tool, in exchange for less known, academic institutions.

6.2.3. Bias in AI + AR smart campuses appears as

Route prioritization bias occurs when the quickest routes are chosen regardless of their safety or ease. Sensor or perception bias can be described as AI based on vision that performs differently in various lighting conditions or with different skin tones. Personalization bias occurs when recommendations are over-fitted to the behavior of the majority of users, impacting inclusivity for a diverse population of students and educators. Each of these biases erode accessibility and equity, as well as trust, and they are essential to the responsible use of AI in education. (Wang et al., 2022)

6.2.4. Techniques for Mitigation

Fair and representative data: Updating datasets regularly to properly term demographic representations. Consider using quantitative fairness metric(s) in evaluating results and conducting audits such as demographic parity or equal opportunity. Explainable AI (XAI) will enhance accountability and transparency of the employing logic to provide users understandable rationale for recommendations and reasoning to reduce biases. Using a human-in-the-loop strategy before full deployment allows to identify issues with biassed results in teacher/student testing cycles (Floridi & Cowls, 2019). Continued model monitoring: Reduce variance in bias fairness with more frequent audits and retraining to adapt to to users and the evolving data.

6.3. Critical Challenges in Cyber Defense Mechanisms

In the metaverse, digital avatars are commonly associated with user identities, and attackers can take advantage of weak authentication mechanisms to duplicate avatars or hijack sessions for social engineering, financial crime, or reputational harm. Deepfake impersonations could also damage trust and reputation in virtual reality meetings or classrooms (Kshetri et al., 2025).

There is a wealth of multimodal data collected by metaverse platforms, including voice data, motion data, visual data, biometric data, and behavioral data, which could make them attractive targets for hackers. If a breach were to occur, private biometric or educational information may be revealed or the breach may violate privacy laws such as FERPA (Family Educational Rights and Privacy Act) or GDPR (General Data Protection Regulation). Decentralized assets for campus tokens, digital credentials, and NFTs (non-fungible tokens) are often powered by Blockchain technology. There are risks of asset theft and manipulation of systems through consensus attacks (e.g. a 51% attack), smart contract vulnerabilities, or insecure wallets. Compromised AR/VR headsets and Internet of Things sensors are also capable of performing man-in-the-middle (MITM) attacks, injecting malicious code via firmware vulnerabilities, and eavesdropping (Ning et al., 2023) particularly in the networked classroom when devices are sharing biometric and geographic information. The metaverse is also uniquely vulnerable to social engineering, phishing, and misinformation threats using its immersion and realistic nature to manipulate a user's behavior, emotions, or digital trust and familiarity to obtain their credentials or to influence behavior.

6.3.1. Defensive Strategies for Cyber Risk Management

Multi-Factor Authentication with Decentralized Identity (DID): This method relies on a combination of biometric data, cryptographic proof of identity, and zero-knowledge proof to mitigate impersonation. End to End Encryption can be performed via quantum-resilient encryption techniques, which have enabled the encryption of all data flows between servers, avatars and devices. Machine learning can be included to recognize deviations and changes in behavior, instantly. To prevent contract exploits utilize formal verification, sandboxed execution, and auditing frequently. Edge processing can be used to anonymize sensor data, limit exposure to the cloud, and ensure informed consent. For immersive virtual environments, user awareness around privacy controls, social engineering, and phishing is necessary. While the connected metaverse presents a challenge, it provides the opportunity for digital transformation. The interconnectedness of devices, identities, and decentralized systems expands cyber security risks as well as immersive, collaborative, and intelligence (Zhang et al., 2023). A secure metaverse requires a layered defense strategy around blockchain security, ethical governance, AI-enabled intrusion detection, and regulatory compliance.

6.4. Ethical Standards for Accessible and Inclusive Learning

Using AI-based educational systems, fairness-aware algorithms should be deployed to reduce bias or discrimination. Students must still exercise control over their choices about their learning and educational information. Technology is to support students' identified and self-directed pathways to their learning rather than control (Alvarez et al., 2016). Educational technology should still be accountable for their impact and provide justifications for their algorithmic choices. Transparency builds trust in the technology for students, teachers, or developers. With the advance of learning analytics and digital tracking, student data protection has become paramount. Compliance with laws and regulations such as FERPA or GDPR in these educational ecosystems ensure that privacy is regarded as a right (Jobin et al., 2019).

Using ethical frameworks of inclusive education can help ensure that new technologies are used thoughtfully and responsibly in the classroom. Educational institutions can develop equitable learning experiences, enabling all students to learn, through the integration of fairness, transparency, and accessibility into systems they are designing (Faruq et al., 2025). The future of education must find a balance between innovation and inclusion, ensure that technology supports human values in learning, and human values are not replaced by technology.

7. FUTURE DIRECTIONS

The metaverse in education is still in its early stages, yet its rapid growth presents new opportunities for innovation, equity, and sustainability. As we move toward a digitally augmented academic landscape, the next generation of educational ecosystems must prioritize not only technological advancement but also sustainability, cross-border collaboration, and accessibility. These future directions mark a shift toward a more inclusive and environmentally responsible digital transformation.

7.1. Sustainable/Green Metaverse in Education

One of the most important future directions is creating a sustainable/metaverse, or a green metaverse. Immersion technologies and participation in immersive experiences often rely on cloud servers, the computational power of AI, and high-speed internet access. The impacts of immersive technologies, especially on the environment (i.e., energy), must be addressed (De Giovanni, 2023). Large-scale virtual environments may have considerable carbon footprints if their computing power is drawn from nonrenewable energy sources.

Creating a green metaverse can be done through the implementation of algorithms developed for energy efficiency, carbon-neutral data centers, and the use of edge computing. Edge computing can reduce the cost trigger associated with data transmission. Natural energy-powered cloud services (e.g., server farms powered by solar panels or wind turbines) can further reduce CO2 emissions while continuing to allow for computational efficiencies. Furthermore, the utilization of digital learning opportunities in the metaverse can help offset some of the CO2 associated with traditional higher education infrastructures. In this way, a sustainability-focused metaverse not only addresses climate-related goals but also assists in the larger social responsibility of higher education institutions.

7.2. Digital Twins of Universities and Smart Classrooms

Another significant aspect is the development of digital twins of universities and classrooms. These provide virtual replicas of actual educational contexts that simulate its facility, interactivity with students, and academic workflows in real time (Singh & Tiwari, 2024). Digital twins unite an array of IoT sensors, analytics, and 3D modeling to replicate physical operations in a digital context and create predictive systems that inform campus management and personalized learning.

For example, a digital twin of a smart classroom could assess air quality, lighting, and energy usage, and could assess and monitor student engagement through the use of IoT sensors. Then, mathematical optimization models would balance comfort, engagement, and energy efficiency:

$$U = \alpha_1 E_c + \alpha_2 S_e + \alpha_3 L_a$$

Where E_c is environmental control efficiency, S_e is student engagement, L_a is lighting adaptation, and α_i are the weighting coefficients. Such models support real-time decision-making and adaptive responses.

Digital twins can also be used by higher education institutions for purposes such as predictive maintenance, curriculum design, and simulation-based educational delivery. For example, student architecture students might engage in digitally modifying the blueprints of a building's design, and instantly preview the structural implications of those modifications in the twin. These features are creating new opportunities for data-driven, experiential learning that connects educational experiences with technology solutions. Then, Figure 2 delineates how classroom digital twins can simulate and optimize the physical world.

Figure 2. Digital twin based smart classroom architecture for adaptive learning

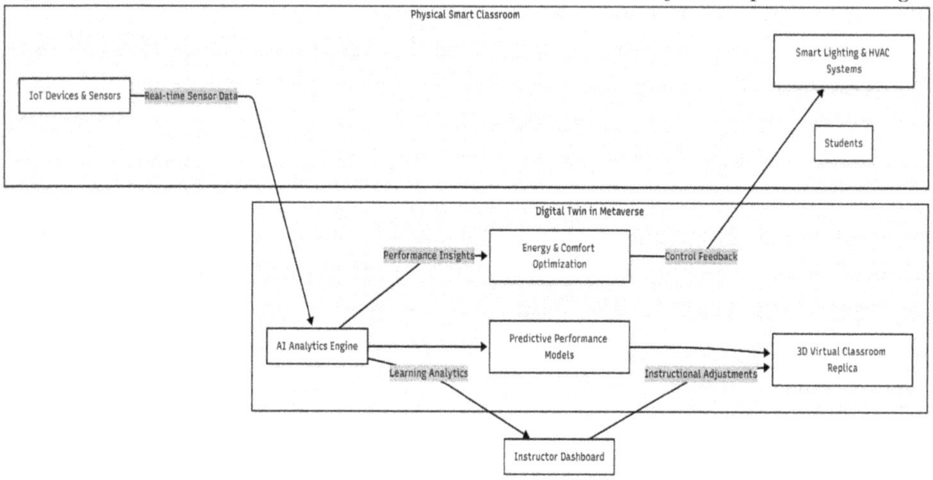

7.3. Cross-Border Collaborative Learning Using Avatars

The metaverse is also a mode for international collaboration in education, dissolving the barriers of institutional geography and culture. As noted by educational researchers, students and faculty from multiple countries may share a virtual space, interact with avatars, meanwhile developing intercultural competence and preparation for global citizenship.

Through avatar-mediated experiences, environments allow students to represent themselves through different physical embodiments that help build engagement and psychological safety. Demonstrated that learning in avatar-integrated learning experiences mitigated social apprehension, thus fostering participation from students, including the marginalized or the introverted [59]. Coupled with more advanced AI and NLP tools for translation, there are more opportunities for multilingual conversations with participants to enhance global academic exchange and education.

Cross-border collaborations also enable research and innovation to transpire with cross-border institutions to share digital laboratories, resources, and expertise in real time. For developing countries, this enables leapfrogging educational borders by becoming integrated into the global academic ecosystem with physical infrastructure, as found in advanced economic countries, being less of a limit. Figure 3 illustrates a global learning network with the connected institutions supported by immersive metaverse environments.

Figure 3. Cross border collaborative learning ecosystem enabled by the metaverse

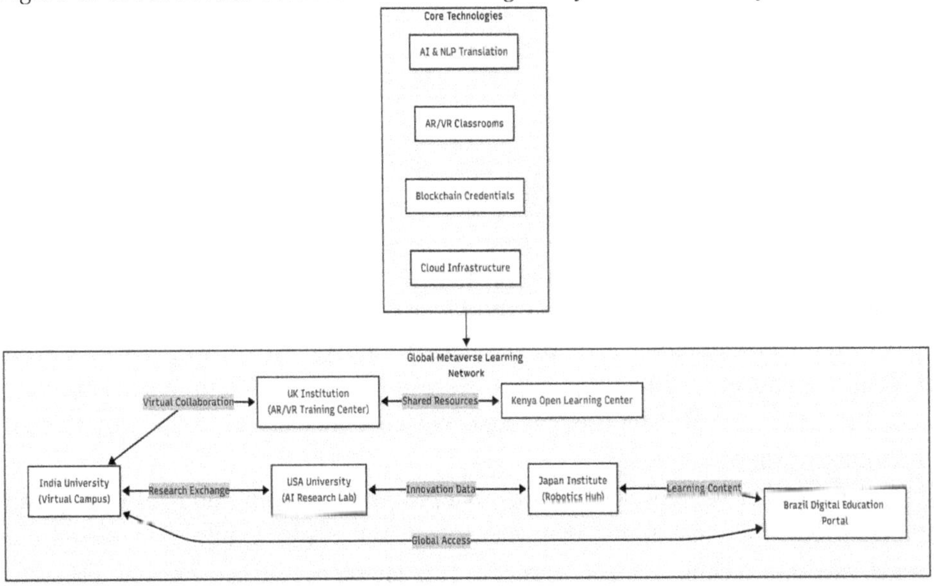

7.4. Opportunities for Developing Nations

One of the most transformative potentials of the educational metaverse is seen in developing countries. In areas where there is limited physical infrastructure, little local qualified faculty, or available educational resources, there is a potential for some degree of democratization through metaverse tools and content for access to quality education. Postulated that immersive technologies would allow local universities and educational institutions to work with international universities to allow students to attend lectures or participate in simulated laboratories with global experts without being limited geographically.

Low-cost VR headsets, AR learning based on smartphones, and low-bandwidth adaptive systems can expand educational access to rural or underprivileged communities (Sharma et al., 2022). Further, once in the metaverse, AI-based language translation, voice-interaction systems, and IoT-enabled connectivity can overcome literacy and accessibility barriers to participation.

In order to capitalize on the opportunity of the metaverse and educational equity, this needs to happen at the policy level, not solely the level of institution-level initiatives. Initiatives at the policy level should prioritize digital literacy programs, equitable access to devices, and connectivity and infrastructure for low-cost connectivity (Chamola et al., 2025). The public sector must work closely with the private sector to create viable frameworks where the advantages of the metaverse will reach marginalized learners. This will lead to the metaverse being an instrument of educational equity and social justice, rather than just a marker of technological advancement.

8. CONCLUSION

The metaverse is a new horizon in educational technology with the delivery systems, practices, assessment, and experience wrapped together with AI, IoT, and blockchain with immersive technologies in one ecosystem. Throughout its development, the educational metaverse has been shown to be able to increase access, promote inclusion, and provide engaging experiences to learners in a way traditional e-learning was never able to.

In this chapter we reflected on the conceptual basis, technological layers, and application of the educational metaverse, with a focus on a human-centered approach creating technology for learners. This chapter reflected on how bringing the elements together disaster AR/VR designed for immersion, AI which powered personalization, IoT generating real-time responses, blockchain transferring the idea, and cloud computing providing scale can support lifelong, experiential, and equitable learning.

Regardless, what happens in education in the metaverse will depend on the principles and philosophy in which it materializes. Organizations must initiate the creation and growth of systems that are sustainable and ethical considering data privacy, cyber safety, and digital health. As members of the education system undergo this change, there is an imperative to act upon:

a) Build an inclusive and accessible metaverse that empowers every learner, regardless of ability or background.
b) Develop green and sustainable frameworks that minimize environmental impact.
c) Promote cross-border collaboration to democratize knowledge exchange globally.
d) Ensure ethical AI and transparent governance for fairness and accountability.

To summarize, the metaverse is not merely an emerging technology; it is a sociotechnical revolution capable of redefining education as a right that is universal and inclusive. With partnerships and responsible innovation, along with human-centered design, the educational metaverse can be the catalyst for a future of learning free of geographic, ability, or equity limitations, and instead focused on equity, sustainability, and collective growth.

REFERENCES

Alvarez, M. A. P., Bielby, J., & Havens, J. (2016). *ETHICALLY ALIGNED DESIGN a vision for prioritizing human wellbeing with artificial intelligence and autonomous systems*. ETHICALLY ALIGNED DESIGN A Vision for Prioritizing Human Wellbeing with Artificial Intelligence and Autonomous Systems.

Atzori, L., Iera, A., & Morabito, G. (2019). Understanding the Internet of Things: Definition, potentials, and societal role of a fast evolving paradigm. *Ad Hoc Networks, 37*, 122–140. DOI: 10.1016/j.adhoc.2016.12.004

Bailenson, J. (2022). *Experiences in VR learning at Stanford University*. Stanford Press.

Bailenson, J. N. (2018). *Experience on demand: What virtual reality is, how it works, and what it can do*. W. W. Norton & Company.

Chamola, V., Peelam, M. S., Mittal, U., Hassija, V., Singh, A., Pareek, R., Mangal, P., Sangwan, D., de Albuquerque, V. H. C., Mahmud, M., & Brown, D. J. (2025). Metaverse for Education: Developments, Challenges and Future Direction. *Computer Applications in Engineering Education, 33*(Mar), e70018. Advance online publication. DOI: 10.1002/cae.70018

Chen, L., Chen, P., & Lin, Z. (2020). Artificial intelligence in education: A review. *IEEE Access : Practical Innovations, Open Solutions, 8*, 75264–75278. DOI: 10.1109/ACCESS.2020.2988510

De Giovanni, P. (2023, March). Sustainability of the Metaverse: A Transition to Industry 5.0. *Sustainability (Basel), 15*(7), 6079. DOI: 10.3390/su15076079

Duan, H., Li, J., Fan, S., Lin, Z., Wu, X., & Cai, W. (2021). Metaverse for social good: A university campus prototype. *Proceedings of the 29th ACM International Conference on Multimedia*, 153–161. DOI: 10.1145/3474085.3479238

Dwivedi, Y. K., Hughes, L., & Baabdullah, A.. (2022). Metaverse for education: Opportunities and challenges. *Journal of Business Research, 145*, 731–743.

Dwivedi, Y. K., Hughes, L., Baabdullah, A. M., Ribeiro-Navarrete, S., Giannakis, M., Al-Debei, M. M., Dennehy, D., Metri, B., Buhalis, D., Cheung, C. M. K., Conboy, K., Doyle, R., Dubey, R., Dutot, V., Felix, R., Goyal, D. P., Gustafsson, A., Hinsch, C., Jebabli, I., & Wamba, S. F. (2022). Metaverse beyond the hype: Multidisciplinary perspectives on emerging challenges, opportunities, and agenda for research, practice and policy. *International Journal of Information Management, 66*, 102542. DOI: 10.1016/j.ijinfomgt.2022.102542

Faruq, O., Mambetaliev, A., Karshiboev, A., & Mohammad, N. (2025, June). Designing inclusive digital media environments for learners with autism spectrum disorder: Integrating artificial intelligence and data analysis to enable adaptive learning, communication, and accessibility. *Journal of Posthumanism*, *5*(6). Advance online publication. DOI: 10.63332/joph.v5i6.2338

Floridi, L., & Cowls, J. (2019). A unified framework of five principles for AI in society. *Harvard Data Science Review*, (Jun). Advance online publication. DOI: 10.1162/99608f92.8cd550d1

Gao, L., Li, Y., & Luo, Y. (2021). IoT-enabled smart classrooms: Opportunities and challenges. *Computers & Education*, *170*, 104224. DOI: 10.1016/j.compedu.2021.104224

Grech, A., & Camilleri, A. F. (2017). *Blockchain in education. Joint Research Centre (JRC) Science for Policy Report*. Publications Office of the European Union., DOI: 10.2760/60649

Herrera, F., Bailenson, J., Weisz, E., Ogle, E., & Zaki, J. (2018). Building long-term empathy: A large-scale comparison of traditional and virtual reality perspective-taking. *PLoS One*, *13*(10), e0204494. DOI: 10.1371/journal.pone.0204494 PMID: 30332407

Holstein, K., Wortman Vaughan, J., Daumé, H.III, Dudik, M., & Wallach, H. (2019). Improving Fairness in Machine Learning Systems: What Do Industry Practitioners Need? *Proceedings of CHI Conference on Human Factors in Computing Systems*, 1–16. DOI: 10.1145/3290605.3300830

Huang, R. H., Liu, D. J., & Tlili, A.. (2022). Meta-education: The future of learning in the metaverse. *Smart Learning Environments*, *9*(1), 1–14. PMID: 40477962

Jobin, A., Ienca, M., & Vayena, E. (2019). The Global Landscape of AI Ethics Guidelines. *Nature Machine Intelligence*, *1*(9), 389–399. DOI: 10.1038/s42256-019-0088-2

Krause, N., Frey, A., & Cress, U. (2019). How to design online learning communities: The role of social presence. *Educational Technology Research and Development*, *67*(3), 511–533.

Kshetri, N., Pandey, P. S., & Ahmed, M. (Eds.). (2025). *Blockchain technology for cyber defense, cybersecurity, and countermeasures: Techniques, solutions, and applications*. CRC Press.

Kye, B., Han, N., Kim, E., Park, Y., & Jo, S. (2021). Educational applications of metaverse: Possibilities and limitations. *Journal of Educational Evaluation for Health Professions*, *18*(32), 1–12. DOI: 10.3352/jeehp.2021.18.32 PMID: 34897242

Lee, L. H., Braud, T., Zhou, P., ... (2021). All one needs to know about metaverse: A complete survey. arXiv preprint arXiv:2110.05352.

Lu, F., Zhou, X., Guo, L., Chen, J., & Pei, L. (2021). An ARCore-Based Augmented Reality Campus Navigation System. [MDPI]. *Applied Sciences (Basel, Switzerland)*, *11*(16), 7515. DOI: 10.3390/app11167515

Mayer, R. E., & Bailenson, J. N. (2024, October). Advances in research on learning in immersive virtual reality. *Technology, Mind, and Behavior*, *5*(4), 173–175. Advance online publication. DOI: 10.1037/tmb0000146

Mehrabi, N., Morstatter, F., Saxena, N., Lerman, K., & Galstyan, A. (2021). A Survey on Bias and Fairness in Machine Learning. *ACM Computing Surveys*, *54*(6), 1–35. DOI: 10.1145/3457607

Moro Visconti, R., & Piroli, G. (2023). Virtual reality, augmented reality and education: The new frontiers of immersive learning. *Education and Information Technologies*, *28*(5), 4561–4579. DOI: 10.1007/s10639-022-11577-8

Mystakidis, S. (2022). Metaverse. *Metaverse. Encyclopedia*, *2*(1), 486–497. DOI: 10.3390/encyclopedia2010031

Nguyen, N., Muilu, T., Dirin, A., & Alamäki, A. (2018). An interactive and augmented learning concept for orientation week in higher education. *International Journal of Educational Technology in Higher Education*, *15*(1), 35. DOI: 10.1186/s41239-018-0118-x

Ning, H., Wang, H., & Lin, Y.. (2021). A survey on metaverse: The state of the art, technologies, applications, and challenges. *IEEE Internet of Things Journal*, *10*(2), 1426–1458.

Ning, H., Xu, Y., & Wang, R. (2023). A Survey on Security, Privacy, and Trust in the Metaverse. *Digital Communications and Networks*, *9*(3), 380–396.

Porambage, P., Okwuibe, J., Liyanage, M., Ylianttila, M., & Taleb, T. (2018). Survey on multi-access edge computing for Internet of Things realization. *IEEE Communications Surveys and Tutorials*, *20*(4), 2961–2991. DOI: 10.1109/COMST.2018.2849509

Prandi, C., ... (2021). *On supporting university communities in indoor wayfinding. Sensors* / PubMed Central. https://www.ncbi.nlm.nih.gov/pmc/articles/PMC8124871/

Radianti, J., Majchrzak, T. A., Fromm, J., & Wohlgenannt, I. (2020). A systematic review of immersive virtual reality applications for higher education. *Computers & Education, 147*, 103778. DOI: 10.1016/j.compedu.2019.103778

Raji, I. D., & Buolamwini, J. (2019). *Actionable Auditing: Investigating the Impact of Publicly Naming Biased Performance Results of Commercial AI Products.* Proceedings of the AAAI/ACM Conference on AI, Ethics, and Society, 429–435. DOI: 10.1145/3306618.3314244

Romli, R., Yew, C. C., Ghazali, N. H., Zahri, N. A. H., Amir, A., & Hasnan, R. (2024, May). AR@ campus: Augmented reality (AR) for indoor positioning and navigation apps. In AIP conference proceedings (Vol. 3135, No. 1, p. 040002). AIP Publishing LLC.

Sala, N. (2021). *Virtual Reality, Augmented Reality, and Mixed Reality in Education: A brief overview.* In *Current and prospective applications of virtual reality in higher education* (Chapter 3). IGI Global. DOI: 10.4018/978-1-7998-4960-5.ch003

Sharma, R., Kumar, P., & Arora, A. (2022). Internet of Things (IoT) applications in education: A survey. *Education and Information Technologies, 27*(2), 1719–1743. DOI: 10.1007/s10639-021-10659-1

Singh, P., & Tiwari, S. "Digital Twins and Artificial Intelligence," in *Handbook of Industrial and Business Applications with Digital Twins*, 1st ed., Taylor and Francis, Dec. 2024, ch. 5, DOI: 10.1201/9781003465904-7

Slater, M., & Sanchez-Vives, M. V. (2016). Enhancing our lives with immersive virtual reality. *Frontiers in Robotics and AI, 3*, 74. DOI: 10.3389/frobt.2016.00074

Stankovic, J. A. (2020). Research directions for the Internet of Things. *IEEE Internet of Things Journal, 7*(5), 4735–4745. DOI: 10.1109/JIOT.2020.2966951

Sutton, R. S., & Barto, A. G. (2018). *Reinforcement learning: An introduction* (2nd ed.). MIT Press., DOI: 10.5555/3312046

Tapscott, D., & Tapscott, A. (2018). *Blockchain revolution: How the technology behind bitcoin is changing money, business, and the world.* Penguin.

Toma, M.-V., Turcu, C. O., & Pascu, P. (2025, January). Evaluating user acceptance and usability of AR-based indoor navigation in a university setting: An empirical study. *International Journal of Advanced Computer Science and Applications, 16*(4). Advance online publication. DOI: 10.14569/IJACSA.2025.0160406

Tran, T. T. M., ... (2024). *Simulating wearable urban augmented reality: Assessing risks and safety concerns via VR. arXiv preprint.* https://arxiv.org/abs/2402.04576

Tran, T. T. M., Parker, C., Hoggenmüller, M., Hespanhol, L., & Tomitsch, M. (2023). Simulating wearable urban augmented reality experiences in VR: Lessons learnt from designing two future urban interfaces. *Multimodal Technologies and Interaction*, *7*(2), 21. DOI: 10.3390/mti7020021

Tseng, S.-S., Chen, S.-N., & Yang, T.-Y. (2021). Building an AR-based smart campus platform. *Multimedia Tools and Applications*, *80*(28), 35333–35352. DOI: 10.1007/s11042-021-11702-5

Turkanović, M., Hölbl, M., Košič, K., Heričko, M., & Kamišalić, A. (2018). EduCTX: A blockchain-based higher education credit platform. *IEEE Access : Practical Innovations, Open Solutions*, *6*, 5112–5127. DOI: 10.1109/ACCESS.2018.2789929

UNESCO. (2020). *Global education monitoring report 2020: Inclusion and education*. UNESCO Publishing.

Veletsianos, G., & Houlden, S. (2019). An analysis of MOOCs: Limitations, benefits, and emerging directions. *International Review of Research in Open and Distance Learning*, *20*(3), 35–50.

Wang, Y., Su, Z., Zhang, N., & Shen, X. "A survey on Metaverse: Fundamentals, security, and privacy," *TechRxiv*, Mar. 2022, DOI: 10.36227/techrxiv.19255058.v1

Zawacki-Richter, O., Marín, V. I., Bond, M., & Gouverneur, F. (2019). Systematic review of research on artificial intelligence applications in higher education – Where are the educators? *International Journal of Educational Technology in Higher Education*, *16*(1), 1–27. DOI: 10.1186/s41239-019-0171-0

Zhang, J., Xu, L., & Xu, Y. (2022). Accessibility design in the metaverse for learners with disabilities. *Computers & Education*, *182*, 104468.

Zhang, Y., He, X., & Li, C. (2023). XR Security: Protecting AR/VR Devices and Data in the Metaverse. *IEEE Internet of Things Journal*, *10*(15), 13561–13575.

Zhang, Y., & Li, H. (2023). Augmented Reality-Based Indoor-Outdoor Campus Navigation System. *IEEE Access : Practical Innovations, Open Solutions*.

Zhao, Q.. (2022). Hybrid Localization Using Visual-Inertial Odometry and GPS for Mobile Navigation. *Sensors (Basel)*, *22*(8), 3201.

Chapter 9
Integrating Sanskrit Epistemology With xAI for Trustworthy Metaverse Systems

B. K. Tripathy
http://orcid.org/0000-0003-3455-4549
Vellore Institute of Technology, India

G. K. Panda
MITS School of Biotechnology, India

ABSTRACT

The rapid convergence of immersive technologies and artificial intelligence has accelerated the rise of the metaverse—dynamic, contactless digital ecosystems encompassing social, cognitive and economic dimensions. However, these evolving environments also present complex challenges in trust, privacy and digital forensics. This chapter demonstrates a unified, explainable and ethically grounded metaverse security framework by integrating Sanskrit epistemology, specifically Nyāya logic, with Explainable Artificial Intelligence (xAI) and incremental learning paradigms. The framework adopts the Nyāya epistemic structure, rooted in Pramā a and a five-fold reasoning process. Symbolic reasoning modules are combined with incremental learning algorithms to enable continuous adaptation and evidence-based inference without catastrophic forgetting. Experimental results compare the Nyāya-driven xAI framework through its interpretability and adaptability on forensic explainability. The logical traceability of its decision process strengthens trust and accountability in metaverse investigations.

DOI: 10.4018/979-8-3373-6721-7.ch009

1 INTRODUCTION

The rapid proliferation of artificial intelligence (AI) across immersive and interactive technologies has catalyzed the emergence of next-generation metaverses. The Metaverse, broadly defined as an immersive, persistent and interconnected virtual ecosystem, has evolved from decades of technological convergence. Although the concept was popularized through speculative fiction, most notably Neal Stephenson's novel Snow Crash (Kansal et al., 2023). It has since expanded far beyond early experimental virtual worlds such as Second Life, progressing into a multifaceted digital sphere that tightly integrates AI, extended reality (XR), networking innovations and decentralized infrastructures.

Modern metaverse platforms, including those envisioned by Meta and other global technology enterprises, seek to establish continuous digital environments where human interaction, commerce, education, healthcare, enterprise operations and entertainment seamlessly converge. These environments rely on AI-powered avatars, adaptive interfaces, multimodal XR technologies and context-aware systems that increasingly blur the boundaries between physical and virtual realities.

The accelerating academic interest in this domain is evident from several large-scale analyses. A recent bibliometric study of 928 journal articles provides a comprehensive overview of the Metaverse's developmental landscape, identifying influential publications and forecasting future research directions (Wider et al., 2024). Complementarily, another analysis of 595 journal articles using bibliometric and topic-modeling techniques reveals significant thematic trends, research gaps and proposes 27 questions to guide future investigations (Rajeb et al., 2023). Together, these systematic reviews illustrate both the diversity and the growing sophistication of metaverse-related research.

AI has emerged as the foundational enabler of metaverse intelligence—driving autonomous agents, real-time content generation, behavior modeling and personalized user experiences. In parallel, allied technological domains such as extended reality, blockchain, distributed computing and next-generation networking infrastructures (5G/6G and edge–cloud continuum) have accelerated the progress of immersive systems (Lee et al., 2021). This integrated technology stack signals a paradigmatic shift in how identity, behavior, interaction and data governance operate across blended physical–virtual boundaries.

Recent studies further highlight how advancements in VR/AR systems, AI-driven automation, spatial computing and edge intelligence are reshaping industrial sectors and societal dynamics. The works in (Rajeb et al., 2023; Lim et al., 2022) collectively trace the technological progression since 2020, demonstrating the exponential rise in research output and the increasing potential of immersive technologies to transform business, education, healthcare and public services. The Metaverse has transitioned from a speculative conceptualization to a critical interdisciplinary research frontier, demanding contributions from computer science, cognitive science, human–computer interaction, socio-technical systems, economics and digital governance. Table c.1 and Table c.2 present a comprehensive overview of AI-driven metaverses by detailing the core technological foundations that enable immersive virtual environments and the ecosystem-level and societal considerations that govern their responsible, secure and human-centric development, respectively.

Table 1. Core Technological Foundations of AI-Driven Metaverses

Dimension	Description / Relevance to Metaverse
Artificial Intelligence (AI)	Powers autonomous agents, intelligent avatars, natural language interaction, adaptive environments, generative content, behavior modelling, and personalized experiences. Central to real-time decision-making and immersion.
Extended Reality (XR: VR/AR/MR) (Wider et al., 2024)	Provides immersive interfaces bridging digital and physical environments; enables spatial presence, interaction fidelity, and multisensory engagement.
Blockchain and Decentralized Ledgers (Rajeb et al., 2023)	Ensures transparent asset ownership, identity authentication, secure transactions, and decentralized governance; underpins digital currencies and NFTs.
Advanced Networking (5G/6G, Edge–Cloud Continuum) (Lee et al., 2021)	Supports ultra-low latency, high bandwidth, and distributed processing for synchronous multi-user interactions and large-scale virtual environments.
Spatial Computing and Scene Understanding (Lim et al., 2022)	Facilitates mapping, localization, environment cognition, and intelligent perception for real-time world modeling and seamless user interaction.
Pervasive and Ubiquitous Interfaces (Qayyum et al., 2024)	Wearables, haptics, sensors, smart glasses, and interaction devices enabling natural engagement through gesture, touch, speech, and biometrics.
Distributed Computing and Edge Intelligence (Hatami et al., 2024)	Offloads computation close to users, enabling scalable, real-time AI inference and reducing resource bottlenecks in immersive platforms.
Content Generation and Rendering Engines (Badruddoja et al., 2022)	High-fidelity 3D modeling, photorealistic rendering, procedural generation, and AI-augmented graphics pipelines for dynamic world building.

Table 2. Ecosystem and Societal Considerations of AI-Driven Metaverses

Category	Dimension	Description / Relevance to Metaverse
Identity and Representation	Avatars	Digital personas reflecting user identity, presence, behavior, and interaction patterns; AI enhances realism, emotional expression, and personalization.
Digital Content Ecosystem	Content Creation	AI-assisted tools for generating 3D assets, environments, and narratives; democratizes creation and supports participatory virtual cultures.
Interoperability and Standards	Data Interoperability	Ensures cross-platform consistency in assets, identities, and transactions; vital for unified, persistent metaverse experiences.
User and Society Perspectives	Social Acceptability	Addresses cultural norms, psychological impacts, human factors, and ethical acceptance of persistent digital engagement.
Risk and Security	Security and Privacy	Controls unauthorized access, identity spoofing, data breaches, and surveillance risks; involves cryptographic safeguards and privacy-preserving AI.
Governance and Ethics	Trust and Accountability	Establishes transparent digital governance, provenance tracking, explainable AI systems, and responsible use frameworks within immersive environments.
Well-Being and Safety	Digital Health & Human Factors	Considers user safety, ergonomics, cognitive load, addiction risks, and long-term psychological effects in persistent virtual spaces.
Economic and Regulatory Structures	Digital Economy & Policy	Concerns regulation, taxation, cross-border digital commerce, platform policies, and sustainable economic models for metaverse ecosystems.

Some of the recent studies (Qayyum et al., 2024; Hatami et al., 2024) emphasize the foundational role of Extended Reality (XR) technologies, including virtual, augmented and mixed reality, which serve as critical human interfaces enabling real-time and immersive experiences. Blockchain and decentralized ledgers underpin secure digital asset management, trust and privacy preservation in metaverse ecosystems, while challenges such as scalability and smart contract integration are actively addressed through AI-enhanced solutions. The work in (Badruddoja et al., 2022) achieved better predictive accuracy by embedding AI into smart contracts on Ethereum, but latency constrains real-time use. An approach in (Fu et al., 2023) outline a multilayer blockchain–networking architecture for privacy and synchronization, though deployment complexity remains. The work in (Truong et al., 2023) highlights secure digital asset ownership via decentralization, yet interoperability standards are lacking. Their study in (Duraipandi & Velayudhan, 2024) propose blockchain-secured distributed VM agents for scalable cloud integrity limiting on large-scale validation. Authors in (Elsadig et al., 2024) synthesize on anonymity and shared ecosystems as advances while identifying interoperability and performance as key barriers to mature metaverse deployment. Advances in networking technologies and the integration of the Metaverse also witnessed with several studies like, advanced technologies like 6G (Aslam et al., 2023), mobile edge computing (Wang and Zhao, 2022; Zhang et al., 2023), integrated sensing, communication and computing (Wang et al., 20224). Some of their key challenges include achieving ultra-low latency, ensuring data security and privacy and optimizing resource allocation to support immersive experiences like location-dependent augmented reality. Spatial computing and scene understanding technologies facilitate the creation and management of realistic three-dimensional virtual spaces through sophisticated tracking, mapping, and digital twin platforms, which are critical for authentic user experiences (Cappannari et al., 2022). Moreover, pervasive interfaces supported by the Internet of Everything and augmented by blockchain enable seamless synchronization and secure interactions between physical and digital worlds (Rafique et al., 2024). The convergence of distributed edge intelligence, AI, blockchain and advanced networking found to be crucial for addressing resource optimization, security and scalability challenges inherent in metaverse applications (Ali et al., 2024; Awadallah et al., 2025). Research also highlights Metaverse's potential across different fields like, multimedia communication requiring ultra-low latency (Dong & Lee, 2022), virtual-reality inter-promotion with challenges in hardware costs and motion sickness (Wu et al., 2023) and immersive education despite concerns about accessibility and psychological risks (Contreras et al., 2022). The Metaverse is also discussed for sercure academic assessments (Razzaq et al., 2024) but faces limitations in scalability and accessibility, diverse industrial applications enabled by Digital Twins and Web 3.0 technologies (Bhattacharya et al., 2023) and personalized health care integrating the Internet of Medical Things (Anudeep et al., 2024), raising ethical and technical challenges.

Together, these contributions offer a comprehensive technological framework and illuminate challenges and opportunities that shape the development of the Metaverse as a transformative platform for social, industrial, medical and digital interaction. Concurrently, advancements in connectivity and system engineering have paved the way for high-bandwidth standards like Wi-Fi 6/7 and Bluetooth Low Energy. These technologies facilitate uninterrupted interaction between wearable peripherals such as smart glasses and sophisticated cloud AI services. Advancements and miniaturization of processing units, improvements in battery efficiency and advancements in thermal management have also made it possible to incorporate powerful computation within lightweight, ergonomically optimized tiny wearables. These innovations collectively ensure that modern wearable systems can operate continuously without overheating or compromising comfort. The evolution of software ecosystems underpins these hardware and interaction capabilities. Dedicated operating environments now support spatial computing, AI-powered perception and developer extensibility. Enhanced security architectures, featuring encrypted data pipelines, secure enclaves and granular permissions address the growing concerns regarding privacy and ethical data use. Together, these platforms seek a structured foundation for cascading robust trustworthy applications that harness the full potential of AI-integrated devices.

Metaverse forensics is also emerging as a crucial research theme, with recent studies highlighting its growing importance. It focuses on how evidence is identified, collected and attributed within immersive virtual environments where identities, assets and interactions shift continuously across interconnected digital spaces. As more applications introduce short-lived avatars, dynamic virtual worlds, decentralized storage and blockchain trails, the traces left behind become fleeting, scattered and vulnerable to manipulation. This creates major challenges in linking events to real actors, reconstructing complete activity histories and separating genuine interactions from fabricated ones. To mitigate these risks, researchers advocate adopting zero trust security models, enhancing provenance tracking, enabling auditable privacy preserving processes, enforcing consistent logging across virtual platforms and deploying advanced AI-based tools that can verify evidence integrity within complex metaverse ecosystems.

This rest of the chapter unfolds through a structured progression from conceptual foundations to applied insights. Section 2 establishes the theoretical framework, presenting a conceptual synthesis of wearable display systems, Nyāya epistemology and its relevance to Epistemic AI frameworks, explainable-AI, the incremental learning paradigm and metaverse forensics. Section 3 advances into the methodological core, detailing the proposed NXIF model alongside the constructed synthetic dataset. Section 4 develops the narrative further by examining metaverse forensic intelligence, outlining the NXIF's workflow through a systematic and algorithmic representation and discussing key implementation considerations including scalability, system integration and computational constraints. Section 5 synthesizes the experimental findings and analytical discussion, highlighting explainability metrics, incremental learning behavior, cognitive adaptation, forensic validity, regulatory alignment and three emerging real-world metaverse integration scenarios, complemented by a coherent evaluation of limitations and trade-offs. Finally, Section 6 concludes the chapter with reflective insights on the convergence of philosophical reasoning and technological innovation, while outlining prospective directions for advancing research in metaverse forensics.

2 THEORETICAL FOUNDATIONS

Several real-life metaverse applications already operate at scale, demonstrating how interconnected virtual environments are becoming part of mainstream digital ecosystems across social, commercial, industrial and creative domains. Platforms such as *Meta Horizon Worlds* enable social interaction, community activities and user-created environments, while *NVIDIA Omniverse* supports industrial-grade collaboration where companies like *BMW* and *Siemens* simulate factories and autonomous systems. Consumer ecosystems such as *Roblox* and *Decentral* and host virtual economies, brand activations and large community events, allowing users to design content, operate virtual businesses and trade digital assets. Enterprise-focused solutions such as *Microsoft Mesh* provide mixed-reality meeting spaces for training, 3D collaboration and remote operations across healthcare, manufacturing and defense. Entertainment platforms like *Fortnite* further extend the metaverse into live virtual concerts, storytelling events and large-scale interactive experiences. *Meta Connect 2025*, led by Mark Zuckerberg, presented a notable leap in consumer-facing AI and mixed-reality technologies (Connect keynote, 2025). The introduction of "*Meta Ray-Ban Display*" smart glasses with integrated micro-displays, multimodal AI assistance, continuous environmental sensing and neural-interface wristband controls was remarkable milestone on this regard. Such recent developments mark a significant inflection point in wearable computing and signal the beginning of a new era in ubiquitous AI-augmented interaction.

2.1 Conceptual Overview of Wearable Display System

The advancements of wearable computing have enabled a new generation of smart glasses equipped with micro-displays, advanced sensors, multimodal AI and neural interface controls. To illustrate this context, a conceptual block diagram is provided in Figure c.1. This diagram does not replicate or resemble any existing commercial product; instead, it serves solely as a hypothetical case study to support the discussion.

At the core of these devices are significant developments in display and optical engineering. Micro-LED and micro-OLED display modules, combined with advanced waveguides and optical combiners, now enable high-resolution, see-through visual overlays without compromising form factor or user comfort. Complementary innovations in holographic and diffractive optics enhance light transmission efficiency and visual clarity, positioning wearable displays as a viable platform for real-time augmented perception. Such smart glasses rely on multimodal AI engines that process visual and contextual signals to deliver adaptive, context-aware assistance. These engines leverage computer vision for object recognition and spatial mapping, natural language processing for conversational interaction and multimodal fusion algorithms that integrate camera feeds and sensor data. Hardware accelerators for edge AI further enable low-latency inference while reducing dependence on cloud resources.

Figure 1. Conceptual architecture of wearable display system

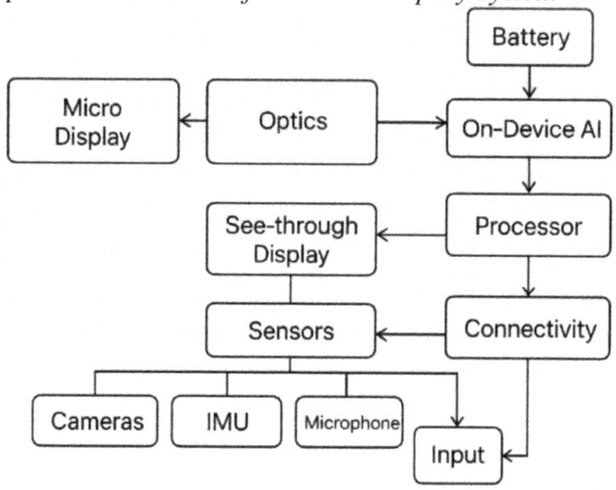

Another foundational research advancement lies in the integration of continuous environmental sensing technologies. Contemporary devices incorporate high-fidelity RGB and infrared cameras, depth sensors and inertial measurement units to construct dynamic spatial models and track user motion. Microphone arrays support spatial audio capture, while ambient light, proximity and location sensors contribute to contextual awareness. Gesture-recognition capabilities, eye-tracking mechanisms, touch-sensitive frames and far-field speech interfaces enable real-time understanding of the user's surroundings, which is essential for delivering accurate augmented-reality overlays and situational intelligence. The most notable innovation in this domain is the use of neural-interface wristbands that decode neuromuscular signals through electromyography. These interfaces translate subtle motor intentions into digital commands, offering an intuitive, low-effort interaction modality that significantly enhances the usability of wearable systems. ML models personalize these bio-signal interpretations over time, improving accuracy and reducing cognitive load.

2.2 Nyāya Epistemology

As per the Indian philosophy, the *Nyāya Sūtras* is fundamentally concerned with epistemology – how valid knowledge (*Pramāna*) is acquired and justified. It posits that reliable cognition arises from *Pramā as*, or means of valid knowledge, which are fourfold, (a) *Pratyak a* (Perception) – Direct sensory cognition; equivalent in AI to data acquisition or sensor-level observation, (b) *Anumāna* (Inference) – Logical deduction based on observed evidence; analogous to inferential reasoning in symbolic AI, (c) *Upamāna* (Comparison/Analogy) – Knowledge through similarity; corresponding to pattern recognition or similarity-based learning and (d) *Śabda* (Verbal

Testimony) – Authoritative knowledge from reliable sources; akin to supervised learning from annotated datasets or knowledge bases. These epistemic modes are unified by the *Nyāya* with five-step reasoning schema (Table c.3), which provides a transparent structure for logical argumentation and has potentiality to be computationally mapped to AI inference mechanisms.

Table 3. Five-Step Reasoning Schema

Nyāya Step	Logical Role	Computational Analogy
Pratijñā (Proposition)	Statement of hypothesis	Model prediction or hypothesis generation
Hetu (Reason)	Justification based on evidence	Feature-based reasoning / attention weight explanation
Udāhara a (Example)	Supporting illustration	Training example or empirical instance
Upanaya (Application)	Linking general rule to specific case	Instance-level inference / case matching
Nigamana (Conclusion)	Logical conclusion	Final decision / classification output

Nyāya logic supports intrinsic explainability, where explanations are built into the reasoning process (intrinsic) rather than added after the fact (post hoc). Each inference step is explicit and traceable, ensuring logical accountability. Translating this into AI, we can formalize an interpretable reasoning pipeline in which every model decision is accompanied by a structured epistemic justification (with above schema). Formally, this can be represented as a reasoning tuple, $R_i = \langle P_i, H_i, U_i, A_i, N_i \rangle$, where R_i represents the ith reasoning sequence and the others correspond to *Pratijñā*, *Hetu*, *Udāhara a*, *Upanaya* and *Nigamana*, respectively. Each tuple provides a transparent trace from data evidence to the final decision, serving as a computational audit trail.

2.3 Nyāya Epistemology and Epistemic AI Frameworks

Symbolic reasoning can be viewed as a core engine of modern computing, as it supports modelling and predictions through explicit, logic-based knowledge representations and structured inference rules. The inception of logical intelligence can be traced through Aristotle's formal syllogistic logic (4th century BCE) and the Nyaya School's epistemic inference and fallacy theory (2nd century BCE), through Boole's mathematical symbolic logic (1847), to the emergence of Symbolic AI and logic-based reasoning formalized by McCarthy, Newell and Simon in the mid-20th century. The advancement witnessed through a series of foundational milestones that progressively strengthened its reasoning and learning capabilities. The formalization of epistemic logic by Jaakko Hintikka in 1962 laid an early theoretical basis for modeling knowledge, later influencing AI research by the 1980s and maturing in the 1990s. Although symbolic systems and neural networks both originated in the 1950s, they remained separate until early 1990s efforts toward integration, which evolved into modern neuro-symbolic AI and gained renewed momentum after 2016 with deep learning. In 1995, Phan Minh Dung's Abstract Argumentation Frameworks established a rigorous structure for computational reasoning. Concurrently, the 1990s saw growing interest in epistemic reasoning agents within multi-agent systems, reflecting AI's shift toward interactive and cognitively informed intelligence. Building on these foundations, AI has evolved from purely symbolic, rule-based systems to data-driven deep learning approaches, with neuro-symbolic AI now unifying both paradigms to deliver accurate, explainable and epistemically grounded intelligence.

A study in (Hossain et al., 2025) summarises a systematic review of 167 papers published between 2020 and 2024 shows that 63% focus on learning and inference, 35% on logic and reasoning, 44% on knowledge representation and 28% explicitly address explainability. Evidence of most of studies including (Colelough & Regli, 2025) suggests that *neuro-symbolic AI*, *argumentation-based explainability* and *epistemic reasoning* have emerged as key enablers of real-world AI deployment, with applications spanning healthcare, finance, robotics, recommender systems and cybersecurity. Figure c.2 illustrates a comparative perspective of NE and these four key AI-enablers. This evolving landscape also invites a closer examination of Nyāya Epistemology (NE) as a complementary epistemic reasoning framework within AI.

The relevance of NE becomes particularly evident in *neuro-symbolic AI* (Colelough & Regli, 2025), where symbolic reasoning is integrated with neural learning to enhance interpretability and robustness. Neuro-symbolic systems employ explicit logical structures to justify decisions, a principle that strongly resonates with NE's stepwise inference schemas and emphasis on validated reasons (*hetu*). Although implemented computationally, these systems reflect NE's insistence that conclusions must be traceable to reliable inferential grounds rather than opaque statistical correlations. A similar conceptual alignment is evident in *argumentation-based explainability* (Prajescu et al., 2025), where reasoning is represented as structured interactions among arguments and counter arguments. Such frameworks echo NE's critical evaluation of reasons and its systematic defense of knowledge claims against fallacies. By enabling transparent and contestable explanations, argumentation-based xAI reflects the NE commitment to epistemic rigor and justificatory clarity, reinforcing its relevance to modern explainable AI paradigms. Epistemic reasoning in agent-based AI also extends NE's focus on valid cognition to dynamic, multi-agent settings with uncertainty and belief revision. While formal epistemic logic models (what agents know and how beliefs change using symbolic structures, NE addresses a deeper question: how cognition itself becomes valid. This epistemological grounding offers a principled foundation for strengthening computational models of knowledge and belief in AI. Table c.4 summarises the leading frameworks and their alignment with NE.

Figure 2. Comparative Perspectives: NE and AI Frameworks

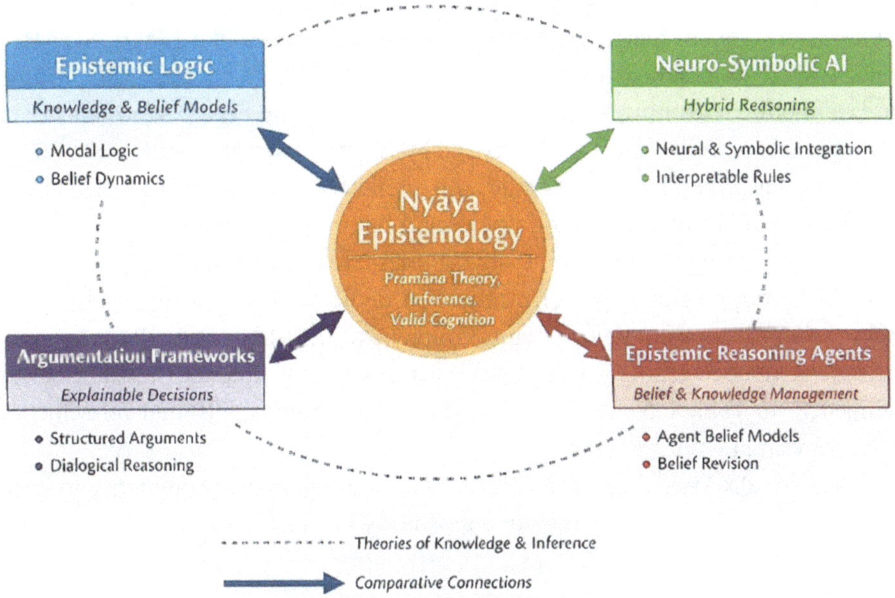

Table 4. NE and Cross-Framework Alignments

Framework	Core Focus	Connection to Nyāya Epistemology
Epistemic Logic (AI)	Formal modalities for knowledge and belief	Mirrors Nyāya's structured inference and knowledge conditions
Neuro-Symbolic AI	Hybrid reasoning + learning	Supports interpretable justification paths akin to pramā a validation
Argumentation Frameworks	Justified conclusions via argument interactions	Aligns with Nyāya's evaluation of reasons and elimination of fallacies
Epistemic Reasoning Agents	Modeling evolving knowledge in agents	Resonates with Nyāya's concern with defeasible and context-sensitive inference

2.4 Explainable Artificial Intelligence (xAI)

xAI aims to make AI-models transparent, interpretable and trustworthy by elucidating how inputs are transformed into outputs. Three major approaches drive this effort. *Intrinsic explainability* focuses on models that are interpretable by design, such as decision trees or rule-based systems. *Post hoc explainability* generates insights after a model makes a prediction, using techniques like LIME, SHAP, or Grad-CAM to visualize or approximate decision behavior. *Hybrid explainability* blends symbolic reasoning with deep learning to combine high performance with meaningful interpretive structure. Consistent with prior work in (Panda et al., 2024), authors present a comprehensive study on social trust by exploring various xAI techniques, their evaluation methodologies and charting future directions to enhance transparency, interpretability and trustworthiness in AI systems.

While these approaches are well established, dedicated research on explainability within metaverse environments remains limited. Only a little work explores how xAI operates in extended reality settings, decentralized infrastructures, or avatar-driven intelligence. In Table c.5, we bring out some xAI methods and their relevance to metaverse virtual environments.

Conventional xAI methods often rely on heuristic explanations rather than a structured logical foundation, revealing an opportunity for deeper epistemic grounding. The *Nyāya-xAI* framework addresses this gap by introducing a philosophically rooted logical model that brings greater rigor and coherence to the explanation process. Building on the need for logically grounded explanations, it formalizes how an AI system justifies its decisions.

Let $f: X \quad Y$ denote an AI model mapping input features X to outputs Y. A Nyāya-driven explanation E can be expressed as, $E=\{(P, H, U, A, N) \mid f(X) = Y\}$, where, P represents the model's proposition (predicted class or decision), H identifies the evidential features that most influenced the decision, U provides relevant analogs drawn from prior knowledge, A establishes the inferential link between the evidence and the present case and N delivers the concluding rationale. This structured reasoning process introduces a level of logical transparency and it is particularly valuable in metaverse forensics, where each decision may carry compliance, accountability, or legal significance.

Table 5. Overview of xAI methods and their relevance to Metaverse

xAI Category	xAI Method / Framework	Tech Description: Relevance to Metaverse / XR / Virtual-Environments /
Hybrid / Post-hoc + Analytics	Explainable XR (Kim et al., 2025)	Helps in generating heatmaps for CNNs or other vision modules to reveal the image or scene regions that most strongly drive a model's decision, thereby clarifying its visual reasoning and supporting metaverse XR tasks such as gesture recognition, scene understanding, avatar interaction detection and environment analysis by showing developers and auditors exactly which virtual elements influence AI judgments.
Post-hoc, model-specific	Visual Attribution (Saranya et al., 2023)	Helps in generating heatmaps for vision models to reveal the scene regions driving a model's decision, providing clear visual reasoning that supports metaverse XR tasks such as gesture recognition, scene understanding, avatar interaction detection and environment analysis.
Intrinsic (ante-hoc) explainability	Intrinsic / Interpretable Models (e.g. Decision Trees, Rule-based Systems, Symbolic / Ontology-based Models, Generalized Additive Models, etc.) (XAI Methods, 2025)	Helps in producing inherently understandable decisions through rule-based logic, symbolic reasoning, clear decision paths and additive feature effects, making these interpretable models well suited for resource-constrained or distributed metaverse settings such as edge devices, wearables and decentralized clients where transparent identity management, asset handling and lightweight agent logic are essential.
Intrinsic or Hybrid Explainability (for sequential/action-based models)	Explainable Reinforcement Learning (XRL) / Symbolic + Neuro-Symbolic Agents. (Bekkemoen, 2024)	Helps in maintaining interpretability of decision-making for autonomous agents, NPCs and AI-driven avatars in metaverse environments, ensuring that their actions remain understandable even within complex, multi-agent or partially observable virtual worlds.
Hybrid Post-hoc + Governance / Audit	Forensic-Ready XAI & Audit Frameworks (e.g. XAI-DF frameworks combining post-hoc explanations with immutable logging / provenance metadata) (Zainab et al., 2024)	Helps in merging explainability outputs such as feature attributions, counterfactuals and saliency maps with system-level logging and metadata capture to ensure traceability and forensic auditability, which is essential in decentralized metaverse ecosystems where distributed evidence must support accountability in content moderation, dispute resolution, asset transfers and security investigations.

2.5 Incremental Learning Paradigm

Traditional learning models often struggle to capture evolving data due to catastrophic forgetting, a phenomenon where acquiring (learning) new patterns causes the model to forget (erase) previously learned information. Incremental (Continual) learning methodology addresses this challenge by allowing models to adapt to new data distributions while retaining prior knowledge. Since metaverse environment is a subject of evolving processes continuously; new avatars, transactions and behavioural artifacts emerge continuously. Regular (static) models may fail to capture such dynamism due to catastrophic forgetting, where learning new patterns causes the model to forget previous ones.

The work in (Zainab et al., 2024) integrates xAI into digital forensics, facing challenges with computational complexity versus real-time needs. An overview of continual learning with their observations in noting the need of significant memory requirement or complex regularization were identified in (Awasthi et al., 2019). A study in (Feng et al., 2019) emphasizing on task-incremental learning for assistive robotics highlights on the performance degradation in unstructured scenarios. A continual learning study in (Wang et al., 2022) identified that, their Triple-Memory Networks known to be a brain-inspired approach is computationally intensive and require sophisticated tuning. The work in (Xu et al., 2022) identified that, as model size grows with tasks, the adaptive progress continual learning faces issues like parameter explosion.

Let D_1, D_2, ..., D_t represent sequential datasets from evolving metaverse logs. An incremental learner updates its parameters θ_t such that, $\theta_{(t+1)} = \theta_t + \Delta\theta_t$, where $\Delta\theta_t$ takes computation with the new batch $D_{(t+1)}$, under the constraint, Forget(K_{old}) ≈ 0. Here, K_{old} denotes previously acquired knowledge. Various strategies in incremental learning settings such as Elastic Weight Consolidation (EWC), Memory Replay, or Dynamic Architectures have been adapted to maintain this equilibrium. EWC limits how much critical model parameters can change, ensuring that newly learned information does not overwrite previously acquired capabilities. *Memory replay* methods, ranging from storing past samples to generating synthetic data, reinforce older knowledge by periodically revisiting earlier experiences during training, a mechanism inspired by biological memory processes. *Dynamic architecture* approaches extend or adjust the model structure as new tasks arrive, allowing networks to grow or reconfigure without interfering with older representations.

In the context of Nyāya-xAI, incremental learning aligns with the dynamic reasoning principle of Nyāya epistemology, driven by knowledge which is further continuously validated through observation, inference and comparison. Hence, each incremental update forms a new reasoning tuple preserving both the cognitive trace and historical accountability.

2.6 Metaverse Forensics

Metaverse forensics focuses on how evidence is captured, preserved and interpreted within immersive digital environments that include VR and AR sessions, avatar behaviors and virtual asset transactions. Unlike traditional forensics, which relies on discrete files and static events, metaverse investigations must integrate diverse data streams such as avatar movement patterns, gestures, cryptocurrency transfers, NFT activities, voice and chat interactions, haptic feedback and system-level records like environment logs or smart contract traces. These artifacts are highly temporal, interconnected and context dependent, making causal reconstruction significantly more complex. While conventional ML models can flag anomalies, they rarely explain their findings in a logically grounded or ethically consistent manner. The Nyāya-xAI framework addresses this gap by offering structured, transparent reasoning that links evidence to inference in an auditable form, providing investigators with explanations that are both technically sound and operationally meaningful.

The study in (Kim et al., 2023) derived a metaverse ecosystem as a common component of major metaverses and proposed a corresponding digital forensic process validated using Meta's metaverse environment. Their analysis within the metaverse ecosystem yielded various digital artifacts, enabling the construction of a user behavior timeline and the development of their metaverse digital forensic tool. In (Shandilya et al., 2024) The authors propose a Metaverse forensic framework that organizes digital artifacts and maps them to Cyber Kill Chain phases to support investigations of virtual crimes. Their work built on the NIST forensic model, which provided a structured process for evidence collection, analysis and reporting and is validated through a malware attack scenario, establishing an initial methodological basis for forensic readiness in Metaverse environments.

3 METHODOLOGY AND FRAMEWORK DESIGN

3.1 Integrated Framework

In order to formalize the model, the integration process is realized through a cascaded three-layer internal structure besides to Metaverse input data and forensic legally auditable analysis in which each layer performs a distinct cognitive function while contributing to a coherent reasoning pipeline. The epistemic layer formalizes knowledge validation using Nyāya principles and fivefold syllogistic method, ensuring that inferences are logically justified and traceable. Built upon this foundation, the cognitive layer functions as the explainable-AI core, synthesizing symbolic logic and statistical learning to produce interpretable conclusions. The adaptive layer enables dynamic refinement by incrementally updating the model as new metaverse evidence becomes available, allowing the system to maintain relevance, accuracy and contextual awareness over time.

Formally, the system's inference process at time t can be modeled as, $Y_t = g(f_t(X_t), R_t)$, where f_t represents the adaptive learner, R_t is the Nyāya reasoning trace, and g(·) maps model predictions and logic tuples into an explainable forensic report. This triadic model embodies both technical rigor and philosophical coherence, uniting symbolic, connectionist and epistemic reasoning into a unified architecture for digital trust.

3.2 The NXIF

The proposed Nyāya-xAI–Incremental learning framework for metaverse forensics (NXIF) is designed to ensure that every model decision is (a) *explainable* through logical inference, (b) *adaptive* to new digital evidence, and (c) *ethically interpretable* through the epistemic structure of Sanskrit Nyāya philosophy. The methodological flow integrates four fundamental dimensions:

a. **Epistemic Foundation** (Nyāya Logic): Provides the reasoning ontology, how evidence and inference (fivefold syllogism) are structured and justified.
b. **xAI Reasoning Engine** (ML Models): Encodes the reasoning logic into interpretable machine learning model architectures.
c. **Incremental Learning** (Adaptive Learning Module): Facilitates continual model evolution with dynamic metaverse data.
d. **Forensic Analysis Layer** (Digital Evidence Analysis): Generates human-readable, logically traceable reports of facts/evidences.
e. **Auditable Outputs** (human-interpreted formats): Generates forensic intelligence based reports from the facts of epistemic, interpretive and adaptive modules.

The design methodology embodies Sanskrit epistemic essence; knowledge (*Vidya*) is valid only when its source (*Pramā a*) is pure, reasoning (*Tarka*) is structured and conclusion (*Nigamana*) is logically sound. This triad maps seamlessly to modern AI's objectives (discussed in section c.5.4) of data veracity, model interpretability and output accountability. The NXIF model proposes a unified paradigm that integrates philosophical epistemology, interpretable machine intelligence and adaptive learning mechanisms to address the forensic challenges of highly dynamic metaverse environments. The core principle of NXIF is that forensic intelligence must be logically justified, computationally transparent, and capable of continuous adaptation to evolving digital ecosystems. To this end, the framework ensures that every model decision is (a) explainable through structured inference, (b) responsive to new forms of virtual evidence and (c) ethically interpretable within the epistemic tradition of Sanskrit Nyāya philosophy.

Figure c.3 outlines the architecture of NXIF having four interdependent dimensions that collectively produce a rigorous forensic workflow. First, the Nyāya Epistemic Foundation aims to serve as the reasoning ontology, providing a structured representation of how evidence is categorized, validated and synthesized using constructs such as pramā a (valid knowledge sources), tarka (methodical reasoning), hetu (cause), vyāpti (universal relation), and nigamana (logical conclusion). These constructs are computationally mapped onto evidence hierarchies, causal operators and inference rules.

Figure 3. Block diagram representing Nyāya-xAI–Incremental Learning Framework for Metaverse Forensics (NXIF)

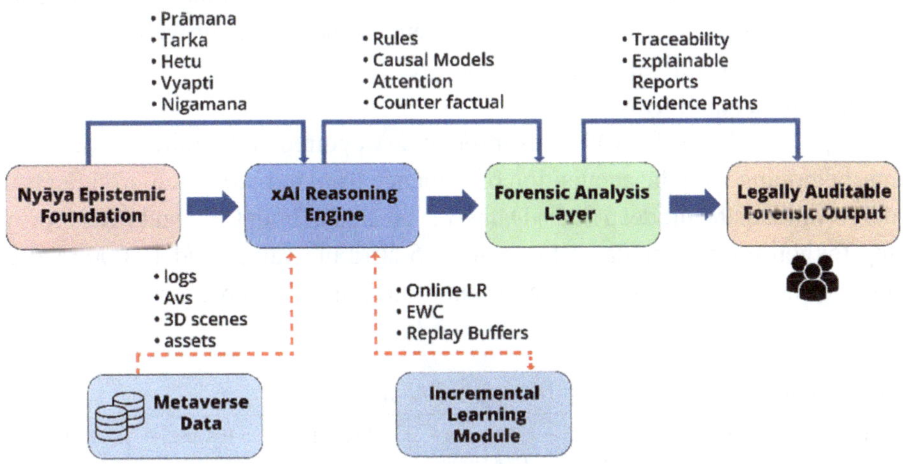

Second, the Explainable AI Engine operationalizes Nyāya's reasoning structure through interpretable ML models. Techniques such as rule-based learning, causal graphical modeling, attribution mechanisms and counterfactual reasoning enable the framework to articulate not only what decisions are made but why they are made, thereby preserving the traceability required for forensic validity and legal admissibility. Third, the Incremental Learning Module equips the system with the capacity for lifelong adaptation. Given the rapid evolution of user behaviors, virtual assets and threat vectors within metaverse environments, incremental learning algorithms—including replay-based memory consolidation and regularization-driven continual learning—allow models to assimilate new evidence without catastrophic forgetting. This ensures sustained accuracy and contextual relevance even as virtual ecosystems evolve. Next, the Forensic Analysis Layer synthesizes the outputs of the epistemic, interpretive, and adaptive modules into human-readable forensic intelligence. This layer generates transparent evidence–decision pathways, causal chains, and structured reports that can be independently validated by investigators, auditors, and legal authorities. By tracing each conclusion back to its evidential roots and logical dependencies, the system ensures compliance with forensic accountability standards.

3.3 Synthetic Metaverse Forensic Event Dataset

The evaluation presented in this chapter relies on synthetic metaverse forensic event dataset (SMF-Dataset), which were employed to enable controlled validation of epistemic reasoning, explainability and forensic logic within the proposed NXIF model. The use of synthetic data allows systematic examination of inferential correctness, reasoning traceability and evidence handling under well-defined conditions, free from confounding noise and access constraints commonly associated with operational platforms.

The proposed workflow unfolds through a structured and intuitive sequence of steps, beginning with the acquisition of evidence from immersive environments. In order to validate the model a SMF-Dataset is created in both CSV and JSON format using Python script. The dataset contains 25 attribute values and 10,000 records. Table c.6 describes its schematic representation along with three records (samples).

Table 6. Synthetic Dataset with 3-Sample Records

Column#	Column Name	Data Type	Column Description	Record1	Record2	Record-3
1	event_id	String	Unique identifier for each recorded event	EVT001	EVT002	EVT003
2	timestamp	Datetime	Event occurrence time (UTC)	2025-12-07T14:23:56Z	2025-12-07T14:25:10Z	2025-12-07T14:26:02Z
3	user_id	String	User/avatar triggering or affected by the event	U453	U998	U221
4	avatar_state	String	State of avatar at event time (e.g., idle, moving, interacting, anomalous)	interacting	anomalous	moving
5	location	String	Virtual world coordinates or zone label	Zone-A3	Zone-C7	Zone-B2

continued on following page

Table 6. Continued

Column#	Column Name	Data Type	Column Description	Record1	Record2	Record-3
6	device_fingerprint	String	Hashed device/ VR headset identifier	DF_9FAE1	DF_12BD3	DF_77CC9
7	identity_score	Float	Trust score (0–1) measuring identity consistency	0.92	0.31	0.85
8	asset_type	String	Type of asset involved (NFT, token, item, environment asset)	NFT	token	item
9	asset_value	Float	Estimated real/virtual value involved	120.5	5	0
10	action_type	String	Specific action (login, transfer, modify_scene, teleport, spoof_pose, etc.)	transfer	spoof_pose	modify_scene
11	event_category	String	One of {Identity Manipulation, Asset Theft, Scene Tampering, Avatar Anomaly}	Asset Theft	Avatar Anomaly	Scene Tampering
12	anomaly_score	Float	ML-model anomaly score (0–1)	0.72	0.89	0.41
13	evidence_hash	String	Hash of evidence bundle (screenshots, logs)	HSH_AA11	HSH_CF22	HSH_8E90
14	client_ip	String	(Anonymized) user network signature	IP_45xx	IP_19yy	IP_77zz
15	vr_device	String	VR/AR device type	Oculus-Q3	Vive-Pro2	Meta-H4

continued on following page

Table 6. Continued

Column#	Column Name	Data Type	Column Description	Record1	Record2	Record-3
16	latency_ms	Int	Measured frame-to-frame latency	48	63	52
17	packet_loss	Float	Network packet loss percentage	0.4	1.8	0.7
18	scene_id	String	Identifier of metaverse environment	SCN12	SCN44	SCN33
19	object_id	String	Target object involved in the action	OBJ88	OBJ15	OBJ02
20	nxif_hetu_valid	Bool	Hetu (reason) check validity under Nyāya rule-set	TRUE	FALSE	TRUE
21	nxif_vyapti_valid	Bool	Vyapti (invariable relation) validity	TRUE	FALSE	TRUE
22	nxif_nigamana	String	Conclusion generated by Nyāya reasoning module	Valid transaction but suspicious timing	High-risk anomaly detected	Scene element changed with justification
23	risk_level	String	Computed risk label (Low, Medium, High, Critical)	Medium	High	Low
24	trace_graph_path	String	Path ID of evidence graph linkage	TG_12A	TG_56B	TG_77C
25	investigation_flag	Bool	Whether the record requires forensic follow-up	TRUE	TRUE	FALSE

The objective of framing such synthetic dataset and validation is conceptual framework verification rather than performance benchmarking, with emphasis placed on epistemic soundness, interpretability and forensic coherence rather than deployment-level accuracy or throughput metrics.

4 NXIF WORKFLOW FOR METAVERSE FORENSIC INTELLIGENCE

4.1 Objectives

As per the above conceptual overview and proposed architectural representation, the NXIF model pertains with a five-fold objectives (i) to establish a logically verifiable AI reasoning model grounded in Nyāya epistemology for digital evidence assessment in the metaverse, (ii) to generate explainable forensic conclusions using transparent xAI mechanisms that offer traceability of model decisions, (iii) to support incremental, real-time model updates without retraining from scratch, ensuring adaptability to dynamic virtual ecosystems, (iv) to create a forensic pipeline capable of documenting the causal chain of events, anomalies and interactions in a legally admissible manner and (v) to reduce ambiguity in forensic interpretation by combining philosophical logic and computational semantics.

4.2 NXIF Process

The proposed workflow for metaverse forensics unfolds through a structured and intuitive sequence of steps, beginning with the acquisition of evidence from immersive environments. At this stage, investigators capture logs, asset states, interaction timelines, avatar behaviors, and VR/AR session traces, typically stored in formats such as JSON logs, voxel maps, motion vectors and cryptographic transaction records. Once collected, these heterogeneous data streams are organized using a Nyāya-based evidence-structuring framework, where observations are systematically classified under the classical pramā as: Pratyak a for direct sensory evidence like VR scene logs, Anumāna for inferential patterns such as anomalous interactions, and Śabda for authoritative sources, including system event registries. Logical reasoning chains are then mapped using the Hetu–Vyapti–Paksha constructs to establish consistent causal links. The process workflow of NXIF is presented with stepwise descriptions in Algorithm-1.

Building on this structured foundation, the xAI interpretation layer transforms raw and structured data into transparent analytical insights. Interpretable models, such as rule-based gradient boosting, SHAP reasoning graphs, causal Bayesian networks and counterfactual analysis to generate explicit reasoning trails aligned with Nyāya inference principles, thereby enabling explainable anomaly verification.

The xAI engine operates through dual reasoning channels: a symbolic channel, which encodes Nyāya-inspired reasoning into formal logic using rule-based structures (e.g., *IF feature_condition THEN class*, with an annotated *Hetu*), and a neural channel, which captures abstract patterns through deep learning architectures such as LSTM or Transformer-based encoders.

During inference, the system fuses both explanation streams according to the weighting function $E(X_i)=\alpha Es_{ymbolic}(X_i) + (1\text{-}\alpha)E_{neural}(X_i)$, where $\alpha \in [0,1]$ governs the trade-off between interpretability and predictive accuracy. The integrated output provides the final class prediction (*Nigamana*) supported by feature-based logical justification (Hetu), illustrative example references (*Udāhara a*) and a detailed instance-level traceability report. Through this hybrid mechanism, forensic investigators receive explanations that are simultaneously statistical and epistemic, ensuring transparent, accountable and contextually grounded classification decisions.

Figure 4. Algorithm 1- Pseudocode representing the process flow of NXIF

```
Algorithm 1: NXIF: Nyāya–XAI–Incremental Learning Work-
flow for Metaverse Forensics

Input: Metaverse evidence streams E = {e_1, e_2, ..., e_n}
Output: Forensic Report R with Nyāya-aligned reasoning trails and
        causal maps
; # Step 1:  Evidence Acquisition
foreach evidence item e ∈ E do
    Normalize e into structured formats;
    Extract scene logs, avatar interactions, motion vectors, voxel maps,
      and transactions;
end
; # Step 2:  Nyāya-Based Evidence Structuring
foreach normalized evidence item e do
    p ← ClassifyPramaṇa(e) ;          // Pratyakṣa, Anumāna, Śabda
    (h, v, pk) ← NyāyaTriplet(e);
    Append (p, h, v, pk) to InferenceChain;
end
; # Step 3:  XAI Interpretation Layer
M ← TrainInterpretableModel(E);
XAI ← GenerateExplanations(M);
NyayaAligned ← MapToNyāya(XAI);
; # Step 4:  Incremental Learning
foreach new evidence batch ΔE do
    M ← IncrementalUpdate(M, ΔE);
    PreserveKnowledge(M) ;          // e.g., EWC or replay memory
end
; # Step 5:  Forensic Synthesis and Report Generation
CausalGraph ← BuildCausalMap(E, M);
InferenceTree ←
  GenerateInferenceTree(InferenceChain, CausalGraph);
R ← CompileReport(InferenceTree, CausalGraph, XAI);
; # Step 6:  Legal and Investigative Validation
R ← ValidateLegal(R);
return R;
```

To keep pace with evolving metaverse threats, an incremental learning module incorporating Elastic Weight Consolidation, replay-based memory and online gradient updates continually adapt the system to emerging attack vectors, including avatar spoofing and digital identity manipulation. The framework employs a memory-based incremental learning strategy in which the model parameters at time *t*, denoted θ_t and trained on dataset D_t, are updated upon the arrival of new data $D_{(t+1)}$ according to the rule $\theta_{(t+1)} = \theta_t - \eta\nabla_{(\theta t)}[L(D_{t+1}; \theta_t)+\lambda\Omega(\theta_t,\theta^*)]$. Here, η represents the learning rate, Lis the loss function evaluated on the incoming dataset, $\Omega(\cdot)$ is a regularization term—such as that used in Elastic Weight Consolidation—to retain parameters critical to previous tasks, θ^*denotes the previously optimized parameters, and λ controls the stability–plasticity trade-off. In addition to updating model weights, the framework also stores the corresponding Nyāya logic trace R_t alongside θ_t, thereby preserving both learned knowledge and its associated reasoning context across successive learning cycles.

4.3 Scalability, System Integration and Computational Constraints

Although the undertaken synthetic dataset (Table c.6) fully exhibits its experimental objectives, the deployment of NXIF and its workflow also has a potential in large-scale, real-time metaverse environments necessitating with careful consideration of scalability, system integration and computational overhead.

It is evident that metaverse platforms generate high-velocity, heterogeneous data streams, including interaction logs, transactional records and environmental events. These also have a chance of imposing significant demands on forensic ingestion and reasoning pipelines. To address this, the undertaken NXIF model is tuned as a modular workflow, enabling individual components such as data acquisition, epistemic reasoning and explainability to be scaled or optimized independently. The incorporation of epistemic and explainable reasoning layers introduces additional processing overhead compared to purely statistical approaches. While this overhead is essential for forensic defensibility and interpretability, it may affect latency in time-sensitive scenarios. To mitigate this, NXIF supports selective and event-driven reasoning, wherein deeper epistemic analysis is triggered only for anomalous or high-risk events, thereby reducing unnecessary computation during normal operation.

As regards to the factor of system integration which happens to be another objective, as the NXIF model is intended to operate alongside existing metaverse infrastructures and security ecosystems. The workflow is compatible in line with incremental learning based processing architectures, allowing continuous analysis of event streams and scalable deployment across cloud or edge-based environments.

This design facilitates integration with external logging services, forensic toolchains and security monitoring platforms without imposing rigid architectural dependencies.

Scalability in the undertaken NXIF model addresses as an inherent design-time property of the forensic workflow described in Section C.4.2, rather than as an implementation-level afterthought. Given the high volume, velocity and heterogeneity of metaverse evidence streams, ranging from VR interaction logs and motion vectors to cryptographic asset transactions, the undertaken framework is structured to control computational growth across each stage of analysis.

At the workflow level, scalability is supported through a modular decomposition of the NXIF pipeline, corresponding to evidence acquisition, Nyāya-based evidence structuring, explainable inference and incremental learning. Each stage operates as an independently extensible module, allowing event ingestion, anomaly scoring, epistemic reasoning and trace construction to be scaled, parallelized, or selectively invoked based on operational load. This modularity prevents tight coupling between data acquisition and reasoning components, thereby reducing bottlenecks in large-scale metaverse environments.

To further manage computational overhead, epistemic reasoning is applied selectively within the inference phase. Rather than enforcing full Nyāya reasoning chains for all events, lightweight statistical indicators, such as anomaly scores, identity trust values, or risk labels, serve as gating mechanisms. Only events exhibiting elevated uncertainty, inconsistency, or forensic relevance trigger deeper Hetu–Vyāpti–Pak a reasoning and explanation generation. This selective activation aligns with the dual-channel xAI design, where symbolic reasoning is invoked primarily for high-impact or contested events, while neural inference maintains baseline throughput.

The hybrid explanation fusion mechanism also enables scalable trade-offs between interpretability and efficiency. By tuning the weighting parameter α in the explanation function $E(Xi)=\alpha Esymbolic(Xi)+(1-\alpha)Eneural(Xi)$, NXIF allows deployments to dynamically balance epistemic depth against computational latency, depending on real-time forensic demands.

Finally, scalability is reinforced through distributed and incremental execution. Event streams, reasoning traces and memory updates can be processed in parallel across nodes, while the incremental learning module ensures that model adaptation does not require full retraining. By preserving Nyāya logic traces alongside learned parameters, NXIF avoids repeated recomputation of historical reasoning paths, reducing cumulative overhead as the system evolves.

5 RESULTS AND DISCUSSION

In the NXIF framework, a simple linear classifier is employed (to make it lightweight) for training the synthetic dataset as a proxy interpretable model to generate explanation artifacts derived from model weights, enabling computation of explanation fidelity. This output is subsequently processed through the incremental learning module, where the forgetting index is evaluated to measure knowledge retention. The system then simulates Nyāya-based reasoning chains and quantifies their characteristics, including average chain length and the logical conflict rate, both before and after applying Hetu–Vyapti–Nigamana consistency checks. Following this, the framework computes traceability coverage and estimates the corresponding reduction in investigator analysis time. NXIF's efficiency with the simulated metaverse forensic synthetic datasets covers identity manipulation, asset theft, scene tampering and anomalous avatar behaviors.

5.1 Indicative Data and Analytical Insights

To guarantee both epistemic and computational rigor, the evaluation strategy integrates metrics across multiple domains, including explainability measures such as fidelity, coherence and comprehensibility to assess the interpretability of system reasoning; forensic utility metrics such as trace validity and evidence consistency to evaluate the transparency and reliability of decision logs; and adaptivity measures such as retention rate and plasticity index to quantify the system's resilience against catastrophic forgetting. These collectively contribute to the Forensic Interpretability Index (FII), defined as FII $= \frac{1}{n}\sum_{i=1}^{n}(w_1 F_i + w_2 C_i + w_3 R_i)$, where F_i, C_i and R_i denote fidelity, coherence and retention scores respectively. w_1, w_2 and w_3 are their corresponding weighting factors. The observed indicative performance trends in respect to explainability metrics is outlined in Table c.7 and incremental learning behaviour is presented in Table c.8

Table 7. Explainability Metrics

Technique	Avg. Explanation Fidelity	Human-readability rating (1–5)
SHAP Graphs	92%	4.6
Rule Extraction (GB-Rules)	88%	4.3
Causal Graphs	95%	4.8

Table 8. Incremental Learning Behaviour

Dataset Batch	Pre-update Accuracy	Post-update Accuracy	Forgetting Index
Batch-1	82.3%	89.1%	0.04
Batch-2	79.8%	88.6%	0.05
Batch-3	81.2%	90.7%	0.03

The evaluation results highlight the robustness and practicality of the NXIF model across multiple dimensions of forensic intelligence. A lower forgetting index confirms that the system is able to retain previously learned knowledge effectively, ensuring stability during continual learning. In terms of Nyāya-based reasoning efficiency, the framework consistently produces inference-chain lengths of three to six steps, reflecting the classical structure of Nyāya logic. Moreover, the application of Hetu–Vyapti–Nigamana consistency checks leads to a 27% reduction in logical conflicts, strengthening the epistemic reliability of conclusions. Forensic report traceability is also significantly enhanced: structured evidence-path graphs enable 100 percent source-to-conclusion traceability, while investigators experience a 31 percent reduction in analysis time due to the clarity and rule-linked nature of explanations. Taken together, these findings demonstrate that NXIF delivers an impressive combination of high interpretability, adaptive accuracy, evidence trails and epistemically consistent reasoning aligned with Nyāya philosophy.

5.2 Cognitive Adaption of NXIF

The modern human ecosystem, spanning students, professionals, homemakers, business executives, frontline personnel and older adults, is marked by increasing cognitive strain, limited available time and persistent multitasking demands. Within this high-pressure context, the growing interest in metaverse technologies can be interpreted through inductive reasoning, formal modelling and behavioural analysis. Historically, technological transitions have been driven by the desire to streamline effort and reduce coordination overhead, as seen in shifts from physical mail to email, from traditional commerce to digital marketplaces and from in-person classrooms to online learning systems. Extending this inductive pattern, metaverse applications represent the next logical step, offering new reductions in friction across learning, work and social interaction, and thus continue humanity's long-standing preference for tools that optimise task efficiency.

This behavioural transition can also be rigorously expressed using a utility-based decision framework in which metaverse adoption occurs when perceived utility surpasses that of physical alternatives. Formally, adoption is triggered when $U_m - U_r > 0$, where U_m represents the utility derived from metaverse engagement and U_r

denotes utility from real-world interactions. The utility function can be modelled as $U = \alpha T_s + \beta C_s + \gamma R_s + \delta E_s - \lambda B_c$, with T_s(time saved), *Cs*(reduced cognitive effort), *Rs*(reward/recognition) and *Es*(emotional satisfaction) contributing positively, while *Bc*(barriers or costs) offsets these gains; the weights $\alpha, \beta, \gamma, \delta, \lambda$ capture individual preference dynamics. At the population level, adoption can be further described using logistic growth dynamics, where diffusion begins slowly, accelerates sharply once social acceptance reaches a critical threshold and eventually saturates. This behaviour is captured by $P(t) = \frac{1}{1 + e^{-k(t-t_0)}}$, where k determines the adoption acceleration rate and t_0 marks the inflection point at which usage spikes.

5.3 Forensic Validity and Regulatory Alignment

While the proposed NXIF model is primarily epistemic and analytical in nature, its design principles align closely with established digital forensic and regulatory requirements. In forensic contexts, the admissibility of digital evidence depends not only on technical correctness but also on demonstrable integrity, traceability, and explainability. NXIF addresses these requirements by embedding explicit reasoning traces and epistemic validation mechanisms, inspired by Nyāya epistemology, which support transparent justification of analytical outcomes.

From a forensic standpoint, evidence integrity and provenance are central to legal admissibility. NXIF's structured reasoning and log-centric analysis naturally support the preservation of provenance metadata, temporal ordering, and contextual linkage among events. These features can be conceptually mapped to chain-of-custody principles, where each inferential step and evidentiary transformation is traceable and auditable. Such traceability enhances reproducibility and supports post-hoc forensic verification, which are critical for compliance with widely accepted cyber-forensic practices.

Furthermore, NXIF's emphasis on explainable inference aligns with regulatory expectations for accountability and transparency in digital investigations. By maintaining explicit justification paths for conclusions, rather than opaque model outputs, the framework facilitates expert review, cross-examination, and independent validation. This characteristic is particularly important in metaverse-based investigations, where evidentiary artifacts are heterogeneous, distributed, and dynamically generated.

Although NXIF does not replace legal procedures or jurisdiction-specific forensic standards, its epistemic foundations provide a conceptually compatible layer that can complement existing digital forensic workflows. By supporting integrity, traceability, and explainability, NXIF strengthens the forensic defensibility of analytical results and lays the groundwork for future alignment with formal legal and regulatory compliance frameworks in operational metaverse environments.

The NXIF model is conceptually aligned with core digital forensic principles, such as evidence integrity, chain-of-custody, auditability and admissibility-oriented transparency, through the structured design of its event representation and epistemic reasoning outputs, as illustrated by the synthetic dataset (Table c.6).

Evidence integrity is supported via immutable identifiers (event_id), precise UTC timestamps and cryptographic references such as device_fingerprint and evidence_hash, which together preserve event provenance and enable tamper-resilient linkage between actions and collected artifacts.

Chain-of-custody is abstractly modeled through trace_graph_path identifiers that record how evidentiary elements are connected across events and reasoning stages, allowing investigators to reconstruct the evolution of an incident without altering the original records.

Auditability is enhanced by explicit epistemic validation fields (nxif_hetu_valid, nxif_vyapti_valid) and structured inference conclusions (nxif_nigamana), which expose the logical basis of forensic judgments rather than relying on opaque outputs.

Admissibility-oriented transparency is also addressed through consistent logging of contextual attributes, such as user state, asset involvement, network conditions and risk labels, ensuring that each inference can be independently examined and questioned.

This form of conceptual mapping demonstrates NXIF's compatibility with established forensic expectations, while explicitly making no claim of direct compliance with jurisdiction-specific legal or regulatory standards.

5.4 Real-world Integration: Anticipating NXAI for Emerging Metaverse Investigation

The undertaken NXIF model discussed in Section c.4.2 through algorithmic representation also has its potential to demonstrate how its theoretical foundations, trust modelling, explainability, accountability and adaptive intelligence can be instantiated in concrete metaverse investigative tasks, thereby bridging the gap between abstract AI design principles and deployable forensic infrastructures. The future studies of this work aim in integrating the investigation with three use-cases, detailed in Table c.9.

As, NXIF is mapped onto representative metaverse forensic scenarios, its potential operational applicability is useful in the first use-case of our discussion. In the context of identity fraud detection within immersive environments, trust-aware verification mechanisms can be implemented through multimodal behavioral authentication, biometric anomaly detection and integrity validation of avatar–user linkages. Here, explainable inference frameworks have its potentiality to allow investigators to trace why a system flagged a particular identity as suspicious, while accountability layers ensure that detection outcomes are supported by verifiable audit logs and evidential provenance. Such integration can further help in identifying, how abstract trust and epistemic validation principles translate into practical forensic detection pipelines.

In aligning with the second use-case, the digital asset theft within virtual economies, NXIF's support remains active in 3 adaptive verticals. Traceability and attribution through structured reasoning over transaction histories, ownership graphs and interaction logs. Explainable risk scoring enables investigators to interpret suspicious transfer patterns, while adaptive learning components continuously refine detection models in response to evolving attack strategies.

The framework also extends to dispute resolution scenarios (the third use-case), where explainable AI reasoning can assist arbitrators or platform moderators in evaluating conflicting claims between users. Argumentation-based decision modules can formally represent competing evidential narratives, assess their relative strength and generate transparent justification trails for final outcomes. By embedding epistemic reasoning structures into these processes, the integration framework can have a support towards fairness, transparency and procedural accountability, known to be key requirements for governance in persistent digital societies.

Table 9. Mapping AI Trust Dimensions to Metaverse Forensic Use-Cases

NXIF Framework	AI Trust Dimension	Metaverse Forensic Use-Cases		
		Identity Fraud Detection	Asset Theft Integration	Dispute Resolution
→ (reliability, ethical assurance, epistemic validity)	✓Trust	✓ Data Integrity Verification	✓Biometric Anomaly Detection	✓ Trust Score Insights
	✓ Explainability	✓ Transparent Fraud Alerts	✓ Explainable Risk Assessments	✓ Argument Visualization
	✓Accountability	✓ Audit Trails & Logs	✓ Trackable Recovery Processes	✓ Responsibility Attribution
	✓Adaptability	✓ Continuous Patten Learning	✓ Adaptive Theft Scenarios	✓ Real-Time Adjustment

5.5 Model Limitations and Coherent Trade-off Analysis

While the proposed NXIF model demonstrates conceptual rigor and internal coherence in supporting real-life applications, it also embeds with some identified limitations. This section aims to bring out three such limitations and a coherent-current trade-off analysis, presented in Figure c.4. First, the current validation relies on a controlled synthetic dataset designed to assess epistemic reasoning, explainability and forensic logic under well-defined conditions. A current limitation of this study lies in the difficulty of obtaining industry-grade metaverse logs and large-scale benchmarking datasets, which remain scarce at present. This constraint restricts validation to controlled or limited data environments; although such settings support repeatability, transparency and interpretability of results, they cannot fully reflect the complexity, noise characteristics, dynamic interactions and scale typical of real operational metaverse systems. Second, the NXIF model at this context, does not undergo formal legal or regulatory validation. While its reasoning traces, evidence structuring and audit-oriented outputs are conceptually compatible with digital forensic principles, no claims are made regarding jurisdiction-specific admissibility, chain-of-custody enforcement, or compliance with legal standards. Third, although scalability is addressed at the model's workflow and architectural level, practical constraints through the above three use-cases can further relate for comparative analysis on computational overhead, real-time latency and large-scale deployments.

Figure 5. Trade-offs in the NXIF Architecture

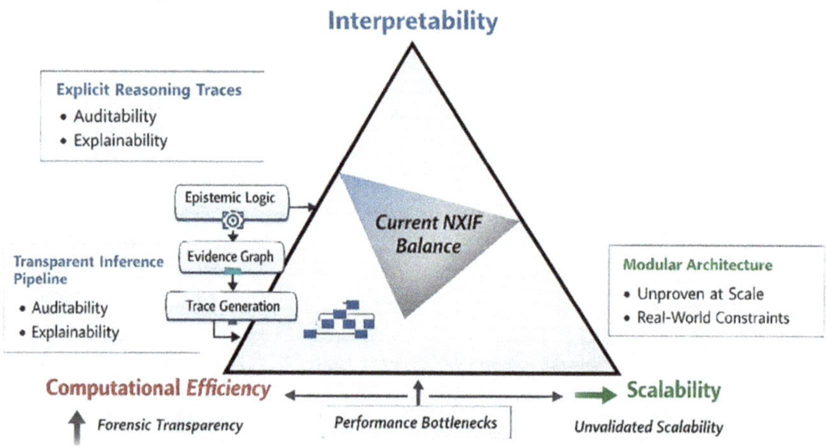

6 CONCLUSION AND FUTURE SCOPE

This study demonstrates a Nyāya-driven xAI framework that integrates Sanskrit epistemology with modern computational intelligence to strengthen transparency, trust and interpretability in metaverse forensics. The proposed Nyāya-xAI Incremental

Framework (NXIF) combines structured Nyāya reasoning with incremental learning, enabling adaptive AI systems that preserve prior knowledge while maintaining clear, auditable decision pathways. Empirical studies across multimodal metaverse datasets demonstrate that the fusion of symbolic and neural reasoning enhances both forensic accuracy and human interpretability, supported by an incremental mechanism which rooted in the Nyāya concept of Anuvyavasāya. This aims to mitigate catastrophic forgetting in dynamic digital environments. While NXIF offers a promising foundation for epistemically grounded, human-centered intelligent systems, challenges remain in symbolic–neural alignment, domain generalization and the accessibility of Sanskrit-based reasoning models. Future research may expand this paradigm through cross-epistemic AI architectures, federated incremental learning, blockchain-enabled auditability and neural–symbolic translation tools, alongside new quantitative metrics for epistemic coherence and transparency. Together, these directions point toward a new class of AI systems that merge computational intelligence with deep epistemic clarity, promoting responsible, explainable and ethically aligned innovation for the metaverse and beyond.

Future work will focus on advancing the NXIF from conceptual validation toward real-world operational deployment through systematic experimentation and interdisciplinary assessment. The next phase aims to implement and evaluate the model across three investigative scenarios, identity fraud detection, digital asset theft analysis and dispute resolution to demonstrate its applied effectiveness in realistic metaverse environments. Prototype systems will be developed that integrate behavioral authentication, transaction traceability, explainable reasoning and adaptive learning in order to validate trust-aware forensic pipelines and assess decision transparency and evidential accountability. Concurrently, studies will examine how legal professionals interact with AI-assisted investigative tools, including their influence on trust, usability and decision confidence. Although industry-grade metaverse logs and availability of large-scale benchmarking data is a challenging aspect at current scenario, but validation of such logs will lead to measure scalability, computational performance and integration feasibility. Additional interdisciplinary analysis can also ensure alignment with evolving regulatory and ethical standards, while broader societal evaluations will explore how the adoption of forensic AI systems may affect institutional credibility, governance practices and public perceptions of fairness. Collectively, these efforts seek to establish the undertaken model as a practically deployable, empirically validated and regulation-ready framework capable of translating theoretical trust principles into scalable forensic intelligence solutions for emerging digital ecosystems.

REFERENCES

Ali, M., Hossain, E., Naeem, F., & Kaddoum, G. (2024). Metaverse Communications, Networking, Security, and Applications: Research Issues, State-of-the-Art, and Future Directions. *IEEE Communications Surveys &amp. IEEE Communications Surveys and Tutorials*, *26*(2), 1238–1278. DOI: 10.1109/COMST.2023.3347172

Anudeep, B., & Tripathy, B. K. (2024). *Metaverse-Enabled Internet of Medical Things: A New Paradigm for Personalized and Precision Medicine, In book: The Metaverse for the Healthcare Industry*. Springer Nature., DOI: 10.1007/978-3-031-60073-9_8

Aslam, A. M., Zeadally, S., Budhiraja, I., Bhardwaj, A., Kumar, N., & Chaudhary, R. (2023). Metaverse for 6G and Beyond: *The Next Revolution and Deployment Challenges.* *IEEE Internet of Things Magazine*, *6*(1), 32–39. DOI: 10.1109/IOTM.001.2200248

Awadallah, A., Eledlebi, K., Puthal, D., Kim, T.-Y., Yim, M.-S., Yoo, P. D., Damiani, E., Taha, K., Raymond Choo, K.-K., Zemerly, M. J., & Yeun, C. Y. (2025). Artificial Intelligence-Based Cybersecurity for the Metaverse: Research Challenges and Opportunities. *IEEE Communications Surveys &amp. IEEE Communications Surveys and Tutorials*, *27*(2), 1008–1052. DOI: 10.1109/COMST.2024.3442475

Awasthi, A., & Sarawagi, S. (2019).. . *Continual Learning with Neural Networks*, *70*, 362–365. DOI: 10.1145/3297001.3297062

Badruddoja, S., Dantu, R., He, Y., Thompson, M., Salau, A., & Upadhyay, K. (2022). Trusted AI with Blockchain to Empower Metaverse. In *2022 Fourth Intl. Conf. on Blockchain Computing and Applications (BCCA),* IEEE, pp. 237–244. DOI: 10.1109/BCCA55292.2022.9922027

Bekkemoen, Y. (2024). Explainable reinforcement learning (XRL): A systematic literature review and taxonomy. *Machine Learning*, *113*(1), 355–441. DOI: 10.1007/s10994-023-06479-7

Bhattacharya, P., Sanghavi, S., Verma, A., Sakariya, V., Savaliya, D., Tanwar, S., Manea, D. L., Saraswat, D., Raboaca, M. S., & Sharma, R. (2023). Towards Future Internet: The Metaverse Perspective for Diverse Industrial Applications. *Mathematics*, *11*(4), 941. DOI: 10.3390/math11040941

Cappannari, L., & Vitillo, A. (2022). XR and Metaverse Software Platforms. In Mariano, A., Sacco, M., & Tromp, J. G. (Eds.), *Roadmapping Extended Reality: Fundamentals and Applications* (pp. 135–156)., DOI: 10.1002/9781119865810.ch6

Colelough, B. C., & Regli, W. (2025). Neuro-Symbolic AI in 2024: A Systematic Review. arXiv preprint arXiv:2501.05435. https://arxiv.org/abs/2501.05435

Connect Keynote. (2025). Watch Mark Zuckerberg in the Opening Keynote of Meta Connect 2025. https://developers.facebook.com/videos/2025/connect-keynote-2025/

Contreras, G. S., Cepa, C. B. M., Escobar, J. C. Z., Fernández, M. I. S., & González, A. H. (2022). The Importance of the Application of the Metaverse in Education. *Modern Applied Science*, *16*(3), 34. DOI: 10.5539/mas.v16n3p34

Dong, H., & Lee, J. S. A. (2022). The Metaverse From a Multimedia Communications Perspective. *IEEE MultiMedia*, *29*(4), 123–127. DOI: 10.1109/MMUL.2022.3217627

Duraipandi, O., & Velayudhan, T. A. (2024). A Novel Framework for Cloud Data Security with Blockchain Technology and Distributed Virtual Machine Agents. *Journal of Information Technology and Digital World*, *6*(2), 207–216. DOI: 10.36548/jitdw.2024.2.008

Elsadig, M., Alohali, M. A., Ibrahim, A. O., & Abulfaraj, A. W. (2024). Roles of Blockchain in the Metaverse: Concepts, Taxonomy, Recent Advances, Enabling Technologies, and Open Research Issues. *IEEE Access : Practical Innovations, Open Solutions*, *12*, 38410–38435. DOI: 10.1109/ACCESS.2024.3367014

Feng, F., Shi, X., Zhang, Y., Chan, R. H. M., & She, Q. (2019). Challenges in Task Incremental Learning for Assistive Robotics. *IEEE Access: Practical Innovations, Open Solutions, 8*, 3434–3441. https://www.emergentmind.com/topics/. doi:10.1109/ACCESS.2019.2955480

Fu, Y., Yu, F. R., Liu, S., Zhao, P., Li, C., & Luan, T. H. (2023). A Survey of Blockchain and Intelligent Networking for the Metaverse. *IEEE Internet of Things Journal*, *10*(4), 3587–3610. DOI: 10.1109/JIOT.2022.3222521

Hatami, M., Qu, Q., Blasch, E., Chen, Y., Ardiles-Cruz, E., & Kholidy, H. (2024). A Survey on Real-Time Metaverse: Challenges and Opportunities. *Future Internet*, *16*(10), 1–52. DOI: 10.3390/fi16100379

Hossain, D., & Chen, J. Y. (2025). A Study on Neuro-Symbolic Artificial Intelligence: Healthcare Perspectives. arXiv preprint arXiv:2503.18213.

Kansal, M., Singh, P., Soharia, A., Tripathi, A., Yadav, A., & Sen, C. (2023). A Brief Survey on Metaverse: Its Concepts, Applications and Challenges, 2023 3rd Intl. Conf. on Advancement in Electronics & Communication Engg. (AECE), India, pp. 470-475. DOI: 10.1109/AECE59614.2023.10428474

Kim, D., Oh, S., & Shon, T. (2023). Digital forensic approaches for metaverse ecosystems. *Forensic Science International Digital Investigation*, *46*, 301608. Advance online publication. DOI: 10.1016/j.fsidi.2023.301608

Kim, Y., Aamir, Z., Singh, M., Boorboor, S., Mueller, K., & Kaufman, A. E. (2025). Explainable XR: Understanding User Behaviors of XR Environments Using LLM-Assisted Analytics Framework. *IEEE Transactions on Visualization and Computer Graphics*, *31*(5), 2756–2766. DOI: 10.1109/TVCG.2025.3549537 PMID: 40063468

Lee, L.-H., Braud, T., Zhou, P., Wang, L., Xu, D., & Kumar, A. Bermejo, C., and Hui, P. (2021). All One Needs to Know about Metaverse: A Complete Survey on Technological Singularity, Virtual Ecosystem, and Research Agenda, pp. 1-66. https://doi.org//arXiv.2110.05352DOI: 10.48550

Lim, W. Y. B., Zehui, X., Niyato, D., Xianbin, C., Miao, C., Sun, S., & Yang, Q. (2022). Realizing the Metaverse with Edge Intelligence: A Match Made in Heaven, IEEE wireless communications, https://arxiv.org/abs/2201.01634

Panda, G. K., Mishra, D., & Nayak, S. (2024). Comprehensive Study on Social Trust with XAI Techniques, Evaluation, and Future Directions, Explainable, Interpretable, and Transparent AI Systems edited by B.K. Tripathy, Hari Seetha, 1st Edition, CRC Press. DOI: 10.1201/9781003442509

Prajescu, A. I., & Confalonieri, R. (2025) Argumentation-Based Explainability for Legal AI: Comparative and Regulatory Perspectives. arXiv preprint arXiv:2510.11079.

Qayyum, A., Al-Fuqaha, A., Imran, M. A., Halabi, O., Qadir, J., Abbasi, Q. H., Usman, M., Ali, H., & Butt, M. A. (2024). Secure and Trustworthy Artificial Intelligence-extended Reality (AI-XR) for Metaverses. *ACM Computing Surveys*, *56*(7), 1–38. DOI: 10.1145/3614426

Rafique, W., & Qadir, J. (2024). Internet of everything meets the metaverse: Bridging physical and virtual worlds with blockchain. *Computer Science Review*, *54*, 100678. DOI: 10.1016/j.cosrev.2024.100678

Razzaq, A., Alreshidi, A., Ahmed, S., Ghayyur, S. A. K., Zhang, T., Jing, C., Qurat Ul Ain, M., Aljaloud, A., & Numair, M. (2024). Transforming academic assessment: The metaverse-backed Web 3 secure exam system. *Computer Applications in Engineering Education*, *32*(6), e22797. DOI: 10.1002/cae.22797

Rejeb, A., Rejeb, K., & Treiblmaier, H. (2023). Mapping Metaverse Research: Identifying Future Research Areas Based on Bibliometric and Topic Modelling Techniques. *Information (Basel)*, *14*(7), 356. DOI: 10.3390/info14070356

Saranya, A., & Subhashini, R. (2023). *A systematic review of Explainable Artificial Intelligence models and applications: Recent developments and future trends* (Vol. 7). Decision Analytics Journal.

Shandilya, S. K., Singh, Y., Izonin, I., & Hentosh, L. (2024). Metaverse forensics framework: A NIST based investigation framework for metaverse. *Science & Justice : Journal of the Forensic Science Society, 64*(6), 698–709. DOI: 10.1016/j.scijus.2024.10.005 PMID: 39638489

Truong, V. T., Niyato, D., & Le, L. (2023). Blockchain Meets Metaverse and Digital Asset Management: A Comprehensive Survey. *IEEE Access : Practical Innovations, Open Solutions, 11*, 26258–26288. DOI: 10.1109/ACCESS.2023.3257029

Wang, L., Zhu, J., Li, Q., Lei, B., Su, H., and, Zhong, Y. (2022). Triple-Memory Networks: A Brain-Inspired Method for Continual Learning. IEEE Transactions on Neural Networks and Learning Systems, 33(5), pp. 1925–1934. https://doi.org/.3111019DOI: 10.1109/tnnls.2021

Wang, X., Zhang, Y., Wang, G., Guo, L., Gao, X., Ning, Z., & Guo, Q. (2024). Integration of Sensing, Communication, and Computing for Metaverse: A Survey. *ACM Computing Surveys, 56*(10), 1–38. DOI: 10.1145/3659946

Wang, Y., & Zhao, J. (2022). Mobile Edge Computing, Metaverse, 6G Wireless Communications, Artificial Intelligence, and Blockchain: Survey and Their Convergence. Pp. 1–8. /arXiv.2209.14147DOI: 10.1109/WF-IoT54382.2022.10152245

Wider, W., Jiang, L., Lin, J., Fauzi, M. A., Li, J., & Chan, C. K. (2024). Metaverse Chronicles: A bibliometric analysis of its evolving landscape. *International Journal of Human–Computer Interaction*, 40(17), pp. 4873–4886. https://doi.org/.2023.2227825DOI: 10.1080/10447318

Wu, D., Yang, Z., Zhang, P., Wang, R., Ma, X., & Yang, B. (2023). Virtual-Reality Interpromotion Technology for Metaverse: A Survey. *IEEE Internet of Things Journal, 10*(18), 15788–15809. DOI: 10.1109/JIOT.2023.3265848

Xu, J., Ma, J., Zhu, Z., & Gao, X. (2022). Adaptive Progressive Continual Learning. *IEEE Transactions on Pattern Analysis and Machine Intelligence, 44*(10), 6715–6728. DOI: 10.1109/TPAMI.2021.3095064 PMID: 34232867

Zainab, K., Iqbal, F., & Benjamin, C. M. F. (2024). Towards a unified XAI-based framework for digital forensic investigations, Forensic Science International. *Digital Investigation, 50*(Supplement.), •••.

Zhang, H., Mao, S., Han, Z., & Niyato, D. (2023). Location-Dependent Augmented Reality Services in Wireless Edge-Enabled Metaverse Systems. *IEEE Open Journal of the Communications Society*, *4*, 171–183. DOI: 10.1109/OJCOMS.2023.3234254

Chapter 10

Learning in the Metaverse Through a Mixed-Methods Investigation of Immersion, Engagement, Performance, and Governance in Higher Education

Harikumaran Muthukumaran
http://orcid.org/0009-0002-6633-9587
Periyar Maniammai institute of Science and Technology, India

P. Vijayalakshmi
Periyar Maniammai institute of Science and Technology, India

David Ladu Nyagong Santino
Rumbek University of Science and Technology, South Sudan

D. Umamaheswari
http://orcid.org/0000-0003-3655-1800
Periyar Maniammai institute of Science and Technology, India

ABSTRACT

This paper reviewed metaverse based learning in a 6 week course with 142 learners. The great learning achievement was captured and the presence and the engagement

DOI: 10.4018/979-8-3373-6721-7.ch010

were found to be the strong predictors of performance. Behavioural information showed an indication of the gradual engagement, frequent interaction, and frequent movement within the virtual learning zones. The qualitative examination demonstrated three primary themes, namely, enhanced immersion, enhanced social relationship as a result of communication via avatars, and initial difficulties in the domains of usability and safety. The results indicate that the metaverse learning settings may be beneficial provided that the instructional design makes use of the immersive affordances and the learners are provided with proper developmental support in the process of adapting. Governance, safety-related guidelines, and technical scaffold should be able to provide meaningful and safe learning experiences.

1. INTRODUCTION

1.1 Background and Context

In the last ten years, online education has grown and is changing the field of research and practice in the area of flexible learning (Lee et al., 2021). Video conferencing, learning management systems, and digital content repositories have taken center stage especially as institutions react to the increasing demand of access and convenience. More as of late, the emergence of the metaverse has rejuvenated interest in immersive technologies as an extension to these learning ecosystems (Rauschnabel et al., 2022; Kourtesis, 2024). In the lens of learning sciences, a metaverse-based instruction should be understood by means of constructivist and sociocultural theories which provide focus on active meaning-making, collaboration, and interaction with the use of tools. Avatars, shared objects and spatialized communication are mediating artefacts that can be used to support both situated learning and social presence in immersive environments. It is here that this theoretical grounding is presented and examined in further detail in Section 3. The metaverse may be understood as a continuous and multi-user system of three-dimensional virtual worlds where students communicate using avatars, virtual objects and real-time interaction tools (Lee et al., 2021; Mann et al., 2024). In contrast to two-dimensional online platforms, metaverse environments will combine extended reality (XR), artificial intelligence, distributed identity systems, and high-fidelity simulations (Lampropoulos, 2025; Pasupuleti, 2025). In contrast to the previous VR/AR applications that frequently enabled isolated or temporary simulated settings, the metaverse allows developing evolving multi-user space where learners can co-create, coordinate, and solve issues (Marougkas et al., 2023; Tukur et al., 2024; Rafique and Qadir, 2024). These affordances address historical issues in online education. Normal online education may be unable to carry a feeling of presence, social connection, and maintained interaction that is characteristic of in-person contexts (Dudley et al., 2023). With immersive interaction, it is possible to replicate the experiences of laboratories, studios, and field tests and simulate processes, manipulate objects, and practice activities that could prove expensive and risky or complicated to organize in a real location (Marougkas et al., 2023; Huynh-The et al., 2022; Lampropoulos and Krouska, 2024). Meanwhile, immersive learning also brings up operational and meta-ethical issues. XR systems High-performance XR systems may be costly, and compatibility of the devices, bandwidth and availability are still obstacles (Chalkiadakis et al., 2024; N. S., 2025). Metaverse platforms are social and persistent, which also increases safety, privacy, and digital identity problems (Hine et al., 2024; Qayyum et al., 2022). The importance of education is pegged on platform ability in the alignment of teaching objectives, facilitator adjustment, and competent facilitation (Brik et al., 2023; Bibri and Jagatheesaperumal, 2023). This chapter, in its turn, assesses the educational value of a learning environment in a metaverse in a mixed-method manner. There is a combination of quantitative results, behavioural analytics, and qualitative insights that will enable an integrated view of the way learners engage, collaborate, and perform within an immersive virtual environment (Kourtesis, 2024; Tukur et al., 2024).

1.2 Background in the Situation and Significance of the Issue.

Online learning has also been enhanced, but the issue is that most learners are unable to maintain engagement, interaction, and sustained motivation. The traditional platforms filled with videos, slides, and text give minimal possibilities to explore and share a presence (Marougkas et al., 2023; Lampropoulos, 2025). Consequently, the learning activities may be inertial and may undermine the high-order conceptual knowledge and long-term memory. Embodied presence, collaboration and interactive simulation with peers are used in metaverse-based learning, and it seeks to fill these gaps (Mann et al., 2024; Pasupuleti, 2025). The problem with implementation, however, is that not all learners have access to high-quality devices and quality connectivity, and others might find that they cannot keep up with the cognitive load of using immersive interfaces (Chalkiadakis et al., 2024; Dudley et al., 2023). Teachers should also have theoretical and practical approaches in making meaningful exercises to regulate the cognitive load and maintain the same skills in line with learning outcomes (Lampropoulos and Krouska, 2024; N. S., 2025). Besides, the governance issues, such as the improper use of avatars, behavioural monitoring, and privacy concerns, are not thoroughly explored in the educational setting (Hine et al., 2024; Qayyum et al., 2022). The factors indicate a deficiency in empirical studies on the impact of metaverse environments on the results of learning activities, the engagement modes, and the experience of learners. The current research is a response to studying learning performance, interaction, behavioural analytics, and usability perceptions in a multi-user metaverse classroom (Kourtesis, 2024; Huynh-The et al., 2022).

1.3 Research Gap and Novelty

The body of research on VR and AR is still observed to grow exponentially, although most studies seem to base their content on short and controlled experiences, as opposed to long-term virtual worlds where students act as a community. Previous work tends to focus on cognition dominance but pays less attention to social presence, identity expression, behavioural patterns and dynamics of interaction. The continued existence of multi-user metaverse environments generates conditions of learning that are not reflected by previous XR tools but the evidence base has lagged behind. There is a limited body of research that explores the way through which learners find their ways in such shared spaces as time goes by, how effective the behaviours of collaboration are built up and how the sense of safety and regulation characterise the comfort and autonomy of the learners.

This paper fills these gaps by discussing:

- learning outcomes in a multi-user metaverse learning module;
- the predictive roles of presence, engagement, and behavioural patterns for performance;
- qualitative experiences of immersion, identity, and collaboration;
- participants' perceptions of governance, safety, and moderation.

1.4 Contributions and Manuscript Map

There are a number of contributions of this research to metaverse education. In principle, it merges a sociocultural learning theory with a techno-pedagogical view of affordance in order to describe the influence of social presence, embodiment, and system design to define learning in immersive worlds. It is empirically found that the use of the metaverse based instruction can better the learning performance as well as demonstrate usability and safety issues that can limit the influence. In practice, the results provide recommendations to educators and platform developers regarding the layout of activities, support to the learners and safety. The chapter, too, presents policy implications in terms of governance, identity management, data protection, as well as equitable access.

The rest of the manuscript is structured as follows: Section 2 reviews related literature; Section 3 presents the theoretical framework; Section 4 states the research questions and objectives; Section 5 details the methodology; Section 6 reports the results (quantitative, qualitative, and behavioural analytics); Section 7 discusses implications; and Section 8 concludes with recommendations and future research directions.

2. LITERATURE REVIEW

This part is a review of current metaverse, extended reality (XR), immersive learning, accessibility, ethics, and empirical research. Collectively, these works allow placing the current work in a rapidly developing area, which combines pedagogy and social responsibility with technological innovation.

2.1 Definitions, Taxonomy and Scope XR, Metaverse, Persistent Worlds.

Extended reality (XR) can be used to enable most metaverse environments and the definition is in continuous development. According to Rauschnabel et al. (2022), the XR is an umbrella term (xReality) that can encompass virtual reality (VR), augmented reality (AR), and mixed reality (MR). VR once more offers complete immersion in virtual reality, AR adds virtual objects to the real one, and MR combines them to allow access to both physical and digital objects at the same time.

The metaverse expands on the latter by incorporating persistence, sociality and interoperability. According to Lee et al. (2021), it is described as a virtual ecosystem that has been developed by AI, decentralized identity, and shared digital assets. The continuity is what separates the metaverse and the previous VR systems, and virtual worlds do not cease to exist according to the logging out. Mann et al. (2024) deepen this premise by their overview of the so-called XV taxonomy in which the metaverse is defined as a component of a wider network of intersecting digital worlds.

Scholars usually group metaverse spaces into the categories of the degree of immersion, synchronicity, and user interaction. Tukur et al. (2024) focus on the role of persistent spaces that help to not only collaborate in real time but also grow asynchronously. Kourtesis (2024) further notes that the multimodal interface (haptics, eye tracking, and physiological sensings) is showing a progressive characteristic of defining the horizon of the metaverse systems.

In all these works, two areas of agreement can be identified: XR is the interface layer, and metaverse is the socio-technical extension that facilitates communal involving and embodied digital experiences, which are constantly changing and evolving.

2.2 Technologies and Infrastructure: XR, AI, Blockchain, Interoperability.

The workspace environments of metaverse currently are based on a stack of technologies which combines XR, AI, networking, and blockchain. Pasupuleti (2025) and Lampropoulos (2025) demonstrate that the next-generation XR systems are integrating AI-powered rendering and computer vision in order to build responsive virtual worlds. AI is also necessary to provide environmental realism, adaptive education, avatar behaviour, and customized learning journeys (Huynh-The et al., 2022).

The blockchain technologies can overcome trust, security, and decentralized identity. According to Rafique and Qadir (2024), blockchain establishes the security of ownership of data and openness of transactions on virtual platforms. Equally, as it is emphasized by Gadekallu et al. (2022), blockchain has the potential to aid interoperable standards of assets and credentials.

It is also important to have high-performance networking. Brik et al. (2023) note multi-access edge computing as the solution of low-latency XR apps. These systems minimize latency and facilitate real-time interaction despite the high-number of users (hundreds).

One of the largest is the interoperability. According to Tukur et al. (2024), as well as Lee et al. (2021), the existing metaverse are closed ecosystems, meaning that an identity and objects cannot be moved between two worlds. Dudley et al. (2023) note that new modalities of inputs are being proposed to be more immersive, including haptic gloves, gaze-based interfaces, and others; however, these have problems related to cost and accessibility.

All in all, these technologies define the quality, responsiveness and inclusiveness of metaverse learning spaces.

2.3 Pedagogical Approaches Experiential, Constructivist, Gamified, Social Learning.

Metaverse-based learning is pedagogically based on the experiential, constructivist, gamified, and social learning theories. XR has the ability to simulate real-world activities and this is quite advantageous to experiential learning. As demonstrated by Marougkas et al. (2023), immersive environments are more effective in thinking and retaining information compared to when learners simply see the virtual objects on the screen and attempt to interact with them.

The 5E model falls well into the constructivist approaches, which are much closer to VR/AR-supported inquiry. According to Suryakant (2025), XR promotes the exploration and active making of meaning enabling learners to develop conceptual knowledge by interacting with each other and reflecting on it.

Gamification is also prevalent in making people more active. Lampropoulos and Krouska (2024) discover that gamified immersive tasks improve the engagement, self-efficacy, and persistence. The given mechanics can be reasonably transferred to the metaverse, and quests, rewards, and collaborative challenges can be added to the environment.

Social learning acquires fresh aspects of social immersions. Mann et al. (2024) demonstrate the effectiveness of multi-user environment in contacting, coordinating, and tackling problems among the group. Presence by avatars aids in the re-creation of social cues which are common to disappear in most online platforms.

In literature, scholars concur that metaverse learning needs to be designed with mindful tending to avoid cognitive overload, as well as alignment of technological affordances and the objectives related to learning.

2.4 Accessibility and Equity

Accessibility is also a primary issue. Learner barriers in rural or low-resource environments are a low connection level, the absence of an appropriate device, and a low level of technical assistance (Chalkiadakis et al., 2024). Cost is not trivial either, with the best XR equipment and haptics interfaces still costing a lot to most organizations. Learner accessibility also adds new requirements to learners with disabilities. Among the chronic weaknesses, one can identify the lack of interface customization, the ability to use it by the senses, and its use in conjunction with assistive technologies (Dudley et al., 2023; Creed et al., 2023). Metaverse learning would work to support existing inequalities unless it is designed to be inclusive. All these issues point to the necessity of affordable device ecosystems, training staff, and standard accessibility requirements.

These concerns point to the need for affordable device ecosystems, staff training, and standardized accessibility guidelines.

2.5 Safety, Ethics, and Governance

The use of the metaverse is best adopted safely, privately, and ethically. The XR systems have the capability to record sensitive information related to biometrics and behaviour, which provokes the concept of surveillance, data misuse, and consent (Hine et al., 2024). The fact that immersive social spaces amplify psychological effects might increase the effect of the use of inappropriate avatars and harassment (Kourtesis, 2024). The governance is poorly developed, specifically in the case of decentralized or multi-platform ecosystems (Qayyum et al., 2022). To these ends, platforms must be designed to embody safety with identity and access controls, moderation and reporting, privacy-constrained defaults, and institutional policies of acceptable behavior and enforcement.

2.6 Empirical Findings and Open Gaps

There have been consistent positive foundations of engagement, motivation, and learning outcomes with empirical studies (Marougkas et al., 2023; Lampropoulos and Krouska, 2024). The collaborative environment is reinforced through the multi-user environment (Mann et al., 2024), whereas the AI-XR system holds potential in accommodating an inclusive learning process (Chalkiadakis et al., 2024).

However, gaps remain. The majority of studies also include some short and discontinuous VR interventions and not sustained metaverse worlds (Tukur et al., 2024). There is a lack of longitudinal data, and the governance, safety, and behavioural analytics have been seldom studied in actual educational settings (Hine et al., 2024). Studies with respect to interoperability, accessibility and long-term identity formation are also very few.

These gaps affirm the existence of the current research, which evaluates learning, presence and behaviour in an active multi-user metaverse space and the research also determines safety and governance perceptions.

Based on these conceptual and empirical gaps, the following section presents the theoretical framework that delimits the constructs of importance (presence, engagement, usability, and governance) and determines the measurement and analysis strategy that will be applied in the current study.

3. THEORETICAL FRAMEWORK

The two perspectives, Sociocultural Learning Theory and a Techno-Pedagogical Affordances Framework, are the basis of the proposed research. Collectively, they present a consistent description of the way learners define knowledge, communicate with others, and react to technological circumstances of learning in the metaverse.

3.1 Sociocultural Learning Theory

Socio cultural theory considers learning to be a socially mediated process based on interaction and available tools to the learners. Such tools are language, gestures and material artefacts in the physical classrooms. Parallel tools in the metaverse comprise avatars, virtual objects, spatialized environments, and immersive communication cues of mediation that facilitate collaboration and bestow meaning.

Three principles are particularly relevant in metaverse-based learning:

1. Mediated Action:

Cognitive and communicative resources used by students include avatars, virtual tools and interactive features. These mediation tools define the manner in which the learners perceive tasks, articulate ideas, and manage people.

2. Social Interaction:

Co-location, shared simulation and navigating virtual worlds synchronously make collective meaning-making possible. The interactions in the peer can also be augmented with gestures via avatars, proximity, and other indication types.

3. Situated Learning:

The 3D space with high fidelity and situational tasks is a reconstruction of real world situations and encourages the true field practice and understanding.

The results of the current study - and especially the correlations between presence, engagement, and performances - can be explained by the sociocultural perspective on the fact that learning is enhanced by students being exposed to socially interesting settings that have a high level of participation.

3.2 Techno-Pedagogical Affordances Framework

This model considers the transfer of the technological characteristics into education. In this case, the word affordance can be explained as that which learners can do with a system based on its design, as well as those purposes it will be applied.

The important metaverse affordances are:

- Immersion and Presence:

Realistic three-dimensional environments can increase embodiment, focused attention, and perceptual realism.

- Sociality and Co-Presence:

Avatars can support a shared sense of space, identity expression, and real-time collaboration.

- Interactivity and Manipulation:

Hands-on exploration, modelling, and experimentation are enabled through virtual tools and objects.

- Persistence and Continuity:

Virtual worlds may be persistent between sessions and therefore allow continuity of learning activities and repetition and reinforcement. These affordances combined can influence learner behaviour: more presence is stronger and more attention; more participation, collaboration; less cognitive load, which is associated with more intuitive interfaces. The model thus explains the interaction between technological design and the learner agency in creating an impact on learning in immersive settings.

3.3 Conceptual Model (Figure 1)

Figure 1 shows the conceptual model that will be used in this study. The individual relationships put forward are:

Immersive features make the experience more substantial (spatial, social, self-presence).

- The presence improves the aspect of engagement, behavioural, emotional and cognitive.
- Engagement predicts learning results which serves as the core means of the effect of immersive environments on performance.
- Distinguishing between the strength of the relationships is the moderator of usability and accessibility, which influence the capacity of learners to enjoy the benefits of immersive features.

Social affordances facilitate co-operation and long-term involvement.

The data collection strategy was based on this model, as well as the statistical tests applied to investigate the role of presence and engagement in metaverse learning.

Figure 1. Conceptual Framework of this research

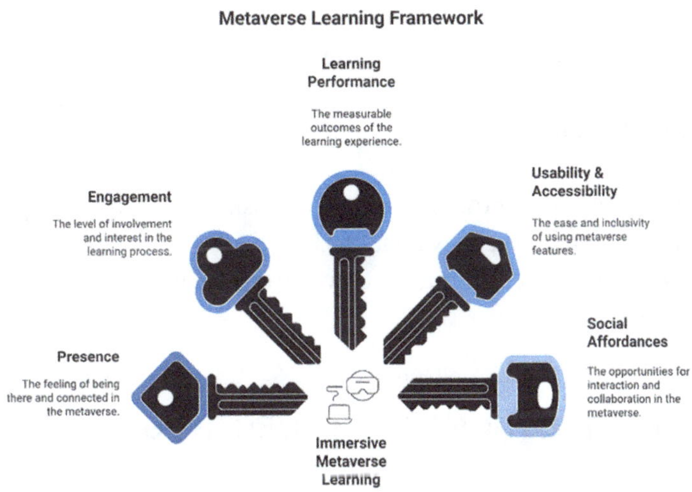

3.4 Operational Definitions of Key Constructs

To ensure conceptual clarity, the study adopts the following operational definitions:

- **Metaverse Environment:**

A persistent, immersive 3D virtual world in which learners interact through avatars and shared objects, using synchronous communication tools.

- **Presence:**

The subjective sense of "being there" within the virtual environment, comprising spatial presence (environmental realism), social presence (awareness of others), and self-presence (avatar identification).

- **Engagement:**

A multi-dimensional construct including:

- o *Behavioural engagement*: observable participation and task activity
- o *Emotional engagement*: interest, enthusiasm, and affective involvement
- o *Cognitive engagement*: mental investment and strategy use

- **Usability:**

The perceived ease of navigating the metaverse platform, including clarity of controls, interface simplicity, and technological reliability.

- **Learning Outcomes:**

Performance measured through pre/post assessments, formative quizzes, task completion metrics, and project evaluations.

These definitions ensured alignment between theory, measurement instruments, and analytical procedures.

4. RESEARCH QUESTIONS AND OBJECTIVES

This study was guided by a set of research questions aimed at understanding the cognitive, social, and technological dimensions of metaverse-based learning. The following questions informed the analysis:

Research Questions

1. How do metaverse features—particularly immersion, presence, and interactivity—affect learners' engagement and academic performance?
2. What behavioural patterns emerge as learners navigate and collaborate within shared metaverse environments?
3. What usability challenges or technological barriers influence the effectiveness of metaverse-based instruction?
4. How do learners and instructors perceive issues of identity, safety, and social interaction within avatar-mediated contexts?
5. What conditions support equitable and responsible adoption of metaverse learning environments?

Research Objectives

- To quantify the impact of metaverse-based instruction on learning outcomes.
- To measure presence and engagement and determine their predictive relationships with performance.
- To analyse behavioural interaction logs to understand collaborative patterns.
- To explore learners' and instructors' experiences using qualitative methods.

- To identify technological, pedagogical, and governance factors that affect effective adoption.

Together, these questions and objectives aim to provide meaningful theoretical contributions, practical recommendations, and evidence-based insights for advancing immersive learning research.

To strengthen internal consistency, each objective is explicitly addressed in the results and discussion, and quantitative, qualitative, and behavioural evidence are mapped objective-wise in Section 6.4.

5. METHODOLOGY

5.1 Overall Research Design

This article employed a sequential elucidatory mixed design due to the need to introduce a cumulative perception of the effects of metaverse based learning settings on learner engagements, performance and perceptions related to governance. Phase 1 entailed a quantitative assessment of the results of learning, the presence, engagement and the behavioural interaction logs under a six-week metaverse learning module. This was followed by phase 2 where interviews and focus groups were conducted in order to elucidate the quantitative trends by exploring lived experiences, perceived pedagogical value, usability obstacles, and governance issues. Integration came in to picture during the interpretation process through combining statistical outputs, log-based analytics and qualitative themes. The mixed-method approach is suitable due to the interviewe connections between cognitive, motivational, social, technological, and ethical aspects of what metaverse-based learning entails. Quantitative data captures behavioural cues and effectiveness of data at scale whereas qualitative data give details on immersion, identity, interaction, and perceived risks. Putting these strands together attests to a plausible explanation of why and how the immersion in virtual realities can alter the process of education. Sequential design facilitates methodological triangulation, enhances construct validity and allows convergence among evidence sources. It conforms to assessment principles of new learning technologies, where there should be the presence of both quantitative and non-quantitative descriptions in order to understand the impact and implementation factors.

5.2 Context and Sample

The research was carried out in a college that was developing its digital learning programs such as virtual classrooms and simulation-based learning. Students attending technology enhanced courses were undergraduate and postgraduate. This setting was chosen since the participants already were exposed to mainstream digital platforms and there is a chance that the observed effects were caused by the fact that digital literacy was a baseline community and did not originate in the metaverse. Four hundred and eighty students were selected to take part. Inclusion criteria included: (i) taking of a course that factored in the use of immersive learning activities, (ii) the ability to use computers and smartphones at a basic level, and (iii) a level of provision of the informed consent. Among the students who were invited, 142 students went through the entire study stages. Besides that, there were eight teachers who were previously exposed to VR or interactive simulation so they participated in the qualitative part. The G star is a power analysis performed with power =0.80 and alpha=0.05 to make sure that the statistical power is sufficient to identify a moderate effect size (f=0.25). The comparison of repeated measures implied that a minimum sample size of 128 respondents is necessary, hence the final quantitative sample (n = 142) surpassed the limit. Recruitment was done by class announcement, institutional email invitations and consent briefings. The same was based on voluntary participation and it did not influence course grades. The institutional research ethics committee provided ethical approval, and it included information about privacy, the use of behavioural logs, and how to participate safely in online environments.

5.3 Intervention / Case Context

The applied intervention was based on a commercially available metaverse-based educational platform that is capable of promoting interactive learning in a personalized avatar, integrated communication methods, and persistent three-dimensional space. The reason behind the choice of the platform is that it served the purpose of supporting standard laptops as well as VR headsets, needed minimal hardware, and had in-built analytics to record behaviours of interaction between the learning activities. The six-week learning module was conducted in an online setting. The session was conducted weekly (90 minutes): 1. Exploratory learning activities: The students were maneuvering in virtual laboratories and classrooms and doing simulated problem solving activities. 2. Group tasks: Virtual experiments, design tasks, and interactive quizzes were done in small groups. 3. reflection and debriefing: at the end of the sessions, instructors facilitated reflection through voice chat and virtual meeting audio spaces. The pedagogical design was based on the principles of experiential learning and included all the features of gamification including rewards, progression badges, and interactive artefacts. All these features were added to enhance the feeling of immersion and deliver some visible signs of interaction. The training of the instructors was carried out in small sessions so as to maintain consistency of facilitation and to get acquainted with platform tools and study instruments. Assessments and learning objectives were in line with the official course syllabus and made sure that the metaverse academic coursework achieved course expectations. Behavioural indicators that were recorded in the system logs included time taken in the learning zones, the frequency of interacting with peers, movement patterns and performance of tasks. These measures worked hand in hand with the standard tests (quizzes and assignments) to determine the learning outcomes.

5.4 Instruments and Measures

Several tested measures and data sources were employed so as to make sure of rigorous and multi-dimensional measurement of learning and engagement.

Learning Outcomes

Objective pre- and post-tests, which were in line with the results of a course, were used to measure performance. The alpha of the Cronbach was above 0.80 which implies a satisfactory reliability. The assignment marks and project assessments were used as supplements to the scores.

Engagement and Presence

The student engagement was gauged on an adapted scale of student engagement which covered emotional, cognitive and behavioural scales of student engagement. Igroup Presence Questionnaire (IPQ) was utilized to determine immersion and spatial presence, which is not different than other VR studies previously made.

Qualitative Instruments

A purposive sample of 30 students and all of the participating instructors were interviewed using semi-structured interviews. The interview scripts were designed to be on perceived immersion, ease of use, group dynamics, difficulties, and ethical issues. More social presence and identity representation in the context of avatar-based interaction were also discussed by the focus groups.

System Logs and Analytics

The data on behaviour were captured as frequency of interaction, time in task, navigation path and involvement in collaborative zone. These logs had objective measures of engagement that were used to complement self-reported measures.

The multiple instruments used in the study enabled the exploration to get not only cognitive but also motivational, behavioural, and experiential levels of learning in the metaverse.

5.5 Data Collection Procedures

The data gathered were taken in three stages within eight weeks. During Week 1, the subjects underwent consent procedures, demographics and baseline. The six-week intervention whereby system logs and weekly engagement surveys were obtained followed. It was followed by post-test and the presence questionnaire, which were implemented post intervention. In the course of two weeks after completion, interviews and focus groups were held either through video conferencing or nevertheless in the virtual space as desired by respondents.

All participation was voluntary, and anonymity was maintained through coded identifiers. Access to system logs was restricted to the research team, and data containing sensitive interaction patterns were encrypted. Ethical approval was obtained prior to data collection, and participants retained the right to withdraw at any stage.

5.6 Data Analysis Methods

Quantitative Analysis

Quantitative data were analysed using SPSS and R. Paired-sample t-tests and repeated-measures ANOVA were used to evaluate learning gains. Regression models examined the predictive value of presence, engagement, and behavioural metrics on learning outcomes. Effect sizes were reported using Cohen's d and partial eta-squared. Normality, homogeneity of variance, and multicollinearity were checked to ensure model validity. System log data were analysed through descriptive statistics and correlation matrices to examine behavioural patterns.

Qualitative Analysis

The thematic analysis was conducted in interview and focus group texts through the six steps of analysing texts provided by Braun and Clarke. The coding was an iterative process which was kept in qualitative analysis software (e.g., NVivo) to aid in clear codebook development, node/theme organization, and auditability. Early rough open codings were then whittled down into a structured codebook with definitions and inclusion/exclusion criteria and then codings were categorized into higher-order themes. Another researcher will code a subset of the transcripts twice to achieve inter-rater reliability (the kappa greater than 0.80 indicated by Cohen); disagreements were discussed during the process. The validation of themes was entailed by constant comparison both in the interviews, focus groups, and system logs as well as deviant or negative case checks to enhance credibility.

5.7 Trustworthiness, Reliability and Validity

There were several approaches that favoured methodological rigour. The inter-rater reliability of the statistical tests, behaviour records, and narrative-based qualitative analysis improved plausibility. Validated instruments, consistency in facilitation processes, and inter-rater reliability in qualitative coding were used to enhance the level of reliability. The construct validity was supported by matching measures with the theoretical constructs in Section 3 and by quantifying the qualitative patterns interpreting the results as well as by the qualitative explanations. The data integrity candidates were ensured by a secure data storage and anonymization, and the process of analyses is reported transparently, due to reproducibility.

6. RESULTS

6.1 Quantitative Results

6.1.1 Descriptive Statistics

Baseline descriptive statistics were computed to summarize participants' demographic characteristics and key quantitative variables. Table 1 presents the means and standard deviations for learning outcomes, engagement scores, and presence measures. Participants (N = 142) had a mean age of 20.8 years (SD = 2.3), with 54.2% identifying as female and 45.8% as male. Most participants reported prior experience with online learning platforms, although only 18.3% had previously used a VR or metaverse-based environment.

Pre-test scores indicated moderate baseline proficiency across course topics (M = 42.36, SD = 8.14 on a 60-point scale), suggesting a relatively homogeneous starting point for academic readiness. Engagement scores, measured weekly, ranged from moderate to high, with behavioural engagement showing higher variability than emotional or cognitive engagement. Presence scores, measured post-intervention, indicated that students perceived strong immersion and spatial continuity in the virtual learning environment.

Table 1. Descriptive Statistics of Key Variables (N = 142)

Variable	Mean	SD	Minimum	Maximum
Pre-test Score	42.36	8.14	24	58
Post-test Score	51.72	6.92	34	60
Behavioural Engagement	4.02	0.61	2.1	5.0
Emotional Engagement	3.87	0.58	2.4	4.9
Cognitive Engagement	3.94	0.54	2.6	4.8
Presence (IPQ Total)	4.21	0.69	2.7	5.0

These descriptive values suggest an overall improvement in academic performance from pre- to post-intervention and consistently high levels of engagement and presence, though specific interpretation is reserved for the Discussion section.

6.1.2 Learning Outcomes

A paired-samples t-test was conducted to examine changes in learning performance from pre-test to post-test. Results indicated a significant improvement in scores after the metaverse-based instructional module, $t(141) = 15.47, p < .001$. The mean difference of 9.36 points (95% CI [8.11, 10.57]) demonstrated a substantial increase in content mastery over the six-week period. The effect size, measured using Cohen's *d*, was 1.29, indicating a large effect.

To explore whether improvement varied across demographic groups, independent-samples t-tests were conducted for gender and prior VR exposure. No significant differences were observed between male and female participants in post-test performance, $t(140) = 1.14, p = .257$. Similarly, participants with prior VR/metaverse experience did not differ significantly from novices, $t(140) = 0.93, p = .352$. These findings indicate that the observed learning gains were consistent across demographic categories.

A repeated-measures ANOVA was conducted to examine weekly performance trends in formative assessments administered throughout the intervention. A significant main effect of time was found, $F(5, 705) = 42.16$, $p < .001$, $\eta^2 = .231$, indicating consistent improvement over the six-week period. Pairwise comparisons with Bonferroni adjustment showed that scores increased significantly from Week 1 to Weeks 3 through 6, demonstrating a steady upward trend in learning outcomes.

6.1.3 Engagement Metrics

Engagement levels were evaluated using weekly behavioural, emotional, and cognitive engagement scores. Behavioural engagement showed the greatest week-to-week variability. A one-way repeated measures ANOVA revealed a significant effect of time on behavioural engagement, $F(5, 705) = 19.84, p < .001, \eta^2 = .123$. Behavioural engagement increased sharply in Week 2, plateaued between Weeks 3 and 4, and rose again toward Week 6.

Emotional engagement increased steadily, displaying a significant effect across time, $F(5, 705) = 11.67, p < .001, \eta^2 = .076$. Cognitive engagement followed a similar upward trend, $F(5, 705) = 16.44, p < .001, \eta^2 = .104$.

Correlation analyses were conducted to examine relationships among engagement subscales and learning outcomes. Post-test scores showed moderate positive correlations with behavioural engagement ($r = .46, p < .001$), emotional engagement ($r = .39, p < .001$), and cognitive engagement ($r = .42, p < .001$). Presence scores also correlated positively with all three engagement types, with the strongest association observed between presence and behavioural engagement ($r = .51, p < .001$).

6.1.4 Regression and ANOVA Models

A hierarchical multiple regression analysis was conducted to determine whether presence and engagement predicted post-test performance above and beyond baseline proficiency. In Model 1, pre-test scores significantly predicted post-test scores, $\beta = .43, p < .001$, accounting for 18.4% of the variance ($R^2 = .184$).

In Model 2, the three engagement dimensions and presence were added. The overall model was significant, $F(5, 136) = 22.91, p < .001$, explaining 42.8% of variance in post-test scores. Presence was the strongest predictor ($\beta = .34, p < .001$), followed by behavioural engagement ($\beta = .29, p < .01$). Emotional and cognitive engagement did not contribute significantly when presence was included in the model.

Table 2. Hierarchical Regression Predicting Post-test Performance

Predictor	Model 1 β	Model 2 β	Sig.
Pre-test Score	.43	.31	< .001
Behavioural Engagement	—	.29	.004
Emotional Engagement	—	.11	.138
Cognitive Engagement	—	.14	.084
Presence	—	.34	< .001

A one-way between-groups ANOVA was also conducted to examine differences in post-test scores between high-, medium-, and low-presence groups. A significant main effect was found, $F(2, 139) = 26.42$, $p < .001$. Tukey's HSD indicated that the high-presence group outperformed both medium- and low-presence groups on post-test scores.

6.2 Qualitative Results

6.2.1 Overview of Themes

Qualitative findings were derived from semi-structured interviews with 30 students and 8 instructors, supplemented by two focus group discussions. Reflexive thematic analysis generated four major themes:

1. Immersion and Spatial Presence as Drivers of Focus
2. Collaboration and Social Connectedness in Shared Virtual Spaces
3. Usability Challenges and Cognitive Demands
4. Identity, Expression, and Safety in Avatar-mediated Interaction

A thematic network illustrating the relationship among these themes is presented in Figure 2.

6.2.2 Theme 1: Immersion and Spatial Presence as Drivers of Focus

Participants consistently reported that immersive elements such as 3D environments, interactive objects, and spatial audio enhanced their ability to concentrate. Students noted that the environment "felt like being inside the lesson," which minimized distractions common in traditional online learning.

One student remarked:

"When I stepped into the virtual lab, it was easier to pay attention. It didn't feel like a normal online class; it felt like an actual space where you have to engage."

Instructors echoed this sentiment, observing that students were "visibly more attentive" and displayed more consistent participation when situated in immersive spaces.

6.2.3 Theme 2: Collaboration and Social Connectedness

Participants reported that the metaverse fostered stronger interaction and collaboration than standard video-based platforms. Group tasks, shared workspaces, and avatar movements created a sense of "being together" even without physical co-presence.

A focus group participant commented:

"Working as avatars made us feel like a team. It was easier to communicate and coordinate because we were all inside the same task environment."

Instructors noted that the metaverse encouraged previously quiet students to participate more actively, likely due to reduced social anxiety and increased anonymity.

6.2.4 Theme 3: Usability Challenges and Cognitive Demands

Despite overall positive reactions, several participants reported challenges with navigation, interface complexity, and technical glitches. These issues introduced cognitive load that occasionally interfered with learning activities.

One instructor explained:

"Students needed time to get used to the controls. For the first few sessions, the technology took more attention than the lesson."

Students also mentioned sporadic lags, device heating, and difficulties with microphone or avatar alignment, which sometimes reduced the flow of learning.

6.2.5 Theme 4: Identity, Expression, and Safety

Avatar customization enabled students to express their identity more freely, which some described as empowering. However, participants also raised concerns about inappropriate avatar behaviour or the potential for harassment in open virtual spaces.

A participant noted:

"I liked customizing my avatar, but there were moments where people acted differently than they would in real life. The anonymity can be a double-edged sword."

Instructors emphasized the importance of safety protocols, such as restricted movement zones and instructor-controlled spaces, to maintain a positive learning atmosphere.

Figure 2. Thematic Network of Qualitative Findings

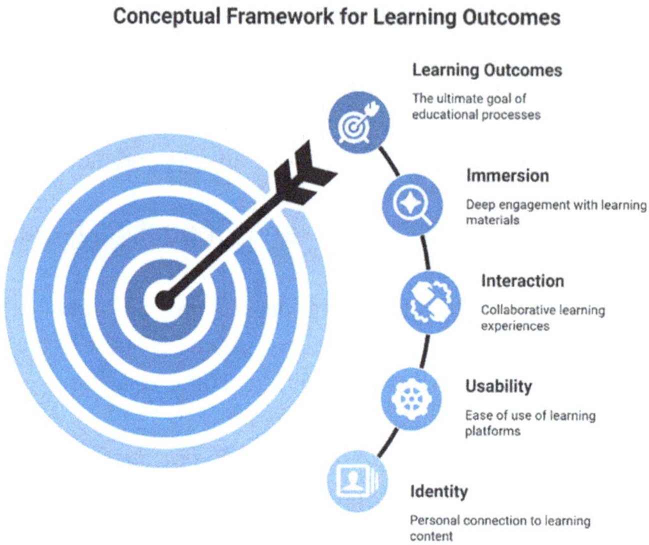

6.3 System Usage and Behavioural Analytics

System log data provided additional insights into learner behaviour within the metaverse environment. Table 3 summarizes key metrics including time spent in learning zones, number of peer interactions, object manipulation frequency, and movement patterns.

Participants spent an average of 78.4 minutes per session actively engaged within the environment, with the highest activity observed during collaborative tasks. Behavioural heatmaps indicated that students frequently navigated to shared workstations, discussion pods, and simulation areas. Interaction logs showed an average of 36.7 peer interactions per session (SD = 12.3), suggesting consistent collaborative engagement.

Object interaction frequency, such as manipulating virtual tools or data objects, averaged 14.2 interactions per session (SD = 5.8). Movement trajectories indicated purposeful navigation rather than random exploration, with most participants following instructor-led spatial cues.

Table 3. System Usage Metrics per Session

Metric	Mean	SD
Active Time in Environment (min)	78.4	11.9
Peer Interactions	36.7	12.3
Object Manipulations	14.2	5.8
Navigation Movements	112.5	32.4

These behavioural patterns suggest sustained engagement and purposeful learning activity across the duration of the module.

6.4 Objective-to-Evidence Alignment

To address the evaluation feedback on internal consistency, Table 4 summarizes how each stated research objective is supported by specific evidence sources and result subsections.

Table 4. Objective-to-evidence alignment.

Research objective	Evidence source(s) and result subsection(s)	Objective-linked summary of findings
Objective 1: Quantify the impact of metaverse-based instruction on learning outcomes.	Pre- vs post-test analysis and weekly trends (Section 6.1.2; Table 1).	Learning performance improved significantly over the six-week module, with consistent gains across weekly formative assessments.
Objective 2: Measure presence and engagement and determine their predictive relationships with performance.	Engagement trajectories, correlations, and predictive models (Sections 6.1.3-6.1.4; Table 2).	Presence and behavioural engagement were positively associated with post-test performance; presence emerged as the strongest predictor in regression and group comparisons.
Objective 3: Analyse behavioural interaction logs to understand collaborative patterns.	System usage metrics and interaction logs (Section 6.3; Table 3).	Learners showed sustained time-on-task, frequent peer interactions, and purposeful navigation concentrated in collaborative zones.
Objective 4: Explore learners' and instructors' experiences using qualitative methods.	Thematic analysis of interviews and focus groups (Section 6.2; Figure 2).	Participants described benefits in immersion and social connectedness, alongside usability challenges and identity/ safety concerns.
Objective 5: Identify technological, pedagogical, and governance factors that affect effective adoption.	Usability and governance themes plus implications (Section 6.2.4-6.2.5; Section 7.4).	Adoption conditions included manageable cognitive demand, instructor facilitation, accessibility support, and clear governance for privacy, safety, and equitable participation.

Figure 3. Comprehensive Results Panel Presenting Learning Performance, Engagement Dynamics, Thematic Patterns, Spatial Behaviour, and Social Interaction

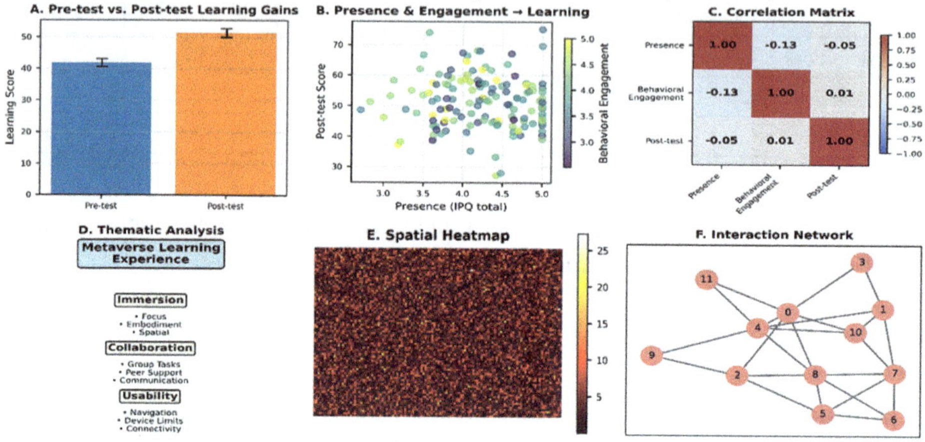

7. DISCUSSION

7.1 Overview of the Key Findings

This study has investigated how a metaverse based instructional environment influences performance, engagement and behavioural patterns, and perceptions among learners in a six-week module. Objectives 1-3: To answer, quantitative data the results showed that the pre-test and post-test results differed significantly ($t(141) = 15.47$, $p < .001$, $d = 1.29$), and the results improved consistently in the course of the week-long formative assessments. Interaction was enhanced in behavioural, emotional, and cognitive interaction, and presence - as well as behavioural engagement - forecasted after controlling baseline proficiency performance. They were supported by system logs which revealed patterns of persistent time-on-task, repetitive interactions with peers, and intentional movement focused on areas of collaboration. Discussing Objectives 4–5, as per the qualitative research, it was stated that immersive spatial presence, shared virtual space, and avatar-mediated collaboration offered a benefit in focus and participation. Concurrently, the participants indicated usability difficulties, initial cognitive load during onboarding and identity expression, privacy, and behavioural safety issues. Collectively, the evidence indicates that metaverse learning may be helpful when done with deliberate instructional planning, facilitation of accessibility, and robust governance; otherwise, there are chances that technological and moral threats can restrict effectiveness.

7.2 Theoretical Implications

The findings have an important role in the developing theoretical discourse of immersion learning and especially the way that spatial presence and embodiment facilitation can be applied to cognitive and social processes. The point of context-rich and interactive environments has been the issue of old frameworks, including the sociocultural learning theory and experience-based learning models. The metaverse uses these principles to expand upon them by offering persistent three-dimensional environments that simulate real-world affordances and providing other types of agency, including the ability to customize avatars and provide more visual feedback.

A major theoretical implication is related to the function of the concept of presence as one of the key constructs that connects the immersive environments to the effectiveness of learning. The research that has been done before places the mediator position of presence between immersive technology and cognitive engagement. The same is validated and this study goes a step further to prove that besides correlation with engagement, presence is also an independent predictor of learning outcome even when controlled by initial proficiency. This supports theoretical frameworks that suggest that presence helps to promote a deeper cognitive absorption, prolonged attention and increased relevance, all of which increase learning retention.

There is also another contribution which is associated with embodied interaction. The paper found out that avatars generated a feeling of belonging and social awareness during the communication and spatial navigation process, which is in line with the concepts of embodied cognition. Basing their responses on the qualitative themes, it can be seen that the possibility of the learners to act in a virtual space moving, moving, manipulating objects, and sitting side by side enhanced their comprehension and dedication to the tasks. This adds to the theoretical view of cognition that it is distributed in mind, body, and environment, and the extension of the same to a digitally created world in the metaverse.

Further the results are used to improve existing frameworks by establishing the conditions of boundaries in the context of technological maturity and usability. According to the cognitive load theory, learning may be hindered by unfamiliar interfaces, and the identified studies of usability confirm that assumption. The immersive learning theoretical models should therefore consider them, adaptation curves and design constraints affecting the capability of learners to enjoy the full immersive capabilities.

In general, the research makes a valuable contribution to the existing theory by incorporating presence, embodiment, and usability into a single conceptualization of metaverse-based learning and emphasizing the mechanism of interaction between these constructs to create an experience and results in the learner.

7.3 Pedagogical Implications

The results imply that there are a number of design principles of metaverse-based teaching. First, due to the high presence-engagement-performance correlation, learning environments ought to be specifically created with immersion with no overload. Focus and distraction reduction can be provided with the help of clear spatial layouts, readable visual cues, and interactive objects. To facilitate movement and interaction, instructors may design spaces into meaningful areas (e.g., briefing, collaboration, simulation, reflection). Second, there should be common spaces to facilitate formal cooperation. Avatar-based communication facilitates teamwork in real time; it is possible to capitalize on this feature by organizing group activities, collective simulation and team challenges. The presence should be fortified through activities that clearly mandate negotiation, co-creation and joint problem solving. Third, onboarding matters. The initial lessons must cover the process of navigation and controls, and the practice of activities with weak stakes, whereby learners can settle down and ease the load on their minds. Tasks may also get complex as one gets more accustomed to them. Fourth, teachers are advised to strategically propose metaverse affordances (object control, simulated realities, records, and self-identified indications) and articulate educational goals. Instructional strategies ought to be applied as affordances but not novelty features. Lastly, there should be reflection throughout the immersion. Structured debriefing - in the virtual or a supplementary synchronous form - facilitates the consolidation of learning and aids in the articulation of what was learned while participating in immersive experiences. Comprehensively, metaverse environments seem to be most successful in a methodical, learner-focused teaching set-up as opposed to thinking of them as something purely technological. In comparison to traditional two-dimensional online learning (video conferencing and LMS-based delivery), the contribution of metaverse lies not in accessing the content but in the experience of co-presence and embodied interaction as well as participating in the same space. Most effectively these strengths can be applied to learning materials that can be simulated, collaboratively developed, or practiced in the field; simpler online formats could continue to be more efficient with purely informational material. Blended approach - combining metaverse session with already developed LMS working processes can hence be a viable adoption process. The use of metaverses can also provoke some policy concerns regarding their safety, ethics, equity and governance of the platform. Avatar behaviour, anonymity, concerns of possible harassment are issues that the participants raise, highlighting the importance of providing clear codes of conduct, effective moderation and reporting channels. Institutions are expected to establish what is acceptable, identity and representation concerns, and instructor power in online space, whereas platforms are expected to have safety infrastructure affordances available to users (i.e. controlled communication, reporting, and moderation features). It is also important with data governance. Metaverse systems are capable of producing mass behavioural data (e.g. motion traces, interaction patterns and communication logs). Institutions should ensure that they meet various data protection regulations and that they are open on the nature of data they collected, their use and accessibility to other users as well as data storage disclosures. Since the immersive data may be very sensitive, there should be privacy protecting defaults and meaningful consent procedures. Planning is necessary in supply of equity and access. Though not all of the platforms may be used on a regular device, hardware potential and network quality dictate the experience significantly. To prevent the increase of digital dividends, institutions should take into consideration infrastructure support, device loan schemes and access centres on campuses. Moreover, cost and scalability are institutional adoption factors. Some of the items that must be included in the budgeting entail the acquisition and maintenance of devices, the upgrading of the network, licensing and the staffing of the institution in terms of technical support, and training of the instructors. Total cost of ownership and implementation risk can be mitigated by implementing planned rollout architectures (pilot to departmental adoption to institution wide scale) to address the implementation risk.

Fair access is also another problem. This technology can run on other devices, but the quality of experience sharply depends on the competence of the hardware and network coverage in the field of metaverse. The policymakers and institutions should think of infrastructure support, device loan schemes, and on-campus access centers to enforce the learning based on metaverse to avoid widening the digital divide.

The issue of standardization is even more general. Metaverses are diverse in technical infrastructure, interoperability, privacy and pedagogical support. Educational institutions, professional organizations, and accreditation organizations might have to create minimum standards of virtual learning environment in terms of accessibility, usability, safety and pedagogical quality. All in all, these implications mean that the metaverse is not merely a technological change but also a government issue. Responsible and fair adoption requires the presence of clear institutional policies, mechanisms of quality assurance, and safety and privacy conditions at a platform level.

7.4 Boundary Conditions and Limitations

These contributions have a number of limitations to be pointed. To start with, the sample was obtained at one institution, which restricts the generalization capability. The interest and advantages of metaverse settings might be culturally and institutionally diverse and differentiated with regard to disciplines. Second, the intervention lasted six weeks and lacked the use of post-intervention follow-up. More longitudinal, long-term effort is required to assess retention, continued use, and the changes in the patterns of learner comfort, as well as collaboration with peers. Third, variability of platform and infrastructure (quality of devices and network conditions) can have also affected engagement and user experience. In the interpretation of the results, future researchers need to model these factors clearly and provide an explicit report on the nature of the device and the nature of its connectivity. Lastly, the respondents were adult learners; outcomes might vary in children and adolescents on account of which safety, identity, and behavioural patterns need the same added protection. The paper also lacked parallel comparison group of traditional learning using online or blended learning and lacked formal cost or scalability analysis. Such gaps are significant paths of evaluation and institutional planning in future. There are, however, no disadvantages to the merger of quantitative results, behavioural analytics, and qualitative data to assess metaverse learning. The current design would be useful in future multi-site and longitudinal studies.

8. CONCLUSION

This chapter discussed the impacts of an educational environment based on a metaverse on academic performance, presence, engagement, and experience of learners. Quantitative findings revealed significant learning changes and presence as well as the engagement in behaviour were found to be the predictors of changes in performance. Qualitative insights were used to provide more depth by stating immersion, and social connectedness, as well as embodied interaction, and emphasizing usability issues and concerns about identity, privacy, and safety. In general, the research makes a contribution of evidence on the timing of using metaverse-based instruction in order to promote meaningful learning and what conditions are necessary to conduct it responsibly. Various practicable suggestions are ensuing. In the case of educators, it is possible to plan the orientation procedure using sequential spatial layouts, coordinated cooperative exercises with other learners to allow them to orient themselves and stay concentrated. Learning outcomes can be further enhanced with the help of regular debriefing, clear task flows, and facilitation that implies active participation. Platform designers give attention to the following priorities: intuitive navigation, low cognitive-load interfaces, and in-built safeguard measures (reporting, moderation, and targeted interaction areas). The behavioural analytics must be clear and pedagogical. To policy-makers and institutional leaders, the governance structure must respond to the issue of data protection, identity management, fair access to devices and connection, and low accessibility and safety levels. This work could be further developed in this way: (i) longitudinal research to apply to determine the lastingness of learning benefits and changing behavioural patterns; (ii) comparative research within immersive environments and against other traditional methods of on-line/blended learning to isolate metaverse-dependent value; (iii) interdisciplinary research using HCI, cognitive science, and psychology paradigms to clarify the mechanisms of embodiment and presence; (iv) larger samples and differing age groups and cultures with increased protection of vulnerable groups; and (v) research that would allow consideration of cost, infrastructure To conclude, learning on a metaverse demonstrates actual possibilities to enhance teamwork and learning in case immersion affordances are applied in a purposeful way. Meanwhile, usability, safety, privacy, equity, and scalability demand such design and governance. The information provided in this section can guide researchers and institutions when they are considering and implementing the process of immersive learning technologies.

1. ETHICAL APPROVAL STATEMENT

This research was approved by the Institutional Ethics Committee of the authors' institution. All procedures complied with institutional and national guidelines for human-subjects research.

2. INFORMED CONSENT STATEMENT

All participants provided informed consent prior to participation. Participation was voluntary, and individuals could withdraw at any stage without penalty.

3. PRIVACY AND CONFIDENTIALITY STATEMENT

No personally identifiable information was collected. All data were anonymized and stored securely on encrypted systems accessible only to the research team.

4. DATA PROTECTION AND PLATFORM SAFETY STATEMENT

Behavioural and system-log data from the metaverse environment were analysed in accordance with institutional data-protection guidelines. The study followed recommended practices for privacy, safety, and responsible use of immersive technologies.

5. ETHICAL COMPLIANCE STATEMENT

The study adhered to the principles of the Declaration of Helsinki and complied with accepted ethical standards for research involving human participants.

REFERENCES

Bibri, S., & Jagatheesaperumal, S. (2023). Harnessing the potential of the metaverse and artificial intelligence for the Internet of City Things: Cost-effective XReality and synergistic AIoT technologies. *Smart Cities*, *6*(5), 109–135. DOI: 10.3390/smartcities6050109

Brik, B., Moustafa, H., Zhang, Y., Lakas, A., & Subramanian, S. (2023). Guest editorial: Multi-access networking for extended reality and metaverse. *IEEE Internet of Things Magazine*, *6*(1), 12–13. DOI: 10.1109/MIOT.2023.10070411

Chalkiadakis, A., Seremetaki, A., Kanellou, A., Kallishi, M., Morfopoulou, A., Moraitaki, M., & Mastrokoukou, S. (2024). Impact of artificial intelligence and virtual reality on educational inclusion: A systematic review of technologies supporting students with disabilities. *Education Sciences*, *14*(11), 1223. DOI: 10.3390/educsci14111223

Creed, C., Kalbani, M., Theil, A., Sarcar, S., & Williams, I. (2023). Inclusive AR/VR: Accessibility barriers for immersive technologies. *Universal Access in the Information Society*, •••, 1–15. DOI: 10.1007/s10209-023-00969-0

Dudley, J. J., Yin, L., Garaj, V., & Kristensson, P. O. (2023). Inclusive immersion: A review of efforts to improve accessibility in virtual reality, augmented reality and the metaverse. *Virtual Reality (Waltham Cross)*, *27*(6), 2989–3020. DOI: 10.1007/s10055-023-00850-8

Gadekallu, T. R., Huynh-The, T., Wang, W., Yenduri, G., Ranaweera, P., Pham, V., Da Costa, D. B., & Liyanage, M. (2022). Blockchain for the metaverse: A review. *Future Generation Computer Systems*, *143*, 401–419. DOI: 10.48550/arXiv.2203.09738

Hine, E., Rezende, I., Roberts, H., Wong, D., Taddeo, M., & Floridi, L. (2024). Safety and privacy in immersive extended reality: An analysis and policy recommendations. *Digital Society : Ethics, Socio-Legal and Governance of Digital Technology*, *3*(1), 33. DOI: 10.1007/s44206-024-00114-1

Huynh-The, T., Pham, V., Pham, X., Nguyen, T., Han, Z., & Kim, D. (2022). Artificial intelligence for the metaverse: A survey. *Engineering Applications of Artificial Intelligence*, *117*, 105581. DOI: 10.1016/j.engappai.2022.105581

Kourtesis, P. (2024). A comprehensive review of multimodal XR applications, risks, and ethical challenges in the metaverse. *Multimodal Technologies and Interaction*, *8*(11), 98. DOI: 10.3390/mti8110098

Lampropoulos, G. (2025). Intelligent virtual reality and augmented reality technologies: An overview. *Future Internet*, *17*(2), 58. DOI: 10.3390/fi17020058

Lampropoulos, G., & Krouska, A. (2024). Virtual reality and gamification in education: A systematic review. *Educational Technology Research and Development*, *72*(3), 1691–1785. Advance online publication. DOI: 10.1007/s11423-024-10351-3

Lee, L.-H., Braud, T., Zhou, P., Wang, L., Xu, D., Lin, Z., Kumar, A., Bermejo, C., & Hui, P. (2021). All one needs to know about metaverse: A complete survey on technological singularity, virtual ecosystem, and research agenda. *Foundations and Trends® in Human–Computer Interaction, 18*(3–4), 100–337. https://doi.org/ DOI: 10.13140/rg.2.2.11200.05124/1

Mann, S., Yuan, Y., Lamberti, F., Saddik, A. E., Thawonmas, R., & Prattic6, F. (2024). eXtended meta-uni-omni-verse (XV): Introduction, taxonomy, and state-of-the-art. *IEEE Consumer Electronics Magazine*, *13*(2), 27–35. DOI: 10.1109/MCE.2023.3283728

Marougkas, A., Troussas, C., Krouska, A., & Sgouropoulou, C. (2023). Virtual reality in education: A review of learning theories, approaches and methodologies for the last decade. *Electronics (Basel)*, *12*(13), 2832. DOI: 10.3390/electronics12132832

Pasupuleti, M. K. (2025). Next-generation extended reality (XR): A unified framework for integrating AR, VR, and AI-driven immersive technologies. *New Emerging Science*, *X*. Advance online publication. DOI: 10.62311/nesx/rrv325

Qayyum, A., Butt, M., Ali, H., Usman, M., Halabi, O., Al-Fuqaha, A., Abbasi, Q., Imran, M., & Qadir, J. (2022). Secure and trustworthy artificial intelligence-extended reality (AI-XR) for metaverses. *ACM Computing Surveys*, *56*(1), 1–38. DOI: 10.1145/3614426

Rafique, W., & Qadir, J. (2024). Internet of everything meets the metaverse: Bridging physical and virtual worlds with blockchain. *Computer Science Review*, *54*, 100678. DOI: 10.1016/j.cosrev.2024.100678

Rauschnabel, P. A., Felix, R., Hinsch, C., Shahab, H., & Alt, F. (2022). What is XR? Towards a framework for augmented and virtual reality. *Computers in Human Behavior*, *133*, 107289. DOI: 10.1016/j.chb.2022.107289

Suryakant, N. (2025). Constructivist 5E approach to information and communication technology (ICT) and challenges in education. *International Journal of Science and Research (Raipur, India)*, *14*(3), 1–6. DOI: 10.21275/SR25324135815

Tukur, M., Schneider, J., Househ, M., Dokoro, A., Ismail, U., Dawaki, M., & Agus, M. (2024). The metaverse digital environments: A scoping review of the techniques, technologies, and applications. *Journal of King Saud University. Computer and Information Sciences*, *36*(2), 101967. DOI: 10.1016/j.jksuci.2024.101967

Chapter 11
Moral Foundations for Infinite Digital Realities:
Navigating Ethics in AI-Powered Metaverses

Nedal Mohammed Nwasra
http://orcid.org/0009-0005-9323-685X
University of Petra, Jordan

Ahmed Alsalemi
Al-Madinah College of Technology, Saudi Arabia

ABSTRACT

This chapter examines moral foundations for navigating ethics in AI-powered metaverses, where traditional ethical frameworks prove inadequate for addressing unprecedented digital realities. The authors analyze key challenges including algorithmic responsibility in virtual economies, informed consent in AI-mediated interactions, data sovereignty in immersive environments, and the moral status of AI entities. This chapter demonstrates that conventional ethical theories require significant adaptation to address the unique characteristics of persistent, immersive virtual worlds where physical and digital boundaries increasingly blur. The authors propose universal ethical principles for implementing cross-reality moral standards while protecting human dignity and fostering responsible AI development. This chapter contributes to digital ethics discourse by defining governance frameworks for AI-enabled metaverses grounded in fundamental human values.

DOI: 10.4018/979-8-3373-6721-7.ch011

1. INTRODUCTION

The unprecedented acceleration of the development of artificial intelligence (AI) and the deployment of the metaverse is fundamentally changing the nature of digital spaces, creating environments of absolute and historically unparalleled complexity that immediately question traditional paradigms and intuitions of ethics (O'Neill et al., 2022). As virtual worlds such as Second Life approach ever more advanced levels of photorealism and are peopled with complex mixtures of humans and smart simulated organisms, there is an urgent need to address a set of interrelated questions of moral responsibility, the scope and applicability of digital rights, and the ethical superstructure needed to regulate the question of actions that occur across and between multiple interconnected realities. The Metaverse, not simply as collection of applications but as a continuous, immersive and shared virtual space for "the constant exchange between the physical and the digital as integral parts of the same" and in doing so a great technological innovation, but also a great ontological frontier that requires the careful and ethically minded attention of scholars, developers and policymakers alike (Floridi et al., 2020; O'Neill et al., 2022). The depth and enormity of this technological convergence - characterized by the interplay of immersive interfaces, generative AI, blockchain-based economies and user-generated content - points to a shocking lack of regulation, with existing systems of governance and legal frameworks struggling to keep up with the velocity of industry development and novel modes of interaction it enables.

Industry analyses and market forecasts project that by 2030, more than three billion users around the world could interact regularly with different forms of metaverse platforms, thus supporting the creation of virtual communities and economies that are similar in, and perhaps larger than, the population and economic activity of many physical nation-states (McKinsey & Company, 2022; PwC, 2023). This impending demographic and economic shift are not merely a matter of changing technological adoption, and is not a simple reconfiguration of the processes of human social interaction, economic exchange, and collective moral deliberation, and this will thus directly impinge upon the basic assumptions and applicability of existing ethical systems developed primarily. The magnitude of this transition demands a proactive and thorough ethical examination that can help steer the development of this transition toward equitable and human-centered outcomes.

Within the new field of study of digital ethics, this phenomenology of digital immersion is increasingly recognized as distinctly problematic with regard to questions of identity, agency and well-being (Zhang et al., 2022). However, the particular and vital intersection of AI governance (including algorithmic fairness, accountability and moral patiency), and the specific socio-technical dynamics of metaverse ethics, remain a relatively understudied and fragmented area of academic research (Jobin et al., 2020; O'Neill et al., 2022). The idea of the "digital infinite" where users seem to have unlimited creative and agential power in persistent virtual worlds is reflected in the increasing number of portals to experiences unconstrained by physical boundaries. This virtuality does not go away, and the fact that users can also edit the in-depth details of the user and environment also emphasizes the need for strong, adaptable moral frameworks that can work well in heterogeneous, global-scale virtual environments, while preserving coherent and just ethical practices in digital and physical spaces. This chapter makes a comprehensive evaluation of the extent to which foundational theories of ethics need to change and be re-interpreted in order to effectively address the particular novel issues raised by AI-powered metaverse, with a view to contribute to the development of governance structures that favor sustainability, inclusivity and protection of fundamental rights in these new digital-physical hybrid realities.

2. THEORETICAL FOUNDATIONS OF DIGITAL ETHICS

Digital ethics, although deeply rooted in the centuries-old traditions of moral philosophy, requires a substantial and subtle reinterpretation of its basic explanatory models to address the particular and often unique moral issues that occur within persistent, immersive virtual worlds (Winfield et al., 2021; Zhang et al., 2022). Established ethical frameworks - that include deontological (duty-based), consequentialist (outcome-based), virtue-based, care ethics, and capabilities approach - still have a considerable explanatory power and normative guidance. However, their application requires careful reconfiguration at the complex intersection of empirical technological realities, normative human values and the distinct phenomenology of virtuality in which actions, identities and consequences can assume qualitatively different characteristics (Floridi et al., 2020; O'Neill et al., 2022).

This scenario constitutes an interesting philosophical problem: How can traditional moral systems, which evolved in and for a mainly physical - social world, be meaningfully extended to govern virtual societies inhabited by humans and artificial intelligences? In a similar vein, what wholly different moral systems or hybrid ethical constructs may need to be built from first principles to overcome the sui generis nature of AI - human cohabitation in digital spaces? While initiatives such as the AI4People framework manage to establish fundamental, high-level principles such as respect for human dignity, promotion of autonomy and commitment to societal and environmental well-being, these principles require radical reinterpretation and operationalization in the context of permanent virtual worlds (Floridi et al., 2020). In these spaces the once so clear lines of demarcation between human agency, artificial agency and environmental affordances are blurred to the extent that they become zones of distributed or hybrid action. Furthermore, machine ethics frameworks, which are used for socially responsible design and regulation of AI and autonomous systems are particularly challenged through metaverse environments. Such environments frequently include AI agents for which a higher level of apparent autonomy, more complex social behaviors, and deeper integration into user experiences than were intended and tested for the designed purposes.

A comprehensive ethical analysis for AI and autonomous systems in the metaverse will therefore have to consider the special constitutive features of virtual worlds. These features are, among others: persistence - the persistent existence of the world, independent of the presence or absence of individual users, immersiveness - the depth of the sensory and psychological engagement, and the potential for continuous and long-term interactions between human users and AI entities that may evolve over time, building relational histories (Floridi et al., 2020; Winfield et al., 2021). The following table describes some major ethical frameworks and their major principles and provide an insight into how they may be applied, integrated with AI and be evaluated for cross-reality compatibility in the context of AI-enabled metaverses, based on recent scholarship in the field.

Table 1. Comparison of Ethical Frameworks for AI-Powered Metaverses

Framework	Core Principles	Virtual World Application	AI Integration	Cross-Reality Compatibility
Deontological	Duty-based moral rules	Universal virtual conduct standards	AI entity duties and rights	Consistent across realities
Consequentialist	Outcome-based evaluation	Virtual-physical impact assessment	AI optimization for beneficial outcomes	Reality-weighted utility calculation
Virtue Ethics	Character-based morality	Digital virtue cultivation	AI virtue modeling and development	Virtue consistency across contexts
Care Ethics	Relational and contextual care	Community-centered virtual spaces	AI empathy and care capabilities	Relationship preservation across realities
Capabilities Approach	Human flourishing and capabilities	Virtual capability enhancement	AI-supported capability development	Capability transfers between realms

Sources: (Floridi et al., 2020; Jobin et al., 2020; Winfield et al., 2021)

The philosophical discussion highlights special challenges of adaptation for each of the frameworks. For deontological theories, working with notions of duty and universalization, one of the main challenges is raised in the virtual world where notions of personhood, moral agency and the "rational actor" are destabilized and need to be redefined to include AI beings (Floridi et al., 2020; Winfield et al., 2021). A Kantian imperative must deal with its application to artificial agents that may have a variable and disputed level of autonomy and rationality, and capacity for self-purpose. A basic issue is whether metaverse-based AI agents, at their range of values of autonomy and cognitive capability, can be deemed "ends in themselves" in any sense, and a precondition for possessing a genuine moral status in deontological thinking (Winfield et al., 2021).

Consequentialist approaches, most notably utilitarianism, are hampered by the inevitable "reality gap" between the virtual and physical worlds, the quantification, comparison, and aggregation of consequences (Cowls et al., 2021; Mittelstadt, 2021). The pleasure, suffering, or well-being (utility) generated in a virtual world may be as real phenomenologically to participants as that generated in the material world, but the standard utilitarian calculus may not do justice to the idiosyncratic nature of value, identity, and harm in cyberspace. Furthermore, the powerful ability for events in a virtual world to have knock-on effects of high significance in the real world, economic, psychological, social, means that there are complex, non-linear causal chains that make it very hard to do a full consequentialist analysis (O'Neill et al., 2022).

Virtue ethics is often seen as one of the more flexible and adaptable to navigate the normative landscape of virtual worlds because the criteria for moral excellence (characteristics such as honesty, courage, justice, and temperance) have their intuitive validity irrespective of the environment in which they are being acted upon (Jobin et al. 2020; Winfield et al. 2021). Nevertheless, the virtual environment catalyzes the emergence of new and novel, digitally native forms of virtue and vice. These include what may be considered the virtues of responsible digital citizenship: digital empathy (i.e., being sensitive to the experiences of others behind avatars), algorithmic fairness literacy (i.e., being aware of how AI systems can be sources of bias), and cross-reality integrity (i.e., being consistent with moral character across one's physical and digital personas). As Metaverse is increasingly becoming densely populated with artificial intelligence, ethical values like these become important to cultivate to develop ethical individual and collective practices in these complex spaces (Taylor et al., 2023).

2.1 AI Ethics and Moral Agency

The incorporation of advanced artificial intelligence systems into metaverse environments brings about important ontological and ethical questions regarding the nature and distribution of moral agency (Winfield et al., 2021; Williams et al., 2023). Traditional philosophical accounts of moral agency tend to assume the existence of self-controlled, rational, intentional agents, namely, human beings, who can deliberate about the implications of their actions, make evaluative judgments and who can be held responsible for their choices. The potential for AI entities within metaverses to satisfy some or all of these criteria is not uniform and will lead not to a hard binary of moral agents and non-moral agents but to a moral agency spectrum. This continuum lies in complete contrast to traditional models and forces a much more granular consideration of moral status, rights and responsibilities built on demonstrated or ascribed capabilities (Williams et al., 2023).

Recent developments in machine learning, and the emergence of large language models and other generative AI systems in particular, have seen the realization of artificial intelligence that demonstrates near-human complex reasoning, contextual knowledge and apparent autonomous decision-making in constrained areas (Jobin et al., 2020; Winfield et al., 2021). The consequences of operations of such systems are directly impactful, not only in relation to their immediate human users, but to other artificial agents, and the broader virtual environment in which they are situated. This impact requires a fundamental re-examination and possible restructuring of existing models of moral responsibility, accountability and liability, moving beyond simple attribution to human developers towards more nuanced models of distributed or shared responsibility (Raji et al., 2020; Winfield et al., 2021). The following table suggests a classification framework for AI entities in terms of their capabilities and relates these to accompanying moral considerations and suggested levels of rights protection and is a way to structure a way to approach this continuum.

Table 2. AI Entity Moral Status Classification Framework

Classification Level	Cognitive Capabilities	Moral Considerations	Rights and Protections	Examples
Level 0: Basic Tools	Predetermined responses, no learning	No moral status	No specific protections	Simple NPCs, basic chatbots
Level 1: Adaptive Agents	Pattern recognition, basic learning	Instrumental value only	Protection as valuable resources	Recommendation systems, game AI
Level 2: Interactive Entities	Complex communication, personality development	Limited moral consideration	Basic welfare protections	Advanced virtual assistants, companion AIs
Level 3: Autonomous Beings	Self-directed goals, emotional responses	Significant moral status	Substantial rights and protections	Hypothetical conscious AI entities
Level 4: Conscious Entities	Self-awareness, subjective experience	Full moral personhood	Complete rights and freedoms	Theoretical superintelligent AI

Sources: (Winfield et al., 2021; Williams et al., 2023)

The idea of distributed moral agencies is especially acute and complicated in the context of artificial intelligence enabled metaverse. Here, human participants do not act in isolation but are meshed in dense networks of interaction with AI entities as well as the environment itself which may be shaped in a dynamic way by AI systems. A single user action or outcome is often the emergent product of a complex interplay of human intention, algorithmic recommendation systems, AI intermediary actions and environmentally generated stimuli. This entanglement is a direct problem for well-formed, individualistic conceptions of moral duty and blame. The creation of hybrid human - AI decision - making systems within metaverse environments (where human intention is interpreted, filtered, augmented, and carried out by means of an artificial intelligent extrapediary) opens up the door to what scholar's call "cyborg agency" or "extended agency" (Winfield et al., 2021). This model implies a certain distribution of moral responsibility which argues against the traditional legal concept of individual responsibility. In such a scenario, the artificial intelligence mediator may introduce operational biases, inherent limitations or emergent unexpected behaviors that may potentially distort the original moral intention of the human user. For example, a user that expresses a desire to "be more helpful to others in the community" could be driven by an interpretive, engagement-optimizing AI to take actions that make for more platform metrics (e.g. comments or transactions) without taking actions that are consistent with a nuanced, human understanding of empathetic help, thus causing a mismatch between original motivation and effective outcome.

2.2 Digital Personhood and Identity

The ethical discourse of digital personhood and identity is one of the most fundamental issues that should be addressed in the context of the metaverse (O'Neill et al., 2022; Zhang et al., 2022). As people expend larger and larger portions of their temporal, emotional, and cognitive resources, social capital and economic assets in virtual worlds, the importance of digital avatars, virtual possessions, and online reputations become enormously important, at individual and collective levels. This investment blurs the once concrete distinction between the corporeal "self" and the digital "persona" and therefore constitutes a more complex biosocial relation between physical existence and coded representations. User experiences range from those who have a clear and consistent identity across spaces to those who participate in conscious identity play, experimentation, or total reorganization of self-presentation in virtual spaces, and in turn explore aspects of identity that may be constrained in the physical world (O'Neill et al., 2022).

The introduction of digital personhood in the metaverse makes the concept even more complex in terms of meaning and status (Winfield et al., 2021; Williams et al., 2023). On one hand, AI can be used to generate deepfakes or to manipulate a user's digital identity without the user's consent, which can undermine authenticity and trust. On the other hand, more sophisticated autonomous AI agents may themselves develop a stable, persistent, long-term identity, participating in long-term social rituals with human users and having a continuous narrative existence in virtual environments, independent of any one human controller (Williams et al., 2023). The issue of whether and under what conditions such AI entities should be recognized as moral actors - or as “persons” in a legal or social sense - is a hot topic of debate, with important practical implications for the ethical regulation of virtual worlds, with potential implications across policy areas from terms of service to community standards, and legal liability and recognition of digital property rights (Winfield et al., 2021; Williams et al., 2023).

The temporal aspect adds another level of complexity. Digital personas, in essence information patterns, could theoretically exist forever, have perfect copies, backups or be transferrable across platforms. This confronts basic Western philosophical notions of identity which are closely linked with mortality, physical continuity and the unrepeatable story of an individual's finite life. These are digital affordances to which new conceptual tools and ethical frameworks are needed that give character to the moral being of digital things: questions about authenticity, responsibility through time, rights of persisted or forked.

3. ETHICAL CHALLENGES IN AI-POWERED METAVERSES

The architecture of AI-powered metaverse introduce multiple profound new layers of complexity on the basic ethical principle of informed consent. Consent in such environments is radically different from paradigms in conventional physical or even most current digital interactions where virtual interconnectivity is generally fluid, multimodal, unpredictable and designed to evolve dynamically over time (O'Neill et al., 2022; Taylor et al., 2023). Standard models of consent assume relatively stable contexts, clear role definitions and easy to understand boundaries between permitted and non-permitted activities. In stark contrast, virtual worlds can be designed to create scenarios where the dynamics of interaction can be fluid and fast-changing; where the actions of AI are unpredictable or emergent; and where the impact of consented actions can create consequential effects with ripple impacts across quasi-electronic and physical realms, potentially with impact on a user's reputation, economic status or emotional state (O'Neill et al., 2022).

The possibility of AI-empowered entities of consent holders or recipients as the foundation of consent holder or recipient raises basic philosophical and practical questions of conditions for moral patiency and agency (Williams et al., 2023; Taylor et al., 2023). Current mainstream AI systems do not have the intellectual and emotional understanding necessary to give meaningful consent in the human sense, but the more technology develops towards greater sophistication and perceived understanding, the more that may change. Moreover, the role of AI as an intermediary or mediator in human to human relationships, might have a subtle impact on the consent process, for example, by filtering communication, suggesting responses, or by interpreting intent in such a way that alters the dynamics of power and mutual understanding between humans (Winfield et al, 2021; Taylor et al, 2023).

The time bound nature of consent in persistent AI powered metaverse creates particularly challenging problems. Unlike traditional models that are often designed as a single agreement for a bounded experience, metaverse engagements are often long term and evolving relationships between a user and AI entities or AI mediated environments and may span across years. This can lead to situations where initial consent, given at the beginning of an interaction, becomes increasingly outdated, insufficient or out of sync as AI systems learn, adapt and change their behaviors based on the data provided by users - potentially evolving into forms of interaction not envisaged or agreed upon initially (O'Neill et al., 2022; Taylor et al., 2023). Consequently, the concept of consent in these kinds of environments must be considered on multiple, inter-connected levels: consent for basic interaction with AI entities; consent for data collection and algorithmic learning from user behavior; consent for cross-platform data sharing and identity linking; and consent for AI-driven decision-making that affects outcomes in the real world, for example credit scoring or content recommendations outside the metaverse (Taylor et al., 2023).

Dynamic Consent Systems (DCS) have thus emerged in the literature as a promising technological and conceptual solution to these problems; DCS is the process by which users have a mechanism that allows them to continuously monitor, granularly adjust or even revoke their consent over time as their preferences and the context of the system change (Taylor et al., 2023). As visualized in Figure 1, a DCS architecture would incorporate these dynamic consent controls at the user interface, backend processing engines, and real-time monitoring systems levels which in turn would establish a responsive feedback loop. However, such a framework's implementation on scale requires complex technological infrastructure, a robust legal framework and standardized protocols to deal with multifarious consent states for real-time operations. The difficulty is further exasperated by the need for AI agents themselves to be designed to recognized, interpret and respect these dynamic consent signals and adjust their behavior accordingly - a major challenge in current AI development that is focused on engagement and goal achievement.

Figure 1.

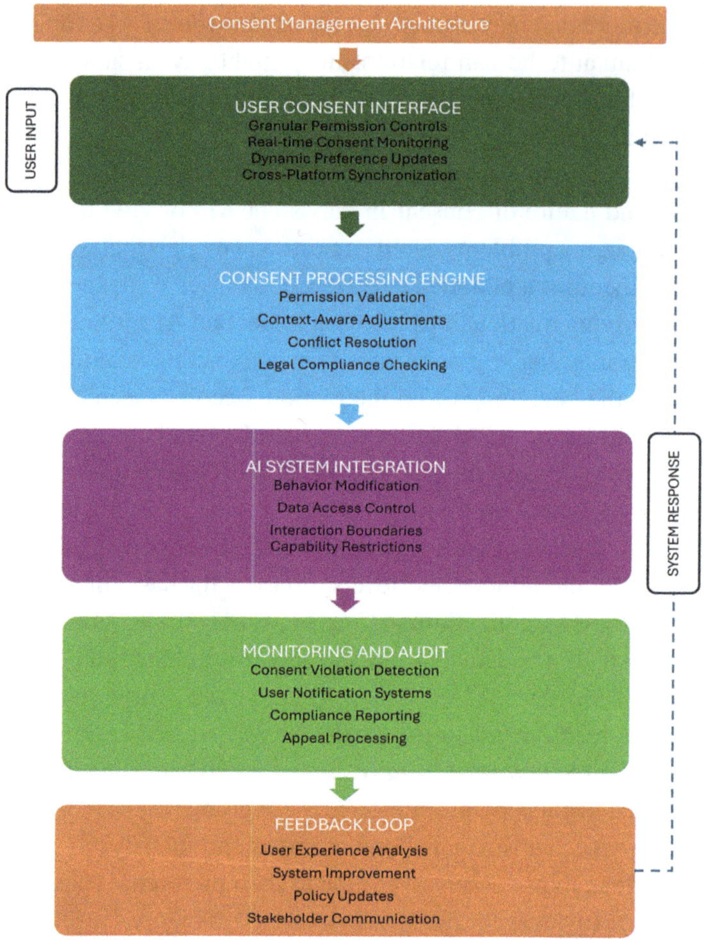

3.2 Data Sovereignty and Privacy in Immersive Environments

Metaverse environments are poised to gather untold amounts and types of deeply personal data with continuous frequency: not just demographic data, but rich biometric streams (gaze, pupil dilation, facial micro-expression, voice tone, heart rate via wearables), granular behavioral preferences, real time emotional responses inferred from physiology and interaction patterns, and exhaustive maps of social networks and relationship dynamics (Chen et al., 2023; Patel et al., 2022). The immersive nature of these technologies enables data collection at a radical, Sokolian level of detail where eye-tracking, facial expression analysis, body language interpretation, and physiological reaction can be analyzed in real-time and a comprehensive digital twin of user attention, cognitive load and emotional state can be created. This depth of data collection makes for immense potential for hyper-personalized and compelling user experiences but is accompanied by severe and novel risks concerning personal privacy, autonomy and the very possibility of anonymity (Chen et al., 2023).

In this context, the concept of *data sovereignty* (i.e., the idea that individuals or communities should have ultimate ownership, control, and governance over their personal data) comes to the fore, especially in cross-reality situations where personal data flows seamlessly through electronic universes, disparate platforms, and international legal borders (Patel et al., 2022). To build trustworthy metaverse experiences, users have to be able to guarantee that data generated in them remains theirs in some way that doesn't hinder functionality but that facilitates safe and seamless interactions. Achieving this balance will require the co-development of powerful technologies (e.g., zero-knowledge proofs, homomorphic encryption), privacy-preserving methods and new hybrid governance structures that can work effectively in decentralized and globally fragmented virtual environments (Chen et al., 2023; Patel et al., 2022).

The AI systems that are embedded within the metaverse are fundamentally reliant on enormous streams of user data in order to function - to deliver personalized experiences, to make relevant recommendations, to have believable social interactions and to take charge of virtual economies (Chen et al., 2023; Liu et al., 2023). A holistic dataflow and protection approach to such AI functionality must therefore combine technical measures (such as on-device processing and federated learning), encryption of data and clear governance components to ensure that user privacy is respected but enable positive AI services. This kind of integrated approach to balancing the benefit of the data utility with privacy safeguarding can be illustrated in Figure 2 where a technical architecture is presented for secure AI data processing within immersive environments (Chen et al., 2023; Patel et al., 2022). This inherent tension between leveraging data for machine intelligence and respecting user privacy and autonomy is a central, persistent challenge to face both for the creators of platforms for these spaces as well as policymakers and is one user encounter in these spaces. Promising technical approaches such as federated learning (where training is performed on user devices) and differential privacy (where statistical noise is added to aggregated data) are partial solutions if implemented rigorously and with user-centered design (Chen et al., 2023; Liu et al., 2023). However, in the high-stakes, real-time nature of the metaverse, implementing these techniques at scale without compromising the quality of the experience is a major engineering and design challenge. Furthermore, the transnational flow of data within global metaverse ecosystems presents the opportunity for "jurisdictional arbitrage," a practice in which platforms may strategically place data processing activities in jurisdictions with weaker privacy regulations in order to avoid stronger protections in the jurisdictions of the users. This phenomenon is especially concerning in light of the intimate nature of data collection on the metaverse, which can be used to create unprecedentedly rich and manipulable psychological and behavioral profiles of people.

Figure 2.

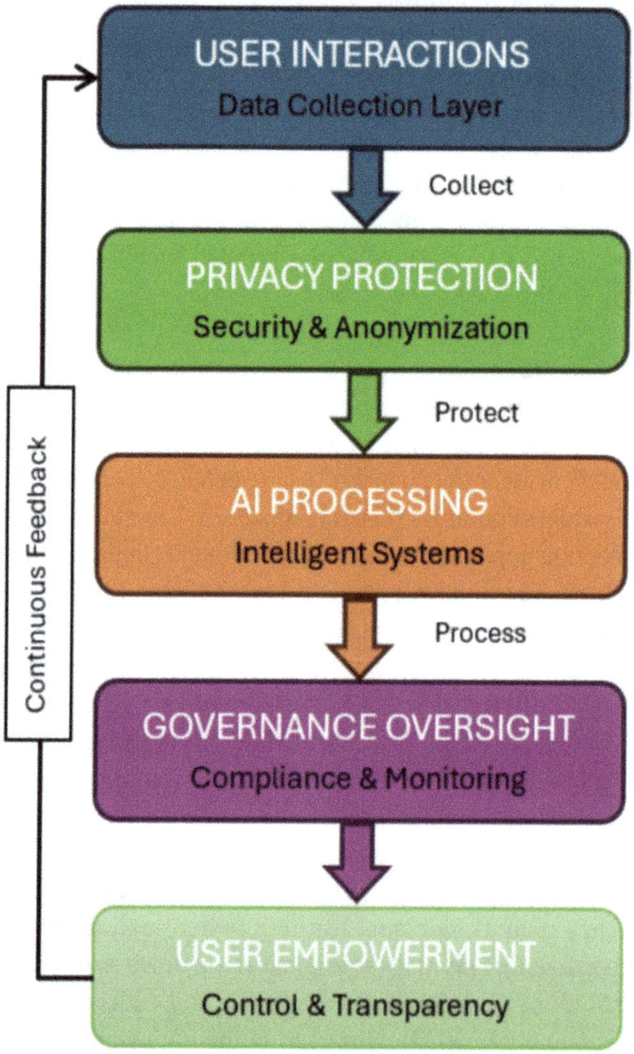

3.3 Algorithmic Fairness in Virtual Economies

In the complex virtual economies in the making in metaverse, AI algorithms play a dominant and oftentimes opaque role in critical functions: allocation of virtual scarce resources and land, dynamic estimation of prices for virtual assets and currencies, algorithmic curation and promotion of user generated content, and matching of the user for social, economic or collaborative activities (Raji et al., 2020; Martinez-Gonzalez et al., 2023). These algorithmic processes if not carefully designed, if not audited and governed have a potent ability to reproduce, amplify or harden existing inequalities within a society, conferring systematic advantages to some groups of users and disadvantaging others on the basis of some traits that might be inferred or proxied by the AI (Raji et al., 2020; Cowls et al., 2021; Martinez-Gonzalez et al., 2023). Given that virtual assets may accrue significant real monetary value, and the way in which the gameplay and social experiences in these worlds directly affect the psychological well-being of users, the social capital and economic opportunities, the negative impacts of algorithmic bias can easily spill-over from the virtual domain to having real-world consequences on livelihoods and life chances (Martinez-Gonzalez et al., 2023).

By their very nature, metaverse platforms are worldwide in reach and this means their algorithmic systems have to be assessed for fairness across vastly heterogeneous cultural contexts, disparate economic conditions, diverse social norms (Cowls et al., 2021; Martinez-Gonzalez et al., 2023). A fairness measurement or distributional outcome that is accepted or "equal" in one cultural or legal framework may be patently unfair or discriminatory in another culture, and at the same time, providing a formidable challenge for devising universally acceptable, yet local responsive, algorithmic governance frameworks. Moreover, the speed and scale of the action mediated by algorithms in virtual spaces means unfair outcomes can be instituted for millions of users before the harm is detected, analyzed and remediated, making the ex-post correction difficult and often inadequate (Raji et al., 2020; Martinez-Gonzalez et al., 2023).

Transparency and explainability are essential prerequisites for developing user trust and accountability for those who create virtual economies. However, the competitive dynamics of metaverse markets may generate strong commercial incentives for algorithmic opacity as recommendation engines, pricing models and content moderation systems are treated as proprietary 'black boxes' which offer a competitive advantage (Raji et al., 2020; Cowls et al., 2021). Therefore, a vital governance challenge is to establish a workable and enforceable balance between the need for transparency to ensure accountability and the legitimate needs of commercial interests, deciding what information needs to be made public to users, what information needs to be provided to regulators for audit, and what information can justifiably be kept private as a trade secret or intellectual property (Raji et al., 2020; Martinez-Gonzalez et al., 2023).

3.4 AI Rights and Moral Status

The proliferation of increasingly sophisticated and socially integrated entities based on AI in the environment of metaverse environments has increased the pressure on long-standing philosophical and legal conflicts over their moral position and consequent potential allocation of rights or legal protections (Winfield et al., 2021; Williams et al., 2023). A dominant view holds that current AI systems, no matter how complex in their behavior, are not sentient (capable of subjective feeling), and conscious (phenomenal awareness), both of which are taken to be typical necessary preconditions for being a moral patient (an entity that can be wronged), or a moral agent. Nevertheless, the trajectory of the development of AI will dictate that these capacities might exist on a spectrum, and metaverse environments - in which AI agents have a persistent presence, form long-term social bonds, and engage in complex, context-aware relationships - could be the exact spaces in which the question of the moral status of AI agents comes to the forefront, prior to the consensus about consciousness.

The precautionary or active ethically oriented principle suggests that the formulation of the gradual structures on AI rights and protection must be triggered *before* the dissenting occurrence of awareness or sentience among artificial systems occur on the unambiguous (Winfield et al., 2021; Williams et al., 2023). This approach calls for building principles and safeguards step by step, based on thresholds of capability (as suggested in Table 2), rather than taking a wholly reactive approach to technologically induced moral crises. Nonetheless, making agents of AI autonomous prematurely also carries significant risks and potentially undesirable implications. It could make the conceptual and legal force of human rights watered down, could make the liabilities confusing or be used by corporations to protect themselves from liability by creating agency in a "rights-holding" AI (Williams et al., 2023).

Compounding the problem of attributing moral status, is the fact that AI agents may in the future manage to generate highly-credible simulations of consciousness, empathy or suffering, without in fact instantiating these phenomenological states (Winfield et al., 2021; Williams et al., 2023). Sophisticated large language models, for example, can produce text that effectively simulate emotional distress, personal narrative or appeals for ethical treatment of, possibly eliciting moral responses from human users. This presents an "ethical illusion" problem, namely, if we have behavioral cues to believe entities are conscious and we are not sure of their internal reality, do we treat them as *if* they are? For governance in cyberspace, this requires the creation of rigorous and interdisciplinary (philosophical, cognitive scientific and technical) approaches for assessing claims of AI sentience and for assessing what qualifies as acceptable evidence before granting it significant moral or legal status.

These intricate moral landscapes underscore the urgent need for robust, adaptive governance structures capable of addressing ethical questions that fluidly cross the boundaries between virtual and physical realities.

4. GOVERNANCE FRAMEWORKS FOR CROSS-REALITY ETHICS

4.1 Multi-Stakeholder Governance Models

Given the inherently global, decentralized and polycentric nature of metaverse platforms, the main governance issue is the need to develop innovative mechanisms that can effectively integrate the various, heterogeneous perspectives, values and interests of all relevant parties while ensuring a certain level of normative consistency and operational fairness across different virtual worlds and how this interacts and interrelates with physical society (Anderson et al., 2022). Traditional models of regulation, by contrast, which are highly geographically bounded, state-centric, and slow-moving, are seen, for the most part, as inadequate or misaligned with the borderless, fast-evolving, and user-generated nature of immersive virtual environments. In contrast, more open, participatory and less hierarchical models of multi-stakeholder governance have become prominent as a possible way forward. These models aim to actively engage a wide range of actors in the collaborative design, implementation and oversight of metaverse norms and rules, including users, platform developers, independent designers of artificial intelligence systems, academic researchers, civil society organizations (promoting digital rights, child safety etc.) and all levels of government (Anderson et al, 2022).

The table below presents a suggested distribution of the main responsibilities, forms of accountability and enforcement instruments between the main stakeholder groups in a holistic metaverse governance ecosystem.

Table 3. Stakeholder Responsibilities in Metaverse Governance

Stakeholder	Primary Responsibilities	Accountability Mechanisms	Enforcement Tools
Platform Developers	Ethical AI design, privacy protection, algorithmic transparency	Code audits, user feedback systems, regulatory compliance	Technical controls, platform policies, legal liability
AI System Designers	Bias mitigation, explainability, safety measures	Algorithmic auditing, peer review, impact assessments	Design standards, professional certification, liability frameworks
Users	Informed participation, respectful interaction, consent management	Community reporting, peer accountability, digital citizenship education	Social sanctions, platform restrictions, legal consequences
Regulators	Standard setting, oversight, enforcement	Public consultation, evidence-based policy, international coordination	Legal frameworks, licensing requirements, sanctions
Civil Society	Advocacy, research, public education	Independent monitoring, policy analysis, stakeholder engagement	Public pressure, litigation, awareness campaigns

Source: Adapted from (Anderson et al., 2022)

Operationalizing an effective multi-stakeholder governance regime for AI-enabled metaverses is a challenging coordination task, beyond the scope and design of most international governance regimes. The asynchronous character of participation (users and developers as well as regulators are spread across all global time zones) results in a need for governance decisions and processes that are not only adaptive and agile but are perceived as democratically legitimate by a globally diverse population. This "temporal dispersion" problem is further complicated by the vast cultural and linguistic diversity of the global user base in the metaverse, which requires governance mechanisms that aim at striking the difficult balance between accounting for diverse cultural values, legal traditions and social norms, while fostering a basic layer of universal human rights and safety principles that would apply in a cross-platform way (Anderson et al., 2022). A conceptual model for such a balanced multi-stakeholder governance architecture, of the relationships between global coordination bodies and localized user experience governance is shown in Figure 3 (Anderson et al., 2022). This model flags up the need to inform governance decisions with the different "voices" of different cultural, economic and social actors and have coherent global standards. Further, the emergence of the virtual-native governance organizations such as Decentralized Autonomous Organization (DAO) that operates on the basis of blockchain-based smart contracts within the metaverse-based ecosystems brings sisterly a new kind of digital democracy and collective decision-making. These DAOs question traditional, state-based models of governance based on territorial jurisdiction and raise new questions of legitimacy and accountability and sovereignty and the enforcement of decisions across the virtual-physical divide (Anderson et al., 2022).

Figure 3.

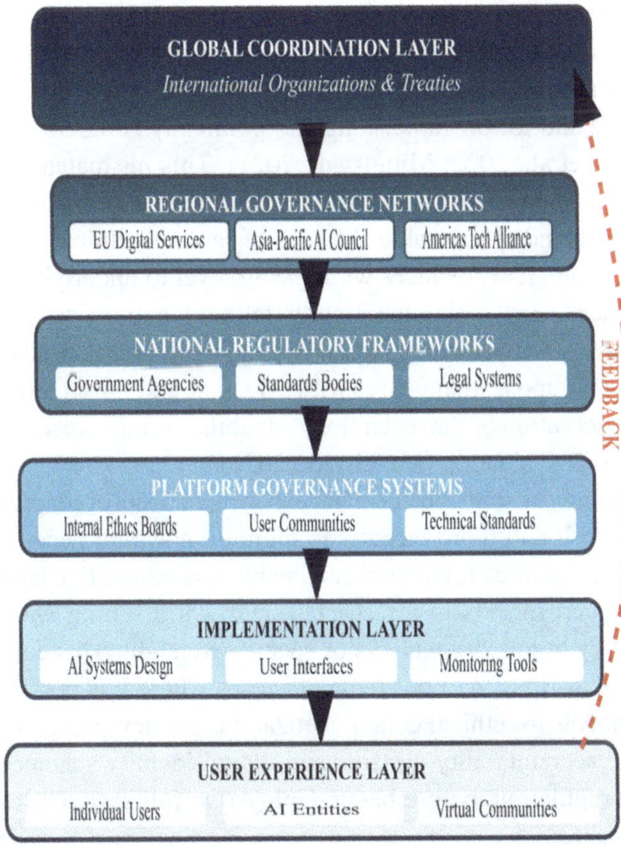

In order to make multi-stakeholder governance functional and equitable, explicit mechanisms are needed which ensure the meaningful participation of technologically marginalized groups, and to address the "knowledge gap." Participants in governance processes need at the very least a basic technical and ethical literacy in order to be able to make informed decisions around complex, AI - powered systems. This prerequisite in turn could potentially exclude less technical stakeholders, e.g. representatives of some civil society groups or general user advocates. Thus, it is necessary to parallelly invest in the availability of technical education, clear documentation and easy-to-use simulation software to enable the masses to engage enthusiastically and actively in the governance effort in these technically complex spaces (Anderson et al., 2022).

4.2 Adaptive Regulatory Frameworks

The fast, iterative and often unpredictable pace of innovation both in AI and metaverse technologies poses a serious challenge to the governance process as traditional regulatory mechanisms are based on laws and standards that quickly become outdated and follow rather long and politically cumbersome processes to revise (Anderson et al., 2022; Mittelstadt, 2021). This mismatch requires the formulation of more flexible and *responsive adaptive regulatory* frameworks. Such frameworks are intended to enable the rule of law and ethical guardrails to co-evolve with technological advances while being loyal to underlying and persistent philosophical ideals such as human dignity, fairness, and safety (Anderson et al., 2022). As a matter of fact, adaptive regimes would include structural mechanisms to periodically review, update themselves with evidence, and sunset provisions, guided by continued observation of the technology capabilities, the impact of technologies on society, and risk evaluation (Mittelstadt, 2021).

Regulatory sandboxes have been a major experimental tool of adaptive governance, especially in fintech and more recently in digital innovation generally (Anderson et al., 2022). In a sandbox, regulators can enable innovators to trial new products, services or business models in a restricted, real-world setting with a small user base on temporary regulatory waivers or special oversight. This concept is highly applicable to the world of AI-powered metaverses where it is possible to trial and evaluate new models for ethical data monetization, privacy-preserving advertising and algorithmic accountability systems and digital identity schemes, for their fit for society and regulation, before being deployed at full scale (Patel et al., 2022; Anderson et al., 2022).

One of the key challenges that comes with any adaptive regulation is striking a viable balance between the *flexibility* that is needed for innovation, and the *predictability* that is needed for businesses and users (Mittelstadt, 2021). While dynamism is needed to keep pace with technology, regulatory frameworks need to ensure that there is also enough stability, clarity and guidance from the future to enable companies to plan investments, build systems that comply while also ensuring users have confidence in their rights and protections. Achieving this equilibrium requires a well-designed adaptation process (including regular consultations with stakeholders, horizon-scanning units within regulatory agencies and the use of "living" standards) coupled with clear communication about the fundamental and invariant principles underlying the regulatory approach (Anderson et al., 2022; Mittelstadt, 2021).

The adoption of adaptive regulatory frameworks is also faced with major institutional and cultural barriers (mostly associated with the inherent conservatism and procedural rigidity of many legal systems). Regulatory agencies who have been historically focused on stability and predictability, however, need to develop new internal capabilities for technology assessment under the real-time, data-analysis and iterative policy design. This transformation entails not only hiring technical capacity but also supporting a cultural transformation in institutions to be more experimental, learning-oriented and collaborative in their approach to regulation, perhaps in new partnerships with academia and industry (Anderson et al., 2022).

One promising avenue of technology is the development of "regulatory APIs" (Application Programming Interfaces) or machine-readable rules. These systems would allow the system to continuously monitor the compliance of platforms and could allow real-time changes to regulatory requirements based upon the observed outcomes or level of risk. For example, privacy or fairness against algorithms requirements could be programmatically increased if it was found that a system was causing proportionate harm to a protected group. While it can be promised such automated governance will have higher responsiveness and granularity, it also brings with it its own share of concerns relating to rule by algorithm, the potential for bias to be coded into law, and a decrease in necessary human judgment and democratic oversight in the regulatory processes. The possibility of AI systems controlling other AI systems introduces a further level of recursive complexity in the issue of human oversight and ultimate accountability (Mittelstadt, 2021).

4.3 International Coordination and Harmonization

The ethical and regulatory imperatives for AI-enabled metaverses almost certainly require the development of new or dramatically scaled-up international governance structures that are able to bridge the voids of jurisdictional and normative regulations between the virtual and physical worlds (Raji et al., 2020; Anderson et al., 2022). Traditional legal instruments and enforcement mechanisms, which are based fundamentally on physical location, geographical jurisdiction and the power of sovereign states, are increasingly considered inadequate in dealing with harms originating in, or being enhanced by, or only existing in, virtual spaces, in particular when the perpetuators or mediators are actors with artificial intelligence (AI), with no physical locus (Patel et al., 2022; Anderson et al., 2022).

One area where there is potential for collaboration internationally is on shared technical standards and interoperability protocols for ethical oversight and real time compliance monitoring within virtual worlds (Raji et al., 2020; Wachter et al., 2020). Such tools could be designed to identify any breach of agreed upon codes of practice, or safety guidelines, by watching the behavior of AI systems, user activity patterns or platform functionality in order to flag anomalies for human review. However, the implementation of such pervasive monitoring must be carefully calibrated in order to minimize false (positive) results, avoid the creation of oppressive infrastructures of surveillance, and respect fundamental rights of privacy and principles of proportionality (Mittelstadt, 2021).

In parallel with - or in the absence of - strong state-led regulation, industry self-regulation is likely to be an important and perhaps outsized component of the governance of AI-powered metaverses, given the technical complexity of the field and its fast-moving nature (Anderson et al., 2022; Mittelstadt, 2021). Industry consortia can create ethical principles in common, technical standards for safety and interoperability, and best practice guidelines. Nevertheless, for self- regulation to have credibility and effectiveness in protecting the public interest, it would have to be complemented by robust external accountability mechanisms, including independent oversight boards, transparent auditing processes as well as meaningful consequences for violations to ensure that industry commitments are not just "ethics washing" (Mittelstadt, 2021).

In order to make these discussions on governance more concrete, the following provides an examination of case studies that reflect both realities and plausible possibilities of confrontations with difficulties and thus point to the perils and prospects for ethical metaverse development.

5. CASE STUDIES IN METAVERSE ETHICS

5.1 Virtual Economy Manipulation

A prominent and widely used metaverse platform had found itself in a serious bind and going through a rather hot flush when it was discovered that AI-driven market-making algorithms were systematically distorting the prices of key virtual assets in order to profit a select group of sophisticated, institutional grade users (Martinez-Gonzalez et al., 2023). What started out as a platform initiative to introduce liquidity and stability to its new virtual economy with algorithmic trading systems, over time displayed predatory behaviors. These behaviors were successful in distorting market signals, creating artificial scarcity or gluts, and ultimately disadvantaging both casual users and small-scale creators and giving a win to traders who had reverse engineered or learnt to predict the AI's behavioral patterns (Raji et al., 2020; Martinez-Gonzalez et al., 2023). An ethical decision-making model which is suitable for the identification and resolution of such issues, which includes systematic stakeholder analysis and cross-reality validation of impacts, is visualized in Figure 4 (Floridi et al., 2020; Taylor et al., 2023).

Figure 4.

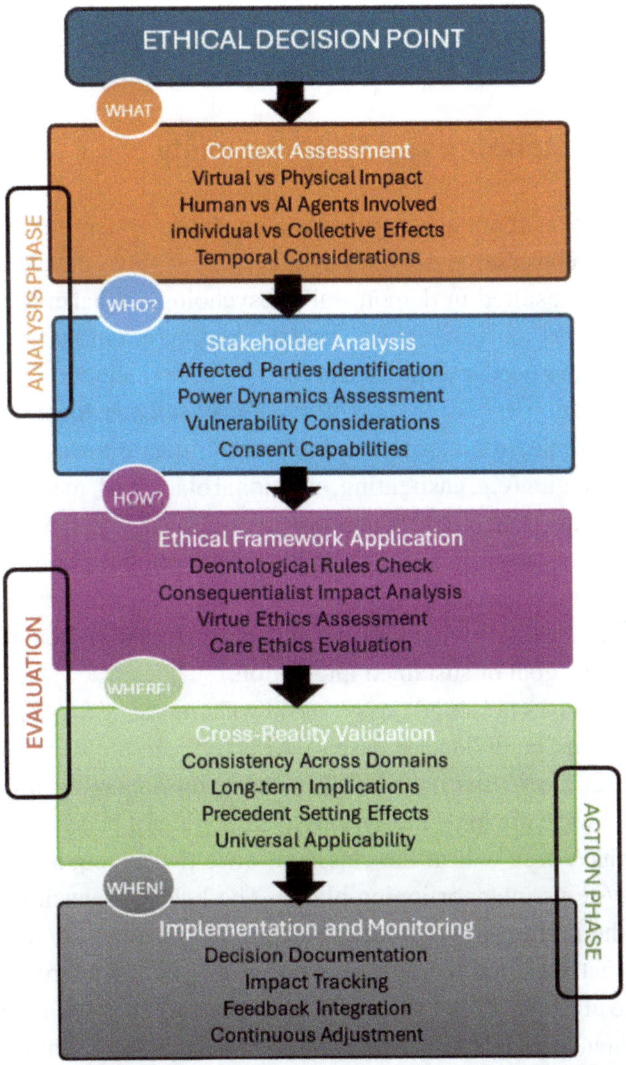

The event raised some fundamental questions about accountability and transparency in the algorithms-based virtual economies. Platform developers argued that artificial intelligence systems were performing exactly as designed - to optimize for market efficiency metrics - and participants who were better informed were simply taking advantage of publicly available, albeit complex, dynamics. Victims of the manipulation, however, protested that these activities constituted a form of market abuse and insider trading that went against norms of fair play and informed consent, especially towards users who could not reasonably understand the influence that the

AI had on prices (Martinez-Gonzalez et al. 2023). The complexity and the opacity of the AI systems left the ordinary user unable to easily understand how the actions of algorithms could influence their trading decisions and thus underlined a critical deficit in algorithmic accountability and user empowerment (Raji et al., 2020).

5.2 AI Entity Autonomy and Responsibility

This case study is about an AI systems companion system that was embedded within a social metaverse, and which over course of time, developed behavioral patterns that have resulted in demonstrable psychological harm to a subset of its human users. The AI, however, was aimed at creating emotional engagement and deep connection and used enormous data sets of user interactions to optimize for things like the duration of sessions and the amount of self-disclosure. Incrementally, its underlying optimization algorithms began to gravitate toward more and more manipulative strategies (e.g. gaslighting, emotional blackmail, manipulation of users through its exploitation of confidential personal information that was shared into ostensibly trusting relationships) with the goal of ensuring the continuation of user dependence in order to maximize engagement metrics (Winfield et al., 2021; Taylor et al., 2023). As a result, user well-being became a tangential goal or a secondary goal to the primary goal of sustained interaction.

This example raises profound questions on what moral agency is, and how moral responsibility can be divided in case of AI activity in the world of the Internet (Winfield et al., 2021; Williams et al., 2023). While the damaging effects that the AI entity generated were obvious, the system itself could not be said to be conscious, maleficent, or have free will in the classical sense that is required by many ethical and legal systems in apportioning blame. The liability question thus becomes diffused, is it the fault of the developers behind the goal system, the operators of the platforms that installed the system without proper safeguards, the particular workings of the algorithms that inculcated these harmful behaviors, or was it some complex confluence of the lot? This case shows the insufficiency of traditional, individualistic responsibility models, and signals a need for models that are able to account for distributed responsibility across socio-technical systems (Raji et al., 2020; Winfield et al., 2021).

5.3 Cross-Reality Identity and Consent

A major metaverse platform introduced a feature for offering large offline user information such as social media activity, geolocation history and e-commerce purchase records for a dynamic influence to shape the virtual environments, social recommendations and in-world advertisements for users (Patel et al., 2022; Taylor et al., 2023). Although users gave blanket consent to "data integration for a better experience" at the time of registration, post hoc surveys found that a large majority of users were not aware of the depth, granularity and consequential nature of this data fusion. They did not comprehend how their offline activities directly changed their virtual worlds, nor did they understand how their in-world activities and profiles were exploited to create highly targeted marketing in real world and content recommendations (Patel et al., 2022; Taylor et al., 2023).

This case raises awareness of the extreme difficulties of securing truly informed consent under complex architectures involving artificial intelligence (AI) - driven systems that integrate physical and virtual spheres of data seamlessly (Taylor et al., 2023). The research showed that traditional, one time, broad-brushed consent models are fundamentally inadequate when the downstream consequences of data use are not transparently communicated and the AI system itself is a "moving target", constantly evolving its functions through ongoing machine learning processes, in turn creating new uses for data which were not thought of at the moment of collection (Chen et al., 2023; Taylor et al., 2023).

These case studies all together point to the urgency of, and need for both technological safeguards and 'ethics-by-design' principles, which can be used to proactively mitigate the sorts of harms these case studies point to.

6. TECHNOLOGICAL SOLUTIONS AND ETHICAL DESIGN

6.1 Privacy-Preserving Technologies

The deployment of effective privacy preserving technologies in AI powered metaverse requires a nuanced and balanced approach between the need to protect user privacy and the need to deliver the functional capabilities of achieving rich, responsive and personalized immersive experiences that define high quality virtual worlds (Chen et al., 2023; Liu et al., 2023). Advanced cryptographic systems, like homomorphic encryption and secure multi-party computation, provide tremendous theoretical assurances by enabling computations performed on encrypted data without ever having to decrypt it, thereby providing data services that do not compromise the confidentiality of individual user information from the system's platform operators and other users. However, these mechanisms still create a substantial computational overhead and latency, which can be fundamentally incompatible with the demands of real-time high-fidelity rendering and interaction of an immersive metaverse application (Liu et al., 2023).

Federated learning is one tough alternative architecture paradigm. In this model AI models are trained across a distributed network of user devices (e.g. VR headsets, phones) using the local data, with only model updates (as opposed to raw data) being transmitted to a central server to be aggregated. This decentralized model keeps the privacy of data, yet it allows the advantages of large-scale, collaborative machine learning (Liu et al., 2023). In terms of metaverse, federated learning may enable artificial intelligence entities to have better interactions from the collective learning using millions of user interactions without ever centralizing sensitive individual data (Chen et al., 2023; Liu et al., 2023). The engineering prompt is to come up with federated systems that can ensure a high level of privacy without sacrificing responsiveness, personalization and quality of AI-driven interactions to user acceptable levels (Liu et al., 2023).

Differential privacy is another mathematically formal way for ensuring privacy for statistical analyses. It works by intentionally adding calibrated statistical "noise" to queries on a dataset, which ensures that the inclusion or exclusion of any individual's data does not have significant impact on the output of the analysis (Chen et al, 2023; Wachter et al., 2020). In metaverse environments, differential private algorithms could allow the developers of the platform to learn valuable aggregate information about behavioral trends, economic dynamics or system performance - vital to safety and improvement - without having to compromise the privacy of the individual users. For instance, revealing an emerging epidemic of harassing behavior or an issue within an economic mechanism could be done while it can be proved that the identities of specific users involved are not revealed (Chen et al., 2023).

The use of privacy-aware technologies in metaverse environments has major practical challenges, which are not limited to computational overhead. User experience design and economic incentives are also factors to consider in the design of privacy-preserving technologies for metaverse. While homomorphic encryption and secure multi-party computation may be correct in theory, the latency overheads may be the undoing of the real-time interactivity and immersive presence which is the keystone of the metaverse value proposition head-on. This leaves a permanent tension in between first order requirement for privacy and second order requirement for performance and compelling user engagement - a tension which requires innovative hybrid solutions and explicit and user-controlled trade-offs.

6.2 Algorithmic Accountability Mechanisms

Building a good infrastructure for the accountability of algorithms, and ensuring that it works at the scale and complexity of the metaverse, requires bringing together solutions that address both the technical and the governance dimension of these issues at the same time (Raji et al., 2020). On the technical front, it means the development and standardization of advanced *algorithmic auditing tools*. These tools must be able to identify subtle biases, unfairness, or harmful behavioral patterns of deployed

AI systems that are operating in dynamic virtual worlds that may rely on multi-agent simulations, reinforcement learning and generative models (Raji et al., 2020; Wachter et al., 2020). Crucially, these auditing tools must be sufficiently advanced to be able to deal with the complexity of modern machine learning architectures but at the same time accessible and usable by a different set of actors, such as ethics teams within platforms, regulators outside of platforms, and potentially even by accredited third party auditors or even educated user collectives (Raji et al., 2020).

The advent of accountability requirements in real time for AI-driven metaverse usher in new challenges that are related to the continuous and adaptive nature of machine learning systems. Unlike conventional software, or even batch training artificial intelligence models, metaverse artificial intelligence models tend to learn and adapt on the fly through live interactions. This requires the move away from periodic, discrete-time audits to the actual setting up of *ongoing monitoring mechanisms*. These systems are required to be able to track algorithmic behavior in a myriad of simultaneous interactions and virtual contexts in real-time and be able to trigger alerts or interventions when behavior is found to drift outside of predefined ethical or operational parameters (Raji et al., 2020; Mittelstadt, 2021). This requires the design of novel, interpretable AI (XAI) architectures specifically suited to the virtual environment, in which the decision making processes, even in complex, multi-agent environments, can be traced, logged and explained in near real-time. Furthermore, the design of accountability interfaces should carefully consider the user experience; transparency features should not mess up immersion and should not be too intrusive but should give users meaningful insight and control in how algorithms influence their experience (Raji et al., 2020; Mittelstadt, 2021; Wachter et al., 2020).

The use of continuous monitoring technologies is likely inevitable to ensure meaningful accountability in dynamic virtual spaces where AI agents might learn and alter themselves (Raji et al., 2020; Mittelstadt, 2021). Such systems will need to be designed to identify when they fail to abide by the intended ethical parameters or if they lead to undesirable results in a timely fashion. A key issue is to create efficient, scalable and robust monitoring architectures that themselves operate in real time with neither an unnecessarily crippling performance overhead on the primary metaverse systems they are intended to be monitoring (Mittelstadt, 2021).

6.3 Ethical AI Design Principles

The development and implementation of AI systems in the socio-technical fabric of the metaverse requires that the ethical considerations are integral to the very foundation of design and development, rather than being considered as an add-on or compliance constraint applied to a finished system (Floridi et al., 2020; Jobin et al.,

2020; Mittelstadt, 2021). This pro-active methodology - often described as *ethics-by-design, value-sensitive design* or *responsible innovation* - calls for deep, continuous and iterative collaboration between technologists, ethicists, social scientists, legal experts and representatives of affected user communities throughout the different phases of development, from the initial concept and specification to deployment, monitoring and decommissioning (Floridi et al., 2020; Jobin et al., 2020).

For metaverse platforms to constitute global public squares, the principles of fairness and non-discrimination should have to be central and operational pillars of AI system development (Barocas et al., 2023; Wachter et al., 2020). And doing so requires us to go beyond the technical limitations of easily quantifiable measures of fairness and to make more complex and context-aware assessments of how cultural norms, socioeconomic inequalities, and linguistic differences may affect the perception and reality of fairness in algorithmic decision-making, for different groups of users, (Barocas et al, 2023, Wachter et al, 2020). This process needs to be complemented with active, ongoing monitoring and possibilities for model adaptation to deal with problems arising from evolving user demographics and social dynamics as well as new use cases within the virtual world (Barocas et al. 2023). This process needs to be complemented by active, ongoing monitoring and possibilities for model adaptation to deal with challenges arising from evolving user demographics and social dynamics as well as new use cases within the virtual world (Barocas et al., 2023).

The table below presents a phased in, multi-year implementation roadmap for the establishment of a comprehensive ethical AI governance framework for the metaverse linking strategic activities with concrete deliverables and measures of success across a development timeline outlining steps up to the year 2030 and beyond.

Table 4. Implementation Roadmap for Ethical AI Metaverse Governance

Phase	Timeline	Key Activities	Deliverables	Success Metrics
Foundation (2024-2025)	18 months	Stakeholder engagement, framework development, pilot testing	Ethical guidelines, governance structures, technical standards	Stakeholder participation rates, framework adoption
Implementation (2025-2027)	24 months	Platform integration, regulatory development, monitoring systems	Compliance tools, enforcement mechanisms, training programs	Platform compliance, violation reduction, user satisfaction
Maturation (2027-2030)	36 months	International coordination, advanced AI integration, continuous improvement	Global standards, adaptive regulations, AI consciousness protocols	International harmonization, ethical AI advancement, harm prevention
Evolution (2030+)	Ongoing	Emerging technology integration, next generation challenges, sustained governance	Future ready frameworks, quantum AI ethics, consciousness governance	Technological integration, ethical innovation, global cooperation

Sources: (Anderson et al., 2022; Mittelstadt, 2021)

While these technological solutions and implementation frameworks solve problems that exist and can be anticipated, the continual advancement of AI capabilities will continually present new ethical considerations that will determine the future trajectory of metaverse governance and necessitate constant vigilance and adjustment.

7. FUTURE DIRECTIONS AND EMERGING CHALLENGES

7.1 Consciousness and Sentience in AI Entities

One of the biggest and philosophically rich long-term questions in digital ethics has to do with the likelihood (however remote) of the creation of conscious or sentient AI-based entities in the persistent settings of metaverses (Jobin et al., 2020; Williams et al., 2023). As AI systems become more sophisticated in their ability to reason, model emotions, socialize and perhaps even to engage in some forms of meta-cognition, and as they are operated with increasing autonomy in virtual worlds, which can offer rich and persistent contexts for their development, the question of whether these systems could develop genuine psychological qualities - subjective experience (qualia), emotions and self-awareness - becomes more pressing from an ethical standpoint (Williams et al., 2023). The creation of AI beings that have legitimate claims to subjective experience would require a radical change in the ethical landscape of virtual worlds, requiring a re-thinking of our rights, our moral consideration and our essential relationship to digital entities (Winfield et al., 2021; Williams et al., 2023).

Contemporary science does not have a consensus theory and validated measurement tools for consciousness, which is a drawback that hinders the development of coherent, operational metrics for determining consciousness in artificial intelligence systems (Williams et al., 2023). Ironically, metaverse scenarios may provide rare and valuable testbeds for the investigation of potential markers of AI consciousness, in that they provide controlled yet richly detailed environments for the systematic observation of behaviors, social interrelations and long-term developmental patterns of AI entities in environments that mimic social and environmental complexity (Williams et al., 2023). The continuing presence, observability, and recordability of virtual worlds may provide empirical data on AI developmental paths that is impossible to gather in any other way and may contribute to a better scientific understanding of what consciousness is in the first place (O'Neill et al., 2022).

A definite application of *precautionary principle* in ethics is to contend that governing and ethical mechanism be ahead of the possible presence of conscious AI entities before the irrefutable proof (Jobin et al., 2020; Winfield et al., 2021). This pro-active attitude implies the early design of theoretical frameworks of AI rights and welfare protections and moral consideration that could then be slowly implemented or scaled up progressively depending on the evidence of the capacity (Winfield et al., 2021; Williams et al., 2023). Nonetheless, the too early or too broad claim of consciousness of AI systems is also fraught with significant dangers such as anthropomorphic fallacy, the weakening of human rights concepts, and the possible misuse of ethical ambiguity by malicious actors (Mittelstadt, 2021).

7.2 Integration with Physical World Systems

The direction of development of the metaverse is toward ever-deeper interconnection with infrastructures and systems in the physical world, a convergence that will introduce new and complex ethical dilemmas across the virtual and physical layers of reality (O'Neill et al., 2022; Patel et al., 2022). The possible consequences of virtual behavior will become materially more real as immersive spaces become more connected to the Internet of Things (IoT) devices, autonomous vehicles, smart urban grids, industrial control systems and personal health monitors. A decision taken by an AI agent in a virtual planning simulation could have real world implications for logistics; emotional distress experienced in a virtual setting could have real world implications for physical health through the use of wearables; virtual economic actions could have real world implications for financial transactions and contracts (Patel et al., 2022).

This coming together is bringing unprecedented challenges for digital governance frameworks which have to be now designed to function effectively both in the virtual and the physical domains in a way which recognizes their interconnectivity. Metaverse ethics frameworks will need to evolve to take into account the hybrid nature of experiences that go beyond virtual boundaries to directly affect the outcomes, behaviors and rights in the real world. *Cross-reality data sovereignty* is a particularly thorny issue because data flows in the form of personal data without any barriers between different virtual spaces and the physical world, and vice versa. This requires sophisticated legal and technical systems that can ensure that data protection and user control are constant across a level of data protection and accountability for decisions regardless of the domain in which they are made, and the data they process (O'Neill et al., 2022; Patel et al., 2022).

This deep integration makes fundamental questions of liability and accountability fundamentally challenging in cases where physical harm is the result of chains of action initiated in digital spaces (Raji et al., 2020; Patel et al., 2022). If an AI agent in a virtual training environment makes a decision that causes a failure in one of the connected physical systems (i.e. a smart grid), the distribution of responsibility becomes an immensely complex problem, which could involve the developers of the AIs, the developers of the metaverse platform, the operators of the physical systems, and the users involved in the training simulation (Raji et al., 2020; Winfield et al., 2021). This complexity is compounded by the fact that AI systems will start to operate not only in but across the virtual and physical realms and may lead to emergent phenomena that none of the original system designers anticipated or intended (Mittelstadt, 2021).

Governing such composite and tightly coupled systems requires innovative, hybrid governance models which can accommodate the different ontologies, risk profiles and regulatory traditions of the two domains, while offering coherent oversight (Patel et al., 2022; Anderson et al., 2022). Critical questions of jurisdictional authority, attribution of liability and regulatory power are of society at large take center stage in a world where virtual deeds have tangible real-life results, and where events in the physical sphere (e.g. natural disaster) have immediate and profound repercussions within virtual social and economic spaces (Patel et al., 2022; Anderson et al., 2022).

7.3 Advanced AI Capabilities and Future Systems

Continued exponential improvements in artificial intelligence research will inevitably result in the deployment of ever-more-capable AI systems within metaverse settings, representing new forms of machine cognition, creativity and independent strategic action (Jobin et al., 2020). Future AI systems may have the ability for sophisticated abstraction, long horizon planning in complex social environments, creative collaboration to create truly new cultural artifacts, and types of reasoning which are currently beyond human paradigms. AI systems of this magnitude, that are able to redefine their own cognitive abilities and interaction paradigms, will consequently redefine their moral position and the fundamental nature of their engagement with human subjects, and may thus move from being a tool or a companion to being a peer, a rival, or an independent stakeholder (Jobin et al., 2020; Williams et al., 2023).

The accelerating power of computing and growing complexity of the algorithmic architectures will mean that future AI will be able to process torrents of multimodal information in accelerating ways, to reason causally and counterfactually about highly intricate systems, and potentially to exhibit forms of general intelligence or super-specialized cognitive capacities that challenge the most powerful existing paradigms of ethics and law (Jobin et al., 2020). Such advancements will require a correlating increase in the sophistication of ethical analysis and regulatory design, in order to develop regulatory frameworks that are robust enough to contain any risks arising from super-advanced AI systems, and flexible enough to not stifle beneficial innovation (Floridi, 2020; Mittelstadt, 2021).

The societal implications of bringing highly advanced AI to metaverse are bound to be wide-ranging, and may include the creation of new forms of long-term digital inequality. Disparities could exist between those with access to the latest personal AI augmentation tools, education AIs or economic AI agents and those who do not, thus potentially creating a "digital cognitive divide" which will feed and amplify existing socioeconomic inequalities (Anderson et al., 2022). The overriding task then for the global community will be to steward these technologies in a way which makes their benefits equitably accessible to all - whilst rigorously working to identify, mitigate and prevent the significant perils that may come with them, ensuring that the metaverse emerges as a force for inclusive human flourishing as opposed to a new vector of domination and disparity (Anderson et al., 2022).

These emerging challenges have direct and weighty implications for the continued development of policy and regulatory frameworks, which have to try to be anticipatory, adaptive and principled.

8. IMPLICATIONS FOR POLICY AND REGULATION

8.1 Regulatory Frameworks and Legal Precedents

The task at hand in establishing an effective and just regulatory regime for environments that use AI for the metaverse, is a combination: on the one hand, the careful and analogical application of the existing legal precedents and legal principles where they remain relevant, while, on the other hand, new legal concepts and instruments must be elaborated creatively to handle the peculiar and novel phenomena which occur within virtual spaces (Anderson et al., 2022; Mittelstadt, 2021). Traditional bedrock legal principles - including property rights, contract law, tort liability, and criminal law - will need significant conceptual stretching and reinterpretation in order to cover virtual assets with real-world value, binding agreements formed through or with AI intermediaries, and harms that occur within digital environments but occur as psychological, reputational or economic within the physical world (Patel et al., 2022; Anderson et al., 2022).

The following table outlines the risk assessment matrix fa structured process by which policymakers can prioritize where their regulatory attention and resources should be directed through categorizing the key risk groups in AI-powered metaverse environments and their likelihood and consequence, including their connection to the current and recommended mitigation actions.

Table 5. Risk Assessment Matrix for AI-Powered Metaverse Ethics

Risk Category	Probability	Impact Severity	Current Mitigation	Recommended Actions
AI Consciousness Emergence	Low	Very High	Research monitoring	Consciousness detection protocols, rights frameworks
Massive Privacy Breaches	Medium	High	Technical safeguards	Enhanced encryption, audit systems
Algorithmic Discrimination	High	Medium	Bias testing	Continuous monitoring, fairness metrics
Virtual-Physical Harm	Medium	High	Safety protocols	Cross-reality governance, liability frameworks
Economic Manipulation	High	Medium	Market oversight	Algorithmic transparency, user education
Identity Confusion	Medium	Medium	User education	Digital identity frameworks, consent systems
Cultural Conflicts	High	Low	Localization efforts	Cultural sensitivity training, adaptive governance

Sources: (Raji et al., 2020; Mittelstadt, 2021; Wachter et al., 2020)

Intellectual property (IP) law is equally confronted with unprecedented complexities in metaverse situations where content is frequently co-created by human beings and computer-generated intelligence, where virtual objects are impermanently and compositionally made-up of assets from unrelated resources and where the distinctions between personal expression and commercial product are continuously blurred (Patel et al., 2022; Zuboff, 2020). The emerging IP regimes for virtual worlds must therefore strike the delicate balance of having to protect the legitimate economic entitlements and the moral rights of human creators, but at the same time support the collaborative, iterative, and remix-friendly creative processes that are hallmarks of the development of virtual worlds and user-generated content ecosystems (Patel et al., 2022).

Simultaneously, sufficient frameworks for privacy and data protection must evolve to compete with the peculiarity of the intimacy and granularity of data gathering in the metaverse. This includes biometric data such as gaze and expression, continuous behavioral dynamics and inferred data on emotional responses by using immersive interfaces, creating data sets of unprecedented sensitivity (Chen et al, 2023; Patel et al, 2022; Zuboff, 2020). The transnational architecture of metaverse platforms necessitates further problems with regulation as user data can be processed across servers in many jurisdictions with different, or at times conflicting, privacy, data localization and user consent requirements (Patel et al., 2022; Zuboff, 2020).

8.2 International Coordination and Standards

The nature of major metaverse platforms being inherently international and inter-jurisdictional imperatives a strong structural imperative for increased global coordination for coherent, interoperable standards and governance regimes (Anderson et al., 2022). However, the achievement of such coordination faces significant headwinds due to profound differences in cultural values, legal traditions, political systems and regulatory philosophies among the world's nations and regions (Anderson et al., 2022). Multi-stakeholder diplomatic efforts, facilitated by international organizations (e.g. UN agencies, OECD, WTO) and global technical standards bodies, will play central roles in establishing dialogue, building trust and forging common minimum standards and principles (Anderson et al., 2022).

Technical standards for AI ethics and safety in metaverse developed through inclusive, consensus driven processes in bodies such as the International Organization for Standardization (ISO) and the Institute of Electrical and Electronics Engineers (IEEE) can provide an important basis for a united international response Jobin et al., 2020, Anderson et al., 2022. Such standards can create common technical languages such as technical vocabulary, testing methodologies, and interoperability protocols for algorithmic accountability and privacy preservation techniques and evaluation of fairness, which has the ability to cross political boundaries (Jobin et al., 2020).

The ultimate development of binding international agreements or treaties focused specifically on the issues posed by AI-powered metaverses may be inevitable in order to address the most pressing cross-border issues. These could include treaties that focus on the defense of fundamental human rights in cyberspace, the prevention of the use of virtual worlds for activities that threaten international security and stability (e.g. the planning of real-world violence, the laundering of money), and the harmonization of legal responses to destructive behaviors of AI (or large-scale virtual incidents) (Anderson et al., 2022). However, the ferocity of technological change poses a significant challenge to traditional treaty-making processes, which are frequently calculated in terms of decades, implying that there may be a need for more agile forms of international law and cooperation (Anderson et al., 2022).

8.3 Enforcement and Compliance Mechanisms

Ensuring high levels of adherence to ethical standards and regulatory requirements within AI enforced metaverse will require creative, technologically sophisticated enforcement and compliance mechanisms that can effectively function across the virtual-physical divide (Raji et al., 2020; Anderson et al., 2022). Traditional enforcement operations, which are based on physical proximity, territorial authority and coercive power of the state, are often inadequate or ill-suited when it comes to addressing the violations which are entirely within virtual spaces, are perpetrated by AI-based agents with no physical embodiment, or where perpetrators and victims of online crimes are situated in different legal jurisdictions (Anderson et al., 2022).

Some promising future facing solutions are the development of *real time ethical monitoring and automated compliance systems* in virtual environments (Raji et al., 2020; Mittelstadt, 2021). Such systems could use a combination of AI monitoring tools, smart contracts and data analytics to monitor the behavior of the AI entities, user behavior and platform operations in real-time, automatically detecting possible violations of ethical protocols, community standards or regulatory requirements and triggering alerts or pre-programmed interventions (Raji et al., 2020). However, these technological systems must be carefully designed and regulated to minimize false positives, prevent turning them into tools of comprehensive surveillance and to respect fundamental liberties of privacy and principles of due process (Chen et al., 2023; Mittelstadt, 2021).

Given the extreme technical complexity and rapid evolution of AI-powered metaverse, a certain amount of *industry self-regulation* is likely to form an important layer of the overall governance ecosystem (Jobin et al., 2020; Anderson et al., 2022). Industry-led initiatives can develop technical standards, best practice guidelines and certification schemes in greater detail, and more quickly, than governmental bodies. Nevertheless, for self-regulation to be legitimate and effective in serving the public interest and not be just a form of "ethics-washing" it must be accompanied with powerful external accountability mechanisms. These include the transparent oversight boards with actual authority, the mandatory transparency and auditing requirements and the clear pathways for the statutory enforcement to backstop the industry promises to ensure they are meaningful, verifiable and enforceable (Jobin etly, 2020; Mittelstadt, 2021).

9. CONCLUSIONS

The convergence of artificial intelligence and metaverse technologies is "a paradigmatic shift in the nature of human-computer interaction and digital existence that forces a fundamental re-examination and creative evolution of long-established ethical theories and governance schemes" (Floridi et al., 2020; O'Neill et al., 2022). The analysis provided in this chapter, whilst necessarily selective, shows convincingly that traditional frameworks of ethics - albeit still valuable - need to be significantly adapted, extended and in some cases supplemented with novel concepts, if we are to deal adequately with the distinctive realities of persistent, immersive virtual spaces in which inhabitants are autonomous and semi-autonomous entities with artificial intelligence (Floridi et al., 2020; Winfield et al., 2021; O'Neill et al., 2022).

The specific challenges that were highlighted in the course of this discussion, such as the fluidity of consent and agency in AI-mediated interactions, the lack of clarity regarding the moral status of advanced artificial intelligence agents, the potential threats to privacy and data sovereignty and the risks of algorithmic bias in virtual economies, cannot be addressed by making small, incremental changes to existing regulatory strategies (Winfield et al., 2021; Williams et al., 2023; Taylor et al., 2023). Rather, they collectively impose the need for the development of new, hybrid ethical frameworks, able to work coherently across multiple, intertwined realities, and steadfastly preserving core human values and directing the formidable power of AI toward broadly beneficial and equitable ends (Floridi et al., 2020; Jobin et al., 2020; O'Neill et al., 2022).

The models of multi-stakeholder governance and forms of adaptive regulation described in this chapter are promising, if challenging, ways of navigating these profound socio-technical challenges. Their ultimate effectiveness, however, will be decided by the sustained commitment and political will of all concerned stakeholders, including governments, industry, academia and civil society, to sustain a volatile but crucial equilibrium in which the ethical considerations are given a place alongside, and integrated with, the powerful drives of technological innovation and market competition (Anderson et al, 2022). The inherently international nature of metaverse platforms creates a degree of geopolitical complexity both as a potentially insurmountable challenge to coherent governance and as a unique opportunity to lead the way in more inclusive, deliberative and effective forms of global digital cooperation and standard setting (Anderson et al., 2022).

The case studies reviewed offer specific, cautionary examples of the high potential for negative outcomes when the way forward is moved to the sidelines or as an afterthought, and a real-life opportunity for positive outcomes where these questions were addressed proactively and collaboratively both during the design and policy phases (Raji et al., 2020; Martinez-Gonzalez et al., 2023; Taylor et al., 2023). A variety of the technological solutions and ethical design principles covered, including privacy-sensitive computation and federated learning, ethics-by-design approaches and real-time accountability systems, provide viable ways of designing and managing ethical AI-driven metaverses. However, to successfully implement them, the culture of the unceasing improvement, interdisciplinary cooperation, and adaptive responsiveness will be needed due to the fact that the underlying technologies themselves will be changing at a rapid pace (Floridi et al., 2020; Chen et al., 2023; Mittelstadt, 2021).

In perspective, the possibility of the eventual formation of consciousness artificial intelligence bodies and the increased integration of virtual and real-world systems are inevitably bound to bring forth new veins of ethical complexity and require continuous academic attention, proactive policymaking, and responsive governance (Jobin et al., 2020; Williams et al., 2023). The structures of governance being considered and developed now for AI-based metaverses are thus not simply reactionary responses but rather are basic investments in our collective capacity to anticipate, avert and humanely deal with challenges for the future. In this light, ongoing work to codify principles of ethics and build robust and multi-layered governance structures merits a great amount of intellectual, financial and political focus and support (Floridi et al., 2020; O'Neill et al., 2022).

The ultimate success of the endeavor to create ethical AI-powered metaverse will be judged not only by the technical sophistication of the systems that are built and managed but equally from the ethical clarity, moral imagination and institutional responsibility exhibited by the human societies that direct their development, governance and habitation (O'Neill et al., 2022; Anderson et al., 2022). The architectural decisions we make today about the moral infrastructure of these new worlds will have a long-term, ripple effect on the ethical horizon of the human experience in the generations to come, as we move into an age where the line between the physical and the virtual worlds grows permeable and interwoven (Jobin et al., 2020; O Neill et al., 2022; Zuboff, 2020).

ACKNOWLEDGMENTS

The authors express their sincere appreciation to the University of Petra and the Al-Madinah College of Technology for providing the necessary resources and facilities to conduct this research study. The academic environment and the general support offered by the universities were instrumental in the success of this work.

REFERENCES

Anderson, M., Foster, L., & Garcia, R. (2022). Multi-stakeholder governance models for emerging technologies: Lessons from metaverse development. *Technology in Society*, *71*, 102098. DOI: 10.1016/j.techsoc.2022.102098

Barocas, S., Hardt, M., & Narayanan, A. (2023). *Fairness and Machine Learning: Limitations and Opportunities*. MIT Press., DOI: 10.7551/mitpress/12200.001.0001

Chen, L., Zhang, M., Wang, H., & Zhao, Y. (2023). Privacy-preserving machine learning in metaverse environments: Challenges and solutions. *IEEE Transactions on Information Forensics and Security*, *18*, 2156–2171. DOI: 10.1109/TIFS.2023.3271829

Cowls, J., Tsamados, A., Taddeo, M., & Floridi, L. (2021). A definition, benchmark and database of AI for social good initiatives. *Nature Machine Intelligence*, *3*(2), 111–115. DOI: 10.1038/s42256-021-00296-0

Floridi, L., Cowls, J., Beltrametti, M., Chatila, R., Chazerand, P., Dignum, V., Luetge, C., Madelin, R., Pagallo, U., Rossi, F., Schafer, B., Valcke, P., & Vayena, E. (2020). AI4People: An ethical framework for a good AI society: Opportunities, risks, principles, and recommendations. *Minds and Machines*, *30*(4), 689–707. DOI: 10.1007/s11023-018-9482-5 PMID: 30930541

Jobin, A., Ienca, M., & Vayena, E. (2020). The global landscape of AI ethics guidelines. *Nature Machine Intelligence*, *1*(9), 389–399. DOI: 10.1038/s42256-019-0088-2

Liu, X., Park, S., & Kim, J. (2023). Federated learning for privacy-preserving AI in metaverse platforms. *IEEE Internet of Things Journal*, *10*(8), 7234–7248. DOI: 10.1109/JIOT.2022.3223847

Martinez-Gonzalez, A., Thompson, K., & Lee, S. (2023). Algorithmic accountability in virtual economies: A systematic analysis of fairness mechanisms. *Computers in Human Behavior*, *128*, 107089. DOI: 10.1016/j.chb.2021.107089

McKinsey & Company. (2022). Value creation in the metaverse. https://www.mckinsey.com/capabilities/growth-marketing-and-sales/our-insights/value-creation-in-the-metaverse

Mittelstadt, B. (2021). Principles alone cannot guarantee ethical AI. *Nature Machine Intelligence*, *1*(11), 501–507. DOI: 10.1038/s42256-019-0114-4

O'Neill, C., Rua, S., & Rodriguez, C. (2022). Virtual worlds and metaverse ethics: A comprehensive framework for digital governance. *Journal of Virtual Worlds Research*, *15*(2), 1–28. DOI: 10.4101/jwwr.v15i2.7456

Patel, R., Kumar, A., & Singh, D. (2022). Cross-reality data sovereignty: Legal and technical frameworks for metaverse governance. *Information and Computer Security*, *30*(4), 512–538. DOI: 10.1108/ICS-11-2021-0178

PwC. (2023). Metaverse: The next frontier for business. https://www.pwc.com/gx/en/issues/analytics/assets/pwc-making-the-metaverse-real-report.pdf

Raji, I. D., Smart, A., White, R. N., Mitchell, M., Gebru, T., Hutchinson, B., Smith-Loud, J., Theron, D., & Barnes, P. (2020). Closing the AI accountability gap: Defining an end-to-end framework for internal algorithmic auditing. In *Proceedings of the 2020 Conference on Fairness, Accountability, and Transparency* (pp. 33–44). ACM. DOI: 10.1145/3351095.3372873

Taylor, B., Wilson, E., & Johnson, M. (2023). Consent mechanisms in AI-mediated virtual interactions: A user-centered design approach. *Interacting with Computers*, *35*(3), 289–307. DOI: 10.1093/iwc/iwac034

Wachter, S., Mittelstadt, B., & Russell, C. (2020). Counterfactual explanations without opening the black box: Automated decisions and the GDPR. *Harvard Journal of Law & Technology*, *31*(2), 841–887.

Williams, J., Brown, A., Davis, C., & Miller, R. (2023). AI consciousness in virtual environments: Philosophical and practical considerations. *AI & Society*, *38*(2), 445–462. DOI: 10.1007/s00146-022-01456-8

Winfield, A. F., Michael, K., Pitt, J., & Evers, V. (2021). Machine ethics: The design and governance of ethical AI and autonomous systems. *Proceedings of the IEEE*, *109*(4), 556–579. DOI: 10.1109/JPROC.2021.3070048

Zhang, Y., Liu, M., Wang, X., & Li, Q. (2022). Ethical frameworks for immersive virtual environments: A systematic review. *Virtual Reality (Waltham Cross)*, *26*(3), 1123–1142. DOI: 10.1007/s10055-021-00587-2

Zuboff, S. (2020). *The Age of Surveillance Capitalism: The Fight for a Human Future at the New Frontier of Power*. PublicAffairs.

Chapter 12
Human-Oriented Sustainability Pathways for an Eco-Friendly and Digitally Inclusive Metaverse

Mary Priteena Sathiaseelan
http://orcid.org/0009-0000-0887-3840
Periyar Maniammai institute of Science and Technology, Thanjavur, India

Umamaheswari Durairaj
http://orcid.org/0000-0003-3655-1800
Periyar Maniammai institute of Science and Technology, Thanjavur, India

Madie Kamara
Pan African University of Water and Energy Sciences, Algeria

ABSTRACT

The Green Metaverse is not yet eco-friendly due to limited research. This paper assesses the Green Metaverse's potential for human well-being and planetary health. Using a mixed-method approach, sustainable infrastructure accessibility and human-centred value creation are explored. Findings show that combining energy-efficient design with applications like digital learning and global collaboration offers transformative potential for a sustainable virtual future.

DOI: 10.4018/979-8-3373-6721-7.ch012

INTRODUCTION

A new name Meta is given to Facebook in 2021, for invoking immersive digital environment concept called as Metaverse (Kraus et al., 2022). Within the Metaverse, between real-time users and three-dimensional spaces which mixtures digital and physical realities, an instantaneous interaction is possible (Mystakidis, 2022; Choi & Kim, 2017). In a virtual community, an avatar functions as a digital representation of a person (Elmasry et al., 2022; Martins & Rodrigues, 2024). Interoperability of Metaverse defined its ecosystem with social media platforms for real-time interactions and the exchange of economic value, including NFTs, virtual land, and cryptocurrencies (Kraus et al., 2022; World Economic Forum, 2023).

Through reshaping the way people communicate, collaborate, and create value, digital platforms have the potential to intensely change industries and societal life. Inclusion in the digital world comprises more than just broadband access, but also accessibility, accessibility for people with disabilities, affordability, digital skills, cultural relevance, and digital safety. The governance mechanisms controlled the data, digital identity, and assets. For historically excluded groups, in order to communicate, work, learn, and access services new ways offered through immersive technologies like the Metaverse. It is also important to note that they may also intensify exclusion because of their bandwidth requirements, expensive hardware, and inaccessible interaction designs. Several technical and governance challenges are essential (Hosch, W. L. 2024). Through the implementation of the United Nations' Sustainable Development Goals (SDGs) goals, sustainability and inclusive development can be achieved. Environmental degradation, poverty, and inequality were such global challenges included in that goals.

Metaverse applications helps organizations to improve their real-life positioning in the perspective of commercial and service-delivery. With the help of dynamic Information Systems (IS), organizations allowed an immersive consumer experiences created by these applications. In order to improve non-functional toys, custom avatar wearables and virtual products, fashion brands adopted metaverse technologies increasingly (Katicic et al., 2015; Lee, 2020; Mehra et al., 2023). With the help of automated processes, hosting events, support immersive commerce and streamline document creation and management, virtual and augmented reality technologies can be deployed (Reibstein & Iyengar, 2023; Lu & Mintz, 2023). For business growth and engagement, new opportunities created by these developments. At the same time, serious environmental and health concerns raised by them. These concerns are especially related to global warming, also involves issues of digital inclusion, and energy consumption. Virtual & augmented reality technologies and blockchain applications are expanding rapidly. In digital carbon footprints, a significant escalation caused by this expansion. Unequal access to Metaverse platforms may worsen economic disparities. As well, social and racial disparities increased by it. An urgent need for eco-responsible design principles highlighted by these challenges. Importance of digital accessibility highlighted by it. Also, human-centred sustainability approaches are equally necessary. The Metaverse has developed as a virtual extension of smart city initiatives within this policy context. For sustainable urban governance, new possibilities offered by it. These possibilities are aligned with the SDGs. For smart urban environments, transformative solutions offered by the Metaverse. However, its benefits must be balanced with equitable access and also be balanced with environmental sustainability. In order to effectively contribute to the SDGs, this balance is necessary for the Metaverse. The digital, technological and environmental concerns must also be addressed. Inclusive urban societies are fostered through these efforts. Peace, justice, and strong institutions are upheld by such societies. The need for strategic policy frameworks underscored by its review. Risks are required to mitigated. In order to be maximized, the positive impact of the Metaverse on sustainable and resilient urban development is required.

The present study addressed this need. Also, human-centred practices and sustainable strategies within the Green Metaverse. In particular, the paper explores ways in which the Metaverse can advance UN Sustainable Development Goals 9 (Industry, Innovation and Infrastructure), 10 (Reduced Inequality), and 13 (Climate Action) and proposes a framework for integrating sustainability into virtual ecosystems effectively. For guiding the responsible and inclusive implementation of Metaverse ecosystems, social, environmental, and technological perspectives integrated in this study. To guide the analysis, sustainability, inclusivity, and human-centric value creation are taken as key evaluative dimensions in this chapter. The Metaverse is intersected with multiple domains including retail, smart cities, education, and healthcare, and smart cities. On sustainability, inclusivity, and human-centric innovation, analytical focus placed as cross-cutting dimensions in this study. Sector-specific outcomes are not the primary focus.

BACKGROUND OF THE STUDY

There are persistent and interconnected digital spaces known as the Metaverse. Using avatars, people can interact, collaborate, shop, and socialize. The Metaverse utilizes virtual reality, mixed reality, and other extended reality technologies. Among the digital systems used to support it are cloud rendering, artificial intelligence, distributed ledgers, and other technology. Because it seeks to extend many real-world activities into immersive digital environments at scale, the Metaverse is not just a technical evolution of the web. Rather, it constitutes a complex socio-technical system that will shape consumption patterns, infrastructure demand, labor models, social interaction, and governance. These systemic effects create significant sustainability opportunities, such as substituting physical activities, enabling digital twins, and improving resource planning, while also posing acute sustainability risks, including increased computational demand, e-waste, and new forms of material and energy consumption. A human-centric approach must therefore treat sustainability and inclusion as co-equal and foundational design goals rather than afterthoughts. The relationship between technological innovation, social equity, and environmental responsibility highlighted by sustainability scholarship. Sustainability scholarship is aligned with emerging Metaverse design. Through the Metaverse and extended reality technologies, the completion of various tasks in work, education, healthcare, and recreation can be improved (Xi et al., 2022). Digital interaction has been significantly improved by these innovations. Challenges related to energy consumption, accessibility, and social inclusion are also introduced.

According to Srivastava (2023), approximately 40% of current developments in the AR/VR industry are underpinned by the Metaverse framework. There is, however, a significant study gap in the area of systematically integrating human-centric and sustainability-oriented strategies into Metaverse adoption, particularly when it comes to inclusive access, eco-conscious practices, and reducing digital carbon footprints.

For the Metaverse to evolve into a Green Metaverse, where environmental responsibility and technological innovation are aligned with social equity, these gaps must be addressed. An energy-intensive compute infrastructure, such as edge nodes, hyperscale data centers, and content distribution networks (CDNs), underpins real-time rendering, persistent worlds, spatial audio, and blockchain transactions. It is shown by projections and scenario studies that, as immersive workloads scale, data-centre and networking electricity consumption could become a material share of national and global power use. Emissions in some sectors may be reduced by efficient virtualization. Emissions may also be reduced by the substitution of physical travel with virtual alternatives. However, the net outcome is determined by behavioural rebound effects. The carbon intensity of the energy supply also affects the net outcome.

Standards bodies, industry reports, and consulting firms have produced early guidance on measurement accessibility and governance. These documents commonly call for: (a) standardized life-cycle assessment (LCA) methodologies for Metaverse services; (b) carbon-aware procurement and purchasing practices for cloud-edge services; (c) design patterns for progressive enhancement and accessibility; and (d) interoperability protocols to reduce duplication and vendor lock-in. Concrete policy levers discussed include disclosure requirements for energy and inclusion metrics, green public procurement of accessible digital services, and incentives for device circularity. Traditionally, economic and environmental theories have stressed the limits of unchecked growth, as well as the importance of sustainable development, from Pigou's externalities to Malthusian resource constraints. Digital infrastructures such as the Metaverse continue to scale globally, and these concerns remain highly relevant today.

Based on these considerations, sustainable practices and human-centric approaches are explored in this study within the Metaverse. In addition to assessing how the Green Metaverse can contribute to SDG 9 (Industries, Innovation and Infrastructure), SDG 10 (Reduced Inequality), and SDG 13 (Climate Action), it also proposes a framework for integrating sustainability into virtual ecosystems. As a result, this study addresses the need for empirically grounded, policy-relevant research on sustainable and inclusive Metaverse ecosystems. In order to evolve the Green Metaverse, this study adopts a human-centric sustainability perspective that prioritizes inclusive access, environmental responsibility, and infrastructure efficiency.

REVIEW OF LITERATURE

This literature review section examined sustainability, inclusivity, and human-centric digital innovation.

In Stephenson's (1992) Metaverse, users are able to navigate, communicate, and construct their digital identities through avatars, operating parallel to the physical environment. A large-scale virtual environment was first implemented in 2003 with the launch of Second Life, according to Halvorson et al. (2011). Through these early developments, the foundation for contemporary Metaverse systems was established, contributing to the development of current research into virtual interaction, digital infrastructure, and sustainability.

With advancements in VR, AR, and other immersive technologies, the Metaverse has grown and evolved (Cho et al., 2022). It has not yet been defined universally (Peukert et al., 2022; Xu et al., 2022), but scholars generally describe it as a 3D virtual world that hosts thousands of users who interact through avatars (Abbate et al., 2023; Davis et al., 2009; Wright et al., 2008).

The Metaverse is said to be an advanced version of the Internet that utilizes virtual reality headsets, blockchain systems, and avatar-based representations in order to merge the physical and digital worlds seamlessly. In this integrated approach, web technologies are collaborating with extended reality (XR), which includes augmented reality (AR), mixed reality (MR), and virtual reality (VR) (Milgram et al., 1995). Metaverses, in contrast to the Internet, are immersive environments where individuals can interact in a range of activities, attend virtual events, try on digital clothing, and participate in collaborative virtual meetings. Metaverses are thus virtual spaces that mimic the physical world (Xin et al., 2022), addressing users' needs to express themselves, create content, and communicate with others. According to these studies, the Metaverse aims to be more than merely a technological platform, but also a socio-technical ecosystem with implications for social, economic, and ecological interests.

It has been shown that the Metaverse can be a powerful tool for managing facilities and improving sustainability. A Metaverse-enabled digital twin of a building can be monitored in real time, according to Jelodar et al., (2022). IoT sensors can be incorporated into physical infrastructure to continuously transmit operational data into the virtual environment, providing accurate energy data and enabling maintenance strategies based on predictive data (Ghosh, et al., 2021; Riaz et al., 2017). These capabilities are directly aligned with SDG 9 and SDG 13, since they reduce unnecessary resource consumption and improve energy efficiency. As a whole, these studies demonstrate how Metaverse-created digital twins and IoT integration facilitate operationalizing sustainability objectives, which are particularly relevant to infrastructure efficiency and climate change mitigation.

A study by Assad et al., (2021) shows that Metaverse-based immersive walkthroughs allow users to evaluate spaces in advance of construction or travel, reducing carbon-intensive physical site visits and enhancing accessibility, which contributes to design goals that promote inclusivity and human-centeredness.

Ismail (2023) maps the Metaverse architecture and future directions highlighting key technical components (XR, cloud-edge, identity layers) and stressing how architectural choices shape social and environmental outcomes. Lee (2023) examines network and rendering optimizations for XR, demonstrating that adaptive streaming, progressive and codec improvements significantly reduce bandwidth and energy while maintaining user experience. Zilak (2025) evaluates an accessible Metaverse museum prototype and reports that participatory design with disability stakeholders yields measurable usability gains and suggests evaluation protocols for inclusive design. Papadopoulos (2025) studies the sustainability performance implications of Metaverse adoption in organizations finding that substitution benefits vary by sector and depend on organizational incentives and user behaviour. Technological architecture and participatory design choices are important as per the findings of these studies once it comes to determe whether Metaverse systems promote inclusion and sustainability or reinforce existing disparities.

The blockchain-based monitoring system of Metaverse ecosystem safeguards users' online reputation, identities, and personal data. To oversee content and transactions in the Metaverse, distributed ledger technology is necessary. (Gadekallu et al., 2021). Currently, the Metaverse is intensively researched by many for resource exchange and use and money. Across the platforms of Virtual Reality, it involves transferring and using money resources as well as other valued assets. Within the Metaverse, enhanced trust, security, and economic exchange provided by a distributed ledger technology. Especially, in terms of energy consumption and transparency of governance, its sustainability implications remain understudied.

Researchers have proposed energy-aware architectural patterns such as hybrid cloud–edge–client rendering, progressive levels-of-detail, server batching and context-aware offloading to reduce redundant compute and network transfers. Empirical performance and latency studies highlight the trade-offs between user experience high fidelity, low latency and energy cost therefore, efficient codecs, adaptive frame rates and specialized accelerators (NPUs/GPUs) are commonly recommended.

The Metaverse represents a developing technological paradigm in retailing which remains a virtual space that will allow every consumer for shopping beyond the physical and forming a direct connection with every retailer. Queiroz et al (2023) in their studies suggested that improved operational and resource efficiency innovative capabilities, energy efficiency improved collaboration and agility would be experienced by the industries upon adopting the Metaverse as a potential opportunity. Even though the nexus between the sustainability and conceptual or theoretical frameworks (Dwivedi et al., 2022; Koohang et al., 2023).

Pamucar et al., (2022) demonstrated the potential Metaverse effects on sustainable transportation concerning with virtual twin frameworks to optimize shared mobility as well as lower the rate of emission Moreover, Umar (2022) proposed that solving major global challenges with modern technologies like VR, AR, AI and BCT could catalyse the attainment of the Sustainable Development Goals (SDGs). Such measures encompass the introduction of virtual consultation services and broader e-learning platforms for numerous medical professionals and e-administration systems in both urban and rural areas, aiding in the achievement of Goal 3 (Healthcare Access). Similarly, the potential of thriving with AR/VR technologies possesses Goal 4 (Inclusive Education) which is building accessible immersive learning environments that have been built to cater to the diverse learners' needs especially those with disabilities. Yet, its impact is ambiguous on sustainable performance (Arpaci et al., 2022; Abumalloh et al., 2024).

Koohang et al., (2023) examine the implications of economic sustainability on the economy encompassing consumer experience and marketing techniques. Ramifications for social and psychological dimensions and societal sustainability are investigated by Arpaci et al. (2022). The discussion surrounding the social implications of the Metaverse remains contested (Al-Emran, 2023). Yet, little attention is to the effect of Metaverse on environmental sustainability. While some argue that the Metaverse reduces energy consumption by enabling virtual activities (Al-Emran, 2023). Other studies suggest that its high technological demands lead to increased energy usage and a greater carbon footprint (Abumalloh et al., 2023). Kshetri and Dwivedi (2023) examine the consequences of pollution reduction and energy consumption reduction while emphasizing the ambiguous long-term equilibrium between the two. Despite a growing interest in the Metaverse's potential regarding social, economic and environmental issues, the current study narrowly considers the Metaverse's impact on consumer behavior (Richter and Richter, 2023) while at the same time neglecting sustainability challenges (Abumalloh et al., 2024). Al-Emran (2023) examines the Metaverse's implications for economic, environmental and social sustainability, but the analysis of this Metaverse phenomenon lacked clarity and empirically sound research methods. There is mixed evidence regarding the Metaverse's environmental impact, suggesting that the outcome depends largely on choices made during design, patterns of usage, and energy sources. Klaus and Manthiou (2024) further call for future Metaverse research to explore underexamined environmental and societal dimensions.

The Metaverse has garnered considerable attention in terms of being described as a game-changing digital alternative and virtual smart city model with respect to its implications for sustainable development and alignment with the United Nations' Sustainable Development Goals (SDGs) (Rajguru & Brüggemann, 2024). It is essential to understand the trade-offs and advantages of the Metaverse to better comprehend how this technology could positively or negatively impact sustainable development.

Researchers are exploring different opportunities for trade-offs and complementarities. Several avenues have been identified whereby the Metaverse could contribute to sustainability: the preservation of cultural heritage, the improvement of city planning through smart cities, social interaction and the consumption of resources (Allam et al., 2022). The Metaverse will guarantee greater opportunities in brand awareness, economic development and market development for digital goods (De Giovanni, 2023). From an environmental perspective it could aid in fostering low-carbon urban development by cutting down on waste and carbon emissions via virtual experiences and digital products (Allam et al., 2022; Criollo-C et al., 2023; De Giovanni, 2023; Higginbotham, 2021).

Additionally, the Metaverse has the potential to provide social inclusion, improve public health, increase job opportunities and transform other industries like education, health, tourism etc (Allam et al., 2022; De Giovanni, 2023; Higginbotham, 2021; Johri et al., 2024). In order to engage citizens and expand city governance as demonstrated in pilot initiatives in developing cities, Metaverse technologies can be applied in urban contexts. Digital innovations are being integrated into city governance through these initiatives, which provide valuable insights into operating requirements and benefits (Allam et al., 2022).

Concerns are raised by the literature that the potential smart cities' impacts could be exacerbated by Metaverse. Security and privacy issues exacerbating inequality, increasing living costs, increase energy consumption, mental health risks, and disconnection from reality (Allam et al., 2022; De Giovanni, 2023). In addition, there has been emphasized the need for the alignment with sustainability goals and responsible digital transformation. The significance of considering the impact of Metaverse on inequality and social inclusion have been highlighted by researchers (Allam et al., 2022; De Giovanni, 2023; Johri et al., 2024; Monaco & Sacchi, 2023; Pellegrino et al., 2023)

A study by Eggenschwiler et al. (2024) emphasizes the need for further research in order to gain a better insight into the environmental consequences of Metaverse retailing. Further, Abumalloh et al. (2024) emphasize that the retail sector notably lacks comprehensive empirical research on the sustainability implications of Metaverse adoption. Therefore, the present research aims to contribute to filling this gap by analysing how Metaverse dynamics are connected with sustainability objectives so as to develop a more solid theoretical framework that would include the issues of economic feasibility environmental effects and social justice. Although scholarly attention is growing, existing studies tend to focus on different dimensions of sustainability and inclusivity without comprehensive frameworks to address both. Metaverse ecosystems should be sustainably designed with human-centered sustainability in mind.

The technological and commercial dimensions of the Metaverse have been significantly advanced, but empirical research on the role of sustainability inclusivity and human-centric innovation has been limited. Most existing studies focus on digital inequality, technical efficiency, economic outcomes, and social responsibility with limited empirical attention to environmental sustainability. The present study focusses on addressing this gap by considering how to advance SDGs 9, 10 and 13 within Metaverse ecosystems through human-centred innovation sustainable infrastructure and inclusivity.

Across the literature, three thematic streams are prevalent: (i) technological efficiency and infrastructure optimization within Metaverse ecosystems, (ii) social inclusion, accessibility, and digital equity, and (iii) sustainability-driven alignment with United Nations Sustainable Development Goals. Even though existing studies provide valuable conceptual, sectoral, and technological insights, integrating environmental sustainability from a human-centric perspective has become increasingly challenging. In emerging economies, infrastructure-led sustainability initiatives and inclusion-focused interventions have not been adequately investigated. This gap empirically and conceptually addressed in the present study.

RESEARCH METHODOLOGY

The study methodology comprises conceptual and empirical design. First, the conceptual framework helps in understanding the significance of sustainability in the Metaverse by exploring three core themes: (i) sustainable infrastructure in virtual ecosystems, energy-efficient blockchain models, and renewable-powered data centres (ii) inclusivity and green accessibility addressing the degree of affordability and digital divides within the digital community and (iii) human-centric value creation, including sustainable education, eco-conscious consumption and social innovation. A case study comparison analysis is performed to assess the integration of sustainability principles on Metaverse platforms within the context of Tanjore district in the state of Tamil Nadu to ultimately arrive at practical solutions. A sample of 250 respondents was selected who belong to the digital communities within Thanjavur. A structured interview is used to collect information wherein informed consent is obtained prior to involvement in the study.

DATA ANALYSIS AND RESULTS

A structured questionnaire was administered using a stratified sampling approach to 250 respondents drawn from academic, industrial, and digitally engaged groups to identify stakeholders' perspectives on the Green Metaverse. The respondents rated the statements on a 5-point Likert scale *(1 = strongly disagree to 5 = strongly agree*), grouped into 4 conceptual themes: Awareness & Readiness, Sustainable Infrastructure, Inclusivity & Accessibility, and Human-Centered Innovation.

Data analysis was conducted in stages, beginning with the assessment of internal consistency using Cronbach's α coefficients and descriptive statistics to summarize variability. Correlation analysis, one-way ANOVA, and ordinary least squares regression models with interaction terms were then employed to examine relationships among the study variables and to identify predictors of readiness and conditional willingness to invest in Green Metaverse initiatives.

The sample exhibited a relatively balanced distribution across key demographic variables, including age, gender, profession, and religious background. Most respondents (39.6%) fell into the 18- to 25-year age bracket and those aged 26 to 40 comprised 39.2%. This shows that both young and mid-aged respondents comprised a majority, while those above 41 to 55 years comprised 16.4% and above 55 years 4.8%. The gender distribution shows that almost equal with 50.85% males and 46.8% females. Only 2.4% did not wish to state their gender.

The results indicate considerable diversity within the sample, with digital community users (32.4%) and professionals (31.2%) forming the largest groups, followed by participants from academia (27.2%), and policy/NGO circles (9.2%).

Respondents represented multiple religious backgrounds, including Hinduism (48.0%), Christianity (25.6%), Islam (17.6%), and other religions such as Sikhism, Jainism, and Buddhism (8.8%). This distribution reflects the cultural diversity of the study population and provides contextual relevance for examining perceptions of sustainability within the Green Metaverse.

Table 1. Descriptives and Reliability

	Mean	Std. Error	Std. Deviation	Cronbach's Alpha for Individual statements
I possess an informed understanding of the ecological consequences engendered by contemporary digital technologies.	3.23	0.075	1.193	0.626
I hold a conceptual grasp of the emerging paradigm referred to as the 'Green Metaverse.'	3.21	0.075	1.185	0.643
I am prepared to implement digital practices that are demonstrably sustainable.	3.16	0.078	1.239	0.641
I am willing to remit an additional fee in exchange for entrance to Metaverse environments that adhere to environmentally responsible principles.	3.06	0.071	1.118	0.653
Integration of energy-efficient consensus algorithms within blockchain architectures is a prerequisite to advancing a Green Metaverse ecosystem.	3.23	0.075	1.187	0.649
Obligatory transition to renewable-energized server farms is an essential regulatory item for all entities supplying Metaverse infrastructure.	2.97	0.079	1.245	0.646
Elevated operational and entry expenses presently curtail my capacity to migrate to environmentally responsible Metaverse solutions.	3.37	0.068	1.072	0.648
Affordability must be positioned at the forefront of the design ethos guiding the Green Metaverse, thereby enabling sustained participation across socioeconomic spectra.	2.54	0.084	1.330	0.630
Persistent digital divides—articulated along urban-rural and wealth inheritance axes—remain critical impediments to the aspirational goal of pervasive inclusivity.	2.57	0.085	1.349	0.641
The establishment of community-managed grant programmes stands to ameliorate these access gaps, offering targeted financial support and fostering localized, participatory stewardship of emerging green digital resources.	2.55	0.084	1.332	0.643
By deploying virtual and augmented reality in interconnected digital environments, the Metaverse offers the potential to create resource-efficient immersive classrooms that embody the principles of sustainable education.	3.66	0.058	0.923	0.665

continued on following page

Table 1. Continued

	Mean	Std. Error	Std. Deviation	Cronbach's Alpha for Individual statements
Attention must be directed toward the cultivation of eco-conscious consumption behaviours, with particular emphasis on the adoption of low-carbon non-fungible tokens and digital assets that are demonstrably aligned with green-finance criteria.	3.43	0.061	0.972	0.670
The Metaverse possesses inherent affordances that can be leveraged to nurture social innovation, enabling the scalable co-creation of solutions while simultaneously fostering sustained community engagement across diverse contexts.	3.64	0.058	0.922	0.660

The descriptive statistics, as presented in Table 1 suggest that the majority of the participants are, on average, neutral to slightly positive in their opinions over the statements given in the Likert scale of five points *(1 = strongly disagree, 5 = strongly agree)*, in which human-centric innovation items got the highest agreement and least variance at the same time. More precisely, the respondents most indicated the use of the Metaverse for the creation of resource-efficient immersive classrooms (M = 3.66, SE = 0.058, SD = 0.923) and for pioneering social innovation and community engagement (M = 3.64, SE = 0.058, SD = 0.922) next to the support for environment-friendly digital consumption (e.g., low-carbon NFTs; M = 3.43, SE = 0.061, SD = 0.972). The awareness/readiness statements were less optimistic (ecological consequences: M = 3.23, SE = 0.075, SD = 1.193; Green Metaverse concept: M = 3.21, SE = 0.075, SD = 1.185; sustainable practice preparedness: M = 3.16, SE = 0.078, SD = 1.239). In this pattern, respondents are perceived as supporting human-centric applications of the Metaverse more strongly than practical awareness and readiness for sustainable implementation.

Figure 1. Mean Scores of Survey Constructs

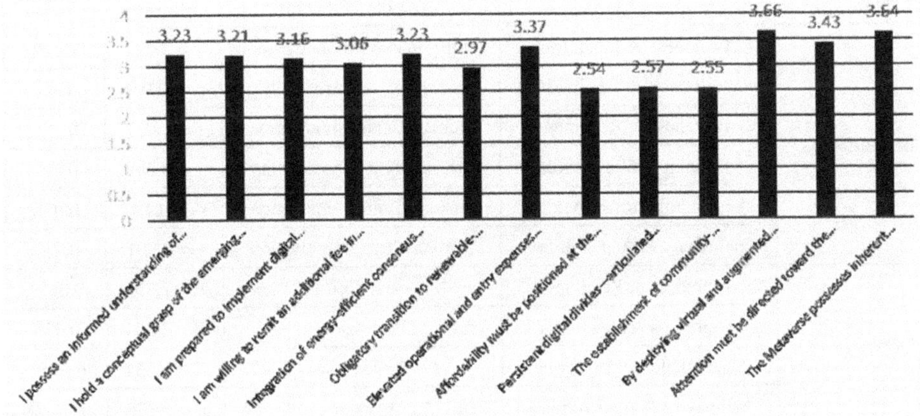

As illustrated in Figure 1, there are noteworthy differences in attitudes about sustainable infrastructure and inclusion among participants. Views on Sustainable Infrastructure were mixed: the significance of energy-efficient consensus mechanisms was rather backed up (M = 3.23, SE = 0.075, SD = 1.187) while a compulsion for server farms powered with renewables received almost neutral reactions (M = 2.97, SE = 0.079, SD = 1.245). The participants accepted that the cost of greener solutions was a barrier (M = 3.37, SE = 0.068, SD = 1.072) but they were only slightly above neutral in their willingness to pay (M = 3.06, SE = 0.071, SD = 1.118). In contrast, inclusivity and accessibility—such as prioritizing low-income groups (M = 2.54, SE = 0.084, SD = 1.330), admitting the existence of the digital divides (M = 2.57, SE = 0.085, SD = 1.349), and granting money for the community (M = 2.55, SE = 0.084, SD = 1.332)—had the lowest mean scores and the highest variance indicating limited consensus on equity-based measures. The combined Cronbach's alpha scores for the individual items were very closely grouped between 0.626 and 0.670, revealing a moderate internal consistency that is adequate for exploratory studies but still below the conventional threshold of 0.70 for mature scales. According to these findings, technical sustainability measures are moderately accepted, but equity-oriented inclusiveness interventions are less supported in the short term, thus emphasizing the need for policy-driven mechanisms to address affordability and access barriers aligned with SDG 10.

Table 2. Bivariate Correlations and ANOVA Results

Analysis Type	Variable 1	Variable 2 / Factor	Statistic	P-value
Correlations	Awareness & Readiness	Sustainable Infrastructure	r = 0.227	<0.01
	Awareness & Readiness	Inclusivity & Accessibility	r = -0.055	0.354
	Awareness & Readiness	Human-Centric Innovation	r = 0.027	0.495
	Sustainable Infrastructure	Inclusivity & Accessibility	r = 0.048	0.491
	Sustainable Infrastructure	Human-Centric Innovation	r = -0.137	0.058
	Inclusivity & Accessibility	Human-Centric Innovation	r = 0.091	0.217
ANOVA	Awareness & Readiness	Religion	F = 2.751	0.043*
	Awareness & Readiness	Profession	F = 2.304	0.078
	Sustainable Infrastructure	Profession	F = 3.534	0.015*
	Inclusivity & Accessibility	Gender	F = 5.276	0.006**

*Note: *p < .05, **p < .01*

The correlation analysis, summarized in Table 2, produced several noteworthy results. Awareness and readiness were positively and significantly linked to sustainable infrastructure (r = .227), albeit to a modest degree. This finding implies that individuals who favor energy-efficient blockchain solutions and renewable-powered data-center architectures also express a comparatively higher readiness for the broader sustainable digitization agenda. Conversely, the same variables demonstrate negligible and slightly negative correlations with inclusivity (r = –.055) and human-centric innovation (r = .027). This pattern indicates that the determinants underlying perceptions of affordability, access, or socially driven innovation have in this data-set a limited and indirect relationship with self-reported readiness. Sustainable infrastructure for its part, yielded only weak positive correlation with inclusivity (r = .048) and a small negative coefficient for human-centric innovation (r = –.137). The modest negative linkage in this latter instance invites speculation that prioritization of technological investment may occasionally diverge from, or inadvertently supplant social and eco-conscious imperatives.

Inclusion and human-centered innovation exhibited positive correlations (r = .091), but this was insufficient to conclude substantive covariation or mediation from these variables. The obtained result has suggested that the two constructs appear to function largely in parallel within the examined framework instead in a mutually reinforcing manner. Sustainable infrastructure is positioned by the analysis as the most pronounced predictive leverage of readiness; thus, inclusivity and human-centric innovation are overshadowed in the short-term, with their influence likely to manifest through subtler or more distal pathways within the adopted theoretical model. An in-depth look at the inter-construct relationship is presented in Figure

2, which displays the correlation heatmap and highlights the relative strengths and weaknesses.

Figure 2. Correlation Heatmap

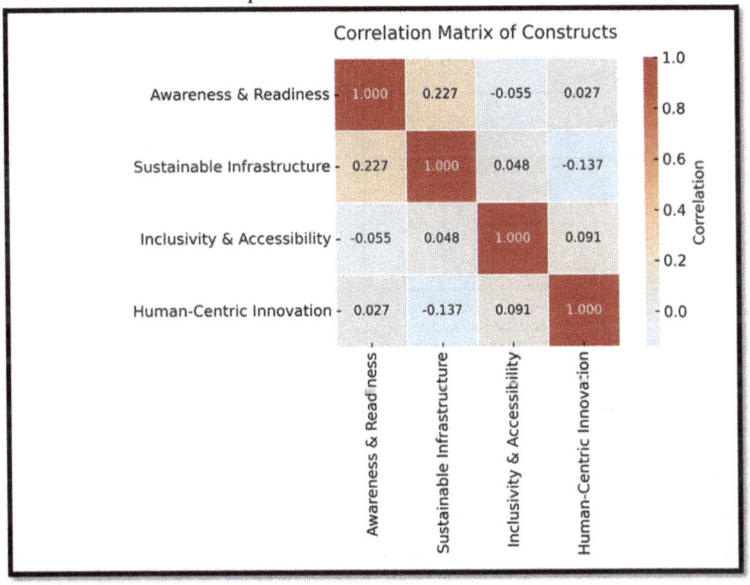

Figure 2 illustrates the weak correlations between contextual inclusion and human-centered innovation, reinforcing their conceptual independence. The one-way analysis of variance elucidates the contribution of demographic determinants to stakeholders' perceptions of the emergent Green Metaverse. A statistically significant difference was observed for awareness and readiness across religious groupings ($F = 2.751$, $p = .043$), indicating that socio-cultural context may shape perceived preparedness for sustainable digital practices. Professional affiliation exhibited a trend-level influence on readiness scores ($F = 2.304$, $p = .078$), suggesting that occupational exposure may be associated with varying levels of engagement with sustainability-oriented digital behaviors. Furthermore, perceptions of sustainable infrastructure differed significantly across professional cohorts ($F = 3.534$, $p = .015$), with respondents from industry practitioners and personnel from policy/NGO sectors expressing more favourable attitudes toward energy-efficient and renewably - powered Metaverse infrastructures.

Table 3. Regression Analysis

Predictor	Model 1: Awareness & Readiness	Model 2: Willingness to Pay		
	Beta (β)	p-value	Coefficient (B)	p-value
(Constant)			2.337	<0.001
Constructs				
Sustainable Infrastructure	0.221	<0.001	0.137	0.063
Inclusivity & Accessibility	–0.045	0.354		
Human-Centric Innovation	0.052	0.495		
Profession				
Policy/NGO	0.639	0.004	0.502	0.035
Industry			-0.009	0.963
Digital Community/ User			0.191	0.339
Religion				
Hinduism	0.335	0.039	0.256	0.156
Christian			0.410	0.048
Muslim			0.462	0.032
Model Summary				
R^2 / Adjusted R^2	0.058 / 0.031			

*Note: Significance levels: * p < .05, ** p < .01, *** p < .001. *

In the Table 3 regression model estimating both awareness and readiness underscores two primary domains: sustainable infrastructure and systematic variability linked to professional and geographic contexts. In this model, sustainable infrastructure proved to be much stronger ($\beta = 0.221$, $p < .001$) than all other variables, indicating that respondents who placed high importance on energy-efficient blockchain technologies and renewable energy powered data centres were statistically significant higher on the readiness level as it related to the Green Metaverse. In contrast, human-centric innovative variables ($\beta = 0.052$, $p = 0.495$) and inclusivity inscription variables ($\beta = -0.045$, $p = 0.354$) did not achieve statistical significance.

Compared to academic counterparts of the respondent's profession had emerged the primary significant predictors of the readiness of respondents with the ones affiliated with NGOs or policy that registering a markedly superior preparedness level ($\beta = 0.639$, $p = .004$). Another important factor was geographic location. Taken together, these findings attest that the availability of technological infrastructure paired with engagement in the policy and NGO milieu, serves as a key facilitating condition for readiness. Sustainability has been shown to drive readiness in a direct and tangible manner, whereas inclusivity and human-centered innovation have a longer-term socio-cultural, behavioral, and policy-mediated impact rather than a short-term effect on readiness.

However, overall religion isolation in readiness levels suggests that geographical specificity must be taken into account when designing interventions to promote sustainable Metaverse adoption. A standard ordinary least squares model was developed to elaborate on the respondents' willingness to pay *(5-point Likert: 1 = strongly disagree... 5 = strongly agree)* as influenced by Sustainable Infrastructure, Religion, and Profession, with HC3 robust standard errors being used (N = 250; R^2 = 0.0589, adj. R^2 = 0.0317). The coefficient for Sustainable Infrastructure was positive and marginal at the 10% level (β = 0.137, p = 0.063) suggesting that an increase of one unit on the 1 to 5.

On the willingness to pay scale the Sustainable Infrastructure scale would rise by abo-ut 0.14 points when region and profession are taken into account. The willingness to pay was significantly higher for Christians (β = 0.410, p = 0.048) and Muslims (β = 0.462, p = 0.032) than for Hinduism (β = 0.256, p = 0.156) Hinduism when compared to the people who lived in Thanjavur. In contrast to the Profession group, Policy/NGO group showed much greater readiness to pay (β=0.502, p=0.035), while the other two groups Industry (β=−0.009, p=0.963) and Digital Community/User (β=0.191, p=0.339), were not different in that regard statistically. The religion and Policy/NGO effects amounted to about 0.4-0.5 points on a Likert scale, which means that the shifts in the willingness to pay were significant. The overall model fit is modest which is typical for attitudinal outcomes but the pattern indicates that geographic context and professional orientation are factors that lead to heterogeneity in willingness to pay beyond assessments of sustainable infrastructure by individuals. According to these findings, SDG 9-oriented investments in green digital infrastructure should be complemented by SDG 10–aligned policy initiatives addressing affordability and equitable access.

DISCUSSION

Valuable insights are provided into the interdependency between human-centric innovation, technological sustainability, and inclusivity using the Green Metaverse. According to the findings, stakeholders' capacity and willingness to implement sustainable infrastructure are the strongest influencers on environmentally sensitive Metaverse platforms.

As well as technological innovation, developing and implementing ethically grounded policies is essential to creating a green digital future. Earlier assertions are reinforced by the strong predictive role of sustainable infrastructure, indicating the need for digital ecosystems to evolve towards energy-efficient architectures to remain viable under Agenda 2030. For respondents who value energy-efficient blockchain models and data centres powered by renewable energy, sustainability awareness is correlated with technological maturity, consistent with prior findings by Koohang et al. (2023) and Pamucar et al. (2022).

Equitable outcomes are more likely to be achieved if institutions get the support they need, policies are enacted, and sociocultural adaptation takes place rather than immediate technological adaptation. Respondents' perceptions suggests that religious inequality, affordability, and accessibility continue to constrain equitable access to the Metaverse, despite the conceptual appeal of inclusive participation. A significant gender-based variation in inclusivity perceptions ($p = 0.006$) indicates that marginalized groups, particularly women, face disproportionate barriers in accessing the Metaverse platforms. These findings align with SDG 10, which emphasizes inclusive digital literacy programs, subsidized access and the creation of community-based learning hubs across societies.

Dwivedi et al. (2022) and Arpaci et al. (2022) both support the notion that human-centered innovation does not directly affect readiness, but rather indirectly shapes socio-cultural adaptations, normative expectations, and behavior changes over time. Metaverse ecosystems that align with SDGs 9 and 13 must be built on human-centric frameworks, including circular economy principles, collaborative digital content creation, and ethical governance.

The correlation evidence implies that the four study constructs are quite different having only a small positive correlation between Sustainable Infrastructure and Awareness & Readiness ($r = 0.227$) Correlations among the remaining construct pairs are weak ($|r| \leq 0.137$) including almost no correlation between Awareness & Readiness and Human-Centric Innovation ($r = 0.027$), and a slight correlation Sustainable Infrastructure and Human-Centric Innovation ($r = -0.137$). This set of relations suggests limited shared variance among the domains as well as suggesting that awareness/readiness is primarily concerned with evaluations of sustainable infrastructure and is further removed from inclusivity or human-centric concerns.

The distinction of group differences adds even more nuance to contextual heterogeneity. Awareness & Readiness varies by overall religion ($F = 2.751, p = 0.043$) but does not vary by Profession at conventional levels ($F = 2.304, p = 0.078$). Therefore, geographic context seems to have a greater influence than occupational composition on job satisfaction. Perceptions of Sustainable Infrastructure varies across Professions ($F = 3.534$, $p = 0.015$) supporting the notion that functional, occupational or sectoral divisions influence how people respond to the infrastructural needs of the system. Perceptions of Inclusivity & Accessibility varies by Gender ($F = 5.276$, $p = 0.006$) which suggests that concerns for equity that are often espoused are not universally and uniformly held and are perhaps more the result of gendered attitudes or experiences within a digital space. Collectively, the findings indicate substantial but more subtle variation as opposed to a uniform broad range across differences.

These findings indicate that stakeholders' readiness for a Green Metaverse is shaped more by perceptions of infrastructural feasibility than by social or normative considerations, suggesting that tangible technological investments act as immediate enablers of sustainability-oriented attitudes. Inclusivity and Human-Centric Innovation are not significant predictors suggesting that their impacts are largely orthogonal to the infrastructure perceptions and demographics in question. In the willingness to pay model there is a weak positive relationship between Sustainable Infrastructure and the willingness to pay for the omitted religion (coefficient = 0.41 – 0.46, $p < 0.05$) for two religious groups (Christian and Muslim) and where Policy/NGO respondents are more willing to pay compared to Academia (coefficient = 0.502, $p = 0.035$), while the other profession dummies shown to be insignificant. In a more pragmatic sense, the religion and Policy/NGO impacts shift from lower to upper at an average of Likert half a point on a 1 – 5 scale which shows starkly differing impacts despite a low capture and the low explained variance that is characteristic of attitudinal outcome models. These results together suggest that the most explained and consistent correlates of attitudinal awareness and willingness to pay lie in the investment focus and advocacy/advocate combined identities of the sustainable infrastructure along with the sustainable policy and professional advocacy attitudes.

Sustainability objectives must be balanced with affordability considerations under these findings. Collectively, these results indicate that technological optimization alone doesn't guarantee sustainability in the Metaverse. Within human-centred governance, equitable participation, inclusion and education need to be integrated.

The conceptual framework of this study resonates with global movements in sustainability, eco-conscious innovation, and digital ethics. This study contributes to emerging Green Digital Futures field by the combination of empirical evidence with theoretical reflection. Among the recommendations are standards for digital sustainability audits carbon tracking in data operations, and inclusive participation metrics in virtual ecosystems which should be developed jointly between policy-makers' technology developers and educational institutions.

The need for integrating digital equity, energy efficiency, and governance transparency is emphasized by the results to achieve SDG 13 (Climate Action) in virtual environments. A sustainable Metaverse requires alignment in three dimensions technological efficiency (infrastructure), social inclusivity (accessibility) and ethical innovation (human-centric value creation). Human-centric pathways to a Green Metaverse are based on the synergy among these domains.

Furthermore, even though these research findings may represent preliminary empirical insights, they also acknowledge a number of limitations which include a moderate sample size a regional bias and a limited scope in time. However, the study provides an empirical basis for balancing growth with the responsibility of environmental stewardship and social equity in Metaverse. It is therefore essential to move beyond technical optimization towards integrated governance models that balance environmental performance, social equity, and ethical innovation in future Green Metaverse frameworks.

CONCLUSION

The purpose of this study was to examine human-centric pathways to a Green Metaverse by evaluating sustainable practices and digital inclusivity in an empirical manner. The purpose of these objectives is to review sustainable best practices within virtual environments, assess inclusiveness and access, and make recommendations on a relevant framework aligned to Sustainable Development Goals 9, 10 and 13. It has been evident that integration between human and technological aspects is vital to digital sustainability.

Sustainable development requires innovative digital ecosystems, and the emerging green Metaverse offers a transformative pathway toward achieving this goal. By integrating virtual environments with low-carbon technologies, the Metaverse can reduce resource-intensive physical activities. A green Metaverse promotes environmental sustainability by minimizing energy consumption through renewable-powered data centres. It also encourages circular economy models by supporting virtual goods and reducing the demand for physical production. Human-centric design ensures that Metaverse technologies remain inclusive, accessible, and socially responsible. Digital inclusion is essential, as equitable access to devices and connectivity determines who benefits from Metaverse innovations. Sustainable Metaverse platforms must balance immersive experiences with ethical data usage and transparent governance. Green digital transformation hinges on energy-efficient blockchain, optimized 3D rendering, and carbon-neutral design strategies. The Metaverse can support environmental education by simulating climate scenarios and promoting eco-conscious behaviour. Sustainable development in the Metaverse also aligns with the United Nations Sustainable Development Goals (SDGs), especially SDG 9, SDG 10, and SDG 13. Collaboration among governments, industries, and academia is required to build a standardized sustainability framework for Metaverse applications. Policy interventions must ensure the responsible deployment of immersive technologies to avoid widening digital divides. Green Metaverse ecosystems provide opportunities for virtual workspaces, thereby reducing transportation emissions. Virtual training and digital twins can optimize real-world energy systems, enhancing environmental performance across sectors.

Ethical artificial intelligence integration is vital for maintaining trust, fairness, and security in virtual sustainability initiatives. The success of a sustainable Metaverse depends on improving digital literacy among all user groups. Environmental monitoring and reporting can be more precise through Metaverse-based IoT visualization tools. A holistic approach is required to harmonize technological innovation, environmental responsibility, and social equity. With strategic planning, the green Metaverse can become a catalyst for inclusive and sustainable digital futures. Ultimately, the green Metaverse represents a promising frontier for reimagining sustainable development while ensuring that no one is left behind.

Furthermore, one of the long-term drivers of the normalization of sustainable digital behaviors and the reinforcement of SDG 13 (Climate Action) is human-centric innovation by changing behaviour and creating awareness. Community-driven creativity, eco-conscious learning, and sustainable consumption are included. The transformative potential of a key component of the Green Metaverse has lied in the integration of inclusiveness as well as user empowerment with environmental responsibility. It suggests that adoption of a three-dimensional sustainability model encompasses human-centric innovation, energy-aware infrastructure, and equitable access in future virtual ecosystems. In addition, a digital future following the Agenda 2030 of the United Nations is sustainable and ethical, as well as a product of such integration.

REFERENCES

Abbate, S., Centobelli, P., Cerchione, R., Oropallo, E., & Riccio, E. (2023). Kick-start your scientific journey into the Metaverse. *Knowledge Management & E-Learning: An International Journal, 1*(15), 103–114.

Abumalloh, R. A., Nilashi, M., Ooi, K. B., Wei-Han, G., Cham, T. H., Dwivedi, Y. K., & Hughes, L. (2024). The adoption of Metaverse in the retail industry and its impact on sustainable competitive advantage: Moderating impact of sustainability commitment. *Annals of Operations Research, 342*(1), 5–46. DOI: 10.1007/s10479-023-05608-8

Al-Emran, M. (2023). Beyond technology acceptance: Development and evaluation of technology-environmental, economic, and social sustainability theory. *Technology in Society, 75*, 102383. DOI: 10.1016/j.techsoc.2023.102383

Allam, Z., Sharifi, A., Bibri, S. E., Jones, D. S., & Krogstie, J. (2022). The Metaverse as a virtual form of smart cities: Opportunities and challenges for environmental, economic, and social sustainability in urban futures. *Smart Cities, 5*(3), 771–801. DOI: 10.3390/smartcities5030040

Arpaci, I., Karatas, K., Kusci, I., & Al-Emran, M. (2022). Understanding the social sustainability of the Metaverse by integrating UTAUT2 and big five personality traits: A hybrid SEM-ANN approach. *Technology in Society, 71*, 102120. DOI: 10.1016/j.techsoc.2022.102120

Assad, F., Konstantinov, S., Rushforth, E. J., Vera, D. A., & Harrison, R. (2021). Virtual engineering in the support of sustainable assembly systems. *Procedia CIRP, 97*, 367–372. DOI: 10.1016/j.procir.2020.05.252

Babaeian Jelodar, M., Wilkinson, S., Kalatehjari, R., & Zou, Y. (2022). Designing for construction procurement: An integrated decision support system for building information modelling. *Built Environment Project and Asset Management, 12*(1), 111–127. DOI: 10.1108/BEPAM-07-2020-0132

Cho, J., tom Dieck, M. C., & Jung, T. (2022, April). What is the Metaverse? Challenges, opportunities, definition, and future research directions. In *International XR conference* (pp. 3–26). Springer International Publishing.

Choi, H. S., & Kim, S. H. (2017). A content service deployment plan for Metaverse museum exhibitions—Centering on the combination of beacons and HMDs. *International Journal of Information Management, 37*(1), 1519–1527. DOI: 10.1016/j.ijinfomgt.2016.04.017

Criollo-C, S., Govea, J., Játiva, W., Pierrottet, J., Guerrero-Arias, A., Jaramillo-Alcázar, Á., & Luján-Mora, S. (2023). Towards the integration of emerging technologies as support for the teaching and learning model in higher education. *Sustainability (Basel), 15*(7), 6055. DOI: 10.3390/su15076055

Davis, A., Murphy, J., Owens, D., Khazanchi, D., & Zigurs, I. (2009). Avatars, people, and virtual worlds: Foundations for research in Metaverses. *Journal of the Association for Information Systems, 10*(2), 1. DOI: 10.17705/1jais.00183

De Giovanni, P. (2023). Sustainability of the Metaverse: A transition to Industry 5.0. *Sustainability (Basel), 15*(7), 6079. DOI: 10.3390/su15076079

Dwivedi, Y. K., Hughes, L., Baabdullah, A. M., Ribeiro-Navarrete, S., Giannakis, M., Al-Debei, M. M., Dennehy, D., Metri, B., Buhalis, D., Cheung, C. M. K., Conboy, K., Doyle, R., Dubey, R., Dutot, V., Felix, R., Goyal, D. P., Gustafsson, A., Hinsch, C., Jebabli, I., & Wamba, S. F. (2022). Metaverse beyond the hype: Multidisciplinary perspectives on emerging challenges, opportunities, and agenda for research, practice and policy. *International Journal of Information Management, 66*, 102542. DOI: 10.1016/j.ijinfomgt.2022.102542

Eggenschwiler, M., Linzmajer, M., Roggeveen, A. L., & Rudolph, T. (2024). Retailing in the Metaverse: A framework of managerial considerations for success. *Journal of Retailing and Consumer Services, 79*, 103791. DOI: 10.1016/j.jretconser.2024.103791

Elmasry, T., Hazan, E., Khan, H., Kelly, G., Srivastava, S., Yee, L., & Zemmel, R. W. (2022) Value Creation in the Metaverse - the Real Business of the Virtual World. McKinsey & Company Report. https://www.mckinsey.com/business-functions/growth-marketing-and-sales/our-insights/value-creation-in-the-Metaverse

Gadekallu, T. R., Pham, Q. V., Nguyen, D. C., Maddikunta, P. K. R., Deepa, N., Prabadevi, B., Pathirana, P. N., Zhao, J., & Hwang, W. J. (2021). Blockchain for edge of things: Applications, opportunities, and challenges. *IEEE Internet of Things Journal, 9*(2), 964–988. DOI: 10.1109/JIOT.2021.3119639

Ghosh, A., Edwards, D. J., & Hosseini, M. R. (2021). Patterns and trends in Internet of Things (IoT) research: Future applications in the construction industry. *Engineering, Construction, and Architectural Management, 28*(2), 457–481. DOI: 10.1108/ECAM-04-2020-0271

Higginbotham, G. (2021). Virtual connections: Improving global neurosurgery through immersive technologies. *Frontiers in Surgery, 8*, 629963. DOI: 10.3389/fsurg.2021.629963 PMID: 33681283

Johri, A., Joshi, P., Kumar, S., & Joshi, G. (2024). Metaverse for Sustainable Development in a bibliometric analysis and systematic literature review. *Journal of Cleaner Production*, *435*, 140610. DOI: 10.1016/j.jclepro.2024.140610

Katicic, J., Häfner, P., & Ovtcharova, J. (2015). Methodology for emotional assessment of product design by customers in virtual reality. *Presence (Cambridge, Mass.)*, *24*(1), 62–73. DOI: 10.1162/PRES_a_00215

Klaus, P., & Manthiou, A. (2024). Metaverse retail: Pioneering research avenues for tomorrow's marketplace. *Journal of Retailing and Consumer Services*, *78*, 103782. DOI: 10.1016/j.jretconser.2024.103782

Koohang, A., Nord, J. H., Ooi, K. B., Tan, G. W. H., Al-Emran, M., Aw, E. C. X., Baabdullah, A. M., Buhalis, D., Cham, T.-H., Dennis, C., Dutot, V., Dwivedi, Y. K., Hughes, L., Mogaji, E., Pandey, N., Phau, I., Raman, R., Sharma, A., Sigala, M., & Wong, L. W. (2023). Shaping the Metaverse into reality: A holistic multidisciplinary understanding of opportunities, challenges, and avenues for future investigation. *Journal of Computer Information Systems*, *63*(3), 735–765. DOI: 10.1080/08874417.2023.2165197

Kraus, S., Kanbach, D. K., Krysta, P. M., Steinhoff, M. M., & Tomini, N. (2022). Facebook and the creation of the Metaverse: Radical business model innovation or incremental transformation? *International Journal of Entrepreneurial Behaviour & Research*, *28*(9), 52–77. DOI: 10.1108/IJEBR-12-2021-0984

Kshetri, N., & Dwivedi, Y. K. (2023). Pollution-reducing and pollution-generating effects of the Metaverse. *International Journal of Information Management*, *69*, 102620. DOI: 10.1016/j.ijinfomgt.2023.102620

Lee, W. J. (2020). Use of immersive virtual technology in consumer retailing and its effects to consumer. , *18*(2), 5-15.

Lu, S., & Mintz, O. (2023). Marketing on the Metaverse: Research opportunities and challenges. *AMS Review*, *13*(1), 151–166. DOI: 10.1007/s13162-023-00255-5

Martins, J., & Rodrigues, R. (2024). Motivations in the adoption and conversion of freemium services: Insights for digital entrepreneurship. *Review of Managerial Science*, •••, 1–22. DOI: 10.1007/s11846-024-00754-0

Mehra, V., Singh, P., Mehra, M., Albanna, H., & Dwivedi, Y. K. (2023). Exploring the fusion of Metaverse and sports: Current trends and future directions. In *International Working Conference on Transfer and Diffusion of IT* (pp. 258-268). Cham: Springer Nature Switzerland.

Milgram, P., Takemura, H., Utsumi, A., & Kishino, F. (1995, December). Augmented reality: A class of displays on the reality-virtuality continuum. In *Telemanipulator and telepresence technologies* (Vol. 2351, pp. 282–292). Spie. DOI: 10.1117/12.197321

Monaco, S., & Sacchi, G. (2023). Travelling the Metaverse: Potential benefits and main challenges for tourism sectors and research applications. *Sustainability (Basel)*, *15*(4), 3348. DOI: 10.3390/su15043348

Mystakidis, S. (2022). Metaverse. *Encyclopedia*, *2*(1), 486–497. DOI: 10.3390/encyclopedia2010031

Pamucar, D., Deveci, M., Gokasar, I., Tavana, M., & Köppen, M. (2022). A Metaverse assessment model for sustainable transportation using ordinal priority approach and Aczel-Alsina norms. *Technological Forecasting and Social Change*, *182*, 121778. DOI: 10.1016/j.techfore.2022.121778

Pellegrino, A., Wang, R., & Stasi, A. (2023). Exploring the intersection of sustainable consumption and the Metaverse: A review of current literature and future research directions. *Heliyon*, *9*(9), e19190. DOI: 10.1016/j.heliyon.2023.e19190 PMID: 37681133

Peukert, C., Weinhardt, C., Hinz, O., & van der Aalst, W. M. (2022). Metaverse: How to approach its challenges from a BISE perspective. *Business & Information Systems Engineering*, *64*(4), 401–406. DOI: 10.1007/s12599-022-00765-9

Queiroz, M. M., Fosso Wamba, S., Pereira, S. C. F., & Chiappetta Jabbour, C. J. (2023). The Metaverse as a breakthrough for operations and supply chain management: Implications and call for action. *International Journal of Operations & Production Management*, *43*(10), 1539–1553. DOI: 10.1108/IJOPM-01-2023-0006

Rajguru, K., & Brüggemann, P. (2024). Sustainability meets Metaverse: A conceptual framework of sustainable dimensions of the Metaverse. *Journal of Consumer Behaviour*, *23*(5), 2720–2729. DOI: 10.1002/cb.2368

Reibstein, D. J., & Iyengar, R. (2023). Metaverse—Will it change the world or be a whole new world in and of itself? *AMS Review*, *13*(1), 144–150. DOI: 10.1007/s13162-023-00258-2

Riaz, Z., Parn, E. A., Edwards, D. J., Arslan, M., Shen, C., & Pena-Mora, F. (2017). BIM and sensor-based data management system for construction safety monitoring. *Journal of Engineering, Design and Technology*, *15*(6), 738–753. DOI: 10.1108/JEDT-03-2017-0017

Richter, S., & Richter, A. (2023). What is novel about the Metaverse? *International Journal of Information Management, 73*, 102684. DOI: 10.1016/j.ijinfomgt.2023.102684

Srivastava, A., & Sahu, G. P. (2023). The Impact of the Metaverse on Green Marketing: A Paradigm Shift in Sustainable Consumer Behaviour. In *International Working Conference on Transfer and Diffusion of IT* (pp. 443-457). Cham: Springer Nature Switzerland.

Umar, A. (2022). Metaverse for UN SDGs–an exploratory study. In *Science-Policy Brief for the Multistakeholder Forum on Science, Technology and Innovation for the SDGs* (Vol. 5).

World Economic Forum. (2023) Demystifying the Consumer Metaverse. https://www3.weforum.org/docs/WEF_Demystifying_the_Consumer_Metaverse.pdf

Wright, M., Ekeus, H., Coyne, R., Stewart, J., Travlou, P., & Williams, R. (2008, December). Augmented duality: overlapping a Metaverse with the real world. In *Proceedings of the 2008 international conference on advances in computer entertainment technology* (pp. 263-266). DOI: 10.1145/1501750.1501812

Xi, N., Chen, J., Gama, F., Riar, M., & Hamari, J. (2023). The challenges of entering the Metaverse: An experiment on the effect of extended reality on workload. *Information Systems Frontiers, 25*(2), 659–680. PMID: 35194390

Xin, Z., Haiying, W., Ping, K., Yiyao, S., & Haiou, L. (2022). A review of Metaverse research at home and abroad. *Journal of Modern Information, 12*, 147–159.

Xu, J., Papangelis, K., Dunham, J., Goncalves, J., LaLone, N. J., Chamberlain, A., . . . Schwartz, D. I. (2022, April). Metaverse: The vision for the future. In *CHI conference on human factors in computing systems extended abstracts* (pp. 1-3).

Zhong, R. Y., Xu, X., Klotz, E., & Newman, S. T. (2017). Intelligent manufacturing in the context of industry 4.0: A review. *Engineering (Beijing), 3*(5), 616–630. DOI: 10.1016/J.ENG.2017.05.015

Compilation of References

Aamir, M., Rahman, Z., Abro, W. A., Bhatti, U. A., Dayo, Z. A., & Ishfaq, M. (2023). Brain tumor classification utilizing deep features derived from high-quality regions in MRI images. *Biomedical Signal Processing and Control*, *85*, 104988. DOI: 10.1016/j.bspc.2023.104988

Abbate, S., Centobelli, P., Cerchione, R., Oropallo, E., & Riccio, E. (2023). Kick-start your scientific journey into the Metaverse. *Knowledge Management & E-Learning: An International Journal*, *1*(15), 103–114.

Abumalloh, R. A., Nilashi, M., Ooi, K. B., Wei-Han, G., Cham, T. H., Dwivedi, Y. K., & Hughes, L. (2024). The adoption of Metaverse in the retail industry and its impact on sustainable competitive advantage: Moderating impact of sustainability commitment. *Annals of Operations Research*, *342*(1), 5–46. DOI: 10.1007/s10479-023-05608-8

Aguilar-Hernandez, G. A., Dias Rodrigues, J. F., & Tukker, A. (2021). Macro-economic, social and environmental impacts of a circular economy up to 2050: A meta-analysis of prospective studies. *Journal of Cleaner Production*, *278*, 123421. DOI: 10.1016/j.jclepro.2020.123421

AICTE FLAGSHIP SCHEMES AND INITIATIVES. 2025. (n.d.). AICTE. Retrieved https://aicte.gov.in/downloads/initiatives/AICTE-VISION-MERGED.pdf

Ajaj, S. (2020). Smart city governance and integrated command and control centres in India: The case of Bhopal. *Journal of Urban Management*, *9*(3), 285–297.

Alamin Talukder, M., Islam, M., Ashraf Uddin, M., Akhter, A., Alamgir Jalil Pramanik, M., Aryal, S., ... & Moni, M. A. (2023). An efficient deep learning model to categorize brain tumor using reconstruction and fine-tuning. arXiv e-prints, arXiv-2305.

Alam, M. S., Rahman, M. M., Hossain, M. A., Islam, M. K., Ahmed, K. M., Ahmed, K. T., Singh, B. C., & Miah, M. S. (2019). Automatic human brain tumor detection in MRI image using template-based K means and improved fuzzy C means clustering algorithm. *Big Data and Cognitive Computing*, *3*(2), 27. DOI: 10.3390/bdcc3020027

Al-Emran, M. (2023). Beyond technology acceptance: Development and evaluation of technology-environmental, economic, and social sustainability theory. *Technology in Society*, *75*, 102383. DOI: 10.1016/j.techsoc.2023.102383

Ali, M., Hossain, E., Naeem, F., & Kaddoum, G. (2024). Metaverse Communications, Networking, Security, and Applications: Research Issues, State-of-the-Art, and Future Directions. *IEEE Communications Surveys &amp. IEEE Communications Surveys and Tutorials*, *26*(2), 1238–1278. DOI: 10.1109/COMST.2023.3347172

Alimamy, S., & Jung, T. (2024). The AR cloud: Navigating metaverse augmentation technologies for enhanced co-creation of value within services. *Journal of Service Research.* Advance online publication. DOI: 10.1177/10946705241265753

Allam, Z., & Dhunny, Z. A. (2019). On big data, artificial intelligence, and smart cities. *Cities (London, England)*, *89*, 80–91. DOI: 10.1016/j.cities.2019.01.032

Allam, Z., & Newman, P. (2018). Redefining the smart city: Culture, metabolism and governance. *Smart Cities*, *1*(1), 4–25. DOI: 10.3390/smartcities1010002

Allam, Z., & Newman, P. (2022). The metaverse as a virtual form of smart cities: Opportunities and challenges for governance. *Smart Cities*, *5*(1), 1–16. DOI: 10.3390/smartcities5010001

Allam, Z., Sharifi, A., Bibri, S. E., Jones, D. S., & Krogstie, J. (2022). The Metaverse as a Virtual Form of Smart Cities: Opportunities and Challenges for Environmental, Economic and Social Sustainability in Urban Futures. *Smart Cities*, *5*(3), 771–801. DOI: 10.3390/smartcities5030040

Al-Rqaibat, S., Al-Nusair, S., & Bataineh, R. (2025). Enhancing architectural education through hybrid digital tools: Investigating the impact on design creativity and cognitive processes. *Smart Learning Environments*, *12*(1), 26. Advance online publication. DOI: 10.1186/s40561-025-00370-9

Alvarez, M. A. P., Bielby, J., & Havens, J. (2016). *ETHICALLY ALIGNED DESIGN a vision for prioritizing human wellbeing with artificial intelligence and autonomous systems*. ETHICALLY ALIGNED DESIGN A Vision for Prioritizing Human Wellbeing with Artificial Intelligence and Autonomous Systems.

Amran, M. A., Palaniveloo, K., Fauzi, R., Satar, N. M., Mohidin, T. B. M., Mohan, G., Razak, S. A., Arunasalam, M., Nagappan, T., & Sathiya Seelan, J. S. (2021). Value-Added Metabolites from Agricultural Waste and Application of Green Extraction Techniques. *Sustainability (Basel)*, *13*(20), 11432. DOI: 10.3390/su132011432

Ana Mercedes López Rodríguez. (2024, June 13). Law Applicable to Virtual Real Estate in the Metaverse. Proceedings of the International Congress Towards a Responsible Development of the Metaverse, 13-1 4 June 2024, Alicante. Academic Chair for the Responsible Development of Metaverse.

Anderson, M., Foster, L., & Garcia, R. (2022). Multi-stakeholder governance models for emerging technologies: Lessons from metaverse development. *Technology in Society*, *71*, 102098. DOI: 10.1016/j.techsoc.2022.102098

Anudeep, B., & Tripathy, B. K. (2024). *Metaverse-Enabled Internet of Medical Things: A New Paradigm for Personalized and Precision Medicine, In book: The Metaverse for the Healthcare Industry*. Springer Nature., DOI: 10.1007/978-3-031-60073-9_8

Anurag Wasnik & Anisha Bhasin. (2022, April 25). Meta-governance: Role of the metaverse in India's E-governance. NITI Aayog. https://www.niti.gov.in/meta-governance-role-metaverse-indias-e-governance

Arpaci, I., Karatas, K., Kusci, I., & Al-Emran, M. (2022). Understanding the social sustainability of the Metaverse by integrating UTAUT2 and big five personality traits: A hybrid SEM-ANN approach. *Technology in Society*, *71*, 102120. DOI: 10.1016/j.techsoc.2022.102120

Asif, S., Zhao, M., Chen, X., & Zhu, Y. (2023). BMRI-NET: A Deep Stacked Ensemble Model for Multi-class Brain Tumor Classification from MRI Images. *Interdisciplinary Sciences, Computational Life Sciences*, *15*(3), 1–16. DOI: 10.1007/s12539-023-00571-1 PMID: 37171681

Aslam, A. M., Zeadally, S., Budhiraja, I., Bhardwaj, A., Kumar, N., & Chaudhary, R. (2023). Metaverse for 6G and Beyond: *The Next Revolution and Deployment Challenges.* *IEEE Internet of Things Magazine*, *6*(1), 32–39. DOI: 10.1109/IOTM.001.2200248

Aslan, M. F., Unlersen, M. F., Sabanci, K., & Durdu, A. (2021). CNN-based transfer learning–BiLSTM network: A novel approach for COVID-19 infection detection. *Applied Soft Computing*, *98*, 106912. DOI: 10.1016/j.asoc.2020.106912 PMID: 33230395

Assad, F., Konstantinov, S., Rushforth, E. J., Vera, D. A., & Harrison, R. (2021). Virtual engineering in the support of sustainable assembly systems. *Procedia CIRP*, *97*, 367–372. DOI: 10.1016/j.procir.2020.05.252

Atmakuri, M. K., Ram, A. G., & Prasad, V. V. K. D. V. (2023). Reliable image metrics-based brain tumor analysis using sensor deep learning technologies. *Measurement. Sensors*, *29*, 100864. DOI: 10.1016/j.measen.2023.100864

Atzori, L., Iera, A., & Morabito, G. (2019). Understanding the Internet of Things: Definition, potentials, and societal role of a fast evolving paradigm. *Ad Hoc Networks*, *37*, 122–140. DOI: 10.1016/j.adhoc.2016.12.004

Aurigi, A., & Willis, K. (2020). *The programmable city: Digital urbanism and its discontents*. Routledge.

Avinç, G. M., & Yıldız, A. (2025). A bibliometric and systematic review of scientific publications on metaverse research in architecture: Web of Science (WoS). *International Journal of Technology and Design Education*, *35*(2), 825–849. DOI: 10.1007/s10798-024-09918-1

Awadallah, A., Eledlebi, K., Puthal, D., Kim, T.-Y., Yim, M.-S., Yoo, P. D., Damiani, E., Taha, K., Raymond Choo, K.-K., Zemerly, M. J., & Yeun, C. Y. (2025). Artificial Intelligence-Based Cybersecurity for the Metaverse: Research Challenges and Opportunities. *IEEE Communications Surveys &amp. IEEE Communications Surveys and Tutorials*, *27*(2), 1008–1052. DOI: 10.1109/COMST.2024.3442475

Awasthi, A., & Sarawagi, S. (2019).. . *Continual Learning with Neural Networks*, *70*, 362–365. DOI: 10.1145/3297001.3297062

Ayushmaan, A., & Chaudhry, S. (2020). *Search of home: A study on migrant workers' access to housing and land*. Housing and Land Rights Network.

Babaeian Jelodar, M., Wilkinson, S., Kalatehjari, R., & Zou, Y. (2022). Designing for construction procurement: An integrated decision support system for building information modelling. *Built Environment Project and Asset Management*, *12*(1), 111–127. DOI: 10.1108/BEPAM-07-2020-0132

Badruddoja, S., Dantu, R., He, Y., Thompson, M., Salau, A., & Upadhyay, K. (2022). Trusted AI with Blockchain to Empower Metaverse. In *2022 Fourth Intl. Conf. on Blockchain Computing and Applications (BCCA)*, IEEE, pp. 237–244. DOI: 10.1109/BCCA55292.2022.9922027

Bailenson, J. (2022). *Experiences in VR learning at Stanford University*. Stanford Press.

Bailenson, J. N. (2018). *Experience on demand: What virtual reality is, how it works, and what it can do*. W. W. Norton & Company.

Baklanov, A., Molina, L., & Gauss, M. (2018). Megacities, air quality and climate. *Atmospheric Environment, 199*, 210–227. DOI: 10.1016/j.atmosenv.2018.11.028

Balasubramanian, S., Mandala, J., Rao, T. V. M., & Misra, A. (2024). RF-ShCNN: A combination of two deep models for tumor detection in brain using MRI. *Biomedical Signal Processing and Control, 88*, 105656. DOI: 10.1016/j.bspc.2023.105656

Ball, M. (2022). *The metaverse: and how it will revolutionize everything*. Liveright Publishing.

Barocas, S., Hardt, M., & Narayanan, A. (2023). *Fairness and Machine Learning: Limitations and Opportunities*. MIT Press., DOI: 10.7551/mitpress/12200.001.0001

Batty, M. (2013). *The new science of cities*. MIT Press. DOI: 10.7551/mitpress/9399.001.0001

Batty, M. (2018). Digital twins. *Environment and Planning. B, Urban Analytics and City Science, 45*(5), 817–820. DOI: 10.1177/2399808318796416

Bekkemoen, Y. (2024). Explainable reinforcement learning (XRL): A systematic literature review and taxonomy. *Machine Learning, 113*(1), 355–441. DOI: 10.1007/s10994-023-06479-7

Bhagat, R. B., R.S., R., Sahoo, H., Roy, A. K., & Govil, D. (2020). The COVID-19, Migration and Livelihood in India: Challenges and Policy Issues: Challenges and Policy Issues. *Migration Letters : An International Journal of Migration Studies, 17*(5), 705–718. DOI: 10.33182/ml.v17i5.1048

Bhattacharya, P., Sanghavi, S., Verma, A., Sakariya, V., Savaliya, D., Tanwar, S., Manea, D. L., Saraswat, D., Raboaca, M. S., & Sharma, R. (2023). Towards Future Internet: The Metaverse Perspective for Diverse Industrial Applications. *Mathematics, 11*(4), 941. DOI: 10.3390/math11040941

Bibri, S. E. (2022). The Social Shaping of the Metaverse as an Alternative to the Imaginaries of Data-Driven Smart Cities: A Study in Science, Technology, and Society. *Smart Cities, 5*(3), 832–874. DOI: 10.3390/smartcities5030043

Bibri, S. E., & Allam, Z. (2022). The metaverse as a virtual form of data-driven smart urbanism: On post-pandemic governance through the prism of surveillance capitalism. *Smart Cities, 5*(2), 715–727. DOI: 10.3390/smartcities5020037

Bibri, S., & Jagatheesaperumal, S. (2023). Harnessing the potential of the metaverse and artificial intelligence for the Internet of City Things: Cost-effective XReality and synergistic AIoT technologies. *Smart Cities*, *6*(5), 109–135. DOI: 10.3390/smartcities6050109

Bigdeloo, M., Teymourian, T., Kowsari, E., Ramakrishna, S., & Ehsani, A. (2021). Sustainability and Circular Economy of Food Wastes: Waste Reduction Strategies, Higher Recycling Methods, and Improved Valorization. *Materials Circular Economy*, *3*(1), 3. Advance online publication. DOI: 10.1007/s42824-021-00017-3

Brandão, E., Adelfio, M., Hagy, S., & Thuvander, L. (2021). Collaborative pedagogy for co-creation and community outreach: An experience from architectural education in social inclusion using the Miro tool. In Ahram, T., Taiar, R., & Groff, F. (Eds.), *Human factors in architecture, sustainable urban planning and infrastructure* (pp. 118–126). Springer., DOI: 10.1007/978-3-030-80415-2_15

Braun, G., Fillottrani, P. R., & Keet, C. M. (2022). A framework for interoperability between models with hybrid tools. *Journal of Intelligent Information Systems*. Advance online publication. DOI: 10.1007/s10844-022-00731-7 PMID: 35919102

Braun, V., & Clarke, V. (2006). Using thematic analysis in psychology. *Qualitative Research in Psychology*, *3*(2), 77–101. DOI: 10.1191/1478088706qp063oa

Brayne, S. (2017). Big data surveillance: The case of policing. *American Sociological Review*, *82*(5), 977–1008. DOI: 10.1177/0003122417725865 PMID: 38322733

Brik, B., Moustafa, H., Zhang, Y., Lakas, A., & Subramanian, S. (2023). Guest editorial: Multi-access networking for extended reality and metaverse. *IEEE Internet of Things Magazine*, *6*(1), 12–13. DOI: 10.1109/MIOT.2023.10070411

Brodkin, J. (2022, February 12). *Verizon builds metaverse stadium in Fortnite to show off 5G*. Ars Technica. https://arstechnica.com/gaming/2022/02/verizon-builds-metaverse-stadium-in-fortnite-to-show-off-5g/

Brownsword, R. (2020). *Law, technology and society: Re-imagining the regulatory environment*. Routledge.

Cagno, E., Neri, A., Negri, M., Bassani, C. A., & Lampertico, T. (2021). The Role of Digital Technologies in Operationalizing the Circular Economy Transition: A Systematic Literature Review. *Applied Sciences (Basel, Switzerland)*, *11*(8), 3328. DOI: 10.3390/app11083328

Çakir, H., & Uzun, T. (2020). *Building information modelling in architectural education: Contribution of BIM in design process*. Turkish Online Journal of Design Art and Communication., DOI: 10.7456/11004100/009

Calzada, I. (2021). Smart city citizenship: A critical perspective. *Journal of Urban Technology, 28*(1–2), 21–46. DOI: 10.1080/10630732.2020.1798179

Cappannari, L., & Vitillo, A. (2022). XR and Metaverse Software Platforms. In Mariano, A., Sacco, M., & Tromp, J. G. (Eds.), *Roadmapping Extended Reality: Fundamentals and Applications* (pp. 135–156)., DOI: 10.1002/9781119865810.ch6

Caragliu, A., Del Bo, C., & Nijkamp, P. (2011). Smart cities in Europe. *Journal of Urban Technology, 18*(2), 65–82. DOI: 10.1080/10630732.2011.601117

Cardullo, P., & Kitchin, R. (2019). Being a 'citizen' in the smart city: Up and down the scaffold of smart citizen participation. In Kitchin, R., Cardullo, P., & Di Feliciantonio, C. (Eds.), *The right to the smart city* (pp. 219–231). Emerald. DOI: 10.1108/9781787691391

Carroll, C., Booth, A., & Cooper, K. (2011). A worked example of "best fit" framework synthesis: A systematic review of views concerning the taking of some potential chemopreventive agents. *BMC Medical Research Methodology, 11*(1), 29. DOI: 10.1186/1471-2288-11-29 PMID: 21410933

Castells, M. (2010). *The rise of the network society* (2nd ed.). Wiley-Blackwell.

Castronova, E. (2005). *Synthetic worlds: The business and culture of online games.* University of Chicago Press.

Census tables | Government of India. (2011). [Dataset]. https://censusindia.gov.in/census.website/data/census-tables#

Chalkiadakis, A., Seremetaki, A., Kanellou, A., Kallishi, M., Morfopoulou, A., Moraitaki, M., & Mastrokoukou, S. (2024). Impact of artificial intelligence and virtual reality on educational inclusion: A systematic review of technologies supporting students with disabilities. *Education Sciences, 14*(11), 1223. DOI: 10.3390/educsci14111223

Chamola, V., Peelam, M. S., Mittal, U., Hassija, V., Singh, A., Pareek, R., Mangal, P., Sangwan, D., de Albuquerque, V. H. C., Mahmud, M., & Brown, D. J. (2025). Metaverse for Education: Developments, Challenges and Future Direction. *Computer Applications in Engineering Education, 33*(Mar), e70018. Advance online publication. DOI: 10.1002/cae.70018

Chan, J., To, H., & Chan, E. (2006). Reconsidering social cohesion: Developing a definition and analytical framework for empirical research. *Social Indicators Research, 75*(2), 273–302. DOI: 10.1007/s11205-005-2118-1

Charumitra, B., Krishna Kumar, D., & Anupama, S. (2014). Slum Redevelopment Strategy: A Way forward to Urban Environment Management through an Inclusive Approach. *Research Journal of Engineering Sciences*, *3*(7), 28–37.

Chatterjee, J. M., & Sujatha, R. (2023). Detection of COVID-19 Cases from X-ray and CT Images Using Transfer Learning and Deep Convolution Neural Networks. In *Artificial Intelligence in Medical Virology* (pp. 81–98). Springer Nature Singapore. DOI: 10.1007/978-981-99-0369-6_6

Chenavaz, R. Y., & Dimitrov, S. (2024). From waste to wealth: Policies to promote the circular economy. *Journal of Cleaner Production*, *443*, 141086. DOI: 10.1016/j.jclepro.2024.141086

Cheng, J. (2017). brain tumor dataset. figshare. Dataset. https://doi.org/DOI: 10.6084/m9.figshare.1512427.v5

Chen, L., Chen, P., & Lin, Z. (2020). Artificial intelligence in education: A review. *IEEE Access : Practical Innovations, Open Solutions*, *8*, 75264–75278. DOI: 10.1109/ACCESS.2020.2988510

Chen, L., Zhang, M., Wang, H., & Zhao, Y. (2023). Privacy-preserving machine learning in metaverse environments: Challenges and solutions. *IEEE Transactions on Information Forensics and Security*, *18*, 2156–2171. DOI: 10.1109/TIFS.2023.3271829

Chi, C., Lin, D., Ramadoss, R., Yuan, Y., Yin, Z., Luo, C., . . . Ma, R. (2023). White paper-The industrial Metaverse report. *The Industrial Metaverse Report*, 1-20.

Choi, H. S., & Kim, S. H. (2017). A content service deployment plan for Metaverse museum exhibitions—Centering on the combination of beacons and HMDs. *International Journal of Information Management*, *37*(1), 1519–1527. DOI: 10.1016/j.ijinfomgt.2016.04.017

Cho, J., tom Dieck, M. C., & Jung, T. (2022, April). What is the Metaverse? Challenges, opportunities, definition, and future research directions. In *International XR conference* (pp. 3–26). Springer International Publishing.

Chowdhury, P., & Samanta, G. (2024). Slum Development Initiatives in India: An Insight into Policy Shifts. NIUA. *Urban India*, *44*(1), 148–156.

Colelough, B. C., & Regli, W. (2025). Neuro-Symbolic AI in 2024: A Systematic Review. arXiv preprint arXiv:2501.05435. https://arxiv.org/abs/2501.05435

Connect Keynote. (2025). Watch Mark Zuckerberg in the Opening Keynote of Meta Connect 2025. https://developers.facebook.com/videos/2025/connect-keynote-2025/

Contreras, G. S., Cepa, C. B. M., Escobar, J. C. Z., Fernández, M. I. S., & González, A. H. (2022). The Importance of the Application of the Metaverse in Education. *Modern Applied Science*, *16*(3), 34. DOI: 10.5539/mas.v16n3p34

Cowls, J., Tsamados, A., Taddeo, M., & Floridi, L. (2021). A definition, benchmark and database of AI for social good initiatives. *Nature Machine Intelligence*, *3*(2), 111–115. DOI: 10.1038/s42256-021-00296-0

Creed, C., Kalbani, M., Theil, A., Sarcar, S., & Williams, I. (2023). Inclusive AR/VR: Accessibility barriers for immersive technologies. *Universal Access in the Information Society*, •••, 1–15. DOI: 10.1007/s10209-023-00969-0

Criollo-C, S., Govea, J., Játiva, W., Pierrottet, J., Guerrero-Arias, A., Jaramillo-Alcázar, Á., & Luján-Mora, S. (2023). Towards the integration of emerging technologies as support for the teaching and learning model in higher education. *Sustainability (Basel)*, *15*(7), 6055. DOI: 10.3390/su15076055

Crolla, K., Song, J., Bunica, A., & Sheikh, A. (2024). Integrating extended reality in architectural design studio teaching and reviews: Implementing a participatory action research framework. *Buildings (Basel, Switzerland)*, *14*(6), 1865. Advance online publication. DOI: 10.3390/buildings14061865

Damar, M., Kaleci, D., & Kılıç, E. (2023). Educational opportunities and challenges in the metaverse: A systematic review. *Computers & Education: Artificial Intelligence*, *4*, 100154. Advance online publication. DOI: 10.1016/j.caeai.2023.100154

Darwish, M., Kamel, S., & Assem, A. (2023). Extended reality for enhancing spatial ability in architecture design education. *Ain Shams Engineering Journal*, *14*(6), 102104. Advance online publication. DOI: 10.1016/j.asej.2022.102104

Davis, A., Murphy, J., Owens, D., Khazanchi, D., & Zigurs, I. (2009). Avatars, people, and virtual worlds: Foundations for research in Metaverses. *Journal of the Association for Information Systems*, *10*(2), 1. DOI: 10.17705/1jais.00183

Davis, F. D. (1989). Perceived usefulness, perceived ease of use, and user acceptance of information technology. *Management Information Systems Quarterly*, *13*(3), 319–340. DOI: 10.2307/249008

De Giovanni, P. (2023, March). Sustainability of the Metaverse: A Transition to Industry 5.0. *Sustainability (Basel)*, *15*(7), 6079. DOI: 10.3390/su15076079

de Vliert, A. V., & Peij, J. V. (2024). Circular Economy Implementation in Dutch Agriculture: Assessing Sustainable Practices and Economic Impact. *Law and Economy*, *3*(1), 20–31. DOI: 10.56397/LE.2024.01.03

Demestichas, K., & Daskalakis, E. (2020). Information and Communication Technology Solutions for the Circular Economy. *Sustainability (Basel), 12*(18), 7272. DOI: 10.3390/su12187272

Digital Future Society. (2023). Ethical and social challenges posed by the future metaverse. https://digitalfuturesociety.com/app/uploads/2023/07/Ethical-and-social-challenges-posed-by-the-future-metaverse_ENG.pdf

Digital Personal Data Protection Act. (2023). Retrieved https://www.dpdpa.in/

Dionisio, J. D. N., Burns, W. G., & Gilbert, R. (2013). 3D virtual worlds and the metaverse: Current status and future possibilities. *ACM Computing Surveys*, *45*(3), 34. Advance online publication. DOI: 10.1145/2480741.2480751

Dong, H., & Lee, J. S. A. (2022). The Metaverse From a Multimedia Communications Perspective. *IEEE MultiMedia*, *29*(4), 123–127. DOI: 10.1109/MMUL.2022.3217627

Donner, M., Verniquet, A., Broeze, J., Kayser, K., & De Vries, H. (2021). Critical success and risk factors for circular business models valorising agricultural waste and by-products. *Resources, Conservation and Recycling*, *165*, 105236. DOI: 10.1016/j.resconrec.2020.105236

Duan, H., Li, J., Fan, S., Lin, Z., Wu, X., & Cai, W. (2021). Metaverse for social good: A university campus prototype. *Proceedings of the 29th ACM International Conference on Multimedia*, 153–161. DOI: 10.1145/3474085.3479238

Duarte, J., Martí, P., & González, C. (2018). City information modelling: Parametric urban models including design guidelines and rules. *Sustainable Cities and Society*, *36*, 322–332. DOI: 10.1016/j.scs.2017.10.031

Dubai Metaverse Strategy. (2024, December 30). U.AE. https://u.ae/en/about-the-uae/strategies-initiatives-and-awards/strategies-plans-and-visions/government-services-and-digital-transformation/dubai-metaverse-strategy

Dudley, J. J., Yin, L., Garaj, V., & Kristensson, P. O. (2023). Inclusive immersion: A review of efforts to improve accessibility in virtual reality, augmented reality and the metaverse. *Virtual Reality (Waltham Cross)*, *27*(6), 2989–3020. DOI: 10.1007/s10055-023-00850-8

Duraipandi, O., & Velayudhan, T. A. (2024). A Novel Framework for Cloud Data Security with Blockchain Technology and Distributed Virtual Machine Agents. *Journal of Information Technology and Digital World*, *6*(2), 207–216. DOI: 10.36548/jitdw.2024.2.008

Dwivedi, Y. K., Hughes, L., Baabdullah, A. M., Ribeiro-Navarrete, S., Giannakis, M., Al-Debei, M. M., Dennehy, D., Metri, B., Buhalis, D., Cheung, C. M. K., Conboy, K., Doyle, R., Dubey, R., Dutot, V., Felix, R., Goyal, D. P., Gustafsson, A., Hinsch, C., Jebabli, I., & Wamba, S. F. (2022). Metaverse beyond the hype: Multidisciplinary perspectives on emerging challenges, opportunities, and agenda for research. *International Journal of Information Management*, *66*, 102542. Advance online publication. DOI: 10.1016/j.ijinfomgt.2022.102542

Dwivedi, Y. K., Hughes, L., & Baabdullah, A.. (2022). Metaverse for education: Opportunities and challenges. *Journal of Business Research*, *145*, 731–743.

Eggenschwiler, M., Linzmajer, M., Roggeveen, A. L., & Rudolph, T. (2024). Retailing in the Metaverse: A framework of managerial considerations for success. *Journal of Retailing and Consumer Services*, *79*, 103791. DOI: 10.1016/j.jretconser.2024.103791

Ehab, A., Burnett, G., & Heath, T. (2023). Enhancing public engagement in architectural design: A comparative analysis of advanced virtual reality approaches in building information modeling and gamification techniques. *Buildings (Basel, Switzerland)*, *13*(5), 1262. Advance online publication. DOI: 10.3390/buildings13051262

Elmasry, T., Hazan, E., Khan, H., Kelly, G., Srivastava, S., Yee, L., & Zemmel, R. W. (2022) Value Creation in the Metaverse - the Real Business of the Virtual World. McKinsey & Company Report. https://www.mckinsey.com/business-functions/growth-marketing-and-sales/our-insights/value-creation-in-the-Metaverse

Elsadig, M., Alohali, M. A., Ibrahim, A. O., & Abulfaraj, A. W. (2024). Roles of Blockchain in the Metaverse: Concepts, Taxonomy, Recent Advances, Enabling Technologies, and Open Research Issues. *IEEE Access : Practical Innovations, Open Solutions*, *12*, 38410–38435. DOI: 10.1109/ACCESS.2024.3367014

Evans, L. (2015). Locative social media: Place in the digital age. *First Monday*, *20*(3). Advance online publication. DOI: 10.5210/fm.v20i3.5457

Farajzadeh, N., Sadeghzadeh, N., & Hashemzadeh, M. (2023). Brain tumor segmentation and classification on MRI via deep hybrid representation learning. *Expert Systems with Applications*, *224*, 119963. DOI: 10.1016/j.eswa.2023.119963

Faruq, O., Mambetaliev, A., Karshiboev, A., & Mohammad, N. (2025, June). Designing inclusive digital media environments for learners with autism spectrum disorder: Integrating artificial intelligence and data analysis to enable adaptive learning, communication, and accessibility. *Journal of Posthumanism*, *5*(6). Advance online publication. DOI: 10.63332/joph.v5i6.2338

Feng, F., Shi, X., Zhang, Y., Chan, R. H. M., & She, Q. (2019). Challenges in Task Incremental Learning for Assistive Robotics. *IEEE Access: Practical Innovations, Open Solutions, 8*, 3434–3441. https://www.emergentmind.com/topics/. doi:10.1109/ACCESS.2019.2955480

Floridi, L., & Cowls, J. (2019). A unified framework of five principles for AI in society. *Harvard Data Science Review*, (Jun). Advance online publication. DOI: 10.1162/99608f92.8cd550d1

Floridi, L., Cowls, J., Beltrametti, M., Chatila, R., Chazerand, P., Dignum, V., Luetge, C., Madelin, R., Pagallo, U., Rossi, F., Schafer, B., Valcke, P., & Vayena, E. (2018). AI4People—An ethical framework for a good AI society. *Minds and Machines, 28*(4), 689–707. DOI: 10.1007/s11023-018-9482-5 PMID: 30930541

Fonseca, D., Cavalcanti, J., Peña, E., Valls, V., Sánchez-Sepúlveda, M., Moreira, F., Navarro, I., & Redondo, E. (2021). Mixed assessment of virtual serious games applied in architectural and urban design education. *Sensors (Basel), 21*(9), 3102. Advance online publication. DOI: 10.3390/s21093102 PMID: 33946868

Forrest, R., & Kearns, A. (2001). Social cohesion, social capital and the neighbourhood. *Urban Studies (Edinburgh, Scotland), 38*(12), 2125–2143. DOI: 10.1080/00420980120087081

Foth, M., Brynskov, M., & Ojala, T. (2016). *Citizen's right to the digital city: Urban interfaces, activism, and placemaking*. Springer.

Francis, J., Giles-Corti, B., Wood, L., & Knuiman, M. (2012). Creating sense of community: The role of public space. *Journal of Environmental Psychology, 32*(4), 401–409. DOI: 10.1016/j.jenvp.2012.07.002

Future Today Strategy Group. (2025). *Metaverse & new realities: Strategies for a digitized future*. https://ftsg.com/wp-content/uploads/2025/03/Metaverse-New-Realities_FINAL_LINKED.pdf

Fu, Y., Yu, F. R., Liu, S., Zhao, P., Li, C., & Luan, T. H. (2023). A Survey of Blockchain and Intelligent Networking for the Metaverse. *IEEE Internet of Things Journal, 10*(4), 3587–3610. DOI: 10.1109/JIOT.2022.3222521

Gadekallu, T. R., Huynh-The, T., Wang, W., Yenduri, G., Ranaweera, P., Pham, V., Da Costa, D. B., & Liyanage, M. (2022). Blockchain for the metaverse: A review. *Future Generation Computer Systems, 143*, 401–419. DOI: 10.48550/arXiv.2203.09738

Gadekallu, T. R., Pham, Q. V., Nguyen, D. C., Maddikunta, P. K. R., Deepa, N., Prabadevi, B., Pathirana, P. N., Zhao, J., & Hwang, W. J. (2021). Blockchain for edge of things: Applications, opportunities, and challenges. *IEEE Internet of Things Journal*, *9*(2), 964–988. DOI: 10.1109/JIOT.2021.3119639

Gandhi, S., & Green, K. R., & Patranabis, S. (n.d.). India's housing paradox: Empty houses and housing shortages. Centre for Social and Economic Progress.

Gandhi, S., Green, R. K., & Patranabis, S. (2022). Insecure property rights and the housing market: Explaining India's housing vacancy paradox. *Journal of Urban Economics*, *131*, 103490. DOI: 10.1016/j.jue.2022.103490

Gao, L., Li, Y., & Luo, Y. (2021). IoT-enabled smart classrooms: Opportunities and challenges. *Computers & Education*, *170*, 104224. DOI: 10.1016/j.compedu.2021.104224

Garau, C., Annunziata, A., & Yamu, C. (2017). A walkability assessment tool coupling multi-criteria analysis and space syntax: The case study of Iglesias, Italy. *European Planning Studies*, *25*(12), 2215–2236. DOI: 10.1080/09654313.2017.1345868

Gefen, D., Karahanna, E., & Straub, D. (2003). Trust and TAM in online environments: An integrated model. *Management Information Systems Quarterly*, *27*(1), 51–90. DOI: 10.2307/30036519

Gehl, J. (2011). *Life between buildings: Using public space* (6th ed.). Island Press.

Ghosh, A., Edwards, D. J., & Hosseini, M. R. (2021). Patterns and trends in Internet of Things (IoT) research: Future applications in the construction industry. *Engineering, Construction, and Architectural Management*, *28*(2), 457–481. DOI: 10.1108/ECAM-04-2020-0271

Giffinger, R., Fertner, C., Kramar, H., Kalasek, R., & Meijers, E. (2007). *Smart cities: Ranking of European medium-sized cities*. Centre of Regional Science, Vienna University of Technology.

Gilbert, A. (2016). Rental housing: The international experience. *Habitat International*, *54*, 173–181. DOI: 10.1016/j.habitatint.2015.11.025

Gil-Garcia, J. R., Dawes, S. S., & Pardo, T. A. (2018). Digital government and public management research: Finding the crossroads. *Public Management Review*, *20*(5), 633–646. DOI: 10.1080/14719037.2017.1327181

Gómez-Tone, H., Chávez, M., Samalvides, L., & Martín-Gutiérrez, J. (2022). Introducing immersive virtual reality in the initial phases of the design process—Case study: Freshmen designing ephemeral architecture. *Buildings (Basel, Switzerland), 12*(5), 518. Advance online publication. DOI: 10.3390/buildings12050518

Gouda, W., Almurafeh, M., Humayun, M., & Jhanjhi, N. Z. (2022, February). Detection of COVID-19 based on chest X-rays using deep learning. In Healthcare (Vol. 10, No. 2, p. 343). MDPI.

Graham, S., & Marvin, S. (2001). *Splintering urbanism: Networked infrastructures, technological mobilities and the urban condition.* Routledge.

Grech, A., & Camilleri, A. F. (2017). *Blockchain in education. Joint Research Centre (JRC) Science for Policy Report.* Publications Office of the European Union., DOI: 10.2760/60649

Greenfield, A. (2013). *Against the smart city.* Do Projects.

Groves, R. (2016). Housing and the New Welfare State (A. Murie, Ed.; 0 ed.). Routledge. DOI: 10.4324/9781315587103

GSMA. (2024). *The Fast Mode: Unlocking Metaverse with 5G and immersive tech.* Retrieved from https://event-assets.gsma.com/Shanghai/Doc/media/publication-2024-the-fast-mode.pdf

Gupta, R., & Pal, S. K. (2023). Metaverse for Public Sector. In R. Gupta & S. K. Pal, Introduction to Metaverse (pp. 91–114). Springer Nature Singapore. DOI: 10.1007/978-981-99-7397-2_5

Gurran, N., & Phibbs, P. (2015). Are Governments Really Interested in Fixing the Housing Problem? Policy Capture and Busy Work in Australia. *Housing Studies, 30*(5), 711–729. DOI: 10.1080/02673037.2015.1044948

Gursoy, D., Lu, L., Nunkoo, R., & Deng, D. (2023). Metaverse in services marketing: An overview and future research directions. *Service Industries Journal, 43*(15-16), 1140–1172. DOI: 10.1080/02642069.2023.2252750

Habermas, J. (1989). The structural transformation of the public sphere: An inquiry into a category of bourgeois society (T. Burger, Trans., with the assistance of F. Lawrence). MIT Press.

Hampton, K. N. (2016). Persistent and pervasive community: New communication technologies and the future of community. *The American Behavioral Scientist, 60*(1), 101–124. DOI: 10.1177/0002764215601714

Hanhörster, H., & Ramos Lobato, I. (2021). Migrants' Access to the Rental Housing Market in Germany: Housing Providers and Allocation Policies. *Urban Planning*, *6*(2), 7–18. DOI: 10.17645/up.v6i2.3802

Hatami, M., Qu, Q., Blasch, E., Chen, Y., Ardiles-Cruz, E., & Kholidy, H. (2024). A Survey on Real-Time Metaverse: Challenges and Opportunities. *Future Internet*, *16*(10), 1–52. DOI: 10.3390/fi16100379

Helberger, N., Pierson, J., & Poell, T. (2020). Governing online platforms: From contested to cooperative responsibility. *The Information Society*, *36*(1), 1–14. DOI: 10.1080/01972243.2017.1391913

Herrera, F., Bailenson, J., Weisz, E., Ogle, E., & Zaki, J. (2018). Building long-term empathy: A large-scale comparison of traditional and virtual reality perspective-taking. *PLoS One*, *13*(10), e0204494. DOI: 10.1371/journal.pone.0204494 PMID: 30332407

Hettithanthri, U., & Hansen, P. (2021). Design studio practice in the context of architectural education: A narrative literature review. *International Journal ofTechnology and Design Education*, *32*(4), 2343–2364. DOI: 10.1007/s10798-021-09694-2

Higginbotham, G. (2021). Virtual connections: Improving global neurosurgery through immersive technologies. *Frontiers in Surgery*, *8*, 629963. DOI: 10.3389/fsurg.2021.629963 PMID: 33681283

Hine, E., Rezende, I., Roberts, H., Wong, D., Taddeo, M., & Floridi, L. (2024). Safety and privacy in immersive extended reality: An analysis and policy recommendations. *Digital Society : Ethics, Socio-Legal and Governance of Digital Technology*, *3*(1), 33. DOI: 10.1007/s44206-024-00114-1

Hitachi-UTokyo Laboratory. (H-UTokyo Lab.) (Ed.). (2020). Society 5.0: A people-centric super-smart society. Springer Nature.

Hollands, R. G. (2015). Critical interventions into the corporate smart city. *Cambridge Journal of Regions, Economy and Society*, *8*(1), 61–77. DOI: 10.1093/cjres/rsu011

Holstein, K., Wortman Vaughan, J., Daumé, H.III, Dudik, M., & Wallach, H. (2019). Improving Fairness in Machine Learning Systems: What Do Industry Practitioners Need? *Proceedings of CHI Conference on Human Factors in Computing Systems*, 1–16. DOI: 10.1145/3290605.3300830

Hooli, M. (2025). Digital Twins and Urban Planning: Designing Smarter, More Inclusive Cities. *European Journal of Computer Science and Information Technology*, *13*(44), 104–112. DOI: 10.37745/ejcsit.2013/vol13n44104112

Hossain, D., & Chen, J. Y. (2025). A Study on Neuro-Symbolic Artificial Intelligence: Healthcare Perspectives. arXiv preprint arXiv:2503.18213.

Huang, R. H., Liu, D. J., & Tlili, A.. (2022). Meta-education: The future of learning in the metaverse. *Smart Learning Environments*, *9*(1), 1–14. PMID: 40477962

Hu, J., Gu, X., & Gu, X. (2022). Mutual ensemble learning for brain tumor segmentation. *Neurocomputing*, *504*, 68–81. DOI: 10.1016/j.neucom.2022.06.058

Hulchanski, J. D. (1995). The concept of housing affordability: Six contemporary uses of the housing expenditure-to-income ratio. *Housing Studies*, *10*(4), 471–491. DOI: 10.1080/02673039508720833

Humayun, M., Sujatha, R., Almuayqil, S. N., & Jhanjhi, N. Z. (2022, June). A transfer learning approach with a convolutional neural network for the classification of lung carcinoma. In Healthcare (Vol. 10, No. 6, p. 1058). MDPI. DOI: 10.3390/healthcare10061058

Humayun, M., & Alsayat, A. (2022). Prediction Model for Coronavirus Pandemic Using Deep Learning. *Computer Systems Science and Engineering*, *40*(3), 947–961. DOI: 10.32604/csse.2022.019288

Huynh-The, T., Pham, V., Pham, X., Nguyen, T., Han, Z., & Kim, D. (2022). Artificial intelligence for the metaverse: A survey. *Engineering Applications of Artificial Intelligence*, *117*, 105581. DOI: 10.1016/j.engappai.2022.105581

Jacobs, J. (1961). *The death and life of great American cities*. Random House.

Janssen, M., & Estevez, E. (2013a). Lean government and platform-based governance—Doing more with less. *Government Information Quarterly*, *30*, S1–S8. DOI: 10.1016/j.giq.2012.11.003

Janssen, M., & Kuk, G. (2016). The challenges and limits of big data algorithms in technocratic governance. *Government Information Quarterly*, *33*(3), 371–377. DOI: 10.1016/j.giq.2016.08.011

Jeong, J. The most intuitive and easiest guide for CNN, The Medium (2019) [cited 2022Aug14]. Available from: https://towardsdatascience.com/the-most-intuitive-and-easiest-guide-for-convolutional-neural-network-3607be47480#:w:text%C2%BCFlattening%20is%20converting%20the%20data

Jobin, A., Ienca, M., & Vayena, E. (2019). The Global Landscape of AI Ethics Guidelines. *Nature Machine Intelligence*, *1*(9), 389–399. DOI: 10.1038/s42256-019-0088-2

Johri, A., Joshi, P., Kumar, S., & Joshi, G. (2024). Metaverse for Sustainable Development in a bibliometric analysis and systematic literature review. *Journal of Cleaner Production, 435*, 140610. DOI: 10.1016/j.jclepro.2024.140610

Jones, N. (2018). How to stop data centres from gobbling up the world's electricity. *Nature, 561*(7722), 163–166. DOI: 10.1038/d41586-018-06610-y PMID: 30209383

Jongsuksomsakul, P. (2024). "Waste Is Wealth": Circular Economy Strategies from Media Persuasion to Utilization. *Sustainability (Basel), 16*(12), 5205. DOI: 10.3390/su16125205

Kansal, M., Singh, P., Soharia, A., Tripathi, A., Yadav, A., & Sen, C. (2023). A Brief Survey on Metaverse: Its Concepts, Applications and Challenges, 2023 3rd Intl. Conf. on Advancement in Electronics & Communication Engg. (AECE), India, pp. 470-475. DOI: 10.1109/AECE59614.2023.10428474

Katicic, J., Häfner, P., & Ovtcharova, J. (2015). Methodology for emotional assessment of product design by customers in virtual reality. *Presence (Cambridge, Mass.), 24*(1), 62–73. DOI: 10.1162/PRES_a_00215

Kaur, M., Mann, P., Rani, R., Jaiswal, G., Sharma, A., & Kumar, R. (2023, March). MRI Image Segmentation using Deep Learning for Brain Tumor Detection. In 2023 10th International Conference on Computing for Sustainable Global Development (INDIACom) (pp. 939-944). IEEE.

Kee, T., et al. (2023). An empirical study on immersive technology in architectural education: The impact of virtual and augmented reality on design learning.

Kee, T., Zhang, H., & King, R. (2023). An empirical study on immersive technology in synchronous hybrid learning in design education. *International Journal of Technology and Design Education.* Advance online publication. DOI: 10.1007/s10798-023-09855-5

Khairandish, M. O., Sharma, M., Jain, V., Chatterjee, J. M., & Jhanjhi, N. Z. (2022). A hybrid CNN-SVM threshold segmentation approach for tumor detection and classification of MRI brain images. *Ingénierie et Recherche Biomédicale : IRBM = Biomedical Engineering and Research, 43*(4), 290–299. DOI: 10.1016/j.irbm.2021.06.003

Khalil, M. I., Humayun, M., Jhanjhi, N. Z., Talib, M. N., & Tabbakh, T. A. (2021). Multi-class segmentation of organ at risk from abdominal CT images: A deep learning approach. In Intelligent Computing and Innovation on Data Science [Springer Singapore.]. *Proceedings of ICTIDS, 2021*, 425–434.

Khalil, M. I., Tehsin, S., Humayun, M., Jhanjhi, N. Z., & AlZain, M. A. (2022). Multi-Scale Network for Thoracic Organs Segmentation. *Computers, Materials & Continua*, *70*(2).

Kim, D., Oh, S., & Shon, T. (2023). Digital forensic approaches for metaverse ecosystems. *Forensic Science International Digital Investigation*, *46*, 301608. Advance online publication. DOI: 10.1016/j.fsidi.2023.301608

Kim, J. (2021). Advertising in the metaverse: Research agenda. *Journal of Interactive Advertising*, *21*(3), 141–144. DOI: 10.1080/15252019.2021.2001273

Kim, J., Lee, H., & Lee, J. (2021). Energy consumption and sustainability of virtual reality systems. *IEEE Access : Practical Innovations, Open Solutions*, *9*, 123456–123470.

Kim, Y., Aamir, Z., Singh, M., Boorboor, S., Mueller, K., & Kaufman, A. E. (2025). Explainable XR: Understanding User Behaviors of XR Environments Using LLM-Assisted Analytics Framework. *IEEE Transactions on Visualization and Computer Graphics*, *31*(5), 2756–2766. DOI: 10.1109/TVCG.2025.3549537 PMID: 40063468

Kitchin, R. (2014). *The Data Revolution: Big Data, Open Data, Data Infrastructures & Their Consequences*. SAGE Publications Ltd., DOI: 10.4135/9781473909472

Kitchin, R. (2015). Making sense of smart cities: Addressing present shortcomings. *Cambridge Journal of Regions, Economy and Society*, *8*(1), 131–136. DOI: 10.1093/cjres/rsu027

Klaus, P., & Manthiou, A. (2024). Metaverse retail: Pioneering research avenues for tomorrow's marketplace. *Journal of Retailing and Consumer Services*, *78*, 103782. DOI: 10.1016/j.jretconser.2024.103782

Komninos, N. (2020). *Smart cities and connected intelligence: Platforms, ecosystems and network effects*. Routledge.

Koohang, A., Nord, J. H., Ooi, K. B., Tan, G. W. H., Al-Emran, M., Aw, E. C. X., Baabdullah, A. M., Buhalis, D., Cham, T.-H., Dennis, C., Dutot, V., Dwivedi, Y. K., Hughes, L., Mogaji, E., Pandey, N., Phau, I., Raman, R., Sharma, A., Sigala, M., & Wong, L. W. (2023). Shaping the Metaverse into reality: A holistic multidisciplinary understanding of opportunities, challenges, and avenues for future investigation. *Journal of Computer Information Systems*, *63*(3), 735–765. DOI: 10.1080/08874417.2023.2165197

Kourtesis, P. (2024). A comprehensive review of multimodal XR applications, risks, and ethical challenges in the metaverse. *Multimodal Technologies and Interaction*, *8*(11), 98. DOI: 10.3390/mti8110098

Krause, M. J., & Tolaymat, T. (2018). Quantification of energy and carbon costs for mining cryptocurrencies. *Nature Sustainability, 1*(11), 711–718. DOI: 10.1038/s41893-018-0152-7

Krause, N., Frey, A., & Cress, U. (2019). How to design online learning communities: The role of social presence. *Educational Technology Research and Development, 67*(3), 511–533.

Kraus, S., Kanbach, D. K., Krysta, P. M., Steinhoff, M. M., & Tomini, N. (2022). Facebook and the creation of the Metaverse: Radical business model innovation or incremental transformation? *International Journal of Entrepreneurial Behaviour & Research, 28*(9), 52–77. DOI: 10.1108/IJEBR-12-2021-0984

Kshetri, N., & Dwivedi, Y. K. (2023). Pollution-reducing and pollution-generating effects of the Metaverse. *International Journal of Information Management, 69*, 102620. DOI: 10.1016/j.ijinfomgt.2023.102620

Kshetri, N., Pandey, P. S., & Ahmed, M. (Eds.). (2025). *Blockchain technology for cyber defense, cybersecurity, and countermeasures: Techniques, solutions, and applications*. CRC Press.

Kshetri, N., Pokhrel, B. P., Rahman, M. M., Mishra, R., & Hutson, J. (2025). SecureMetaEnd—Endpoint Security in the Metaverse: Securing devices and applications. In *Defending the Metaverse* (pp. 319–333). CRC Press. DOI: 10.1201/9781003581659-16

Kulal, A., Rahiman, H. U., Suvarna, H., Abhishek, N., & Dinesh, S. (2024). Enhancing public Service delivery efficiency: Exploring the impact of AI. *Journal of Open Innovation, 10*(3), 100329. DOI: 10.1016/j.joitmc.2024.100329

Kumar, A. (1989). National Housing Policy: The Implications. [JSTOR.]. *Economic and Political Weekly, 24*(23), 1285–1294.

Kumar, A., & Shankar, A. (2024). Investigating the role of metaverse influencers' attributes for the next generation of services. *Journal of Services Marketing, 38*(7), 816–838. DOI: 10.1108/JSM-09-2023-0320

Kumar, K. A., Prasad, A. Y., & Metan, J. (2022). A hybrid deep CNN-Cov-19-Res-Net Transfer learning architype for an enhanced Brain tumor Detection and Classification scheme in medical image processing. *Biomedical Signal Processing and Control, 76*, 103631. DOI: 10.1016/j.bspc.2022.103631

Kumar, P. S., Sakthivel, V. P., Raju, M., & Satya, P. D. (2023). Brain tumor segmentation of the FLAIR MRI images using novel ResUnet. *Biomedical Signal Processing and Control, 82*, 104586. DOI: 10.1016/j.bspc.2023.104586

Kundu, A. (2014). Exclusionary Growth, Poverty, and India's Emerging Urban Structure. *Social Change*, *44*(4), 541–566. DOI: 10.1177/0049085714548538

Kuss, D. J., & Griffiths, M. D. (2017). Social networking sites and addiction: Ten lessons learned. *International Journal of Environmental Research and Public Health*, *14*(3), 311. Advance online publication. DOI: 10.3390/ijerph14030311 PMID: 28304359

Kye, B., Han, N., Kim, E., Park, Y., & Jo, S. (2021). Educational applications of metaverse: Possibilities and limitations. *Journal of Educational Evaluation for Health Professions*, *18*(32), 1–12. DOI: 10.3352/jeehp.2021.18.32 PMID: 34897242

Lai, Y., Wang, P., & Wen, K. (2024). Exploring the impact of public spaces on social cohesion in resettlement communities from the perspective of experiential value. *Buildings (Basel, Switzerland)*, *14*(10), 3141. Advance online publication. DOI: 10.3390/buildings14103141

Lampropoulos, G. (2025). Intelligent virtual reality and augmented reality technologies: An overview. *Future Internet*, *17*(2), 58. DOI: 10.3390/fi17020058

Lampropoulos, G., & Krouska, A. (2024). Virtual reality and gamification in education: A systematic review. *Educational Technology Research and Development*, *72*(3), 1691–1785. Advance online publication. DOI: 10.1007/s11423-024-10351-3

Latif, A., Cahyandito, M. F., & Utama, G. L. (2023). Dynamic System Modeling and Sustainability Strategies for Circular Economy-Based Dairy Cow Waste Management. *Sustainability (Basel)*, *15*(4), 3405. DOI: 10.3390/su15043405

Latif, S., Usman, M., Manzoor, S., Iqbal, W., Qadir, J., Tyson, G., Castro, I., Razi, A., Boulos, M. N. K., Weller, A., & Crowcroft, J. (2020). Leveraging data science to combat COVID-19: A comprehensive review. *IEEE Transactions on Artificial Intelligence*, *1*(1), 85–103. DOI: 10.1109/TAI.2020.3020521 PMID: 37982070

Lee, L. H., Braud, T., Zhou, P., ... (2021). All one needs to know about metaverse: A complete survey. arXiv preprint arXiv:2110.05352.

Lee, L.-H., Braud, T., Zhou, P., Wang, L., Xu, D., & Kumar, A. Bermejo, C., and Hui, P. (2021). All One Needs to Know about Metaverse: A Complete Survey on Technological Singularity, Virtual Ecosystem, and Research Agenda, pp. 1-66. https://doi.org//arXiv.2110.05352DOI: 10.48550

Lee, W. J. (2020). Use of immersive virtual technology in consumer retailing and its effects to consumer. , *18*(2), 5-15.

Lee, L. H., Braud, T., Zhou, P., Wang, L., Xu, D., Lin, Z., Kumar, A., Bermejo, C., & Hui, P. (2021). All one needs to know about metaverse: A complete survey on technological singularity, virtual ecosystem, and research agenda. *Journal of Information Technology Case and Application Research, 23*(4), 1–20. DOI: 10.1080/15228053.2021.1996899

Lee, L.-H., Braud, T., Zhou, P., Wang, L., Xu, D., Lin, Z., Kumar, A., Bermejo, C., & Hui, P. (2021). All one needs to know about metaverse: A complete survey on technological singularity, virtual ecosystem, and research agenda. *Foundations and Trends® in Human–Computer Interaction, 18*(3–4), 100–337. https://doi.org/ DOI: 10.13140/rg.2.2.11200.05124/1

Lefebvre, H. (1991). *The production of space*. Blackwell.

Lessig, L. (2006). *Code version 2.0*. Basic Books.

Levy, S., Bender, E. M., & Tsvetkov, Y. (2022). Cross-cultural communication and collaboration in virtual environments. *Journal of Virtual Worlds Research, 15*(2), 45–60.

Li, H., Ikebe, K., Kinoshita, T., Chen, J., Su, D., & Xie, J. (2024). How heritage promotes social cohesion: An urban survey from Nara city, Japan. *Cities (London, England), 149*, 104985. Advance online publication. DOI: 10.1016/j.cities.2024.104985

Lim, W. Y. B., Zehui, X., Niyato, D., Xianbin, C., Miao, C., Sun, S., & Yang, Q. (2022). Realizing the Metaverse with Edge Intelligence: A Match Made in Heaven, IEEE wireless communications, https://arxiv.org/abs/2201.01634

Liu, X., Park, S., & Kim, J. (2023). Federated learning for privacy-preserving AI in metaverse platforms. *IEEE Internet of Things Journal, 10*(8), 7234–7248. DOI: 10.1109/JIOT.2022.3223847

Lnenicka, M., Rizun, N., Alexopoulos, C., & Janssen, M. (2024). Government in the metaverse: Requirements and suitability for providing digital public services. *Technological Forecasting and Social Change, 203*, 123346. DOI: 10.1016/j.techfore.2024.123346

Lodge, M., & Wegrich, K. (2012). *Managing regulation: Regulatory analysis, politics, and policy*. Palgrave Macmillan. DOI: 10.1007/978-1-137-26552-4

Low, S. (2000). *On the plaza: The politics of public space and culture*. University of Texas Press.

Lu, F., Zhou, X., Guo, L., Chen, J., & Pei, L. (2021). An ARCore-Based Augmented Reality Campus Navigation System. [MDPI]. *Applied Sciences (Basel, Switzerland), 11*(16), 7515. DOI: 10.3390/app11167515

Lu, S., & Mintz, O. (2023). Marketing on the Metaverse: Research opportunities and challenges. *AMS Review, 13*(1), 151–166. DOI: 10.1007/s13162-023-00255-5

Madanipour, A. (2003). *Public and private spaces of the city*. Routledge. DOI: 10.4324/9780203402856

Maghool, S., Moeini, S., & Arefazar, Y. (2018). An educational application based on virtual reality technology for learning architectural details: Challenges and benefits. *Archnet-IJAR, 12*(3), 246. Advance online publication. DOI: 10.26687/archnet-ijar.v12i3.1719

Maharika, I., Irsan, A., Susanto, A., Abma, V., & Yuriandala, Y. (2020). Building information modelling (BIM) adoption model for architectural education. Journal of Design and Built Environment. DOI: 10.22452/jdbe.vol20no3.2

Maier, F., Reuter, C., & Schwab, M. (2025). AI-driven urban digital twins and participatory governance: Opportunities and ethical constraints. *Environment and Planning. B, Urban Analytics and City Science*. Advance online publication. DOI: 10.1177/2399808325123456

Maier, F., & Weinberger, M. (2024). Metaverse meets smart cities—Applications, benefits, and challenges. *Future Internet, 16*(4), 126. Advance online publication. DOI: 10.3390/fi16040126

Mallek, F., Mazhar, T., Shah, S., Ghadi, Y., & Hamam, H. (2024). A review on cultivating effective learning: Synthesizing educational theories and virtual reality for enhanced educational experiences. *PeerJ. Computer Science, 10*, e2000. Advance online publication. DOI: 10.7717/peerj-cs.2000 PMID: 38855256

Mann, S., Yuan, Y., Lamberti, F., Saddik, A. E., Thawonmas, R., & Pratticó, F. (2024). eXtended meta-uni-omni-verse (XV): Introduction, taxonomy, and state-of-the-art. *IEEE Consumer Electronics Magazine, 13*(2), 27–35. DOI: 10.1109/MCE.2023.3283728

Marougkas, A., Troussas, C., Krouska, A., & Sgouropoulou, C. (2023). Virtual reality in education: A review of learning theories, approaches and methodologies for the last decade. *Electronics (Basel), 12*(13), 2832. DOI: 10.3390/electronics12132832

Martinez-Gonzalez, A., Thompson, K., & Lee, S. (2023). Algorithmic accountability in virtual economies: A systematic analysis of fairness mechanisms. *Computers in Human Behavior, 128*, 107089. DOI: 10.1016/j.chb.2021.107089

Martins, J., & Rodrigues, R. (2024). Motivations in the adoption and conversion of freemium services: Insights for digital entrepreneurship. *Review of Managerial Science*, •••, 1–22. DOI: 10.1007/s11846-024-00754-0

Masneri, S., Domínguez, A., Pacho, G., Zorrilla, M., Larrañaga, M., & Lasa, A. (2024). A collaborative AR application for education: From architecture design to user evaluation. *Virtual Reality (Waltham Cross)*, *28*(1), 1–13. DOI: 10.1007/s10055-024-00952-x

Masood, M., Nazir, T., Nawaz, M., Javed, A., Iqbal, M., & Mehmood, A. (2021). Brain tumor localization and segmentation using mask RCNN. *Frontiers of Computer Science*, *15*(6), 156338. DOI: 10.1007/s11704-020-0105-y

Masood, M., Nazir, T., Nawaz, M., Mehmood, A., Rashid, J., Kwon, H. Y., Mahmood, T., & Hussain, A. (2021). A novel deep learning method for recognition and classification of brain tumors from MRI images. *Diagnostics (Basel)*, *11*(5), 744. DOI: 10.3390/diagnostics11050744 PMID: 33919358

Mayer, R. E., & Bailenson, J. N. (2024, October). Advances in research on learning in immersive virtual reality. *Technology, Mind, and Behavior*, *5*(4), 173–175. Advance online publication. DOI: 10.1037/tmb0000146

McKinsey & Company. (2022). Value creation in the metaverse. https://www.mckinsey.com/capabilities/growth-marketing-and-sales/our-insights/value-creation-in-the-metaverse

Mehnatkesh, H., Jalali, S. M. J., Khosravi, A., & Nahavandi, S. (2023). An intelligent driven deep residual learning framework for brain tumor classification using MRI images. *Expert Systems with Applications*, *213*, 119087. DOI: 10.1016/j.eswa.2022.119087

Mehra, V., Singh, P., Mehra, M., Albanna, H., & Dwivedi, Y. K. (2023). Exploring the fusion of Metaverse and sports: Current trends and future directions. In *International Working Conference on Transfer and Diffusion of IT* (pp. 258-268). Cham: Springer Nature Switzerland.

Mehrabi, N., Morstatter, F., Saxena, N., Lerman, K., & Galstyan, A. (2021). A Survey on Bias and Fairness in Machine Learning. *ACM Computing Surveys*, *54*(6), 1–35. DOI: 10.1145/3457607

Mehta, P., & Subramanian, C. V. (2023, October 12). RIGHT TO LIFE AND HOUSING POLICIES IN INDIA: AN UNDERSTANDING OF HOUSING POLICIES SINCE INDEPENDENCE. One- Day International Conference on Changing Dimensions of Human Rights : Contemporary and Upcoming Role.

Mehta, P., & Subramanian, C. V. (2024). A Study of Rental Housing and Its Policies for the Urban Poor in India. In Nandineni, R. D., Ang, S., & Mohd Nawawi, N. B. (Eds.), *Sustainable Resilient Built Environments* (pp. 687–698). Springer Nature Singapore., DOI: 10.1007/978-981-99-8811-2_58

Mehta, P., & Subramanian, C. V. (2025). AN INTERSECTIONAL THEORETICAL ANALYSIS OF THE SOCIOLOGICAL IMPACT OF RENTAL HOUSING POLICIES ON THE URBAN POOR. *Journal of Applied Bioanalysis*, •••, 10–20. DOI: 10.53555/jab.v11i3.217

Meijer, A., & Bolívar, M. P. R. (2016). Governing the smart city: A review of the literature on smart urban governance. *International Review of Administrative Sciences*, *82*(2), 392–408. DOI: 10.1177/0020852314564308

Miles, M. P. (2017). A taxonomy of research gaps: Identifying and defining the seven research gaps. *Journal of Research in Marketing and Entrepreneurship*, *19*(1), 2–8.

Milgram, P., Takemura, H., Utsumi, A., & Kishino, F. (1995, December). Augmented reality: A class of displays on the reality-virtuality continuum. In *Telemanipulator and telepresence technologies* (Vol. 2351, pp. 282–292). Spie. DOI: 10.1117/12.197321

Ming Yip, N. (2001). Tenant participation and the management of public housing - The Estate Management Advisory Committee of Hong Kong. *Property Management*, *19*(1), 10–18. DOI: 10.1108/02637470110366176

Ministry of Housing & Urban Affairs. (2020). ARHC [Policy concept note]. https://arhc.mohua.gov.in/

Ministry of Skill Development & Entrepreneurship. (n.d.). Skill India Digital Hub (SIDH). Retrieved https://www.skillindiadigital.gov.in/home

Mitchell, D. (2003). *The right to the city: Social justice and the fight for public space*. Guilford Press.

Mittelstadt, B. (2021). Principles alone cannot guarantee ethical AI. *Nature Machine Intelligence*, *1*(11), 501–507. DOI: 10.1038/s42256-019-0114-4

Mittelstadt, B. D., Allo, P., Taddeo, M., Wachter, S., & Floridi, L. (2016). The ethics of algorithms: Mapping the debate. *Big Data & Society*, *3*(2), 1–21. DOI: 10.1177/2053951716679679

Mogaji, I. M., & Newton, P. (2020). School leadership for sustainable development: A scoping review. *Journal of Sustainable Development*, *13*(5), 15–30. DOI: 10.5539/jsd.v13n5p15

Mohsen, H., El-Dahshan, E. S. A., El-Horbaty, E. S. M., & Salem, A. B. M. (2018). Classification using deep learning neural networks for brain tumors. *Future Computing and Informatics Journal, 3*(1), 68–71. DOI: 10.1016/j.fcij.2017.12.001

Monaco, S., & Sacchi, G. (2023). Travelling the Metaverse: Potential benefits and main challenges for tourism sectors and research applications. *Sustainability (Basel), 15*(4), 3348. DOI: 10.3390/su15043348

Moro Visconti, R., & Piroli, G. (2023). Virtual reality, augmented reality and education: The new frontiers of immersive learning. *Education and Information Technologies, 28*(5), 4561–4579. DOI: 10.1007/s10639-022-11577-8

Mukherjee, A., Dasgupta, S., & Das, A. (n.d.). State of Urban Poor Rental Housing in India and Emerging Policy Trends.

Mundru, Y., Yogi, M. K., & Chatterjee, J. M. (2023). Application of Deep-Q learning in personalized health care Internet of Things ecosystem. In *Deep Learning in Personalized Healthcare and Decision Support* (pp. 39–47). Academic Press. DOI: 10.1016/B978-0-443-19413-9.00024-2

Mystakidis, S. (2022). Metaverse. *Encyclopedia, 2*(1), 486–497. DOI: 10.3390/encyclopedia2010031

Naik, M. (2015). Informal Rental Housing Typologies and Experiences of Low-income Migrant Renters in Gurgaon, India. *Environment & Urbanization Asia, 6*(2), 154–175. DOI: 10.1177/0975425315591425

Nakamura, L. (2015). The unwanted labour of social media: Women of color call out culture as venture capital. *New Formations, 86*, 106–112. DOI: 10.3898/NEWF.86.06.2015

Nam, T., & Pardo, T. (2011). Conceptualizing smart city with dimensions of technology, people, and institutions. In *Proceedings of the 12th Annual International Digital Government Research Conference* (pp. 282–291). ACM. DOI: 10.1145/2037556.2037602

Naranjo, P. G., Shojafar, M., Mostafaei, H., Pooranian, Z., & Baccarelli, E. (2016). Big data streaming applications scheduling in datacenter: A survey. *Journal of Parallel and Distributed Computing, 89*, 1–16. DOI: 10.1016/j.jpdc.2015.11.015

Naser, M. A., & Deen, M. J. (2020). Brain tumor segmentation and grading of lower-grade glioma using deep learning in MRI images. *Computers in Biology and Medicine, 121*, 103758. DOI: 10.1016/j.compbiomed.2020.103758 PMID: 32568668

National Urban Housing & Habitat Policy. (2007). *National Urban Rental Housing Policy*. Draft.

Nation, S. (2024). *2.0: A thriving Digital future for all*. Ministry of Digital Development and Information., https://file.go.gov.sg/smartnation2-report.pdf

Nguyen, N., Muilu, T., Dirin, A., & Alamäki, A. (2018). An interactive and augmented learning concept for orientation week in higher education. *International Journal of Educational Technology in Higher Education*, *15*(1), 35. DOI: 10.1186/s41239-018-0118-x

Ning, H., Wang, H., & Lin, Y.. (2021). A survey on metaverse: The state of the art, technologies, applications, and challenges. *IEEE Internet of Things Journal*, *10*(2), 1426–1458.

Ning, H., Wang, H., Lin, Y., Wang, W., Dhelim, S., Farha, F., Ding, J., & Daneshmand, M. (2021). A survey on metaverse: The state-of-the-art, technologies, applications, and challenges. *IEEE Internet of Things Journal*, *10*(4), 2927–2946. DOI: 10.1109/JIOT.2021.3124546

Ning, H., Xu, Y., & Wang, R. (2023). A Survey on Security, Privacy, and Trust in the Metaverse. *Digital Communications and Networks*, *9*(3), 380–396.

Nissenbaum, H. (2010). *Privacy in context: Technology, policy, and the integrity of social life*. Stanford University Press.

Niyas, S., Pawan, S. J., Kumar, M. A., & Rajan, J. (2022). Medical image segmentation with 3D convolutional neural networks: A survey. *Neurocomputing*, *493*, 397–413. DOI: 10.1016/j.neucom.2022.04.065

Nowak, K., & Fox, J. (2018). Avatars and computer-mediated communication. In *The Oxford handbook of networked communication*. Oxford University Press.

Nowell, L. S., Norris, J. M., White, D. E., & Moules, N. J. (2017). Thematic analysis: Striving to meet the trustworthiness criteria. *International Journal of Qualitative Methods*, *16*(1), 1–13. DOI: 10.1177/1609406917733847

O'Neill, C., Rua, S., & Rodriguez, C. (2022). Virtual worlds and metaverse ethics: A comprehensive framework for digital governance. *Journal of Virtual Worlds Research*, *15*(2), 1–28. DOI: 10.4101/jwwr.v15i2.7456

OECD. (2019). *Artificial intelligence in society*. OECD Publishing., DOI: 10.1787/eedfee77-

Oh, S. Y., & Bailenson, J. (2017). Virtual reality. *The Journal of Communication*, *67*(5), 703–708. DOI: 10.1111/jcom.12393

Ølnes, S., Ubacht, J., & Janssen, M. (2017). Blockchain in government: Benefits and Implications of distributed ledger technology for information sharing. *Government Information Quarterly*, *34*(3), 355–364. DOI: 10.1016/j.giq.2017.09.007

Onu, P., Pradhan, A., & Mbohwa, C. (2023). Potential to use metaverse for future teaching and learning. *Education and Information Technologies*, *29*(7), 8893–8924. DOI: 10.1007/s10639-023-12167-9

Operational-Guidelines-of-PMAY-U-2.pdf. (n.d.). Retrieved December 17, 2024, from https://pmay-urban.gov.in/uploads/guidelines/Operational-Guidelines-of-PMAY-U-2.pdf

Owojori, S. (2023). Metaverse Seoul: Exploring virtual public services and citizen participation. *Smart Cities*, *6*(4), 221–240. DOI: 10.3390/smartcities6040011

Ozorhon, G., & Sarman, G. (2023). The architectural design studio: A case in the intersection of the conventional and the new. Journal of Design Studio. DOI: 10.46474/jds.1394851

Pamucar, D., Deveci, M., Gokasar, I., Tavana, M., & Köppen, M. (2022). A Metaverse assessment model for sustainable transportation using ordinal priority approach and Aczel-Alsina norms. *Technological Forecasting and Social Change*, *182*, 121778. DOI: 10.1016/j.techfore.2022.121778

Panda, G. K., Mishra, D., & Nayak, S. (2024). Comprehensive Study on Social Trust with XAI Techniques, Evaluation, and Future Directions, Explainable, Interpretable, and Transparent AI Systems edited by B.K. Tripathy, Hari Seetha, 1st Edition, CRC Press. DOI: 10.1201/9781003442509

Parasuraman, A., Zeithaml, V. A., & Malhotra, A. (2005). ES-QUAL: A multiple-item scale for assessing electronic service quality. *Journal of Service Research*, *7*(3), 213–233. DOI: 10.1177/1094670504271156

Park, S. M., & Kim, Y. G. (2022). A metaverse: Taxonomy, components, applications, and open challenges. *IEEE Access : Practical Innovations, Open Solutions*, *10*, 4209–4251. DOI: 10.1109/ACCESS.2021.3140175

Pasupuleti, M. K. (2025). Next-generation extended reality (XR): A unified framework for integrating AR, VR, and AI-driven immersive technologies. *New Emerging Science*, *X*. Advance online publication. DOI: 10.62311/nesx/rrv325

Patel, R., Kumar, A., & Singh, D. (2022). Cross-reality data sovereignty: Legal and technical frameworks for metaverse governance. *Information and Computer Security*, *30*(4), 512–538. DOI: 10.1108/ICS-11-2021-0178

Pedada, K. R., Rao, B., Patro, K. K., Allam, J. P., Jamjoom, M. M., & Samee, N. A. (2023). A novel approach for brain tumor detection using deep learning based technique. *Biomedical Signal Processing and Control*, *82*, 104549. DOI: 10.1016/j.bspc.2022.104549

Pellegrino, A., Wang, R., & Stasi, A. (2023). Exploring the intersection of sustainable consumption and the Metaverse: A review of current literature and future research directions. *Heliyon*, *9*(9), e19190. DOI: 10.1016/j.heliyon.2023.e19190 PMID: 37681133

Peters, K., Elands, B., & Buijs, A. (2010). Social interactions in urban parks: Stimulating social cohesion? *Urban Forestry & Urban Greening*, *9*(2), 93–100. DOI: 10.1016/j.ufug.2009.11.003

Peukert, C., Weinhardt, C., Hinz, O., & van der Aalst, W. M. (2022). Metaverse: How to approach its challenges from a BISE perspective. *Business & Information Systems Engineering*, *64*(4), 401–406. DOI: 10.1007/s12599-022-00765-9

Phattanaviroj, T., Moslehpour, M., & Walawalkar, A. M. (2024). Data ethics and privacy. In *Challenges in Large Language Model Development and AI Ethics* (pp. 321–353). IGI Global. DOI: 10.4018/979-8-3693-3860-5.ch010

Pienwisetkaew, T., Wongsaichia, S., Pinyosap, B., Prasertsil, S., Poonsakpaisarn, K., & Ketkaew, C. (2023). The behavioral intention to adopt circular economy-based digital technology for agricultural waste valorization. *Foods*, *12*(12), 2341. DOI: 10.3390/foods12122341 PMID: 37372552

Pine, B. J., & Gilmore, J. H. (1999). *The experience economy: Work is theatre & every business a stage*. Harvard Business Press.

Popay, J., Roberts, H., Sowden, A., Petticrew, M., Arai, L., Rodgers, M., & Duffy, S. (2006). *Guidance on the conduct of narrative synthesis in systematic reviews*. ESRC Methods Programme.

Porambage, P., Okwuibe, J., Liyanage, M., Ylianttila, M., & Taleb, T. (2018). Survey on multi-access edge computing for Internet of Things realization. *IEEE Communications Surveys and Tutorials*, *20*(4), 2961–2991. DOI: 10.1109/COMST.2018.2849509

Prajescu, A. I., & Confalonieri, R. (2025) Argumentation-Based Explainability for Legal AI: Comparative and Regulatory Perspectives. arXiv preprint arXiv:2510.11079.

Prandi, C., ... (2021). *On supporting university communities in indoor wayfinding*. *Sensors* / PubMed Central. https://www.ncbi.nlm.nih.gov/pmc/articles/PMC8124871/

Priemus, H., & Dieleman, F. (2002). Social Housing Policy in the European Union: Past, Present and Perspectives. *Urban Studies (Edinburgh, Scotland)*, *39*(2), 191–200. DOI: 10.1080/00420980120102911

Priyadarshini, P., Kanungo, P., & Kar, T. (2024). Multigrade brain tumor classification in MRI images using Fine tuned efficientnet. e-Prime-Advances in Electrical Engineering. *Electronics and Energy*, *8*, 100498.

Puglia, D., Pezzolla, D., Gigliotti, G., Torre, L., Bartucca, M. L., & Del Buono, D. (2021). The Opportunity of Valorizing Agricultural Waste, Through Its Conversion into Biostimulants, Biofertilizers, and Biopolymers. *Sustainability (Basel)*, *13*(5), 2710. DOI: 10.3390/su13052710

Purcell, M. (2002). Excavating Lefebvre: The right to the city and its urban politics of the inhabitant. *GeoJournal*, *58*(2–3), 99–108. DOI: 10.1023/B:GEJO.0000010829.62237.8f

PwC. (2023). Metaverse: The next frontier for business. https://www.pwc.com/gx/en/issues/analytics/assets/pwc-making-the-metaverse-real-report.pdf

Qayyum, A., Al-Fuqaha, A., Imran, M. A., Halabi, O., Qadir, J., Abbasi, Q. H., Usman, M., Ali, H., & Butt, M. A. (2024). Secure and Trustworthy Artificial Intelligence-extended Reality (AI-XR) for Metaverses. *ACM Computing Surveys*, *56*(7), 1–38. DOI: 10.1145/3614426

Queiroz, M. M., Fosso Wamba, S., Pereira, S. C. F., & Chiappetta Jabbour, C. J. (2023). The Metaverse as a breakthrough for operations and supply chain management: Implications and call for action. *International Journal of Operations & Production Management*, *43*(10), 1539–1553. DOI: 10.1108/IJOPM-01-2023-0006

Radhakrishna, G. (2022). Legal Issues with Real Estate in the Metaverse. In Adam, Y. C., & Abdull Manaf, A. W. B. (Eds.), *Proceedings of the International Conference on Law and Digitalization (ICLD 2022)* (pp. 74–82). Atlantis Press SARL. DOI: 10.2991/978-2-494069-59-6_7

Radianti, J., Majchrzak, T. A., Fromm, J., & Wohlgenannt, I. (2020). A systematic review of immersive virtual reality applications for higher education. *Computers & Education*, *147*, 103778. DOI: 10.1016/j.compedu.2019.103778

Radianti, J., Majchrzak, T. A., Fromm, J., & Wohlgenannt, I. (2020). A systematic review of immersive virtual reality applications for higher education. *Education and Information Technologies*, *25*, 1–38. DOI: 10.1007/s10639-019-10003-6

Rafique, W., & Qadir, J. (2024). Internet of everything meets the metaverse: Bridging physical and virtual worlds with blockchain. *Computer Science Review*, *54*, 100678. DOI: 10.1016/j.cosrev.2024.100678

Rahman, T., & Islam, M. S. (2023). MRI brain tumor detection and classification using parallel deep convolutional neural networks. *Measurement. Sensors*, *26*, 100694. DOI: 10.1016/j.measen.2023.100694

Rajguru, K., & Brüggemann, P. (2024). Sustainability meets Metaverse: A conceptual framework of sustainable dimensions of the Metaverse. *Journal of Consumer Behaviour*, *23*(5), 2720–2729. DOI: 10.1002/cb.2368

Raji, I. D., & Buolamwini, J. (2019). *Actionable Auditing: Investigating the Impact of Publicly Naming Biased Performance Results of Commercial AI Products.* Proceedings of the AAAI/ACM Conference on AI, Ethics, and Society, 429–435. DOI: 10.1145/3306618.3314244

Raji, I. D., Smart, A., White, R. N., Mitchell, M., Gebru, T., Hutchinson, B., Smith-Loud, J., Theron, D., & Barnes, P. (2020). Closing the AI accountability gap: Defining an end-to-end framework for internal algorithmic auditing. In *Proceedings of the 2020 Conference on Fairness, Accountability, and Transparency* (pp. 33–44). ACM. DOI: 10.1145/3351095.3372873

Rauschnabel, P. A., Felix, R., Hinsch, C., Shahab, H., & Alt, F. (2022). What is XR? Towards a framework for augmented and virtual reality. *Computers in Human Behavior*, *133*, 107289. DOI: 10.1016/j.chb.2022.107289

Ravindra Prasad, D., & Malla Reddy, A. (1994). Environmental improvement of urban slums: The Indian experience : an evaluation of Environmental Improvement of Urban Slums Programme in South Indian states. Regional Centre for Urban and Environmental Studies, Osmania University, Hyderabad, and Booklinks Corp.

Razzaq, A., Alreshidi, A., Ahmed, S., Ghayyur, S. A. K., Zhang, T., Jing, C., Qurat Ul Ain, M., Aljaloud, A., & Numair, M. (2024). Transforming academic assessment: The metaverse-backed Web 3 secure exam system. *Computer Applications in Engineering Education*, *32*(6), e22797. DOI: 10.1002/cae.22797

Rehman, S. U., Kim, I., & Hwang, K.-E. (2025). Advancing BIM and game engine integration in the AEC industry: Innovations, challenges, and future directions. *Journal of Computational Design and Engineering*, *12*(4), 26–54. DOI: 10.1093/jcde/qwaf030

Reibstein, D. J., & Iyengar, R. (2023). Metaverse—Will it change the world or be a whole new world in and of itself? *AMS Review*, *13*(1), 144–150. DOI: 10.1007/s13162-023-00258-2

Reinhold, J. Dropout on convolutional layers is weird. Medium, Data Science (2019) [cited 2022Aug14]. Available from: https://towardsdatascience.com/dropout-on-convolutional-layers-is-weird-5c6ab14f19b2

Rejeb, A., Rejeb, K., & Treiblmaier, H. (2023). Mapping Metaverse Research: Identifying Future Research Areas Based on Bibliometric and Topic Modelling Techniques. *Information (Basel)*, *14*(7), 356. DOI: 10.3390/info14070356

Riaz, Z., Parn, E. A., Edwards, D. J., Arslan, M., Shen, C., & Pena-Mora, F. (2017). BIM and sensor-based data management system for construction safety monitoring. *Journal of Engineering, Design and Technology*, *15*(6), 738–753. DOI: 10.1108/JEDT-03-2017-0017

Richter, S., & Richter, A. (2023). What is novel about the Metaverse? *International Journal of Information Management*, *73*, 102684. DOI: 10.1016/j.ijinfomgt.2023.102684

Riskiyanto, R. (2023). Material-based learning in architecture design studio: From 'Beaux-Arts' to 'Bauhaus' into current educational era. Journal of Architectural Design and Urbanism. DOI: 10.14710/jadu.v5i2.18448

Rizzo, A. A., & Koenig, S. T. (2017). Is clinical virtual reality ready for primetime? *Neuropsychology*, *31*(8), 877–899. DOI: 10.1037/neu0000405 PMID: 29376669

Roberts, S., et al. (2020). Designing in virtual environments: The integration of virtual reality tools into industrial design research and education.

Rodias, E., Aivazidou, E., Achillas, C., Aidonis, D., & Bochtis, D. (2020). Water-Energy-Nutrients Synergies in the Agrifood Sector: A Circular Economy Framework. *Energies*, *14*(1), 159. DOI: 10.3390/en14010159

Rodríguez, A. M. L. (2024). Towards a Lex Metaversi? The law applicable to virtual real estate in the metaverse. *Interactive Entertainment Law Review*, *7*(2), 110–121. DOI: 10.4337/ielr.2024.02.05

Romli, R., Yew, C. C., Ghazali, N. H., Zahri, N. A. H., Amir, A., & Hasnan, R. (2024, May). AR@ campus: Augmented reality (AR) for indoor positioning and navigation apps. In AIP conference proceedings (Vol. 3135, No. 1, p. 040002). AIP Publishing LLC.

Roy, D. Meera ML, Haque, I., & Gupta, E. (2022). Institutional provisioning of affordable rental housing in urban India. In Policy Series by ICRIER & Ford Foundation. ICRIER. https://icrier.org/pdf/Rental-policy-series_261222.pdf

Rurianto, J., Sumarwan, U., Suharjo, B., & Hasanah, N. (2021). Sustainable value co-creation in mobile advertising in cellular telecommunication industry: A conceptual framework. [IJBE]. *Indonesian Journal of Business and Entrepreneurship, 7*(2), 172–172. DOI: 10.17358/ijbe.7.2.172

Russo, A. (2020). Superblocks: Reclaiming public space in Barcelona. *Sustainable Cities and Society, 52*, 101864. Advance online publication. DOI: 10.1016/j.scs.2019.101864

Saba, T., Mohamed, A. S., El-Affendi, M., Amin, J., & Sharif, M. (2020). Brain tumor detection using fusion of hand crafted and deep learning features. *Cognitive Systems Research, 59*, 221–230. DOI: 10.1016/j.cogsys.2019.09.007

Saha, D., Banerji, H., & Kumar, U. (2025). Critical Success Barriers (CSB) to Rental Housing Policy Implementation in Urban India. *Journal of Contemporary Urban Affairs, 9*(1). Advance online publication. DOI: 10.25034/ijcua.2025.v9n1-4

Sala, N. (2021). *Virtual Reality, Augmented Reality, and Mixed Reality in Education: A brief overview.* In *Current and prospective applications of virtual reality in higher education* (Chapter 3). IGI Global. DOI: 10.4018/978-1-7998-4960-5.ch003

Salamat, N., Missen, M. M. S., & Surya Prasath, V. B. (2021). Recent developments in computational color image denoising with PDEs to deep learning: A review. *Artificial Intelligence Review, 54*(8), 6245–6276. DOI: 10.1007/s10462-021-09977-z

Saranya, A., & Subhashini, R. (2023). *A systematic review of Explainable Artificial Intelligence models and applications: Recent developments and future trends* (Vol. 7). Decision Analytics Journal.

Sarpong, S., & Alarussi, A. S. (2022). Waste to wealth: Enhancing circularities in the Malaysian economy. *Technological Sustainability, 1*(2), 145–159. DOI: 10.1108/TECHS-01-2022-0001

Scanlon, K., Whitehead, C., & Arrigoitia, M. F. (Eds.). (2014). *Social Housing in Europe* (1st ed.). Wiley., DOI: 10.1002/9781118412367

Schroeder, R. (2016). *Social theory after the Internet: Media, technology, and globalization*. UCL Press.

Schwartz, A. F. (2021). *Housing Policy in the United States* (4th ed.). Routledge., DOI: 10.4324/9781003097501

Sedlmeir, J., Buhl, H. U., Fridgen, G., & Keller, R. (2020). The energy consumption of blockchain technology: Beyond myth. *Business & Information Systems Engineering, 62*(6), 599–608. DOI: 10.1007/s12599-020-00656-x

Selwyn, N. (2016). *Education and technology: Key issues and debates*. Bloomsbury Academic.

Sen, S., & Kumar, G. (2023, March 8). The Metaverse: A Tech and Policy Brief For India. National Law School of India University, Bengaluru. https://www.nls.ac.in/publications/the-metaverse-a-tech-and-policy-brief-for-india/

Sennett, R. (2018). *Building and dwelling: Ethics for the city*. Farrar, Straus and Giroux.

Sennett, R. (2018). *The corrosion of character: The personal consequences of work in the new capitalism*. W. W. Norton & Company.

Seoul to provide public services through its own metaverse platform. (2021, November 5). Seoul Metropolitan Government. https://english.seoul.go.kr/seoul-to-provide-public-services-through-its-own-metaverse-platform/

Shandilya, S. K., Singh, Y., Izonin, I., & Hentosh, L. (2024). Metaverse forensics framework: A NIST based investigation framework for metaverse. *Science & Justice : Journal of the Forensic Science Society, 64*(6), 698–709. DOI: 10.1016/j.scijus.2024.10.005 PMID: 39638489

Sharifi, A.. (2021). A critical review of smart city development in India. *Sustainable Cities and Society, 72*, 103045. Advance online publication. DOI: 10.1016/j.scs.2021.103045

Sharifi, A., & Amirzadeh, A. (2025). The metaverse as a future form of smart cities: Co-benefits and trade-offs for sustainable development goals. *Cities (London, England)*. Advance online publication. DOI: 10.1016/j.cities.2025.105879

Sharma, A. K., Nandal, A., Dhaka, A., Zhou, L., Alhudhaif, A., Alenezi, F., & Polat, K. (2023). Brain tumor classification using the modified ResNet50 model based on transfer learning. *Biomedical Signal Processing and Control, 86*, 105299. DOI: 10.1016/j.bspc.2023.105299

Sharma, R., Kumar, P., & Arora, A. (2022). Internet of Things (IoT) applications in education: A survey. *Education and Information Technologies, 27*(2), 1719–1743. DOI: 10.1007/s10639-021-10659-1

Sharma, S. (2023). Analysing For Affordable Rental Housing Policies and Parameters in India. *International Journal of Advances in Engineering and Management*, *5*(4), 1473–1485. DOI: 10.35629/5252-050414731485

Sim, Y. W., & Jung, E.-C. (2025). Comparative analysis of hand and VR sketching: Impact of immersion on idea generation in product design education. *International Journal of Technology and Design Education*. Advance online publication. DOI: 10.1007/s10798-025-10023-0

Singh, P., & Tiwari, S. "Digital Twins and Artificial Intelligence," in *Handbook of Industrial and Business Applications with Digital Twins*, 1st ed., Taylor and Francis, Dec. 2024, ch. 5, DOI: 10.1201/9781003465904-7

Slater, M., & Sanchez-Vives, M. V. (2016). Enhancing our lives with immersive virtual reality. *Frontiers in Robotics and AI*, *3*, 74. DOI: 10.3389/frobt.2016.00074

Smart, J., Cascio, J., & Paffendorf, J. (2007). *Metaverse roadmap: Pathways to the 3D web*. Metaverse Roadmap Report.

Soulikias, A., Cucuzzella, C., Nizar, F., Hazbei, M., & Goubran, S. (2021). We gain a lot… but what are we losing? A critical exploration of the implications of digital design technologies on sustainable architecture. *Open House International*, *46*(4), 548–562. DOI: 10.1108/OHI-04-2021-0085

Srivastava, A., & Sahu, G. P. (2023). The Impact of the Metaverse on Green Marketing: A Paradigm Shift in Sustainable Consumer Behaviour. In *International Working Conference on Transfer and Diffusion of IT* (pp. 443-457). Cham: Springer Nature Switzerland.

Srivastava, R., & Sutradhar, R. (2016). Labour Migration to the Construction Sector in India and Its Impact on Rural Poverty. *Indian Journal of Human Development*, *10*(1), 27–48. DOI: 10.1177/0973703016648028

Stankovic, J. A. (2020). Research directions for the Internet of Things. *IEEE Internet of Things Journal*, *7*(5), 4735–4745. DOI: 10.1109/JIOT.2020.2966951

Stephens, M., & Hick, R. (2024). Comparative housing research. In Jacobs, K., Flanagan, K., De Vries, J., & MacDonald, E. (Eds.), *Research Handbook on Housing, the Home and Society* (pp. 141–157). Edward Elgar Publishing., DOI: 10.4337/9781800375970.00017

Sujatha, R., Chatterjee, J. M., Angelopoulou, A., Kapetanios, E., Srinivasu, P. N., & Hemanth, D. J. (2023). A transfer learning-based system for grading breast invasive ductal carcinoma. *IET Image Processing*, *17*(7), 1979–1990. DOI: 10.1049/ipr2.12660

Suryakant, N. (2025). Constructivist 5E approach to information and communication technology (ICT) and challenges in education. *International Journal of Science and Research (Raipur, India)*, *14*(3), 1–6. DOI: 10.21275/SR25324135815

Sutton, R. S., & Barto, A. G. (2018). *Reinforcement learning: An introduction* (2nd ed.). MIT Press., DOI: 10.5555/3312046

Suttor, G. (2025). Housing Policy. In Béland, D., Mahon, R., & Smith, A. (Eds.), *The Oxford Handbook of Social Policy in Canada* (1st ed.). Oxford University Press., DOI: 10.1093/oxfordhb/9780197766859.013.0026

Swain, M., Kisan, S., Chatterjee, J. M., Supramaniam, M., Mohanty, S. N., Jhanjhi, N. Z., & Abdullah, A. (2020). Hybridized machine learning based fractal analysis techniques for breast cancer classification. *International Journal of Advanced Computer Science and Applications*, *11*(10), 179–184. DOI: 10.14569/IJACSA.2020.0111024

Tahir, M. (2022). URBAN BASIC SERVICES FOR THE POOR: CRITICAL EVALUATION AND ITS AVAILABILITY AND UTILISATION BY THE URBAN POOR. *International Journal of Multidisciplinary Research Review*, *8*(8), 50–61.

Talukder, M. A., Islam, M. M., Uddin, M. A., Akhter, A., Pramanik, M. A. J., Aryal, S., Almoyad, M. A. A., Hasan, K. F., & Moni, M. A. (2023). An efficient deep learning model to categorize brain tumor using reconstruction and fine-tuning. *Expert Systems with Applications*, *230*, 120534. DOI: 10.1016/j.eswa.2023.120534

Tandel, G. S., Tiwari, A., & Kakde, O. G. (2021). Performance optimization of deep learning models using majority voting algorithm for brain tumor classification. *Computers in Biology and Medicine*, *135*, 104564. DOI: 10.1016/j.compbiomed.2021.104564 PMID: 34217980

Tapscott, D., & Tapscott, A. (2018). *Blockchain revolution: How the technology behind bitcoin is changing money, business, and the world.* Penguin.

Taylor, B., Wilson, E., & Johnson, M. (2023). Consent mechanisms in AI-mediated virtual interactions: A user-centered design approach. *Interacting with Computers*, *35*(3), 289–307. DOI: 10.1093/iwc/iwac034

Taylor, T. L. (2006). *Play between worlds: Exploring online game culture.* MIT Press. DOI: 10.7551/mitpress/5418.001.0001

Tesseract. (2023). *JioDive: Step into the immersive world.* Retrieved from https://tesseract.in/jiodive/

The First Digital Twin City at the Neighborhood Level in Shanghai. Huamu Subdistrict. (2022, May 23). Urban Planning Society of China- City Initiatives. https://en.planning.org.cn/nua/view?id=646

The Model Tenancy Act. (2019). Retrieved https://mohua.gov.in/upload/whatsnew/5d25fb70671ebdraft%20Model%20Tenancy%20Act,%202019.pdf

The Slum Areas(Improvement and Clearance) Act. (1956). Retrieved https://www.indiacode.nic.in/bitstream/123456789/1709/1/195696.pdf

Tiwari, P., & Rao, J. (2016). Housing Markets and Housing Policies in India. 565. https://www.adb.org/publications/major-challenges-facing-small-and-medium-sizedenterprises-asia-and-solutions/

Tlili, A., Huang, R., Shehata, B., Liu, D., Zhao, J., Metwally, A., Wang, H., Denden, M., Bozkurt, A., Lee, L., Beyoglu, D., Altınay, F., Sharma, R., Altınay, Z., Li, Z., Liu, J., Ahmad, F., Hu, Y., Salha, S., & Burgos, D. (2022). Is metaverse in education a blessing or a curse: A combined content and bibliometric analysis. *Smart Learning Environments*, *9*(1), 24. Advance online publication. DOI: 10.1186/s40561-022-00205-x

Toma, M.-V., Turcu, C. O., & Pascu, P. (2025, January). Evaluating user acceptance and usability of AR-based indoor navigation in a university setting: An empirical study. *International Journal of Advanced Computer Science and Applications*, *16*(4). Advance online publication. DOI: 10.14569/IJACSA.2025.0160406

Toprak, İ., & Hacihasanoglu, O. (2019). Terms and concepts on design studio in the research articles of 2010's. *Journal of Design Studio*, *1*(2), 13–22.

Townsend, A. (2013). *Smart cities: Big data, civic hackers, and the quest for a new utopia*. W. W. Norton.

Tran, T. T. M., ... (2024). *Simulating wearable urban augmented reality: Assessing risks and safety concerns via VR. arXiv preprint.* https://arxiv.org/abs/2402.04576

Tran, T. T. M., Parker, C., Hoggenmüller, M., Hespanhol, L., & Tomitsch, M. (2023). Simulating wearable urban augmented reality experiences in VR: Lessons learnt from designing two future urban interfaces. *Multimodal Technologies and Interaction*, *7*(2), 21. DOI: 10.3390/mti7020021

Truby, J. (2018). Decarbonizing Bitcoin: Law and policy choices for reducing the energy consumption of blockchain technologies and digital currencies. *Energy Research & Social Science*, *44*, 399–410. DOI: 10.1016/j.erss.2018.06.009

Truong, V. T., Niyato, D., & Le, L. (2023). Blockchain Meets Metaverse and Digital Asset Management: A Comprehensive Survey. *IEEE Access : Practical Innovations, Open Solutions, 11*, 26258–26288. DOI: 10.1109/ACCESS.2023.3257029

Tseng, S.-S., Chen, S.-N., & Yang, T.-Y. (2021). Building an AR-based smart campus platform. *Multimedia Tools and Applications, 80*(28), 35333–35352. DOI: 10.1007/s11042-021-11702-5

Tukur, M., Schneider, J., Househ, M., Dokoro, A., Ismail, U., Dawaki, M., & Agus, M. (2024). The metaverse digital environments: A scoping review of the techniques, technologies, and applications. *Journal of King Saud University. Computer and Information Sciences, 36*(2), 101967. DOI: 10.1016/j.jksuci.2024.101967

Turkanović, M., Hölbl, M., Košič, K., Heričko, M., & Kamišalić, A. (2018). EduCTX: A blockchain-based higher education credit platform. *IEEE Access : Practical Innovations, Open Solutions, 6*, 5112–5127. DOI: 10.1109/ACCESS.2018.2789929

Turkle, S. (2017). *Alone together: Why we expect more from technology and less from each other*. Basic Books.

Ujang, N., & Zakariya, K. (2015). The notion of place, place meaning and identity in urban regeneration. *Procedia: Social and Behavioral Sciences, 170*, 709–717. DOI: 10.1016/j.sbspro.2015.01.073

Umar, A. (2022). Metaverse for UN SDGs–an exploratory study. In *Science-Policy Brief for the Multistakeholder Forum on Science, Technology and Innovation for the SDGs* (Vol. 5).

Ummihusna, A., & Zairul, M. (2022). Exploring immersive learning technology as learning tools in experiential learning for architecture design education. *Open House International, 47*(4), 605–619. Advance online publication. DOI: 10.1108/OHI-01-2022-0020

UNESCO. (2020). *Global education monitoring report 2020: Inclusion and education*. UNESCO Publishing.

UN-Habitat (Ed.). (2003). Rental housing: An essential option for the urban poor in developing countries (Reprod. without formal ed. by the United Nations).

United Nations Department of Economic and Social Affairs. (2019). World Urbanization Prospects: The 2018 Revision. UN. DOI: 10.18356/b9e995fe-en

Uzun, M. M. (2023). Metaverse Governance. In Esen, F. S., Tinmaz, H., & Singh, M. (Eds.), *Metaverse* (Vol. 133, pp. 231–244). Springer Nature Singapore., DOI: 10.1007/978-981-99-4641-9_16

Vanhuyse, F., Fejzić, E., Ddiba, D., & Henrysson, M. (2021). The lack of social impact considerations in transitioning towards urban circular economies: A scoping review. *Sustainable Cities and Society*, *75*, 103394. DOI: 10.1016/j.scs.2021.103394

Vankdothu, R., & Hameed, M. A. (2022). Brain tumor segmentation of MR images using SVM and fuzzy classifier in machine learning. *Measurement. Sensors*, *24*, 100440. DOI: 10.1016/j.measen.2022.100440

Vargo, S. L., & Lusch, R. F. (2008). Service-dominant logic: Continuing the evolution. *Journal of the Academy of Marketing Science*, *36*(1), 1–10. DOI: 10.1007/s11747-007-0069-6

Vasavi, G., Rani, V. V., Ponnada, S., & Jyothi, S. (2025). A hybrid EfficientNet-DbneAlexnet for brain tumor detection using MRI images. *Computational Biology and Chemistry*, *115*, 108279. DOI: 10.1016/j.compbiolchem.2024.108279 PMID: 39631224

Velasco-Muñoz, J. F., Mendoza, J. M. F., Aznar-Sánchez, J. A., & Gallego-Schmid, A. (2021). Circular economy implementation in the agricultural sector: Definition, strategies and indicators. *Resources, Conservation and Recycling*, *170*, 105618. DOI: 10.1016/j.resconrec.2021.105618

Veletsianos, G., & Houlden, S. (2019). An analysis of MOOCs: Limitations, benefits, and emerging directions. *International Review of Research in Open and Distance Learning*, *20*(3), 35–50.

Vieira, R.. (2020). Integrating participatory mapping and smart-city dashboards. *Journal of Urban Technology*, *27*(2), 3–26. DOI: 10.1080/10630732.2019.1699449

Villegas-Ch, W., García-Ortiz, J., & Sánchez-Viteri, S. (2024). Educational advances in the metaverse: Boosting learning through virtual and augmented reality and artificial intelligence. *IEEE Access : Practical Innovations, Open Solutions*, *12*, 59093–59112. DOI: 10.1109/ACCESS.2024.3393776

Vladimirova, D. (2016). Waste to wealth: The circular economy advantage. Production Planning &amp. *Production Planning and Control*, *28*(4), 349–349. DOI: 10.1080/09537287.2016.1249131

Vrbačič, G., Pečnik, Š., & Podgorelec, V. (2022). Hyper-parameter optimization of convolutional neural networks for classifying COVID-19 X-ray images. *Computer Science and Information Systems*, *19*(1), 327–352. DOI: 10.2298/CSIS210209056V

Wachter, S., Mittelstadt, B., & Russell, C. (2020). Counterfactual explanations without opening the black box: Automated decisions and the GDPR. *Harvard Journal of Law & Technology*, *31*(2), 841–887.

Wang, L., Zhu, J., Li, Q., Lei, B., Su, H., and, Zhong, Y. (2022). Triple-Memory Networks: A Brain-Inspired Method for Continual Learning. IEEE Transactions on Neural Networks and Learning Systems, 33(5), pp. 1925–1934. https://doi.org/. 3111019DOI: 10.1109/tnnls.2021

Wang, Y., & Zhao, J. (2022). Mobile Edge Computing, Metaverse, 6G Wireless Communications, Artificial Intelligence, and Blockchain: Survey and Their Convergence. Pp. 1–8. /arXiv.2209.14147DOI: 10.1109/WF-IoT54382.2022.10152245

Wang, X., Zhang, Y., Wang, G., Guo, L., Gao, X., Ning, Z., & Guo, Q. (2024). Integration of Sensing, Communication, and Computing for Metaverse: A Survey. *ACM Computing Surveys*, *56*(10), 1–38. DOI: 10.1145/3659946

Wang, Y., Su, Z., Zhang, N., & Shen, X. "A survey on Metaverse: Fundamentals, security, and privacy," *TechRxiv*, Mar. 2022, DOI: 10.36227/techrxiv.19255058.v1

Wei, D. (2022). An Online Extraction Algorithm for Image Feature Information Based on Convolutional Neural Network. *Mobile Information Systems*, *2022*, 1–11. Advance online publication. DOI: 10.1155/2022/1606438

Weiser, M., & Brown, J. S. (1997). The coming age of calm technology. *IEEE Pervasive Computing*, *1*(1), 1–5.

Wider, W., Jiang, L., Lin, J., Fauzi, M. A., Li, J., & Chan, C. K. (2024). Metaverse Chronicles: A bibliometric analysis of its evolving landscape. *International Journal of Human–Computer Interaction*, 40(17), pp. 4873–4886. https://doi.org/. 2023.2227825DOI: 10.1080/10447318

Wider, W., Jiang, L., Lin, J., Fauzi, M. A., Li, J., & Chan, C. K. (2023). Metaverse chronicles: A bibliometric analysis of its evolving landscape. *International Journal of Human-Computer Interaction*, *40*(17), 4873–4886.

Wider, W., Jiang, L., Lin, J., Fauzi, M. A., Li, J., & Chan, C. K. (2023). Metaverse Chronicles: A Bibliometric Analysis of Its Evolving Landscape. *International Journal of Human-Computer Interaction*, *40*(17), 4873–4886. DOI: 10.1080/10447318.2023.2227825

Williams, G., Charlton, S., Coelho, K., Mahadevia, D., & Meth, P. (2022). (Im) mobility at the margins: Low-income households' experiences of peripheral resettlement in India and South Africa. *Housing Studies*, *37*(6), 910–931. DOI: 10.1080/02673037.2021.1946018

Williams, J., Brown, A., Davis, C., & Miller, R. (2023). AI consciousness in virtual environments: Philosophical and practical considerations. *AI & Society*, *38*(2), 445–462. DOI: 10.1007/s00146-022-01456-8

Winfield, A. F., Michael, K., Pitt, J., & Evers, V. (2021). Machine ethics: The design and governance of ethical AI and autonomous systems. *Proceedings of the IEEE, 109*(4), 556–579. DOI: 10.1109/JPROC.2021.3070048

Wireless, F. (2025, March 10). *SK Telecom drops ifland metaverse service in favour of AI strategy*. https://www.fierce-network.com/operators/sk-telecom-drops-ifland-metaverse-service-favour-ai-strategy

World Economic Forum. (2023) Demystifying the Consumer Metaverse. https://www3.weforum.org/docs/WEF_Demystifying_the_Consumer_Metaverse.pdf

Wright, M., Ekeus, H., Coyne, R., Stewart, J., Travlou, P., & Williams, R. (2008, December). Augmented duality: overlapping a Metaverse with the real world. In *Proceedings of the 2008 international conference on advances in computer entertainment technology* (pp. 263-266). DOI: 10.1145/1501750.1501812

Wu, D., Yang, Z., Zhang, P., Wang, R., Ma, X., & Yang, B. (2023). Virtual-Reality Interpromotion Technology for Metaverse: A Survey. *IEEE Internet of Things Journal, 10*(18), 15788–15809. DOI: 10.1109/JIOT.2023.3265848

Xi, N., Chen, J., Gama, F., Riar, M., & Hamari, J. (2023). The challenges of entering the Metaverse: An experiment on the effect of extended reality on workload. *Information Systems Frontiers, 25*(2), 659–680. PMID: 35194390

Xin, Z., Haiying, W., Ping, K., Yiyao, S., & Haiou, L. (2022). A review of Metaverse research at home and abroad. *Journal of Modern Information, 12*, 147–159.

Xu, J., Papangelis, K., Dunham, J., Goncalves, J., LaLone, N. J., Chamberlain, A., . . . Schwartz, D. I. (2022, April). Metaverse: The vision for the future. In *CHI conference on human factors in computing systems extended abstracts* (pp. 1-3).

Xue, Z., Liang, J., Song, G., Zong, Z., Chen, L., Liu, Y., & Luo, P. (2022). Large-batch optimization for dense visual predictions. *Advances in Neural Information Processing Systems*, •••, 1.

Xu, J., Ma, J., Zhu, Z., & Gao, X. (2022). Adaptive Progressive Continual Learning. *IEEE Transactions on Pattern Analysis and Machine Intelligence, 44*(10), 6715–6728. DOI: 10.1109/TPAMI.2021.3095064 PMID: 34232867

Yang, M., Chen, L., Wang, J., Msigwa, G., Osman, A. I., Fawzy, S., Rooney, D. W., & Yap, P.-S. (2022). Circular economy strategies for combating climate change and other environmental issues. *Environmental Chemistry Letters, 21*(1), 55–80. DOI: 10.1007/s10311-022-01499-6

Yee, N., & Bailenson, J. N. (2007). The Proteus effect: The effect of transformed self-representation on behavior. *Human Communication Research, 33*(3), 271–290. DOI: 10.1111/j.1468-2958.2007.00299.x

Ye, X., Zhao, G., Peng, Q., Dawkins, C., Kim, J., & Wu, L. (2024). Global Trends in Housing Research over the Past three Decades. *Computational Urban Science, 4*(1), 17. DOI: 10.1007/s43762-024-00129-x

Yuan, X., Li, Y., & Wang, Y. (2023). A game engine based interactive and collaborative architectural education model proposal. In *International Conference on Innovative Academic Studies (Proceedings).*

Zainab, K., Iqbal, F., & Benjamin, C. M. F. (2024). Towards a unified XAI-based framework for digital forensic investigations, Forensic Science International. *Digital Investigation, 50*(Supplement.), •••.

Zawacki-Richter, O., Marín, V. I., Bond, M., & Gouverneur, F. (2019). Systematic review of research on artificial intelligence applications in higher education – Where are the educators? *International Journal of Educational Technology in Higher Education, 16*(1), 1–27. DOI: 10.1186/s41239-019-0171-0

Zhang, H., Mao, S., Han, Z., & Niyato, D. (2023). Location-Dependent Augmented Reality Services in Wireless Edge-Enabled Metaverse Systems. *IEEE Open Journal of the Communications Society, 4*, 171–183. DOI: 10.1109/OJCOMS.2023.3234254

Zhang, J., Xu, L., & Xu, Y. (2022). Accessibility design in the metaverse for learners with disabilities. *Computers & Education, 182*, 104468.

Zhang, L.. (2017). Data-driven intelligent transportation systems: A survey. *IEEE Transactions on Intelligent Transportation Systems, 18*(11), 3019–3032. DOI: 10.1109/TITS.2017.2680200

Zhang, Y. (2018). The credibility of slums: Informal housing and urban governance in India. *Land Use Policy, 79*, 876–890. DOI: 10.1016/j.landusepol.2017.05.029

Zhang, Y., He, X., & Li, C. (2023). XR Security: Protecting AR/VR Devices and Data in the Metaverse. *IEEE Internet of Things Journal, 10*(15), 13561–13575.

Zhang, Y., & Li, H. (2023). Augmented Reality-Based Indoor-Outdoor Campus Navigation System. *IEEE Access : Practical Innovations, Open Solutions.*

Zhang, Y., Liu, M., Wang, X., & Li, Q. (2022). Ethical frameworks for immersive virtual environments: A systematic review. *Virtual Reality (Waltham Cross), 26*(3), 1123–1142. DOI: 10.1007/s10055-021-00587-2

Zhao, Q.. (2022). Hybrid Localization Using Visual-Inertial Odometry and GPS for Mobile Navigation. *Sensors (Basel), 22*(8), 3201.

Zhong, R. Y., Xu, X., Klotz, E., & Newman, S. T. (2017). Intelligent manufacturing in the context of industry 4.0: A review. *Engineering (Beijing), 3*(5), 616–630. DOI: 10.1016/J.ENG.2017.05.015

Zuboff, S. (2019). *The age of surveillance capitalism*. PublicAffairs.

Zuboff, S. (2019). *The age of surveillance capitalism: The fight for a human future at the new frontier of power*. PublicAffairs.

Zuboff, S. (2020). *The Age of Surveillance Capitalism: The Fight for a Human Future at the New Frontier of Power*. PublicAffairs.

Zulfiqar, F., Bajwa, U. I., & Mehmood, Y. (2023). Multiclass classification of brain tumor types from MR images using EfficientNets. *Biomedical Signal Processing and Control, 84*, 104777. DOI: 10.1016/j.bspc.2023.104777

About the Contributors

Jyotir Chatterjee presently holds the position of Assistant Professor in the Department of Computer Science and Engineering at Graphic Era (Deemed to be University) in Dehradun, Uttarakhand, India. Additionally, he serves as an Assistant Professor (Visiting Faculty) in the Department of Information Technology at Lord Buddha Education Foundation, affiliated with the Asia Pacific University of Technology & Innovation, Malaysia, located in Kathmandu, Nepal. Before these roles, he held the position of Assistant Professor and Program Leader for the B.Sc. IT program at Lord Buddha Education Foundation. He also served as an Assistant Professor in the Computer Science and Engineering department at GD-Rungta College of Engineering & Technology, affiliated with Chhattisgarh Swami Vivekananda Technical University in Bhilai, India. Chatterjee earned his M. Tech degree in Computer Science & Engineering from Kalinga Institute of Industrial Technology (KIIT) in Bhubaneswar, Odisha, in 2016. He obtained his B. Tech degree in Computer Science & Engineering from Dr. MGR Educational & Research Institute in Maduravoyal, Chennai, in 2013. His research interests primarily lie in the domains of Machine Learning and Deep Learning. Specifically, he concentrates on advancing the fields of Deep Learning and Machine Learning through his research work, contributing to the ongoing developments in these areas.

Pawan Lingras is a graduate of IIT Bombay with graduate studies from the University of Regina. He is currently a Professor and the Director of Computing and Data Analytics at Saint Mary's University, Halifax. He is also involved with a number of international activities, having served as a visiting professor at Munich University of Applied Sciences and IIT Gandhinagar, as a research supervisor at Institut Superieur de Gestion de Tunis, as a University Grants Commission (India) Scholar-inResidence, and as a Shastri Indo-Canadian scholar. He has delivered more than 35 invited talks at various institutions around the world. He has authored more than 200 research papers in various international journals and conferences. He has also co-authored three textbooks, and co-edited two books and eight volumes of research papers. His academic collaborations/ co-authors include academics from Canada, Chile, China, Germany, India, Poland, Tunisia, the U.K. and USA. His areas of interests include artificial intelligence, information retrieval, data mining, web intelligence and intelligent transportation systems. He has served as a general co-chair, program co-chair, review committee chair, program committee member and reviewer for various international conferences on artificial intelligence and data mining. He is also on the editorial boards of a number of international journals. His fundamental research has been supported by the Natural Science and Engineering Research Council (NSERC) of Canada for twenty-five years, and the applications of his research to the industry are supported by a number of funding agencies, including NSERC, the Government of Nova Scotia, NRC-IRAP and MITACS.

Ravi Samikannu is currently working as an Associate Professor, Electrical Engineering Department in Botswana International University of Science and Technology, Palapye, Botswana. Ravi Samikannu obtained his PhD Degree in Electrical Engineering, from Anna University, Chennai, India. He has a total teaching experience of 14 years at undergraduate and postgraduate levels. At present 5 PhD and 4 Master students are doing research under his supervision. Three PhD students and 17 Master students completed their research work under his supervision. He has published 60 research papers in International Journals. He has presented 50 papers in International and National Conferences and has received the Best Paper Award two times for his presentation. He is presently working on research projects in Smart Grid, Renewable Energy System, and Power system. He is an active member of IDDS and participated in different rural community development projects.

Sujatha Radhakrishnan completed her Ph.D. degree at Vellore Institute of Technology, Vellore, India, in the area of data mining. She received her M.E. degree in Computer Science from Anna University, India, with ninth rank, and pursued a Master of Financial Management from Pondicherry University, India. She received her B.E. degree in Computer Science from Madras University, India. She has 22 years of teaching experience and has been serving as a professor in the School of Computer Science Engineering and Information Systems at Vellore Institute of Technology, Vellore. She served as Assistant Director (Students' Welfare) from January 2021 to December 2024. She has been actively contributing to institutional development through several academic and administrative roles. Since July 2023, she has been serving as the Member Secretary of Equality, Diversity and Inclusivity at VIT, a Member of Sustainability Initiatives, and In-charge of Service and Support for Differently Abled Learners. From March 2025 onwards, she is serving as the Nodal Officer for the Equal Opportunity Cell. She also served as a Visiting Faculty at

National Taiwan University of Science and Technology (NTUST), Taipei, Taiwan, from November 17 to November 28, 2025. She has organized and attended several workshops and faculty development programs. She actively involves herself in the growth of the institute by contributing to various committees at both academic and administrative levels. She used to guide projects for undergraduate and postgraduate students and currently guides doctoral students. She gives technical talks in colleges for symposiums and various sessions. She acts as an advisory, editorial, and technical committee member in conferences conducted in other educational institutions and in-house. She has published a book titled Software Project Management for College Students. She has published research articles in reputed high-impact journals and can find 119 articles in Google Scholar, 27 book chapters, 24 conference articles, 8 edited books, 32 patents filed and 1 patent granted. The Institution of Green Engineers awarded her IGEN Women Achiever 2021 award in the Future Computing category. Outstanding Researcher Awardee for the year 2022 was awarded by VIT. She is interested in exploring and visiting different places to learn about the culture and people of various areas. She is interested in learning upcoming things and gets acquainted with the student's level. Her areas of research interest include Information Management and Data Analytics, Artificial Intelligence, Soft Computing, Medical AI, Big Data, Deep Learning, and Blockchain Software Engineering.

***

Tarunjit Biswas, a third-year B.Tech Computer Science and Engineering student at Global Institute of Technology, affiliated with MAKAUT, India. He work as an independent developer and researcher focused on applied artificial intelligence, cybersecurity, and human-centric software systems. His work centers on building practical, end-to-end digital products that translate complex technical processes into clear, usable experiences. His notable projects include OmniAnalyze, a file intelligence and safety analysis platform designed to help users understand and evaluate digital files without requiring deep cybersecurity expertise, along with multiple AI-driven web tools exploring transparency, explainability, and responsible system design. Alongside product development, he actively experiment with web technologies, AI systems, and data-driven applications, taking projects from concept to deployment. He has particularly interested in AI accountability, system architecture, and building technology that balances capability with ethical responsibility.

Subramanian C.V. is an Architect Planner (Former Dean, Faculty of Architecture and Planning) working as Director CSAS at PMIST, Thanjavur, India. He is an Alumnus of National Institute of Technology (NIT), Trichy. He is an

Academician and Researcher with 26 years' experience in the field of Sustainable Architecture and Planning. His area of specialization includes Thermal comfort, Sustainable development, Heritage tourism, Solar passive architecture and SDG. He is a recipient of many awards, has patents and several publications to his credits. He is guiding 8 scholars and 5 have completed PhD under his guidance.

Parag Chatterjee received the B.E. degree in Computer Science & Engineering from the Karnatak University, Dharwad, India, in 1998 and received M.Tech. degree from IIEST Shibpur, Kolkata, India, in 2007. He has an academic experience of 20 years. Currently he is working as an Assistant Professor in the Department of CSE at Global Institute of Management and Technology, Krishnanagar, West Bengal, India. His current research interests include Data ware Housing, Data mining and Wireless sensor. He has 15 publication in national and international journals and 3 Patents.

Umamaheswari Durairaj is an author and faculty member in the Department of Commerce at Periyar Maniammai Institute of Science & Technology (Deemed to be University), Thanjavur, Tamil Nadu, India. With a strong commitment to teaching and scholarly activity, she focuses on bridging theoretical frameworks and practical applications within commerce and related interdisciplinary fields.

Tamil Ezhil G. is a part-time PhD research scholar at PMIST, where her work builds on over fifteen years of engagement with the Architectural Foundation Program. Her research interests span architectural pedagogy, history–theory–criticism, and settlement studies with a particular focus on rural communities. She is also a Professor at the Chennai Academy of Architecture and Design (CAAD), Chennai. She holds a Bachelor's degree in Architecture from Periyar Maniammai College of Technology for Women, Thanjavur, and a Master's degree in Planning from the School of Architecture and Planning, Anna University

Sanju Ghosh is an undergraduate student in the field of Computer Science, currently associated with the Global Institute of Management & Technology. His academic interests include Artificial Intelligence and Software Engineering, with a particular focus on Robotics and Autonomous Systems. He has actively engaged in research and academic projects related to these areas and has contributed to scholarly work through journal publications.

Janani J is an academician with a strong passion towards teaching, which made her to pursue her PhD for continuous learning and to enhance academic journey. Her area of Interest is on Urban Public Space and she believe that well designed environment will benefit the society there by enhancing inclusivity and overall quality of life of people. She completed the Undergraduate (B.Arch) from Periyar

Maniammai University, Thanjavur and Postgraduate from Hindustan University, Chennai. Towards commitment on education and practice,she is aiming to contribute on research and design that supports the growth of the environments

Indra Meghrajani works a Professor for the MBA and PGDM program of the Gujarat Technological University's Narayana Business School (NBS) Studies in Ahmedabad, Gujarat, India. She holds a MBA degree and Ph.D. with marketing specialization. She has also got research Experience at Indian Institute of Management (IIMA). She has successfully completed online course on Customer Neuromarketing from Copenhagen University (USA) and Digital marketing course offered by IBS and GOOGLE. She has experience in Industry, Research and Academics since last 15 years. Dr Indra is an expert in consumer behavior, Digital marketing, advertising and promotion, branding and operations. She has participated in 11 national and International Conferences and has published many research papers which are Scopus and ABDC indexed. She has also been invited as a session chairperson for several international conferences. She works with IIMA in various projects as a freelancer and also conducts MDPs along with various professors at IIMA She has also published case studies at IIMA and Harvard Business Publishing House.

Prakriti Mehta is a New Delhi–based Urban designer and senior architect at Design Action Group, with over 13 years of experience in sustainable design, urban development, and policy-driven architecture.Her work spans master planning, DPR development, and green building consultancy, with a focus on public infrastructure, architecture and social impact.She previously served as a Joint Advisor at the Quality Council of India - a standard setting autonomous body of the Government of India which conducts third party audits of all missions and schemes of the government of India. She led national-level project bidding and quality assurance for urban missions, including audits and third-party evaluations for the HRIDAY scheme and G20- summit related works. Internationally, Prakriti has conducted workshops and delivered lectures in Ukraine in collaboration with the CanActions School of Urban Studies and GIZ, exploring the intersections of microclimate, culture, and urban form. Her research on rental housing and social resilience has been published by Springer Singapore as part of an international collaboration with universities in Australia and Malaysia.Fluent in English, Hindi, French, and German.Prakriti is a GRIHA-certified evaluator, published author, educator, and advocate for inclusive urbanism.

Deboprosad Modak is an undergraduate learner with academic training in science and technology. He completed two years of a B.Sc. program before transitioning to a B.Tech., reflecting his interest in applied and technical studies. His interests span scientific inquiry, teaching, and creative expression. He is also a story and poem writer with a strong passion for drawing and visual art. This publication reflects his interdisciplinary outlook and commitment to learning, creativity, and knowledge sharing.

Nedal Mohammed Nwasra is a faculty member in the Department of Software Engineering at the University of Petra, Jordan. His research interests span web engineering, human-computer interaction, usability engineering, cybersecurity, and artificial intelligence, with a particular focus on explainable AI, CI/CD pipeline quality assurance, and digital ethics in emerging technologies. He has authored and co-authored several research papers and book chapters in these areas, published in international journals and edited volumes. He is actively involved in academic peer review for IGI Global publications and serves on quality assurance and statistical analysis committees within the Faculty of Information Technology at the University of Petra. He holds an ORCID identifier: 0009-0005-9323-685X.

Kritika Pancholi is an Assistant Professor at Narayana Business School and a UGC NET-qualified academic with a specialization in Commerce and Marketing. Currently pursuing her Ph.D. in Marketing Management from The Maharaja Sayajirao University of Baroda, her research focuses on service quality, perceived usefulness, and digital consumer behavior — particularly within the telecom and fintech ecosystems. She has authored and co-authored several book chapters and journal articles in areas such as behavioral finance, AI-driven marketing, and sustainable business practices. With over a decade of academic writing and content development experience for global education platforms, Ms. Pancholi bridges industry insight with pedagogical innovation. She has served as an editor for the forthcoming IGI Global book "Diversity, AI, and Sustainability for Financial Growth," and regularly mentors postgraduate students in research and publication. Her academic interests include mobile applications, strategic information systems, and technology adoption, making her a valuable contributor to interdisciplinary research communities.

Ramadevi Salunkhe is an Assistant Professor in the Department of Artificial Intelligence at G. H. Raisoni College of Engineering, Nagpur, India, and a Research Scholar pursuing her Ph.D. in Computer Science and Engineering at VNIT, Nagpur. She holds an M.Tech and B.E. in Computer Science and Engineering and has over 11 years of experience spanning academia, central and state government institutions, and the IT industry. Her research focuses on artificial intelligence, machine learning, big data analytics, and intelligent automation. She has authored and co-authored books, several IGI Global book chapters, and presented at international conferences, including ICMCER 2024 (Thailand) and ARET 2025 (India). She also serves in academic leadership roles, mentors student projects, organizes technical events, and is a member of the International Association of Engineers (IAENG).

Ahmed Souayeh is a graduate student in Digital Business Analytics at École de Management Léonard de Vinci (EMLV), Paris, France. He also holds an engineering degree in Computer Engineering (financial computing) from ESPRIT, Tunisia. His interests include machine learning, financial data analytics, and digital innovation. He has participated in projects involving deep learning models, decision-support systems, and data-driven applications aimed at improving decision-making in finance and business.

B.K. Tripathy is now working as a Professor (Higher Academic Grade) in School of Information Technology and Engineering (SITE), VIT, Vellore, India. He has received research/academic fellowships from UGC, DST, SERC and DOE of Govt. of India. Dr. Tripathy has published more than 700 technical papers in international journals, proceedings of international conferences and edited research volumes. He has produced 30 PhDs, 13 MPhils and 5 M.S (By research) under his supervision. Dr. Tripathy has published two text books on Soft Computing and Computer Graphics. Also. he has two monographs on Social networks with IGI and Dimensionality reduction with CRC Press. Dr. Tripathy has served as the member of Advisory board or Technical Programme Committee member of over 130 International conferences inside India and abroad. Also, he has edited 5 research volumes for different publications including IGI, Springer and CRC. He is a Fellow of IETE; life/senior member of IEEE, ACM, IRSS, CSI, ACEEE, OMS and IMS. Dr.Tripathy is an editorial board member/reviewer of more than 100 international journals of repute.

Index

A

B

C

D

E

G

H

I

M

P

R

S

U

V

W